MW00848770

THE I TATTI
RENAISSANCE LIBRARY

*James Hankins, General Editor*

# PETRARCA

# SELECTED LETTERS

VOLUME II

ITRL 77

# FRANCESCO PETRARCA

✦ ✦ ✦

# SELECTED LETTERS

VOLUME II

TRANSLATED BY

ELAINE FANTHAM

THE I TATTI RENAISSANCE LIBRARY
HARVARD UNIVERSITY PRESS
CAMBRIDGE, MASSACHUSETTS
LONDON, ENGLAND
2017

Printed in the United States of America

Series design by Dean Bornstein

*Library of Congress Cataloging-in-Publication Data*

Names: Petrarca, Francesco, 1304–1374, author. |
Fantham, Elaine, translator. |
Petrarca, Francesco, 1304–1374. Correspondence. Selections. |
Petrarca, Francesco, 1304–1374. Correspondence. Selections. English.
Title: Selected letters / Francesco Petrarca ; translated by Elaine Fantham.
Other titles: I Tatti Renaissance library ; 76–77.
Description: Cambridge, Massachusetts : Harvard University Press, 2017. |
Series: The I Tatti Renaissance library ; 76 | This is a facing-page volume:
Latin on the versos; English translation on the rectos. |
Includes bibliographical references and index.
Identifiers: LCCN 2016011703 |
ISBN 9780674058347 (v. 1 : alk. paper) |
ISBN 9780674971622 (v. 2 : alk. paper)
Subjects: LCSH: Petrarca, Francesco, 1304–1374 — Correspondence. |
Poets, Latin — Correspondence.
Classification: LCC PQ4496.E29 E21 2016 | DDC 856/.1 — dc23 LC record
available at https://lccn.loc.gov/2016011703

# Contents

## PART VII. RELIGION AND THE CHURCH



## PART VIII. LETTERS TO THE ANCIENTS

# SELECTED LETTERS

[Volume II: Parts V–IX]

# [PART V]

: I :

## *Ad eundem Thomam Messanensem, de studio eloquentie.*

1 Animi cura philosophum querit, eruditio lingue oratoris est propria; neutra nobis negligenda, si nos, ut aiunt, humo tollere et per ora virum volitare propositum est. Sed de priore alibi; magna enim res est et labor ingens, sed messis uberrima; hoc loco, ne in aliud exeam quam quod me ad calamum traxit, exhortor ac moneo ut non vitam tantum et mores, quod primum virtutis est opus, sed sermonis etiam nostri consuetudinem corrigamus, quod artificiose
2 nobis eloquentie cura prestabit. Nec enim parvus aut index animi sermo est aut sermonis moderator est animus. Alter pendet ex altero; ceterum ille latet in pectore, hic exit in publicum; ille comit egressurum et qualem esse vult fingit, hic egrediens qualis ille sit nuntiat; illius paretur arbitrio, huius testimonio creditur; utrique igitur consulendum est, ut et ille in hunc sobrie severus, et hic in illum veraciter norit esse magnificus; quanquam ubi animo consultum fuerit, neglectus esse sermo non possit, sicut, ex diverso, adesse sermoni dignitas non potest, nisi animo sua maiestas affuerit.

# PART V

## EDUCATION AND THE PRINCE

: I :

### *To Tommaso of Messina, the study of eloquence.*

1 The care of the mind requires a philosopher, but learning in speech is peculiar to the orator; we should not neglect either activity, if, as the saying goes, it is our intention to raise ourselves from the ground and fly freely on the lips of men.[1] But I will write about the former elsewhere, since it is a great subject involving immense toil, but it brings a most abundant harvest. Here, so as not to digress to a theme other than the one which drew me to my pen, I am urging and advising you that we should correct not only our life and behavior, which is the first task of virtue, but our practice in speaking, which attention to artful eloquence will pro-
2 vide for us. Indeed, speech is no small reflection of the mind, nor does the mind play a small part in controlling speech. The one depends on the other; however the one is hidden in the breast, the other comes out in public. The mind grooms speech as it is about to emerge, and shapes it as it wants, whereas speech as it emerges announces the nature of the mind; it obeys the mind's judgment, and speech provides the evidence we trust. We must therefore take thought for each, so that the mind knows how to be soberly severe in speech and speech knows how to be true to the grandeur of the mind. However, once we have paid attention to the mind, we cannot neglect speech, just as, from the opposite point of view, there can be no dignity in speech unless the mind too has its own

3 Quid enim attinet quod ciceronianis te fontibus prorsus immer-
seris, quod nulla te neque Grecorum neque nostrorum scripta
pretereant? ornate quidem, lepide, dulciter, altisone loqui poteris;
graviter, severe sapienterque et, quod super omnia est, uniformiter
certe non poteris. Quoniam nisi primum desideria invicem nostra
conveniant, quod preter sapientem scito nemini posse contingere,
illud necesse est ut, dissidentibus curis, et mores et verba dissi-
deant. At bene disposita mens instar immote serenitatis placida
semper ac tranquilla est: scit quid velit, et quod semel voluit, velle
non desinit; itaque, tametsi oratorie artis ornamenta non suppe-
tant, ex se ipsa magnificentissimas voces atque gravissimas et certe
4 sibi consonas elicit. Negari autem nequit quiddam singularius
emergere quotiens, compositis primum animi motibus, quibus es-
tuantibus nichil feliciter eventurum sperare licet, eloquentie studio
tempus impenditur. Que si nobis necessaria non foret et mens,
suis viribus nisa bonaque sua in silentio explicans, verborum suffragiis non egeret, ad ceterorum saltem utilitatem, quibuscum vivimus, laborandum erat; quorum animos nostris collocutionibus
plurimum adiuvari posse non ambigitur.

5 Instabis autem et dices: 'Heu quantum et nobis tutius et illis
efficacius fuerat suadere, ut eorum oculis nostre virtutis exempla
preberemus, quorum illi pulcritudine delectati ad imitationis
impetum raperentur! Natura enim hoc habet, ut multo melius
multoque facilius factorum quam verborum stimulis excitemur
perque hanc viam expeditius ad omnem virtutis altitudinem con-
surgamus.' Ego vero non adversor; quid enim de hoc sentirem,
iam tunc intelligere potuisti, cum in primis animum componen-

majesty. Otherwise what use is it to bathe yourself in Ciceronian springs, to let no writings either of the Greeks or our own Latin writers pass you by? You can speak with a handsome style, with charm, sweetness and lofty tone, but you surely will not be able to speak with weight, seriousness and wisdom, and, most important of all, with consistency. This is because, unless our desires agree with each other (and be sure that this cannot happen to anyone except the wise man), inevitably, as our concerns are in conflict, both behavior and language will also be in conflict. But the well-ordered mind is like undisturbed sunshine, always peaceful and calm: it knows what it wants and does not cease to want what it has once wanted. So even if the adornments of rhetorical skill are not in supply, the mind draws the most grandiose and weighty utterances from itself, sentiments with which it is undoubtedly in 3
harmony. On the other hand it cannot be denied that something 4
rather exceptional comes forth whenever a great mind devotes time to eloquence—provided we have ordered the emotions of the spirit, since we may not hope for anything to turn out successfully as long as they are seething in us. If we did not need eloquence, and the mind had no need for the support of words, relying on its own powers and unfolding its bounties in silence, we would still have to toil for the benefit of the other people with whom we live; there is no doubt that their minds can be considerably helped by our eloquence.

Now you will insist on the point and say: "Alas, how much 5
safer it would be for us and more effective for them to offer examples of our virtue to their eyes, to delight them with its nobility and carry them off with the urge to imitate it! Nature has this quality, that we are roused much better and more easily by the goads of deeds than of words, and so soar more swiftly by this approach to every height of virtue." Not that I disagree; you could have understood my opinion about this long since, when I warned

dum esse premonui. Non equidem sine causa reor dixisse Satyricum:

> Prima michi debes animi bona;

6 non essent autem prima, siquid illa precederet. Veruntamen quantum quoque ad informationem humane vite possit eloquentia, et
apud multos auctores lectum et quotidiana experientia monstrante
compertum est. Quam multos, quibus nichil omnino loquentium
exempla contulerant, etate nostra velut experrectos agnovimus et a
sceleratissime vite cursu ad summam repente modestiam alienis
7 tantum vocibus fuisse conversos! Non referam tibi nunc que de
hac re Marcus Cicero in libris *Inventionum* copiosius disputat—est
enim locus ille notissimus—, nec fabulam Orphei vel Amphionis
interseram, quorum ille beluas immanes, hic arbores ac saxa cantu
movisse et quocunque vellet duxisse perhibetur, nonnisi propter
excellentem facundiam, qua fretus alter libidinosos ac truces bru-
torumque animantium moribus simillimos, alter agrestes et duros
in saxi modum atque intractabiles animos, ad mansuetudinem et
8 omnium rerum patientiam creditur animasse. Adde quod hoc studio multis in longinqua regione degentibus prodesse permittimur;
ad quos enim nostri copia et convictus nunquam forte venturus
est, sermo perveniet. Iam vero quantum posteris collaturi simus,
optime metiemur, si quantum nobis contulerint maiorum nostrorum inventa, meminerimus.

9 Sed hic rursus occurres: 'Quid enim est opus amplius elaborare, si omnia que ad utilitates hominum spectant, iam ante mille annos tam multis voluminibus stilo prorsus mirabili et divinis ingeniis scripta manent?' Pone, queso, hanc solicitudinem; nunquam te res ista trahat ad inertiam; hunc enim metum et quidam ex veteribus nobis abstulerunt et ego post me venturis aufero. Decem adhuc

you that the mind must be set in order first of all. I don't believe the satirist wrote without cause:

> First of all you should count the talents of the mind,[2]

since they would not have been first if anything had preceded them. But we have read in many sources and discovered from the 6
demonstration of daily existence just how much eloquence can contribute to the shaping of human life. How many men do we see in our time who had gained no benefit from the models offered in other men's speech, suddenly aroused, as it were, and converted from the most criminal career to the greatest moderation just by other men's voices! I will not repeat to you now what Cicero ar- 7
gues rather fully in his books *On Invention*—after all the passage is famous—nor will I work in the myths of Orpheus or Amphion; the first supposedly moved monstrous beasts and the other, trees and rocks with song, leading them wherever he chose, simply on account of his extraordinary eloquence; with this eloquence Orpheus is believed to have inspired lustful and violent men of brutish and animal natures, and Amphion moved boorish minds as intractable and hard as a rock, to mildness and endurance of all things.[3] Add that by this skill we are enabled to help many people 8
living far away, where neither access to us nor our company would perhaps ever have come near them, but our speech will reach them. Again we will be able to take precise measure of how much we shall contribute to our successors, if we recall how much the discoveries of our ancestors have conferred upon us.

But here again you will confront me: "What need is there to 9
develop a theme further if everything that works to men's advantage has survived from a thousand years ago, written by divine intellects in so many volumes and in an utterly wonderful style?" I beg you, cast off this anxiety; never let that problem cow you into inactivity; some of the men of old have removed this fear from us and I am going to remove it from those who will come after me.

redeant annorum milia, secula seculis aggregentur: nunquam satis
laudabitur virtus; nunquam ad amorem Dei, ad odium voluptatum
precepta sufficient; nunquam acutis ingeniis iter obstruetur ad
10 novarum rerum indaginem. Bono igitur animo simus: non laboramus in irritum, non frustra laborabunt qui post multas etates
sub finem mundi senescentis orientur. Potius illud metuendum
est, ne prius homines esse desinant, quam ad intimum veritatis
11 archanum humanorum studiorum cura perruperit. Postremo, si
ceterorum hominum caritas nulla nos cogeret, optimum tamen et
nobis ipsis fructuosissimum arbitrarer eloquentie studium non in
ultimis habere. De se alii viderint; de me autem, quid mereantur
in solitudine quedam voces familiares ac note, non modo corde
concepte, sed etiam ore prolate, quibus dormitantem animum excitare soleo; quam preterea delectet vel aliorum vel mea nonnunquam scripta revolvere; quantum ve ex ea lectione exhonerari me
sentiam gravissimis acerbissimisque molestiis, non facile dicturum
12 me speraverim. Eoque magis propriis adiuvor interdum, quo illa
langoribus meis aptiora sunt, que conscia manus medici languentis
et ubi dolor esset sentientis, apposuit. Quod nunquam profecto
consequerer, nisi verba ipsa salutaria demulcerent aures, et me ad
sepius relegendum vi quadam insite dulcedinis excitantia sensim
illaberentur atque abditis aculeis interiora transfigerent. Vale.

*Kalendis Maiis.*

Let the past ten thousand years return, let ages be heaped on ages, virtue will never be adequately praised; instructions will never be enough to do justice to the love of God or to hatred of pleasures. The way will never be blocked for shrewd intellects to investigate
new subjects. So let us be of good cheer: we are not working to no 10
effect, nor will those men work in vain who come to birth after many ages just before the end of our aging universe. Rather we should fear that men will cease to exist before the zeal for humane studies has broken through to the innermost secret of the truth.
Finally, if no affection for other men compelled us, I would still 11
judge it to be best and most fruitful for us not to put the study of eloquence in last position. Let others decide for themselves, but I don't think I could easily express how much some familiar and well-known ideas, not only formed in my heart but also expressed on my lips, have served to support me when I am alone, when I use them to rouse my sleeping soul, nor again how much it delights me to open up either other men's writings or sometimes my own, and how greatly I feel relieved by such reading from the
heaviest and most bitter distresses. And I am helped all the more 12
by my own writings, just as remedies are more suited to my times of weakness, because they are applied by the informed hand of a doctor who in his own weakness understands where the pain is situated. Surely I would never achieve this if the actual healing words did not soothe my ears and stimulate me by some power of inherent sweetness to reread them again and again, slipping in gradually so as to pierce my inner being with hidden goads. Farewell.

*May 1.*

## : 2 :

## *Ad Iohannem de Columna ordinis predicatorum, quid exempla valeant exemplis ostenditur.*

1 Exemplis abundo, sed illustribus, sed veris, et quibus, nisi fallor, cum delectatione insit autoritas. Possem, aiunt, paucioribus uti. Fateor, possem et sine exemplis agere; nec istud infitior, quippe
2 cum et tacere possem, et forte consultius. Sed in tot mundi malis, inter tam multa dedecora tacere difficile est; satis patientie prestitisse videor, quod nondum satyre calamum applicui, cum, diu ante hec monstra, scriptum videam:

> difficile est satyram non scribere.

Multa passim loquor, multa etiam scribo, non tam ut seculo meo prosim, cuius iam desperata miseria est, quam ut me ipsum con-
3 ceptis exhonerem et animum scriptis soler. Veruntamen si ratio queritur cur exemplis interdum affluam, curioseque in his videar immorari, dicam: puto lectorem eo animo esse quo sum ego. Me quidem nichil est quod moveat quantum exempla clarorum hominum. Iuvat enim assurgere, iuvat animum experiri an quicquam solidi habeat, an generosi aliquid atque adversus fortunam indo-
4 miti et infracti, an sibi de se ipse mentitus sit. Id sane, preter experientiam que certissima magistra rerum est, nullo melius modo fit, quam si eum his quibus simillimus esse cupit, admoveam. Itaque, sicut omnibus quos lego, gratiam habeo, si michi sepe propositis exemplis hanc experiendi facultatem dederint, sic michi gratiam

: 2 :

## *To Giovanni Colonna of the Order of Preachers, demonstrating the power of examples by means of examples themselves.*

Yes, I do spill over with examples, but they are brilliant and true, 1
carrying authority along with enjoyment, if I don't deceive myself. They say I could make use of fewer. I admit it—and I could argue even without examples; I don't deny that either, since I could also
keep silent, and perhaps it would be wiser. But amid so many evils 2
of this world, among so many scandals, it is difficult to keep quiet; I think I have shown enough patience if I have not yet directed my pen to satire, although I find the following written long before the present enormities:

> It is difficult not to write satire.[1]

I say a great deal incidentally and write a great deal, not so much to benefit my own generation, whose wretchedness is now beyond hope, as to unload myself of my ideas and comfort my spirit by
writing. But if the question is really why I overflow with examples 3
from time to time and I seem to linger too precisely on them, I will tell you. I think the reader has the same reaction as I do. For me there is nothing so moving as the examples of famous men. In fact I like to soar, I like to test whether my spirit contains any solid value, or some nobly born element untamed and unshattered
by fortune, or whether it has been lying to itself about itself. Cer- 4
tainly, besides experience, the most reliable instructor in things, there is no better way of achieving this than by directing my spirit to those whom it is most eager to emulate. So just as I give thanks to every writer whom I read if they have given me this chance of experience by often setting examples before me, so I hope those

habituros spero qui me legent. Fallor forsan in hac spe; tu tamen
5 in hac narratione non falleris; hec enim una vera rei causa est. Altera est, quod et michi scribo, et inter scribendum cupide cum
maioribus nostris versor uno quo possum modo; atque hos, cum
quibus iniquo sidere datum erat ut viverem, libentissime oblivis-
cor; inque hoc animi vires cuntas exerceo, ut hos fugiam, illos sequar. Sicut enim horum graviter conspectus offendit, sic illorum
recordatio magnificique actus et clara nomina incredibili me affi-
ciunt atque inextimabili iocunditate, que si omnibus nota esset,
multos in stuporem cogeret, quid ita cum mortuis esse potius
6 quam cum viventibus delectarer. Quibus veritas responderet, illos
vivere qui cum virtute et gloria diem obierunt; hos inter delitias et
falsa gaudia exultantes, luxu somnoque marcidos, vino graves, etsi
vivere videantur, esse tamen adhuc quidem spirantia sed obscena
iam et horrenda cadavera. Verum hec inter doctos et indoctos
7 eterna lis maneat; ego sequar inceptum. Habes ergo quod inter-
rogationi tue, quodque quorundam qui tecum sunt, admirationi
modo responsum velim, cur exemplis abundem veterum illustrium: quod et aliis profutura spero, et michi scribenti ac legenti
profuisse admodum certe scio. Deinceps, quoniam nichil ab uno
homine quod omnibus hominibus placeat fieri potest, mirentur
improbentque, si libet; certe ego, ne propter alienum murmur
intermisisse videar morem meum, inserere huic etiam epystole
aliquot exempla non desinam et quid exempla possint, exemplis
ostendam.

8 Omnes qui ante Marium a medicis secabantur, vinciri mos fuerat; quia enim dolorem corporis animi robore superari non posse
persuasum erat, vinculorum auxilio utebantur. Primus Marius

who read me will give thanks to me too. Perhaps I am deceived in
this expectation, but you will not be deceived, since this is my one
true motive for the practice. Another reason is that I am also writ- 5
ing for myself, and, as I write, eagerly keep company with our ancestors in the only way I can, and forget most gladly these contemporaries with whom a hostile star had destined me to live: I
exercise all my spiritual strength to this purpose, to escape from
them and follow those men of old. Just as the sight of these moderns deeply offends me, so the memory of those ancients and their
grand achievements and glorious names affect me with unbelievable and incalculable pleasantness: indeed, if everyone knew this, it
would drive many to wonder why I should take pleasure in associating with the dead rather than with the living. The truth would 6
give them their answer: it is the men who have met their death
with valor and glory who live on; those others, rejoicing amid
these self indulgences and false joys, languid with luxury and sleep
and heavy with wine, even if they seem alive, are still breathing,
but loathsome and awful corpses. But let this dispute between the
educated and uneducated persist without end; I will follow the
argument I started. So you have the answer I would like to give to 7
your question and to the surprise of some of your associates, wondering why I overflow with examples of famous men of old; I hope
these examples will do good to others, and I know for sure that
they have done me good as I write and read. Finally, since one man
can do nothing to please all men, let them wonder and criticize if
they choose: I, at least—so I will not seem to have suspended my
practice because of outsiders' criticism—will not stop inserting in
this letter too a number of examples, and I will show by examples
how much examples can achieve.

Before Marius all the men who suffered surgery from doctors 8
used to be tied up, because men were convinced that bodily pain
could not be overcome by the strength of the mind, so they used
the aid of bonds. Marius was the first to be operated on unbound,

solutus sectus est, sed post eum plurimi; cur, queso, nisi quia
exemplum viri constantissimi atque fortissimi ad imitandum ani-
9 mos erexit, et ut compatriote sui verbo utar, valuit autoritas? Bello
latino, ad Veserim Decius consul se ipsum pro legionibus et pro
populi romani victoria devovit; res dictu quam executione facilior,
sponte tua mortem appetere ut alteri victoriam queras; tam efficax
tamen exemplum fuit et tam validum, ut bello samnitico ac gallico
filius Decius, et ipse consul, patris imitator existeret, et nomine
patrem vocans, securus iret ad mortem, quam pro salute suorum
civium contemnere illo autore didicerat; quos bello tarentino adversus Pyrrum imitatus nepos, tertia tandem uno de grege victima,
etsi non eodem infularum habitu, pari tamen animi virtute ea-
10 demque reipublice pietate, procubuit. Nunquam talis vir Themistocles fieret, nisi Miltiadis exemplis accensus, fieri illi par in animum induxisset; nunquam Iulius Cesar in illud glorie culmen
ascenderet, nisi mirari et imitari Marium ab adolescentia didicisset; quin et Alexandri profuit imago in templo Herculis Gadibus
conspecta, qua mox ad cupiditatem magnas res agendi non exarsit
11 modo, sed, ut ait Tranquillus, ingemuit. Profecto autem, si statue
illustrium possunt nobiles animos ad imitandi studium accendere,
quod Q. Fabium Maximum et P. Cornelium Scipionem dicere solitos Crispus refert, quanto magis ipsa virtus hoc efficit, claro dum
proponitur non marmore sed exemplo? corporum nempe linia-
menta statuis forsan expressius continentur, rerum vero gestarum
morumque notitia atque habitus animorum haud dubie plenius
atque perfectius verbis quam incudibus exprimuntur; nec improprie michi videor dicturus statuas corporum imagines, exempla

but very many came after him; why, I ask, unless because the example of this exceptionally brave and steadfast man stimulated their minds to imitate him, and to use a phrase of his compatriot, his authority was effective?[2] In the Latin War the consul Decius, 9
at the battle by the river Veseris, vowed his own life in sacrifice for the legions and the victory of the Roman people; it is easier to name this than to carry it out, voluntarily to seek death so as to obtain victory for another, but his example was so effective and so powerful that in the Samnite and Gallic Wars his son Decius, also a consul, became his father's imitator, and calling on his father by name went confidently to his death, which he had learned on his father's authority to despise on behalf of his fellow citizens' welfare; then in the Tarentine war against Pyrrhus the grandson imitated them both, as a third victim from a single flock, even if he was not wearing the same ritual garland: yet he laid down his life with equal moral courage and loyalty to the state.[3] Themistocles 10
would never have become so great a leader if he had not been inflamed by the precedent of Miltiades and persuaded his mind to become the other's match;[4] Julius Caesar would never have climbed to that summit of glory if he had not learned from his youth to admire and imitate Marius: even the statue of Alexander in the temple of Hercules at Gades did him good service. When he saw it he was not only inflamed with desire to achieve great feats, but as Suetonius says, "he let out a groan."[5] And if the stat- 11
ues of famous men could actually kindle noble spirits with desire for imitation, as Fabius Maximus and Cornelius Scipio used to say, as reported by Sallust,[6] how much more does virtue achieve this when it is set before us, not in brilliant marble but as a brilliant example? Perhaps men's physical features are more precisely conveyed in statues, but without doubt knowledge of their deeds and character and the nature of their spirits are more fully and perfectly expressed by words than on the anvil; indeed I don't think I will be speaking out of place in saying that statues are

12 virtutum. Quid de ingeniis loquar? imitatio unum insigne par si-
derum lingue latine, Ciceronem ac Virgilium, dedit, effecitque ne
iam amplius Grecis ulla in parte eloquentie cederemus; dum hic
Homerum sequitur, ille Demosthenem, alter ducem suum attigit,
13 alter a tergo liquit. In omni hominum genere licet idem ostendere,
sed in eo quod in me reprehenditur a tuis, nolim hodie nimius videri. Unum etiam nunc exemplum tibi notissimum quominus interseram, temperare nequeo. Siquidem, quem vite callem arriperet diutissime fluctuanti Augustino, et Antonii Egiptii et Victorini rethoris ac martyris profuit exemplum, nec non et illorum duorum in rebus agentium apud Treveros repentina conversio; quam cum sibi Pontianus miles imperatorius enarrasset—ipsius Augustini verba tenes, octavo, nisi me memoria frustratur, *Confessionum* libro posita—, 'Exarsi' inquit, 'ad imitandum; ad hoc enim et ille narraverat.'

14 Hec ergo consilii mei ratio est, propter observatores ac miratores meos sepius iteranda; video enim quam multis exempla contulerint ad virtutem, et quid in me agant sentio, et de aliis idem spero. Si fallor, res periculo abest; quibus exempla non placent, non legant; neminem cogo; et si me rogas, a paucis legi malim. Vale.

*Avinione, VII Kal. Octobris.*

likenesses of bodies, but examples of minds. What need I say about intellects? Imitation gave us the one conspicuous pair of stars in the Latin language, Cicero and Vergil, and brought it about that we no longer had to give way to the Greeks in any field of eloquence: while the latter followed Homer and the former Demosthenes, the latter matched his forerunner, and the former left his behind.[7] One can show the same result in every category of men, but today I would not want to seem excessive in the aspect of my writing reproached by your friends. Even so, I can't refrain from inserting one more example well known to you. Indeed when Augustine was long wavering as to what path of life to follow, the example of Anthony of Egypt and Victorinus, the rhetorician and martyr did him a service, not to mention the sudden conversion of those two men of affairs among the Treveri; when Pontianus, an imperial soldier, had told this story to Augustine—you have Augustine's own words in the eighth book of the *Confessions,* unless my memory deceives me—he said: "I was ardent to follow his example; he had indeed told it to me with this object in view."[8]

12

13

Therefore this is the motive for my policy, which should be constantly reiterated on behalf of my spectators and admirers: I see how many men examples have converted to virtue and I feel what examples achieve in me, and hope for the same effect in others. If I am deceived there is no danger incurred. Those who don't like examples should not read them; I am forcing no one and if you ask me I would rather be read by a few. Farewell. 14

*Avignon, September 25.*

## : 3 :

## *Ad Gibertum grammaticum parmensem, institutio puerilis et scolastica.*

1 Adolescentulum nostrum, consilii inopem et etatis agitatum stimulis, paterne solicitudinis ope complectere. Iam, ut vides, ad bi-
vium pithagoricum vivendo pervenit; nusquam prudentie minus,
nusquam periculi magis est. Leva quidem ad inferos fert, ad celum
dextera; sed illa facilis prona latissima et multarum gentium trita
concursibus, hec ardua angusta difficilis et paucorum hominum
2 signata vestigiis. Non ego hoc dico; dixit Dominus omnium et
magister: 'Spatiosa via que ducit ad perditionem, et multi sunt qui
intrant per eam; arcta via que ducit ad vitam, et pauci sunt qui
3 inveniunt eam.' Puerum sane nostrum, si hic sibi dimiseris, quid
acturum putas? nempe vel ceci more vulgarem strepitum sequetur,
vel ferrato, ut aiunt, ibit itinere, et que gravium corporum natura
est, deorsum suis ponderibus feretur. Nunc tu, oro, vir optime,
succurre et incautum ac nutantem adiuva rege sustenta; discat te
magistro dextrum sequi callem, discat ascendere.

4 Quod promptius faciet, si peculiariter in eum oculos defixeris,
et adolescentie sue morbis singularis quedam tue providentie me-
dicina subvenerit. Scis quam in partem pendeat, unde sit ruine
5 proximus; illinc oportuno presidio fulciatur. Vetus medicorum re-
gula est, contraria contrariis curari. In letitiam effuso triste quidlibet, mestitia contracto letum aliquid obicito; intentione nimia si

: 3 :

## *To Giberto, teacher of grammar from Parma, the training of boys and school education.*

Please embrace our young lad, who lacks purpose and is being 1
driven by the goads of his age, in the generosity of your fatherly concern. As you see, he has already reached the Pythagorean crossroads;[1] at no other stage does a boy have less sense or run more risk. The left path leads to the underworld, the right to heaven, but the former is easy, downhill and very broad, worn by the crowded traffic of many nations, this right hand one is steep, narrow and difficult, marked by the tracks of few men. It is not I who 2
says this but the Lord and master of us all: "The way leading to ruination is wide and there are many who enter onto it, but the way that leads to life is narrow and there are few who find it."[2]
What do you think our boy will do if you leave him to himself at 3
this point? Surely like a blind man he will follow the common clamor, or, as they say, go by the iron path,[3] and, given the nature of heavy bodies, will be swept downward by his own weight. Now, I beg you, best of men, come to his aid while he is unwary and wavering, help him, direct him and sustain him; let him learn under you as teacher to follow the right pathway; let him learn to climb.

He will do this more readily if you fix your gaze on him person- 4
ally, and that exceptional remedy of your good judgment comes to the aid of his youthful sicknesses. You know his tendency, and the source of his brush with ruin; let him be propped up by timely protection from that side. Doctors have an old rule that opposites 5
are healed by opposites.[4] So when a boy overflows with joy, put something grim in his view; when he is withdrawn with gloom

obtusum erit ingenium, more solertis agricole alterna intermis-
sione reparabitur; si rubiginem situ traxerit, exercitio splendescet,
atque ita fiet ut labor quietem condiat, laborem quies, vicissimque
6 nunc otio nunc negotio recreetur animus. Innumerabiles preterea
sunt morum differentie, et tam diversa remedia non magis morborum corporis quam animi passionum, ut quod uni pestiferum est,
7 alteri sit salubre; in hoc tota discretio preceptoris vertitur. Iuvenilis
pavor familiaritate ac blanditiis mulcetur, insolentia minis et seve-
ritate comprimitur; nec una scolastice censura militie est: levia
verbis, gravia verberibus castiganda; hic laudibus erigendus, hic
coercendus infamia; hic opere fatigandus, hic domandus est ferula;
generoso animo perseverantie studium, affecto solatium, desperanti subsidium, fervor algenti, precipiti frenum, lento calcar ad-
8 dendum. Notissima scienti ingero, ut attritu memoria recalescat;
et de comunibus magna pars artium constat, et aliquando iocundius assueta loca revisimus, et sepe non tam novis quam notis
cantibus delectamur.

9 Puero huic, ut ad rem redeam, vel invito manum inice ne cor-
ruat, ne deviet ad sinistram; doce quanto periculo processurus,
quanto inde labore quantoque dispendio regressurus sit. Ostende
illi quanto tutius iam hinc rectum iter sequi quam spe reditus, que
multos in abruptum egit, ultro divertere; facilem casum esse para-
tumque omnibus, in assurgendo autem magnis viribus, magno
10 nisu, magno auxilio opus esse. Monstra ei vana esse vulgi somnia,
falsamque de omnibus sed presertim de voluptate sententiam; nic-

put something happy before him; if his intellect is blunt with too much concentration it will be restored by alternating fallow like a shrewd farmer, but if he grows rusty from neglect, exercise will make him bright, and so work will season rest and rest work and his spirit will be refreshed in turn, now by idleness and now by
being kept busy. Besides there are countless differences of charac- 6
ter, and the cures are so varied, as much for the passions of the mind as for the disease of the body, that what is deadly to one brings health to another: this is the sole concern of an instructor's
discrimination. Youthful fear is soothed by intimacy and endear- 7
ments, arrogance is suppressed by threats and severity; and the discipline of scholastic soldiering is not uniform: trivial offenses should be chastised by words, but serious ones by blows; one boy should be raised up by praise, the other repressed by shame; one boy should be tired out by assignments, the other tamed by the rod. We should apply the desire for perseverance to a noble spirit, comfort to a discouraged spirit, help to one in despair, warmth to
one shivering, a bridle to the headlong, a spur to the sluggish. I am 8
imposing well known methods on an expert, so that his memory may be reheated by friction: a majority of technical skills consists of commonplaces, and at times we revisit familiar places with more enjoyment, and often we are less charmed by new songs than by known ones.

To return to my business, lay your hand on this boy even when 9
he is reluctant, so he does not stumble nor diverge to the left; teach him how great the danger is as he advances, and with what great toil and expense he will have to return. Show him how much safer it will be to follow the right path, starting here and now, than to attempt to change direction in the hope of being able to turn back, which has led so many to the pit. A fall is easy and ready for all, but in picking yourself up you need great strength, great effort
and great help. Show him that the dreams of the crowd are vain 10
and their beliefs false about everything but especially about plea-

hil ad levam vie huius, nisi fedum fuscum fragile caducum; nichil
11 ad dexteram, nisi pulcrum lucidum validum immortale; et quam proprie illam sequentibus conveniat quod scriptum est: 'Derelinquunt iter rectum et ambulant per vias tenebrosas,' atque illud: 'Vie eorum et tenebre et lubricum,' et illud: 'Via impiorum tenebrosa; nesciunt ubi corruant'; hanc vero alteram sectantibus illud potius convenire: 'Vie illorum pulcre et semite pacifice,' et illud: 'Via iustorum sine offendiculo'; de utraque autem simul dictum: 'Vias que a dextris sunt, novit Dominus, perverse vero sunt que a sinistris sunt'; neque solum uni dictum populo: 'Ecce ego do co-
12 ram vobis viam vite et viam mortis.' Fac ista consideret, fac videat quam reprehensibilis, post tot duces, quamque error ambiguus per inextricabiles vite brevis anfractus; unde sepe redeuntibus seu re-
13 dire meditantibus mors occurrit; denique, dum res integra dumque ipse suus est necdum peccati iugum subiit, doce quanto facilius iugum illud declinare quam excutere, et poeticum illud teneris auribus frequenter inculca: 'hac itur ad astra'; et illud

Hac iter Elysium nobis, at leva malorum
Exercet penas et ad impia Tartara mittit;

in quo poete nostro sapientium hebreorum unus consonat; sic enim ait: 'Via peccantium complantata lapidibus, et in finem illo-
14 rum inferi et tenebre et pene.' His hac etate consuescat monitis, has hauriat disciplinas; facile quamvis formam recens excipit materia, facile quivis habitus nondum duratis mentibus imprimitur; ubi falsis opinionibus aditum prebueris, operosius excluduntur.

sure; there is nothing on the left of this path but what is vile, dark, brittle and transient, nothing on the right that is not handsome,
gleaming, strong and everlasting. Tell him how well what is writ- 11
ten in the Scriptures fits those who follow that course:[5] "They abandon the right path and walk along dark ways" and "Their paths are darkness and slippery," "The way of the impious is dark; they don't know where they are falling down." Indeed what best fits those who follow this other path is the following comment: "Their ways are lovely and their pathways peaceful," and again "The way of the just is without a stumbling block"; and comment is made on both at the same time: "The Lord knows the paths to the right, but those which are on the left are distorted." Nor is this said just for one people: "See, I shall set in your sight the way of
life and the way of death."[6] Make him reflect on these things, 12
make him see how culpable, after using so many guides, and how misleading it is to stray along through the baffling twists of our short life, from which death often confronts those turning back or
planning to return. Finally, while the matter is uncompromised 13
and he is his own master and has not yet undergone the yoke of sin, teach him how much easier it is to avoid that yoke than to shake it off, and often instill that poetic saying into his unformed ears "this is the way to reach the stars,"[7] and that saying:

> This way is our path to Elysium, but the left fork imposes
> evil men's punishment and sends them to impious Tartarus.[8]

In this one of the Hebrew wise men agrees with our poet, for this is what he says: "The way of sinners is strewn with boulders and at their end are the underworld and darkness and punishments."[9]
Let the boy be accustomed to such warnings at this age, let him 14
absorb these rules: raw material easily accepts any mold, any attitude is impressed on minds not yet hardened; once you offer access to false beliefs, they are more laborious to drive out.

Insta ergo, dum votivi spem successus tractabile tempus prefert; et sic habeto, plus te illi puero hoc beneficio collaturum, quam si omnes simul ingenuas artes in pectus suum sedulo ore transfuderis. Magna quedam res est, fateor, scientia literarum, sed maior virtus animi, etsi utranque ex te discipulus docilis sperare queat. Nosti ingenium quid possit, nosti melius expertus; ego id unum novi, paucorum esse ut literati fiant, omnium ut boni, modo se bonis ducibus exhibeant obsequentes. Fastidiosior quidem est scientia quam virtus, cum sit illa nobilior; hec paucorum dignatur ingenia; illa nullius animum contemnit, nisi a quo prius ipsa contempta est. Vale.

*Patavi, VII Kal. Aprilis.*

## : 4 :

## *Ad Paganinum Mediolanensem, temperandum imperii appetitum, et de optimo reipublice statu.*

1 Quamvis non sim nescius quanto plus sub multorum quam sub
unius imperio romana res creverit, multis tamen et magnis viris
visum scio felicissimum reipublice statum esse sub uno eodemque
iusto principe: ita pugnare simul autoritas et experientia videntur.
Sed maior est questio quam ut tam brevi sit explicanda literula.
Certe ut nostrarum rerum presens status est, in hac animorum
tam implacata discordia, nulla prorsus apud nos dubitatio relinqui-
tur, monarchiam esse optimam relegendis reparandisque viribus
2 italis, quas longus bellorum civilium sparsit furor. Hec ut ego novi,
fateorque regiam manum nostris morbis necessariam, sic te illud

So press on while a malleable phase offers hope of the success
we pray for; and consider that you will contribute more to this boy
by this good service than if you were to pour all the gentlemanly
arts with dutiful speech into his breast. I admit the knowledge of 15
book learning is a great thing, but virtue of spirit is greater, even if
a teachable pupil can hope to learn both from you. You know the
power of the intellect, you know better having experienced it; I only
know this one thing, that it is given to few to become educated in
literature but to all to become good, provided they present themselves obediently to their good guides. Knowledge is more demanding than virtue, although virtue is more noble; the one deems
few intellects worthy, the other does not despise the spirit of any
man, except someone who has already despised her. Farewell.

*Padua, March 26.*

## : 4 :

## *To Paganino of Milan, that one should restrain one's desire for power, and on the best condition of the state.*

Although I am well aware how much more the Roman state in- 1
creased under the rule of many than under one man, I know many
great men have thought that the happiest condition of any state
was under one leader who was also just, so much do authority and
experience seem in conflict. But this problem is too great to be
analyzed in one short letter. Certainly given the present condition
of our affairs, amid such unappeasable discord of men's spirits,
absolutely no doubt remains that monarchy is the best for recuper-
ating and repairing the strength of Italy, which the long frenzy of
civil wars has dissipated. While I know this and admit a royal 2
hand is necessary for our sicknesses, still I do not doubt you believe that I would prefer no king to our own ruler, under whose

credere non dubito nullum me regem malle quam hunc nostrum,
cuius sub ditione vivimus adeo suaviter ac tranquille, ut nec Pyrri
humanitatem, nec fortunam Alexandri, nec Zaleuci iustitiam, nec,
ut romanis potius exemplis utar, Romuli ardorem, nec Nume religionem, nec Tullii militiam, nec Anci magnificentiam, nec Tarqui-
3 nii habitum, nec Servii providentiam requiramus. Et profecto si
regem a tyranno sola iustitia discernit, iste rex verus est, quamlibet
tyrannum vocent verissimi omnium tyranni, qui se patres patrie
dici volunt, cum quibus nullus Phalaris, nullus Agathocles, nullus
Dyonisius, nullus denique Gaius aut Nero omniumque fedissimus
Eliogabalus possit de impudicitia et feritate contendere.

4 Sane, quoniam prudentis est non tam quid delectet quam quid
expediat advertere, inque hoc ipso non principia rerum sed exitus
contemplari, tibi, cuius ille consiliis agitur optimo consilio, cuius
de prudentia et fide dubitari nusquam sinis, tibi, inquam, amice,
cui animus meus notus est, hoc rusticum forte sed fidele consilium
dedisse velim, ut suadeas sibi fines suos satis patere, sive opes sive
gloriam spectet. Cupiditati nichil est satis; illa eum non fallat pro-
missis ingentibus; aurea mediocritas est in omni fortuna; humana
quidem felicitas, nullo sibi fine proposito, progrediendi avida et in
infinitum tendens, ut solicitudinis plurimum sic nichil solidi, nic-
5 hil certi, nichil quieti habet. Ideoque semper michi placuit Africani modestia iunioris, qui censor lustrale carmen, quo a diis romane felicitatis augmentum poscebatur, velut nimie cupiditatis
plenum et ipsis importunum deis mutari et ex illo non aliud quam
status qui tunc erat, stabilitatem solam iussit exposci. Sobrie quidem ac prudenter, si et mortalia consistere scirent et ab omnipotenti Deo petitum esset quod a diis fallacibus petebatur.

authority we live so sweetly and calmly that we do miss neither the humanity of Pyrrhus nor the fortune of Alexander nor the justice of Zaleucus; nor, to use Roman examples instead, the fiery passion of Romulus, the religion of Numa, the military expertise of Tullus, the lavishness of Ancus, the demeanor of Tarquin nor the
foresight of Servius.[1] Indeed, if only justice distinguishes the king 3
from a tyrant, our man is the true king, although he is called a tyrant by the most genuine tyrants of all, who want to be named fathers of their country, men with whom no Phalaris nor Agathocles nor Dionysius, in short no Gaius nor Nero nor Heliogabalus, most loathsome of all, can compete in immorality and savagery.[2]

Obviously, since it is not the wise man's role to note what gives 4
pleasure but what is advantageous, and in this very matter to consider not the beginnings of things but their outcome, I would like to give this country-dweller's loyal advice to you, dear friend, who know my mind, and on whose advice he is now acting on the best counsel, and whose wisdom and loyalty you never allow to be in question; so I am advising you, I say, to convince him that his territory is wide enough, whether he is aiming at wealth or glory. Nothing is enough for greed; let it not cheat him with vast promises. There is a golden moderation in every fortune, but human happiness, setting itself no limit and eager to advance, stretching out infinitely, contains the greatest anxiety and nothing solid, fixed
and calm. This is why the moderation of the younger Africanus 5
always pleased me, when as censor he ordered a change to the lustral hymn, in which an increase of Roman blessedness was demanded from the gods, on the grounds that it was full of greed and an imposition on the gods themselves: he wanted nothing else to be demanded from it than the current condition and stability.[3] This was discreetly and wisely said, if mortal affairs knew how to stand still, and if it had been sought from Almighty God rather than from the false gods.

6 Multa hic dici posse video, sed quid opus est verbis? vides animum meum; quid cupiam et quid metuam nosti. Audio illum novas res moliri: opto feliciter, si pergit, sed malo desinat; tutior enim via est. Oppone te, oro, principiis; ingere sibi illud abstinentissimi ducis: 'Romanos non tam aurum habere, quam imperare
7 aurum habentibus, voluisse.' Id si de auro recte dicitur, quod abdi potest, quid de terris atque urbibus? Itemque, si de hostibus recte dicitur, quid de amicis dices, quos non coacto sed spontaneo moderereris imperio, quorum non terras modo vel aurum, sed corpora, sed animos pleno iure possideas? Cum honestius, tum tutius est amicos habere quam patrimonium amicorum; et ubi volentibus possis, stultum est velle nolentibus imperare. Philosophorum, quin potius nature vox est: 'Nichil violentum, diuturnum.' Modestos regni fines facile tueare; immensum imperium difficile queritur, difficillime custoditur. Vale.

: 5 :

## *Ad Nicolaum Azarolum, magnum Regni Sicilie senescallum, institutio regia.*

1 Iantandem, vir clarissime, perfidiam fides avaritiam largitas superbiam vicit humilitas; iam caritati odium, desperatio spei cessit, perseverantie difficultas; iam sub malleo veritatis pertinax mendacium et mendax obstinatio votis tuis obstantium fracta est. Immortale bellum est inter invidiam et gloriam, inter nequitiam et virtutem, gratias Illi qui est dominus virtutum et rex glorie, quod eo duce in presenti certamine victa parte deterrima, cuius sepe

I see there is much that could be said on this, but what need 6
have we for words? You see my mind, you know what I desire and what I fear. I hear that he is attempting new initiatives;[4] I hope they may be fortunate if he persists, but I prefer him to stop, since this is the safer course. I beg you, oppose its beginnings, and thrust on him that saying of that most restrained leader: "The Romans did not want to possess gold but to to command its possessors."[5] If it is right to say this about gold, which can be con- 7
cealed, what about lands and cities? If it is right about enemies, what about friends whom you guide not by coercive but by spontaneous power, when you lawfully possess not just their lands and gold but their bodies and spirits? It is both more honorable and safer to have friends than have their property, and when you could command them with their good will it is stupid to want to command them against their will. It is the utterance of philosophers, or rather of nature: "Nothing violent is lasting." You could easily protect a modest territory under your rule; but an unlimited empire is difficult to win and difficult to keep. Farewell.

## : 5 :

## *To Niccola Acciaiuoli, Grand Seneschal of the Kingdom of Sicily, the education of a prince.*

At last, most distinguished friend, good faith has overcome treach- 1
ery, generosity avarice, and humility arrogance; now hatred has given way to affection, desperation to hope, and difficulty to perseverance; now persistent falsehood and the deceitful obstinacy of those obstructing your prayers have been shattered by the hammer of truth. There is an everlasting war between envy and glory, between wickedness and virtue, thanks to Him who is master of the virtues and king of glory,[1] because with Him as leader in the

2 contrarium videmus, optima pars triumphat. Ecce nunc, unica tua cura, gloriosissimus Siculi regis vertex negatos honores invito livore suscipiet; peccatores videbunt et irascentur, dentibus suis frement et tabescent; ipse autem solito augustior multumque serenior, avito solio residens, pulsis Latio mestitie nubibus atque imbribus lacrimarum, orbem nostrum fronte siderea et stellanti dyademate serenabit, ereptam restituens regno pacem, tranquillita-

3 tem populis exoptatam. In quam rem ut fecisti hactenus, mundo notissimum tuum illud ostendes ingenium, eoque vigilantius quo maioris est laudis iuste modesteque regnum regere quam feliciter adipisci. Nunc siquidem tempus est ut omnes animi tui vires colligas atque ingentibus negotiis accingaris; nichil est actum, siquid Cesarei moris habes, cum et multa supersint et supremam tua ce-

4 lebris gloria manum poscat. Vidimus te adverse fortune magnificentissime reluctantem; iam cernimus te victorem; sed en totiens victa revertitur aspectu mitior et aurate cassidis, ut ita dixerim, fulgore suavior. Vicisti adversam; prospera redit in prelium: quid putas? mutata sunt arma, non hostis, et tibi quoque novo armorum genere est opus; nolo enim extimes minus esse negotii quoniam hostis est blandior; nullum insidiosius bellum est quam ubi

5 blanditiis credulitas oppugnatur. In arcto quidem egregie rem gessisti; qualem te in aperto exhibeas expectamus. Multos in angustiis indefessos campestris pugna lassavit, multos in adversitatibus fortes viros fortuna prosperior stravit; Hanibal Cannis victor, victus est Capue et ardorem, quem Trebia glacialis accenderat, tepor

present conflict—contrary to what we often see—the worse side
has been defeated, and the better side is triumphant. Look! Now 2
the person of the most glorious Sicilian king, your sole care, will enter on the honors denied him, in despite of envy; the sinners will see this and grow angry and will gnash their teeth and wither away,[2] while he, more august than before and much more serene, seated on his ancestral throne, having driven off the clouds of gloom and the showers of tears from Latium,[3] will calm our world with stellar brow and starry diadem, restoring to the kingdom the peace snatched from it and the tranquility longed for by the nations. This is the purpose for which, as you have done up to this 3
time, you will display to the world your famous intellect, and all the more watchfully since it is a matter for greater praise to rule the kingdom justly and with moderation than to win it by good fortune. Now it is surely time to rally all the powers of your spirit and gird yourself for mighty actions: nothing has been done if you measure things by Caesar's standard,[4] as many tasks remain
and your renowned glory demands the finishing touch. We have 4
watched you wrestling most magnificently with opposing fortune, and already behold you as victor, but see! though so often defeated, Fortune is returning milder in appearance and sweeter, so to speak, in the gleam of her gilded helmet. You conquered her in adversity, but in success she is returning to battle. What do you think? Her weapons have changed, but not the enemy, and you too need a new kind of weaponry, since I do not want you to think there is less trouble because the enemy is more beguiling: no war is more treacherous than when credulity is attacked by compliments.
In difficult straits you handled the task brilliantly, and we are now 5
waiting to see how you handle yourself in open combat. A pitched battle has exhausted many warriors unwearied in times of hardship and a favoring fortune has laid low many men gallant in adverse circumstances: Hannibal, victor of Cannae, was overcome by Capua, and the ardor for battle which icy Trebia had kindled was

baianus extinxit; sepe pax periculosior bello fuit, multis nocuit
6 adversario caruisse. Quorundam virtus otio latuit; quorundam vero prorsus emarcuit, locum submoti hostis occupante luxuria. Nulla homini pertinacior lis quam cum animo moribusque suis; nusquam minus indutiarum; intra murum pugna est; hoc genus hostium bello languidum pace fervidum experimur et sub toga plus ausurum quam sub galea. Ut ceteras gentes sileam, Romanos bello indomitos et omnium gentium victores pax tranquilla perdomuit, et ut quidam illius evi scriptores elegantissime lamentantur,
7 victum orbem victorum victrix luxuria ulta est. Quod presagire videbatur Scipio, ille vir optimus a senatu habitus, dum tam enixe Catonis sapientissimi licet senis adversante sententia, deleri Carthaginem prohibebat, non quod illam parcius odisset, sed 'ne' ut ait Florus, 'metu ablato emule urbis, luxuriari felicitas nostre urbis inciperet.' Qui utinam consilio valuisset mansissetque potius nobis cum hostibus et cum Carthagine quam cum vitiis et cum voluptate certamen! meliori loco res nostre starent, ut puto, rariusque pugnatum esset et crebrius triumphatum.

8 'Quorsum hec?' forsan interroges. Quia scilicet multos auguror futuros quibus quiescendi iam tempus esse videatur. Michi penitus diversa mens est; si me audire volueris, scies unum esse laboris et vite finem tibique et omnibus claris viris usque ad extremum spiritum vel cum visibili vel cum invisibili hoste luctandum fore; quin etiam—vide quantum a comuni opinione dissentio—geminatum
9 tibi laborem et senties et gaudebis. Nullo unquam tempore tam magno conamine consurgendum tibi tamque supra se ipsum attollendus animus fuit. Ad summa certamina ventum est ut univer-

extinguished by the warmth of Baiae;[5] often peace was more dangerous than war, and it harmed many fighters to be without an adversary. Some heroes' valor went unnoticed in idle peace, and 6
other men's utterly withered away, as indulgence took the place of the ousted enemy. There is no more obstinate conflict for any man than with his own character and behavior, nowhere is there less chance of armistice, for the battle is inside the fortifications; we are experiencing this kind of enemy, idle in war but passionate in peace: one who will dare more in the toga than in his helmet. To pass over other peoples, an undisturbed peace tamed the Romans, untamed in war and victors over all nations, and as some writers of that age complain most elegantly, indulgence, triumphant over the victors, avenged a defeated world upon them.[6] Scipio seems to 7
have foreseen this: that hero, considered best by the senate, while the vote of Cato, wise old man as he was, opposed him so urgently, forbade Carthage to be destroyed, not because he was more moderate in his hatred, but to ensure, as Florus says, "that when fear of the rival city was removed, the success of our city would not begin to indulge itself."[7] If only he had prevailed in his advice and our struggle had continued to be with the enemy and with Carthage rather than with vices and pleasure! Our affairs would be a better condition, as I think, and there would have been fewer battles and more frequent triumphs.

"Where is this taking us?" you may ask. Because I suspect that 8
there will be many who think it is now time to rest. But my view is utterly contrary to this:[8] if you are willing to listen to me, you will know that there is a single aim in both toil and life for you and for all men of distinction up to the last breath, and it will be to wrestle with the enemy whether visible or invisible; indeed—see how far I disagree with the common opinion—you will both feel that your toil has been doubled and rejoice at the doubling of it. At no other time must you rise up with so mighty an effort or 9
your spirit be lifted so far above itself. The heights of conflict and

sus orbis intelligat in utraque fortuna qualis quantusque vir fueris,
neque tu tantum sed qui tuis etiam consiliis obsequuntur.

Habes regem, animo senem annis adolescentem, cum quo terra
marique iactatus es, quem per multa precipitia cogente fato in
10 summum status humani fastigium perduxisti. Ostende illi quibus
gradibus in hunc fortune verticem sit evectus, quibus artibus con-
sistendum sit, neque tam deinceps enitendum ut ascendat altius
quam ut ascensu se se approbet non indignum et hereditarium
sceptrum non magis sanguini debitum quam virtuti. Non facit
virum sed detegit principatus, et honores non mutant mores atque
11 animum sed ostendunt. Persuade illi minus esse regem nasci quam
iudicio regem fieri; esse enim fortune illud, hoc meriti; doce:
Deum colat, patriam amet, iustitiam servet, sine qua regnum licet
opulentum ac validum stare nequit; discat violentum nichil esse
longevum et amari multo tutius esse quam metui; assuescat nichil
in terris optare nisi bonam mentem, nichil sperare nisi bonam fa-
12 mam, nichil nisi dedecus formidare. Cogitet quo altior est eo se
clarius videri eoque minus occultari posse que gesserit, et quo potentie plus est eo minus esse licentie. Noverit regem a populo non
magis habitu differre quam moribus; studeat, ab extremis equo
spatio discedens, virtutem in medio sitam sequi; cesset prodigali-
tas, absit avaritia: illa opes vastat, hec gloriam; sit sane tenax fame
proprie, sit parcus honoris, sit avarus temporis, sit largus pecunie,
et illud romani ducis modestissimum animosissimumque responsum semper in auribus eius sonet, nolle aurum sed aurum habenti-
13 bus imperare. Malit subiectos abundare quam fiscum, et intelligat

crisis have been scaled so that the whole world may know what a great man you have been in both kinds of fortune, and not just you in person, but those who obey your advice.

You have a king mature in spirit but youthful in years, with
whom you have been buffeted on land and sea,[9] whom you have
led to the highest peak of human dignity through many steep
places under the coercion of fate. Show him the steps by which he 10
has been carried to this summit of fortune and the arts he must
use to stay there, striving henceforward not so much to climb
higher but to show himself worthy of rising and to prove that his
inherited scepter is due no less to his virtue than to his blood. Being a prince does not make a man but exposes him, and honors do
not change our behavior and spirit but display it. Persuade him 11
that it is less important to be born a king than to become a king
by men's judgment; the first is a gift of fortune, the other of merit;
teach him these things: let him worship God, love his country,
observe justice, without which a kingdom, however sturdy and
wealthy cannot stand firm. Let him learn that nothing violent is
long-lived, and it is much safer to be loved than to be feared; let
him grow accustomed to desire nothing on earth except good
sense, hope for nothing except a good repute, and fear nothing
except disgrace. Let him reflect that the higher he is, the more 12
clearly he is observed and so his actions can less easily be hidden,
and the greater his power, the less his license. Let him know that
a king is no more distinguished from his people by his clothing
than by his behavior; shunning extremes equally, let him pursue
the virtue which is a model to us all; let extravagance subside, and
avarice be far from him: the first ravages a man's resources, the
other his glory. Let him be concerned with his own reputation,
and protective of honor; let him be economical with time, generous with money, and may that most moderate and spirited reply of
the Roman leader always echo in his ears, that he did not want to
command gold, but those who possessed it.[10] He should prefer 13

divitis regni dominum inopem esse non posse; calamitatum semper meminerit ac laborum quos calamitosa Terra Laboris his temporibus passa est; tunc se felicem, tunc se voti compotem, tunc se vere regem putet quando criminibus alienis invectas miserias propria virtute discusserit, damna restituerit, ruinas erexerit, pacem reformaverit, tyrannidem oppresserit, reddiderit libertatem; inducat in animum amare quos regit, nam et amando amor queritur et nullum certius regnum est quam preesse volentibus.

14 Salustianum illud dogma regium nunquam exeat ex animo regis
tui: non exercitus neque thesauros presidia regni esse sed amicos
eosque nec armis cogi nec pecunia parari sed officio et fide, et que
in eandem sententiam sequuntur: concorditer vivendum esse cum
suis, concordia enim parvas crescere, discordia maximas res dilabi;
exemplo Menenii Agrippe plurimum huic sententie debeat, per
15 quam et frater et sotius et amicus et rex bonus fiet. Amicitiis post
Deum, post virtutem nichil carius habeat; quem semel amicitia
dignum duxerit, nulla consilii parte submoveat sequensque Senece
consilium, omnia cum amico deliberet, sed de illo prius; multum
fidat sed non multis, et insistat verum amicum a blando hoste
discernere; veras laudes accipiat ut virtutum stimulos, blanditias
16 horreat ut venenum. Tarde eat in amicitiam, tardius inde discedat
et si fieri potest nunquam; id ipsum non precipitanter sed pedetentim faciat, et ut est in antiquo proverbio, dissuat amicitiam non discindat. Qualem prestat, talem ab aliis animum speret, nec a quoquam diligi sibi fingat quem ipse non diligit: error iste poten-

abundance among his subjects rather than in his treasury. He should understand that the master of a rich kingdom cannot be penniless; let him always keep in mind the disasters and the toil that the disastrous "Land of Laboring" suffered in our time;[11] he should think himself fortunate and fulfilled and truly a king when he has driven off by his own virtue the wretchedness imported by other men's offenses; when he has compensated for losses, rebuilt ruins, remodeled the peace, put down tyranny and restored freedom; let him persuade his mind to love those he rules over, since love is earned by loving, and no monarchy is more sure than one in authority over the willing.

Let that fine Sallustian concept of monarchy never leave the 14
spirit of your king:[12] it is not armies nor treasures that are the
guarantees of the kingdom but friends, and these are not coerced
by force nor obtained by money but by dutiful behavior and loyalty; then what follows in the same sentence, that one should live
harmoniously with one's associates, since small things grow by
harmony, whereas the greatest enterprises disintegrate through
discord. Following the example of Menenius Agrippa,[13] let him
owe most to this precept which will make him a good brother and
friend and ally and king. After God and virtue he should have 15
nothing dearer to him than friendship. If he has once thought a
man worthy of friendship, he should always include him in his
counsels; and following Seneca's advice, he should reflect over everything with his friend, but first deliberate about his friend.[14] Let
him trust strongly but not in many and concentrate on distinguishing a true friend from a flattering enemy; let him welcome
true praise as goads to virtue but shun wheedling like poison. Let 16
him move slowly toward friendship and leave it more slowly, and if
possible never; and he should do it, not in headlong haste but step
by step. As it says in the old proverb, let him unstitch a friendship,
not tear it apart.[15] Let him hope to receive from others the same
feelings he offers them, nor imagine he is loved by anyone whom

tum est; liberrimi autem sunt affectus, iugum non ferunt, dominum non agnoscunt; nunquam amor nisi amore cogitur, nunquam amore non cogitur. De amico sane nichil mali cogitet, nichil temere cuiquam credat; pellat suspitiones, delatoribus aurem neget, pertinacius instantes arguat, non desinentes puniat. Imperatoria vox est: 'princeps qui delatores non castigat, irritat.'

17 Alexander Macedo, licet impetuosissimus adolescens, eximia tamen fidutia contempsit accusatorem et felix fuit eventus ut debuit. Morbo siquidem quem patiebatur accomodum farmacum accepturo supervenerunt a Parmenione litere quibus admonebatur Philippum medicum, Darii muneribus expugnatum, necem eius hosti promisisse; itaque cavendas insidias et mortiferam potionem. Has ille perlectas occuluit dissimulansque subticuit, donec, ingresso ad se medico, et oblatum poculum exhausit et tum demum coniectis in illum oculis accusationem sibi suam obtulit: sero quidem inutiliterque si vera esset, sed quoniam falsa erat, efficaciter et tempestive.

18 Obtrectatores alto animo despiciat et sic vivat ut eos vel in silentio redarguat probetque mentitos, memorans Augustum rescripsisse Tiberio non esse indignandum quod de se quisquam male loqueretur; 'satis est enim' inquit, 'si hoc habemus, nequis nobis male facere possit.' Preclare; alioquin plus haberet homo quam Deus, qui licet inaccessibilis sit offense, humanis tamen sepe
19 convitiis attentatur. Hac in re igitur rex tuus exerceat animum atque aures, in qua non tantum huius omnium maximi ac modestissimi principis cuius modo mentionem feci, sed et Magni Pompeii civis amplissimi et Pyrri regis et Pisistrati Atheniensium tyranni patientia commendatur. Secretum vero suum ab aliis inquiri equo

he does not himself love. This is the blunder of the powerful; for men's emotions are completely free and do not endure a yoke or acknowledge a master: love is never compelled except by love, but never fails to be compelled by love. Let him think no ill of his friend, yet not rashly trust anyone; let him drive away suspicions, deny his ear to informers, refute those who press too obstinately, and punish those who do not stop it. It was an emperor who said: "A prince who does not punish informers provokes them."[16]

Alexander of Macedon, although he was a most impulsive young 17
man, despised an informer with conspicuous confidence and was happy in the outcome as was proper. When he was going to take a drug for the sickness he was suffering, a letter came from Parmenio warning him that Philip the doctor had been overcome by the bribes of Darius and had promised that enemy to kill him, so he should be wary of treachery and a deadly potion. After reading this letter he hid it and kept quiet in pretense, until the doctor had come in to him and he had drained the cup the man offered: only then did he turn to the fellow and produce the accusation against him. This would have been too late and useless if it had been true, but since it was false he did this effectively and in good time.[17]

Let him despise slanderers with a lofty heart and so live that he 18
either refutes them in silence or proves that they lie, remembering how Augustus wrote back to Tiberius that he should not resent the fact that others spoke badly about him: "for it is enough," he said, "to have the means to prevent anyone doing us any harm."[18] This was splendid. Otherwise a mere man would have had more power than God, who is often challenged by human abuse, though
he is far beyond offense. So your king should exercise his mind 19
and ears in this respect, which won admiration for the patience, not only of this greatest and most moderate prince of all whom I just mentioned, but also of Pompey the Great, that most imposing citizen, and of King Pyrrhus and of Pisistratus the tyrant of Athens.[19] Let our prince endure with calm the investigation of his

animo ferat, alienum non magnopere scrutetur; magni animi est talia non curare, contra autem prope par utrobique diffidentia.

20 Talis fiat qualis videri vult; tum demum in se nichil occultum volet, nec magis horrebit hostis oculum quam amici, nec pluris faciet consilium quam testimonium emulorum. Pari fidutia Scipio totis castris exploratores Romanorum atque Carthaginiensium circumduxit; pari animi magnitudine Iulius Cesar et captum Domitium dimisit et transfugam Labienum sprevit rerum licet conscium suarum, et non semel archana hostium inventa nec unquam lecta
21 combussit. Ad hec non temere neque fortuito serenissimi titulum sibi impositum arbitretur, sed ut in animum eius, Deo proximum et humanis passionibus altiorem, nulla meroris nebula, nullus flatus letitie gestientis, nulla pavoris glacies, nullus libidinum terrenarum fumus possit ascendere. Iram in principe turpissimam non ignoret, crudelitatem vero nominari etiam nefas esse, eo funes-
22 tiorem quo nocendi plura suppeditant instrumenta. Sentiat verum esse quod ait Tragicus,

Omne sub regno graviore regnum

esse; atque ideo minaci tumore deposito comunem se subiectis exhibeat et quicquid in illos statuerit, de manu sui superioris expectet. Superbiam, nec minus invidiam, plebeium malum credat esse, non regium: cur enim vel superbire regem oportere qui debitor munerum tantorum et tanto sit obnoxius creditori, vel cur etiam invidere qui supra se neminem, tam multos autem infra se videat?

23 Veritatem totius fidei fundamentum esse non dubitet et mendacio provenire ut vera loquentibus non credatur; plurimum enim

secrets by others, but not examine thoroughly another man's secrets; it is proof of a great spirit not to concern oneself about such things, whereas mistrust grows almost equal on both sides.

He should be as he would wish to appear, since only then will 20
he want to hide nothing in his nature, and will no more shudder at the enemy's eye than that of a friend, putting no more value on the advice of rivals than on their evidence. It was with this level of confidence that Scipio led the spies of both the Romans and Carthaginians all around his encampment; with equal greatness of spirit Julius Caesar both released the conquered Domitius and spurned the deserting Labienus, although Labienus was accessory to his plans; similarly Caesar on more than one occasion burned the secret correspondence of his enemies without ever reading it.[20]
In this respect he should not believe the title of Most Serene was 21
rashly or randomly bestowed on him, but so that in his spirit, close to God and more lofty than the passions, no fog of gloom, no gust of excited joy, no ice of terror, no smoke of earthly lusts can rise. He should not be unaware that anger in a prince is most shameful, and for cruelty even to be mentioned is an abomination, the more deadly as he has access to more means of doing harm.
Let him realize that the saying of the tragic poet is true: 22

Every kingship is set under a weightier rule,[21]

and on this account discard blustering arrogance and show himself openly available to his people and expect from the hand of someone higher than himself whatever treatment he has decided against them. He should believe pride and envy alike are the evil of common folk, not of royalty: for why should a king be arrogant who is debtor for such great gifts and indebted to so great a Creditor; or why should he even feel envy when he sees no one above him but so many beneath him?

He should not doubt that truth is the basis of all credit, and 23
the consequences of lying are that when men speak truth they are

veri parva falsitatis aspersione fuscari. Itaque si credi sibi aliquid
cupit, omnia vera loqui in consuetudinem trahat atque ita linguam
instituat ut mentiri nesciat. Quid enim ridiculosius dicam an peri-
culosius rege mendaci, sub quo necesse est incertam trepidamque
24 rempublicam fluctuare? Stabile prorsus ac solidum verbum esse
debet in quo fundata est tantorum spes ac tranquillitas populorum. Cur autem mentiatur cui maxime expediat nullum, si fieri
possit, usquam esse mendacem? cur aduletur qui nullum metuat,
nichil speret, quos adulatorum stimulos non improprie videor dicturus? contra etiam cur se iactet, cum laudare se ipsum rebus
deceat non verbis? cur minetur cum sola valeat fronte terrere? cur
in quempiam excandescat, cum possit etiam tranquillus ulcisci,
25 possit et parcendo vindicte genus nobilissimum exercere? Caveat
preterea immoderantius exultare, occupationes circumspiciens im-
mortales; desinat tristari, honores suos et divinam erga se munificentiam recognoscens; nulli se negare audeat cum non sibi soli sed
reipublice natus sit; compertum habeat se res suas agere quotiens
subditis opem fert.

26 Sit equitate temperatus rigor, sit severitas mixta clementie, prudentie insit alacritas, maturitas celeritati, securitati cautio, modestie iocus, autoritas lenitati. Sit in gestu decor, in convivio sobrietas,
suavitas in sermone, in reprehensione caritas, in consilio fides, in
iudicio libertas, in risu tarditas, modus in accubitu, gravitas in in-
27 cessu. Sit ei calcar in premio, frenum in supplicio: ad illud ardenter, ad hoc pigrius accedat. Alio vultu superbum hostem, alio
civem noxium feriat; illic exultet, hic doleat, exemploque ducis

not believed, since a great quantity of truth is obscured by a small sprinkling of falsity. So if he is eager to be believed, he should make it his custom to speak everything truly and so train his tongue that it does not know how to lie. For what should I call more absurd or more dangerous than a lying king, under whom
inevitably the state will waver in uncertainty and trembling? A 24
word on which is based the hope and peace of great peoples must be reliable and solid. Then why should he lie when it is most in his interest that that there be no liar, if this is possible? Why should he flatter when he fears no one, hopes for nothing, rejects what I am justified in calling the goads of flatterers? On the other hand why should he vaunt himself when it is proper for him to do himself credit through deeds, not words? Why should he threaten when he has the power to terrify with his mere frown? Why should he flare up with anger against anyone when he can avenge himself calmly and by forbearance exercise the noblest form of
vengeance? And he should be wary of gloating too much, consid- 25
ering his never-ending occupations, nor be downcast, recognizing his own honors and divine generosity toward him; let him not dare to deny himself to any man, since he has been born not for himself alone but for the state. Let him know that he is doing his own business whenever he brings aid to his subjects.

Let his rigor be modified by fairness, let his severity be mixed 26
with mercy, let there be eagerness in his caution, timeliness in his speed, caution in his freedom from care, jesting in his moderation, authority in his gentleness. There should be grace in his gesture, sobriety in his conviviality, sweetness in his talk, affection in his rebuke, good faith in his advice, freedom in his judgment, measure
in his laughter, restraint in his dining, dignity in his gait. Let him 27
use the spur in rewarding but the bridle in punishing; let him move passionately to the former but more reluctantly to the other. Let him strike the arrogant enemy with a different expression than when he is striking a guilty citizen: let him exult in one case and

eximii suorum scelera 'invitus tanquam vulnera *attingat, que* nisi
tacta tractataque sanari non possunt,' ut Livius ait, et cum gemitu
28 ac lacrimis haud secus quam viscera secet sua; affigatque animo
regem misericordia simillimum Deo fieri et penitus errasse philosophos qui misericordiam damnaverunt; magnanimitatem peculia-
rem regibus esse virtutem, sine qua nec regno nec regio nomine
digni sunt; humanitatem si assit, non virtutem esse hominis sed
naturam, si desit, monstrum potius esse quam vitium; eo magis
regi debitam quo magis reliquos homines debet excellere is qui
primum in hominibus locum tenet; eam que in omnibus pulcra
sit, esse pulcerrimam in principe, castitatem; nil pudico rege for-
29 mosius nil obscenius impudico; gratitudinem mutis etiam animan-
tibus insertam, turpiter humanis abesse pectoribus; eam ceteris
ornamento, regi etiam presidio fore; ingratitudinem regni nervos
roburque corrumpere, dum et oblivioso piget obsequi et ingrati
animi voraginem fundo carentem perituris explere muneribus.

30 Denique honeroso honore et honorato se pressum honere fatea-
tur, eumque qui rex fiat, etsi ante fuerit expeditus ac liber, ex illo
tamen honestam suscipere sed laboriosam ac solicitam servitutem
et sub qua publica sit libertas; vivendumque sibi deinceps exempla-
riter: exemplo enim regum regna componi et requiri solere de
31 manibus presidentium quicquid vulgus erraverit. Nichil sibi proprium velit preter sceptrum et dyadema, et que hinc oritur curam
de salute omnium, gloriosam sed difficilem ac multorum capitum
hydreque non dissimilem renascenti. Prestet acrimoniam ingenio
debitam, verecundiam etati, virtutem generi, imperio maiestatem;

grieve in the other, and following the example of that exceptional commander, touch on his own men's crimes "unwillingly, like wounds that cannot be healed unless they are handled and manipulated," as Livy says, and hurt them with groans and tears, as if
cutting his own flesh.[22] He should fix firmly in his heart that a 28
king is like God in his pity and the philosophers who have cursed pity are utterly astray;[23] that generosity is a virtue peculiar to kings, without which they are worthy neither of the kingdom nor the royal title; that if a man has humanity, this is not a virtue but human nature; if he lacks it, this is a portent rather than a vice; it is all the more an obligation to a king, as he ought to excel all other men who occupies the foremost place among men; and that chastity which is noble in all is most noble in a prince. Nothing is more handsome than a modest king, but nothing more disgusting
than one without modesty. Gratitude has even been imparted to 29
dumb animals, and its absence from a human breast is a disgrace. It is an ornament to other men and to a king even a protection; ingratitude corrupts the sinews and strength of a kingdom, as men are reluctant to obey a thankless ruler and fill the bottomless pit of an ungrateful spirit with gifts that will be wasted.

Finally let him acknowledge that he is weighed down by a bur- 30
densome honor and by honorable burdens, and that the man who becomes a king, even if he was previously noble and free, from that time takes on an honorable but laborious and anxious servitude, beneath which there is the public freedom, and that henceforth he must live in an exemplary fashion; for kingdoms are constituted on the example of kings, and it is usual to seek restitution from the hands of those in power for whatever blunders the crowd
has made. He should want nothing peculiar to himself except his 31
scepter and diadem, and the care for all men's well being which arises from this glorious but difficult role, many-headed and not unlike the constantly reborn hydra. Let him display the keenness due to his intellect, the modesty of his age, the virtue of his blood-

purpuram spernat, contemnat gemmas, despiciat voluptates et irrideat universa que fugiunt, eterna sola suspiciat ac miretur. Arma equi litere supellex regia, pax et bellum exercitatio regis sint; utrobique romanis artibus regnet, que sunt, ut Maro meminit,

pacisque imponere morem,
Parcere subiectis et debellare superbos,

32 Postremo norit hanc vitam aleam esse magni discriminis, non ad ludum iocumque, non ad iners otium, non ad degenerem luxum, ad nichil aliud demum hominibus datam quam ut brevi merito eternitatis aditum pandat et fame materiam sempiterne. Itaque rerum se bonarum docilem prebeat, cupide legat atque audiat maiorum gesta nostrorum et exemplorum illustrium sit scrutator solici-
33 tus et fervidus imitator. Illud nominatim domi teneat quod olim ab illo magnifico inimicarum urbium eversore servatum in exercitu numantino, multis deinde romanis ducibus discipline militaris exemplum fuit, ut sicut ille castris sic iste urbibus ac regno instrumenta luxurie depellat et mores longa licentia depravatos corrigat,
34 sine quo spes salutis, ne dicam victorie, nulla est. Hoc ab illo, alia sumat ab aliis, e quibus omnibus perficiat clarum virum; quotque insignia nomina precesserunt, tot sibi magistros vite, tot duces ad gloriam datos sciat; non minus interdum accendunt generosos animos exempla quam premia, nec minus verba quam statue; iuvat laudatis se se conferre nominibus et pulcra emulatio est que de
35 virtute suscipitur. Ac ne curiosa inquisitione tempus teram, habet ante oculos rex tuus non peregrinum vetustumque sed recens ac

line, the majesty of his command; let him spurn the purple, despise jewels, hold pleasures in contempt and scorn everything that is transient, respecting and admiring only what is eternal. Arms, horses and dispatches are the king's equipment, peace and war his exercise; let him rule in both respects by Roman arts which are, as Vergil reminds us:

> To impose the ways of peace,
> To spare the submissive and crush the arrogant.[24]

Finally he should know that this life is a game of dice at a high 32
stake, not for sport and play, not for idle leisure, not for degenerate luxury, but given to men for no other purpose than to open up the access to eternity through a short-lived merit and provide material for everlasting glory. So let him show himself teachable in good disciplines, and let him read and listen to the achievements of our ancestors and be a keen and passionate observer and imitator of
illustrious examples. Let him in particular observe in civilian life 33
the practice observed on campaign by Aemilianus, the mighty overthrower of enemy cities in the Numantine campaign, who was later an example of discipline to many Roman leaders, so that, as that commander acted in camp, so our prince would expel from cities and his kingdom the tools of luxury, and correct behavior perverted by long license:[25] without all this there is no hope of
survival, let alone victory. Let our prince take this from Scipio and 34
other merits from others, thanks to whom he may incarnate a glorious man to perfection. Let him know that he has been given as many teachers of life and as many leaders and guides toward glory as the distinguished names that have gone before him; sometimes examples inflame noble spirits as much as rewards, and words no less than statues;[26] it is a joy to compare himself to much-praised names, and the emulation which competes in virtue
is noble. And there is no need for me to waste time in diligent in- 35
vestigation: your king has before his eyes not a foreign and ancient

domesticum virtutum omnium, nisi me amor fallit, exemplar ydoneum: illustrem ac divinum eius patruum Robertum, cuius quam regno utilis vita esset, mors damnosissima declaravit. Illum intueatur; ad illius regulam se conformet; in illo se nitidissimo speculo contempletur; ille sapiens, ille magnanimus, ille mitis, ille rex regum erat; illum ut tempore, ut sanguine sic animo sequatur et moribus. Sepe enim cum ceterarum rerum tum precipue ingeniorum imitatio felix fuit; iam bonus est qui bono similis fieri studet.

36 Multa dixi, sed pre magnitudine rerum pauca; plura etenim sunt que restant. Tu quidem prope omnia, preclarissime vir, humeris tuis sentis incumbere; verum magno amori nichil est arduum, nichil durum, nichil grave, nisi non amari. Id tu causari non potes, de alumni tui amore iudicioque certissimus, duxque et auriga consiliorum eius; non Chiron Achilli gratior, non Palinurus
37 Enee, non Philotetes Herculi, non Lelius Africano. Eia ergo perfice quod cepisti; omnia fert enim caritas. 'Omnia vincit amor.' Profecto autem qui glorie partęm petit, consequens est ut solicitudinis partem ferat. Aurum profunde foditur; de longinquo vehuntur aromata; thus sabeis sudat arboribus; muricem Sidon, ebur India, margaritas mittit occeanus; difficile paratur omne quod in precio est; non est quesitu facilis preciosissima rerum virtus; auro splendidior fama est; labore queritur, studio detergitur, diligentia custoditur. Rosa inter spinas habitat, inter difficultates virtus, inter
38 curas gloria; illic digitus periclitandus, hic animus. Hunc tu igitur gloriosissimis accinge primordiis; dum enim consummasse putas, tunc incipies; hunc optimis et regis et reipublice curis exerce,

example but a suitable, fresh and household model of all virtues, unless love deceives me: his glorious and divine uncle Robert, whose life of useful service to his kingdom was shown by the ruinous effect of his death. Let him gaze on Robert; let him shape himself to Robert's design, let him contemplate himself in that most shining mirror; he was wise, he was noble-hearted, he was mild, he was the king of kings; let him follow Robert in spirit and behavior as in time and blood; for often imitation of intellects as of other things has been fortunate, and the man who is eager to become good is already good.

I have said a great deal, but little in comparison with the impor- 36
tance of the topic, since there is more left to say. Certainly you, my distinguished friend, feel that almost all of this rests on your shoulders. But to a great love nothing is difficult, nothing hard, nothing burdensome, except failing to be loved. This you cannot allege, being most sure of the love and good judgment of your pupil, and acting as guide and charioteer of his purposes. Chiron was not more beloved of Achilles, nor Palinurus of Aeneas, nor
Philoctetes of Hercules, nor Laelius of Africanus.[27] So then com- 37
plete what you have undertaken, for affection brings everything: "Love conquers all."[28] Surely the man who seeks a share in glory must in consequence have a part in anxiety. Gold is excavated from the depth of earth, perfumes are transported from a distance, incense exudes from the trees of Sheba, Sidon sends purple, India ivory, the Ocean pearls; everything valuable is procured with difficulty; virtue, that most precious of things, is not easy to win; fame, more glittering than gold, is sought by toil and polished by diligence and guarded by scruple. A rose grows among thorns, virtue among difficulties, glory among cares: there the hand must
be at risk, here the spirit. So do you gird him about with most 38
glorious beginnings; for while you think you have completed them, then you will be beginning; exercise him with the best cares of king and state so that he is driven on by them to act more success-

quibus exagitatus et felicius hic aget et postquam hinc abierit, ut Cicero opinatur et nos scimus, velocior ad sedes ethereas pervolabit. Vale, patrie decus ac nostrum.

*X Kal. Martias, Avinione.*

## : 6 :

## *Ad magnificum Franciscum de Carraria Padue dominum, qualis esse debeat qui rempublicam regit.*

1 Dudum tibi, vir clarissime, scribere aliquid meditor et tu me interdum more tuo leniter admones, et indignum esse video, inter tot mediocrium et magnorum nomina, preteriri tuum nomen et paternis et tuis beneficiis ita de me meritum ut nunquam michi e memoria dilabi sine ingenti possit ingratitudine, nec unquam certe hactenus lapsum sit. Scribere igitur est animus, sed unde incipiam quero nec invenio; nam neque unus est aditus ad intentum, et pluralitas herere animum cogit ut ambiguum in bivio viatorem.
2 Hinc crebra nimis in me liberalitas tua ad agendas gratias stilum vocat, et est sane mos percelebris, susceptis amicorum et maxime principum muneribus, grates agere. Quem aliquandiu ipse tecum tenui, donec, perpetuis et in dies auctis beneficiis atque honoribus tuis pressus et pro rebus verba remittere ingenuo pudore prohibitus, munerum magnitudinem, quam sermone non assequor, mente complecti memorique silentio metiri potius quam verbis inanibus consilium cepi. Hinc exclusus, vertor ad amplissimam pronamque materiam tuarum laudum.

fully here on earth; and after he has departed from here, as Cicero believes and we know, he will fly more swiftly to the heavenly dwellings.[29] Farewell, our country's glory and our own.

*February 20, from Avignon.*

## : 6 :

## *To the magnificent lord of Padua, Francesco da Carrara, the sort of man one should be to govern a state.*

Most distinguished friend, I have long been planning to write 1
something for you and in the mean time you have gently reminded me in your usual way, and I see it is not right that among so many moderately well-known and great names, your name should be passed over, though you have deserved so well of me by your father's and your own kindnesses,[1] such that it could never slip from my memory without enormous ingratitude, and in fact it has never yet slipped away. So I have a mind to write, but I am searching for where to begin, without finding it, for there is more than one approach to my purpose and that multiplicity makes my mind
stick fast, like a traveler uncertain at a fork in the road. Your too 2
frequent generosity to me summons my pen to give you thanks, and of course it is a very widespread practice to give thanks when you have received gifts from friends, and especially princes. I maintained this practice for some time until loaded daily by you with continuing and increasing kindnesses and honors; but prevented by my inborn modesty from returning words adequate to the circumstances, I decided to embrace in my mind the greatness of those gifts which I cannot match in speech and measure them in grateful silence rather than by hollow language. So barred from this, I am turning to the immense and easy material of your praises.

3 Nam et hic quoque nonnullorum mos est principes laudare, quod et ipse nonnunquam feci, non tam laudati gratie quam veritati obsequens et virtutem laudum stimulis excitans, quibus nichil generosum animum urgerem potentius. Qua in re, hinc laudantis adulatio, hinc vel maxime inconstantia me offendit: sunt enim et qui indignos laudent et qui laudatos mira mox animi levitate vitu-
4 perent, quo nichil inhonestius, nichil est turpius. In quo quidem maxime Ciceronem noto, usqueadeo ut, quem inter omnes scriptores gentium miror ac diligo, in hoc uno pene oderim: ita ille aliquos, sed in primis Iulium Cesarem, laudum fasce dicam an preconio honerat an honorat, eundemque post probris ac maledictis insequitur. Lege illius epystolas ad Quintum fratrem: omnia ibi de Cesare honorifice dicuntur atque amice. Eiusdem ad Athicum epystolas percurre: prima, ibi, ambigua; ultima queque odiosa videbis et infamia. Lege ipsius orationes quas vel ad ipsum Cesarem vel eo presente ad senatum habuit: tante ibi cesaree laudes sunt, ut nec mortali debite nec a mortali profecte ingenio videantur. Sed progredere. Lege libros Officiorum orationesque Philippicas: invenies nec affectibus odia nec laudibus inferiora convitia; utque sit indignior hec tanta varietas, et viventi laus et defuncto vituperatio omnis attribuitur. Pati possem equanimius si vivum vituperasset extinctumque laudasset: solet enim mors invidiam at-
5 que odium vel extinguere vel lenire. Habet tamen, sortem suam quo soletur, Cesar unum ex omnibus magnum comitem, nepotem filiumque suum adoptivum Cesarem Augustum, qui, licet virtute minor bellica, certe imperio maior fuit, cui immodice laudato Cicero idem, in hoc animosior, vivo etiam et ad ipsum scribens

For here too it is the common custom to praise princes, as I too have often done, not paying homage to the influence of the man I praise, but showing respect for the truth and rousing virtue with the goads of encomium; there is no more powerful way of urging on a noble spirit. But in this both the flattery and above all the inconsistency of praising offends me, since there are men who praise the undeserving and soon abuse those they have praised with a strange frivolity of mind — nothing is more dishonorable, nothing more shameful. I censure Cicero most of all for this, so 3
much so that on this one count I almost loath the man whom I admire and love among all pagan writers. He so honors, or rather onerously burdens, some figures, but especially Julius Caesar with a bundle of praises or with public commendation, then after a short time, persecutes the same man with abuse and curses.[2] Read his letters to his brother Quintus: everything that concerns Caesar is said in honorific and friendly terms. Then run through his letters to Atticus; there you will find the early ones ambiguous, but the last ones all full of hatred and shameful. Read his own speeches, made either to Caesar himself or to the senate in his presence; there are such lavish praises of Caesar in them that they seem neither due to a mortal nor coming from a mortal mind. But move on. Read the books *On Duties* and the *Philippics:* you will read words of hatred no less powerful than those expressions of affection, and insults no less powerful than those praises; and to make this great inconsistency more outrageous, every praise is assigned to the living man and every abuse to the deceased. I could bear this more calmly if he had abused the living man and praised the dead, since death usually either extinguishes or mitigates envy and hatred. But Caesar has as consolation for his doom one great 5
companion among them all, his nephew and adoptive son Augustus, who, though weaker in military valor, was surely greater in authority: Cicero, after having praised him to excess, certainly showed more spirit in this, slandering him to excess while writing

immodice maledixit. Invitus de dilecto michi viro maximo hec loquor, sed dilectior et maior est veritas. Equidem sic esse doleo, sed sic est, nec sum dubius ad hec illum, si adsit, suo illo omnipotenti eloquio facile responsurum. Sed verbis veritas non mutatur.

6 Id michi nequaquam eventurum reor ut, morbo animi, laudata vituperem, verum, ut unde digressus eram redeam, hac ad tuum colloquium ingressuro illud occurrit in limine: etsi vera virtus dignam gloriam non recuset eamque vel invitam ut corpus umbra sequi soleat, hic vir tamen, quod inditiis multis percipere potuisti, presens argui maluerit quam laudari, multoque facilius fuerit iustis hunc reprehensionibus quam veris etiam laudibus promereri. Quid igitur faciam? Quo me vertam? Quem laudare sum veritus, reprehendere non vererer si tam lata esset reprehendendi materia quam laudandi. Est, fateor, conditio ista mortalium, ut nullus omnino sit irreprehensibilis. Ille perfectus atque optimus dici potest, qui paucis ac parvis obnoxius est. Age ergo gratias Deo, qui te talem fecit ut, si equis ingeniis reprehensor tuus laudatorque convenerint, multo disertior sit laudator, sicut e duobus agricolis, et arte equis et robore, ille apparebit insignior cui arvum sors dedit uberius, sicut e duobus nautis omni ex parte paribus, felicior erit illius na-
7 vigatio cui prosperiores aure fuerint et mare tranquillius. Ut te autem reprehendere et hanc colloquii literalis materiam eligere decrevissem, nil in te reprehensione dignum noveram nisi unum illud de quo aliquando multa tecum, nullo teste, disserui. Qua in re, si humiles ac fideles monitus meos exaudire dignabere, rem hauddubie et corpori et anime et fame tue presenti et venture glorie saluberrimam feceris, unde, ut ita ego te nunc alloquar sicut in

directly to him in his lifetime.[3] I am reluctant to say this about a great man whom I love, but truth is greater and I love it more.[4] I am pained that it is so but so it is, and I don't doubt that if he were with us he would easily answer this with his all-powerful eloquence. But words cannot change truth.

I do not think it will in any circumstance be my lot to de- 6
nounce from some weakness of the mind what I have praised, but to return to my point of departure, when I entered conversation with you this thought confronted me at the threshold: even if true virtue would not reject real glory, following it even against her will as the shadow follows the body, yet the man I am honoring,[5] as you have been able to discern from many signs, would rather be accused than praised in his presence, and it would be much easier to serve him with rebuke than with praise, even real praise. So what am I to do? Where shall I turn? I would not be afraid to reproach the man I was afraid to praise if there was as much scope for reproach as there is for praise. I admit that it is the human condition that none of us is utterly irreproachable. He who is guilty of few and trivial faults can be called perfect and most excellent. So give thanks to God who made you such that if a critic and an encomiast of equal talent gathered to blame and to praise you, the encomiast would be much more eloquent, just as between two farmers equal in skill and strength, the man whom chance has given a richer soil would seem more notable, just as between two entirely well-matched sailors, the voyage of the man who has enjoyed more favoring breezes and a calmer sea will be more successful. Now even if I had I decided to criticize you and to select this 7
kind of material for our epistolary conversation, I knew no characteristic in you worthy of criticism except the one element about which I have sometimes talked to you privately at length. So if you will condescend to listen to my humble and loyal warnings on this matter, you will undoubtedly be following the course most beneficial for your body and soul and present reputation and future

campo thesalico Cesarem Crastinus alloquitur, 'aut michi vivo aut mortuo gratias agas.' Hic non agam pluribus: intelligenti enim et scienti omnia quid opus est verbis? Scis quid velim, et nil nisi bonum tuum velle debeo aut possum, teque hoc ipsum scire non sum dubius. Sed et hec transeo, sciens nec michi honestas nec tibi placitas esse blanditias.

8 Que cum ita sint, labor, ut video, michi nunc historie longioris eripitur (quod et tibi, ut dixi, minime placitura et publice omnibus nota est) ut, sub ipsum scilicet adolescentie tue florem, glorioso et magnanimo patre spoliatus sub quo preclara omnia atque magnifica discere et doctrina poteras et exemplo, eo ipso tempore quo rectoris adhuc vel maxime indigus videbaris, ad regimen omnium conscendisti, commissamque tibi rempublicam, immaturos superante annos industria, tanta maturitate tamque senili consilio rexisti, ut, in primis, nullus tumultus in patria tanta mutatione rerum, nulli motus exarserint; ex multa dehinc inopia, quam eris insuper alieni pondus urgebat, brevi ad magnas divitias pervenires; ut deinde paulatim, et etate et experientia rerum crescens, non civibus tantum tuis egregium te rectorem, sed exemplar aliarum urbium rectoribus exhiberes, ita ut sepe ego finitimos populos tibi subesse votis optantes audierim et tibi subditis invidentes; ut tu interim, nec tumide insolentie nec inerti deditus voluptati, in hoc unum vigilantissimo studio incubueris, ut te omnes agnoscerent sine desidia tranquillum, sine superbia gloriosum, utque in te mo-
9 destia cum magnanimitate contenderet. Inter multa igitur decora, cum te pene ex equo etiam minimis adeundum incredibili humanitate prestares, filias tamen tuas conquisitis ab extremo terre

glory. Hence I shall speak to you as Crastinus spoke to Caesar on the Thessalian battlefield: "You will thank me whether I live or die."[6] Here I will not go into details; what need for words to a man who understands and knows it all? You know what I want and I must and can wish only your benefit, and I don't doubt you know this. But I pass over this too, knowing that flattery is neither honorable in me nor pleasing to you.

In the circumstances I see that the toil of a longer historical ac- 8
count (which would not at all please you and is already known to all in the community) has been snatched from me: to relate how, just before the flower of your adolescence, you were robbed of your glorious and greathearted father, under whose guidance you could have learned, from his teaching and example, every distinguished and magnificent principle, at the very time when you seemed most in need of a guide;[7] how then you rose up to take on the direction of all your fellow citizens and ruled the state entrusted to you with an energy triumphing over your unripe years, with such maturity and such veteran judgment that, first of all, there was no alarm in your country at such a change of affairs, and no disturbances. Then, emerging from a severe scarcity and also burdened by a load of debt, you quickly reached great wealth, and gradually thereafter, growing in both age and experience, you not only showed yourself an exceptional ruler to your own citizens, but an example to the rulers of other cities, to such an extent that I often heard of neighboring peoples longing to be under your authority and envying your subjects; while you, without yielding to swollen insolence or idle pleasure, gave your full attention with ever watchful concern that everyone should recognize you as tranquil without idleness, confident without pride, and that modesty
should compete with greatheartedness in you. In this way among 9
many creditable actions, while making yourself accessible on almost equal terms even to the lowest with your unbelievable humanity, you placed your daughters in glorious marriages, sought

preclarissimis nuptiis collocasti; perque idem tempus, quamvis ante alios quietis publice studiosus—quod nunquam tamen aut populo dum civitas comuni consilio regebatur, aut cuiquam tuorum dum tam diu frena reipublice tenuerunt in animum venit—solus tu patriis in finibus, oportunis locis, arces multas ac validas erexisti; atque ad summam sic te in omnibus habuisti, ut et cives, te duce, liberi fuerint ac securi nec ullius sanguis innoxius funderetur, vicinosque omnes, vel metu vel amore tueque virtutis admiratione, pacaveris, totque iam per annos florentem patriam serena tranquillitate et constanti pace tenueris, donec tandem adversarius humani generis, hostis pacis, unde tale nil timebas, bellum tibi repente gravissimum excitavit, quod—tantus amor pacis—intrepidus excepisti diuque ingenti animo gessisti, speratis licet destitutus auxiliis; cumque tibi id utilius visum esset, pacem pristinam alto consilio reformasti, uno ex actu laudem geminam et fortitudinis et prudentie consecutus. Hec, inquam, et similia multa pretereo, quibus te omnibus tue reipublice aliarumque multarum rectoribus magno spatio, rebus ipsis nec tam tuo quidem quam omnium iudicio, pretulisti. [*§§11–14 omissis*]

Nunc peragam quod promisi, et qualis esse debeat patrie rector expediam, ut hoc velut in speculo tete intuens, ubi te talem videris qualem dico, quod persepe facies, gaudeas, et virtutum bonorumque omnium largitori devotior fias atque in dies obsequentior, et ingenti nisu per difficultatum obices assurgas usque ad illum gradum quo ire altius iam non possis; siquando autem deesse tibi

from almost the ends of the earth,[8] and at the same time, though
you were devoted beyond all others to public calm—you alone
erected many strong fortresses at appropriate places within your
ancestral boundaries, a measure which never occurred either to the
people while the city was being ruled by a communal council, or to
any of your family during the long period when they held the reins
of the state.[9] In short you behaved toward everyone in such a way
that under your leadership your citizens were both free and saved
from anxiety, and no innocent blood was shed, while you pacified
all your neighbors either through fear or love and admiration of
your virtue, and have held your country flourishing for so many
years in serene calm and constant peace. This lasted until finally 10
that antagonist of the human race,[10] the enemy of peace, suddenly
stirred up a most serious war against you, from a direction you
least expected, and so great was your love of peace that you fearlessly tackled and waged this war for some time with great courage, although you were abandoned by the expected allied forces,[11] and when it seemed more advantageous to you, you reconstituted the old peace with far-seeing purpose, deriving a double credit from a single action, for both courage and shrewdness. I am passing over these events, I say, and many such decisions by which you surpassed by far all the rulers of your state and many others in real achievements, and not so much in your own judgment as in that of others. [*§§11–14 omitted*]

Now I will carry out my promise, and explain what should be 15
the nature of the guide[12] and leader of his country, so that, looking at yourself as if in a mirror, when you see yourself as I describe, as you will do often, you may rejoice and become more devoted and daily more attentive to God, the bestower of virtues and all good things, and rise with an immense effort through obstructions and difficulties up to the level where you can no longer tread higher. But if you ever feel anything, you can, so to speak, brush your face

aliquid senseris, faciem ipse tuam, ut sic dicam, perfrices et manu operum fame frontem tergas teque ipso formosior vel certe nitidior fieri cures.

16 Sit ergo hic rector in primis amabilis nec bonis formidabilis; malis enim formidabilis necessario sit oportet, si iustitie est amicus. 'Non enim sine causa gladium portat. Dei enim minister est,' ut ait Apostolus. Nichil est autem stultius, nichil a principatus stabilitate remotius quam velle ab omnibus formidari, quamvis quidam et veterum principum et novorum nil magis optaverint quam timeri, et nulla re alia posse imperium teneri quam metu et crudelitate crediderint, quod nominatim de Maximino imperatore barbarico lectum est. Quorum opinionibus nichil est a veritate remotius. Amari expedit non timeri, nisi eo modo forsitan quo pius filius bonum patrem timet; omnis metus alius eorum proposito est
17 adversus. Regnare enim diu volunt securique vitam agere: utrique contrarium est metui, utrique consentaneum est diligi. Et diuturnitatem et securitatem aufert metus, confert utramque benivolentia, quoque plus fidei dicto sit, audiendus Cicero, imo quidem Ciceronis ore loquens Veritas audienda est. 'Omnium,' inquit, 'rerum nec aptius est quicquam ad opes tuendas ac tenendas quam diligi, nec alienius quam timeri,' nec multo post: 'Malus enim,' inquit, 'custos diuturnitatis metus contraque benivolentia fidelis vel ad perpetuitatem.' Utque esse sibi rem cordi scias, idem alibi: 'Carum esse civem, bene de republica mereri, laudari, coli, diligi gloriosum est; metui vero et odio esse invidiosum, detestabile, im-
18 becillum, caducum.' Iam loqui de securitate non attinet, quam metu tolli atque extingui nemo tam rudis ignarusque rerum est qui nesciat. Hic occurritur a quibusdam metum hunc in subditis esse non in regnante affirmantibus, quo non ipsius sed illorum

and wipe the brow of your fame with that hand of yours, taking pains to become more handsome than you are, or at least more glowing.

So this guide should be particularly lovable and not cause fear 16
in good citizens, since he must rather cause fear to bad ones, if he is the friend of justice. "He does not bear a sword without reason, for he is the servant of God," says the Apostle.[13] Now nothing is more foolish, nothing more distant from the stability of princely rule than to want to be feared by all, although some of the ancient and the modern emperors wanted nothing more than to be feared, and believed empire could not be maintained by any other force than fear and cruelty: I have read this explicitly attributed to the barbarian emperor Maximin.[14] But nothing is further from the truth than their opinions. It is in our interest to be loved, not feared, except perhaps in the way a loyal son fears a good father: certainly any other kind of fear is opposed to their intentions.
Some men want to rule for a long time and spend their life free of 17
risk, and being feared is opposed to both conditions, while being loved is in harmony with both. Fear takes away both duration and freedom from anxiety, while kindness bestows both, and to give more credit to the saying we should hear Cicero, or rather Truth speaking through Cicero's mouth:[15] "Of all things nothing is more suited to protect and retain one's wealth than being loved, nor more contrary than being feared," and soon after he says: "For fear is a bad preservative, whereas kindness is faithful unto eternity." And so you know that this is dear to his heart, he says elsewhere: "It is glorious to be a beloved citizen, to serve the state well, to be praised, respected and loved; but to be feared and hated is loathsome, detestable, weak and transient."[16] It is not relevant to talk 18
about freedom from anxiety here, since no one is so inexperienced or ignorant that he does not know this freedom is destroyed and extinguished by fear. At this point some people object, declaring that this fear is in the subjects but not the ruler, so that it is not

securitas quatiatur. Quibus ego pro responso notissimum illud obiciam Laberii, equitis romani, docti viri ac prudentis, in Iulium Cesarem:

Necesse est multos timeat quem multi timent.

19 Quod dictum, quo plus habeat virium, dicto alio simili et ipsius quem sepe nomino Ciceronis auctoritate firmandum est. 'Etenim,' inquit, 'qui se metui volent, a quibus metuantur, eosdem metuant ipsi necesse est.' Huius sententie rationem ne nos imitari pudeat, ab Ennio mutuatur. 'Preclare enim,' inquit, 'Ennius:

Quem metuunt oderunt, quem quisque odit perisse expetit.'

Addo ego: quod quisque expetit, fieri studet; ad quod multi autem
20 validis urgentur affectibus, vix differri potest. Que quamvis ita
sint, fuerunt tamen et sunt usque hodie qui dicant: 'Oderint dum
metuant.' Fuit hoc Atrei verbum crudelissimi tyranni ab Euripide
relatum. Id quotidiano usu Gaius Caligula nichilo Atreo mitior
21 suum fecit, nec inventori faustum nec sequacibus. Quo etiam uti
solitum Iulium Cesarem opinari aliqui et dicere voluerunt. Mirum
certe si verum. Nam ipse quidem, preter glorie et imperii appetitum, in quo multus, ne dicam nimius, fuit, omnia fecit quibus esset amabilis potius quam timendus, quadam hinc mansuetudine
atque clementia, hinc munificentia ac liberalitate mirabili, cum e
toto imperio omnibusque victoriis nichil sibi retinuerit, quod
magni testantur auctores, preter dispensandi potestatem, ad veniam vero tam facilis fuerit, ut de eo Cicero idem scribat quod
22 nichil soleret nisi iniurias oblivisci. Nobile quidem vindicte genus

his freedom but theirs that is shaken. I will offer as answer that notorious saying of Laberius the Roman knight, a learned and shrewd man, to Julius Caesar:

> That man whom many fear must fear them all.[17]

And to give more strength to that saying, it should be reinforced by another similar utterance and the authority of Cicero (whom I keep mentioning).[18] "For those" he says, "who want to be feared must themselves fear the same crowd of those who fear them." And so we are not ashamed to imitate the logic of this saying which he has borrowed from Ennius: "Ennius spoke splendidly," he says, "declaring: 19

> Whom people fear they hate; whom each man hates he wants to die."

Furthermore each man works to bring about what he wants; and the goal that many are driven to by powerful emotions can hardly
be forestalled. Though this is true, there have been and are still 20
men who say: "Let them hate, provided that they fear!" This was the motto of Atreus, that most cruel tyrant, reported by Euripides.[19] And Caligula, not a whit milder than Atreus, made it his own by daily use, a saying ill-omened to both its inventor and his
followers. Some have chosen to believe and declare that Julius 21
Caesar used to employ this maxim. This would be surprising if it were true. For besides his greed for glory and empire, which he indulged greatly, not to say excessively, he did everything to make himself lovable rather than an object of fear, in one case with mildness and clemency, in another by amazing lavishness and generosity, keeping back nothing for himself from the entire empire and all his victories, as great authors affirm,[20] except the power of distribution; indeed he was so ready to give pardon that Cicero writes about him that he used to forget nothing except wrongs.[21]
It is a noble form of vengeance to spare a man, and the most noble 22

est parcere, nobilissimum oblivisci, ut id sibi pro supremo nature bono suus ille nunc amicus nunc hostis attribuat. Quid multa? Usqueadeo his virtutibus, ut sileam reliquas, abundans fuit ut nemo magis, etsi ex his premia non sat digna perceperit, siquidem ab his ipsis quos opibus atque honoribus summis expleverat, quibus victor omne ius victorie, omnes inimicitias iniuriasque remiserat, interfectus est; nec eum liberalitas iuvit nec clementia, ut non immerito sibi pacuvianum illud in funere caneretur:

Men servasse, ut essent qui me perderent?

23 Quibus ita se habentibus, queri potest quenam sibi odium causa conflaverit; nempe odio coniuratio illa non caruit. Ego nullam invenio nisi insolentiam quandam elationemque animi, quod supra patrium morem sese attolleret, quod nimiis gauderet honoribus et dignitates indebitas usurparet. Nondum assueverat Roma cesareos fastus pati, quos postea longe disparium tales tulit, ut, facta collatione, mira illa videri possit humilitas. Si illum igitur talem virum nulla potentia, nulle opes adversus multorum odia protexerunt, restat inquirere quibus amor artibus sit querendus, quoniam, ut odium ruine, sic amor contrarii causa est: illud preci-
24 pitat, hic sustentat. Quid hic dicam nisi unam eandemque rationem esse amoris publici que privati est? 'Ego,' inquit Anneus Seneca, 'tibi monstrabo amatorium sine medicamento, sine herba, sine ullius venefice carmine: si vis amari, ama.' Sic est hercle. Et quamvis hic multa et varia dici possint, tamen hec omnium summa est: quid magicis opus est artibus? quid precio aliquo aut labore? Gratuita res est amor; solo queritur amore. Quis tam ferrei pectoris inveniri potest quem honeste amanti vicem reddere pigeat? Inhonestus enim amor non est amor, sed honesto nomine velatum

to forget, so that Cicero, sometimes his friend and sometimes his enemy, attributes this to him as the highest good of his nature. Need I say more? Caesar was so overflowing in these virtues, to pass over the others, that no other man could surpass him, even if he received an unworthy reward for them, since in fact he was killed by those whom he had heaped with wealth and honors, men for whom he as victor had renounced all the rights of victory, and all enmities and wrongs; neither his liberality nor his clemency came to his aid, so that the famous verse of Pacuvius was rightly sung at his funeral:

To think I saved them to survive and be my death.[22]

In this case one can ask what cause had generated hatred for 23
him, since that conspiracy was not free of hatred. I find no cause except a certain insolence and conceit of mind, because he exalted himself beyond ancestral custom, because he rejoiced too much in honors and claimed titles not owed to him. Rome had not yet accustomed herself to endure the arrogance of Caesars, which the city later endured from very different persons, such that once the comparison was made, Caesar's behavior seemed a marvelous humility. So if no power, no resources could protect him against the hatreds of many, it is left for us to investigate the art of winning love, given that, as hatred is the cause of ruin, so love causes its
opposite. The one casts down, the other raises up. What can I say 24
here except that there is one single way to public as to private love? Seneca says: "I will show you a love potion without a drug, without a plant, without the incantation of any poisoner; if you want to be loved, then love!"[23] That is surely so. And although there are many different points to mention here, this is the total of them all; why do you need magic arts? Why any fee or toil? Love comes for free; it is won only by love. Who could be found so iron-hearted that he grudges responding to an honorable lover? For dishonorable love is not love, but hatred disguised under an honorable

odium, non amore sed odio compensandum. Nam turpiter amantem redamare quid est aliud quam scelere scelus confovere et alieni flagitii fieri velle participem? Igitur hoc omisso ad honestum illum amorem alterum redeamus.

25 Ex quo utique magnum tibi et honestum gaudium nasci debet, qui te tuis ita carum sentias quasi non civium dominus sed patrie pater sis. Quod cognomen antiquorum principum fere omnium fuit, sed quorundam iuste admodum, quorundam iniuste adeo ut nichil iniustius. Pater patrie dictus est Augustus Cesar, pater patrie dictus est Nero; ille verus pater, iste verus hostis et patrie et pietatis. Tibi verum hoc cognomen obtigerit. Nullus est civium, eorum dico quibus pax ac requies patrie grate sunt, qui te aliter aspiciat, aliter cogitet quam parentem. Id ut factis meritum evoque perpetuum sit, eniti debes: et facies spero; facies admonitus oratusque quod iampridem per te ipsum facis. Scito autem hoc tibi pre-
26 stare solam posse iustitiam et civium caritatem. Vis esse verus civium pater? Quod filio tuo vis, et civibus tuis velis. Non iubeo ut tantundem unumquemque civium ames quantum filium, sed ut filium. Nam et Deus ipse summus legifer non dixit: 'Diliges proximum tuum' quantum te ipsum, sed 'sicut te ipsum'; hoc est pure, sine fictione, sine utilitatis aut premii respectu, nuda ac gratuita caritate. Audebo tamen dicere sine preiudicio verioris sententie: etsi non quemque civium, omnes tamen simul cives universamque rempublicam, non quantum filium modo vel parentes, sed quantum temet ipsum amare debes. In singulis enim caris capitibus singuli sunt affectus, in republica autem omnes. Amandi tibi sunt igitur cives tui ut filii, imo, ut sic dixerim, tanquam corporis tui membra sive anime tue partes: unum enim corpus est res publica

name, to be recompensed not with love but with hatred. To return love to someone loving shamefully is simply nourishing crime with crime and wanting to share in another's dirty deed. So let us leave this and return to that other honorable love.

At all events you should derive a great and honorable joy from 25
this, feeling yourself so dear to your people that you are not the citizens' master but the father of your country. This was the title of almost all the ancient emperors, but quite justly in some cases, whereas for certain others it was so unjust that nothing could have been more so. Augustus was called "father of his country."[24] Nero too was called father of his country, but the former was a true father, the latter the true enemy of both his country and of piety. But this title will fall to you in truth. There is no citizen, not among those who welcome the peace and repose of their country, who looks to you or thinks of you in anyway except as a father. You must strive to keep this deserved and long-lasting through your actions; and you will do so, I hope; you will do in response to advice and petition what you have long been doing on your own initiative. Know then that only justice and the affection of your
citizens can guarantee this. Do you want to be the citizens' true 26
father? Then you should want for your citizens what you want for your son. I am not bidding you love each and every citizen as much as your son, but like a son. For God, our highest legislator, did not say "love your neighbor" as much as yourself, but "like yourself,"[25] that is, sincerely, without pretense, without thought of utility or reward, out of bare unforced affection. However, I will dare to say, without prejudice to a truer sentiment: even if you cannot love each citizen, you ought still to love all your citizens together and the entire community, not like a son or parents, but as much as yourself. For toward beloved individuals we have individual affections, but we give all our affections to the community. So you must love your citizens like sons, or rather, so to speak, like the limbs of your body or parts of your soul, since the

27 cuius tu caput es. Amor autem hic et lenibus verbis et multo maxime piis panditur actibus, atque in primis, ut dicebam, iustitia et pietate. Quis non amet enim quem pium, quem iustum, quem innoxium, quem sui amantem opinetur? Quod si amori beneficia accesserint, qualia sunt bonorum principum in subiectos, tunc exardescit incredibilis quedam benivolentie magnitudo, quo nexu ad perpetuum dominatum nullus pulcrior, nullus firmior texi potest. Secedant arma satellites stipendiarii tube buccine; in hostes ista vertantur; tibi cum civibus non nisi benivolentia opus est. 'Caritate' enim, inquit Cicero, 'et benivolentia civium septum oportet esse, non armis.'

28 Eos autem cives intelligo qui civitatis amant statum, non eos qui quotidianas mutationes rerum querunt; illi enim non cives sed rebelles atque hostes publici extimandi sunt. Sepe Augustum ipsa in medium res adducit. Huius est notissimum illud: 'Quisquis presentem statum civitatis commutari non vult, et civis et vir bonus est.' Itaque qui contrarium vult, proculdubio malus, nec civium nec virorum bonorum nomine dignus aut consortio. His te autem artibus natura tua instruit abunde, quibus amor et benivolentia queri possint. He sunt autem non ad gloriam modo sed ad celum scale, unde ille bonus pater optimum filium alloquens: 'Cole,' inquit, 'iustitiam et pietatem, que, cum sit magna in parentibus et propinquis, tum in patria maxima est; et ea vita via est in celum.' Quis amator celi viam, qua ad celum pergitur, non amaret? [§29–35 *omissis*]

36 Illud iustitie de qua loquor, munus eximium lateque latissimum, ius suum cuique tribuere, nulli sine ingenti causa nocere, et, causa quamvis affuerit, ad misericordiam inclinare imitantem celestis iudicis eternique regis morem. Cum misericordia enim

community is one body, and you are its head. This love expresses itself in gentle words and most of all in pious actions, particularly, as I said, in justice and piety. Who would not love the man he thinks pious and just, honest and fond of him? And if kindnesses are added to love, like the actions of good princes to their subjects, then an incredible quantity of goodwill is kindled, unsurpassed by any other bond that can be woven in the splendor and firmness of lasting lordship. Away with weapons, henchmen, mercenaries, trumpets and bugles; let them turn on the enemy; you need nothing but kindness in dealing with your citizens. Cicero says: "One ought to be surrounded by the affection and goodwill of citizens, not by weapons."[26] 27

I consider those men as citizens who love the stable condition of the state, not those who aim at daily transformations of affairs; they should not be thought citizens but rebels and public enemies. Often this very topic naturally brings Augustus into the argument. That famous comment comes from him: "Whoever does not want the present condition of the state to be changed is a citizen and a good man."[27] Hence the man who wants the opposite is undoubtedly bad, unworthy of the name or association with citizens or decent men. Your nature has equipped you abundantly with these arts by which love and goodwill can be won. These are also steps not just to glory but to heaven, from which that good father addressed his excellent son, saying: "Cultivate justice and piety, which, great as it is toward parents and kinsmen, is also greatest toward one's country, and such a life is the way to heaven."[28] What lover would not love the way that leads to heaven? [§§29–35 *omitted*] 28

The exceptional and by far the broadest service of justice that I am talking about is to render to each man what is his right, harming no one without a serious reason, and even if there is a reason, to tend toward mercy, imitating the behavior of the Heavenly Judge and Eternal King.[29] While mercy is necessary for all because 36

omnibus necessaria eo quod a peccato nemo prorsus immunis sit et, propter fragilitatem nostre conditionis, omnibus ferme sit debita, consequens est ut, qui vere iustus esse voluerit, et misericors sit. Quamvis ergo misericordia et iustitia prima fronte contrarie videantur, recto iudicio inseparabiliter sunt coniuncte; imo quidem 'liquet iustitiam esse misericordiam et misericordiam esse iustitiam' (quod preclare in libro *De obitu Theodosii* imperatoris sacer ait Ambrosius), ut iam non coniuncte tantummodo sed unum
37 sint. Nec ideo tamen illud exigitur ut sicariis proditoribus atque veneficis ceterisque id genus impunitas tribuatur, ne, dum in paucos misericors vis videri, sis crudelis in plurimos; sed, ut levitate lapsis atque errore, si sine exempli periculo fieri potest, misericordia non negetur. Alioquin fieri potest ut nimia misericordia et
38 indiscreta lenitas sit magna crudelitas. Illud preterea ad amorem civium promerendum efficax, si rector populi non iustus modo, sed beneficus sit in suos, quod si non possit in singulos, at saltem in universos: vix est enim qui diligat a quo boni nichil vel publice vel privatim speret. De amore illo loquor quo amantur principes. Amicorum enim alius quidam amor est sese contentus, nilque vel
39 postulans vel expectans. Hoc in genere est templorum refectio et publicorum edificiorum, in quo quidem ante omnes laudatus est Augustus Cesar, ut eum merito Titus Livius 'templorum omnium conditorem aut restitutorem' dicat, et ipse, quod Tranquillus ait, 'iure sit gloriatus urbem se marmoream relinquere quam lateritiam accepisset.' His accedit et murorum urbis edificatio, que res in primis clarum nomen Aureliano peperit, truculento alioquin et sanguinario principi. Qui cum non amplius quam sex annos eosque non integros imperaverit, in tam parvo tempore 'muros urbis Rome,' quos usque nunc cernimus, 'sic ampliavit ut,' sicut Flavius Vopiscus historicus, illorum credo temporum mensuram secutus, ait, 'quinquaginta prope milia passuum murorum eius ambitus

no one is quite immune from sinning, and given the frailty of our condition it is due to virtually everyone, it follows that whoever wants to be truly just should also be compassionate. Now although mercy and justice seem at first sight to be opposed, in correct judgment they are inseparably joined together; in fact "it is clear that justice is pity and pity justice" (as Saint Ambrose expresses it splendidly in his book *On the Death of Theodosius*),[30] so
that they are not just joined together but a unity. Yet what is re- 37
quired is not that cutthroats and traitors and poisoners and such may be offered impunity—you don't want to be cruel to the majority just so you may seem compassionate to the few—but that mercy will not be denied to those who have failed through carelessness and error, if this is possible without risk of setting a precedent.[31] Otherwise it is equally possible that excessive compassion
and indiscriminate leniency entails great cruelty. Besides, it is an 38
effective way of winning the citizens' love if the people's ruler is not simply just but kind toward his people, and if he cannot achieve this for individuals, he should at least show kindness to the people as a whole. Indeed, hardly anyone will love a man from whom he expects neither public nor private good. I am talking of the kind of love shown toward princes. For the love of friends is different, content with itself, neither expecting nor demanding
anything. In this category comes the restoration of sacred and 39
public buildings, for which Augustus was praised beyond all others, so that Livy rightly calls him "founder and restorer of all temples" and according to Suetonius he himself "was justified in boasting that he left a marble city behind him when he had found it made of brick."[32] Add to this the construction of city walls, the chief source of fame and glory to Aurelian, who was otherwise a savage and bloodthirsty prince. Although he ruled no longer than six years, and those incomplete, in such a short time "he so expanded the walls of the city of Rome," which we see to this day, "that they had a perimeter of almost fifty miles," as the historian

teneant.' Qua in re, maiorum industrie gratiam habe, qui hanc tibi partem solicitudinis abstulerunt; ut nesciam an ulla usquam, vel externarum urbium vel nostrarum, muris nobilioribus cincta sit quam patria tua est.

40 Nec minorem ego illos curam viarum quam murorum habuisse arbitror; etsi enim muri tutum presidium bello sint, vie sunt pacis gratissimum ornamentum. Hoc interest: quod muri in longum evum mole sua stant, vie autem, assiduo usu hominum et presertim equis atque ante omnia nostris his tartareis curribus, deteruntur quos ego, fateor pro virili parte, optarem nondum Erithonius invenisset; ita non vias tantum sed domorum fundamenta atque in eis habitantium et boni aliquid mente volventium corda concutiunt. His tu nunc igitur opem fer, longa etate convulsis tuumque auxilium, tacita deformitate, poscentibus; non te his difficilem
41 prebere debes. Huius enim non tantum patrie civibusque tuis es debitor, cui et patrie decor et civium honesta solatia cure esse debent—suntque, non dubito—sed id ipsum tibi etiam debes. Ex omnibus namque, non modo principibus sed cuiuscunque status hominibus, alium non videor vidisse, preter unum clare memorie genitorem tuum, qui tam diu et tam sepe equo patriam permearet. Neque in vobis morem improbo, quibus unum studium unaque reipublice cura est; civibus nempe fidelibus conspectus boni principis periocundus est. Curare igitur debes ut quod libentissime facis, securissime facias; ut, periculo et difficultate cessantibus, ex equestri vectatione facilem atque honestam percipias voluptatem. Committe igitur rem istam alicui viro bono tuique et reipublice studioso, neu metuas ne famoso ornatoque homini officii vilioris iniuriam inferre videaris. Animo enim bene instituto et egregio civi nichil vile videbitur quod ad obsequium patrie iubeatur.

Flavius Vopiscus says, following the calculations of those times.[33] In this matter be thankful to the energy of your ancestors who took away this part of your cares, so that I doubt any city anywhere, either among our Italian cities or foreign ones, is surrounded with more noble walls than your country.

And I do not think they showed less concern for roads than for 40
fortifications: even if walls are a safe protection in war, roads are
the most welcome adornment of peace. The difference is that walls
stand for a long period by their own mass, but roads are worn
away by men's constant use and especially by horses and beyond all
else by these infernal chariots of ours which I wish, as I will
stoutly admit, that Erithonius had not yet invented,[34] so badly do
they shake up not only roads but the foundations of houses and
the hearts of their occupants and men trying to deliberate on some
good purpose. So do now bring aid to these roads, broken down
by the long passage of time and in their silent disfigurement demanding your help; you ought not to oppose them. You owe this 41
debt not only to your country and citizens, since the beauty of your country and the honorable comfort of your citizens should be your concern—as they are, I don't doubt—but you owe just this to yourself. Indeed I don't believe I have seen anyone else, not only among all princes but all men of any rank—except your father of glorious memory—who traveled over his country on horseback so long and so often as you. Not that I reproach your practice, since your one object of devotion and concern is for your state; in fact the sight of a good prince is most pleasant to loyal citizens.[35] Hence you should take pains to do what you most enjoy doing with the utmost concern for safety, so that when danger and difficulty retreat, you may enjoy an easy and honorable pleasure from your riding. Accordingly, entrust this task to some good man devoted to you and the community, and don't be afraid of seeming to impose the insult of a lower office on an honored and distinguished man. Nothing ordered as service to his country will seem

42 Historiam locus hic exigit. Fuit Thebis vir fortissimus simulque doctissimus Epaminondas quem, si seposita fortuna que indignos sepe concelebrat sola virtus attenditur, aut Grecie principem aut unum ex paucissimis dixisse non verear. Huic tali viro, cum quo 'manifestum est patrie gloriam et natam et extinctam fuisse' (sic enim de illo verissime scriptum est), infensi cives, quod crebrum liberis in urbibus est malum, 'sternendarum viarum,' quod apud eos vilissimum habebatur, officium commisere, ut vel sic spectatam viri gloriam obscurarent. Ille nec ferro nec saltem verbo ultus iniuriam, prompto animo commissum munus excipiens: 'Curabo, ait, ne tam michi delati ministerii obsit indignitas, quam ut mea illi dignitas prosit, ut ex abiecto atque ignobili meas inter manus nobilissimum fiat.' Id enim vero splendida mox administratione sic prestitit, ut, despectum plebeis quoque, negotium illustribus etiam exoptandum linqueret. Idem ego, nunc, cuicunque industrio ac fideli viro opus hoc mandaveris eventurum spero ut certatim multi postea idem petant atque ita, paulatim caritate civium, vetus patria iuvenescat.

43 Unum michi nunc pene ridiculum occurrit ut scribam, de quo scilicet presens nuper tecum egi nostros inter libellos, cum ad me visendum tunc venisses, quem honorem michi indigno sepe dignatio tua prestat. Ante oculos autem res erat unde oblata materia est sermoni. Est autem talis patria quidem tua et nobilitate civium et fertilitate locorum et vetustate venerabilis, et ipsa etiam urbe Roma seculis multis antiquior; denique et Studio ornata et clero ac religionibus et sacris, et insignibus locis, et, ad ultimum, Prosdocimoque pontifice et Antonio iuniore et Iustina virgine,

low to a well-educated mind and distinguished citizen. There was 42
a most gallant and learned man at Thebes called Epaminondas, and if virtue alone is considered, setting aside fortune which often makes famous the unworthy, I would not have feared to call him either the leading man of Greece or one of the very few.[36] But the hostility of his fellow citizens (a frequent evil in free cities) against so fine a person, "with whom it is clear the glory of his country was both born and extinguished" (so it was most truly written of him)[37] entrusted to him the role of "road maker," which was thought by them to be extremely humble: they hoped to eclipse the man's established glory in this way. He did not avenge the insult either by violence or even abuse, but taking up the duty with willing spirit said: "I shall make sure that the indignity of the task delegated is not as much of a detriment to me as my dignity is an asset to it, so that from being base and humble it becomes most noble in my hands."[38] And truly he guaranteed by his splendid administration that he left a job despised even by the common people in a state that even distinguished men found it desirable. So I hope now that, no matter which hardworking and reliable man you entrust with this task, it will turn out that hereafter there will be many competing for it and so the old city will gradually regain its youth through the affection of its citizens.

Now I come to writing about something almost absurd, which 43
I recently discussed with you in person among our little books on the occasion when you came to visit me, an honor which your condescension frequently offers me, unworthy as I am. For the subject providing the material of our discussion was in front of us. Your country is splendid in the nobility of its citizens and fertility of its landscape and venerable in its antiquity, being many centuries older than the city of Rome itself; furthermore it is adorned by a university and clergy and religious rites and holy and prestigious places, and finally by Bishop Prosdocimus and the younger Antonius and the virgin Justina, and—not, I think, as you also

quodque nec ego reor contemnendum nec tu reri debes, et te do-
44 mino ac rectore, et virgiliano tandem carmine nobilis; hec urbs,
inquam, talis, tot preclara fulgoribus, te spectante nec obstante
cum possis, ceu rus horridum ineptumque, porcorum gregibus
deformatur: passim, quocunque te verteris, grunnientes audias so-
lumque suffodientes aspicias; fedum spectaculum, tristis sonus.
Que nos utcunque iam longa consuetudine toleramus, advene sunt
qui arguunt et mirantur. Quod cum merito omnibus odiosum sit,
nulli tamen odiosius quam equitantibus esse debet, quibus cum
semper importunum sepe quoque periculosum est, dum occursu
fedi et intractabilis animantis equi in stuporem et nonnunquam in
45 precipitium impelluntur. De hoc ergo cum tecum agerem, dixisti
statutum populi vetus esse ne id fieret, penamque additam ut porcos in publico repertos auferre volentibus liceret. Sed an nescis, ut
homines, sic humana cunta senescere? Senescunt pene iam romane leges, et nisi in scolis assidue legerentur, iam proculdubio
senuissent: quid statutis municipalibus eventurum putas? Ut statutum igitur illud antiquum valeat, renovandum, et voce preconia
publicandum est, penis vel eisdem vel gravioribus appositis. Sub-
mittendi aliqui preterea qui vagantes porcos eripiant ut, vel damno
admoniti, urbani isti pastores intelligant non licere eis quod publice leges vetant omnibus. Qui porcos habent, rure eos alant; qui
rus non habent, domi eos includant; quibus autem non est domus,
nec civium domos nec honorabilem aspectum patrie dehonestent,
nec famosam urbem Patavum aram fecisse porcorum, quia libitum
46 et licitum, arbitrentur. Frivola ista fortasse dicat aliquis; ego nec

should, to be treated contemptuously—with you as its lord and
guide and in its renown for Vergil's poetry.[39] This fine city, I say, 44
glorious with so many brilliant monuments, is disfigured, even as you look on without hindering it, as you might, by herds of pigs, like some rough and clumsy country place: wherever you turn you may hear them snorting at random and see them uproot the ground; a loathsome sight and an ugly noise. We at any rate have come to endure this after habituating ourselves to it over such a long time, but there are visitors who condemn it and express amazement. While this is rightly distasteful to all, it must be most detestable to those on horseback: an encounter is always unwelcome but often dangerous, as horses are sent into a daze and sometimes stumble headlong at the encounter with this vile and
unmanageable creature. Hence, when I was discussing this with 45
you, you said there was an ancient statute of the people to forbid it, with a penalty attached, authorizing anyone who wanted to, to carry off pigs found wandering in the public way: but don't you know that, like human beings, all human sanctions grow old? Now even Roman laws are aging and if they weren't read constantly in class would undoubtedly have become obsolete; what do you think will become of municipal statutes? To give strength to that old statute it must be repeated and broadcast by the herald, attaching to it either the same or heavier penalties. And men must be sent out to catch those wandering pigs; and once reminded by their losses, those urban grazers must understand they are not allowed to do what public laws forbid to everyone. If men keep pigs, let them fatten them in the countryside; if they don't have a country place let them shut the pigs up at home; if they don't have a home they should not dishonor either the houses of citizens or the distinguished appearance of their country, nor think they should make their celebrated country of Padua a sty for pigs, just
because it is allowed and they choose to do it. Someone may per- 46
haps call this trivial, but I maintain it is neither trivial nor beneath

frivola nec spernenda contendo. Restituenda maiestas sua est urbi nobili et antique, non in magnis tantummodo, sed in parvis, nec in his solum que ad intimum reipublice statum sed que ad exteriorem quoque pertinent ornatum, ut oculi etiam partem suam de comuni felicitate percipiant, et cives mutata civitatis facie glorientur et gaudeant, nec se villam sed urbem ingressos sentiant peregrini. Hoc patrie debitum, hoc te dignum maximeque tuum censeo. Et de hoc quidem, pro re, satis est dictum.

47 Unum subinde nunc aliud ex his oritur, ut, viis publicis intra et circa urbem reformatis, paludum in circuitu proxime siccandarum studium solicita pietate suscipias. Nullo enim modo alio pulcerrime regionis faciem sic ornare potes, et paludibus his obsessos colles euganeos, late notos ac Minerve ramis et Bachi insignis uberrimo palmite nobiles, sic in veram telluris optime speciem reformare, quin et Cereri excluse pinguia arva restituere, que nunc fedus et supervacuus humor premit. Ita undique utilitas cum decore certabit, tuque multiplicem tibi laudem unico labore conflave-
48 ris. Arripe, queso, et hanc glorie partem quam maiores tui omnes seu non viderunt seu spreverunt seu aggredi timuerunt. Tibi tam pio in opere Deus aderit. Nam natura adest utique, quod paludes pene omnes altioribus locis sunt, ut ad infima derivari vel in flumina proxima vel vicinum in mare perfacile valeant, quo et presentibus terre uber et locorum forma et celi serenitas salubritasque proveniat, et posteris vel ob hoc unum tui nominis eterna memoria. Etsi autem, quod indignans sepe audio, his otii inertis amatoribus res impossibilis videatur, est tamen, quod sensus ipse indicat quodque incole testantur, non possibilis modo sed facilis.

notice. The reverence due this noble and ancient city must be restored, not just in great aspects but in small, and not just in those that concern the innermost condition of the city but also those affecting its external grooming, so that the eyes too may receive their share of the common felicity and the citizens be proud and rejoice in the changed appearance of the community, and foreigners will realize they have not entered a country house, but a city. We owe this to our country and I hold this worthy of you and your role in particular. And that is enough and proper to this topic.

Next another issue arises from this, that once the public roads 47
are restored inside and outside the walls, you must take up conscientiously the task of draining the marshes in the immediate vicinity. There is no other way that you can adorn the appearance of this most handsome region so as to remodel these Euganean Hills, now beset by marshes but known far and wide and ennobled by Minerva's olive branches and the most fertile tendrils of Bacchus' finest wine, making them into a genuine display of the best landscape. You can even restore the fertile fields of Ceres whose grain has been excluded from fields that are now sodden with a loathsome flood of moisture.[40] So utility will compete everywhere with
beauty and you will earn many kinds of praise from one effort. I 48
beg you, seize on this contribution to glory which all your ancestors either did not see or disregarded or feared to tackle. God will support you in so pious a task. Nature is on your side. Almost all the marshes are on higher ground so that they can easily be channeled into either low-lying nearby rivers or the neighboring sea, so as to produce fertility in the soil and a contoured landscape and a sunny and healthy climate for men of this generation, and an everlasting memory of your name with posterity, thanks this one measure. Even if, as I often hear with indignation, the enterprise seems impossible to these lovers of sluggish idleness, it is still not just possible but easy, as our good sense suggests and the

Aggredere tandem, vir magnanime: pium conatum prosper eventus excipiet. [§§49–50 *omissis*]

51 Neque enim infitior neque ignoro ei, cui reipublice cura commissa est, summo opere providendum ut inutilibus ac superfluis impensis abstineat, ne exhaustum vanis erarium necessariis non sufficiat. Nichil igitur effundat, nil omnino faciat nisi quod ad decus aut commodum pertineat civitatis cui presidet aut regni; sic ad summam agat omnia ut administrator non ut dominus. Philosophicum nempe consilium est in *Politicis* latius expositum, et usu utile deprehensum et consonum equitati. Ceteri enim non rectores
52 atque conservatores urbium sed predones sunt. Semper illud ergo meminerit quod ab Hadriano principe, iuste nescio magis an civiliter, dictum est. De quo Elius Spartianus ita scribit: 'Et in contione et in senatu sepe dixit ita se rempublicam gesturum, ut sciret populi rem esse, non propriam.' Ita, inquam, agat omnia ut rationem de omnibus redditurus; utique enim rationem reddere habet, etsi non hominibus, at Deo. Et certe rationarium imperii Augustum Cesarem egrotantem senatui reddidisse notissimum est; et quisquis bonam honestamque vitam agere instituit, quocunque in statu sit, ita se gerit, ita cunta circumspicit, ut, etsi nulli teneatur, possit tamen omnibus reddere rationem causamque probabilem: hec est enim fere, ut vult Cicero, 'descriptio officii' quod
53 qui negligit, et virtutem ipsam negligat oportet. Quid autem refert alteri non teneri, cum sibi ipsi sueque conscientie animus teneatur, cui nisi satisfaciat, tristis et anxia vita sit? Iure ergo laudatur illud non optimi licet principis, optimum tamen et generose fidutie

locals bear witness. So tackle it, greathearted man, and a prosperous outcome will follow from your pious undertaking. [*§§49–50 omitted*]

51 I don't deny and am well aware that the prince who has been entrusted with care of the state must take great pains to refrain from unprofitable and superfluous expenses, to ensure that the treasury is not emptied by follies and unable to meet essential needs. So he should not squander anything or take any action at all except what concerns the beauty or advantage of the state or kingdom over which he presides; in short let him act in all respects as an administrator, not a master. In fact there is a philosophical recommendation set out rather fully in Aristotle's *Politics*, recognized as both useful and consistent with fairness.[41] All other
princes are not guides and preservers of cities, but brigands. So he 52
should always remember what the emperor Hadrian said, whether with greater justice or greater civility I am unable to say. Aelius Spartianus writes about this emperor: "Both in the assembly and the senate he often said he would conduct affairs of state knowing that it was the people's state and not his own."[42] I am saying, let the prince carry out all decisions just as if he is going to render an account of them all, for necessarily he must render an account, if not to men, then to God. Certainly it is a well known fact that when Augustus was taken ill he handed over his accounting tablets of the empire to the senate;[43] and whoever has begun to live a good and honorable life, whatever his condition, conducts himself and pays attention to everything so that even if he is indebted to no one he can still render an account and convincing explanation to all; this is more or less, as Cicero puts it, "the definition of a
duty," and anyone who neglects it must neglect virtue itself.[44] For 53
what is the advantage of not being beholden to another, when each man's heart is bound to himself and his conscience? Life would be grim and anxious if he did not satisfy himself. So that saying deserves praise and, though not from a great emperor, these are still

plenum verbum in senatu habitum: 'Dabo,' inquit Tiberius, 'operam ut rationem factorum meorum dictorumque reddam.' En plus
aliquid quam quod querebamus, non factorum modo sed dic-
54 torum ratio. Circa publicorum sane sumptuum parcitatem illud
Vespasiani principis considerare profuerit, qui, licet multa publice
decora liberaliter fecisset, tamen artifici columnas ingentes parvo
sumptu se in Capitolium pervecturum promittenti, dignum quidem ingenii precium dedit, at operam non admisit, et 'Sine,' inquit, 'me plebeculam meam pane pascere.' Pia prorsus boni principis et laudabilis cura omni studio famem plebis arcere sobriamque
simul copiam comitemque illius honestam letitiam procurare. Siquidem illud Aureliani principis dictum: 'Neque enim populo romano saturo quicquam potest esse letius,' eque ad omnes populos
trahi potest, quos non tam virtutum, quam victualium contristat
inopia: sic populorum omnium felicitas in corpore potius quam in
55 animo sita est. Ex hac nempe solicitudine non modo gaudium
popularium procedit, sed etiam securitas presidentium. Nichil est
enim terribilius plebe famelica de qua dictum est:

nescit plebs ieiuna timere.

Idque non tantum veteribus scriptis, sed exemplis sepe recentibus et presertim Rome nuper innotuit. Hoc in genere maxime Iulii Cesaris laudatur industria, quod et bellis gallicis atque germanicis huic cure semper intentissimus fuerit, et reversus Romam nichilo segnior, ad conquirendum frumentum necessitatibus populi succursurum, navigia per frugiferas insulas sedula intentione disperserit; neque minus Augusti Cesaris, de quo scribitur quod 'frumentum in annone difficultatibus sepe levissimo, interdum nullo precio

great words pronounced in the Senate and full of generous confidence: "I will see to it," Tiberius said, "that I render an account to you of my actions and sayings."[45] Here is something beyond what we were looking for, an account not only of one's actions but of one's words. As to economy in public expenses, it will be beneficial 54
to keep in mind the thrift of Vespasian, who despite generosity in providing many public embellishments, demurred when a craftsman said he would convey huge columns cheaply onto the Capitol. He gave the man a fee worthy of his talent, but did not commission his work, saying: "Let me feed my humble folk their bread."[46] It is utterly pious and praiseworthy on the part of a good prince to strive with all his power to keep hunger from his common people and at the same time to provide a sober sufficiency and the cheerfulness that is its honorable accompaniment. Indeed that saying of the emperor Aurelian, "nothing can be more cheerful than the Roman people when well fed,"[47] can be applied to all nations, since they are made gloomy less by a shortage of virtues than of victuals; so the happiness of all peoples rests in their body rather than their soul. From this princely concern comes not only the rejoicing of 55
the people but the freedom from anxiety of those holding office over them. For nothing is more terrible than a starving populace, as the poet said:

The hungry rabble knows no fear.[48]

And this is known not just from ancient writings but often from recent instances and particularly at Rome.[49] Julius Caesar's energetic action meets the greatest praise in this respect; in the Gallic and German wars he was always most focused on this responsibility and no more remiss when he returned to Rome: in order to import grain that would relieve the need of the people he sent out vessels to the islands productive of grain with keen attention.[50] This was no less a concern of Augustus; it is reported about him that "he distributed to each man grain during difficult periods

viritim' populo distribuit. Et hec quidem ita demum vera principis laus est si non adulandi animo, ut multi solent populos mulcere quo patientiores habeant liberiusque decorient, sed vera et patria
56 fit pietate. Quod in ipso Augusto clare patuit, qui cum populum fame laborantem nunc, ut dixi, levi precio nunc gratuita liberalitate relevasset, de vini inopia lamentantes acri et sobria oratione redarguit, ut constaret non blandum principem sed salubrem esse et amantem populi. Dixit enim urbem Romam aque ductibus abundare quibus siti hominum esset occursum: idque a Marco Agrippa, genero suo, factum ait, et siluit Tiberim menibus illabentem. Et revera non est par frumenti ratio et vini: cum illud vite necessarium sit semper, hoc sepe damnosum. Neque tamen hoc minus populo placuisset, voluptaria prope quam necessaria plus amanti; verum optimus ac providentissimus princeps non quod delectaret,
57 sed quod prodesset attendit. Hec nimirum cura frumentaria tam principum sua est, ut eam malis quoque et inertibus fuisse comperiam: ex quo quanta bonis esse debeat, pronum sit advertere. Qua te tamen, magna ex parte, Deus liberat ac natura earum regionum quibus presides, ubertate que prestat, ut sepius aliis subvenire soleas quam ab aliis mendicare. Consilium est tamen, ut, in prosperis quoque, paratus sit animus ad adversa, et velut e specula, non quid est tantum, sed quid esse possit vigili cogitatione prospiciat, nequa eum inopina mutatio rerum turbet.

Hactenus necessaria, nescio an pluribus an paucioribus quam
58 necesse erat, attigerim. Nam illa in viscerationibus ac ludis circensibus et ferarum peregrinarum exhibitione luxuria, ad nichil utilis, delectationem solam ac libidinem oculorum habens brevem nec honestam quidem nec honestis dignam oculis, quamvis insano

of supply, often at the lowest price and sometimes at no cost."[51] In
fact this is the true praise of a prince if he does this, not as a blan-
dishment, as many often soothe the people to increase their patience and strip them more freely, but as an act of true and ancestral piety. This was openly revealed in Augustus: when he had 56
relieved the people suffering from hunger now by cutting prices, as
I said, and now by free gift, and they lamented a shortage of wine,
he retorted with a sharp and sober speech, so that he was clearly
not a wheedling prince but a beneficial one who loved the people.
For he said the city of Rome was overflowing with aqueducts to
counter men's thirst and this had been taken care of by his son-in-
law Agrippa, and he passed over in silence the Tiber which glided
beneath its walls. And really the supply of bread and wine are very
different issues: if bread is always necessary to life, wine is often
ruinous. This would not have appealed to the people, who love
their pleasures more than necessities, but that excellent and most
prudent emperor paid attention, not to what gave pleasure, but to
what would do them good. This concern for grain supplies is so 57
much peculiar to princes that I find it existed even in bad and lazy
ones; and it is easy to argue from this how great this must be in
good princes. However, God and the nature of the districts over
which you rule free you largely from it, thanks to the exceptional
fertility that nature provides, so that you more often come to others' aid than beg from others. Nevertheless, my advice is that your
spirit should be ready for adversity even in times of prosperity, and
look out as if from a watchtower with alert calculation to see not
only what is happening but what could happen, so that a sudden
reversal cannot cause a disturbance.

So much for necessities; I don't know whether I have covered
them in more or fewer words than was needed. Indeed that parade 58
of luxury in the distribution of meat and chariot races and the
display of foreign wild beasts to no purpose offers only the amusement and lust of the eyes, short and not even honorable, nor

pessimoque rerum iudici vulgo grata, repudianda tamen est penitus. [§§59–67 *omissis*]

68 Nisi autem vel belli, ut nuper tibi, vel aliqua ineluctabilis difficultas inciderit, quicunque dominis lucra de suorum damnis ostentant, qui est aulicorum fere omnium mos vulgaris, ita illos ut anime fameque sue hostes aspiciant. Incitant dominos ut cum illorum invidia furentur et rapiant, genus hominum nequissimum populos torquentium dominosque fallentium, simulque alios se-
69 que perdentium. De quibus vera et memorabilis est illa sententia Marii Maximi cuius Elius Lampridius meminit in historia Alexandri principis (ipsa enim verba posui): 'meliorem esse rempublicam, et prope tutiorem, in qua princeps malus est, ea, in qua sunt amici principis mali, siquidem unus malus potest a plurimis bonis corrigi, multi autem mali non possunt ab uno, quamvis bono, ulla ratione superari.' Idcirco idem Alexander bonus princeps fuit, quod, preter insitam animo virtutem, amicos, ut ibidem scribitur, 'sanctos et venerabiles habuit, non malitiosos, non furaces, non factiosos, non callidos, non ad malum consentientes, non bonorum inimicos, non libidinosos, non crudeles, non circumventores sui, non irrisores, non qui illum quasi fatuum circumducerent, sed sanctos venerabiles continentes religiosos amantes principis sui et qui de illo nec ipsi riderent nec eum risui esse vellent, qui nichil venderent, nichil mentirentur, nichil fingerent, nunquam decipe-
70 rent extimationem principis sui, ut se amarent.' Et hec quidem ille: tales ergo amici optandi principibus querendique; alii autem, ut et principum pestis et publica, quasi hostes excludendi vitandique sunt. Malarum artium doctores, ut qui bonas et nesciunt et oderunt, in primis eam, qua ipsi estuant, avaritiam dominos suos
71 docent ut, si persuaserint, discipulos se peiores faciant. Est enim

worthy of honorable eyes, although it is welcome to the mad crowd, vicious judge of events: but it must be utterly rejected. [*§§59–67 omitted*]

So unless some troubles of war—as in your case[52]—or other inescapable difficulty befalls you, the men who boast to their princes of profits at the expense of his people, which is the common behavior of most courtiers, should be seen as enemies of his life and repute. They urge their lords to steal and rob to their discredit, a most worthless group of fellows who torment the common people and cheat their lords, ruining others and themselves 68
together. In their case the saying of Marius Maximus, quoted by 69
Aelius Lampridius in the story of the emperor Alexander, is both true and unforgettable (I have recorded the actual words):[53] "The state is better and safer in which the prince is bad than the one in which he has bad friends, since in fact one bad man can be set right by several good ones, but many bad men cannot be overcome by one individual, however good." That is why this Alexander was a good emperor: because, besides his innate virtue, he had, as is written in the same passage, "holy and reverend friends, not spiteful nor thieving nor quarrelsome nor cunning, not agreeing to a bad purpose, not enemies of good men, not lustful, not cruel, not cheating him nor mocking him, not men who led him around by the nose like a fool, but holy, reverend, controlled, religious, loving their emperor, neither laughing at him nor wanting him to be laughed at, who sold nothing and told no lies and invented nothing, never deceiving the judgment of their emperor for the love of
their own selves." That is the comment of Maximus; so princes 70
should desire and seek out such friends, whereas those others, like a plague on emperors and the people, should be shut out and shunned like enemies. They are teachers of evil arts, since they do not know and they shun good ones: they particularly teach their lords that avarice with which they seethe, so that if they convince
them, they can make their pupils more rotten than themselves. For 71

avaritia privatorum mala, principum vero longe pessima, quo et plus licentie habet ad nocendum et, quo pulcrior est rerum vilium contemptus in principe, eo admiratio atque aviditas est turpior. [*§§72–73 omissis*]

74 Et de aulicis quidem (quibus bonis nichil est melius, sed id rarum; quibus malis nichil est peius, et id crebrum), de his, inquam, ultimis sententiam meam habes; imo non meam sed Dioclitiani, qui, nisi tam impius fuisset in religionem nostram, ascribi non immerito claris principibus potuisset. Eius ergo de his verba sunt hec, memorabilia nisi fallor, sic ad literam descripta in libro de vita Aureliani: 'Colligunt se,' inquit, 'quattuor vel quinque atque unum consilium ad decipiendum imperatorem capiunt, dicunt quid probandum sit. Imperator, qui domi clausus est, vera non novit; cogitur hoc tantum scire quod illi loquuntur; facit iudices quos fieri non oportet; amovet a republica quos debeat obtinere. Quid multa? Ut Dioclitianus ipse dicebat, "bonus, cautus, optimus venditur imperator,"' His atque aliis inductus, cum iam deposuisset imperium, concludebat 'nichil esse difficilius quam bene imperare.' Et vere sic est. Non putent principes felicitatem sibi simulque facilitatem obtigisse; felicitatem qualemcunque, certe difficillimam consecuti sunt. Qui michi non credit, principi saltem experto credat.

75 Hac in parte, unum hoc monere satis atque hortari vix sufficio, nequem talium sic commisse tibi patrie preficias, ut alius dominus sit quam tu. Fuerunt enim multi in imperio qui, dum suos attollere cupiunt, sese depresserunt et contemptibiles atque invisos populis effecerunt, per eos ipsos, quos ad alta promoverant, venditi et irrisi. In quo maxime Claudius, qui Neronem precessit in imperio, vilis est habitus, qui libertos suos, nullius precii homines, Posiden

the avarice of private men is bad, but that of princes is far worse, since they have more license to do harm and, just as contempt for worthless possession is nobler in a prince, so admiration and greed is more shameful. [*§§72–73 omitted*]

And you have my judgment now about courtiers (nothing is 74
better than good ones, but that is rare: nothing is worse than bad ones and they are frequent) that is, about these last mentioned. No, not my judgment but that of Diocletian, who would have deserved to be listed among the distinguished emperors if he had not been so impious against our faith. These are his remarks about them, memorable, if I am not mistaken, and copied out to the letter in the book on the life of Aurelian: "Four or five men gather and form a single plan to deceive the emperor, and say what must be approved. The emperor, shut up in his palace, does not know the truth, but is compelled to know only what they say: he makes judges men who should not become judges, and sends away from the state those he ought to keep. Need I say more? As Diocletian himself said: 'the good, cautious, and excellent commander is put up for sale.'" Misled by these and others when he had already resigned the empire, he concluded: "Nothing is harder than to rule well."[54] And this is so. Princes should not think they have found both prosperity and ease; they have won some sort of prosperity but an extremely challenging one. Anyone who does not believe
me should at least believe a prince with the experience. On this 75
topic I am hardly able to issue this one precept and exhortation strongly enough: do not put anyone like this in command of the country that has been entrusted to you, making someone other than yourself lord. For many men have held the principate who in wanting to exalt their friends have lowered themselves and made themselves contemptible and loathed by their people, having been sold and mocked by the very men whom they had promoted on high. In particular Claudius, who held the principate before Nero, was despised for exalting his base and worthless freedmen, Posides

et Felicem, Narcissum et Pallantem, usque adeo evexit ut provincias regerent eumque ipsum atque imperium spoliarent, et ille infelix, servis suis affluentibus, indigeret. 'His et uxoribus addictus,' ut Tranquillus ait, 'non se principem sed ministrum egit'; horumque consilio et impulsu multa stulte gessit, multa crudeliter. [*§§76–78 omissis*]

79 Unum te igitur dominum sciant omnes, unum colant, unum diligant, unum denique vereantur; reliquos non ut potentes, sed ut a te missos aspiciant, qui, ubi iussus tuos executi fuerint, privati sint, nulla prediti dignitate aut potestate. Non loquor sine causa: vidi et observavi magnis in populis miram erga dominos patientiam, quamvis asperos et immites; nec minus miram indignationem atque impatientiam in eo quod plures suspicere ac metuere cogerentur, de quo ipso tecum quoque videor egisse, dum me ultimo, nisi fallor, anno altero rure solitarium, dignatus es invisere. [*§80–97 omissis*]

98 Multa nunc etiam occursant ni vererer ne, qui te fortasse fastidio his affeci, cunta prosequendo conficiam. Unum hoc nullo modo pretereundum reor, quod preclaros maxime ac verendos principes facit, in quo tu quidem hortatore non indiges, viros egregios ut honores tibique familiarissimos efficias. In hoc enim per te ipsum adeo pronus es ut, contrarium facere si velis, natura ipsa prohibeat; nichil autem fit melius quam quod duce fit natura. Efficax consuetudo, efficax doctrina, efficacior est natura; omnes si iunguntur, efficacissime. Egregios autem viros dico, quos e grege hominum vulgarium aliqua abstraxit excellentia, et vel iustitia insignis ac sanctitas — quod, heu, nostra etate perrarum est — vel rei militaris experientia ac doctrina, vel literarum copia rerumque
99 notitia, singulares fecit. Quamvis autem 'plerique arbitrentur res

and Felix, Narcissus and Pallas, so high that they ruled provinces and robbed him and the empire, and the wretched man suffered poverty while his slaves were thriving.[55] "Enslaved to those man and to his wives," Suetonius says, "he didn't act as a prince but as a servant." Upon their advice and prompting he did many foolish things and many cruel ones. [*§§76–78 omitted*]

So let all men know you as their sole lord, let them respect only 79
you, love only you, and revere only you, looking on the rest not as men in power but as your emissaries, who once they have carried out your orders are private men equipped with no rank or power. I do not speak idly. I have seen and watched in great peoples a strange submission toward their lords, although they were harsh and merciless, and an equally strange indignation and lack of patience in situations where they were compelled to look up to and fear many men. This is something I think I discussed with you in person, when you deigned last year, if I am not mistaken, to come to see me living my solitary life in the country. [*§§80–97 omitted*]

Many thoughts occur to me even now, or would do if I did not 98
fear that having perhaps bored you with these reminders, I would weary you outright by following every issue through. There is one thing I think I must not pass over, which makes princes distinguished and respected, in which you certainly need no encouragement, that is, in your honoring exceptional men and making them most intimate with you. In this you are so naturally inclined that if you wanted to do the opposite your nature itself would bar you; and nothing is better done than what occurs with nature as guide. Practice is effective, learning is effective, but nature is more effective; and if all are combined, this is most effective of all.[56] I mean by exceptional men those whom some excellence has separated from the herd of vulgar men and whom some distinguished traits of justice and holiness—which is alas very rare in our generation—or experience and learning with regard to warfare or a wealth of reading and knowledge of events, has made unique. For although men 99

bellicas maiores esse quam urbanas, minuenda est tamen hec opinio,' ut Officiorum primo ait Cicero. Ponit exempla greca et latina, Themistoclem et Solonem, Lisandrum et Lycurgum et, ex nostris, Gaium Marium et Marcum Scaurum, Gneum Pompeium et Quintum Catulum, Africanum minorem et Publium Nasicam; denique se ipsum, homo glorie appetentissimus, his exemplis interserit. Nec iniuste tamen id quidem; sine dubio enim non plus egit Antonius dum armis et acie Catilinam fregit, quam Cicero ipse dum coniurationem impiam alto consilio patefecit et coniuratos oppres-
100 sit in carcere. Et in hoc quidem urbanarum rerum studio, literati homines excellunt. In hoc autem numero literatorum hominum magnum locum iurisconsulti tenent, utilissimi semper rei publice, si iuris notitie iustitie quoque amor et cultus accesserit et sint, ut Ciceronis utar verbo, 'non magis iuris consulti quam iustitie.' Sunt enim qui ius atque iustitiam, quam profitentur, oppugnant, professionis sue nomine prorsus indigni. Non enim satis est scire nisi et velis, et voluntas bona rectam scientiam comitetur. Talibus sane multi principum suum imperium exornarunt: Hadrianus Iulio Celso, Salvio Iuliano, Neratio Prisco; Antoninus Scevola; Severus Papiniano; Alexander Domitio Ulpiano, Fabio Sabino, Iulio Paulo aliisque compluribus. His tu semper, quantum etas hec patitur, patrie tue Studium honestasti.

101 Sunt et literatorum species alie ex quibus et oportuna consilia sperari possunt et docta colloquia et, ut dicere solebat Alexander, 'fabule literate.' Itaque et medicos et 'liberalium artium' magistros civitate donasse Iulius Cesar legitur. Quibus omnibus hauddubie preferendi sunt qui eam, quam theologiam vocant, sacram scientiam profitentur, modo illam ab inanibus sophismatibus incorruptam servent. Faciebat hoc autem princeps prudentissimus ut et

generally believe that warfare is more important than civil life, this
opinion should be modified, as Cicero says in his first book *On
Duties*. He offers both Greek and Latin examples:[57] Themistocles
and Solon, Lysander and Lycurgus, and from our Romans, Gaius
Marius and Marcus Aemilius Scaurus, Pompey the Great and
Quintus Catulus, the younger Africanus and Publius Nasica, finally he includes himself, being a man most eager for glory. And
that is not unjustified, for without doubt Antonius did not achieve
more when he broke Catiline in war and battle than Cicero himself when he laid open the conspiracy by his penetrating intelligence and suppressed the conspirators in the prison. And in this 100
pursuit of city life it is men of letters who excel. The legal experts
are counted among lettered men and occupy a great place, being
always most valuable to the state if they add love and reverence for
justice to the knowledge of the law, and they are, to use Cicero's
words, "as expert in justice as in law."[58] For there are men who attack the law and justice which they claim as their business, utterly
unworthy of their profession. For knowledge is not enough unless
you have the will to use it, and good will accompanies correct
knowledge. Many emperors adorned their power with such men:
Hadrian with Julius Celsus, Salvius Julianus and Neratius Priscus,
Antoninus with Scaevola, Septimius Severus with Papinianus,
Alexander Severus with Domitius Ulpianus, Fabius Sabinus, Julius Paulus and many others.[59] You have always, as far as this generation allows, honored the university of your country with them.[60]

There are also different kinds of men of letters from whom you 101
can expect appropriate advice and learned conversations, and as
Alexander Severus used to say "literary stories."[61] This is why Julius Caesar, as we read, bestowed the citizenship on medical doctors and teachers of the liberal arts.[62] And among all of these we undoubtedly should give preference to those who profess the sacred knowledge which they call theology, provided they keep it unspoiled by hollow quibblings. Now that most prudent prince

literati homines libentius Rome essent et ceteros ad studendum,
tanti spe premii, invitarent. Erat enim cara res admodum civilitas
tunc romana, unde et Paulo apostolo se romanum civem asserenti,
tribunus in cuius ille potestate tunc erat: 'Ego,' ait, 'multa summa
102 civilitatem hanc consecutus sum.' Tu, vir inclite, qui rem tantam
dare non potes, hoc saltem prestabis ut doctos honestisque studiis
claros viros loco civium tuorum habeas, et civili urbanitate prose-
quaris sic ut urbem tuam, virorum illustrium incolatu, Studium-
que iam vetustum, renoves et exornes. Nichil enim eque eruditos
homines allicit ac principum familiaritas atque dignatio. Familiam
illam nempe clarissimam, non tam Augustus Cesar imperio, quam
103 convictu et morum comitate contraxerat. Habuit ergo in sodalitio
Marcum Tullium Ciceronem primo; consequenter Asinium Pol-
lionem, Valerium Messalam, Parium Geminum florentissimos oratores; Publium quoque Virgilium, Horatium Flaccum poetas egregios, ad quos sunt ipsius principis familiares epystole quibus ille,
summus hominum mundi dominus, duobus illis rusticanis man-
tuane ac venusine originis, non se equat tantummodo sed submit-
tit quodammodo, nequem plebeie familiaritatis unquam pudeat
quam ingenium ac doctrina nobilitent. Quem puderet enim, queso,
104 cuius Augustum non puduerit? Tuccam preterea et Varum cre-
monensem habuit et Ovidium sulmonensem, quamvis hunc ultimum, suo indignum contubernio iudicans, relegarit; habuit et
Marcum Varronem, doctissimum ut perhibent Romanorum, his-
torieque patrem Titum Livium patavinum, qui tuus, nunc si vive-
ret, civis esset; habuit et alios multos uno tempore, non minus
quam omnibus romanis legionibus illustratus hoc doctorum homi-
105 num comitatu. Nam quid tantum sibi conferre potuerant vel triginta quinque tribus populi romani vel quadraginta quattuor legiones bellatorum — tot enim habuisse illum invenio — quantum

Caesar made sure that men of letters were glad to be at Rome and
invited others to study in hope of so great a reward. For at that
time Roman citizenship was very dear. Hence when Paul affirmed
his Roman citizenship, the tribune who had him in his power said
"I obtained this citizenship at great cost."[63] Now, renowned friend, 102
though you cannot give so great a gift, you will at least treat
learned men and those distinguished in honorable studies as equal
to your citizens, and compliment them with the courtesy due to
citizens so as to renew and adorn your city and your already ancient University as the residence of distinguished men. For nothing entices learned men so much as the friendship and condescension of princes. And Augustus had built up that most glorious
household of his not so much by his imperial authority as by living in common and the affability of his person. So he had in his 103
brotherhood of companions first Cicero, and following him Asinius Pollio and Valerius Messalla, Parius Geminus, the most successful orators, also the distinguished poets Vergil and Horace:[64]
intimate letters to them survive from the prince himself in which
the highest lord of the human world does not just condescend to
these two country folk from Mantua and Venusia but in a sense
subordinates himself, so that no man should feel shame at a plebeian friendship when intellect and learning make it noble.[65] I ask
you, whom would it shame when it did not shame Augustus? He 104
also had as friends Tucca and Varius of Cremona,[66] and Ovid
from Sulmona, although he judged this last man unworthy of associating with him and sent him into exile.[67] He also had Varro,
the most learned of the Romans as they say, and Livy, father of
history, from Padua, who would have been your citizen if he lived
now,[68] and Augustus had many others at the same time: he was
made no less glorious by this retinue of learned men than by
all the Roman legions. For what honor could those thirty-five 105
tribes bestow upon him or his forty-four legions of fighting men—
I find that this is the number he had[69]—comparable to what

Virgilius solus contulit ad eternam famam? Vivit illa utique, cetera periere. Neque vero tantum ex Italia, sed ex Grecia quosdam quoque cesaree fama lenitatis allexerat. Nam quid, oro, benemeritis et insignibus viris potest esse iocundius quam sub iusto et miti principe ac favorabili extimatore meritorum vitam agere? Unde illud opinor, multos horum interdum tua e patria digressuros ni tu illos, tue notissime benignitatis vinclis, astringeres. Laudo equidem et probo. Armati enim tibi ad horam utiles esse possunt et temporale obsequium prestare, literati autem et temporale consilium et mansurum nomen; insuper ascendendi ad superos rectum iter ostendere atque ascendentem lingue ulnis attollere aberrantemque retrahere. [*§§106–10 omissis*]

*Arquade, IV Kalendas Decembres.*

Vergil alone contributed to his eternal glory? Certainly that lives on, whereas the rest has perished. Nor did the renown of Augustus' mildness attract only men from Italy but some also from Greece.[70] For I ask you, what can be more pleasant to deserving and distinguished men than to live under a just and mild prince and a favorable critic of their achievements? Hence this is my belief, that many of these would at times leave your country if you did not bind them by the bonds of your well-known generosity. I praise and approve of this. For armed men can be useful to you in a crisis and provide occasional defense, but educated men offer both advice in the present and a lasting name, showing you as well the right path to ascend to the gods and supporting you as you rise with the aid of their tongue and drawing you back when you stray. [*§§106–10 omitted*]

*Arquà, November 28.*

# [PART VI]

: I :

## *Ad Dyonisium de Burgo Sancti Sepulcri, congratulatio super eo quod ad Robertum isset, summum et regem et philosophum, et quid clarorum virorum conversatio prosit ad quietem animi.*

1 Nil dulcius audierant aures mee, postquam vocem tuam audire desierunt, quam quod ad regem vocatus accesseris. 'Rationem' in-
2 quis, 'expecto.' Non possum breviter; itaque longius incipiam. Optavit aliquando tibi genitrix longitudinem dierum, innumerabilibus periculis et calamitatibus obiectam; aliquando divitias, humanarum mentium non mediocrem laqueum ac funestam sarcinam libertatis; aliquando formam corporis, deformitatis anime plerunque materiam. Quid de sodalibus, quid de nutricula tua dicam? muliercularum omnium una lex est: inepta cupiunt, ridenda formi-
3 dant. De patre libet altiora credere; optaverit ergo filio quod ait Satyricus,

> Eloquium et famam Demosthenis aut Ciceronis,

que quanti sepe periculi plena sint, utriusque exitus est testis. Multis et inanibus vel tuis vel aliorum pro te votis fatigate sunt
4 aures Dei. Horum tibi aliquid anxie non opto: quare? quia stultum est vehementer appetere quod potest pessimo fine concludi. Illud bonum tibi cupio quod michi, beatam vitam, ad quam multi suspirant, pauci perveniunt. Est enim salebrosum iter atque

# PART VI

## ROME, ITALY AND ITS RULERS

: I :

*To Dionigi da Borgo Sansepolcro, congratulating him on going to Robert, a very great king and philosopher; also how association with distinguished men benefits tranquility of mind.*

My ears had heard nothing sweeter, after they ceased to hear your 1
voice, than the news that you had gone to the king on his invitation. You say: "I am waiting for the explanation." I can't tell you
quickly, so I will begin indirectly at greater length. Your mother 2
once wished you longevity of days,[1] something exposed to countless dangers and disasters; and another time wealth, no trivial snare for human minds, and a deadly burden on liberty; and on some other occasion, beauty of body, which is generally the source of ugliness of mind. What about your playmates and your nurse? All women conform to one law: they want foolish things and fear
absurdities. I prefer to think more respectfully of your father, so 3
let us suppose he wished for his son what the satirist calls:

> The eloquence and renown of Demosthenes and Cicero.[2]

Yet the death of each orator bears witness to the great dangers of their talents.[3] The ears of God have been wearied by many foolish
wishes either from you or from others on your behalf. I don't anx- 4
iously desire any of these things for you. Why? Because it is stupid to seek out passionately what can come to a wretched end. I want the same good thing for you as for me: the blessed life for which many sigh, but which few attain. For it is a rough and narrow and

angustum et difficile, et amena ac prona circum devia; est autem,
ut in sagittando, sic in alia qualibet operatione mortalium, aberrare
perfacile. Signum attingere, is demum artificii finis est; idcirco
difficilior, quia ad illum una tantummodo, ad errorem innumera-
5 biles sunt vie. Hanc sane quam dico beatam vitam, quanquam
ingeniosissimis atque doctissimis viris forte aliter visum sit, in hoc
corporis ergastulo mereri quidem utcunque potest labor humanus
et sperare, amplecti autem ac tenere non potest. Hoc ergo stadio
decurritur; finis est ubi quiescit intentio. Neque nobis hoc solis
persuasum est; quid enim aliud Cicero sentiebat, ubi ait quod hec
vita via est in celum?

6 Habet tamen interdum illi eterne quiddam hec mortalis vita
simillimum, ut etsi beata nondum sit — id enim beatum est duntaxat cui nichil valet accedere — iam tamen humanas miserias longe
infra se videat et in imo stans adhuc superne felicitatis luce re-
splendeat. Hoc sane non divitie prestant, non insanientis vulgi
plausus, non potentia, non voluptas, sed virtutum comitatus atque
animi tranquillitas, ad quam adipiscendam, diversum fortasse aliis
videbitur, sed, quantum opinio mea fert, nichil eque adiuvat ac
nobilium ingeniorum familiaritas et clarorum virorum conversatio.
7 Cernis, ut arbitror, quid intendam; dicam tamen expressius. 'Quis
in Grecia clarior Themistocle?' ait Tullius; ego fidentissime: 'Quis
in Italia, imo vero quis in Europa clarior Roberto?' in quo sepe
cogitans soleo non tam dyadema quam mores, neque tam regnum
8 quam animum admirari. Illum ego vere regem dixerim, qui non
subditos modo, sed se ipsum regit ac frenat; qui exercet in passiones suas imperium, que sunt animo rebelles, illum, si cesserit,
oppressure. Ut nulla est quidem clarior victoria quam se ipsum
9 vincere, sic nullum regnum altius quam se ipsum regere. Quomodo ille michi rex erit, in quem regnat ambitio? quomodo invic-

difficult path, and there are pleasant tracks on all sides running
downhill to lead you away from it: as in archery so in any other
mortal skill it is most easy to miss the mark. To hit the mark is the
ultimate goal of this art; so it is more difficult, because only one
shot will reach it, but there are countless ways of missing the target. Now this life which I call blessed, though the most talented 5
and learned men may have thought otherwise,[4] is something human effort can earn somehow in this prison house of the body and
hope for, but it cannot embrace it and hold it fast. So this is the
track on which we race; the finishing post is where our desires may
find rest. And this is not just our conviction alone; what else did
Cicero mean when he said: "This life is the path to heaven"?[5]

However, this mortal life has at times a feature very similar to 6
that eternal one, so that even if it is not yet blessed—for only that
is blessed which lacks nothing—yet it already sees human wretchedness far below and, even if still standing down below, will glitter
with the light of celestial happiness. Clearly wealth does not provide this, nor the applause of the raving crowd, nor power nor pleasure but the company of virtues and tranquility of mind. As far as
my opinion goes, though it may seem otherwise to others, nothing
is as helpful for obtaining this as intimacy with noble intellects and
association with distinguished men. You can perceive, I think, what 7
I have in mind, but I shall say it more explicitly. "Who in Greece
is more glorious then Themistocles?" says Cicero.[6] I in turn shall
declare most confidently: who in Italy, indeed who in Europe, is
more glorious than Robert? And often when I think about him I
have in mind not his diadem but his character, and I admire not
his kingdom but his spirit. I would call him truly a king, who rules 8
and reins in not only his subjects but himself, who wields authority over his passions which rebel from the spirit, and would overwhelm it if it yielded. Just as there is no more glorious victory than
to be victor over oneself, so there is no loftier rule than to rule
over oneself. How shall any man be a king in my eyes, in whom 9

tus quem sternit adversitas? quomodo serenus quem meror ob-
nubilat? quomodo magnanimus quem minimarum etiam rerum
pavor exanimat? et ut fulgida virtutum nomina taceamus, quis
michi liberum dicet eum qui cupidinum variarum iugo premitur
10 multiplici? Infra omnia ista descendam: qua fronte hominem dicimus, quem scimus ex homine nichil preter nudam effigiem reti-
nere, beluarum moribus deformem et sevorum animantium feritate terribilem? Mira ergo, licet publica, dementia regem eum
dicere, qui nec rex nec liber et sepe ne homo quidem sit.

11 Magnum est regem esse, perexiguum regem dici; rariores sunt
reges quam vulgus existimat; non est titulus iste vulgaris. Minus
gemmarum atque eboris sceptra consumerent, si soli reges illa
portarent. Veri reges intra se gerunt quod eos venerabiles facit:
semotis licet satellitibus et abiectis insignibus reges sunt; ceteros
cultus exterior facit horribiles. Robertus vere inclitus et vere rex
est; qui quam sit imperiosus in se ipsum exempla inaudite patientie et moderationis indicant, de quibus alter forte dicendi locus
fuerit. Quam vero late regnet in alios, dissonantes lingua et mori-
12 bus populi et disiunctissimi regionum fines ostendunt. Seneca
tuus in quadam tragedia quid regem faciat et quid non faciat,
egregie recollegit his versibus:

Regem non faciunt opes,
Non vestis tyrie color,
Non frontis nota regie,
Non auro nitide trabes;
Rex est qui posuit metus
Et diri mala pectoris.

ambition reigns? How can he be unconquered if adversity lays him
low? How can he be calm if grief clouds his brow? How can he be
magnanimous if the dread of the least things terrifies him? And
to pass over the glittering names of virtues, who will speak to me
of a man as free if he is weighed down beneath the multiple yoke
of various desires? I shall stoop lower than that: with what coun- 10
tenance shall we call him a man whom we know to have nothing
of a man except his bare likeness, disfigured with the behavior of
wild beasts and terrible with the bestiality of savage creatures? So
it is a strange, though common, madness, to call a man king who
is neither a king nor free and often not even a human being.

It is great to be a king, but insignificant to be called a king. 11
Kings are more rare than the crowd assumes; that is no common
title. Scepters would waste fewer jewels and less ivory, if only true
kings carried them. True kings carry within them what makes
them worthy of reverence; they are kings even when their attendants are removed and their emblems cast away; as for the others,
it is their costume that makes them inspire fear. Robert is truly
distinguished and truly a king, and examples of his unheard-of
patience and moderation demonstrate how harshly he exercises
command over himself, and perhaps I shall have another place to
speak of these virtues. The peoples so diverse in their speech and
behavior and the most remote boundaries of the regions show
how widely he rules over others.[7] Your Seneca[8] expressed in a cer- 12
tain tragedy what makes a king and what does not; he has brilliantly assembled these qualities in these verses:

> Wealth does not make a king,
> nor the hue of his Tyrian robe,
> nor the brand on his royal brow,
> nor beams glittering with gold,
> He is a king who has put down fear
> and the evils of a doomed breast.

Nec longe post:

> Mens regnum bona possidet;
> Nil ullis opus est equis,
> Nil armis et inertibus
> Telis, que procul ingerit
> Parthus, cum simulat fugas.
> Admotis nichil est opus
> Urbes sternere machinis
> Longe saxa rotantibus.
> Rex est qui metuit nichil.

13 Hec ille. Ad hunc itaque regem, ut principio conveniat finis, vocatus ivisti; quod ut ille iuberet et ut tu pareres, quid aliud quam studiorum summa conformitas fecit? Ille quidem quantum curis suis solamen asciverit, dicerem si apud alium loquerer; tibi certe ad interni hominis pacem, quam, uti sepe querebaris, tuscarum rerum fragor impulerat, qua compendiosius pergeres non erat.
14 Congratulor ergo seu prudentie seu fortune tue, et vocem que tunc michi fuit in ore, aliquanto nunc fidentius repeto. Ubi enim fama primum, deinde per literas tuas accepi te Florentia digressum isse Neapolim, et mecum et cum amicis dixi: 'Dyonisius noster ad tranquillitatem animi magnis passibus contendit et ad beatam vitam rectum iter ingressus est.'

15 De me autem sic habe: brevi te consequar, nosti enim quid de laurea cogito, quam singula librans, preter ipsum de quo loquimur regem, nulli omnino mortalium debere constitui. Si tanti fuero ut vocer, bene est; alioquin fingam nescio quid audiisse, vel epystole sue sensum, quam ipse michi summa hominis incogniti et familiarissima dignatione transmisit, quasi dubitans, in eam

And soon after:

A mind that is good possesses royal power;
it has no need for horses,
nor armor and idle weapons,
that the Parthian hurls from afar
when he pretends to flee.[9]
There is no need to raze cities,
applying siege machines
that cast rocks at a distance,
He is a king who has no fears.

This is what he says. So you have gone invited to this king, to 13
make my ending match my beginning; and what else if not the highest harmony of your studies made him bid you come and you obey? If I were speaking to another man I would say how great a consolation he had adopted for his cares; as for you there was surely nowhere you could resort more swiftly for the peace of your inner self, which, as you often lamented, the crash of Tuscan affairs had assaulted.[10] So I congratulate either your prudence or 14
your good fortune, and I am returning a little more confidently to the comment that was in my heart then. Indeed when I learned, first from rumor, then from your letter, that you had left Florence for Naples, I said to myself and to my friends: "Our Dionigi is marching with great strides toward tranquility of mind, and has embarked on the direct road to the blessed life."

As for me, hear my news: I shall follow you shortly, for you 15
know my plans about the laurel crown, and how, weighing arguments up, I have decided to owe it to no mortal man besides the king himself of whom we are talking. If I am thought worthy of invitation, that is good; otherwise I shall pretend I have heard something; or, as if doubting the meaning of his letter which he personally sent me with the highest and most intimate respect toward a man unknown to him, I shall stretch it to the effect that I

potissimum partem traham, ut vocatus videar. Et regio quidem stilo quiddam modo plebeium reddidi, fulgore attonitus, nec equis ingenii viribus, et lyra, ut aiunt, longe impari. Vale.

*II Nonas Ianuarias, ad fontem Sorgie.*

: 2 :

## *Ad inclitum regem Sicilie Robertum.*

1 Prestrinxit oculos meos fulgor insolitus; felix calamus visus est, cui talia crederentur. Quid primum mirer? eximiam brevitatem an maiestatem sententiarum an divinam eloquii venustatem? Nunquam, rex inclite, fateor, credidi rem tantam dici posse tam breviter, tam graviter, tam ornate, nec iam tale aliquid ex humanis
2 ingeniis expectabam. Equidem ut constaret te corda hominum in manibus habere, quo tota illustrium oratorum suspirat intentio, legentis animum tam variis affectibus impulisti, ut sine luctamine in omnem partem stili tui vestigia sequeretur volubilitate mirabili.
3 Ecce enim in prima sobrii fronte sermonis, dum summam humane miserie acerrimasque molestias laborum et necessitatem mortis acerbissimam, tractim ex radicis labe ramis ac frondibus obrepentem, magnificentissime deplorasses, movebar usque adeo ut crebro inter legendum suspirans et ineluctabili sorte perterritus totumque hoc nomen hominis perosus, pene nec natus esse nec unquam nasciturus optaverim. Actum erat et michi iam tranquillitas omnis exciderat, nisi que lethale vulnus inflixerat manus, ea-
4 dem mox remedium attulisset. Sensi unum et repentini meroris et

seem to have been invited. And I have answered in rather ordinary language compared with his royal style, dazzled by his brilliance, and with unequal intellectual power, and on a far inferior lyre, as men say. Farewell.

*January 4, by the source of the Sorgue.*

: 2 :

## *To Robert, renowned king of Sicily.*

The unaccustomed brilliance of your person has dazzled my eyes, 1
and I deem that pen happy which was entrusted with such words. What should I marvel at first? Its exceptional brevity or the majesty of its sentiments or the divine charm of its eloquence? Renowned king, I admit I could never have believed so great a matter could be expressed so succinctly, so weightily, so richly, nor did I
expect any such writing from human intellects. As it was evident 2
that you held the hearts of men in your hands, the goal to which the whole aim of orators aspires, you have swayed the reader's spirit with such a mixture of emotions that it followed with marvelous swiftness and without effort the traces of your style in every
way. Indeed, see how in the first part of your sober discourse, 3
while you most splendidly deplored the total of human wretchedness and the sharp distress occasioned by our labors and the most bitter necessity of death creeping up gradually from the corruption of its root to its branches and foliage, I was so deeply moved that I frequently sighed as I read and was terrified by our inevitable lot. Hating entirely the name of man, I almost wished I had not been born nor might ever come to birth. The end would have come and all my calm have fallen from me if the hand which had inflicted
the deadly wound had not quickly brought a remedy. I realized 4

consolationis artificem, nec unquam certius quid eloquentia posset, agnoveram; tam potenter enim paucorum ope verborum sub immortalis anime futureque reparationis obtentu egrum atque labantem animum erexisti, ut gaudio michi fuerit genitum esse mortalem. Nam quid beatius excogitari potest, quam exutum veste corporea et de compedibus istis explicitum, ad illam diem, exactis temporum curriculis, pervenire, que nos, absorpta morte, immortalitatem induat, reparans indissolubiliter ac reformans putrem et semesam tineis atque undique fluentem tunicam carnis nostre?

5 Quam spem etsi philosophorum gentilium nullus attigerit, vetustissima tamen est immortalitatis opinio; nec nostris solum, sed
6 illis etiam probata quibus Cristi nomen inauditum est. Preter Epy-
curum enim et nescio quot ex illo infami grege, immortalem esse
animam nemo est qui neget. De qua re, ut Pherecidem, primum
apud Syros sententie huius auctorem, discipulumque Pherecidis
Pithagoram totamque pithagoream familiam et Socratem omnesque socraticospreteream, Plato ipse, summus vir, clarissimum vo-
lumen edidit, quo Uticensis Cato moriturus suprema illa nocte
sua pro consiliario usus perhibetur, ut ad contemptum vite huius
7 animosior et ad amorem decrete mortis accederet. Quam sententiam postea Marcus Cicero et in *Tusculano* suo et in sexto *Reipublice*
divino genere orationis asseruit; necnon et in dyalogo *Lelii*, qui de
amicitia vera est, et in eo libro qui *Cato Maior* inscribitur, defensio-
nem continens senectutis, aliisque preterea tam multis in locis attigit, ut valde michi quidem solicitus videatur ne quem veritas tam
8 comperta pretereat. Sed cui hec insipiens loquor? profecto non
modo regum nostri temporis sed philosophorum regi. Ignosce autem, queso, si hactenus me dicendi calor evexit, ut regium dogma,

that there was one creator of both my sudden gloom and my consolation, nor had I ever recognized more surely the power of eloquence; you lifted up my weary and failing mind so powerfully with the aid of a few words, through the promise of an immortal soul and future restoration, that I rejoiced to have been born mortal. For what can be imagined more blessed than for the soul, freed from its bodily clothing and disentangled from those shackles, to reach the day when the cycles of the ages have been completed, which once we have absorbed death will cloth us with immortality,[1] restoring and remodeling beyond any dissolution the tunic of our flesh, rotten and half eaten away by worms and melting in every part?

Even if none of the pagan philosophers has achieved this hope, 5
the belief in immortality is very ancient, approved not only by our
fellow Christians but by those who have not heard the name of
Christ. For besides Epicurus and an unknown number of his ill- 6
famed flock, there is no one who denies that the soul is immortal.
On this topic, to pass over Pherecydes, the first source of this belief among the Syrians, and Pythagoras, the pupil of Pherecydes
and the whole brood of Pythagoras and Socrates and all the So-
cratics, Plato himself, that great man, published a most famous
volume which Cato of Utica when about to die is said to have
used as a counselor on that last night of his life, in order to approach with more courage contempt for this life and love of the
death he had determined on.[2] After that, Cicero affirmed this be- 7
lief both in the *Tusculans* and in the sixth book *On the Republic* in a
divine form of speech; and in the dialogue *Laelius* too, on true
friendship, and in the book entitled *Cato the Elder,* which contains
a defense of old age,[3] and he touched on it besides in so many
other passages that he seems to me deeply worried lest such assured truth should escape any man's notice. But fool that I am, 8
whom am I addressing? The king not only of kings in our time
but of philosophers. Now forgive me, please, if my passion in
speaking has carried me so far that I not only embrace the royal

cui plurimum me debere fateor, non amplecterer solum, sed testibus adhibitis confirmarem; quod ita michi animum affecit, ut securus iam ac spei plenus formidatum gentibus diem mortis expec-
tem.

9 Hunc diem transvecta neptis tua, quam finis epystole canit ac
predicat, invidiosa potius, ut michi quidem videtur, quam miserabili sorte defungitur. Quamvis enim in ipso etatis et forme flore
subtracta sit, publica fere totius orbis querimonia multisque precipue populorum utriusque regni, et unde ortum et in quod transla-
tum illud rarum et eximium decus erat, lacrimis ac lamentis, ipsa
tamen felix est, non solum quod ad eterne vite delitias per horrificum illud mortis limen ingressa est, sed etiam quod tu eam nobi-
10 lissimo elogio omnibus seculis illustrasti. Quis enim mortuam,
imo vero quis non gloriosissime viventem dicere audebit, quam
Deus in celo, tu in terris vivere voluisti? O, inquam, felix mulier, o
iterum felix, que pro una temporali vita, eademque brevi et incerta
et mille semper casibus exposita, duas eternitates, ut ita dixerim,
consecuta est, quarum alteram celesti, alteram terreno regi, illam
11 Cristo debeat, hanc Roberto! Ingentia duo munera a munificentis-
simis largitoribus accipiens, eo felicior videri debet, quod in celo et
in terra gratiam dignissimis relatura est; plurimum enim ex persona tribuentis muneribus ipsis accedit; multum interest a quo
12 beneficium acceperis et cui inde sis obnoxius. Sane quesitam illi
celitus immortalitatis conditionem beatissimamque vite mutationem sileo, ne ineffabilia prosequentem destituant vires. Quanta
demum gloria est quam tu sibi supremis laudibus peperisti! certe,
dum illud tuum sive epygramma sive epythaphium dici mavis,
quod eterne mansurum esse confido, nuper defuncte neptis memoriam celebrabit, semper illa tecum et cum clarissimis omnis evi
13 nominibus vivet. Erunt qui mortem immaturam et iacturam

decree to which I owe so much,[4] but confirm it by adducing witnesses; it has so deeply affected my mind that I now await calmly and full of hope the day of death dreaded by all nations.

This is the day your niece, whom the end of your letter honors 9
and proclaims, passed away, experiencing a destiny as it seems to
me more enviable than pitiable. For although she was taken in the
very flower of her youth and beauty, among the public lamentation
of the whole world and amid many tears and plaints, especially of
the peoples of the two kingdoms—both the country of her birth
and that to which her rare distinction had passed[5]—she herself is
happy, not just because she has entered the delights of eternal life
across that horrendous threshold of death, but also because you
have illuminated her for all ages by your most noble eulogy. For 10
who shall dare to call her dead, or indeed anything but living most
gloriously, since God has wished her to dwell in heaven, and you
to live on earth? O happy woman, I say, and again happy, to have
won in exchange for a single temporal life, short and unsure and
exposed to a thousand mischances, two eternities, so to speak, one
owed to the heavenly King, the other to a king on earth, the one
to Christ, the other to Robert! Receiving two immense gifts from 11
most lavish givers and benefactors, she should seem all the more
happy because in heaven and on earth she is going to confer grace
upon the most worthy, since a great deal is added to gifts by the
character of the giver; it makes a great difference from whom you
have received a kindness and to whom you are indebted for it.
Obviously I keep silent about the condition of immortality which 12
she has won and her most blessed exchange of life, lest my strength
fails me as I try to convey ineffable qualities. But how great is just
the glory that you have produced for her by your last words of
praise! Certainly whether you prefer it to be called an epigram or
epitaph, which I am confident will last for eternity, it will celebrate
the memory of your newly deceased niece: she will always live with
you and the most glorious names of every age. There will be those 13

modici temporis tali cupiant compensasse pangerico, quique, quod de Achille dixisse fertur Alexander Macedo, suspirantes dicant: 'O fortunatam, que talem preconem tue virtutis invenisti!'

14 Sed iam metuo ne prolixitas in fastidium vergat; elegantissima quoque brevitas tua ne longius vager, admonuit. Subsistam igitur Deum orans cuntosque celicolas, ut serenitatem tuam, geminis tam bellorum quam studiorum laureis ornatam, diu iubeant in statu felicissimo florere.

*VII Kal. Ianuarias, ad fontem Sorgie.*

## : 3 :

## *Ad Barbatum Sulmonensem, de Roberti Siculi regis obitu.*

1 Quod verebar accidit, quod timebam patior; in dolorem metus, vota in gemitum abiere. Non multo antequam presagirem, deseruit nos inclitus ille rex noster, cuius etsi matura etas esset, tamen
2 peracerba mors est. Et, heu me miserum, Barbate optime, quam vereor ne illa quoque presagia confirmet eventus, que michi suggerit anxius et malorum suorum semper nimis certus vates, animus meus! Ita me regine iunioris novique regis adolescentia, ita me regine alterius etas ac propositum, ita me tandem territant
3 aulicorum ingenia et mores. Mendax hic utinam sim propheta; sed agnos duos multorum custodie luporum creditos video, regnumque sine rege. Nam quid ego eum qui ab alio regitur, regem dicam, multorum avaritie—mestus addam—multorumque sevitie expositum? Itaque, si quo die Plato rebus humanis excessit, sol celo cecidisse visus est, quid illo moriente videatur, qui et Plato

who desire to compensate for her premature death and loss of a short time with such a panegyric, and who will say with a sigh, as Alexander of Macedon is reported to have said of Achilles: "Fortunate woman, to have found so great a herald of your virtue!"[6]

But I am beginning to fear that my verbosity is tending to bring 14
satiety; and your most elegant conciseness has warned me not to stray too far. So I shall pause, praying to God and all the saints that they bid your serenity, adorned by twin laurels of warfare and learning, to flourish in the most blessed condition.

*December 26, by the source of the Sorgue.*

: 3 :

## *To Barbato da Sulmona, on the death of King Robert of Sicily.*

So what I dreaded has happened, and I am suffering what I 1
feared; my fears have turned into grief and my prayers to a groan. Our glorious king has abandoned us not much earlier than I anticipated; even if his age was ripe, his death is very bitter. And woe 2
is me, my good friend Barbato, I fear that those forebodings may be confirmed by the outcome, which my mind, a prophet anxious and always too accurate in its forebodings, piles up before me! The immaturity of the younger queen and the new king, the age and resolve of the older queen, and finally the nature and behavior of
the courtiers all terrify me.[1] If only I may be a false prophet in 3
this; but I see two lambs entrusted to the guardianship of many wolves and a kingdom without a king. For why should I call king someone who is directed by another, and who, I may add, is exposed to the greed and savagery of many? So if on the day Plato departed mortal life the sun seemed to have fallen from the sky,[2]

alter ingenio fuit et regum nulli aut sapientia secundus aut gloria, cuius preterea mors tam multis hinc inde periculis viam fecit? Secundet hec omnipotens Deus et solicitudinem meam piam magis quam necessariam rebus probet.

4 At, ut aliis cunta supra spem eveniant et metus iste supervacuus
fuerit, michi tamen, amice, quis consulet? aut quis medebitur dolori meo? cui de cetero vigilabo? cui quantulumcunque hoc ingenium aut studium consecrabo? quis spes collapsas eriget, quis
torpentem animum excitabit? Duos ingenii duces habui: utrunque
michi annus hic abstulit, et de altero quidem, nuper, dum adhuc
essem in Italia, — utrobique consortem fletus ydoneum querens —
nostro cum Lelio questus sum, de hoc hodie tecum queror querar-
que dum vixero; et qui solari alios interdum soleo, nunc qua me
5 ipsum ratione vel oratione consoler, non invenio. Hinc ergo conso-
landi desperatio, hinc flendi pudor, hinc ad utrumlibet stili diffidentia, sed supra omnia illico te videndi spes silentium iubet.
Parebo, tecum propediem fleturus ex commodo; hec interea tibi
flens ad fontem Sorgie dictabam, notum procellarum animi mei
portum, quo heri ad vesperam solus fugi, cum mane me Rodani ad
ripam rumor mestissimus invenisset.

*IV Kal. Iunias.*

how do we understand the death of this king, a second Plato in character and second to no king in either wisdom or glory; besides this, his death has made way for so many dangers. May immortal God favor this and prove by events that my anxiety is more a matter of piety than necessity.

But even if everything in all other respects turns out above my 4
expectation and my fear proves unwarranted, who will take thought for me, dear friend? Or assuage my grief? For whom shall I keep watch henceforward, to whom dedicate this talent or learning of mine, such as it is? Who will raise up my fallen hopes, who arouse my dulled spirit? I had two guides in my intellectual life; this year has taken both of them from me, and I lamented about one with Laelius only recently when I was still in Italy[3]—seeking in each case a fit companion for my weeping—and now I lament with you about the other, and shall lament as long as I live. I who usually console others, now cannot find argument or speech to
console myself. So this has caused my despair of being consoled, 5
this my embarrassment in lamenting, this my insecurity of style in either mode; but above all it is the hope of seeing you promptly that bids me be silent. I shall obey and weep with you shortly at our convenience; meanwhile I am dictating this in tears by the source of the Sorgue, the familiar harbor from the hurricanes of my life: I fled here alone yesterday toward evening, after that most grievous rumor found me in the morning by the bank of the Rhône.[4]

*May 29.*

## : 4 :

## *Ad Nicolaum tribunum urbis Rome, de fama eius immutata indignatio precibus mixta.*

1 Fecisti, fateor, ut sepe per hoc tempus illud apud Ciceronem loquentis Africani dictum multa cum voluptate repeterem: 'Quis est hic qui complet aures meas, tantus et tam dulcis sonus?' Quid enim in tanta claritate tui nominis, ad tam letos et tam crebros rerum tuarum nuntios convenientius diceretur? Idque quam cupide fecerim, inscriptus tibi exhortationum mearum liber indicat, sti-
2 mulis meis ac laudibus tuis plenus. Noli, queso, committere ut dicam: 'Quis est hic qui vulnerat aures meas, tantus et tam tristis fragor?'; cave, obsecro, speciosissimam fame tue frontem propriis manibus deformare. Nulli fas hominum est, nisi tibi uni, rerum tuarum fundamenta convellere; tu potes evertere qui fundasti: so-
3 let architectus esse optimus propriorum operum demolitor. Nosti quibus tramitibus ad gloriam ascendisti; versis retro vestigiis inde descenditur, et natura facilior est descensus; latissime enim patet neque solum apud Inferos locum habet, quod a poeta dicitur:

facilis descensus Averni.

4 Tantum ab illorum desperata miseria presentis vite varietate differimus, quod quandiu hic sumus, cadimus quidem et resurgimus, descendimus et ascendimus; inde autem nullus est reditus. Quid vero dementius quam, cum stare possis, cadere fiducia resurgendi? Semper ex alto periculosior casus est; et quid, oro te, virtute altius ac gloria, quarum in vertice consederas nostris temporibus inaccesso? tamque impigre et tam insueto calle ad summa perveneras,

## : 4 :

### *To Nicola, tribune of Rome, a rebuke mixed with urgent requests, over his changed reputation.*

Lately I admit you have made me often repeat with great pleasure 1
the saying of Africanus in Cicero: "What is this great and sweet sound which fills my ears?"[1] For what could be said more befitting such glory as is attached to your name, in response to such happy and abundant news of your achievements? How eagerly I did this, my work called *Exhortations*, dedicated to you, makes clear, filled as
it is with my encouragements and your praises.[2] Please don't make 2
me say "what is this great and grim crash which wounds my ears?" Beware, please, of disfiguring with your own hands the glorious brow of your fame. It is not right for any man except you alone to uproot the foundations of your power; you can overthrow them since you laid down these foundations. An architect is the best
man to demolish his own constructions. You know by what paths 3
you climbed to glory. The descent comes once you have turned your steps back, and the descent is easier by nature. It lies wide open and has a place not only in Hades, as the poet says:

> Easy is the descent into Avernus.[3]

We differ so much from that desperate wretchedness in the variety 4
of our present life that as long as we are here we fall and rise again, descend and ascend, but from there we have no return. Now what is more crazy than to fall in confidence that you will be capable of getting up again, when you could have remained standing? The fall is always more dangerous from on high, and what, I ask you, is loftier than virtue and glory, on whose summit, not reached in our times, you were settled? You had reached the summit so energetically and by so unprecedented a path that I doubt whether there

5 ut haud sciam cui usquam formidolosior sit ruina. Pedem figere
oportet obnixius ut consistas neque spectaculum prebeas riden-
dum hostibus, lugendum tuis. Non queritur gratis clarum nomen
nec servatur quidem;

Magnus enim labor est magne custodia fame.

6 Permitte michi meo versiculo tecum uti, qui adeo michi placuit ut
eum ex quotidianis epystolis non puduerit ad *Africam* transferre; et
hanc michi quoque durissimam necessitatem exime, ne lyricus apparatus tuarum laudum, in quo — teste quidem hoc calamo — mul-
7 tus eram, desinere cogatur in satyram. Neu me casu in hanc narra-
tionem incidisse aut de nichilo locutum putes. E curia digressum
amicorum litere consecute sunt, in quibus ad me rerum tuarum
discolor et prime multum dissimilis fama pervenit: non te populum, ut solebas, sed partem populi pessimam amare, illi obsequi,
illam colere, illam admirari. Quid dicam nisi quod Ciceroni scri-
8 bens Brutus? 'Pudet conditionis ac fortune.' Mundus ergo te videbit de bonorum duce satellitem reproborum? sic nobis subito tur-
bata sunt sidera, sic infensa divinitas? ubi nunc ille tuus salutaris
genius, ubi, ut usitatius loquar, ille bonorum operum consultor
spiritus, cum quo assidue colloqui putabaris? neque enim aliter
talia fieri posse per hominem videbantur.

9 Quid autem torqueor? ibunt res quo sempiterna lex statuit;
mutare ista non possum, fugere possum. Itaque non parum michi
negotii remisisti: ad te animo properabam, flecto iter, certe te alterum non videbo. Tu quoque longum vale, Roma; si hec vera
10 sunt, Indos ego potius aut Garamantes petam. Sunt ne autem vera
hec? o multum principio dissimilem finem et o nimium delicatas
aures meas! assueverant magnificis rumoribus, pati ista non

would ever be a collapse more dreadful to anyone. You should 5
plant your foot more vigorously to stay still and not provide a sight
laughable to your enemies but grievous to your friends. A glorious
name is not earned freely nor preserved:

Great is the toil in guarding a great fame.[4]

Let me use my own verse to you, since it pleased me so much that 6
I was not ashamed to transfer it from my daily letters to the *Africa*.
Spare me this harsh necessity that the lyric adornment of your
praises, on which topic I was abundant — my pen bears witness to
it — must now end as satire. And don't think I came to this narra- 7
tive by chance or am speaking without cause. After I left the Curia
my friends' letters reached me,[5] in which an ugly rumor, very different from your earlier fame, came to me, that you did not love
the people as you used to but the worst part of the people, that
you obeyed them, heeded them and admired them. What am I
to say except what Brutus said when writing to Cicero: "I am
ashamed of your circumstances and situation."[6] Shall the world 8
see you turned from a leader of patriots to a henchman of the
wicked? Have the stars so suddenly been disturbed and divinity
grown so hostile? Where is that beneficent genius of yours, or
to speak in more common terms, that spirit, counselor of good
works, with which you were thought to exchange constant talk?
For such things did not seem possible by human agency.

So why am I tormented? Events will turn out as everlasting law 9
has determined; I cannot change them, but I can shun them. So
you have spared me no little toil: I was hurrying to you in spirit
but I am turning away and will surely not look toward you as you
have changed. To Rome also, a long farewell; if these things are
true, I will seek out the Indians and Garamantes instead.[7] But are 10
these things true? O how different the end from its beginning and
how delicate my ears. They had become accustomed to magnificent reports and cannot endure your present behavior. But what I

possunt. Sed et possunt falsa esse que loquor, et falsa sint utinam; nunquam libentius erraverim. Magna quidem apud me est scribentis autoritas, sed cognite michi multis indiciis—generose di-
11 cam an animose?—cuiusdam invidie non parva suspitio. Igitur etsi plura loqui dolor imperet, frenabo tamen impetum; quod profecto non possem, nisi quia solicitudinem meam incredulitate consolor. Secundet hec Deus et letiora faciat quam narrantur, potiusque me amicorum alter mendacio, quam impietate alter flagitioque leserit; siquidem consuetudine pessima effectum est ut mendacium iam quotidianum et vulgare peccatum sit; proditorem patrie nullius evi
12 licentia, nulla consuetudo, nulla libertas criminum excusat. Potius ergo ille mentiendo paucos michi mestos dies, quam tu patriam deserendo mestam omnem vitam feceris; ille siquid verbo deliquerit, verbo purgabitur; tuum si—quod fictum cupio—verum scelus est, quibus unquam piaculis abolendum speres? Immortale decus est, immortalis infamia.

13 Quamobrem si—quod opinari nequeo—tuam fortasse negligis, at saltem fame mee consule; scis quanta michi impendeat procella, quanta, si labi ceperis, in caput meum reprehensorum turba conspiret. 'Proinde, dum tempus est,' ut terrentianus loquitur adolescens, 'etiam atque etiam cogita'; circumspice, oro, summo studio quid agas, excute acriter te ipsum, examina tecum, nec te fallas, qui sis, qui fueris, unde, quo veneris, quorsum inoffensa libertate progredi fas sit, quam personam indueris, quod nomen assumpseris, quam spem tui feceris, quid professus fueris: videbis te non dominum reipublice, sed ministrum.

*Ianue, III Kal. Decembris.*

am speaking of could be false—if only they were! For I would never be more glad to be mistaken. The source of this information has great authority with me but I have no small suspicion of a certain ill will, known to me by many signs—shall I say springing from generosity or hatred?[8] So even if pain bids me say more, I 11
shall rein in my urge, which I could not do if I did not console my anxiety by disbelief. May God favor this and make what is reported more happy and let one of my friends hurt me more by lying than the other by impiety and criminal action; even if it has come to pass that by a wicked habit lying is now a daily and common offense, no license of the age, no customs, no excess of offenses will excuse the traitor to his country. Rather let my friend 12
bring me some days of sadness by this falsehood than that you by deserting your country should make my whole life sad. If he has offended in speech he will be excused in speech, but if your crime is real—as I hope is not true—by what expiation do you hope to wipe it out? Honor is immortal; but so is disgrace.

So if, as I cannot believe, you are neglecting your glory, at least 13
take thought for my reputation; you know how great a storm hangs over me, and if you stumble, how great a crowd of moral censors will converge upon my head. "Accordingly while there is time," as the young man says in Terence: "think again and again."[9] Look round, I beg you, with keenest concern at what you are doing, shake yourself clean. Examine yourself and do not deceive yourself about what you are, what you have been and whence and whither you have come, to what end it is right to advance without offending liberty, what role you have put on, what name you have claimed, what hope you have created of yourself, what oath you have taken:[10] you will see that you are not the master of the state but its servant.

*Genoa, November 29.*

: 5 :

## *Ad Franciscum Sanctorum Apostolorum, de poetice nomine inter vulgares et indoctos profanato.*

1 Quid expectas audire nisi reliquum proxime ad te superioris epystole, unde fleas et rideas? nil certe nunc maius habeo quod agam; imo vero multa, sed maioribus incumbere breve tempus vetat idque non sat liberum sed obicibus miris implicitum; nam et ego totus in motu et multa circumstrepunt simulque hic et alibi atque
2 ita nusquam sum; familiare malum loca mutantium. Babilone ultima digressus ad fontem Sorgie substiti, notissimo mearum procellarum portu. Hic vie comites opperior et autumni exitum aut illud saltem a Marone descriptum tempus, quando

iam breviorque dies et mollior estas.

Interim ergo ne inanis rusticatio mea sit, cogitationum consumptarum fragmenta recolligo, ut omnis dies, si fieri possit, aut aliquid maioribus ceptis adiciat aut minutum aliquid absolvat.

3 Quod hodiernum est, his ad te prolatum literis, accipies: poesis divinum munus et paucorum hominum, iam vulgari, ne profanari dicam ac prostitui, cepit; nichil est quod indignantius feram; tu, amice, si stomacum tuum novi, ferre indignitatem hanc nullo pos-
4 ses modo. Nunquam Athenis aut Rome, nunquam Homeri Virgiliique temporibus tantus sermo de vatibus fuit quantus est ad ripam Rodani etate hac, cum tamen nullo unquam loco aut tempore tam nullam rei huius notitiam fuisse arbitrer. Volo bilem risu

: 5 :

## *To Francesco of the Holy Apostles, about the name of poetry, now promiscuously used among the common and uneducated.*

What do you expect to hear, apart from the rest of my most recent letter to you, to make you weep and laugh?[1] Now I certainly have nothing more important to do, or rather a lot of tasks, but the short time forbids me to weigh in on greater duties, and even that is not free enough, but entangled in amazing hindrances, for I am entirely distracted by the prospect of travel and there are many disturbances around me and I am simultaneously here and there and so nowhere—the familiar misfortune of those changing 1
places. Having left this modern Babylon just now I have paused at 2
the source of the Sorgue, that notorious haven from my storms.[2] I am waiting here for my traveling companions and the end of autumn, or at least the time described by Vergil when

> now the day is shorter and the summer heat more kind.[3]

Meanwhile, so my time in the country may not be empty, I am gathering up the pieces of past deliberations, so that if possible every day either adds something to my larger enterprises or finishes some small one.

You will receive today's theme, presented by this letter: that po- 3
etry, the divine gift of a select few, is now made commonplace, not to say vulgarized and prostituted. There is nothing I endure with more indignation, and as for you, friend, if I know your temper,
you will be quite unable to put up with this outrage. Never was 4
there so much chatter about bards at Athens or Rome or in the times of Homer and Vergil as on the banks of the Rhône in this age,[4] and yet there has never been such a total lack of understanding of this art in any place or time. I want you to ease your bile

5 lenias et discas inter tristia iocari. Venit ad curiam nuper, imo vero
non venit sed captivus ductus est, Nicolaus Laurentius, olim late
formidatus tribunus urbis Rome, nunc omnium hominum miserrimus, et quod extremum mali genus est, nescio an, ut valde miser
sic minime miserabilis, qui cum in Capitolio tanta cum gloria mori
posset, bohemicum et mox lemovicensem carcerem subire tanto
6 suo et romani nominis ac reipublice ludibrio sustinuit. In quo
laudando monendoque quantus hic calamus fuerit, notius est forte
quam vellem. Amabam virtutem, laudabam propositum, mirabarque animum viri; gratulabar Italie, alme Urbis imperium, mundi
totius requiem providebam; tot ex radicibus oriens gaudium dissimulare non poteram videbarque michi totius glorie particeps, si
currenti sibi stimulos addidissem, quos, ut nuntii eius testabantur
7 et litere, in verbis meis acutissimos sentiebat. Tanto ego magis ardebam acuebamque animum siquid excogitare possem quod fer-
vens illud ingenium inflammaret, et qui probe nossem nulla re
magis quam gloria et laudibus generosum pectus inardescere, inse-
rebam laudes, magnificas et multorum forte iudicio nimias sed
mea opinione verissimas, preteritumque commendans hortabar ad
8 reliqua. Extant aliquot mee ad illum epystole, quarum me hodie
non penitus pudet; divinare enim non soleo, atque utinam nec ipse
etiam divinasset! profecto autem quod, dum scriberem, agebat
acturusque videbatur, non mea tantum sed totius humani generis
laude et admiratione dignissimum erat; an tamen ob hoc unum
eradende sint, nescio, quod turpiter vivere maluit quam honeste
mori; sed de impossibilibus non est consultatio; etsi enim delere
illas valde velim, non potero; in publicum egresse mei iuris esse
desierunt. Itaque ceptum sequor.

with laughter and learn to joke in grim circumstances. Recently 5
Cola di Rienzo came to Curia—or rather he didn't come but was
brought there: once the widely feared tribune of the city of Rome,
but now most wretched of men; and—what is the worst feature of
his misfortune—I don't know whether he isn't as unworthy of pity
as he is utterly wretched. He who could have died so gloriously on
the Capitol first endured a Bohemian imprisonment, then one at
Limoges,[5] with such great mockery of himself and of the Roman
name and of the Republic. Perhaps the effect of my pen in prais- 6
ing and advising him is better known than I would wish. I loved
his virtue and praised his purpose and marveled at the man's
spirit; I congratulated Italy and foresaw the empire of our mother
city as a requiem for the whole world; I could not conceal my joy,
springing from so many roots; and I saw myself as sharing in all
the glory if I goaded him on when he was in action; and as his
messages and letters bear witness, he felt this most keenly in my
words. So I was all the more eager and sharpened my wits to see 7
if I could discover anything to inflame his passionate nature; and
knowing full well that his noble breast was heated by nothing
more keenly than glory and praise, I included praise that was grandiose and perhaps excessive in the judgment of many but true in
my opinion, and in recommending his past actions urged him to
complete them. Some of my letters to him survive[6] of which I am 8
not utterly ashamed today, for I am not accustomed to prophesy,
and I just wish he himself had not made prophecies. Certainly
what he was doing, and seemed about to do at the time when I was
writing that, was worthy not only of my praise and admiration but
of that the whole human race. I don't know whether the letters
should be deleted for this reason alone, because he preferred living
shamefully rather that dying honorably; but there is no deliberation about what is impossible. Even if I were desperately eager to
destroy them I shall not be able to; they have become public and
have ceased to be under my control. So I continue where I began.

9 Intravit curiam humilis atque contemptus is qui malos orbe
toto tremefecit ac terruit, bonos spe letissima atque expectatione
complevit et universo quondam populo romano italicarumque urbium primatibus comitatus, nunc duobus hinc illinc stipatus satellitibus ibat infelix, plebe obvia videndique avida faciem eius, cuius
10 modo tam clarum nomen audierat. Erat autem a romano rege ad
romanum pontificem missus. O mirum commercium! Non audeo
quod sequitur dicere, neque hoc ipsum dicere volebam, sed quod
inceperam. Ut ergo pervenit, illico Pontifex Maximus tribus e numero principum Ecclesie causam eius discernendam dedit, quibus
impositum est: 'Videant quo supplicii genere dignus sit qui rempublicam liberam esse voluit.' O tempora o mores, o sepe michi ex-
11 clamatio repetenda! Est quidem, fateor, omni supplicio dignus
quia quod voluit non adeo perseveranter voluit ut debuit et ut rerum status necessitasque poscebant; sed libertatis patrocinium
professus, libertatis hostes, cum opprimere simul omnes posset,
quam facultatem nulli unquam imperatori fortuna concesserat, di-
12 misit armatos. O diram tetramque caliginem, sepe in mediis maximarum rerum conatibus mortalium se luminibus ingerentem!
nempe si alteram tantum cognominis sui partem, et non illam que
morbo reipublice necessaria erat—dici enim se Severum Clemen-
temque volebat—, si ergo clementiam solam in publicos parricidas
exercere decreverat, poterat eos nocendi instrumentis omnibus ex-
13 cussos precipueque superbis artibus exarmatos, vite relinquere, atque ita urbi romane vel de hostibus cives vel de timendis hostibus
contemnendos facere, de qua re non otiosam me sibi tunc epystolam scripsisse sum memor, cui si habita fides esset, alio loco respu-
14 blica staret nec Roma hodie serva foret nec ipse captivus. Certe
neque hoc neque quod sequitur, qualiter excusari possit intelligo;

The man who had made the wicked tremble throughout the 9
world and terrified them and had filled good men with joyous
hope and expectation, came humble and despised into the Curia.
Once escorted by the entire Roman people and leaders of the Italian cities, he was now flanked by two attendants to right and left,
unhappy fellow, as the common folk met him, eager to see the face
of the man whose glorious name they had so recently heard. Now 10
he had been sent by the Roman king to the Roman pontiff. What
a strange bargain![7] I do not dare to say what follows, nor had I
meant to say this, but rather what I had begun. So when he arrived, the Pontiff assigned three princes of the Church to judge his
case. Their charge was "to see what punishment a man deserved
who wanted the state to be free." "O, these times and their behavior!"[8] — an exclamation I must repeat so often. I admit he deserves 11
every punishment because he did not want what he wanted as
persistently as he should have and as circumstances and necessity
demanded; but having claimed patronage over liberty he let the
enemies of liberty go free when he could have overwhelmed them
all together, an opportunity which fortune had never granted to
any commander. O, what dread and loathsome darkness, which 12
often heaps itself on mortal eyes in the midcourse of the greatest
enterprises! For if he had used only half of his name and not the
half needed by the sickness of the state — since he wanted to be
called Severus Clemens[9] — if he had determined to use only clemency against the murderers of the state, he could have left them to
live stripped of all the instruments of doing harm, and especially
disarmed of their proud tricks, and so made them either citizens 13
instead of enemies of the city of Rome, or contemptible instead of
formidable enemies. Indeed, I remember sending him a far from
idle letter on this topic:[10] if he had believed it, the republic would
be standing in a different position, and neither would Rome have
been a slave today nor he a prisoner. Surely I do not understand 14
either how this or what follows could be excused: that after he had

quod cum in se bonorum tutelam et malorum exterminium susce-
pisset, post non longum tempus—ipse forte causam noverit; ego
enim eum postea non vidi; sed malefacti ratio proculdubio, etsi ab
homine diserto aliqua fingi possit, vera tamen esse penitus nulla
potest—repente mutatus animo ac moribus, non sine gravi periculo metuque bonorum malis favere totumque se illis credere ince-
pit. Atque utinam ex malis non pessimos elegisset! de quo alia
etiam ad eundem epystola mea est, nondum prolapsa iam nutante
republica.

15 Sed hec hactenus; loquor enim ardentius et per singulos orationis mee passus subsisto, mestus, ut vides, ut qui in illo viro ultimam libertatis italice spem posueram, quem diu ante michi cogni-
tum dilectumque, post clarissimum illud opus assumptum colere
ante alios mirarique permiseram, ideoque quanto magis speravi
tanto nunc magis doleo spe prerepta, fateorque, qualiscunque sit
16 finis, adhuc non possum principium non mirari. Venit autem non
vinctus—hoc unum defuit publico pudori—, ceterum eo habitu ut
spei nichil esset in fuga, inque ipso civitatis ingressu de me quesivit
infelix an in curia essem, seu opem forte aliquam ex me sperans—
que in me, quod ego quidem noverim, nulla est—, seu sola veteris
17 eisque ipsis in locis contracte olim amicitie memoria. Nunc ergo
viri salus, de cuius manu tot populorum salus incolumitasque
pendebant, de manibus pendet alienis; vita simul et fama eius in
ambiguo sunt. Non advertes quando, vibrante sententia, vel intes-
tabilem illum audies vel extinctum; et extingui quidem cuiuscunque mortalis, licet sanctissimum, corpus potest; at neque mortem neque infamiam virtus timet: inviolabilis est, nulli prorsus
18 iniurie, nullis telis obnoxia. Utinam non ipse suum decus vel desidia vel mutatione propositi deformasset! nil sibi nisi in corpus ab

taken on the protection of good men and the banishment of evil
men, after a short time (he will know the reason, but I have not
seen him since; yet certainly the justification for this crime, even if
a justification could be invented by an eloquent man, cannot be
truthful by any means), suddenly changing his attitude and behavior, not without causing risk and fear to the good men, he began
to support bad men and completely entrusted himself to them. If
only he had not chosen the worst of these bad men! On this subject I wrote another letter to the same Cola, when the republic was
not yet fallen but tottering.[11]

But enough of this, since I am talking too passionately and 15
pausing over individual passages in my argument, grieving as you
see, because I had placed in him the last hope of Italian liberty, a
man I had long before known and loved and had allowed myself,
after he had taken on this most glorious task, to worship and admire before all others; and so the more I hoped, the more I now
grieve at the snatching away of my hope, and I admit, whatever
the outcome, that I still cannot avoid admiring his beginning. So 16
he came, not in chains — this one thing was lacking to public
shaming — but in such a state that there was no hope of his escape,
and in the moment of entering the city the poor wretch asked
about me, whether I was in the Curia, either hoping for some help
from me — which, as far as I know, I have none to give — or just in
memory of the old friendship conceived in that very place.[12] So 17
now the survival of this man, upon whose hands the undamaged
survival of so many nations depended, depends on other men's actions; his life and reputation together are in doubt. You will not
notice when, according to the shifting verdict, you hear of him as
either disgraced or dead — indeed the body of any mortal, however
holy, can be destroyed, but virtue fears neither death nor disgrace;
it is inviolable, vulnerable to no injustice or violence. If only he had 18
not disfigured his own glory either from inertia or a change of intention! He had nothing to fear from this verdict, except for his

hac sententia metuendum esset, quamvis ne nunc quidem ullum
inde sibi fame discrimen impendeat apud eos qui veram gloriam
falsumque dedecus, non opinione vulgari, sed quibusdam certiori-
bus suis notis examinant et eventus virorum illustrium virtutis
19 non fortune iudicio metiuntur. Quod ita esse, ex obiecti criminis
qualitate perpenditur; nichil enim ex his que bonis omnibus in illo
viro displicent, arguitur, neque omnino finis sed principii reus est;
non sibi obicitur quod malis adheserit, quod libertatem destitue-
rit, quod e Capitolio fugerit, cum nusquam honestius vivere, nus-
20 quam gloriosius mori posset. Quid ergo? illud unum sibi crimen
opponitur, unde si condemnatus fuerit, non michi quidem infamis
sed eterna decoratus gloria videbitur: quod scilicet cogitare ausus
sit ut salvam ac liberam vellet esse rempublicam et de Romano
21 imperio deque romanis potestatibus Rome agi. O cruce vulturibus-
que dignum scelus, civem romanum doluisse quod patriam suam,
iure omnium dominam, servam vilissimorum hominum videret;
hec certe criminis summa est, hinc supplicium poscitur.

22 In hoc statu, ut iantandem audias cur incepi habeasque quod
rideas post dolorem, unam sibi relictam spem salutis amicorum
literis edidici, quod vulgo fama percrebuerit poetam illum esse
clarissimum; itaque nefas videri talem et tam sacro studio deditum
hominem violare, illa quidem preclara sententia iam in vulgus ef-
fusa, qua pro Aulo Licinio Archia preceptore suo apud iudices
23 usus est Cicero; quam non apposui quoniam orationem illam, ab
extremis olim Germanie advectam, dum loca illa visendi ardore
iuveniliter peragrarem et anno altero in patriam vobis optantibus
transmissam, habetis studioseque legitis, quod in literis inde ve-
24 nientibus recognosco. Quid vero nunc dicam? gaudeo equidem et
plusquam dici posset gratulor, tantum etiam nunc honorem Musis

body, although there is no risk even now to his repute in the minds of those who test true glory and false shame not by vulgar opinions but by some more reliable signs, who measure the ends of distinguished men by the judgment of virtue, not of fortune.
That this is so can be weighed by the quality of the charge leveled 19
at him, for no act is charged against that man which displeases all good men, and he is accused not for the ending of his career but for its beginning; he is not being reproached with associating with bad men, with deserting liberty, with fleeing from the Capitol, when he could not have lived more honorably nor died more gloriously in any other place. What then? This one charge is leveled 20
against him, and if he is found guilty of it, he will not seem to me disgraced but adorned with eternal glory, that is, that he dared to entertain the wish for the republic to be safe and free and for decisions of Roman authority and Roman magistracies to be made at
Rome. O what a crime worthy of the cross and vultures, that a 21
Roman citizen should grieve to see his native country, rightly mistress of all, as the most despised slave of all! This is surely the total of the charge, and from this the demand for his execution.

In these circumstances, so that you can finally hear why I began 22
to write, and have a reason for laughter after your sorrow, I learned of one hope of survival left to him from the letters of friends: that the rumor has become widespread that he was a distinguished poet; so it seemed wrong to violate such a man dedicated to so holy a pursuit; that splendid opinion was already diffused among the crowd, which Cicero used to the jury on behalf of his instructor Aulus Licinius Archias.[13] I have not quoted it because you 23
have that speech, brought from the remotest part of Germany when I was traveling in youthful enthusiasm for seeing those parts, and imported to our country a year ago at your request; and you
are now reading it attentively, as I gather from your letters. So 24
what shall I say now? I rejoice and give thanks more than can be expressed that such honor is given to the Muses, and—something

esse, quodque magis mireris, apud Musarum inscios, ut hominem
alioquin ipsis iudicibus invisum salvare possint solo nomine. Quid
plus sub Augusto Cesare meruissent, quando illis summus honor
habitus, quando ille vatum ex omni regione concursus Rome fuit
ad spectandam preclarissimam illam faciem unici principis et amici
25 poetarum et regum domini? quid amplius, queso, tunc tributum
Musis esset quam ut hominem, non laboro quanto dignum odio,
odiosum certe, neque cuius reum criminis, reum tamen convic-
tumque et confessum concordique voto iudicum capitali sententia
feriendum, periculo mortis eriperent? Iterum dicam, gaudeo gra-
tulorque sibi et Musis: sibi hoc esse presidium, Musis hunc honorem; neque ancipitis spei reo in extremis casibus hoc saluti-
26 ferum poete nomen invideo. Si me tamen interroges, Nicolaus
Laurentii vir facundissimus est et ad persuadendum efficax et ad
oratoriam pronus, dictator quoque dulcis ac lepidus non multe
quidem sed suavis colorateque sententie; poetas, puto, qui comu-
niter habentur, omnes legerit: non tamen ideo magis est poeta
27 quam textor ideo quia manibus alienis texta chlamyde induitur; et
licet ad poete nomen promerendum non sufficiat solum carmen
sitque verissimum illud Horatii

neque enim contexere versum
Dixeris esse satis, nec siquis scribit uti nos
Sermoni propiora, putes hunc esse poetam,

iste tamen nunquam vel unicum carmen quod ad aures meas venerit, contexuit; neque enim ad id animum applicuit, sine quo nichil
28 quantumlibet facile bene fit. Hoc tibi notum facere placuit, ut
de assertoris olim publici fortuna doleas, de insperata gaudeas

to make you wonder all the more—among people ignorant of the
Muses, that they can save a man otherwise hated by the judges
just by invoking this name. What more would poets have earned
under Augustus Caesar, when they were paid the greatest honor
and there was an assembly of bards at Rome from every region in
order to gaze on the glorious presence of this unique emperor,
who was both friend of poets and master of the world? What 25
more, I ask, was done in homage to the Muses than to rescue from
the danger of death a man certainly worthy of hatred (I do not
trouble over the degree of hatred he deserved) nor about the
charge of which he was guilty, but nonetheless a defendant, confessed and convicted to be struck down with capital punishment
by the unanimous vote of the jury? So, I repeat, I rejoice and give
thanks to him and the Muses for the protection given him and the
honor given the Muses, nor do I begrudge the lifesaving title of
poet to a defendant of dubious hope in extreme cases. But if you 26
ask me, Cola di Rienzo is a most eloquent man and effective in
persuasion and disposed to oratory, and equally a sweet and appealing writer, not of an abundant expression but one pleasant and
colorful; he has read, I think, all those generally thought of as
poets, but this does not make him any more a poet than a man
who wears a cloak woven by others is himself a weaver; and 27
though a poem is not enough to earn the name of poet, and that
sentiment of Horace is most true:

> You would not call it enough to weave a poem,
> Nor if anyone writes like us, verse closer to speech,
> Would you think this man a poet,[14]

he still never composed even one poem that reached my ears, nor
did he direct his spirit to this aspiration, without which nothing,
however easy, is well made. I wanted to make this known to you so 28
that you might grieve over the lot of the former public champion
and rejoice over his unexpected survival, but share my indignation

salute, de salutis autem causa mecum pariter indigneris et rideas,
cogitesque: si — quod utinam accidat — sub clipeo poetico Nicolaus e tantis periculis evaserit, unde non evasurus esset Maro? sed
ille sub his iudicibus aliam ob causam periret, quoniam scilicet
29 non poeta sed nigromanticus haberetur. Dicam quod magis rideas:
ipse ego, quo nemo usquam divinationi inimicior vivit aut magie,
nonnunquam inter hos optimos rerum iudices propter Maronis
amicitiam nigromanticus dictus sum. En quo studia nostra dilapsa
sunt! o nugas odibiles ridendasque! et ut multiplici gustu cunta
cognoscas quid ve de minoribus opinandum sit maiorum concipias
ab exemplo, addam aliud illustre ridiculum.

30 Magnum amicum cultuque precipuo colendum Babilone habeo;
utor enim prisco et ingenuo loquendi more quo Cicero Magnum
Pompeium familiarem suum vocat et Plinius Secundus Vespasiano
suo salutem dicit; nam si moderno servili atque adulatorio sermonis genere utendum est, habeo singularem verendumque domi-
31 num. Utcunque tamen hoc dixerim, illud vere dici potest: unum
esse ex paucis, principem inter principes, excellentissimum inter
summos, romuleique clarum decus cardinis, virum rare prudentie,
cuius consilio perfacile terrarum orbis regi posse videatur, literarum preterea multarum et excelsi ingenii; sed verum est quod Sa-
32 lustius Crispus ait: 'ubi intenderis ingenium valet.' Ille ergo vir
tantus inter familiares sermones quibus me sepe dignatur, quotiens mentio incidisset alicuius qui vel tria verba ad populum facere vel securi conductus epystolam dictare didicisset, me attentus,
ne dicam attonitus, percontari solebat in hunc ferme modum: 'Est
ne hic de quo loquimur poeta?' Ego autem tacebam; quid enim
33 aliud facerem? Id enim vero cum ex me sepe de quibusdam scolas-
ticis pingue quiddam et rancidum usu potiusquam ratione dictan-
tibus quesivisset, et ego semel egre risum continerem, animadvertit

at the cause of his survival and laugh and think that if Cola escaped from such great dangers—and may that happen—under the shield of poetry, from what dangers would Vergil have not been able to escape? But Vergil would have perished with this jury for another reason, since he would be thought not a poet but a wizard.[15] I will pass on a better cause for laughter: I myself, more 29
hostile to divination and magic than any other living man, am sometimes called a wizard among these excellent judges of life, because of my affection for Vergil. See what has become of our studies! O loathsome and absurd nonsense! And so that you recognize everything from more than one sampling, and may conceive what to think about lesser matters from a greater example, I will add another conspicuous absurdity.

I have a grand friend here in Babylon to be cherished with 30
special reverence—for I am using the ancient style of language by which Cicero called Pompey the Great his friend and Pliny greeted Vespasian as his;[16] but if we must use the modern servile and flattering kind of talk, I have a unique and venerable master.
Yet whatever I would call him, it can be truly said that he is one 31
among few, a leader among leaders, most excellent among the greatest, and brilliant glory of the Romulean college—a man of rare good sense, by whose advice the world seemingly could be most easily ruled, and what is more a man of much reading and lofty intellect; but then it is true, as Sallust says, that "where you
direct your intellect it flourishes."[17] So among the intimate conver- 32
sations which he often deigns to have with me, this great man used to question me more or less like this, whenever there was a reference to someone who could utter three words to the people or a hired secretary who had learned to dictate a letter: "Is this man we are talking about a poet?" I would keep quiet, for what else
could I do? So as he often asked me about some schoolmen who 33
composed clumsy and tasteless verse from habit rather than conviction, there was one time when could barely hold in my laughter.

oris mei habitum vir ille cautissimus; itaque magis ac magis instare
34 cepit ut dicerem quid rei esset. Tunc ego familiaritate illa qua secum fidenter loqui omnia, eo sic volente, sum solitus, ignorantiam
rei pulcerrime in tanto ingenio reverenter increpui, quod non saltem primos atque latissimos terminos nosset artis illius in qua
olim, licet publicis occupatos curis, mundi dominos altissima inge-
35 nia cupide et diligenter exercuisse constaret; propositisque aliquot
exemplis, quibus tu non eges, in hanc sententiam conclusi, ut
ostenderem sibi pauciores poetas esse quam crederet et pro tempore pauca strictim de poetice primordio, de viis ac termino et
presertim de ipsa incredibili poetarum raritate disserui; quem no-
vissimum articulum in *Oratore* suo Tullius attigit. Que cum ille vir
magnus inque aliis doctus et in his minime indocilis intentis auribus audivisset, sitienter amplecti visus crebroque dehinc singula
36 repetens post eum diem huiusmodi questionibus abstinuit. Tu vive
feliciter et vale, et nisi tibi aliter videtur, epystolam hodiernam
hesternamque, postquam legeris, mitte Neapolim ad Zenobium
nostrum, ut ipse Barbatusque meus, si forsan e portu Sulmonensi
Parthenopeas repetiit procellas, risum nostrum indignationemque
participent.

*Ad fontem Sorgie, IV Idus Augustas.*

: 6 :

## *Ad quattuor cardinales reformando Romane Reipublice statui deputatos.*

1 Fragilibus humeris grande honus imponitur ab illo et pro illa quibus negare nil potui; nequid ergo reicerem, iussit anime dominus

That cautious man noticed the look on my face and began to press me more and more to explain the problem. Then I, with that inti- 34
macy with which I spoke of everything confidently to him and was accustomed to do so at his wish, respectfully rebuked ignorance of this most noble subject in so great an intellect, since he did not even know the basic and broadest terms of the art in which once, though occupied by public concerns, the lords of the earth exercised the loftiest intellects eagerly and scrupulously; and after put- 35
ting forward some examples which you don't need, I finished to this effect: I showed him there were fewer poets than he believed, and I gave a concise lecture on the foundations of poetry, on its methods and terms and especially on the incredible rarity of poets — the last topic being that which Cicero touched on in his books *On the Orator*.[18] So when that great man, quite learned in other matters and by no means unteachable in these, heard these remarks with ears alert, he seemed to embrace them thirstily and often thereafter repeated them, refraining from that kind of question from that day forward. As for you, live happily and fare well 36
and unless you choose otherwise, send today's and yesterday's letter, after you have read them, to Naples to Zanobi so that he and my Barbato, if he happens to seek the storms of Parthenope from the harbor of Sulmona, can share our laughter and indignation.[19]

*By the source of the Sorgue. August 10.*

## : 6 :

## *To the four cardinals delegated to reform the condition of the Roman Republic.*

A great burden has been set upon my frail shoulders by that man 1
and on behalf of that republic to whom I can deny nothing, and

amor mee. Comunis patrie et parentis publice salus in ambiguo vertitur; non est filius quem pie matris non tangit iniuria. Accedit ad humani generis universale debitum singulare quoddam erga me meritum urbis Rome, que et suum me insigni privilegio civem vocat et fortasse non ultimum hoc tempore nominis sui et fame
2 presidium senescentis in me repositum arbitratur. Denique sic semper de me meruit, ut ubi de statu eius queritur, non modo turpe silentium meum sit sed inhumanum etiam et ingratum. Hec idcirco prefari libuit nequis me insanum aut mei ipsius oblitum putet, qui maiora viribus meis sim aggressus contraque consilium Sapientis altiora me quesierim et fortiora me scrutatus fuerim; seu indignanter audiat quod romana libertas pio quidem sed humili prorsus et subito ac pedestri et forsan impertinenti elogio defenda-
3 tur. Magna res, fateor, et coram magnis agitur et ad maximum referenda. Ego vero parvitatis mee michi sum conscius, sed ad loquendum animos dat innata devotio; itaque, patres optimi, quibus huiusce rei cura mandata est, si a vobis, ut spero, hactenus mee procacitatis excusatio faventibus animis est admissa, pias, oro, dehinc aures fidelibus adhibete sermonibus, non quis ego sed quenam intentio mea sit, neque tam qualiter quam quid dicam, imo vero non tam quid dicam quam quid dicere velim et quid super tanta materia dici potest, misericorditer attendentes.

4 Primum hoc animis vestris reor insitum, nullius humane rei nomen esse sonantius quam Reipublice Romanorum; hoc michi nulla regio, nulla gens, nulla barbaries negabit, sed orbis ipse terrarum, si loqui possit, uno ore fatebitur, et suum caput ingenue recognoscet, impexum licet neglectumque miserabiliter et incultum.

so love, the lord of my soul, has bidden me not to reject it. The common welfare of our country and the parent of us all is in danger and uncertainty; no son can be untouched by wrong done to his loving mother. In addition to the universal debt of our human race I recognize the unique service of the city of Rome toward me, since it calls me its citizen by a special privilege[1] and perhaps believes me to be an important protector of her name and aging reputation at this time. In short she has so greatly obliged and 2
served me that when there is discussion of her condition my silence would be not merely shameful but inhuman and ungrateful. I have chosen to declare this as a preliminary for fear anyone might think me crazy or forgetful of myself in tackling problems greater than my strength and, contrary to the advice of the wise king, more lofty and examining things stronger than myself,[2] or for fear that someone might be indignant to hear that Roman liberty is being defended by a devout but humble and improvised and prosaic and perhaps irrelevant eulogy. I admit it is a great matter, 3
and heard by great judges and to be referred to the greatest of them all. Indeed I am aware of my insignificance, but my innate loyalty gives me courage to speak; so best of Fathers, to whom this business has been entrusted, if you have accepted my excuse for outspokenness with a well-disposed mind, I beg you to offer your devout attention to my loyal arguments, paying compassionate attention not to who I am but to what my purpose is, and not so much how well I argue but what is my argument, in fact not so much what I am saying as what I mean to say and what else can be said on such a great topic.

I think the first principle instilled in your hearts is that no 4
name of any human creation is more resounding than the Roman republic.[3] No land, no nation, no barbaric masses will deny this, but the very world itself, if it could speak, will unanimously admit and honestly recognize that Rome is its head, though it may be unkempt and wretchedly neglected and ungroomed.

5 Quamobrem et si nichil aliud esset Roma quam nomen, esset tamen regine olim nomen urbis, ut arbitror, quadam cum veneratione tractandum; illius, inquam, urbis quam Deus omnipotens tot tantisque prerogative temporalis ac spiritualis insignibus adornasset, penes quam et vere fidei basim et Ecclesie fundamenta et supremum totius orbis imperium statuisset. Nunc vero et plus aliquid quam nomen Roma est et unde vel sperari possit aliquid
6 vel timeri. Illud ex ordine cogitantibus occurrat non frustra nec temere sed divinitus factum esse ut vobis potissimum ex omni sacro collegio Romanus Pontifex gloriosum hoc et meritorium, quamvis equa lance librantibus minime grave, pondus iniungeret; e quibus tres preter profundissimam sapientiam uberrimamque doctrinam, romanarum quoque rerum notitiam experientia docuisset; quartus vero non modo romane esset originis sed genus etiam, ut quidam putant, ex altissima ac vetustissima traheret gente Cornelia, et tamen — o vera pietas, o patrie dulcis amor! — adversus superbam nobilitatem athleta fortissimus indefense causam plebis ageret et oppresse patrocinium libertatis. Piam igitur ad causam a Deo iudices dati, nullum secordie locum, nullum humanis preci-
7 bus aut gratie relinquatis. Sed ut iantandem questionis et sententie mee summam brevi sermone complectar, lis antiqua repetitur atque utinam prisce superbie nil nove tyrannidis accessisset. Ignava placensque sibi de nichilo et spernens cunta nobilitas humilitate nimia romane plebis abutitur, nec aliter quam totidem Penos aut Cimbros captos et sub iugum missos, ignominiosum pertrahit ad triumphum; atqui nulla lege cautum, nullo more servatum, nunquam alias fando auditum est ut domitis civibus triumphetur.
8 Unum hoc etiam loco non alienum fuerit interfari, nequa sit orationi mee vel levis odii permixta suspitio, me scilicet harum

So even if Rome was nothing else but its name, this would be the 5
name of the one-time queen of cities, to be treated, as I believe,
with a certain reverence; that city, I say, which Almighty God had
adorned with so many great ornaments of temporal and spiritual
primacy, and in whose power he had set up the base of the true
faith and foundations of the Church and supreme empire over the
world. But now surely Rome is something more than a name, and
a source from which something is to be either hoped or feared. If 6
we think about it systematically, it should occur to us that it is not
in vain nor casually, but by divine ordinance that the Roman pope
imposed upon you, out of the whole sacred college, this glorious
and deserved responsibility, although it is not heavy for those bal-
ancing it in fair scales; and shared among three men who, beside
their deep wisdom and abundant learning, have been taught by
experience of Roman history, while the fourth is not only of Roman origin but derived his birth, as some think, from the most
exalted and ancient family of the Cornelii, and yet—O true piety,
O sweet love of country—has been a most gallant champion
against the arrogant nobility, pleading the case of the undefended
common people, as patron of downtrodden liberty.[4] So being appointed by God as judges of this devout case, you should leave no
room for lethargy or human pleas and influence. But to cover 7
briefly the main purpose of my inquiry and verdict, this is the return of an old grievance—would there had been no new tyrannical
feature in ancient arrogance! The nobility, idle and self-satisfied
without cause and contemptuous of everything, is exploiting the
excessive humbleness of the Roman people, dragging them, like so
many Carthaginians and Cimbrians taken prisoner and sent beneath the yoke, to a shameful triumph;[5] yet it has been required by
no law, observed by no custom, nor heard of at any other time for
a triumph to be held over defeated fellow citizens. At this point it 8
would not be out of place to insert the claim that no suspicion of
even trivial hatred is mingled with my words; in fact, that of the

unde ea lis oritur familiarum, alteram non odisse, alteram vero, quod commemorare superfluit, non amare solum, sed familiari quodam semper obsequio coluisse, nullamque michi toto orbe principum familiam cariorem; carior tamen michi respublica, carior Roma, carior Italia, carior bonorum quies atque securitas.
9 Itaque ut defunctorum atque viventium pace loquar, hec, nisi fallor, causa fuit cur in hanc magnitudinem urbem unam crescere consenserunt Deus virtus labor pariter ac fortuna, ut Ecclesie et Imperii caput esset, non ut regnum fieret paucorum civium, imo — si verum, petita venia, loqui licet — nec civium quidem romanorum nec romanum nomen amantium. Non insistam in utriusque gentis origine recensenda; nota res est et Rheni vallibus et Spoletinis
10 etiam decantata pastoribus. Ita domina gentium, in omnes lapsa miserias nullique miserabilis, non, ut quondam, propriis sed alienis manibus lacerata, vetus illud solatium perdidit malorum:

nullos admittere reges
Sed civi servire suo.

Et an huic iniurie occurrendum sit, ambigitur; illud autem omittitur, quod ante omnia quesitu dignum erat, quibus seu quam exquisitis suppliciorum gencribus predones publici puniendi, aut saltem in libera civitate libertatis hostes quam procul a muneribus
11 publicis sint arcendi. Id unum queritur, stupendum dictu, an dominator olim populorum omnium populus romanus eousque restitui debeat libertati ut in Capitolio suo, unde Senonum flammas atque arma submovit, ubi reges captos ante triumphales currus vidit, ubi legatos gentium supplices audivit, unde precipitans superba civium atque hostium colla confregit, hodie possit una

two families who are the source of this conflict I do not hate the one, and truly, as hardly needs mention, I do not merely love the other family but have always been devoted to it with the attention of an intimate friend:[6] no noble family in the whole world has been dearer to me, yet the republic is dearer still, Rome is dearer, Italy is dearer, and the repose and freedom from anxiety of good
people is dearer. So, to speak with the indulgence of the dead and 9
living, this was the reason why God, virtue, toil and fortune alike worked together for one city to grow to this greatness, to become the capital of the Church and Empire, not the dominion of a few citizens, and even—if I may speak the truth with your leave—persons who are neither Roman citizens nor lovers of the name of Rome. I shall not linger over reviewing the origin of either noble house, for this is known in the valleys of the Rhine and chanted by
the shepherds of Spoleto.[7] Thus Rome, mistress of nations, hav- 10
ing sunk into every kind of wretchedness yet not pitied by any man, torn apart not by her own folk as she once was but by foreign action, has lost the old consolation of her misfortunes:

> To allow no kings,
> but serve one of her own citizens.[8]

And yet there is doubt whether to confront this injustice; indeed the question is left out which deserved investigation before all else, by what or how refined varieties of torture these public brigands are to be punished, or at least how far the enemies of freedom should
be kept away from public service in a free community. The one 11
issue, amazing to relate, is whether the Roman people, once conqueror of all nations, should be restored to such a point of liberty that in its Capitol, from which it drove the flames and weapons of the Senones, where it saw captured kings led before the triumphal chariots, where it heard the envoys of nations in supplication, from which it hurled down and smashed the proud bodies of enemies and citizens,[9] it may share in any part of the public admin-

cum domesticis tyrannis partem ullam publice administrationis
12 attingere. O bone Iesu, ubinam gentium habitamus? aspicis ista,
Salvator, aut quonam piaculis nostris offensus solite pietatis oculos
avertisti? Miserere iam et tanti maculas absterge dedecoris. Hucne
igitur vivendo decidimus, hic erat erumnarum terminus ut in publico vel, quod publico maius est, coram Cristi vicario et coram
Apostolorum successoribus quereretur liceat ne romanum civem in
senatum eligi, cum tandiu alienigenas regnare et tot Tarquinios
Superbos in Capitolio videamus?

13 En questio ad quam solvendam quattuor celi cardinum labor
invigilet. Certe ego, si consular, respondere non dubitem romano
more senatum romanum nonnisi ex romanis civibus constare et
externos a limine secludendos, non tantum quos miserint longinqua terrarum, sed Latinos etiam, gentem proximam atque conti-
guam Romanis et pene cum eis unum corpus, neque illos solum
verbo vel calamo sed si fieri possit, etiam gladio deterrendos;
14 exemplo Auli Manlii Torquati, qui cum Latini quondam peterent
ut ex eis alter consulum et senatus pars dimidia legeretur, tanta
indignatione permotus est ut iuraret se in curiam cinctum gladio
venturum et siquem ibi Latinorum cerneret, manu propria pe-
rempturum. Quonam ille animo spectasset senatum totum a Rheni
ripis vel ab Umbria venientem, qui solam partis dimidie mentio-
15 nem tam indignanter pertulit a Latinis? Nostri autem peregrini,
ne sine causa furere videantur, hanc usurpati senatus rationem af-
ferunt, quod potentiores sunt ad honus tanti officii perferendum.
Que ista potentia est, nunquam nisi damno civitatis cognita? unde
autem, quantulacunque est, nisi e sanguine populi et reipublice
conflata visceribus? Ut magna tamen sit et iusta potentia, quid ad

istration together with its homegrown tyrants. Gentle Jesus, where 12
on earth are we living? Savior, do you see this or have you, in offense at our offenses, turned away your gaze of customary kindness? Take pity now and wipe away the stains of such disgrace.[10] Have we lived merely to sink to this, was this the end of our losses, that in a public hearing or—something greater than a public hearing—before the Vicar of Christ and the successors of the Apostles, the question should be raised whether a Roman citizen may be elected to the Senate, when we can see foreign-born men ruling for so long and so many Proud Tarquins on our Capitol?[11]

This is the problem which the labor of four cardinals will watch 13
over for its solution. I surely, if I am consulted, would not hesitate to answer in the Roman fashion that the Roman senate cannot consist of any but Roman citizens and that foreigners should be driven from the threshold, not only those sent from remote regions of the earth but even Latins, that race nearest and even neighboring on the Romans and almost a single body with them, and they should be driven off not just by speech or pen but if possible even with the sword. Take as your model Aulus Manlius 14
Torquatus: when the Latins once requested that one of the consuls should be from their number and half the senate, he was stirred by such indignation that he swore he would come into the senate house girt with his sword and slay with his own hand any Latin whom he saw there.[12] What would have been his mood if he had looked on an entire senate coming from the banks of the Rhine or from Umbria,[13] since he took with such indignation just the mention of one half by the Latins? But our foreigners, so as not to 15
seem to rage without reason, give this justification for usurping the senate, that their power makes theme more able to carry the burden of so great a function. What power is this, never met without cost to the city? Whence does it come, however small it may be, except brewed from the people's blood and the republic's flesh? If their power is great and just, how does this affect the argument?

16 rem? Certe dum illa, cuius proxime memini, Romam venisset legatio Latinorum, armis virisque et opibus florens Latium describitur, nec minus ideo repulsi sunt qui potentie fidutia ad honorem indebitum aspirarent, ne virtutis premia fortune tribuerent immerenti. Profecto enim, si nude potentie senatoria Rome dignitas deberetur nec respectus esset vel originis vel virtutis, poterant et Macedonia tunc temporis et Carthago et nunc alia per orbem magnis viribus regna pollentia, multum sibi iuris hac in re multumque preminentie vendicare.

17 Sed dicent: 'Et nos Romani sumus et longa vel detentione magistratuum vel libertatis oppressione, romanorum civium iura prescripsimus.' Ego vero profecisse me non modicum arbitrarer, si ad hoc elatissimos animos inclinassem ut cives et non vastatores civium esse vellent, neque tunc illos ab honorum gradibus Manliano rigore depellerem. Sed per miserantem res humanas Deum, mitissimi patres, siqua romani nominis miseratione tangimini, percontor vos an eo proposito capessere illos rempublicam extima-
18 tis, ut comuni penurie propriis opibus opem ferant. Utinam id in animum inducerent! possem munifice ambitioni veniam dare et undecunque venientes candidatos admittere. At michi credite, contrarium meditantur, ut scilicet de reliquiis sparse urbis insatiabilem avaritie sue famem non tam mitigent quam accendant. Verum et hoc negare forsitan audebunt et unius verbi impudentia notam mundo totius vite seriem occultare et romani cives et amantes
19 patrie dici volent. Non ita est; quippe quos cives, imo quos homines et non principes aut dominos vocare, capitalis offensa est. Quia vero, licet sub equis iudicibus, iniqua rerum sorte contendimus, detur concordie gratia quod facillimum est negare, et cives et

16 Certainly when that embassy of the Latins which I mentioned just now came to Rome, Latium is described as flourishing with weapons, manpower and resources,[14] but they were none the less rejected for aspiring to an unjustified honor out of confidence in their power, for fear they might assign the rewards of virtue to mere undeserving fortune. For surely, if the rank of senator at Rome was the due of bare power and there was no consideration for origin or merit, at that time Macedonia and Carthage[15] and now other kingdoms around the world, powerful through their great strength, would claim great rights for themselves and great preeminence in this matter.

17 But they will say: "We too are Romans and by virtue of our long tenure of magistracies or oppression of liberty we have appropriated the rights of Romans." In fact I would believe I had gained no small advantage if I had swayed distinguished minds to want to be citizens and not the mass killers of citizens, and I would not then thrust them down from the ranks of honor with the rigor of Manlius. But in the name of God who pities human life, most gentle fathers, if you are touched by any compassion for the name of Rome, I ask you whether you think they entered political life so as to bring aid to the common poverty with their own
18 resources? If only they would persuade themselves of this idea! I could give lavish pardon to their ambition and admit candidates coming for any and every place. But believe me, they are planning the opposite, that is not to dilute but to inflame the insatiable hunger of their greed from the remains of the scattered city. But perhaps they will dare to deny this and hide with the shameless use of one word the events of their whole life known to the world,
19 and want to be called Roman citizens and patriots. Hardly, since it would be a capital offense to call them citizens or even mortals, and not princes and lords. But since we are contending on unfair terms, albeit with fair judges, for the sake of harmony let the proposition be granted which it is most easy to deny, that they are

pacificos cives esse. Indigni veniant ad honores, ita tamen ut dig-
nissimos non excludant. Ut enim iam ex equo cum Romanis externi litigent et sint omnes uno nomine Romani, quid est cur illi
soli honorari debeant quibus hoc precarium nomen est, imo vero
cur ulla in re suis contribulibus anteferri? An propter nobilitatem?
20 Sed quid sit vera nobilitas, non parva disputatio est; tum demum
ergo quam sint nobiles intelligent, cum intelligere ceperint quam
sint etiam virtuosi.

An propter divitias? quas nunc extenuare verbis nolo; illud tantum moneo ut non ideo tenuiores despiciant sciantque illas omnino bonis moribus nil conferre, et quas de fecundis Ecclesie matris uberibus suxerunt, eis sobrie et pro transitoriis utantur, vel si
libet — ad maiora pigriores animi non assurgunt — fruantur etiam
pro eternis, modo unum prestent ut quas de comuni liberalitate
21 percipiunt, in comunem pernitiem non convertant. Quodsi ad
publicum regimen privatas divitias necessarias opinantur, velim
michi respondeant quam dives erat Valerius Publicola dum adiutor
Bruti superbos reges eiceret, dum primo consulatu de Tuscis, tertio de Sabinis, vir sepeliendus e publico, triumpharet; quam dives
Menenius Agrippa dum discordem scissamque rempublicam sacro
22 conglutinaret eloquio; quam dives Quintius Cincinnatus dum deserto rure inopi Romam metu et obsidione consulem romanum
atque exercitum liberaret; quam dives Curius, quam dives Fabri-
tius dum Pyrri regis ac Samnitium signa prosternerent; quam
dives Atilius Regulus dum Carthaginiensium funderet legiones;
quam dives Appius Claudius dum luminibus captus rempublicam
consilio gubernaret. Operosum est omnia gloriose paupertatis

both citizens and peace loving citizens. Give unworthy men access
to office but only provided that they do not exclude the deserving.
for even if outsiders now litigate on equal terms with Romans and
are all Romans under a single name, why should they alone deserve to be honored who have this name merely on the basis of
favor, or why should they be preferred to their fellow tribesmen in
any matter? Is it on account of their nobility? But there is no 20
trivial dispute about what is true nobility; hence they will only
understand how noble they are when they have begun to understand how virtuous they are.

Is it because of their wealth? I don't want to diminish this in
argument; I just warn you that they should not for that reason
scorn the less well off and know that wealth confers absolutely
nothing in good behavior, and they should use soberly and for the
sake of transitory things what they have sucked from the fertile
breasts of mother Church, or if they choose — those lazy spirits do
not rise to greater endeavors — they could enjoy them as eternal,
provided they guarantee one thing, not to misuse for universal
ruin what they have won from communal generosity. But if they 21
think private wealth necessary for public government I would like
them to answer me: how rich was Valerius Publicola when he
drove out the arrogant kings, as Brutus' supporter, when he triumphed in his first consulship over the Etruscans, and in his third
over the Sabines, a man worthy of his public burial? How rich 22
was Menenius Agrippa when he bonded together the discordant
and schismatic republic with his holy eloquence? How rich was
Cincinnatus when, after abandoning the countryside, he freed
Rome from helpless fear and the Roman consul and his army from
blockade? Or how rich Fabricius when the Romans laid low the
standards of King Pyrrhus and the Samnites? How rich was
Atilius Regulus when he routed the Carthaginian legions? How
rich was Appius Claudius when he guided the Republic by his
advice though deprived of his sight?[16] It would be laborious to

23 exempla colligere. Audeo autem affirmare, licet obstrepat multi-
tudo, nil magis quam supervacuas divitias obesse virtutibus; et ne
ceteras nationes a radicata medullitus opinione convellam, quod
inter scriptores rerum constat, Romam victricem gentium vicere
divitie, nec dubium est una eademque via et paupertatem romanam exivisse et peregrina subintrasse flagitia. Ita quod maxime
nocet rectoribus civitatum, id isti maxime profuturum putant sive,
quod potius reor, putare se simulant.

24 Reliquum est ut veriorem causam presidendi cupidinis inqui-
ramus. Ea vero non alte fodientibus presto est. Omitto avaritiam,
que etsi magnis indiciis suspecta sit, propter honestatem quandam
nominari in hoc sermone michi quidem videtur indigna, eo quod
in animis nobilibus turpissime habitat, imo vero procul inde exu-
25 lat; sed loquor nunc de nobilitate vulgari. Superbiam igitur solam
dico 'comune nobilitatis malum,' ut Salustius ait, non utique novam pestem in republica, siquidem et veros illos et veteres Romanos attigit interque virtutes maximas lividus tumor obrepsit, semper tamen humilitatis gravitate compressus, vestro etiam nunc, ut
spero, gloriosissimi patres, arbitrio comprimendus. Egere videtur
res exemplo.

26 Iam ab initio plebs romana inhumanis iniuriis affecta, suos magistratus et libertatis ambigue patronos ac vindices poscebat; acri
nobilitas adversata luctamine; hinc in Sacrum Montem prima se-
cessio; vicit tandem superbiam nobilium plebeia iustitia et recla-
mantibus nequaquam patritiis, tunc primum calcar unicum ac
27 frenum illorum violentie, tribunatus plebis est inventus. De hoc
quoque graviter altercatum; instante plebe ut novus magistratus
suis, hoc est tribunitiis, comitiis crearetur, et hic quoque plebs
victrix, Appio Claudio, viro licet acerrimo, pertinacius obluctante.

gather all the models of splendid poverty. But I dare to affirm, 23 though the crowd may heckle, that nothing obstructs the virtues more than superfluous wealth, and not to uproot the other nations from their entrenched opinion, I assert what is agreed among historians, that riches conquered Rome, the conqueror of nations, and there is no doubt that poverty left Rome by the same road on which foreign vices made their way in. So these men think that what most harms the leaders of cities will be of most benefit, or as I am more inclined to think, they pretend to believe this.

So it remains for us to seek out a more genuine cause for their 24
greed for government. Indeed it is ready to hand without digging deeply. I leave aside avarice, even if major evidence leads us to suspect it; it seems to me unworthy of mention in this discussion out of respect for honorable status, because it is most disgraceful when found in noble spirits; in fact it is exiled far from them; but now I
am talking about the common nobility. Hence I affirm that pride 25
alone is "the common vice of nobility," as Sallust says,[17] certainly not a new plague of the state, since it touched even those genuine old Romans, and discoloring envy crept in among the greatest virtues; yet it is always crushed by the weight of humility, as it is even now to be crushed by your decision, most glorious fathers. The matter seems to need an example.

Now from the beginning the common people of Rome suffered 26
inhuman wrongs, and demanded its own magistrates and patrons as champions of their fluctuating and uncertain liberty, while the nobility opposed this in a fierce struggle: hence the first secession to the Sacred Hill; and finally plebeian justice overcame the nobles' arrogance, and when the patricians protested in vain, the tribuneship of the plebs was created, the first and only spur and
bridle to control the nobles' violence.[18] There was bitter dispute 27
over this too, because the people insisted that the new magistracy should be elected by its own, that is the tribunician, elections, and here too the people was victorious, though Appius Claudius, a

Nova dehinc orta contentio, primoribus superbo fastidio negantibus inter plebem patritiosque matrimonia, et sic abrupto sanctissimo vinculo generis humani, in duas iterum partes scindentibus
civitatem. Indignata plebs restitit: sic invitis adversariis, lege lata,
28 promiscua sunt permissa coniugia. Decemviratus sacrorum causa,
questura, curulis edilitas nonnisi patritie gentis erant. Animadvertit plebs se ludibrio haberi; annisa est evicitque ut harum quoque
particeps dignitatum fieret; qua in re non est silentio supprimen-
dum parvum illud per se, sed superbie nobilium et plebeie liberta-
29 tis evidentissimum argumentum a Tito Livio relatum. Gneus Flavius, scribe filius, humillime vir fortune, ceterum vafer ac disertus,
edilis curulis factus erat. Ea res nobilibus novitatem eius horrenti-
bus tantum stomacum excitarat ut in illius honore, velut in luctu
proprio, plurimi ex eis anulos aureos et ornamenta deponerent;
contra ille, nichil motus, adversus eorum insolentiam liberrimam
30 contumaciam exercebat. Itaque dum visitandi gratia egrotantis
collega thalamum intranti nobiles iuvenes, qui tum forte aderant,
unanimi contemptu non assurgerent, confestim sellam curulem
iussit afferri, atque ita suorum nobilium contemptorum contemptor ipse nobilior illos invidia tabescentes non de privato
scamno sed publica de sede despexit; qua unica libertate michi
quidem videtur non edilitatis modo, sed consulatas etiam honore
dignissimus.

31 De quo loqui sciens ad ultimum reservavi, quod scilicet sena-
tores duo qui e tanta conscriptorum patrum frequentia supersunt,
videri possunt in locum duorum consulum successisse. Ut enim
hic habet, sic ille finem habuit magistratus; senatorum potestas
terminum non habebat. De hoc igitur consulatu quotiens et

most fierce man, resisted rather obstinately.[19] From this a new conflict arose, when the nobles with arrogant contempt refused marriages between the people and the patricians, and as a result, since the most sacred bond of human life was broken, the state again broke into two parties. The people were indignant and resisted; so against the will of their antagonists a law was passed and
mixed marriages permitted.[20] There was a board of ten for the 28
administration of public rites; the quaestorship and the curule aedileship were only awarded to men of patrician birth. The people realized it was being mocked; it wrestled and won the right of sharing in these ranks; and in this we should not suppress in silence an episode small in itself but the most obvious proof of the nobles' arrogance and plebeians' freedom reported by Livy.[21]
Gnaeus Flavius, the son of a scribe, and a man of humble condi- 29
tion but otherwise shrewd and eloquent was elected curule aedile. This raised such resentment in the nobles in their horror at his being a "new man," that on his election, as if in personal mourning, most of them took off their gold rings and adornments; he was unmoved and exercised the most outspoken obstruction
against their abuse. Indeed, when he was visiting a sick colleague 30
and entered his bedchamber, the noble young men who happened to be sitting there, unanimous in their contempt, refused to rise; so he instantly ordered his magistrate's chair to be brought in and thus, as the more noble despiser of the nobles who despised him, as they sickened with envy, he looked down on them not from a private man's bench but from an official seat; and in this freedom he seems to me to have been most worthy, not just of the aedileship but of the honor of a consulship.

I knowingly held back speaking about this consulship since the 31
two senators who are prominent in so great a crowd of conscript fathers may seem to have taken over the place of the two Roman consuls. In fact this office has a term limit as did the consulship, whereas the power of the senators of old had no term.[22] So if I

quanta cum indignatione certatum sit, si retexere incipiam, elonga-
32 bor ab epystole fine, ad quem festinat oratio. Hoc nosse sufficiat,
quod cum plebs romana summi etiam loci partem posceret, idque
nobilitati summum dedecus videretur, summa vi obstitit; ad extremum ut in reliquis victa succubuit; multisque hinc inde contentionibus agitatis, primo quidem ad id deventum est ut non consules
sed consulari potestate permixtim tribuni militum quattuor crea-
rentur; cumque ne hic etiam plebis animi quiescerent, quod diu
tumore superbie negatum erat, iustitie viribus est obtentum, ut
plebeius consul iuxta patritium sederet et comunem patriam et
comuni opera partum imperium pari regeret maiestate.

33 Que si vera, si apud clarissimos historicos nota sunt, quid dubi-
tamus adhuc longe, providentissimi patres, aut quid hortatoribus
indigemus? Si Romanorum calamitatum misereminì, si pios hu-
meros immense ruine subicere decrevistis, eius temporis exempla
sequimini quo urbs illa de nichilo surrexit ad sidera, non huius,
34 quo de tante fastigio fortune pene ad nichilum est redacta. Dubitari non oportere arbitror, quin urbs Roma multos et nobiliores et
meliores habeat his qui soli nobilitatis cognomine gloriosi celum
terrasque fastidiunt; quos ego si boni erunt, nobiles non negabo;
romanos certe non ego solus sed ipsa etiam negat Roma. Esto autem: sint nobiles, sint romani; an maioribus nostris, cultoribus
iustitie, subiectorum protectoribus, debellatoribus superborum,
fundatoribus imperii preferendi sunt? hoc dicere quantalibet im-
35 pudentia non audebunt. Quodsi illi cesserunt, non pudeat hos
etiam plebi cedere dignissima postulanti, ne in urbe scilicet sua
exulet neu velut infecta de publico repellatur; qua in re aristotelici

were to recall how often and how angrily men have contended about this consulship I would increase my distance from the end of this letter to which my argument is hastening. Let it be enough 32
to know this: that when the Roman people demanded even a share in this highest rank and this seemed the greatest dishonor to the nobility, the nobles resisted with all their strength, but finally, as in the other cases, they were defeated and crumbled. And when there had been many disputes this way and that, first they resorted to electing not consuls, but four military tribunes with consular power. Since the spirits of the people did not calm down even then, the goal that had long been frustrated by bloated patrician pride was ensured by the force of justice: that a plebeian consul should sit alongside a patrician and rule with equal majesty their common native land and empire won by common effort.[23]

If these tales are true and reported by the most distinguished 33
historians, why, most prudent fathers, are we hesitating so long, or why do we need encouragement? If you pity the misfortunes of the Romans, if you have decided to set your devout shoulders beneath this vast, collapsing ruin, follow the examples of that period when that city rose from nothing to the stars, not this time at which it is reduced from such a summit of fortune almost to nothing. I think we should not doubt that this city of Rome has many 34
nobler and better men than these fellows who, boastful of their nobility alone, despise heaven and earth. If they behave well, I will not deny that they are noble; but that they are Roman, not just I but Rome herself will deny. But let it be so: let them be noble, let them be Roman: are they to be privileged before our ancestors, worshippers of justice, protectors of their subordinates and defeaters of the proud,[24] even founders of empire? They will not dare to say this, however great their shamelessness. And if they have 35
given way, let them feel no shame to yield to the people which is claiming what is its own by right: not to be exiled in its own city nor rejected from public life as if infected. In this it will be right

dogmatis meminisse conveniet ut, quod dirigentes tortuosa lignorum solent, cogatis hos nobiles non modo senatoriam et reliquas dignitates participare cum aliis, sed diu etiam ab his penitus abstinere, quas diu soli per arrogantiam suam et plebis patientiam usurparunt, donec in partem alteram deflexa respublica sensim ad equalitatem debitam revertatur.

36 Hoc censeo, hoc supplex oro; hoc senex Roma cum lacrimis obtestatur, quodsi segnes in eius instauranda libertate fueritis, ad tribunal tremendi iudicis vos appellat; hoc Cristus iubet, qui dum consultabitis, in medio vestrum erit, ut quos elegit a principio, eorum usque in finem se prebeat spectatorem; hoc apostoli Petrus et Paulus flagitant, qui Romano Pontifici ut non alteri quam vobis ista committeret inspirarunt; quorum tacitas et internas preces si audire volueritis, quorumlibet contrarias preces ac gratiam facillime contemnetis, non quid aliene superbie libeat, sed quid vestram deceat honestatem, quid urbi quid Italie quid mundo expediat, cogitantes.

*XIV Kal. Decembris.*

: 7 :

## *Ad Laelium, disceptatio super quibusdam que contra urbis Rome gloriam dicta videntur a multis.*

1 Iam vale dixeram signatoque die epystolam complicabam, dum nova clam obrepens cogitatio scripture longioris admonuit. Quid facerem? prior papirus plena nec addendi aliquid locus erat,

summusque in margine versus adheserat,

to recall Aristotle's statement that like men controlling crooked logs,[25] you should compel these nobles not only to share with others the dignity of senator, and other offices, but to step back for a long time from these privileges which they have so long usurped by means of their arrogance and the longsuffering of the people, until the republic bends back in the other direction and gradually returns to an appropriate state of equality.

This is my vote, this my suppliant prayer; this aged Rome begs 36
from you with tears. But if you are sluggish in renewing her liberty she summons you before the tribunal of the dread judge. This is the order of Christ, who will be in your midst while you deliberate, so that until the end he may present himself as a spectator of those whom he first chose. This is the demand of the apostles Peter and Paul, who inspired the Roman pope not to entrust that business to others than to you; if you are willing to hear their silent internal prayers you will easily scorn the opposing prayers and influence of anyone else, thinking not what is the choice of another man's arrogance but of what becomes your honor, and what is good for the city, for Italy and for the world.

*November 18.*

## : 7 :

*To Laelius, a dispute on several arguments which are apparently alleged by many against the glory of Rome.*

I had already said farewell and folded the letter with the day's seal 1
when a new thought creeping up stealthily urged me to a longer composition. What was I to do? The first sheet of paper was full with no room to add anything,

and the last line had clung to the margin,

2 ut ait Naso; certe quod illic omissum fuit, hic exequar. Tanto quidem nobis accuratius agenda sunt omnia, quanto plurium subitura
iudicium sepiusque inter livorem ignorantiamque versanda sunt.
Id minime negligendum ut superioris epystole ratione reddita,
quantum fieri potest contra sentientibus satisfaciat appareatque
3 me ut magno sic haud indigno desiderio Romam trahi. Sileo bella
civilia et implacate semper plebis ardorem, omitto multa que illi
urbi cum toto orbe comunia mala sunt, pretereo voluptates longe
lateque regnantes; non voluptuosum quero domicilium sed honestum, memorans Scipionem exilio suo literninum horrorem baianis
pretulisse delitiis, et de hoc laudatum; ad illud unum venio quod
ea michi cogitatio recens attulit, qua nunc ultra destinatum scri-
4 bendo rapior ut audisti. Occurrit enim electioni mee multorum
sententias adversari, apud quos Babilon Roma et, ut ita stomacer,
feda virtus, infamis est gloria; nec negaverim esse huius quoque
5 sententie magnos duces. Nam et Augustinus, civitatem Dei edifi-
cans, quodam loco dum nativitatis Abrahe tempus attingeret,
quem natum constat regnante apud Assyrios Nino, 'habebat' inquit, 'in regno annos quadraginta tres quando natus est Abraham,
qui erat annus circiter millesimus ducentesimus ante conditam
Romam.' Vellem quod sequitur tacuisset: 'veluti alteram' inquit, 'in
6 occidente Babiloniam.' Nec semel hoc dixisse contentus, alio quodam loco, dum per Albanorum successionem ac progeniem regum
ad Romulum pervenisset, 'ne multis' inquit, 'morer, condita est
Roma velut altera in occidente Babilon.' Ecce non tantum quod
dixerat supra repetiit, sed processit ulterius: 'et velut prioris' inquit,
7 'filia Babilonis.' Verum enimvero hoc loco tacitum nullo modo
vellem esse quod sequitur: 'per quam' inquit, 'Deo placuit orbem
debellare terrarum et in unam sotietatem reipublice legumque

as Ovid says;[1] so I will complete here what was omitted there. We 2
must argue everything all the more precisely as my words will suffer the judgment of more people and circulate quite often amid envy and ignorance. I must in no way neglect, once I have justified the earlier letter, giving satisfaction to opponents as far as possible and showing that I am drawn to Rome, not just by a strong desire
but one by no means undeserved. I pass over the civil wars and the 3
passion of the never placated crowd,[2] I omit many disadvantages shared by that city with the whole world, I pass over pleasures dominating far and wide; I am not looking for a luxurious home but an honorable one, recalling that Scipio in his exile preferred the roughness of Liternum to the indulgences of Baiae, and was praised for it.[3] Now I come to the one point which my recent reflection brought me, which has carried me on to write beyond my
intent, as you heard. For it comes to mind that the votes of many 4
are opposed to my choice, men for whom Rome is Babylon, and (to vent my anger), virtue is vile and glory infamous, and I would
not deny that important predecessors also share this opinion. For 5
Augustine, when he was building his City of God, and touched on Abraham's birth in a certain passage, born as he was under Ninus, king of Assyria, says: "Ninus had reigned forty-three years when Abraham was born, that is about twelve hundred years before Rome was founded." I wish he had suppressed what follows: "like
a second Babylon in the West."[4] And not content with saying this 6
once, in another passage, while he was passing through the succession and descent of the Alban kings to reach Romulus, he adds: "not to delay you with many arguments, Rome was founded, like a second Babylon in the West."[5] You see he doesn't just repeat what he had said, but goes further: "and like a daughter of the earlier
Babylon."[6] But here I would in no way want to suppress what fol- 7
lows: "through whom it pleased God to conquer the world and pacify it far and wide, bringing it into one common society that

perductum, longe lateque pacare.' Ecce audis almam urbem ut nomine Babilonis infamem, sic causa originis et dignatione precipua celestis providentie gloriosam, dum dicit: 'per quam Deo placuit orbem debellare terrarum.' Poterat nempe per aliam, sed per hanc voluit, quam scilicet tanto operi pre cuntis ydoneam ab eterno
8 previderat. Neque enim mediocre negotium erat orbi indomito et effreni caput dare, quod Augustinus ipse non dissimulat quando sententiam illam suam ratione confirmans, 'Erant enim' inquit, 'iam populi validi et fortes et armis gentes exercitate que non facile cederent, quas opus esset ingentibus periculis et vastatione utrin-
9 que non parva atque horrendo labore superare.' Ecce quibus effectibus divina providentia romanum imperium fabricata est, ut esset scilicet mundo caput; et regno quidem Assyrio sive finium spatio breviore sive rudi et imbelli domandarum gentium barbarie, ut Augustinus idem pluribus verbis ostendit, facile contigerat non ut
10 orbis, sed ut Asie caput esset. Romano autem imperio quia maiora quedam et difficiliora restabant, tale illud Deus esse voluit quale quantitas laborum et complanandarum rerum asperitas exigebat. In his omnibus adhuc nichil, ut puto, preter nomen Babilonis obscurum est, quo multi, sed in primis, Augustinum sequens, in
11 historia utitur ille mundi malorum coacervator Orosius. Certe Ieronimus in epystola quadam otium suum Bethleemiticumque silentium laudans gratioremque Deo volens ostendere inopem illum locum quam Capitolii arcem tot triumphis insignem, dicit arcem ipsam sepe fulminibus de celo tactam, nec fallitur; quod historias percurrenti promptum est agnoscere. Neque illam modo sed et reliquas arces romanas pari infamia premi posse non nego,

shared both state and laws." Look, you hear that the mother city, although shamed by the name of Babylon, was also glorious because of its origin and the special respect of heavenly providence, when he says: "through whom God chose to conquer the world." Clearly God could have done this through another city, but he wanted this one, which he thought suited from eternity beyond all
others for so great a task. Nor was it an ordinary business to set a 8
head over the unconquered and ungovernable world, as Augustine himself does not conceal when he declares, confirming his judgment with a reason: "For there were then stout and brave nations and races practiced at arms which would not yield easily; they would have to be overcome with huge dangers and no small devastation on both sides and dreadful toil." See with what outcome the 9
Roman Empire was constructed by Divine Providence to become the capital of the world, whereas the Assyrian kingdom, either because of the smaller extent of its dominions or the raw and unwarlike barbarism of the nations to subjugate, as Augustine again demonstrates more fully, could only achieve becoming capital not
of the world, but of Asia. But because greater and more difficult 10
tasks remained for the Roman Empire, God wanted it to be such as was demanded by the quantity of tasks and difficulty of the affairs to be smoothed down. In all this, I think nothing is obscure except the name of Babylon, which many and especially Orosius, that heaper up of the woes of the world, uses in his history, following Augustine.[7] Surely Jerome was praising his retreat and si- 11
lence at Bethlehem and wanted to show that this impoverished place was more welcome to God than the citadel of the Capitol, distinguished by so many triumphs, when he said that the citadel itself was often struck by thunderbolts from heaven;[8] and he is not wrong, as it is easy to recognize if you run through the histories. And I don't deny that not just this citadel but the other Roman hilltops may have been afflicted with the same calamity, and more

Celiumque conspectius montem, non suopte quidem infortunio
neque odio fulminantis, sed claritate patientis, que sepe futuram
12 in altero mediocrem cladem, insignem fecit in altero. Illum igitur
de quo loquor collem, infamasse potuit vel unus abunde mestus et
horrificus Tulli Hostilii romani regis eventus, quem post impetuo-
sam vereque fulmineam vitam usque ad extremum uno tenore
traductam—o vite hominum consentaneum finem!—fulminis incendio tota ibi cum domo conflagrasse legimus. Mitto alios romano nomini insultantes; non pauci enim sunt et veteres et novi et
nostre etiam etatis aliqui, quorum nonnulli—quod ipsis in verbis
elucescit—non tam veri studio quam urbis odio et invidia trahun-
tur; quibus nichil respondendum puto; satis est illos veneno suo
13 confici. Si literati homines sunt et libros legunt, credo, suspirare
illos coget per singulas lineas occurens clarissimum Rome nomen,
idque, nequid calumnientur, in libris non romana manu scriptis
sed externa; populo enim romano, ut ait Crispus, nunquam scrip-
torum copia fuit, quippe honestius ac gloriosius ducebant alios de
se quam se de aliis scribere, res ipsas rerumque famam querentes
14 potiusquam verborum. Quid multa? quisquis urbem Romam
eventus exceperit, nomen vivet quandiu grecarum aut latinarum
memoria literarum ulla supererit, nec unquam deerit invidis materia tabescendi. Augustino sane ac Ieronimo, quos contemnere fas
non est, hoc modo responsum sit.

15 Romam velut alteram Babilonem in occidente fundatam non
infitior, ut scilicet iubente Deo imperium orientale, quod in Babilone multis seculis fuit, inde ablatum cum tempore pariter ad occasum iret, ubi Romam esse perspicuum sit; interesse autem quod
et mores urbium diversi et de orientali non occidentale, sed universale imperium sit effectum omniumque sola verissima monarchia.

conspicuously the Caelian Hill, suffering not from its own misfortune and the hatred of the Thunderer, but from its glory, which often made conspicuous in one place a disaster that would have been ordinary in another. The gloomy and horrifying death of the Roman king Tullus Hostilius was enough in itself to disgrace that hill I am speaking of;[9] we read that after his violent and truly stormy life, maintained without variation to its last moments—O end matching the life of men!—he was set ablaze with his whole house by the fire of the thunderbolt. I pass over others who mock 12
the Roman name; they certainly are not few, both ancient and modern, and even some of our own generation, not a few of whom—as shines out in their very words—are propelled not so much by desire for truth but envy and hatred of the city. I think they deserve no reply: it is enough for them to perish by their own poison. If men are educated and read books, I believe the glorious 13
name of Rome will make them sigh as it meets them on the page, and to prevent them uttering any slander, this happens in books written not by a Roman but a foreign hand; for as Sallust says, the Roman people never had a great abundance of writers because they thought it more honorable and glorious to have others write about them than they themselves, seeking deeds and fame for deeds rather than for words.[10] Need I say more? Whatever out- 14
come shall overtake the city of Rome, its name will live as long any memory of Greek and Roman writing survives, and there will never be a shortage of fuel to sicken the envious. Let this be the answer to Augustine and Jerome, whom it is not right to scorn.

I don't deny that Rome was founded like a second Babylon in 15
the West, expressly so that at God's command the eastern empire which was in Babylon for many ages should be taken from it and go likewise with time to the West, where Rome was obviously situated; but there was a difference, since the ways of life of these cities were opposed and from the eastern empire what developed was not a western but a universal empire, and the only true mon-

16 Quodsi propter totius domiti orbis in una urbe concursum et con-
fusionem rerum maximam ac super omnia deorum turbam sacro-
rumque, Babilon, hoc est confusio, dici potest, non obluctor neque
contendo; sed audeo dicere illud sibi nomen excidisse quo primum
die fallacibus diis exclusis, unius veri Dei cultum nomenque susce-
pit et, ut Leonis pape verbum mutuer, de 'magistra erroris facta *est*
discipula veritatis.'

17 Iam illud quod sepe fulminibus ictum Capitolii saxum dicunt
idque in argumentum trahunt non acceptum Deo locum, sanctissimi literatissimique viri pace dixerim, non id divine iracundie tri-
buendum sed nature. Alioquin multum inter omnes terras amat
Egiptum Deus, sedem omnis impietatis omniumque malarum superstitionum, que non modo Isim et Osirim sed Apim et Serapim
et cocodrillum adoravit ac coluit, nunc minime sanctiorem coco-
drillo Maometum colit, et tamen vel raro ibi vel nunquam tonare
18 fama est; multum contra Pireneos montes odit, ubi Cristus adora-
tur et ubi quam terrifice tonet et quam crebro, quis nobis melius
novit, qui illic viridioris evi unam egimus estatem et fulminum
19 flammis totiens fumantia rura conspeximus? Etsi omnis quidem
cogitatio opinioque omnis pium sobriumque excitans timorem
utilis ac laudanda sit, vere tamen sonus atque ignis ille non tam ire
quam nature est et 'fortuitus et ventorum rabie cadit in terras,' ut
Satyrici utar verbo, et rei huius causam esse nobilitatem aeris volunt quidam, inter quos Plinius Secundus, vir doctissimus; quod si
20 verum est, valde nobilis ille Pirenei tractus aer credi potest. Ipse
tamen hanc causam ponit cur sepe tonet in Italia, que si iterum
vera est, pro virili mea parte libentissime nobilitatem hanc permu-
tatam velim cum ipsis Egiptiis aut Hibernis, apud quos perraro

archy of them all. And if because of the crowding and convergence 16
of the whole conquered world into one city and the huge crowd above all of gods and rites, it can be called Babylon, which means confusion, I am not disputing or challenging this, but I dare to say that this name fell from it on the day when first the false gods were shut out and it took on the worship of the one true God and, to borrow the words of Pope Leo, "from being the teacher of deception was made the pupil of Truth."[11]

Now about their statement that the rock of the Capitol was 17
often struck by lightning and their use of it as an argument that the place was not acceptable to God, I would say, with all respect to the most holy and learned man, that it should not be attributed to divine wrath but to nature. Otherwise God loves Egypt much among all lands, the seat of every impiety and all evil superstitions, which has adored and worshipped not only Isis and Osiris and Apis and Serapis and the crocodile but now worships Mahomet, scarcely more sacred than the crocodile, and yet the story is that it
seldom or never thunders there. Far in the contrary direction God, 18
it seems, loathes the Pyrenees where Christ is revered and where no one knows better than us how dreadfully it thunders and how often (we spent a summer of our green youth there and so often
saw the countryside alight with the flames of thunder). Even if ev- 19
ery thought and opinion which arouses a pious and sober dread is useful and praiseworthy, truly that sound and fire is not so much the product of wrath as of nature and caused "by chance, falling with the rage of the winds onto the earth," to use the Satirist's phrase,[12] and some, including that learned man Pliny, want to believe the cause of this is the nobility of the air;[13] and if this is true, the air over the Pyrenean zone can be thought immensely noble.
But Pliny himself sets down the cause why it often thunders in 20
Italy, and again if this is true, I personally would most gladly want to exchange this nobility with the Egyptians and Irish, among whom those who write on this topic and who come from there

etiam et leniter tonare, et qui de his scribunt et qui inde veniunt testantur; sed revertor Romam.

21 Non amat Deus Tarpeiam rupem, gloriose Ieronime, quam sepe, ut maroneo utar versu,

> Fulminis afflavit ventis et contigit igni?

Liceat, oro, reverenter pro veritate tecum colloqui. Non amat Tarpeiam rupem Deus? quomodo ibi caput orbis esse voluerit, valde miror, quod ipse michi non infitiaberis. Quid vero sis responsurus video; quamobrem huic patrocinio non innitor. Esto igitur: oderit Deus locum illum, qui, nisi amaret illum Deus, certe non staret; sed oderit idque compertum sit. An hinc tamen hoc elicis, quod eum fulminando persequi visus sit? vide, queso, argumenti huius
22 vim. Nolo exempla longe petere nec oportet; profecto si Tarpeiam rupem non amat Deus, quam fulminavit quamque — quod apertius divini odii signum putem — de capite terrarum orbis latronum receptaculum fieri sepe nostris quoque temporibus passus est, at saltem suum lateranense domicilium, at saltem Virginis Matris et suorum domos Apostolorum amat, quibus an pepercerit videmus.
23 Lateranum, nostra etate flammis absumptum, nunc etiam multo labore infinitaque reficitur impensa; verum id non Dei odium dicet aliquis, sed culpa hominum fuit. Quartus annus agitur ex quo terremotu terribili et apostoli Pauli templum pene funditus ruit et Virginis domus supremo colle consistens graviter concussa est; nisi forte dicat quispiam non tam clarum celestis iracundie indicium
24 terremotum esse quam fulmen. Ecce autem presens annus turrim illam Petri apostoli ita fulmine conflagrantem atque collapsam vidit — incredibile quidem dictu — ut vix tanti edificii vestigium extet

both bear witness that it thunders only most rarely and gently. But I come back to Rome.

21 So does God, glorious Jerome, not love the Tarpeian rock? The rock which often, to use the words of Vergil:

> He has blown with the winds of thunder and struck with
> fire?[14]

I beg you, let me argue respectfully with you on behalf of the truth. God does not love the Tarpeian rock? Then I am very much amazed how he could have wanted the capital of the world to be there, which you yourself will not deny to me. I see what you are going to answer; and for this reason I don't rely on this patronage. So be it: suppose God hates that place, which, if God did not love it, would not be standing; but suppose he hates it and this is confirmed. Then do you infer this from the fact that he seems to be persecuting it with thunder? Consider, pray, the force of this
argument. I don't want far-fetched examples nor should I, but 22
surely if God does not love the Tarpeian rock which he has struck and which—something I consider a more open sign of divine hatred—from being capital of the world has often in our time suffered becoming a refuge for brigands, at least God loves his Lateran dwelling and the homes of the Virgin mother and his
Apostles, and we see whether he has spared them. The Lateran, 23
consumed with fire in our generation, is now being restored with great toil and unlimited expense;[15] but no one will call this the hatred of God, but the guilt of mankind. It is the fourth year now since the temple of the Apostle Paul was almost utterly ruined by a terrible earthquake, and the Virgin's home standing on the highest hill was grievously struck[16]—unless perhaps someone will claim that an earthquake is not as obvious a sign of heavenly
wrath as a thunderbolt. See next how this year witnessed that 24
tower of the Apostle Peter so consumed and collapsed with a thunderbolt—amazing to relate—that scarcely a trace survives of

turrimque ibi fuisse vix putet nisi qui viderit; quinetiam, quod in stuporem religionemque multorum vertit, campana illa percelebris, Bonifacii VIII opus et nomen, ita liquefacta dicitur ut ne reliquie quidem superfuerint.

25 Quem ultimum casum non ut plane compertum ignoranti sciens narro, sed ut ignarus a sciente percontor; nos enim fame credidimus que tu cernis; ego post iubileum annum Rome non fui, qui nunc tertius retro est; sed si verum est quod de hac re omnium Roma venientium una vox loquitur, que mentiri non solet, certe nunquam rupes Tarpeia tale aliquid passa est. Credo ego Deum nichil omnium odisse que fecit; sin locum unum altero plus amat, arbitror Eum plus amare ubi se plus amari novit, interdum vero
26 loca sanctissima ferire ut profana perterreat. Accedit quod nec ego, ut soleo, tonitrua pavesco sive quia quo magis vixi minus mori timeo, sive quia ex quo conscientiam abditis suis malis exhonerare cepi, externos tumultus minasque non metuo. Nec si successerit quod cogito, Tarpeiam rupem in qua habitem elegi, non ne populo sim suspectus, quod fecisse legimus Publicolam, sed ne tedio affectus in id quod fugere est animus, sponte recidam; nosti autem e septem collibus qui omnibus montibus ac vallibus prefuerunt, quisnam longe gratissimus sit michi studiisque meis aptissimus.
27 Itaque ut ad propositum redeam atque concludam, non moveor sententia, magno Urbis desiderio teneor; eventus in manibus Dei est. Certe si unquam sanctam civitatem intravero, verum dices quod superior spondet epystola. Vale.

that great building, and a man would hardly think it had existed unless he had seen it; indeed, something that has turned to the astonishment and awe of many, that very famous bell, the work and renown of Boniface VIII, is said to have been so melted that no traces survive.[17]

I am not reporting this last disaster as one in the know would 25
announce a definite discovery to the ignorant, but asking you as an
uninformed man asks one who knows; for we have believed from
rumor what you can see for yourself. I have not been in Rome
since the year of the Jubilee, which is now three years back; but if
the unanimous voice of all who come from Rome is true, and it
does not usually lie, surely the Tarpeian rock never suffered any
blow of this kind. I believe God does not hate any of all the things
that He has made; but if He loves one place more than another, I
think He loves more greatly places where He knows He is more
greatly loved, but sometimes strikes the most sacred places in order to terrify profane ones. Moreover, I do not usually dread thun- 26
derbolts, either because the longer I live the less I am afraid to die
or because, since I began to unburden my conscience of its hidden
evils, I no longer fear external disruptions and threats. And if
what I think of comes to pass, I have chosen to live on the Tarpeian rock, not to avoid being suspect to the people, as we read
Publicola once did,[18] but so as not to lapse spontaneously out of
boredom into the condition my spirit wants to escape; for you
know which of all the seven hills, that excelled all mountains and
valleys, was by far the most welcome to me and fitted to my studies.[19] So to return to my argument and round it off, I have not 27
changed my judgment, but am held fast by a great longing for the
city: the outcome is in God's hands. But surely if I ever enter the
holy city you will call my promise in the earlier letter true. Farewell.

## : 8 :

## *Ad Andream Dandulo ducem Venetorum, exhortatio ad pacem cum Ianuensibus.*

1 Ut aliquid ad te scribam, inclite dux, hinc mea fides hinc humanitas tua suggerit, illinc rerum presentium ac temporum status cogit; hec quidem prestat ut loqui velim, hec ut audeam, ille autem ut
2 tacere nequeam. Quis enim ab amante solicito silentium requirat? libertas amoris verecundie frenum nescit; os licet obstruxerit rationis manus et magnitudini rerum se imparem recognoscens animus quiescendum tacendum ve denuntiet, erumpet tamen anxium pectus in voces, non peregrinas sententias aut verba venabitur, quicquid ad manum venerit, quicquid dolor metusque suaserint, loquetur; festina trepida tumultuaria et quod natura rerum fert,
3 simillima mentis fluctibus exibit oratio. Id si unquam alias, nunc michi presertim evenire noveris. Moveor equidem, dux illustris, et valde permoveor, et si proprium affectus mei nomen exigis, permetuo frementes in circuitu procellas et quos undique cernimus rerum motus; sed ut totius humani generis lamenta preteream,
4 italicus homo ad italicam querelam venio. Surgitis nunc ad arma duo potentissimi populi, due florentissime urbes, duo ut dicam breviter, Italie lumina, que ut michi quidem videtur, peroportune adeo hinc illinc circum Ausonii orbis claustra distribuit natura parens, ut vobis ad arthon et ad ortum solis, illis ad meridiem et ad occasum versis, vobis Superum, illis Inferum Mare frenantibus, post debilitatum inclinatumque iam, ne dicam prostratum prorsus

: 8 :

## *To Andrea Dandolo, doge of Venice, exhorting him to make peace with the Genoese.*

Most renowned doge: my loyalty first and your humanity second 1
encourage me to write to you, while, third, the condition of present times and circumstances compels me to do so. The first gives me the desire to address you, the second the daring to do so, and
the last forbids me to stay silent. For who would demand silence 2
from an anxious devotee? The liberty of love does not know the bridle of bashfulness, even if the hand of reason blocks the mouth; and the mind, recognizing it is unequal to the greatness of the situation, demands calm and silence: yet my anxious breast will break out in speech. It will not hunt for imported opinions or language, but will utter whatever comes to hand, whatever pain and fear urge upon it. My speech will reveal its utter likeness to the stormy waves besetting my mind: it will be hasty, frightened, chaotic. Now above all, if ever, you will know what I am experiencing. 3
For I am disturbed, illustrious doge, deeply disturbed, and if you want to know the proper name of my emotion, I am terrified of the storms rumbling around us and the political tumult we see everywhere; but to pass over laments for the whole human race, I
come as an Italian to protest what affects Italy. Two most powerful 4
nations, you are rising up to arms. You are Italy's two most flourishing cities—to speak shortly, her two beacons—which (as it seems to me) Mother Nature has set most opportunely on either side of the enclosures of the Ausonian world, so that that world, divided into its four quadrants, might still recognize Italy as their sovereign, given the way that you face the north and east, while the Genoans face the south and the west, and given how, after the Roman Empire was weakened and tottering if not prostrate and

et extinctum, romanum imperium, adhuc reginam Italiam quadri-
5 partitus orbis agnosceret. De qua re, etsi quarundam forte gentium
superbia in terris litem factura videatur, in alto certe nullius usquam impudentia controversiam movebit.

Ceterum si in vosmet ipsos, quod nedum spectare sed ominari
horreo, victricia nunc arma convertitis, hauddubie nostris propriis
manibus saucii perimus, nostris propriis manibus spoliati et nomen et multis quesitum laboribus imperium maris amittimus; ita
tamen ut quod sepe alias malorum solamen habuimus, non perda-
mus; calamitatibus enim nostris gaudere poterunt hostes, sed mi-
6 nime gloriari. Inter cunta nimirum quibus angor aut terreor, nil
magis quam intractabiles animos et consilia iuvenum pavesco;
ignara etas est ac fortune volubilis inexperta et cuius impetu magna
olim imperia corruerunt; omnia sibi que cupiunt, pollicentur
7 eoque sepissime falluntur. Ut enim verum est quod ait apud Livium ille clarissimus bello vir: 'Non temere incerta casuum reputat
quem nunquam fortuna decepit,' sic et quod sequitur verum est:
'Nusquam minus eventus respondere quam in bello.' Falli proculdubio necesse est eos quibus unus duntaxat isque serenus ac
tranquillus fortune vultus apparuit; bifrons est enim aliquantoque
sepius violenta quam mitis. Ideoque letus audivi te res ambiguas
8 ad senile consilium reiecisse. Hoc providentiam moresque tuos
decuit, quorum gravitas atque maturitas te in illa acie primum fecit, cum adhuc in altera sis etate. Adolescentie ferociam, senio
prudentiam attribuunt, ut non immerito illi quondam romane
reipublice magistri, quorum virtuti nichil inaccessum fuit, sive ob
honorem sive ob similitudinem paterne solicitudinis patres dicti,
9 ob etatem certe senatorum nomen acceperint. Qua cura iuvenibus

lifeless, you controlled the Upper Sea and they the Lower.[1] Even if 5
the arrogance of some nations seems intent on creating a conflict
on land, no such shamelessness will rouse a quarrel on the high
seas.

But if—something I dread to anticipate let alone behold—you
now turn your triumphant forces against yourselves,[2] we are undoubtedly perishing, wounded by our own hands; and robbed by
our own hands, we are losing both our renown and our sea empire, earned by many toils, but on these terms, that we are not
losing what has often been a comfort in misfortune on other occasions; our enemies will be able to exult over our disasters but
hardly boast of them. Among all the other reasons for my anguish 6
or terror I fear nothing more than the unmanageable temper and
designs of young men; their youth is ignorant and inexperienced
in the revolutions of Fortune, whose onslaught has brought low
once mighty empires; they promise themselves everything that
they covet and are most often deceived in this. For as that glorious 7
warrior rightly says in Livy: "The man whom Fortune has never
tricked does not randomly reflect on the uncertainty of chance."[3]
So also what follows is true, that "outcomes never match expectations worse than in war." Men undoubtedly deceive themselves
when they have been shown only one face of fortune, calm and
serene. She is two-faced and more often violent than lenient. So I
was overjoyed to hear that you had referred these problematic circumstances to the council of elders.[4] This matched your caution 8
and your character, whose gravity and maturity made you first in
the line of battle, even if you ought in terms of age to take your
place in the reserves. They attribute boastfulness to youth and
caution to age, so that those lords of the old Roman Republic, to
whose virtue nothing was out of reach, called "fathers" either to
honor them or because of their affinity with a father's concern,
certainly received the name of Senators because of their seniority.[5]
I only wish it were not public knowledge from what heights we 9

primum, mox etate nostra pueris quoque permissa, ex quam alto
ceciderimus, utinam non tam publice notum foret! Sed de hoc
alibi; neque enim leve est dolori ac pavori simul obsequentem et
deflere preterita et venientia providere, dare damno lacrimas et
periculo cautionem.

10 Ad id ergo quod venturi metu cruciat, revertor. Solicitum,
fateor, atque attonitum me habet patrie tue status; de te quid dicam? cuius enim glorie gratulor, si compatiar labori, parum ipse
michi consentiam. Ingenio tuo non compati non possum; sentio
namque quid intersit inter armorum strepitum et pyeriam quietem
quamque tenuiter inter Martis tubas plectrum sonet Apollinis.
11 Quia vero nichil patrie negare potes, que de te sic in pace merita
est ut eam nec belli tedio nec mortis terrore desereres, si relicto
tantisper Elicone ac feriantibus libellis secutus es publici fati viam,
et grati civis et boni viri et egregii ducis officio functus es, ita tamen ut armatus pacem cogites, pacem ames atque ita persuasum
habeas nullos te triumphos clariores, nulla opimiora patrie spolia
12 referre posse quam pacem. Libenter ubi de pace agitur Hanibalis
verbo utor, quod scilicet ex ore bellicosissimi viri veritas ipsa videatur loquentis adversum studiis testimonium extorsisse. Is ergo
apud eundem Livium quid ait? 'Melior tutiorque' inquit, 'est certa
pax quam sperata victoria.' Hec ille vincendi desiderio ardens et
qui pacem toto orbe turbaverat. Quid igitur amicus pacis? Nonne
potius dicat: 'Melior sanctiorque est certa pax quam certa victoria'?
propterea quod illa quietis et caritatis et gratie, hec laboris et
13 criminum et insolentie plena est. Quid autem pace iocundius,
quid felicius, quid dulcius? quid vero sine pace vita hominum, nisi

have fallen, since their supervision was opened up to young men
and then, in our generation, even to boys. But I will talk of this
elsewhere, since it is no light task to obey pain and fear at the
same time, and weep for the past and take thought for the future,
to grant tears to loss and caution to danger.

So I return to what torments me with fear for the future. I ad- 10
mit that the condition of your country keeps me anxious and
thunderstruck. What should I say about yourself? I congratulate
your glory, so if I share your suffering and toil I am at variance
with myself. I cannot but sympathize with your intellect, for I
know the difference between the din of warfare and the calm of
the Muses, and how thinly Apollo's plectrum sounds out among
the bugles of war. But since you can deny nothing to your country, 11
which has served you so well in times of peace that you would not
desert it either from weariness of war or fear of death, if you have
left Helicon and, allowing your books a holiday, have taken the
path of public destiny, you have performed both the duties of a
grateful citizen and patriot and the task of an exceptional leader.
But you have done so acting from love of peace while under arms
and in the conviction that you have no more glorious triumphs, no
richer spoils to bring back to your country than peace. When we 12
talk of peace I am glad to adopt Hannibal's saying, which truth
itself seems to have forced from the lips of a most warlike man
against his preferences. What then does he say in Livy? "A sure
peace is better and safer than a hoped-for victory."[6] This is what
Hannibal said, although he was burning with eagerness to conquer and had disrupted peace worldwide. So what does a friend of
peace say? Would he not rather say: "A sure peace is better and
more holy than a sure victory"? The former in fact is full of calm
and affection and goodwill whereas the other is full of toil and accusations and insolence. Now what is more pleasing than peace, 13
more happy, more sweet? What indeed is the life of man without

periculum pavorque perpetuus ac tristis curarum immortalium
officina? quenam ista voluptas, oro, est sub divo pernoctare, clas-
sico somnum frangere, corpus lorica atque, ut ait Maro, canitiem
galea premere, ferreis semper vinculis arctatum mori subito et que
14 ultima virorum fortium cura est, inhumatum abici? Iuvat mordaci
solicitudine, iuvat metu et odio miserum cor atterere, et his studiis
incertum huius brevissime vite tempus impendere. Siccine tutum
est cum pelago simul et cum hoste certare, hoc est gemina pariter
cum morte luctari? Nemo enim, queso, vos fallat: cum asperrima
atque invictissima et, quod tristius dico, cum italica gente bellum
geritis. Utinam inimice urbes vobis essent Damascus aut Susis,
utinam Memphis potius aut Smyrna quam Ianua, utinam adversus
Persas aut Arabes, utinam adversus Tracas aut Illirios pugnaretis!
15 Nunc vero quid agitis? Siqua latini nominis reverentia est, quos
delere molimini, fratres sunt, et heu non tantum apud Thebas
fraterne acies sed per Italiam instruuntur, amicis flebile, letum hostibus spectaculum. Quis autem belli finis ubi seu victores fueritis
seu victi — anceps est enim alea fortune — necesse est ut alterum e
duobus Italie luminibus extinguatur, obscuretur alterum? De tanto
enim hoste incruentam sperare victoriam, vide ne non tam gene-
16 rose fidutie quam incuriose dementie signum sit. Sane vos videritis, viri magnanimi et prepotentes populi, — quod enim uni dico,
dictum ambobus intelligo, nisi quia, ut ad te potissimum hec
scripta perveniant, et devota familiaritas, que michi cum virtutibus
tuis est, et ipsa locorum vicinitas causam prebuere — vos, inquam,
videritis quorsum pergatis animis, quis sit irarum modus, quis
terminus odiorum, quid de salute propria, quid denique, cuius

peace, except danger, unceasing terror and a grim forge of immortal troubles. What pleasure is it, I ask you, to pass the night in the open, break off one's sleep with the bugle, and cover one's body with a breastplate and, as Vergil says "burden our old age with a helmet,"[7] or to be always cramped in iron armor, to die suddenly, and—the last distress of armed men—to be cast away unburied?
If it is a pleasure to wear away the poor heart with biting anxiety 14
and fear and loathing, and waste the brief time of life with these pursuits, is it safe to struggle simultaneously with the sea and the enemy, that is, to struggle equally with two kinds of death? I beg you, let no one deceive you, you are waging war with a most fierce and unconquered and—something I say with great sadness—with an Italian race. If only your enemies were the cities of Damascus and Susa! If only Memphis or Smyrna rather than Genoa, if only you were fighting against Persians and Arabians, Thracians or Il-
lyrians![8] But what are you actually doing? If there is any respect 15
due to the Latin name, those whom you are striving to destroy are your brothers, and alas, these battle lines of brothers are drawn up, not just in remote Thebes[9] but through Italy, a sight lamentable to our friends and joyful to our enemies. For what end will there be of war if you are either victors or defeated—for the throw of fortune's dice is unpredictable—and inevitably one or other of the two shining lights of Italy will be put out and the other dimmed. You will surely see then how hoping for a bloodless victory from so great an enemy is less a sign of noble confidence than careless
madness. You surely will see this, great men and most powerful 16
nations—for what I say to one city is said to both, except that this letter has reached you first, because the loyal intimacy which I feel with your virtues, and the very proximity of our localities[10] has provided a cause—both your communities will see, I say, whither you are driven by your temper, what will be the outcome of your anger, what the end of your feuding, what you are to think about your own safety and about the condition of the state, no small part

17 non parva portio pendet ex vobis, de statu publico cogitetis; modo
ne illud excidat quod, nisi gliscentis belli ardor fonte aliquo pietatis extinguitur, de vulneribus que parantur, non numantinus aut
penus sed italicus sanguis fluet et eorum qui, siqua nunc repentina
vis ingruat aut siqua barbaries — quod interdum sed nunquam
gratis ausa est — fines nostros irrumpat, primi vobiscum arma pro
comunium fortunarum defensione suscipient, qui simul pectora
sua morti atque hostilibus telis obicient, qui et vestris tegentur et
vos clipeis ac corporibus suis tegent, qui profugos hostes vinctis
classibus persequentur, pariter vivent, pariter morientur, pariter
18 pugnabunt, pariter triumphabunt. Tales igitur hos viros propter
levis forsan iracundie stimulos invadere et quanquam impune possis, evertere, quid delectationis habeat non intelligo; norunt fortasse melius incensi quorundam animi, qui supplicio amicorum et
vindicta quarumlibet offensarum more femineo delectantur! Pro-
19 fecto nec utile nec honestum, denique nec humanum est: satius est
oblivisci iniuriam quam ulcisci, et inimicum placare quam perdere,
illum precipue cuius et merita precesserunt et, si in gratiam redi-
erit, sequi possunt; nempe etsi utrobique par labor esset, tamen
mansuetudo hominum est, ferarum rabies, eaque non omnium sed
ignobilium et quas sinistra nature manus attigit.

20 Si igitur inter consiliarios tuos, quos plurimos gravissimosque
non dubito, mea vox auditur, non modo venientem non repelles
pacem, sed ultro illi obviam ibis et avidissime complexus inventam,
ut apud vos eternum maneat curabis; quod facilius assequeris si,
quicquid erit, sobriam venerandamque canitiem in consilii partem
21 voces. Illos audi qui et fortune ludos nosse et amare rempublicam

of which depends on you. Only do not forget that, unless the pas- 17
sion of swelling war is extinguished by some spring of piety, no lives of alien Numantines or Carthaginians,[11] but Italian blood will be shed from the wounds that are being prepared, and if some sudden attack or barbarous force should invade our territory—something that happens at intervals but never accidentally—the men of Genoa will be first to take up arms along with you for our common fortunes and will thrust their breasts along with you against death from enemy missiles: they will be protected by your shields and bodies and protect you with theirs: they will pursue the enemy, routed when its fleet has been defeated, they will live
and die and fight and triumph equally with you. I do not under- 18
stand what pleasure there is in attacking such men on account of some trivial cause of anger and overthrowing them, even if you can do it with impunity, although perhaps some inflamed spirits know better, taking delight like women in the suffering of friends and
vengeance for trivial offenses. Surely this is neither advantageous 19
nor honorable, in short not even human; it is better to forget a wrong than avenge it and better to appease an enemy than assail him, especially an enemy who has previously done services to us and, if he is reconciled, will renew them; for even if both reactions brought equal trouble, still, mildness is proper to man and mad anger to beasts, and not even to all the beasts but to the lower creatures on whom Nature has laid a harmful touch.

So if my voice is heard among your counselors, whom I do not 20
doubt are many and weighty, you will not merely not reject the approaching peace but move spontaneously toward it, and once you have found and eagerly embraced it, see to it that it stays permanently with you; and you will achieve this more easily if, whatever happens, you invite the sober and reverend white hair of old
age into a share of your counsels. Listen to those who have learned 21
to recognize the tricks of fortune and to love the state, for the

didicerunt; his enim dulcedo pacis est gratior qui contrarii amari-
tudinem pregustarunt; ceteri ergo tanquam pacis hostes a limine
arceantur. Neque tamen illos admitto quibus nulla sunt senectutis
insignia preter rugas canos ac calvitium et incurvum tergum na-
sique madentis infantiam et cum voce trementia membra, ut Satyricus ait; suas sibi haud equidem invidiosas dotes habeant; nos
22 enim non putres querimus sed maturos. Neque rursus illos ex-
cludo, siqui sunt, qui florentibus annis animi preoccupaverunt senectutem, neque quod in te miror, in aliis sperno, sicubi precox
indoles affulserit. Non sum nescius quantum Africanus meus adolescens afflicte reipublice non manu solum sed consilio profuerit;
aut dum secretum senatus celat, Papirius Pretextatus quonam matrem ioco luserit. Quid pedagogo suo Portius Cato, quid seni
23 anxio puer suasit Alcibiades? Sed michi crede, perrarum genus
hominum quibus tenera etate contingat sapere; ubi sane tale aliquid et pregressum annos adolescentem videris — nec enim infitior
fieri posse — senum choris ascribito. His consultoribus, neque pre-
cipites irruent sententie neque sub amictu veri mendacium clam
subrepet. Tu qui et consilii prima vox et rerum caput esse meruisti,
hoc semper tecum cogita, primas ad te partes vel glorie vel infamie
24 pertinere; ideoque sopitis omnibus solus vigila. Neque enim, quod
illustribus viris placet, par imperatoris et militis labor est; promp-
tior ad actum venit quem maior premii spes impellit, et quanquam
multe et varie sint premiorum species ad quas pro varietate affec-
tuum non uniformiter inclinamur, hauddubium tamen quia nobilibus animis post virtutem summum calcar est gloria.

Hoc igitur excitatum animum curis optimis exerce; 'sunt autem
25 optime cure de salute patrie,' ut ait Cicero. His tibi nunc in celum

sweet appeal of peace is more welcome to those who have sampled the bitterness of its opposite; so let the rest be kept away from the threshold as enemies of peace. Nor would I let in those who have no emblems of old age except wrinkles, white hair, and baldness and a bent-over back "and the infancy of a wet nose and limbs that tremble with their speech," as the satirist says.[12] Let them keep their hardly enviable assets, for we are not looking for rotting creatures but mature men. I am not shutting out those, if there are 22
any, who in their prime years have staked advanced claim on the maturity of old age, nor do I despise in others what I admire in you, wherever a precocious intellect has shone upon them. I am well aware how my Scipio as a young man benefitted the stricken state as much with his advice as with his bodily strength, or how Papirius Praetextatus teased his mother when the senate was keeping a secret. Or what Porcius Cato urged on his pedagogue,
what the boy Alcibiades urged on the anxious old man.[13] But be- 23
lieve me, the kind of man who in tender youth has the fortune to be sensible is very rare; so when you see something like that and a young man advanced beyond his years—for I don't deny it is possible—enroll him in the bands of old men. With such counselors headstrong opinions will not rush in nor falsehood sneak in under the guise of truth. You, who deserve to be first voice in council and head of affairs, always think that the first share in glory or shame falls to your lot, and so when all others are drowsy keep your
watch alone. For the task of the general and the common soldier 24
is not equal, as distinguished men believe.[14] The man whom a greater hope of reward drives on will come faster into action, and although there are many varieties of reward to which we are not uniformly attracted, given the variety of our emotions, there is no doubt that, after virtue, glory is the sharpest spur for noble souls.

So roused by these considerations employ your spirit with the best concerns, and "the best concerns are for the welfare of one's
country" as Cicero says.[15] Now that, thanks to such commitments, 25

iter facturus, assurge teque supra te ipsum erige; vide circumspice contemplare omnia et felices bellorum exitus cum infelicibus confer et damna cum commodis et gaudium cum merore; et quoniam, ut dixi, in causa pacis aptissimus testis est Hanibal, diligenter cave 'ne' ut ait ille, 'tot annorum felicitatem in unius hore dederis discrimen.' Quantis enim, putes, laboribus hec collecta potentia
26 est! quantis gradibus ad hoc fortune fastigium est ascensum! Pervetusta, si nescis, gentis tue fama est, quod plerique non putant, multisque ante urbem conditam seculis non Venetorum modo, sed quod magis mirabere, Veneti etiam ducis clarum nomen invenio; quo diligentius advertendum est, ne virtutem casibus et tot anno-
27 rum consilio partum decus, fortune vastatricis subdas imperio. Et quoniam, ut sapientibus visum est, nullo maiori quam fame precio virtus constat, optime et e republica te facturum noveris, si ubi res exigat, iactura etiam proprie laudis bonum publicum redemeris, frementique turbe tuta magis quam speciosa consilia et profutura potius quam placitura prebueris, cuntatorque dici malueris quam preceps, Maximi ducis exemplo de quo ait Ennius:

Non ponebat enim rumores ante salutem,

neque virtutis studio quesitam infamiam aut stultorum odium horrueris. Quod enim eidem duci accidit, et cumulatior gloria et cum admiratione omnium amor te publicus sequetur; que si etiam spes abesset, quid virtuti tamen, quid et glorie debeamus, et per te ipsum scis et a philosophis didicisti.

28 Quanto autem cum dolore, nequid omnino tibi subtraham, audivisse me putas recens vobis cum Aragonie rege fedus initum? ergo ne ab Italis ad Italos evertendos barbarorum regum poscuntur

you will make your way to heaven, rise up and lift yourself above yourself: see, examine and contemplate everything and compare the happy outcomes of wars with unhappy ones and losses with advantages and joy with grief; and since, as I said, Hannibal is the best witness in the cause of peace, take great care that, as he says, "you do not put at risk in a single hour the successes of so many years."[16] How many ordeals would you think one must endure to assemble such power! By how many steps does one climb to such
a peak of fortune! If you don't know this, there is a very ancient 26
tradition of your race which most men do not keep in mind, and it was many ages before the founding of Rome that I find that not only the name of the Veneti but that of their leader Venetus was glorious,[17] so one must pay extra attention not to subordinate virtue to chance, and glory won with wise counsel over so many years
to the empire of devastating Fortune. And since, as men believe, 27
virtue meets no greater reward than fame, you will know you are acting for the best and most patriotically if, when circumstances demand, you ransom the public good even at the loss of personal glory, giving the fretful crowd sound rather than glamorous advice, and offer what will do good rather than give pleasure, preferring to be known as "the delayer" rather than "the precipitate," on the model of the general Fabius Maximus whom Ennius describes:

> for he never put gossip before the public weal.[18]

And do not fear, in your zeal for virtue, to earn shame or the hatred of many. For as happened to this same leader, a more lavish glory and public affection will follow with universal admiration, and if even that hope were missing, we should think what we owe to virtue and to glory: you know this on your own account and have learned it from the philosophers.

Don't you think I felt great distress (to keep nothing from you) 28
to hear of your recent treaty with the king of Aragon?[19] So you are even demanding the help of barbarian kings in order that Italians

auxilia? unde infelix opem speret Italia, si parum est quod certatim
a filiis mater colenda discerpitur, nisi ad publicum insuper parrici-
29 dium alienigene concitentur? Dicet aliquis: 'Idem mali genus prius
ab hoste tentatum.' Iam dixi; etsi unum alloquor utrunque redar-
guo. Quanto dignius fuerat, irarum detersa rubigine, a qua non
ullius amicitie sinceritas, non fraternus amor, non suprema demum parentis ac natorum pietas prorsus immunis est, Venetos
cum Ianuensibus unum fieri, quam formosum corpus Italie lacerari, vobis occidentalium, illis, ut audio, dextras orientalium tyran-
30 norum in partem furoris implorantibus. O ferales et supervacuas
cautelas, o malivolentie genus ultimum, quod manu propria non
possis, ad id circumspicere quos irrites, et argumentum odii pre-
bente vicinia, vicarios scelerum subrogare! Atqui multarum hinc
miseriarum fluxere primordia, dum indigno et nescio unde pro-
deunte fastidio nostrarum rerum, in admirationem rapimur externarum, et iampridem consuetudine pestifera italicam fidem barba-
31 rice perfidie posthabemus. Insani, qui in venalibus animis fidem
querimus quam in propriis fratribus desperamus. Quo effectum est ut iure optimo in has calamitates inciderimus quas iam sero et inefficaciter lamentamur, postquam Alpes ac maria, quibus, non menibus, natura vallaverat, et interiectas obseratasque divino munere claustrorum valvas, livoris avaritie superbieque clavibus aperiendas duximus Cimbris Hunnis Pannoniis Gallis Theutonis et Hispanis. Quotiens illud pastorium Maronis flendo cecinimus:

may not be overthrown by Italians? Where shall unhappy Italy
look for help if it is not enough that the mother who should be
revered by her sons is torn apart by them in competition, unless
foreigners too are aroused to the murder of our common parent?
Someone will say: "The same kind of wickedness was formerly 29
tried by our enemies." I have already made my point: even if I am
addressing one side, I am accusing both. How much more worthy
it would be if the Veneti, having rubbed away the rust of anger,
from which the sincerity of no friendship or brother's love, nor the
ultimate piety between parents and children is utterly immune,
should become one with the Genoans, rather than that the lovely
body of Italy should be mutilated, as you invite the troops of western tyrants to a share in your madness, and the Genoese, as I hear,
invite the troops of eastern ones.[20] O deadly and superfluous pre- 30
cautions, if in the last stroke of malice you look around to incite
others to the harm you cannot do with your own hands, and with
proximity supplying a reason for hatred, to provoke substitutes to
implement your crimes! But this has been the origin of many
wretched events, when from an unwarranted disgust with our circumstances proceeding from an unknown source we are swept into
admiration of outsiders, and by a longstanding destructive habit
we put Italian loyalty second to barbarian treachery. We are mad 31
to seek loyalty in souls for sale which we despair of in our own
brothers. The result has been that we rightly sink into these calamities which we are now lamenting too late and to no effect after
we chose to lay open the Alps and seas, which nature had made
our rampart instead of walls, and unbar the bolted doorways
which God has set between, opening them with the keys of envy,
greed and arrogance, to the Cimbri, Huns, Pannonians and Gauls,
Teutons and Spaniards.[21] How often we have wept, singing the
lament of Vergil's shepherd:

Impius hec tam culta novalia miles habebit,
Barbarus has segetes? en quo discordia cives
Perduxit miseros!

32 Sed ut ad rem redeam, quid vos deliberaturi sitis ignoro; illud scio quod in emulatione olim pari sed conditione longe impari, dum evertendi infestissimam Athenarum urbem Lacedemoniis oblata esset occasio, nec de potentia iam sed de sola voluntate superesset questio, e duobus Grecie luminibus eruturos se alterum negaverunt; preclarissimum sane responsum et prisca illa Sparthanorum dignissimum disciplina. Quodsi ex ore illorum sonuit quos victoriarum principandique libidinis notat Plato, quid vobis mitissimis ac modestissimis viris visum iri arbitrer? certe ego, qui in tantis motibus non moveri nequeo et diversis affectibus, amore metu spe, unum pectus urgentibus secumque certantibus, pace animi careo, iusta me reprehensione cariturum credidi, si cum hi silvas in classem traherent, hi gladios acuerent ac sagittas, illi muros ac navalia communirent, quod unum michi telorum genus erat, ad calamum confugissem, non belli auctor sed suasor pacis.

34 Finem facere iandudum cogito, non ignarus quanto verborum freno uti deceat cum superioribus colloquentem; sed nullus est amore superior. Ille te coget ad veniam qui ad multiloquium me coegit; hoc unum in finem coram duorum populorum ducibus affusus et lacrimosus obsecro: infesta manibus arma proicite, date dextras, miscete oscula, animis animos signis signa coniungite. Sic navigantibus occeanus et Euxini maris ostia patebunt nullusque regum aut populorum nisi venerabundus occurret; sic vos Scitha,

An impious soldier will hold these carefully tended fallow fields,
a barbarian these crops: see to what extreme discord has driven
our unhappy citizens.[22]

But to return to the issue, I do not know what deliberation you 32
will reach, but I do know that once in a similar competition but in very different circumstances, when the opportunity was offered to the Spartans to overthrow the hostile city of Athens, and there was no longer any question of power but only of will, they refused to gouge out one of the two eyes of Greece—a glorious reply most worthy of Sparta's old discipline.[23] If this saying rang out from 33
those whom Plato condemned for their victories and lust for primacy,[24] what should I think would seem good to your mild and modest people? Certainly I cannot be unmoved amid such great upheavals and lack peace of mind, being afflicted with the conflicting emotions, love, fear, and hope, pressing down in one breast as they clash with each other. So I believed I would not incur a fair rebuke if, when this side felled the forests for their fleet and others sharpened their swords and arrows, while yet others fortified their docks and arsenals, I took refuge in my pen, my only weapon, not as a sponsor of war but as an advocate of peace.

I have for some time been thinking how to end, not unaware 34
how fierce a bridle one should impose on words when debating with superiors. But no one is superior to love. That god will compel you to pardon me, just as he drove me to verbosity; this is the one outcome for which I appeal at last, prostrate and in tears, before the leaders of two peoples. Cast away the hostile weapons from your hands,[25] offer your right hands and mingle your kisses, join minds with minds and standards with standards. When you 35
sail on these terms the Ocean and the mouth of the Euxine will lie open and no king or people will come to meet you except in

sic Britannus Aferque permetuet; sic Egiptum sic tirium litus et armenium, sic formidatos olim Cilicum sinus et Rhodon quondam pelagi potentem, sic sicanios montes et maris monstra trinacrii, sic infames antiquis et novis latrociniis Baleares, sic denique Fortunatas Insulas Orchadasque famosamque sed incognitam Thilen et omnem australem atque yperboream plagam securus vester nauta transiliet; modo invicem tuti sitis, nil aliunde trepidandum est. Vale, ducum ac virorum optime.

## : 9 :

## *Ad Carolum quartum Romanorum regem, exhortatio ad transitum in Italiam.*

1 Precipitium horret epystola, serenissime Cesar, auctoris sibi conscia, dum cogitat unde digrediens quo ventura sit; in tenebris enim orta, quid mirum si clarissimi tui nominis splendore confunditur? sed quoniam omnem pavorem amor excutit, in lucem veniet etsi nichil aliud, at saltem fidelis affectus mei nuntia. Perlege, oro, decus nostrum, perlege, neu quas odiosas tibi ac molestas audio, ex me blanditias verearis, publicam regum pestem, lamentis potius aurem para; non tam blanda quam querula oratione pulsaberis.
2 Quid enim nostri et, si dici fas est, tui ipsius immemor factus es? quonam abiit Italie tue cura? Nos equidem sperabamus te, celitus nobis missum, libertatis nostre promptissimum assertorem; tu refugis et ubi facto opus est, longissimis consultationibus tempus

veneration; thus the Scythian, African and Briton will fear you, and your seamen will pass free of care through Egypt and the Tyrian shore and Armenia, the once dreaded gulfs of Cilicia and Rhodes, formerly powerful by sea, the Sicilian mountains and the monsters of the three-cornered island, the Balearics notorious for their ancient and modern piracy; he will pass through the Fortunate Islands and Orkneys and famous but unknown Thule and the whole Antipodean and Hyperborean region.[26] Provided you are safe from each other, nothing is to be dreaded from any other source. Farewell, best of doges and of men.

## : 9 :

## *To Charles IV, king of Rome, an appeal urging him to come to Italy.*

My letter is terrified of collapsing in utter failure, most gracious 1
Caesar, when it considers its humble author, its origin and its destination. It has come from dark obscurity, so it is not surprising that it is dumbfounded by the splendor of your glorious name. But since love dispels all panic, if nothing else, the loyal message of my affection will see the light. I beg you, source of our glory, to read it, to read it through and not to have any fear of flattery, which I hear you loathe as offensive and tiresome, the public scourge of kings: instead you should prepare your ear for complaints. You will be assailed with speech less beguiling than complaining. For why have you become forgetful of us and if it is right 2
to say this, your own self? Where has your concern for Italy disappeared? We were hoping that you, sent to us as you were from heaven, would be a swift and ready champion of our liberty, but you step back and, when action is needed, drag out the time in

trahis. Vide, Cesar, quam fidutialiter tecum ago, homo pusillus et
incognitus. Tu, queso, ne libertati mee succenseas, sed nature
moribusque tuis gratulare, qui hanc michi fidutiam subministrant.
3 Quid enim, ut ceptum sequar, quasi venturi certus, tempus in consiliis expendis? Nescis in quam brevi spatio maximarum rerum
momenta versentur; que multis elaborata sunt seculis, sepe dies
unus conficit; crede michi, si famam propriam, si reipublice statum cernis, videbis tuas itidem res ac nostras dilationibus non
4 egere. Quid, quod ambigua et fugacissima vita est et quamvis in-
tegerrima etas tua sit, est tamen instabilis assidueque volat ac rapi-
tur? itaque non sentientem omnis te in senium dies trudit; dum
circumspicis, dum cuntaris, improvisa furtim aderit canities. An
forte dubitas ne ante tempus inceperis ad quod peragendum vix
humane vite longissimum tempus intelligis suffecturum? neque
5 enim vulgaris aut mediocris tibi negotii cura est. Romanum imperium multis diu iactatum tempestatibus sepe delusam et pene iam
proiectam spem salutis in tua tandem virtute reposuit, et post in-
numeros casus sub umbraculo tui nominis utcunque respirat; sed
sola iam spe diutius pasci nequit. Sentis quantam et quam piam
curarum sarcinam suscepisti; perfer ad exitum, precamur, idque
6 quamprimum facito. Preciosissima, imo vero inextimabilis res est
tempus et cuius solius avaritiam doctorum hominum commendat
autoritas. Pelle moras igitur, et quod grande aliquid aggressis uti-
lissimum est, singulos dies magni extima; ea te cogitatio parcum
temporis efficiet, ea te coget ut venias et inter adversitatum nostrarum nubila speratum nobis augustissime tue frontis lumen osten-
7 das. Non te transalpinarum solicitudo rerum, non te natalis soli
dulcedo detineat; quotiens Germaniam respexeris, Italiam cogita.

tedious consultations. See Caesar, how confidentially I am arguing
with you, though I am a petty and unknown fellow. In return I
beg you not to be angry with my frankness, but congratulate your
nature and character which supply me with this confidence. To 3
pursue what I have begun, why do you spend time in deliberating,
as if you were sure of what will come? Don't you know how
swiftly the crisis points arrive of the most important affairs? A
single day often puts an end to things worked out over many generations; believe me, if you observe your own fame and the condition of the state you will see that your affairs and ours do not need
procrastination. Think how life is doubtful and fleeting, and al- 4
though your age is at its prime,[1] it is still unstable and constantly
flies and is swept onward? So every day thrusts you toward old age
unawares: while you look around and hesitate, hoary old age will
suddenly overtake you. Or do you perhaps hesitate to begin prematurely an undertaking you realize even the longest extent of
human life is scarcely adequate to complete? For your responsibility is not for any ordinary or average business. The empire of 5
Rome, so long tossed by many storms, often disappointed and almost abandoned, has finally entrusted its hope of salvation to your
virtue, and after countless misfortunes at least draws breath under
the shade of your name, but it cannot feed any longer on mere
hope. You know how great and devout a burden of cares you have
taken up; carry it to its outcome, we beg, and do so as soon as
possible. Time is a most precious, indeed invaluable thing, and the 6
only thing which the authority of the most learned men urges us
to cherish like misers. So put away delays and do what is most
useful to men tackling some great enterprise, put a high value on
each day; this thought will make you sparing of time, it will compel you to come and show us among the cloudy skies of our misfortunes the long awaited brilliance of your majestic countenance.
Do not let any anxiety for affairs beyond the Alps nor any charm 7
of your native land hold you back: whenever you look back at

Illic natus, hic nutritus; illic regnum, hic et regnum habes et imperium, et quod nationum ac terrarum omnium pace dixerim, cum
ubique membra, hic ipsum caput invenies monarchie. Nullus igitur ignavie locus est, ut ad nutum cunta succedant; magnum fuerit
8 tantarum rerum fragmenta colligere. Sentio quidem novitatem rerum omnium esse suspectam; sed ad nova non traheris, neque tibi
aliter Italia quam Germania nota est. Ab infantia enim tua, nobis
divinitate propitia repromissus, altum incliti patris iter mira indole
prosecutus, sub eo et italicas urbes et mores hominum et terrarum
9 situs et gloriose rudimenta militie didicisti. Quin etiam adhuc
puer—quod plusquam humane virtutis fuerit—preclaras hic sepe
victorias meruisti, sub quibus, etsi magna erant que gerebas,
maiora tamen puerilis expeditionis mysterio velabantur, ne scilicet
eam patriam vir timeres, que tibi puero tantarum victoriarum materiam prebuisset, et quid hinc sperare debeas imperator, primevi
10 tyrocinii auspicio provideres. Adde quod nullius unquam externi
principis adventum letius expectavit Italia ut que nec aliunde remedium vulneribus suis sperat nec tuum tanquam alienigene iugum timet. Hoc singulare, si nescis, habet apud nos maiestas tua;
quid enim verear loqui quod sentio et quod iudice te probari posse
confido? miro quidem Dei favore nunc primum in te nobis post
tot secula mos patrius et Augustus noster est redditus; te enim
utlibet sibi Germani vendicent, nos te italicum arbitramur.

11 Propera igitur, quod sepe iam dixi et sepius est dicendum; propera. Scio tibi actus placere cesareos, nec immerito: Cesar es.
Atqui primus ille opifex imperii tante celeritatis fuisse dicitur, ut

Germany, think of Italy. You were born there, but bred here; you have a kingdom there, but both a kingdom and empire here,[2] and to speak with the indulgence of all nations and lands, while you will find the limbs of your monarchy spread everywhere, you will find its actual head here. So to ensure that everything succeeds at your command, there is no room for slackness; it will be a great task to gather together the pieces of such important matters. I 8
know that novelty is suspect in all enterprises, but you are not being drawn into new business nor is Italy less known to you than Germany. From your infancy you have been promised us by a propitious deity; following your distinguished father's lofty journey with marvelous talent, you learned under his guidance the cities of Italy and the customs of men and the geography of the lands and the elements of glorious warfare. Indeed while still a boy 9
you often earned splendid victories here — an achievement beyond human valor — and in them, even if your successes were great, greater successes were clothed in the mystery of your boyish exploits, so that you would not as a man fear the country which had provided you as a boy with material for such victories, and you foresaw by the omen of your early apprenticeship what you should expect here as emperor. What is more, there was no foreign ruler 10
whom Italy awaited more gladly since she cannot hope for a remedy for her wounds from elsewhere and does not fear your yoke as if it were foreign. This is the unique quality of your majesty in our eyes, if you do not know it; for why should I fear to say what I think and am confident I can prove with you as judge? By a marvelous favor of God our ancestral tradition and our Augustus are now finally restored to us in your person;[3] however the Germans may claim you for themselves, we believe you to be Italian.

So make haste, as I have often said and must say more of- 11
ten, make haste. I know that Caesar-like actions please you and rightly; you are our Caesar.[4] Indeed that primary craftsman of empire is said to have been so swift that he often anticipated the

ipse sepe adventus sui nuntios preveniret. Idem fac et quem titulis
12 equasti, rebus equare satage. Noli amplius benemeritam Italiam
tui desiderio fatigare; noli ardorem nostrum nuntiis et expectatione restinguere; te unum poscimus, tui siderei vultus intuitum
postulamus. Si virtutis amicus es, si glorie studiosus, cuius—ut sic
ego Carolum nostrum alloquar, sicut Iulium Cesarem Marcus
Tullius alloquitur—'avidissimum te, quamvis sis sapiens, non ne-
gabis,' noli, obsecro, laborem fugere; nam qui laborem fugit, fugit
et gloriam et virtutem, ad quas nunquam nisi arduo et laborioso
13 calle pertingitur. Tu vero quem et honesti laboris et vere laudis
appetentissimum scimus, surge, age, et equus magnorum pon-
derum distributor, graviora quelibet etati prevalide et fortioribus
humeris impone; iuventus labori apta, otio senectus; profecto autem ex omnibus optimis ac sanctissimis curis tuis nulla gravior
quam ut italicum orbem tranquilla pace componas; ea sarcina
huius evi viribus par est, cetera leviora quam ut tantum et tam
14 generosum animum occupare mereantur. Hoc igitur primum fac,
reliqua suum tempus invenient, quanquam placata ad plenum et
composita Italia, nichil aut modicum putem negotii superesse.
Finge nunc animo almam te Romane urbis effigiem videre; cogita
matronam evo gravem, sparsa canitie, amictu lacero, pallore miserabili, sed infracto animo et excelso, pristine non immemorem
maiestatis, ita tecum loqui:

15 'Ego, Cesar,—ne despexeris etatem meam—multa olim potui,
multa gessi; ego leges condidi, ego annum partita sum, ego docui
militie disciplinam, ego quingentis annis in Italia consumptis,
ducentis ordine sequentibus—cuius rei fide dignissimi testes
sunt—Asiam Africam Europam totum denique terrarum orbem
bellis et victoriis peragravi, multo sudore multo sanguine multoque

messengers of his coming.[5] Do just this, and begin to match in deeds him whom you have matched in titles. Do not weary Italy, 12
which has served you well, with any further longing for you: do not quench our passion with messengers and waiting; we ask only for you and the chance to gaze upon your starry features. If you are a friend of virtue and eager for glory—glory, for which, to address our Charles as Cicero addresses Julius Caesar, "you will not deny you are most hungry, despite your wisdom,"[6] do not avoid the toil; for the man who avoids toil avoids glory and virtue, which cannot be reached except by a steep and toilsome pathway. Rise 13
up, then, you whom we know to be most eager for honorable toil and true praise, and as fair distributer of great weights, put the heavier burdens on your own powerful shoulders, strong even for your age. Youth is suited for toil and age for leisure; so as is proper, let none of all your best and most holy concerns be more weighty than to settle the Italian world in tranquil peace. That burden is matched to the strength of your present prime, while the rest are too trivial to deserve the attention of so great and noble a spirit. So achieve this first, and your other tasks will find their 14
proper time—although once Italy is fully calmed and settled, I think either no trouble or very little will remain. Now imagine you see the motherly image of Rome: think that a lady mature with age, with hoary locks spread out, torn clothing, pitiable pallor, but of unbroken and lofty spirit, not forgetful of her original majesty, is speaking to you like this:

"Caesar, do not despise my age—I once was very powerful and 15
achieved much; I founded laws, I divided the year, I taught the discipline of warfare,[7] and after spending five hundred years in Italy I traversed during the two hundred which followed—something about which there are witnesses most worthy of belief—Asia, Africa and Europe, indeed the entire world—in wars and victories, strengthening the foundations of my rising empire with much sweat and blood and deliberation;[8] I saw Brutus the first

16 consilio surgentis imperii fundamenta communiens; ego primum libertatis auctorem Brutum, dum michi obsequitur, interfectis filiis superbo hosti mutuis commorientem vulneribus aspexi; ego natantes armatum virum et inermem puellam stupui; ego pium Camilli exilium et Cursoris laboriosam militiam et incomptum Curii caput et electum ab aratro consulem et ruricolam dictatorem et regiam Fabritii paupertatem et Publicole clarum funus et insolitam viventis Curtii sepulturam et gloriosum carcerem Atilii et insigni devotionis habitu procumbentes Decios et Corvini spectabile duellum et mitem patri durum filio Torquatum et profusum una Fabiorum sanguinem et attonitum Porsennam et fumantem genero-
17 sam Mutii dextram vidi; ego Senonum flammas et Pyrri elephantes et opes Antiochi et pertinaciam Mithridatis et Siphacis amentiam et Ligurum difficultates et bella samnitica et Cimbrorum motus et Macedonum minas et punicas fraudes pertuli; ego Carras Egiptum Persidem Arabiam Pontum et utranque Armeniam et Galatiam et Cappadotiam et Trachiam et maurum litus et ethiopicas arenas; ego Lybie campos et Hispanie; ego Aquas Sextias Ticinum Trebiam Transimenum Cannas et claras persico cruore Termophilas;
18 ego Danubium et Rhenum, Indum et Hydaspem, Rodanum et Hiberum, Eufratem Tigrim Gangem Nilum et Hebrum, Tanaim et Araxem; ego Taurum et Olimpum; ego Caucasum et Atlanta; ego Ionium et Egeum, scithicum atque carpathium mare; ego hellespontiacum sinum et euboicas angustias; ego Adriaticum ac Thirrenum, denique perdomitum nostris classibus occeanum, hostium simul et natorum sanguine cruentavi, ut tantam scilicet bellorum seriem pax eterna sequeretur et per multorum manus ad te

creator of liberty, who slew his sons in obeying me, himself dying
in mutually inflicted wounds from the arrogant enemy; I was 16
amazed to look on the armed man and the unarmed girl swimming; I saw the pious exile of Camillus and the wearisome warfare of Cursor and the unshorn head of Curius and the consul appointed from behind the plow who became farmer-dictator and the royal poverty of Fabricius and the glorious burial of Publicola and the unique burial of the living Curtius and the glorious imprisonment of Atilius Regulus and the Decii falling to their knees in the conspicuous clothing of self-dedication, and the spectacular combat of Corvinus, and Torquatus mild to his father but harsh to his son, and the blood of all the Fabii shed at one time and Porsenna thunderstruck and the noble hand of Mucius burning in
smoke.[9] I endured the flames of the Senones and the elephants of 17
Pyrrhus and the wealth of Antiochus and the obstinacy of Mithridates and the madness of Syphax and the resistance of the Ligurians and the Samnite wars and the migrations of the Cimbri and the threats of the Macedonians and the frauds of the Carthaginians;[10] I saw Carrhae, Egypt, Persia, Arabia, Pontus and both Armenias and Galatia and Cappadocia and Thrace and the Moorish coast and Ethiopian sands; I saw the plains of Libya and Spain, I saw Aquae Sextiae, Ticinus, Trebia, Trasimene, Cannae and Thermopylae glorious in Persian bloodshed;[11] I saw the Danube and 18
Rhine, Indus and Hydaspes, Rhône and Ebro, Euphrates, Tigris, Ganges, Nile, the Hebrus, the Don and Araxes; I saw Taurus and Olympus, the Caucasus and Atlas range, I saw the Ionian and Aegean, Scythian and Carpathian seas, I saw the Hellespontine gulf and Euboean straits, I saw the Adriatic and Tyrrhenian seas, finally Ocean tamed by our fleets;[12] I made its waters crimson at the same time with the blood of our enemy and ourselves, so that an eternal peace might follow such a series of wars, and so that the empire, destined to come to you through many hands, might be

19 venturum stabiliretur imperium. Nec mea me fefellit intentio; voti compos, omnia sub pedibus meis vidi. Inde sensim nescio quonammodo, nisi quia mortalium opera decet esse mortalia, in labores meos irrepsit aliena segnities, ac ne lacrimabilem ordiar historiam, quorsum res redierint, vides.

20 'Tu michi prope iam desperanti divinitus destinatus, quid cessas, quid cogitas, quid expectas? Nunquam aut ego tui egentior aut tu ad opem ferendam aptior aut Romanus Pontifex clementior aut expectatio populorum maior aut favor Dei et hominum propensior aut illustrior res agenda. Differs? inimica semper magnis mora principiis. Moveant animum tuum exempla clarissima eorum qui nichil in senium differentes oblatam semel occasionem impi-
21 gerrime rapuerunt. Alexander Macedo ea etate qua nunc es, Oriente pererrato Indorum regna pulsabat, aliena rapturus; tu tuum repetens, devotam tibi non intrabis Italiam? Eadem hac etate tua Scipio Africanus in Africam transgressus, senum quamvis retrahente sententia, nutanti iam et ruinam minanti imperio pias adhibuit manus atque incredibili virtute impendens michi iugum
22 carthaginiense discussit. Magna res in primis et periculi novitate memorabilis, nostris ardentibus hostium fines invadere et Hanibalem, Italie tunc Galliarumque et Hispanie victorem ac iam totius orbis imperium tumida mente versantem, hinc vi detractum illic
23 armis vincere. Tibi nulla quidem transeunda sunt maria, nullus Hanibal vincendus; pronum iter, plana et aperta sunt omnia; que enim obserata quidam putant, presentie tue tonitru patescent. Ingens, nisi respuis, nove tibi glorie campus ostenditur; ingredere

established. Nor did my intention betray me: I achieved my prayer 19
and saw everything beneath my feet. Then gradually, I know not how, except that it is fitting for the achievements of mortals to be themselves mortal, an alien sloth crept into my striving, and, not to begin on a lamentable history, you see how far matters have sunk.

"You were destined by divine will for me, who am now close to 20
despair, so why do you hesitate, deliberate and keep waiting? I was never more in need of you or you more fit to bring me aid or the pope of Rome more well-disposed[13] or the eagerness of the peoples greater, or the favor of God and men more inclined to us or a more noble task ours to perform. Are you postponing it? Delay is always hostile to great enterprises. Let your spirit be stirred by the most brilliant examples of men who postponed nothing to old age
but seized most energetically the opportunity offered them. At 21
your present age Alexander of Macedon had traversed the East and was assailing the Indian monarchies, intending to sweep away other men's possessions; and will you in reclaiming your own possessions not enter an Italy that is devoted to you? At the same age as you Scipio Africanus was about to cross into Africa, despite the opinions of the old men dragging him back, and laid loyal hands on my empire, tottering and threatening collapse, and with unbelievable valor shook off the Carthaginian yoke hanging over me.[14]
It was an exceptionally great achievement and memorable for the 22
newness of the risk, to invade the enemy when our own lands were on fire, and defeat Hannibal, at the time victor over Italy and the Gauls and Spain, and brooding with his arrogant spirit over an empire of the whole world, and to pull him away from Italy by
force and conquer him in arms on his own territory. But you have 23
no seas to cross, no Hannibal to defeat; the path is level, all is smooth and open; even the roads which some men believe are barred will open at the thunder of your presence. Unless you reject it a huge field for new glory is being shown to you; enter it boldly

fortiter intrepide; iustorum comes et adiutor principum, Deus aderit; aderunt armate bonorum acies duce te libertatem perditam reposcentes.

24 'Possem nunc exemplis te solicitare contrariis eorum qui gloriosa primordia seu mortis seu insignis cuiuspiam impedimenti
obice nequaquam ad exitum perduxerunt; sed ubi domestica sup-
25 petunt, externa non querimus. Unus tibi, non procul, non ex an-
nalibus querendus, unus tibi pro omnibus satis erit: Henricus,
eterne memorie serenissimus avus tuus, cui si ad explenda que sacra mente conceperat, vite spatium suffecisset, versa rerum sorte et
afflictos hostes et me regnantem et liberrimos Italie populos ac fe-
licissimos reliquisset. Spectat ille nunc celorum perpes incola, dies
computat horasque dinumerat teque mecum increpitans alloqui-
26 tur: "Nepos amantissime, quo superstite nec bonorum spes nec
ego totus interii, Romam nostram atque illius lacrimas precesque
dignissimas amplectere reformandeque reipublice propositum,
quod mea mors, mundo quam michi damnosior, prevertit, et inef-
ficacem animi mei zelum pari ardore prosequere, sed felicius sed
letius. Incipe; ne moreris; et nostri memor scito te esse mortalem.
27 I celer et gaudentia Alpium claustra transcende; Roma sponsum,
sospitatorem suum vocat Italia et tuis pedibus tangi cupit; expectant te leti colles ac flumina, expectant urbes et oppida, expectant
bonorum agmina; et si te nil aliud urgeret nisi quod malis nunquam satis distulisse, bonis nunquam satis festinasse videberis, sat
cause est ut his gaudium, illis penam vel si resipiscere maluerint,

and fearlessly; God, the companion of the just and supporter of princes, will be there to aid you; so will the battle lines of patriots under arms, with you as leader reclaiming their lost liberty.

"I could harass you now with counter examples of those who 24
forestalled by death or by some conspicuous hindrance were in no way able to bring their glorious beginnings to completion, but when family examples are in supply we are not looking for foreign
cases. One man, not far from you, nor to be sought in ancient 25
histories—this one man will be enough. Henry, your most gracious grandfather of immortal memory, who if the extent of his life had been sufficient to fulfill the policies he had conceived in his holy mind, if only the chance of events had changed, would have left the enemy smitten and me as their ruler and the peoples of Italy most free and blessed.[15] Now as an everlasting dweller in the heavens he watches and lists the days and counts the hours
and speaks, rebuking you along with me: 'Devoted grandson, in 26
whose survival neither the hopes of patriots nor I myself have utterly perished, embrace our Rome and her most worthy prayers and tears and the purpose of reshaping the republic which my death, more ruinous to the world than to me, has overthrown, and follow the unsuccessful dedication of my spirit with equal passion, but more successfully and joyously. Begin! Do not delay. Mindful
of my fate, know that you are mortal. Go swiftly and cross the 27
barriers of the rejoicing Alps; Rome summons you as her groom, Italy as her savior, longing to be trodden by your feet; the hills and rivers await you in joy, the cities and towns await you; so do the battle lines of patriots. And if nothing else pressed upon you—except that to wicked men you never seem to have delayed your action enough but to patriots never to have hastened enough—this is reason enough to give patriots rejoicing and the wicked punishment, or if the latter prefer to recover sanity, hasten to bring them

veniam laturus acceleres. Solus enim es cui Deus omnipotens interrupti consilii mei dilatam gloriam reservavit.'"

*VI Kal. Martias, Patavi.*

## : 10 :

## *Ad Carolum quartum, gratulatio seri licet adventus.*

1 Et gaudium ingens verba precidere solitum; quidni autem est ubi spiritum abrumpat? Idem ego in tua totiens exhortatione multiloquus, en ut in gratulatione perbrevis sum. Quid enim dicam? unde ordiar? vacuasti cor meum multis angoribus atque implesti gaudio, quodque ait Psalmista, 'adimplebis me letitia cum vultu tuo,' sola iam fama tui nominis adimpletum est. Quid vultus ergo
2 cesareus, quid augusta frons faciet? Longanimitatem, inter expectationes, ac patientiam exoptabam; ecce optare incipio ut tante felicitatis capax tantoque gaudio par sim. Iam michi non Boemie sed mundi rex, iam romanus imperator, iam verus es Cesar; invenies, ne dubita, que tibi pollicitus sum, parata omnia: dyadema, imperium, immortalem gloriam apertumque celi aditum, et ad sum-
3 mam quicquid optare aut sperare datum homini. Nunc te excitasse qualibuscunque sermunculis glorior atque exulto; iam iuga Alpium transcendenti occurro animis, haud equidem solus; infinita mecum acies, quin ipsa nostrum omnium publica mater Italia et Italie caput Roma, tibi obvie altis vocibus virgilianum illud exclamant:

pardon. For you alone are the person for whom Almighty God has reserved the postponed glory of my unfinished plan of action.'"

*Padua, February 24.*

## : 10 :

## *To Charles IV, congratulating him on his coming, however late.*

Immense joy is wont to cut off speech, so what is the emotion that 1
cuts off breath itself? See how I, so often longwinded in exhorting you,[1] am shortness itself in my congratulation. For what shall I say? Where begin? You have emptied my heart of many torments and filled it with rejoicing and, as the Psalmist says, "You will fill me with joy with your countenance."[2] My heart has been filled simply with the renown of your name. What, then, will Caesar's
countenance, what his Augustan brow, bring to pass? I was long- 2
ing for endurance of spirit and patience in awaiting you; see now I am beginning to wish instead that I may be capable of such great happiness and equal to such rejoicing. Now for me you are not king of Bohemia but of the world, now you are emperor of Rome, now the true Caesar; you will find, never doubt it, what I promised you, everything ready: a diadem, imperial command, immortal glory and the way to heaven laid open, in short whatever is
granted to a man to wish or hope for. Now I feel pride and exulta- 3
tion that I aroused you by my modest talks, such as they were; now I run to meet you in my spirit as you cross over the Alpine range, and by no means alone: there is an uncountable throng with me, indeed Italy, the mother of all our people, and Rome, her capital, will go out to greet you and cry out in full voice that famous Vergilian welcome:

Venisti tandem tuaque expectata parenti
Vicit iter durum pietas.

4 Neque vero Germanie obtentu hanc fastidias aut repellas matrem, cum qua et vite primordia egisti et si tuum decus amas, extrema exiges. Nos te, Cesar, ut ab initio dicebam, ubicunque ortum, italicum arbitramur, neque vero magni interest ubi sis natus, sed ad quid. Vive et vale, Cesar, et propera.

## : II :

## *Ad Lelium suum, ut falsam non querendam sic veram gloriam non spernendam.*

1 Credulum amorem, ait Naso, nec fallitur; utramvis in partem experientia testis adest. Quam facilis enim et quam prona est caritas amicorum ad amplissimas spes opinionesque clarissimas? aut quid tam magnificum fingi potest quod de amato non facile credat amans? Credo ego labores herculeos nulli magis creditos quam Philoteti; credo famam victe Carthaginis nulli profundius hesuram
2 fuisse quam Lelio. Patule sunt aures amicorum: omnia ante omnes excipiunt; magna fides amicitie: omnia statim credit nec credidisse contenta est nisi de proprio aliquid auditis adiecerit. Contra autem comes amoris zelus ardens quam preceps est ad credendum omne quod displicet! non rebus tantum sed umbris etiam terretur ac somniis.

Sed ad piam illam amicitie credulitatem redeo, de qua michi
3 nunc sermo est. Equidem, quantum ingenio assequor, Rome olim

> You are come at last, and piety, long awaited by your parent,
> has conquered the harsh journey.[3]

Nor indeed should you disdain or reject for the claims of Germany this mother with whom you spent your life's beginning and, if you love your glory, will spend your last moments. As I said from the beginning, Caesar, we hold you to be Italian, wherever you were born,[4] and it is of little importance where you were born, but for what destiny. Live and thrive, Caesar and make haste. 4

## : II :

### *To his dear Laelius, just as false glory is not worth seeking, so true glory is not to be despised.*

Ovid says love is credulous,[1] and he is not mistaken; experience is 1
our witness to both sides of the argument. How easy and prone is the affection of friends to grandiose hopes and opinions, and what can be imagined so magnificent that a lover does not easily believe it about the one he loves? I believe no one had more faith than Philoctetes in Hercules' labors. I believe the glory of conquering Carthage was not more deeply planted in any man than in Laelius.[2] The ears of friends are wide open and they welcome all good 2
news more than other men. Great is the trust of friendship; it believes everything good immediately and is not content to believe unless it has added something of its own to whatever it has heard. In contrast how headlong is the passion that is love's companion to believe every kind of unwelcome news! It is terrified not just by events but by ghosts and dreams.

But I come back now to that pious trust belonging to friendship which is my present topic. As far as I can divine there were 3

duo fuerunt Lelii, Scipionibus amicum nomen; ille avum coluit, hic nepotem; ille tributariam vidit Carthaginem, hic eversam. Certe et michi Lelius meus est, quem tot seculis interiectis urbs eadem, senex nondum sterilis, genuit. Miraris? sed te etiam fallit amor; credidisti perfacile, mi Leli, quod de me tibi ab obvio quodam forte narratum est, nec quanta narranti fides esset, exegisti.
4 Quis enim tam sobrius, ne dicam durus, ut quod multum delectat libenter abiciat, cum presertim delectatio honesta sit et amicitie velo non modo error excusabilis sed laudandus?

Credidisti igitur nescio cui — vix etenim suspicari ausim famam, etsi sepissime mendax sit, id nunc publice fuisse mentitam — me scilicet ad italicam pacem novo cum Cesare sanciendam singulariter preelectum, feliciter rebus actis et pace reipublice quesita,
5 magna cum gloria remeasse. Nolo erres aut inanem voluptatem ex errore percipias; non ita est, amice. Neque enim unum caput res tanta poscebat; primi procerum missi sunt. Si enim Argivos delectos viros ad petendam pellem auratam et forsitan fabulosam arietis olim missos legimus, non multo nunc delectiores Italos mitti dignum erat ad vere auream procurandam pacem? Illi equidem parva spe magno et procelloso mari Colchon barbaricam petiere, ubi regnabat incognitus rex Oethes; isti Mantuam, quo iam Cesar pervenerat late notus, magno et prorsus incomparabili premio il-
6 lecti atque exiguo et plano calle non peterent? Iverunt itaque, quod res docuit, felicibus ac letis auspiciis; et ut Graii magam veneficamque famosissimam, sic nostri dulce bonum patrie reportarunt.

once two men called Laelius at Rome. It was a name friendly to the Scipios. The elder Laelius worshipped the grandfather, the other the grandson; the first saw Carthage made tributary, the other saw it overthrown. Certainly I too have my Laelius whom the same city, old but not yet sterile, brought to birth after the lapse of so many ages.[3] Are you surprised? But love deceives even you. And you believed with great ease, my dear Laelius, something that must have been told you about me in some random encounter, and did not challenge the credibility of the teller. For what 4
person is so sober, not to mention hardheaded, that he will freely reject what gives him great pleasure, especially when that pleasure is honorable and the cloak of friendship makes a mistake not just excusable but praiseworthy?

So you believed some unknown person — I can hardly dare to suspect Rumor, even if she most often lies, has now spread the story in public — that I was singled out to sanction the Italian peace agreement with the new Caesar,[4] and having completed negotiations successfully and won peace for the state, returned with great glory. I don't want you to be misled or to derive empty plea- 5
sure from the tale. That is not how it happened, dear friend. For so great a matter required more than one person; the foremost nobles were commissioned. If we read that select men of the Argives were once sent to seek the Golden (and perhaps mythical) Fleece,[5] then wasn't it proper to send much more exceptional Italians to obtain the truly golden peace? The Argonauts made for barbaric Colchis with little hope over a mighty and stormy sea, where the unknown king Aeëtes reigned. So should not the Italians also go to Mantua, which the widely known Caesar had already reached, enticed by a mighty and utterly incomparable reward and by a short and level road? So they went, as events have 6
proven, with successful and happy omens, and as the Greeks won a poisoner and notorious witch,[6] so our men brought back a sweet

Quorum tamen ex numero non fui; nemo tibi mendacio blandia-
tur; quamvis autem tanto negotio longe impar, iudicio tamen beni-
gniore mittentium gloriosum laborem effugere nequivissem, nisi
publicis votis private quedam obstitissent cause, quas nunc siluisse
7 prestiterit. Ne vero forsan his dictis omnis glorie contemptorem
putes, sed intelligas me ut falsam respuere sic veram gloriam non
horrere, dicam quid multis diebus post profectionem legatorum
nostrorum et prope iam omnibus ibi conventis ac firmatis, acciderit. Cesari enim interea mei desiderium incessit et cuius animum
mores ac studia noverat, optavit et faciem videre.

8 Iam hiems miris modis induruerat; misit tamen nec occupatio-
nibus meis parcens nec labori, et misit nuntium solemnem; quique
regibus imperat me rogavit ut ad se pergere festinarem; ei insuper
preces misit, cui nil negaturum me putabat, nec errabat. Quid vis?
illo vocante atque hoc urgente proficiscor, nec unquam alias
evidentius intellexi quid est quod ait Augustinus: 'Italicum glaciale
9 solum.' Ad. II° Idus Decembris hinc movi, neque tam terreum
quam adamantinum atque chalybeum iter erat, et glaciei metus
non nisi nivis solatio levabatur, que ipsa etiam preter morem nescio quid horrificum habebat. Captabamus tamen omni studio ubi
nequicquam armati in glaciem equorum pedes utcunque consiste-
10 rent, et ruine pavor assiduus vie laborem fecerat non sentiri. Ad
hec et brume et algori nebula, qualis in memoria hominum non
est, et celo immiti terrarum vastitas accesserat et solitudo horrida,
qualem non Musis et Apollini sed Marti convenire diceres ac Bellone. Strate passim domus, habitator nullus fumosaque tecta villarum et dumosa novalia et hinc illinc erumpentes e latebris armati,
quanquam sine noxa, ut qui nostri essent, non tamen sine horrore

benefit to their country. But I was not one of them; let nobody beguile you with lies; although I was far beneath such a great task, by the more generous judgment of those sending me I would not have been able to escape this glorious toil if private motives, about which it is wiser now to keep silent, had not obstructed public
desires. But to ensure that these comments do not lead you to 7
think me contemptuous of all glory, and to show that I am not afraid of true glory, just as I reject the false form, I will tell you what happened many days after the departure of our envoys, when virtually all the terms were agreed and confirmed. In that time Caesar felt a longing to see me, and knowing my attitude, character and enthusiasms, he also wanted to see my features.

Winter had already set in to an extreme degree but he sent for 8
me, not sparing my preoccupations nor my effort, and sent a formal messenger:[7] he who commands kings asked me to hasten to come to him, and he entrusted an additional request to a man whom he thought I would not refuse, nor was he mistaken. What do you expect? When he summoned me and the messenger urged this request, I set out, and I never understood more manifestly
what Augustine calls "Italy's icy soil."[8] I left here on December 11, 9
and the path was not so much earthy as made of diamond and iron, and only the consolation of snow softened my terror of ice—though the snow itself had an unusually frightening aspect. So we searched out with great care where the feet of our horses, vainly shod against the ice, could somehow stand, and the constant terror of falling prevented us from feeling the hardship of the journey. In addition to the midwinter and frost there was a fog such as 10
is not known to human memory, and the merciless weather was intensified by the wildness of the land and a dreadful solitude, that you would say befitted not Apollo and the Muses but Mars and Bellona.[9] There were ruined dwellings here and there with no inhabitant and the smoking roofs of houses and fallow fields of scrub and armed men bursting out of hiding all around: though

quodam, presentis adhuc belli vestigia preferebant. Sed veteri fato meo mos gerendus fuit interque difficultates et pericula incedendum.

11 Mediolano autem digressus, quarta luce, imo vero quartis seu certe continuis tenebris, Mantuam veni, ubi ab illo nostrorum cesarum successore plusquam familiaritate cesarea et plusquam imperatoria lenitate susceptus sum; et ut comunia pretermittam, aliquando soli ambo ab initio prime facis ad noctis silentium intempeste colloquendo et confabulando pervenimus; in summa nichil illius principis maiestate suavius, nichil humanius: hoc unum scito; de reliquis, quoniam, ut ait Satyricus,

Fronti nulla fides

est, nondum diffinitive pronuntio. Expectabimus, quantusque sit Cesar, non verba non vultum, ne fallamur, sed actus hominis atque exitum consulemus.

12 Quod ipse sibi non tacui; dum enim ad id forte mecum sermo cesareus descendisset, ut aliqua sibi de opusculis meis exposceret atque in primis librum cui *De viris illustribus* nomen dedi, illum inexpletum esse respondi et temporis atque otii egentem; dumque ille pacisci vellet in posterum, occurri libertate illa mea qua cum maioribus magis uti propositum est, quam michi quidem contulit natura, auxit vero vicina iam senectus, in immensum auctura cum venerit, et 'Ita,' inquam, 'id tibi promissum credito, si tibi virtus
13 affuerit, vita michi.' Mirantique et dicti causam requirenti: 'Quod ad me' inquam, 'attinet, tanto operi iustum vite spatium debetur; egre enim magna in angustiis explicantur. Quod autem ad te, Cesar, ita demum hoc te munere et eius libri titulo dignum scito, si non fulgore nominis tantum aut inani dyademate, sed rebus gestis

harmless, being on our side, they displayed the traces of lingering warfare, causing a certain horror. But I had to humor my old fate and advance amid difficulties and dangers.

Having left Milan I came to Mantua at the fourth dawn, or 11
rather after four periods of continuous darkness, and was welcomed there by this successor to our Caesars with more than Caesarean intimacy and more than imperial gentleness, and to pass over commonplaces, we walked alone together for some time, passing from the first dawn to the silence of dead of night in discussion and conversation. In short nothing was sweeter than the dignity of this emperor, nothing more humane: for the rest, you should know just this one thing, since as the satirist says

> you cannot trust men's faces,[10]

I am not yet making a final assessment. We shall wait, and consider the greatness of Caesar not from his words or expression, but from the man's actions and their outcome.

I did not keep this quiet from him; for while Caesar's conversa- 12
tion had relaxed to the point that he wanted to know some of my works and especially the book I called *On Illustrious Men*, I answered that it was incomplete and needed time and leisure:[11] while he wanted to bargain for a future gift I met him with the frankness which I have resolved to use with important men beyond what comes naturally to me; it has been enhanced by the approach of old age, and will increase immensely when old age comes. So I said: "So believe it is promised to you on these terms, if virtue
stands with you and life with me." When he expressed amazement 13
and asked the motive for my comment, I said: "As far as I am concerned the full space of a life is needed for such a work, for it is very difficult to explain great matters in a narrow compass. As for you, Caesar, know that you are worthy of this gift and the title of this book if you do not just enroll among these heroes with the glitter of your name and an empty diadem but with achievements

et virtute animi illustribus te te viris ascripseris et sic vixeris ut
14 cum veteres legeris, tu legaris a posteris.' Quod dictum serenis oculorum radiis et auguste frontis leto probavit assensu. Itaque peroportunum aggredi visum est quod iandudum facere meditabar; sumpta igitur ex verbis occasione, aliquot sibi aureas argenteasque nostrorum principum effigies minutissimis ac veteribus literis inscriptas, quas in delitiis habebam, dono dedi, in quibus et Augusti Cesaris vultus erat pene spirans.

15 'Et ecce' inquam, 'Cesar, quibus successisti; ecce quos imitari studeas et mirari, ad quorum formulam atque imaginem te componas, quos preter te unum nulli hominum daturus eram. Tua me movit autoritas; licet enim horum mores et nomina, horum ego res gestas norim, tuum est non modo nosse sed sequi; tibi itaque debebantur.' Sub hec singulorum vite summam multa brevitate perstringens, quos potui ad virtutem atque ad imitandi studium aculeos verbis immiscui; quibus ille vehementer exhilaratus, nec ullum gratius accepisse munusculum visus est.

16 Quid te in singulis morer? multa ibi mecum ille que sileo; unum quod ut puto miraberis, non silebo. A die ortus usque ad hanc etatem totam vite mee, fabulam dicam an historiam?, ex ordine voluit audire, quamvis ego longam nimis inamenamque testarer; et ita me diuticule loquentem animo atque auribus intentus audivit, ut sicubi vel oblivione vel brevitatis studio aliquid preterirem, protinus ille suppleret ac sepe me melius ipse res meas nosset, quarum fumum—stupor!—usque trans Alpes nescio quis flatus impegerat oculosque compleverat intuendis mundi defectibus
17 occupatos. Denique dum ad hoc tempus narratio pervenisset conticuissemque parumper, ille me de sequentis vite proposito

that are glorious for virtue of spirit, and live so gallantly that, just as you have been a reader of the ancient sources, you yourself will
be read about by future ages." He accepted this saying with calm 14
glances of his eyes and the glad agreement of his revered brow. So it seemed most opportune to take action, as I had long since planned to do; so I seized the chance offered by his words and showed him some gold and silver portrait coins of our emperors inscribed with tiny and ancient letters. These I kept as treasures, and I made a gift of them to him including the face of Augustus Caesar, almost breathing with life.

"Look, Caesar, see the man in whose succession you stand; see 15
the men you should strive to imitate and admire, to whose form and image you should shape yourself, on the coins I would not have given to any one except to you. Your authority has moved me; for although I know these men's characters and names and achievements, it is your duty not just to know them but to follow them, so they were destined for you." In this way I shrank within a brief compass the total of their individual lives, mixing goads with my words to provoke virtue and imitation. Greatly excited, he seemed never to have accepted any little gift with more appreciation.

Need I delay you over details? He talked to me a great deal, 16
which I will pass over. But one thing I will not let pass, as I think you will marvel at it. From the day of my birth to my present age he wanted to know my life story—or shall I call it a legend?—all in due order, although I declared it was too long and unappealing; and so as I went on chattering, a little on the long side, he listened to me with such attentive spirit and ears that when, out of forgetfulness or desire for brevity I passed over anything, he immediately supplied it and he often knew my affairs better than I—since (amazing as it is) some gust had driven the smoke of rumors across the Alps and filled his eyes, strained with gazing on the
failures of the world. Finally when the story had reached the pres- 17
ent time and I fell briefly silent, he asked me about my plans for

percontatus: 'Fare' inquit, 'de futuro quid cogitas quem ve tibi finem mente constituis?' 'Intentio,' inquam, 'Cesar, optima est, quamvis adhuc actus meos ad limam expolire nequiverim; preteriti enim temporis consuetudo violenta et presenti intentione potentior, cor adversus recens propositum, quasi contra novum ventum
18 aliis flatibus impulsum mare, precipitat.' Ad hec ille: 'Credo sic esse' inquit, 'ut dicis, sed aliud percontabar: quenam tibi vite semita placeret.' Ego autem incuntanter et intrepide: 'Solitarie' inquam, 'qua nulla tutior, nulla tranquillior, nulla denique felicior vita est, que iudice me tui quoque gloriam principatus fastigiumque transcendit; illam ego, si dabitur, in sede sua, hoc est in silvis ac montibus quod sepe iam feci, alioquin, quantum possibile fuerit, ut nunc facio, ipsis in urbibus consectabor.'

19 Hic ille subrisit et 'Sciebam' inquit, 'sciensque ad hanc te confessionem pedetentim interrogando perduxi, ubi tuum, quod in multis probo, iudicium reprobarem.' Sic inter nos ingens disputatio est exorta, sepe me interpellante: 'Vide, Cesar, quo progrederis; mecum non equo quidem Marte contendis, cui in hac questione non tu tantum sed sillogismis armatus Crisippus ipse succumberet.
20 Diu enim nil aliud cogitavi plenumque caput rationibus et exemplis habeo; magistra rerum experientia mecum sentit, ineptum et indocile vulgus adversum est; noli secum partes facere. Vincam te, Cesar, sub quocunque iusto licet urbano iudicio, quippe qui hoc ipso tam plenus sim ut de parte vel exigua libellum unum nuper
21 ediderim.' Intercepit ille promptissime et: 'Hoc ipsum scio' inquit, 'et si unquam ad manus meas liber ille pervenerit, ignibus eum tradam.' 'Providebo' inquam, 'Cesar, ne perveniat.' Ita longis iocosisque sermonibus protracta altercatio est, ut fatear ex omnibus

the life ahead. "Tell me," he said, "what you are planning for the future and what end you have set up in your mind for yourself?" "I have an excellent plan, Caesar, although I have not yet been able to smooth my actions with the polishing file: for as I said the habits of the past are violent and more powerful than my current intention, driving my heart to confront the fresh project like the sea
stirred up with contrary gusts against a new wind." He answered: 18
"I think it is as you say, but I was asking a different question. What path of life would you choose?" So I replied without hesitation or fear: "I will choose a life of solitude, since no other life is safer or calmer or more blessed, indeed in my judgment it surpasses the glory and summit of your imperial power. If it is granted I shall live like this in its proper setting, that is, in the woods and hills as I have often done, but otherwise, as far as possible, as I do at present, I shall pursue it even in cities."

Here he smiled and said: "I knew it, and was deliberately lead- 19
ing you gradually by my questioning to this confession, so that I might criticize your judgment, although I approve it in many others." So a great dispute arose between us, with me often interrupting: "See, Caesar, where you are advancing: you are not disputing with me on equal terms, since in this investigation not just you but
Chrysippus himself armed with syllogisms would give way.[12] For a 20
long time I thought of nothing else and I have my head full of reasons and precedents. Experience, mistress of life, agrees with me, but the foolish and unteachable crowd is opposed. Don't join their party! I shall overcome you, Caesar, under any just if sophisticated judgment, because I am so full of this that I have just
published a whole book on a small part of this issue."[13] He readily 21
interrupted me and said: "I know this and if ever that book comes into my hands, I shall consign it to the flames." I said: "I shall take care it does not, Caesar." The exchange was extended in our long and jesting conversations so much so that I shall admit that of all

quos oppugnatores solitarie vite sum expertus, nullum audisse contra id vite genus efficacius disputantem.

22 Finis is fuit ut—si dicere Cesarem aut credere victum licet—verbis et ratione nisi fallor victus, opinione autem sua non modo invictus sed etiam palam victor, hoc ultimum precaretur ut secum Romam peterem; hanc enim fuisse primam causam me quietis avidum tam adverso tempore fatigandi; optare se tantam urbem non suis modo sed meis, ut ita dicam, oculis videre; egere etiam se mei presentia in quibusdam Tuscie urbibus, de quibus ita locutus est ut italicum hominem et italicum credere posses ingenium.
23 Quod etsi michi admodum placeret—pergrata enim duo nomina, Roma et Cesar, ita convenerant ut nil animo meo dulcius quam cum Cesare Romam ire—multis tamen ex causis partim iustis partim necessariis negavi; unde nova iterum lis exarsit, que in multos dies producta, finiri usque ad supremum vale non potuit, quando Mediolano scilicet abeuntem ultra Placentie muros ad quintum lapidem prosecutus, vix ab ipso tandem multa verborum
24 colluctatione divulsus sum. Quo tempore tusci militis ex comitatu cesareo grave verbum et liberum insonuit, qui me manu tenens oculis in illum versus, 'Ecce' inquit, 'imperator, de quo tibi sepe dixeram, qui siquid laude dignum gesseris, nomen tuum tacitum non sinet; alioquin et loqui didicit et tacere.'

25 Redeo autem ad inceptum. Non igitur oblatam gloriam fugio quod invisa sit, sed quod veritas cuntis rebus amicior: non sequester pacis ego sed amator fui, neque petitor sed hortator et laudator, neque principio eius interfui sed fini; cum enim in conclusione tractatuum publicis monimentis pacis firmitas fundaretur, inter-
26 esse me Cesar et fortuna voluerunt. Profecto autem in hoc genere

those I have heard attacking the solitary life, I have not heard any man disputing more effectively against that way of living.

The outcome was that if one may say or believe Caesar to have 22
been defeated, he was defeated in words and argument, but in his own opinion not only undefeated but even openly the victor: this was his last prayer, that I should travel to Rome with him, since this was his main reason for harassing me, eager for rest as I was, at such an unfavorable time; he desired to see so great a city not just with his own eyes but through mine, so to speak. And he would need my presence in certain Tuscan cities,[14] about which he spoke in such a way that you could tell he was an Italian with an Italian mind. And even though this pleased me a great deal—since 23
two names, Rome and Caesar, particularly welcome to me, merged so that nothing was sweeter to my spirit than to go to Rome with Caesar—yet from many fair or necessary motives I refused. So a new quarrel arose, which was extended for many days, and could not be ended until the last "farewell." In fact when he was leaving Milan I escorted him beyond the walls of Piacenza to the fifth milestone, and was barely torn away from him with a great wrestling match of words. At this time a serious and frank saying of a 24
Tuscan soldier from Caesar's bodyguard resonated with me. Holding me by the hand and turning his eyes toward the emperor he said: "This is the emperor who I often said will not leave your name unmentioned if you do anything deserving praise: in fact he knows both how to speak and how to be silent."

So now I come back to my beginning. I am not shunning glory 25
offered to me because I dislike it, but because truth is dearer to me in all matters. I was not the agent of peace but its lover, and I did not petition for it, but urged it and praised him for it, and if I was not part of the opening negotiations I shared in their outcome. For when firm peace was established by public record in the sealing of treaties, Caesar and Fortune wanted me to be involved. Surely I know that in this kind of negotiation no Italian was 26

nulli italo plus tributum scio: vocari et rogari a Cesare, iocari et disputare cum Cesare. 'Platoni quidem, sapientie antistiti' ut Plinius ait, 'Dyonisius tyrannus vittatam navem misit obviam; ipse quadrigis albis egredientem in litore excepit'; hec ut magnifica referuntur in gloriam Platonis.

27 Vide nunc, amantissime Leli, quo tendam et ut nullam oblate vere glorie materiam pretermittam. Quid vero non ausurus sim, qui Platoni me conferre non verear? sed absit ut me illi conferam cui maximorum hominum et in primis Tullii Augustinique iudicio nec Aristotiles conferendus sit; non ingeniorum sed eventuum ista
28 collatio est. Ille Platoni a siracusia forsitan arce prospecto per aliquantulum freti spatium vittatam navem misit obviam; iste autem generosum ac militarem et strenuum quendam virum aliquot dierum spatio honustum precibus ad me misit; ille ultro venientem excepit; oravit hic etiam ut venirem. Confer modo singula, et armato militi vittatam navem, et cesaree lenitati Dyonisii quadrigas, postremo romano principi siculum tyrannum: credo fateberis me-
29 rito Platonem precellere me fortuna. Sed iam satis glorie ludendo captavimus; quod ipsum levitatis vitio non careret, nisi ita tecum loquerer ut mecum. Epystolam quam ad Cesarem ipsum tuis me de rebus scribere voluisti, qua comitatus illum fidentius atque familiarius adeas, cum hac simul accipies; utraque tibi Pisis occurret, ubi tu occursurus es principi. Illa quidem, ut spero, sed multo maxime tua virtus et nostrorum heroum recordatio cesareum tibi limen aperiet. Vale.

granted a greater role—to be summoned and consulted by Caesar, to joke and dispute with him. "Dionysius the tyrant sent a garlanded ship to Plato, as the representative of wisdom," according to Pliny, "and welcomed him in person as he disembarked on shore, with a chariot of four white horses"; these details are related as grandiose and glorifying Plato.[15]

But consider now, most affectionate Laelius, where I am taking 27
my account, to leave no material of glory offered to me unmentioned. What would I not dare, since I am not afraid to compare myself with Plato? But far be it from me to compare myself with the man with whom in the judgment of the greatest men, like Cicero and Augustine, not even Aristotle is to be compared;[16] this is
not a comparison of intellects but of outcomes. Perhaps Dionysius 28
sent the garlanded ship from the citadel of Syracuse across the modest distance of the straits to meet Plato, but our Caesar sent a noble and military and vigorous man over the space of several days, weighed down with requests; Dionysius welcomed Plato when he decided to come, while Caesar begged me to come. Just compare the individual details, the garlanded ship to the armed soldier, the chariot of Dionysius to Caesar's gentleness, and finally the Sicilian tyrant to the Roman emperor, and I believe you will
admit that I deserved to exceed Plato in fortune. But now we have 29
spent enough time chasing glory in sport, which itself would not escape the fault of frivolity if I was not talking to you as if to myself. As for the letter which you wanted me to write to Caesar himself about your business, so that you may approach him with greater confidence and familiarity, you will receive it along with this letter, and both will meet you at Pisa where you are going to meet the emperor.[17] As I hope, that letter, but far more your own virtue and the memory of our heroes, will open up Caesar's threshold for you. Farewell.

## : 12 :

*Ad Cesarem hunc nostrum, primo dulcis gratulatio privatim pro sui familiaritate, post acerrima increpatio pro republica atque imperio desertis et exhortatio in finem vehementissima.*

1 Letum me fecit epystola tua, Cesar. Quidni autem, cum sola tui recordatio letum facere soleat, dum subit animum me, nescio quidem unde, nisi ex tua humanitate et fortuna mea sive, ut hoc ultimum sanius loquar, non certe solari virtute sub qua essem natus—qua michi adhuc puero famosus quidam predixit astrologus futurum ut fere omnium principum atque illustrium virorum quos mea tulisset aut latura esset etas, familiaritates eximias atque insignem benivolentiam habiturus essem—, sed Eius qui solem fecit et stellas, omnipotentis Dei, munere, maiestati cesaree carum fore?
2 Cuius rei argumentum habeo unum ex multis, quod e tam longinquo seu temporum seu locorum tibi, magnanime imperator, usqueadeo mei memoria recens est, ut prope ex equo summus hominum humillimo vices amoris reddere dignum putes: nostra etate monstrum ingens, qua, ut vides, quisque pro exigui gradus eminentia solet esse superbior atque infra se positos gravi fastu vel
3 fastidire vel premere. Quod ipse tacitus mecum librans, sentio quanti precii apud me hec dignatio tua sit; nam si pro fortune fastigio, ut mos est, animi quoque fastidium assumpsisses, nec nosse me dignareris; sed generosum pectus vereque cesareum nec inflat certe nec contrahit, nec attollit fortuna nec deicit. Itaque tu me non tantum familiari notitia, sed dulcibus insuper dignaris epystolis, que res inter meos, siqui sunt aut erunt tituli, non

## : 12 :

*To our Caesar, first a sweet offering of private thanks for his friendly intimacy, then a severe rebuke for deserting the republic and his empire, and finally a most urgent exhortation.*

Your letter made me rejoice, Caesar. And why should it not, since 1
the mere remembrance of you usually makes me rejoice, as it
somehow comes to my mind that I don't know how I would become dear to Caesar's majesty except through your humanity and
my good fortune, or to express the last idea more sensibly, not by
virtue of the sun under which I was born (so that when I was still
a boy a famous astrologer predicted that I would come to have
exceptional friendships and the conspicuous goodwill of virtually
every prince and man of distinction whom my age had borne or
would give birth to) but by the gift of Him who made the sun and
stars, Almighty God.[1] And I have one proof of this out of many, 2
that from so great a distance of time or space, most noble emperor,
your memory of me is so fresh that you think fit to exchange re-
ciprocal love on more or less equal terms, you the highest of men,
with me the most lowborn. This is a mighty portent in our age in
which, as you see, each man tends to be prouder in proportion to
his small degree of eminence, and either to scorn or oppress those
set beneath him with heavy disdain. Weighing this up silently in 3
my thoughts I realize the high value to me of this condescension
of yours; for if you had put on a disdain of spirit to match the
summit of your fortune, as men do, you would not even deign to
know me. But fortune neither swells nor shrinks your noble and
truly Caesarean heart, neither exalting it nor casting it down. So
you think me worthy not only of intimate acquaintance but of
delightful letters, something which occupies and will occupy by no
means the last place among any claims I have or shall come to

4 extremum tenet aut tenebit locum. Si enim Virgilio, si Flacco gloriosum fuit Augusti Cesaris et notitiam et convictum et epystolas promereri, cur ego, illorum etsi non ingenio successor, at tempore et opinione hominum fortasse, aliqua ab illius principis successore
5 similia promeritum me fuisse non glorier? Nimirum et humanitatis et literarum tuarum non minor michi uni quam illis duobus sui imperatoris est copia; ut convictu superer non in te imperii altitudo, quam supra modum humane conditionis extantem, benemeritis aut certe tuum nomen amantibus attollendis, facile soleas libenterque submittere, sed in me vel animi tarditas vel amor patrie verior causa est. Ridebis forte mollitiem et cognosces quantum ad
6 veram philosophiam michi nunc etiam desit. Potui interdum, sed iam, fateor, non possum equanimiter esse diu procul ab Italia, sive ea natalis soli sola dulcedo est, sive rerum extimatio, nescio quam vera sed constans et immobilis et a prima etate pectori meo insita, nichil omnino terrarum sub celo esse quod Italie comparari queat,
7 seu nature seu hominum consideres ornamenta. Quod nisi sic michi penitus persuasissem, facilior proculdubio fuissem et tibi olim, quem sensi quamvis immeriti presentiam optare, et nudiustertius cognato tuo Francorum regi, vere serenissimo mitissimoque regum omnium, qui non modo prece fervida sed manu amica pene michi iniecta, tenere me voluit abeuntem, denique literis prosecutus ardentibus ad hos vicarios ac fideles tuos ut suasu placido inflexum me sibi remitterent; postremo nichil omnium omisit quibus nichil michi mentitus multa mentiri solitus astrologus vi-
8 deretur. Nec eram nescius sine insolentie quadam nota negligi non posse desiderium tanti regis, ni me, validior uncus, obstringeret

have. For if it was a source of glory for Vergil and for Horace to 4
earn the familiarity and company and letters of Augustus Caesar,[2]
why should I, their successor if not perhaps in talent, yet in the
time and opinion of men, not boast that I earned something similar from that prince's successor? For certainly I alone have had no 5
inferior access to benevolence and correspondence from my emperor than those two had from theirs; so that if I am outdone in
companionship, it is not the loftiness of your imperial prestige—
though rising above the limits of the human condition, you are
wont to condescend easily and freely by elevating those who have
served you well or at least love your name—but in my case either
slowness of wit or love of my country is the cause. Perhaps you
will laugh at this softness and recognize how much I fall short
even now of true philosophy. I have been able from time to time 6
but now, I admit, I can no longer stay far from Italy in good spirits, whether because the only real sweetness is that of one's native
soil, or because of my own judgment of the world, perhaps not
true but firm and immovable and planted in my breast from my
infancy—that there is nothing under the skies that can be compared with Italy, whether you consider the embellishments of nature or of men. Had I not completely persuaded myself of this I 7
would certainly have been more affable both previously to you
when I realized you were seeking my undeserving presence, and
just recently to your kinsman the king of France, truly the most
calm and mild of all kings, who wanted to detain me not only with
a fervent request when I was leaving, but almost laying upon me
the hand of friendship, then followed this with passionate letters
to your representatives and loyal servants to sway me and send
me back with calm persuasion;[3] in short he omitted no actions to
show that the astrologer, whose habit was to lie abundantly, had
not told me any lies. Indeed I knew full well that the desire of so 8
great a king could not be overlooked without some touch of arrogance, if it had not been the case that the love of my native land, a

ille quem dixi, patrie amor, nequid ve dissimulem, animi sarcina quam evi flexus iam ingravescentis exaggerat, ut non facile totus loco movear.

9 Accedit opinio illa, cuius paulo supra memini, de Italie principatu, que una michi animum fecit ut te sepe hactenus verbis aggrederer, non tantum hortari ausus sed arguere, quod sic ultimam
facere videreris quam natura parens, me iudice, primam fecit. Et si
pergis, scripto etiam, ne non predictum queri possis, te notatum
posteris tradere sim ausurus. Quid enim agis, oro te, Cesar? quid
moliris, quid cuntaris? unde autem nisi tuo de labore gloriam
speras? Mirum, tanti animi vim, tanti acumen ingenii non dicam
obtusum esse — absit ut id verear —, sed situ nimio rubiginem con-
10 traxisse. Undecimus, nisi fallor, annus agitur ex quo primum
moras tuas increpui, homo tunc incognitus tibi sed et nosci cupiens et amator imperii; et si libertatem meam tunc non tantum tu-
listi sed laudasti, certe, iam senioribus, et michi plus libertatis et
tibi excusationis aliquanto est minus. Relege que tunc scripsi.
Videbis quanto tibi nunc singula convenientius dici possint, eo
quod et occasio ingens pretermittitur et plus vite abiit, minus re-
11 stat. Nonne vides fluxum temporis et prerapidam etatis fugam?
non sentis quanto studio virtuti primum conscientieque, dehinc
glorie tue et posteritatis iudicio vacandum sit? non cogitas ubi
abieris solioque descenderis — quod utique faciendum est — neque
tibi reditus ullam spem neque successoris tui virtutem, quod
Traiano dixisse fertur anus illa miserabilis, pudori tuo posse consulere?

more powerful hook, as I mentioned, constrained me, and to conceal nothing from you, that burden of spirit which the onset of increasingly heavy old age intensifies, so that I cannot easily and wholeheartedly move from any place.

In addition there is my judgment, mentioned a little before, 9
about exercising your role as prince over Italy, the only thing which gave me the courage to assail you often with speech, daring not only to exhort but to condemn you for seeming to treat as last in this way what Mother Nature, in my judgment, made first. And if you persist in this, I shall dare to pass you on to posterity branded by my writing, so that you cannot complain you were not warned. For what are you doing, pray, Caesar, what are your contriving, why do you delay? What source do you expect for your glory unless it is from your own effort? It is most strange that such force of spirit, such keenness of intellect, should be, not blunted—far be it from me to fear this—but rusted by an accumulation of disuse.
Unless I deceive myself, this is the eleventh year since I first 10
scolded you for your delays.[4] I was unknown to you then, but eager to be known and devoted to the empire; and if you not only tolerated but praised my frankness, surely now that we are older I have more frankness and you have rather less excuse. Read again what I wrote then. You will see how much more appropriately each of those charges can be laid against you now, since a great opportunity is being let slip, and more of your life has passed,
leaving less to come. Don't you see the course of time and the too 11
swift flight of your age? Don't you perceive how eagerly you must now give heed to your virtue and conscience, and hence your glory and the verdict of posterity? Don't you think that when you have departed and left your throne—which surely must happen—there is neither any hope of return nor can the virtue of your successor take thought for your shame? As that wretched old woman supposedly said to Trajan:[5]

Cum semel occideris et de te splendida Minos
  Fecerit arbitria,
Non, Torquate, genus, non te facundia, non te
  Restituet pietas,

12 inquit Flaccus. Non audis Virgilium:

Optima queque dies miseris mortalibus evi
Prima fugit?

eundemque:

Stat sua cuique dies: breve et irreparabile tempus
Omnibus est vite; sed famam extendere factis,
Hoc virtutis opus?

Non audis Flaccum ipsum:

Truditur dies die,
  Noveque pergunt interire lune:
Tu secanda marmora
  Locas sub ipsum funus et sepulcri
Immemor struis domos?

Non audis Lucanum:

  veniet que misceat omnes
Hora duces: properate mori?

Et eundem:

  me non oracula certum,
Sed mors certa facit: pavido fortique cadendum est.
Hoc satis est dixisse Iovem?

13 Non audis Statium:

'Utere luce tua longamque' ait 'indue famam'?

Once you are gone and Minos makes
his brilliant verdict,
not birth, nor eloquence nor piety shall
set you right, Torquatus.

So Horace says.[6] Don't you hear Vergil? 12

Every best day of life for wretched mortals
is the first to flee.

And again:

Each man's day of doom is fixed, life's time is short for all
beyond renewal; but making fame great by feats,
this is the task of virtue.[7]

Don't you hear Horace in person?

Each day is displaced by the next
and the new moons persist in waning
while you commission marble facing
in the shadow of death, and without thought
of your tomb, construct your residence.[8]

Don't you hear Lucan?

The hour will come that makes confusion
of all the leaders: make haste to die.

And again:

No oracles assure me,
but death is sure: the coward and the brave must fall.
It is enough that Jupiter has laid this down.[9]

Don't you hear Statius? 13

Exploit the light, and cloak yourself in lasting fame.

Et eundem:

> Immites scis nulla revolvere Parcas
> Stamina?

Non audis Iuvenalem:

> festinat enim decurrere velox
> Flosculus anguste misereque brevissima vite
> Portio: dum bibimus, dum serta, unguenta, puellas
> Poscimus, obrepit non intellecta senectus?

Hanc si forte longam tibi seramque pollicitus, ut multi solent iacturam temporis levem ducis; an eundem ipsum non audis: olim, inquit,

> Prodigio par est in nobilitate senectus?

14 Id si olim, quid hodie? Et si in nobilitate, quid in imperio suspicemur? Percurre annales: multi senes ad imperium pervenerunt, pauci in imperio senuerunt; cum omnium mortalium sit brevis, tum brevissima principum vita est, et interno curarum prelio oppressa et externis insidiis circumventa; itaque cum in cuntis segnis cuntatio feda sit, tum in imperatore fedissima est, cui et rerum plus et minus est temporis atque, ut dici solet, via longior et bre-
15 vior dies. Ecce nunc, Cesar, — sentio enim hinc quid ibi agitur: magnus quidem explorator amor est, et magnus excubitor — in consiliis vitam teris. Consilia vero nisi in actum prodeant, nudi sunt cogitatus et inanes cure. 'Cras incipiam, postridie movebor.' Cur non, queso, hodie? ita ne semper lux ventura serenior pre-
16 sensque nubilosior? Nempe vatum maximus, ut audisti, optimam primam dicit; prima autem presens est, quando in preteritis preter memoriam nil habemus, neque impossibilium consultatio ulla est;

And again:

> You know the Fates unmerciful
> unwind no threads[10]

Don't you hear Juvenal?

> Man's swift bloom races to reach its end
> and the scant share of wretched, cramped life:
> just as we drink and summon garlands, scent and girls,
> old age creeps up unnoticed.

If you perhaps have promised yourself this long and late life, like many others, and think the loss of time trivial, don't you hear the same poet say that for some time now

> Old age in noblemen has been a kind of miracle?[11]

And if this was true in the past, what about nowadays? And if this 14
applies to nobility, what are we to expect in the possessor of empire? Run through the records: many men came old to empire but few grew old in it; although the life of all mortals is short, the lives of princes are shortest of all, weighed down by the interior battle of anxieties and beset by external treachery; so although sluggish delay is loathsome in anyone it is most loathsome in an emperor, who has more business and less time and as men say, a longer
journey and a shorter life. See now, Caesar—for I sense from here 15
what is happening there: love is a great spy and a great watchman—how you are wasting time in deliberations. But unless deliberations issue in action, calculations are unarmed and cares futile. "Tomorrow I shall begin; the next day I shall move forward!" Why not today, I ask? Is the coming dawn always more sunny and
the present more clouded? As you have heard, the greatest of po- 16
ets said the first day was the best,[12] and the first is here now, since we have nothing of the past except our memory, and there is no deliberation about what is impossible; in the future there is only

in futuris nichil preter augurium et spei fallacis illecebras. Ut sint pares in reliquis hec et sequens dies, num saltem ista presentior eoque certior negari nequit? et illa quidem ventura utique nos an
17 inventura sit dubium; hec certe cum abierit non redibit. Quid semper absentia querimus? presentia complectamur neu nobis inutiliter effluant, enitamur. Id cum omnibus utile, tibi necessarium adeo, Cesar, est ut sine hoc quantalibet industria seu virtute rationarium imperii non absolvas. 'Et cui' inquies, 'rationem imperii
18 redditurus sum?.' Tibi, Cesar, ipsi, quam non dubitem quin a te sepe exigas—parum dura tibi videtur exactio? nulla quam sui ipsius increpatio acrior, nulla salubrior—; quin et huic etati, que te suspicit, in te unum oculos defixit, et sequentibus seculis, quorum et diuturniora erunt et liberiora iudicia, demum et Imperatori illi eterno, qui huic temporali imperio te prefecit, non ut solium non ut sceptrum non ut imperii nudum nomen occupes, sed ut regnes
19 ut imperes ut afflictis opem rebus feras. Quid te subtrahis, quid in crastinum prominens hodiernum prodigis? Nullus in hodierna necessitate crastino locus est; fac tu hodie quod incumbit; cras siquid emerserit, vel tu facies vel alius; non deerunt temporibus sui duces, et ut desint, nunquam aliene ignavie reus fies. Tu ne tempori tuo desis, cura; porro cras istud quod suspensos tenet et inertes facit, quodque quasi venturum expectatur, iam preteriit;
20 nullus enim, preter primum, dies non diei alterius cras fuerit. Vis audire quid hic adolescens poeta quidam dicat?

'Cras hoc fiet.' Idem cras fiet. 'Quid? quasi magnum,
Nempe diem donas?' Sed cum lux altera venit,

prophecy and the traps of treacherous hope. Even if this day and
the next are equal in other respects, surely it can't be denied that
this one is more present and so more sure. It is doubtful whether
that other day will come or find us; but for sure when this day has
departed it will not return. Why are we always seeking what is far 17
away? Let us embrace the present and strive to make sure it does
not seep away to no avail. This is useful to all but so necessary to
you, Caesar, that without it you will not balance the account book
of your empire by the greatest possible effort or virtue. You will
say: "To whom should I render this account of my empire?" Does 18
this demand not seem harsh enough, Caesar? I don't doubt you
often demand this from yourself—no rebuke is fiercer than self-
rebuke, none more beneficial. But you also owe an accounting
both to this generation, which has turned and now fixes its gaze
on you, and the following generations whose judgments will be
both more lasting and more frank, and finally to that eternal Commander who put you in charge of this worldly empire, not to take
possession of the throne, the scepter, and the bare name of empire,
but to rule and command and bear aid to the afflicted. Why 19
shrink away, why squander today while concentrating on the morrow? There is no room for tomorrow in today's need; do what
presses on you today; if something else surfaces tomorrow, either
you or another will handle it; there will be no lack of leaders for
the times, and even if they fall short you will never be accused of
another man's sloth. See that you yourself do not fail your time;
that tomorrow, which holds us in suspense and makes us idle,
which we wait for as if it were coming, has already passed; for no
day except the first is not the morrow of another day. Do you 20
want to hear what a certain young poet says on this?

> "This will be done tomorrow." Tomorrow it will be just the
> same.
> "What, as if granting a day is something great?"

Iam cras hesternum consumpsimus; ecce aliud cras,
Egerit hoc annos, et semper paulum erit ultra;
Nam quamvis prope te, quamvis temone sub uno
Vertentem se se frustra sectabere tantum,
Cum rota posterior curras et in axe secundo.

Quid igitur? An etate Persius inexperta et acerba publicam cecitatem funditus introspexit, nostra id etas maturior non videbit? Aperire oculos et figere animos oportet ne fallamur, et errore qui
21 corrigi nequeat, implicemur. Quid vero nunc ostiatim poetarum domos ambio, nisi ut quem forsitan mea vox autoritatis inops non movisset, tantorum testimonio moveare? Nemo poetarum aut philosophorum fuit, qui non idem et diceret et sentiret; discordes in multis, hic conveniunt. Quodsi omnes taceant aut negent, certe, ut dici solet, ipsa res loquitur, et si dissimulare quisquam velit, sentiet vel invitus; sic in foribus experientia est, seque vel conniventibus
22 veritas ingerit. Proinde ut reliqua sperni possint, que quidem sperni tali ingenio tamque incorrupto iudicio non possunt, an in ea ipsa saltem, quam michi dictabas epystola, non animadvertisti sextum imperii tui annum agi? Quid tu igitur? An sextum forsan et quinquagesimum expectas? Augusto Cesari duntaxat id contigit; nescio an optandum, sed sperandum minime.

23 Venisti, Cesar, post exhortationes illas meas ad Italiam, cuius ego michi particeps glorie visus eram eo quod animosum quoque cornipedem calcar impellit; venisti, inquam, atque ut tibi de celesti ope confisus repromiseram, invenisti aperta et prona omnia que obstrusa et ardua videbantur. Intrasti Mediolanum, inde Romam,

But when the next day comes, we have already spent
yesterday's morrow; here is another morrow,
this will go on for years with ever a bit beyond;
for though it be near to you and turning under the same shaft
you still will chase the front wheel in vain, while you run as
back wheel on the rear axle.[13]

Well then? Shall our riper age not see deep down into public blindness when Persius did so at a raw and inexperienced age? We should open our eyes and focus our attention so as not to be cheated and entangled in a blunder which cannot be corrected. So 21
why am I going the rounds of the poets door by door, except so that, if perhaps my voice lacks authority and has not moved you, you will be roused by the authority of such great men? There was no poet or philosopher who did not say and believe the same thing; quarreling over so many matters, they agree on this. But if all of them were silent or denied it, surely as the saying goes, the facts themselves speak out, and if anyone wanted to pretend otherwise, he will realize it even against his will; such is the experience of the law courts, that Truth will thrust herself even on those who overlook her. Accordingly, even if other arguments can be 22
scorned—and they cannot in fact be scorned by such an intellect and such an uncorrupted judgment as yours—did you not notice in that very letter which you wrote to me that this was now the sixth year of your reign?[14] So what are you doing about it? Are you perhaps waiting for the fifty-sixth year? That luck befell Augustus Caesar;[15] I don't know whether it is to be desired but certainly not to be expected.

You came to Italy, Caesar, after my exhortations, and I saw my- 23
self as sharing in your glory because a spur drives on even a spirited steed; you came, I say, and as I had promised you in my confidence in heavenly aid, you found open and downhill whatever seemed obstructed and steep. You entered Milan and from there

in quibus geminum dyadema sortitus, erectis in spem magnam
24 populis atque urbibus, subito in Germaniam remeasti. Cur autem
aut quis te error seu quis horror perculit? an forte quorundam se-
ditiosorum motiunculas timuisti? at hoc affixum animis esse debet, ut quisque navigaturus tempestatem cogitet. Nesciebas quod
nullum sine fluctibus mare est, nullus sine ventis mons, nullum
25 sine curis imperium? Sileo Scipiones ab exercitibus desertos suis
militumque perfidiam, nunc proditorum nunc quando ita res tulit,
propria etiam morte, vincentes; Alexandrum taceo suorum sedi-
tiones et latentes dolos ac molimina comprimentem; iocundius
tuorum exempla lecturus sis. Iulius Cesar unus a toto circumvalla-
tus exercitu, non modo non timuit sed timeri etiam presentissimo
animo atque indomita virtute promeruit, paucorumque supplicio
uniusque legionis ignominia et saluti omnium consuluit et decori
proprio. [*§§26–30 omissis*]

31 Quid, quod patriam ipsam tuam nullo modo magis amaveris,
nullo studio magis ornaveris, quam nomen ipsius quam latissime
divulgando? Si Alexander se intra fines Macedonie tenuisset, non
tam notum Macedonum nomen esset. Quis putas magis amet ux-
orem, an qui omnium negligens die noctuque in illius heret amplexibus, an qui ut illam honeste ubertimque educet, nullam pere-
32 grinationem refugit nullum renuit laborem? Est ubi magnus amor
odium sit. Nunquam Romam magis amavit Africanus quam dum
illa relicta adiit Carthaginem. Molles affectus et externi monitus
coniugum natarumque ac vulgarium amicorum altis consiliis semper adversi sunt; obserande aures ulixeum in morem, ut in portum
glorie sirenum inter scopulos evadamus. Quid, quod hec ipsa,
quam tuam dicis, fuit quidem sed iam non patria tua est, ex quo

Rome, places where you won a double diadem while peoples and cities were roused to a mighty expectation, then instantly returned to Germany.[16] Why then, what confusion or dread struck you? 24
Did you perhaps fear the petty disturbances of some disloyal folk? But this must stay fixed in our minds: that anyone about to sail should take a storm into account. Did you not know that no sea is without breakers, no mountain without winds, no empire without anxieties? I am not mentioning the Scipios, deserted by their 25
armies and overcoming the soldiers' treachery according to circumstances, now by the death of traitors, now even by their own death. I pass over Alexander controlling the mutinies of his men and their hidden deception and intrigues; you will read more pleasant examples among your own ancestors. Julius Caesar alone, besieged by a whole army, not only felt no fear but made himself feared by his acute presence of mind and unquenchable valor, and by the punishment of a few and the disgrace of one legion took thought for the well-being of all and for his own dignity.[17] [*§§26–30 omitted*]

What about the fact that you have never loved your own coun- 31
try nor honored it more than by spreading its name as widely as possible? If Alexander had stayed within the boundaries of Macedon, the name of the Macedonians would never have been so well known. Who do you think loves his wife more, the man who clings to her embraces night and day, neglecting all else, or the man who to provide her with honor and abundance shuns no journey and demurs at no effort?[18] There are situations in which a great 32
love is also hatred. Africanus never loved Rome more than when he left it to attack Carthage.[19] Soft affections and the warnings from outside of wives and daughters and common friends are always the enemies of lofty designs. We must stop our ears like Ulysses so that we may escape the reefs of the Sirens to reach the harbor of glory. What about the fact that the land itself which you call yours was indeed your country, but is no longer, since the time when you

primum ad imperium pervenisti, aliamque nascendo atque aliam
33 renascendo patriam es adeptus? Audisti ut Alexander idem Macedo, regno accepto, non Macedonie se sed mundi regem dici iussit; a quo ut multa precipiti, sic unum hoc magno animo gestum non infitier. Idem ne tu olim feceris, patrii regni viduitas inhibebat, quod abitu tuo deseri videbatur et siquid tibi humanitus accidisset, ad alienas manus perventurum. Hanc seu iustam seu iniustam excusationem propitia divinitate sublatam vides, que tibi et imperio expetitum votis infantem ex augusta tori consorte lar-
34 gita est. Habet iam Boemia suum regem; tu Italie mundique rex, post tergum linquendi orbis iam securus, et patriam et solium tuum pete. Nam etsi secundum apostolicam sententiam manentem hic non habeas civitatem, siqua tamen in terris patria est tua, propria Cesarum domus ac vera patria Roma est; quin et comunis omnium est patria, rerum caput, orbis atque urbium regina, nobiliumque tam fertilis exemplorum, ut conspecta facile animos excitet detergatque rubiginem.

35 Quas vero nunc more causas aucupabere quibus ve deinceps te compedibus tentum dices? Nescio quid Romano Pontifici pollicitus, iureiurando interposito, quasi muro valido seu monte invio, romane urbis aditu prohiberis; sic et summo principi suum imperium et summo imperio suus princeps, queque iacturarum omnium maxima est, tua tibi libertas eripitur. Sed iurasti, quod uti-
36 nam non fecisses!, sed fecisti; dispensatione opus est. Quid in plano hesitas? Quem unus vinxit, sepe idem, sepe alius solvit. Quid refert unde redeat libertas? redeat modo. Qui impedivit expediet; si is nolit, veniet qui volet; quomodo autem, nichil ad rem, modo ut velit, seu tua virtus amorem, seu stuporem gloria, seu

first reached the summit of empire and you obtained a different country by birth and then by rebirth? Have you heard how the 33 same Alexander of Macedon, once he received the kingship, ordered himself to be called king, not of Macedon but of the world?[20] Although he did many things recklessly I would not deny that he did this in a noble spirit. The bereavement of your father's kingdom prevented you from doing the same thing long ago, since it seemed to be deserted by your departure, and if any mortal accident had befallen you it would have come into foreign hands. You see that this excuse, just or unjust, has been removed by the favor of God, which has lavished on you the infant heir longed for by the empire, born of the august consort of your bed. Now Bohemia 34 has its king;[21] you are king of Italy and the world; now free of care at leaving the world behind you, go seek your country and your throne. For even if according to the view of the Apostle you do not have any abiding city here on earth,[22] if any country is yours, Rome is the proper seat of the emperors and their true country. Nay, Rome is the common country of us all, the capital of the world, queen of the world and its cities, so rich in examples of nobility that the sight of her easily rouses the spirits and rubs away their rust.

But now what reasons will you seek for your delay or by what 35 shackles will you claim to be bound? You made some promise to the Roman Pontiff, reinforced by an oath like a stout wall or impassable mountain, and are forbidden access to the city of Rome;[23] in this way the highest prince has been robbed of his empire and the highest empire of its prince, and, greatest loss of all, you are being robbed of your liberty. But you swore—if only you had not done so! But you did that, and you need a dispensation. Why 36 hesitate with level ground before you? The man bound by one pope has been set free often by the same pope, often by another. What matter the source of liberty's restoration? Just let it be restored. The man who obstructed it will release it; if he refuses, another will come who is willing. How it happens is immaterial,

timorem paritura felicitas; nemo est qui iustum ac famosum et felicem principem non vel amet mireturque vel metuat. Incipe. Vetus est verbum multis itineribus Romam peti. [§§37–43 *omissis*]

*Mediolani, XII Kal. Aprilis.*

## : 13 :

## *Ad fratrem Iacobum Augustinensium ordinis et Ticinensium tyrannum, increpatio gravis ac multiplex.*

1 Sepe te, frater, admonui ut status et officii tui memor, paci operam dares, qua sublata quid aliud vita hominum quam mors est, seu quid mundus hic aliud quam laborum immortalium ac discriminum officina? Preces quoque et obsecrationes immiscui ut si te
2 ratio non movisset, amici caritas moveret. Oravi perque omnes te celicolas adiuravi atque in primis per sacrum et venerabile Augustini ducis tui nomen, cui et ego quamvis peccator in spiritu meo
3 servio et cuius opem apud Cristum spero, ut aliquando, sopitis aut lenitis odiorum flammis et compresso tumore superbie, qui animorum oculos atque aures sanioribus consiliis obstruxerat, illud acumen ingenii tui et eloquentiam celitus datam tibi, quam irritandis animis tuorum civium, quod pace tua dixerim, plausibiliter hactenus potiusquam salubriter intendisti, iantandem ad meliora converteres et quod maxime te decebat, religiosam animam pacifi-
4 cis tractatibus applicares. Non dura quidem neque difficilia postulabam, ut Augustini miles ac discipulus, pacem velles, precipue

provided he is willing, whether your virtue provokes love, or your glory amazement or your success gives birth to fear: there is no one who will not either love and admire or fear a just and celebrated and successful emperor. [*§§37–43 omitted*]

*Milan, March 21.*

## : 13 :

### *To Brother Giacomo of the Augustinian Order and tyrant of Pavia, an earnest and many-sided rebuke.*

I have often warned you, brother, to be mindful of your status and 1
duty and devote yourself to peace; once peace is taken away what else is human life but death, or what else is this world than the workshop of immortal toils and dangers? I have included some prayers and supplications too so that if reason did not move you,
the affection of a friend might do so. I have begged and adjured 2
you by all the saints—and especially in the holy and reverend name of your leader Augustine, whom, though a sinner, I too
serve in spirit and whose support I hope for with Christ—that fi- 3
nally when the flames of hatred have been lulled and eased and the vaunt of arrogance has been suppressed which had blocked the eyes and ears of men's spirits to more healthy intentions, you would now at last divert to a better policy the keenness of your wit and the eloquence granted you by heaven that up to now you have strained more successfully than beneficially to provoke the spirits of your fellow citizens (if I may say so with your indulgence): now at last you should apply your religious mind, as would be most
fitting, to peace-bringing negotiations. I was not demanding any- 4
thing harsh or difficult: just that as a soldier and disciple of Augustine you should want peace, especially when you heard your

dum audires ducem ac magistrum tuum, cum sepe alias tum
expressius in eo libro in quo celestis et eterne reipublice leges trac-
5 tat, quodam loco de pace sic loquentem: 'Tantum est enim' inquit,
'pacis bonum ut etiam in rebus terrenis atque mortalibus nichil
gratius soleat audiri, nichil desiderabilius concupisci, nichil post-
6 remo possit melius inveniri.' Et post paululum: 'Sicut nemo' inquit,
'est qui gaudere nolit, ita nemo est qui pacem habere nolit, quandoquidem et ipsi qui bella volunt, nichil aliud quam vincere volunt; ad gloriosam ergo pacem bellando cupiunt pervenire.' Et
rursus: '*Paci* igitur geruntur' inquit, 'et bella ab his etiam qui virtutem bellicam student exercere imperando *aut* pugnando, unde pacem constat belli esse optabilem finem; omnis enim homo etiam
7 belligerando pacem requirit.' In quo quidem Ciceroni consentit,
ubi suscipienda bella ait 'ob eam causam ut sine iniuria in pace vi-
vatur.' Non exequor que ibidem Augustinus idem divino strinxit
ingenio, quod et tibi notissima sunt et michi providendum ne si
cunta complecti velim, magnitudo rerum modum vincat epystole.
Quorum tamen illa conclusio est ut omnem usum rerum tempora-
lium ad fructum terrene pacis in terrena civitate, in celesti autem
ad pacis eterne fructum referendum esse diffiniat.

8 Que cum ita essent, sperabam, fateor, ut omne quidem, licet
ferox sed in primis ratione utens, animal, hoc est hominem cui
vera scilicet insit humanitas, sic ante alios homines te, cui et ratio
esse deberet uberior et singularis religio ac pietas, pacem amare,
pacem querere; nempe qui tibi dictum crederes daviticum illud
quod sepissime decantares: 'Inquire pacem et persequere eam,' nisi
forte dicas te illam utique persequi, qui eam, ut videmus, finibus
9 tuis pulsam exulare coegeris. Sed quid eidem regio prophete dicimus clamanti: 'Rogate que ad pacem sunt Ierusalem'? qui sciens

leader and master speaking in this wise about peace, in many other
places but more explicitly in the book where he discusses the laws
of the heavenly and eternal city:[1] "So great is the blessing of peace 5
that even in earthly and human affairs nothing usually can be
heard more welcome, nothing longed for with greater desire, nothing, in short, can be found superior." And a little later: "Just as 6
there is no one unwilling to rejoice, so there is no one unwilling to
have peace, since even those who want wars only want to be victorious: they want to reach the glory of peace through warfare." And
again: "Even wars are waged for peace, even by men who are eager
to exercise their merit in warfare by commanding or fighting;
hence it follows that peace is the desirable end of war, for every
man seeks for peace even in waging war." In this he agrees with 7
Cicero, when he says wars should be undertaken "for this reason,
that one may live in peace without being wronged."[2] I shall not
follow the arguments which Augustine touched on with his divine
intellect, things that are very well known to you, and I must take
care lest, if I wanted to encompass everything, the great scale of
things might surpass the limits of a letter. But his conclusion defines every use of temporal matters as for the enjoyment of earthly
peace in the earthly city, whereas the heavenly city he defines as
oriented to the enjoyment of eternal peace.

In these circumstances I hoped, I admit, that just like every liv- 8
ing creature, even if fierce, but primarily a rational one—that is, a
man possessed of true humanity—so you, whose reason should
be more fertile and whose religion and piety exceptional, would
love peace before all other men, and seek peace, inasmuch as you
thought that saying of David intended for you, which you so often
chanted: "Seek out peace and pursue it"[3]—unless perhaps you
would claim to be pursuing it anyway, since you have driven it
from your territory and compelled it to be an exile. But what shall 9
we say to the same royal prophet when he cries out: "Ask for what
conduces to the peace of Jerusalem"?[4] Knowing that in peace there

in pace omnem bonorum abundantiam esse, omnem iustitiam,
omnem delectationem ac sanctarum animarum requiem, vide quid
addidit: 'Et abundantia diligentibus te,' et iterum: 'Fiat pax in virtute tua,' et intulit: 'Et abundantia in turribus tuis,' et alio loco:
'Orietur in diebus eius iustitia et abundantia pacis,' et alio: 'Man-
sueti hereditabunt terram et delectabuntur in multitudine pacis,' et
10 rursus alio: 'In pace in id ipsum dormiam et requiescam.' Longum
est singula prosequi, ex quibus elicitur bonorum omnium atque
optabilium hunc unicum fontem esse, quo arescente succedant
egestas tedium et labor. Quid autem et Ieremie dicimus, cuius illa
vox miror nisi tuis semper auribus insonet: 'Querite pacem civitatis et orate pro ea ad Dominum quia in pace illius erit pax vobis'?
11 Ex his atque similibus sacrarum testimoniis scripturarum, in
quibus apprime doctum te putabam, bene de te, frater, opinabar
teque pacis amicum michi persuaseram; sed fallebar ut intelligo: tu
enim sub Cristi tunica Marti sacer et Bellone devotior quam Ma-
rie, sub religiosi habitu tegens propositum bellatoris, nec id quoque iam tegens sed dictis et factis aperiens — relatu mirum, terri-
12 bile cogitatu —, in eo tibi summam meritorum et felicitatis et
glorie sitam putas, si hoc videat etas nostra, hoc posteritas audiat
te multis gentibus et toti pene Italie pestiferum, populo autem tuo
funestum et fortasse ultimum bellum ingenio fovisse, exacuisse
consiliis, eloquio inflammasse, ut tibi, quem sequestrum pacis et
quietis auctorem credidi, iam merito dici possit, quod ipsi olim
Ieremie immerito dictum est: 'Siquidem homo hic non querit pa-
13 cem populo, sed malum.' Heu, care michi in Cristo frater, quam
valde vereor ne tibi quoque conveniat quod ille vir sapiens ait in

is an abundance of all good things, there is all justice, all enjoyment
and repose for holy spirits, see what he added: "And there is abundance for those who love you," and again "Let there be peace in
your virtue,"[5] and he adds "And abundance in your towers," and in
another passage "The justice and abundance of peace will arise in
his days,"[6] and elsewhere "The meek shall inherit the earth and be
delighted by the many examples of peace,"[7] and again in another
place "I shall sleep and rest in peace."[8] It would be a long business 10
to list each of his sayings from which we deduce that peace is the
only source of all good and desirable things; if it dries up, need,
boredom and toil will take its place. Again, what shall we say to
Jeremiah, since I shall be surprised if this saying of his does not
always echo in your ears: "Seek the peace of your community and
pray to the Lord for it, because there will be peace for you in His
peace."[9]

From these and other witnesses of the Sacred Scriptures, in 11
which I thought you exceptionally learned, I thought well of you,
brother, and had persuaded myself that you were the friend of
peace. But I was deceived, as I recognize. For under Christ's tunic
you are dedicated to Mars and more devoted to Bellona[10] than to
Mary, hiding the intent of a warrior beneath your religious dress
and not even hiding that but displaying it by your words and
deeds — strange to report, and dreadful to contemplate. You think 12
the sum of your services and blessedness and glory is placed in
this, if our age sees and posterity hears that you have nursed in
your mind a war-dealing plague to many communities and almost
all Italy, but deadly and almost fatal to your own people, and you
have sharpened it by your policies and inflamed it by your eloquence. Thus you whom I believed to be the arbiter of peace and
instigator of calm can fairly be told what was once unjustly said to
Jeremiah: "Truly this man is not seeking peace for the people, but
evil."[11] Alas, my dear brother in Christ, how greatly I fear that 13
what the wise king said in the Book of Proverbs may fit your case:

parabolis: 'Vir impius fodit malum et in labiis eius ignis ardescit; homo perversus suscitat lites et verbosus separat principes,' et quod alter ait in *Ecclesiastico*: 'Homo iracundus incendit litem et vir peccator turbabit amicos, in medio habentium pacem immittet
14 inimicitiam.' Nam si equis auribus et pacato animo audire verum potes ab amico, quis est usquam hominum qui dubitet quin — si tu unus non esses, tot hominum milia, que hanc non modo Italie sed totius orbis pulcerrimam atque optimam partem tenent, in tran-
15 quilla et exoptata pace nunc viverent — quicquid per squalidos et incultos agros armorum aut signorum volitat, quicquid incendiorum desertis villarum tectis exestuat, quicquid formidinis aut fuge amplas ac nobiles alternis motibus urbes quatit, quicquid denique sanguinis hoc bello ultro citroque fusum fundendumque est, totum e tuorum consiliorum scatebris et fecundi pectoris fonte processerit?

16 O felicem te, qui ad hanc rei militaris gloriam sine ullo armorum exercitio sedendo loquendoque perveneris, ut unus e numero sis illorum qui, ut ait Psalmista, 'cogitaverunt iniquitates in corde, tota die constituebant prelia'; idque ut de te, quamvis in aciem non prodeas, perproprie dictum scias, sequitur non, quod erat proprium bellatorum: 'induerunt arma, conscenderunt equos, ordinarunt agmina,' sed quid? 'acuerunt linguam suam sicut serpentes;
17 venenum aspidum sub labiis eorum.' Heu michi, fratrer, quanto melius quantoque professione tua dignius fuit, linguam Deo dicatam divinarum laudum occupare preconiis, quam delinimentis anilibus et ventosis adhortationibus populorum, quibus te non uno aut altero, ut ceteri, sed omnibus omnium flagitiis inquinares, omniumque quibus abundare bellum solet, particeps delictorum,
18 nec tantum particeps fieres sed magister! Ita ne tibi, cura consci-

"The impious man digs out evil and a flame burns on his lips; the perverse man stirs up lawsuits and the man of words drives apart princes."[12] And another sage says in Ecclesiasticus: "The angry man kindles a lawsuit and the sinner will disturb his friends, and shall send enmity into the midst of those enjoying peace."[13] For if 14
you can hear the truth from your friend with impartial ears and a peaceable spirit, who has ever doubted that, if it were not for you alone, so many thousands who inhabit this best and most lovely region, not just of Italy but of the whole world, would now live in calm and longed-for peace. Who doubts that whatever arms and 15
standards hover over the neglected and uncultivated lands, whatever conflagrations soar from the deserted roofs of villas, whatever dread or flight shakes prosperous and noble cities with alternating panics, in short, whatever blood has been shed and is still to be shed in this war all around us, has all emerged from the fountains of your policies and the spring of your fertile breast?

Blessed art thou, who hast advanced to this military glory with- 16
out any training in arms by sitting and talking, so that you are among those who according to the Psalmist "have thought wicked deeds in their heart and were setting up battles the whole day."[14] And so that you may know that, although you did not enter the battle line, this is very properly said of you, what follows is not the proper activities of warriors such as: "They put on their armor, mounted their horses, and arrayed their battle columns," but rather: "They sharpened their tongues like serpents; the venom of asps was beneath their lips."[15] Woe is me, brother, how much bet- 17
ter and how much more worthy of your profession it would have been to occupy your tongue, dedicated to God, with the announcing of divine praises, than with old women's enticements and windy exhortations of the peoples, in which you had sullied yourself, not with one sin or another like other men, but with all sins, sharing all the offenses in which war usually overflows, in fact not just sharing but acting as instructor! As you put care for your 18

entie posthabita, fama duntaxat inanis eloquentie satis est, ut propter hanc unam fons et principium et causa horum malorum omnium dici velis? Nam quis ulla etate bellum hoc aut meminerit aut narrabit, qui non tuum in primordio flebilis historie nomen ponat? quis hanc pinget historiam, que iam per aulas porticusque magnatum pingi incipit, qui non et inter consiliarios et inter ipsos
19 etiam bellatores tuam fingat effigiem? Mirum prorsus nec unquam alias visum spectaculum, inter galeas clipeosque et micantes gladios et tela trementia, venenoso afflatu animos inficiens et verbis incendens bellum, nigra succinctus veste fraterculus!

20 Gaude igitur et exulta, qui e tribus Catonis magni et Scipionis Emiliani laudibus consecutus es duas, ut scilicet et imperator sis et orator optimus, quippe qui exercitum nutu solo, populum voce regas. Nequa autem in re summis illis viris cedas, eorum quoque laudem tertiam usurpare quis prohibet, ut optimus etiam sis senator, quando omnis patrie fortuna, omnes primorum civitatis sententie de consiliis tuis pendent? Tres enim in homine summas res uterque illorum prestitisse fertur, 'ut esset optimus orator optimus
21 imperator optimus senator.' Sed vide, oro, nequa te glorie cupiditas obliquis tramitibus huc impellat; profecto enim nemo vel senator vel imperator bonus est, ne dicam optimus, nisi qui domi militieque ea consulit atque agitat non que sibi speciosa sed que populo atque exercitui fructuosa sunt; a quo te quam longissime abesse quis non videt, qui pacis dulcedine relegata, ultro in pa-
22 triam bellum amarissimum atque anceps attraxeris? Restat oratoris nomen solum, quod ipsum mala et noxia suadendo mereri equidem non potes, cum, sicut summis oratoribus visum est, orator sit 'vir bonus dicendi peritus.' Vides in quantas angustias te

conscience behind you, is even the renown for hollow eloquence enough to make you want this one talent to be called the source and origin and cause of all these woes? But who in any generation will either recall this war or relate it without putting your name in the preamble to this lamentable history? Who will depict this history, which is already beginning to be painted in the courts and porticoes of powerful men, without shaping your likeness among the advisers and actual warriors? That is certainly an 19
utterly strange sight never seen elsewhere, a little black-robed brother among the helmets and shields and flashing swords and trembling missiles, infecting men's minds with venomous miasma and inflaming war with words!

So rejoice and exult to have earned two of the three excellences 20
of Cato the Elder and Scipio Aemilianus,[16] to be both a commander and an excellent orator, since you control the army just by your nod, and the people by your voice. But not to yield to those great men in any respect, who prevents you from claiming the third credit, to be also an excellent senator, since the entire fate of your country, and all the votes of the city's leaders depend on your policies? For each of those men of old is said to have shown three great excellences: "to be the best of orators, the best of generals, and the best of senators." But consider, I beg you, whether the 21
desire for glory is not dragging you to this behavior by devious paths, since surely no senator nor general is good, not to say excellent, unless he chooses thought and action at home and abroad that does not bring glamour on himself, but is fruitful for the people and its army. But who does not see that you are very far from this, since you have discarded the sweetness of peace and brought down on your native land a most bitter and uncertain war.
So only the name of orator remains, which you cannot earn by 22
urging bad and harmful actions, since in the judgment of the greatest orators an orator is "a good man experienced in speaking."[17] You see the narrow space to which I am confining you: that

coarctem, qui ex omnibus titulis quos sperabas, ne unum quidem tibi concesserim, nisi pro parte dimidia. Etsi enim dicendi peritum non infitier, oratorem nego; neque etenim aut bonus vir es aut esse potes quandiu te publicis bonis, ut facis, et pacis consiliis adver-
23 sum prebes. O quanto felicius vel tibi vel patrie mutus esses, quam facundiam pestilentem tanto studio quesivisses! Ergo si tu loqui aut nescires aut nequires, nec laboraret Italia nec lugeret; ergo in lingua tua publice miserie radix est, quam si Deum, si proximum, si patriam, si te ipsum diligeres, commorsicatam dentibus proiecisse decuerat, profuturam potius corvis aut canibus quam hominibus nocituram.

24 Tu tamen hoc agis, ad hoc niteris, hoc magnificum ducis, quod te more aucupis mulcente aures, credulum vulgus in tendiculas tuas cadat quodque aliquid erumnarum novarumque in dies ruinarum titulis tuis accrescat, quibus iam pene nichil accrescere intra miserabilis patrie fines potest, que exterius vastitatem miseram et hostilem tuis attractum, ut sic dicam, manibus exercitum, intus
25 vero lingue tue arietem duraque patitur imperia. Dirceo siquidem Amphioni per contrarium simillimus evasisti; ille Thebas suo struxit eloquio, tu Ticinum sternis tuo, pervetustam, ut fama est, nobilissimamque urbem et nisi te unum civem levo sidere genuisset, felicissimam, te autem cive miseram, te duce miserrimam, nisi te illud excusat quod obsessam patriam magne partis civium exilio et multa domorum strage laxaveris atque una contentam crebris muniens plateis, obsidionis horrenda solatia, mestam tota urbe solitudinem et diversoria sane bonis inamena paraveris.

of all the titles you hoped for, I have not granted you even one, except perhaps halfway. For even if I would not deny you are experienced in speaking, I would not call you an orator, given that you are not and cannot be a good man as long as you show yourself opposed to the public weal as you do, and to policies of peace.
How much more blessed for either yourself or your country if you 23
were mute, rather than refining your destructive fluency with such eagerness! If you either did not know or have the power to speak, Italy would neither be suffering nor mourning, so the root of public wretchedness is in your tongue. If only you loved God, your neighbor, your country or even yourself, it would have been more fitting to chew your tongue up with your teeth, and spit it out, doing good to crows and dogs instead of doing harm to men.

However, this is what you are pursuing and striving for and 24
hold magnificent, that, while you sooth men's ears like a fowler, the gullible crowd may fall into your nets and some of the losses and new ruinations each day may be added to your credits, since now almost no woes can be added within the territory of your pitiable country, which suffers from outside wretched devastation and an enemy force drawn here by your hands, so to speak, and from within the battering ram and harsh commands of your
tongue. So you have become very like Dircaean Amphion in re- 25
verse.[18] He constructed Thebes by his eloquence; you bring Pavia to the ground with yours, that most ancient and noble city, as fame has it, and one that would have been most blessed too, if it had not given birth to you, a single citizen, under a sinister star. But it is wretched with you as its citizen and most wretched with you as its leader, unless you are excused for having relieved your besieged city with the exile of a majority of citizens and the destruction of many houses; and by paving with many open spaces the city formerly content with one — a dreadful consolation for siege — you have set up a grim solitude in the whole city and lodgings most disagreeable to good men.

26 Hoc ne autem seu quid aliud, queso, est propter quod ut labia
tua aperiat, quotidie Deum rogas? Vide, oro, quid postulas, quid
promittas. Petis ut aperiat, puto, non ut hominum cladem sed
ut Dei laudem nuntiet os tuum, quod quam fideliter impleas, tu
cogita; certe Ille pacem, tu contrarium predicas, ad literam fortassis intelligens evangelicum illud: 'Non veni pacem mittere sed gla-
27 dium.' Cur non potius ad id respicis, quod sine allegorico tegmine
nuda veritas clamat: 'Hoc est preceptum meum ut diligatis invicem'; 'diligite inimicos vestros, benifacite his qui vos oderunt'; 'pacem habete inter vos'; quod quotiens aliquem salvasset, hoc fere
eum alloquio dimittebat: 'vade in pace,' et ad discipulos ingressus
hoc salutationis genere uti solebat: 'pax vobis,' eodem illos uti debere precipiens; postremo quod eisdem, quos valde dilexerat et
diligebat, in finem iam morti proximus supremo elogio pacem dedit ac reliquit?

28 Tu populo tuo quid sis moriens relicturus, nescio; certe vivens
bellum illi et labores et impensas et multiforme periculum acer-
vasti. Quantum michi videris oblitus omnia quecunque conferre
potuerant ad salutem! illam in primis parabolam Salvatoris, quam
fortassis ideo despicis quia Lucas solus eam posuit, seu turrim
erecturi seu ad bellum profecturi atque antequam opus aggredia-
29 tur, sumptus operis aut militiam computantis. Que negligentia
que ve precipitatio non rogantem ea que pacis sunt, sed maiora
viribus ausum te merito perdet, ut auguror; bene quidem, modo
ne unius hominis ruina populum premat immeritum, quem audire
non sinis, quo salvus et innocens permansisset, illud apostolicum
ad Hebreos: 'Pacem sequimini cum omnibus et sanctimoniam,
sine qua nemo videbit Deum.' O ingens extimatio parve rei, tam

Is it for this or some other purpose, I ask, that you daily pray to 26
God to open your lips? See, I beg you, what you are asking for,
what you are promising! I suppose you are asking Him to open
your mouth, not to announce human disasters but the praises of
God. So think how faithfully you carry this out! Certainly He
preaches peace and you its opposite, perhaps understanding literally that Gospel saying: "I have come not to bring peace but a
sword."[19] Why don't you look instead at what the bare truth cries 27
out without the cloak of allegory? "This is my instruction, that
you should love one another";[20] "Love your enemies and do good
to those who hate you";[21] "Keep peace among yourselves";[22] and
whenever the Lord had saved anyone He let him go with this saying: "Go in peace."[23] And coming in to join His disciples He used
this kind of greeting: "Peace to you,"[24] instructing them that they
should use the same greeting; finally at the end, coming close to
death, He gave peace with his last speech to the same disciples
whom He had greatly loved and still loved, and then left them.

As for you, I don't know what you will leave your people when 28
you die. Surely while you live you have given them war and toils
and expense and heaped up danger of many kinds. How forgetful
you have been, it seems to me, of anything that could have contributed to salvation!—especially that parable of our Savior (which
perhaps you despise because only Luke set it down)[25] of the man
either about to build a tower or set out for war and calculating the
expense of the enterprise and the campaigning before tackling the
task. This carelessness and haste, as I guess, will deservedly de- 29
stroy you, for not asking what belonged to peace, but daring something beyond your powers. Well and good, provided the ruin of
one man does not destroy an innocent people, whom you do not
allow to hear that saying of the Apostle to the Hebrews, by which
it could have stayed safe and innocent: "Follow peace with all men
and piety, without which no man shall see God."[26] O exaggerated
valuation of a small thing, that so many men should be ruined in

multos esse calamitosos ut tu disertus appareas et unius lingue
falsam gloriam tot mortibus atque vulneribus constare!

30 Quanquam, quid ego hanc frivolis et inanibus coniecturis malorum presentium causam quero? que si vera esset, hauddubie plus
sit vanitatis habitura quam criminis; alia quidem et verior et gravior causa est; aliquantoque altius quam ad solam eloquentie famam tendis. Atqui romanos duces externosque considera: nullum
apud nos propositi talis exemplum, nullum similis audacie ducem
31 habes. Quis enim inermis lingue fidutia tale unquam aliquid aggressus est? nisi Ciceronem michi forsan obicias, qui licet, ut
scimus, omnipotenti facundia terruerit atque urbe propulerit Catilinam, tamen et consulatus illum suus et senatus ac civium con-
sensus armabat, nec privatim ipse sibi imperium querebat, sed
32 reipublice libertatem. Obicies Pisistratum, Atheniensium tyrannum, quem licet eloquentissimum non ignorem, ille tamen et lingua armatus et gladio, servire sibi patriam coegit. Unus ex omnibus Pericles, qui postea locum eius arripuit, tibi magna ex parte
similis videtur; siquidem tantum inermi facundia valuit quantum
ille valuerat armata; itaque florentissimam urbem, summum Gre-
33 cie decus, fando pessumdedit. Sed et hic quoque diversitas multa
est; ille enim magnis principiis, nulla religiose servitutis compede
obstrictus; tu e radice humili veniens et paupertatem et obedien-
tiam professus, qui subesse pauperibus novisti, divitibus vis preesse, et ut voti huius iniquissimi compos sis, prestat tibi non tam
tuus lepos — ne hinc tibi valde complaceas — quam tuorum civium
mira simplicitas, quos ex ore tuo pendentibus hamis captos, eo
trahis unde, michi crede, non retrahes.

order for you to seem eloquent and for the false glory of one
tongue to cost so many wounds and deaths!

But why am I seeking out with trivial and hollow guesswork 30
this cause for our present evils? If it were the true cause it would
surely contain more vanity than guilt. However, there is another
more true and serious explanation: you are aiming rather higher
than at the mere fame for eloquence. But just consider Roman and
foreign leaders: you have no example of such a purpose among us,
no leader of equal shamelessness. What unarmed man has ever 31
attempted such a deed relying on his tongue? Unless perhaps you
make Cicero a counterexample to me, who certainly, as we know,
terrified Catiline with his all-powerful eloquence and drove him
from the city, but was armed by the consulship and the unanimous agreement of senate and citizens and was not seeking power
for himself without office, but the freedom of the state.[27] You will 32
offer as a counterexample Pisistratus the Athenian tyrant, but although I am not unaware that he was most eloquent, he still
forced his country to obey him armed with both tongue and
sword. Alone of them all Pericles, who subsequently seized his
place, seems largely like you, that is, provided he was as strong
with unarmed fluency as his predecessor had been with arms; and
so he ruined by speaking that most flourishing city, the greatest
glory of Greece.[28] But here too there is a great difference, for he 33
started from great beginnings, bound by no shackle of religious
servitude; you, coming from a humble stock and professing poverty and obedience, knowing how to be humble before the poor,
wish to be preeminent above the rich, and it is not your charm
which enables you to be possessed of this wish—in case you
should be highly satisfied with yourself—but the strange simplicity of your citizens, whom you have caught hanging from your lips
with hooks, and are dragging them, believe me, where you will not
be able to draw them back.

34 Quid hic dicam? utinam tam fidei tue possem quam ingenio gratulari! profecto si patriam amares, matrem et altricem tuam, illi potius te quam illam tibi subiceres; nunc ut contrarium velle damnabile, sic tantum posse mirabile est. Gaude iterum; unus tu e cuntis terris ac seculis incomitatus nudus pauper ignobilis novis et inauditis artibus tyrannidem occupasti, et que Longobardorum regum quondam regia fuerat, nunc tui imperii sedes est. Robustum
35 populum qui talem dominum ferre queat! Bellicis quoque successibus tuis letor et quod giganteum illum exulem, triumphis ac victoriis clarum, providentissimi cives tuo freti consilio receperunt, qui velut alter Alcides non duodenos tantum sed millenos obeat labores et heroycis actibus cunta terrarum monstra conculcet, et quod circa Nançani castrum, ubi maxime fervida illa vis animi et ille tuus acerrimus conatus exarserat, saltem semel egit ut debuit
36 fortuna. Videto autem ut et arcis illius exactam custodiam et piam captivorum curam habeas. Hoc magnitudinem tuam decet, ne per insolentiam attollatur, sed inter vinctos tuos, quos ante triumphalem currum es acturus, summum et precipuum sit insigne clementia.

37 Proinde ut omittam iocos et finiam quod incepi, oro te, amice, et obtestor ut ad te reversus examines non quid iuvet sed quid deceat, neque quid esse cuperes, sed quid es; quem te fecerit natura, quem fortuna, quem professio, quem vite series anteacte; intelliges, nisi fallor, nullum inter hec ambitioni ac iactantie, nullum
38 inepte et indigne tyrannidi locum esse. Quotiens ista tua dominandi cupiditas inardescet, non dico celum aspice, quod quidam bene instituti et modesti homines faciunt dum tentationibus perurgentur, sed in te ipsum verte oculos ac vicissim calceos zonam

What am I to say at this point? I only wish I could congratulate you as much on your good faith as on your intellect! Surely if you loved your country, your mother and nurse, you would submit yourself to her rather than her to yourself. Now just as it is damnable to want the opposite, so it is amazing that you have so much power. So rejoice a second time, you alone from all lands and ages, without supporters, naked, poor and ignoble, have seized the tyranny by new and unheard of tricks, and what was once the palace of the Lombard kings is now the seat of your empire.[29] A sturdy nation indeed to endure such a master! I also rejoice in your military successes, and that your most shrewd fellow citizens, relying on your guidance, have recovered that giant exile glorious in triumphs and victories: like a second Hercules he undergoes not twelve but a thousand labors and with heroic feats tramples on all the monsters of the earth; and near the fortress of Nazzano, where that passionate power of spirit and your fiercest attempts had burst into flames, Fortune at least acted once as she ought.[30] Now see that you keep careful guard of that citadel and devout care of your prisoners. This befits your greatness, not to be puffed up with arrogance, but for mercy to be the chief and conspicuous emblem among your captives whom you are going to drive before your triumphal chariot. 34 35 36

So, to drop jesting and finish what I began, I beg and beseech you, my friend, to come back to your senses and consider not what is in your interest but what is proper, and not what you would desire to become but what you are; how nature, how your fortune, how your holy orders, how the sequence of your past life shaped you. You will realize, if I am not mistaken, that there is no place for ambition and boasting, none for a foolish and unworthy tyranny. Whenever your desire to tyrannize flares up, I do not say "look up at the sky," as well trained and modest men do when they are hard-pressed by temptations, but turn your eyes on yourself and contemplate keenly in turn your shoes, your girdle and your 37 38

amictumque tuum contemplare acriter: videbis nil tibi purpureum et sub Cristo famulatum redolere omnia, non super homines prin-
39 cipatum. Ad summam, si nullis ad hoc seu iurgiis seu monitis seu precibus flecti potes ut ridiculum tyrannidis appetitum exuas, at saltem pacis amorem indue, ne vel a consortio exul hominum bone voluntatis, quibus pacem angelicus preco denuntiat, vel in testamento quo Cristus pacem suis legat, exheredatus aut preteritus
40 videare. Cura, si sapis, ut quod cupide facis, diu facias. Dominandi avidus, servire cupientibus impera; dominare, frater, dominare volentibus sed in pace, que sola quidem et parva augere potens est et dissipata colligere et exsanguia refovere; dominare, sed integra in urbe, sive, id iam quoniam fieri nequit, his ipsis in ruinis dominare placatior, nec laceram iam amplius lacerandam implacabili censeas
41 feritate. Ne accingaris lingue tue gladio semper, sed prudentia et facundia tua intende prospere, procede et quando ita vis civesque volunt tui, regna et attende sequentia; 'propter veritatem *enim* et mansuetudinem et iustitiam,' que pacis utique sunt sorores, 'deducet te mirabiliter dextera tua.' Memento ut Gedeon, cum audisset a Domino: 'Pax tecum, ne timeas,' erexit altare Domino et domi-
42 nice pacis nomen imposuit. Noli tu de tuis bellis, quod supremo vite tempore Iulius Cesar meditatus fertur, Marti templum extruere; aliud namque bellicosum principem, aliud pacificum fratrem decet. In finem, si exemplo cesareo delectaris et dominus mavis esse quam frater, etsi nichil monstruosius a seculis auditum sit, si tamen astra consentiunt, imo si patitur Deus, esto dominus, sed clemens et mitis et amator pacis, quod illum fuisse constat omnibus in quorum manus illius epystole, quas per ipsum civilis belli tempus scripsit, forte pervenerint.

robe: you will see that nothing of yours suggests the purple, but
everything your servitude under Christ, not imperial power over
men. Finally, if you cannot be swayed by any rebukes or warnings 39
or prayers to cast off your absurd lust for tyranny, at least put on
the love of peace so that you will not be an exile from the association of men of good will, to whom the angel herald announces
peace, or seem to have been disinherited or passed over in the
testament by which Christ bequeaths peace to his disciples. If you 40
have sense, see to it that what you do eagerly, you do for a long
time. If you are greedy for domination, command those who want
to be slaves; rule, good brother, rule over the willing, but in peace
which alone is able to make the small great and rally the scattered
and restore the unconscious; rule, but in an undamaged city or,
since this is impossible now, rule more mildly in these actual ruins,
and do not think the mutilated state should be mutilated any further by your unappeasable savagery. Do not gird yourself always 41
with the sword of your tongue, but aim successfully with prudence
and eloquence; go forth and, since you wish it and your citizens
are willing, rule and pay attention to the consequences. For "on
account of truth and mildness and justice," which are the sisters of
peace, "your right hand will lead you in wondrous wise."[31] Remember how when he heard from the Lord "Peace be with you, do
not fear," Gideon raised an altar to the Lord and gave it the name
of the Lord's peace.[32] Do not erect a temple to Mars to honor your 42
wars, as Julius Caesar is said to have contemplated in the last period of his life.[33] The one thing is fitting to a warlike commander,
the other to a pacific brother. Finally, if you are charmed by the
example of Caesar and would prefer to be a master than a brother,
even though nothing more unnatural has been heard through the
ages, yet if the stars agree, rather if God allows, be master, but
merciful and mild and a lover of peace, as it is agreed Caesar was
by all into whose hands the correspondence that he wrote during
that period of civil war happened to come.[34]

43 Hoc ultimum quasi celeste oraculum ausculta. Stude potius ut tibi bene sit quam ut aliis male, et cave ne odiorum aut invidie stimulis populum tibi subiectum in extrema miseriarum, que iam vicina sunt, ultimamque perniciem impellas; neve, quod tibi, si saperes, summopere providendum erat, honestissimum ordinem quem professus es, supra gloriosum Augustini nomen et sacras heremitice vite delitias multorum religiosorum hominum devotione humili fundatum, tua tyrannica et urbana superbia vel
44 concutias vel infames; sed memor sub eodem tecto venerabiles ipsius Augustini reliquias tecum esse eumque solicitum sui ordinis et amantem; fingens tibi semper imaginarium, ut dicitur, testem atque omnibus que gesseris aut dixeris aut demum cogitaveris interesse, tandem timeas tanto sub teste peccare atque ea committere quibus et tuus ille dominus ac magister et omnium magister ac dominus, Cristus, offenditur. Vale.

*Mediolani, VIII Kal. Aprilis.*

Listen now to this last injunction as if it were a heavenly oracle. 43
Work to enjoy good conditions rather than make others suffer bad, and beware of driving the people under your rule with the goads of hatred or envy to the extremes of wretchedness, which are now imminent, and the worst ruination. And do not, as you should most urgently have foreseen and averted if you had any sense, either shatter or disgrace by your tyrannical and citified arrogance the honorable order which you have entered, founded by the humble dedication of many religious men in the glorious name
of Augustine and the holy pleasures of the hermit's life. But stay 44
mindful that the remains of the most venerable Augustine are under the same roof as you,[35] and that he is concerned for and devoted to his order; conceive him always as an imaginary witness, as they say, present at everything you do or say or even think:[36] at last, fear to commit a sin with such a witness or to do such things as offend the lord and master of your order, and the Master and Lord of all, Christ himself. Farewell

*Milan, March 25.*

# [PART VII]

## : 1 :

## *Ad Anibaldum Tusculanum epyscopum cardinalem, contra avaritiam pontificum.*

1 Infelicem invidiam dixit Maro, nec immerito; quid enim infelicius, quam suis malis alienisque simul bonis affligi? Non ineleganter quidem in Mutium nescio quem, apprime invidum atque malivolum, lusisse legitur Publius quidam; cum enim tristiorem solito vidisset: 'Aut Mutio, inquit, nescio quid incommodi accessit, aut nescio cui aliquid boni.' Prorsus ita est; invidus alterius bonum suis ascribit incommodis et, ut ait Flaccus,

alterius rebus macrescit opimis.

Magna miseria, non aliter saturitate alterius quam fame propria torqueri, atque alio pinguescente non secus ac se esuriente macres-
2 cere. Sed haud temere diffinierim annon invidia tantum, sed vitiis omnibus infelicior avaritia sit. Invidia enim mesta sepe sed otiosa est, avaritia tristis et occupata; superbia, dum se aliquid magnum putat, falsa licet opinione delectatur, avaritia semper se famelicam et egenam sentit, neque fallitur; verissimum enim est poeticum il-
3 lud: 'Semper avarus eget.' Nam si avarus est, cupit, quod ipsum

# PART VII

## RELIGION AND THE CHURCH

: I :

*To Annibaldo, cardinal bishop of Tusculum, against the greed of prelates.*

Vergil called envy unfortunate[1] and rightly so, for what could be more unfortunate than to be simultaneously distressed by one's own hardships and other men's prosperity? And we read that a certain Publius made elegant sport against someone called Mucius who was exceptionally envious and malicious; when he saw Mucius more grim than usual he said: "Either Mucius has suffered some setback, or some success has come to another fellow."[2] That's just how it is; the envious man counts another's success among his own setbacks and, as Horace puts it, 1

> grows thin upon another's fattening profits.[3]

It is an enormous wretchedness to be tormented just as badly by another man's self-indulgence as by one's own hunger and to grow just as thin when another man grows plump, as if one were himself starving. But I would not be too quick to decide whether 2
greed is not more unfortunate, not only than envy, but than all other vices.[4] For envy is often gloomy but inactive, whereas greed is grim and preoccupied. Arrogance thinks itself important, but it is made happy by a false belief; greed on the contrary always feels itself to be hungry and needy, and is not mistaken: for that poet's
saying is very true that "the greedy man is always needy."[5] Indeed if 3
he is greedy, he feels desire, as the very name of the vice shows;

vitii nomen indicat; sane, quod ait Seneca, 'non qui parum habet sed qui plus cupit, pauper est.' Et hoc inde concluditur, quod non paucitas rerum inopem facit, cum paucis natura contenta sit, cui qui rite satisfecerit dives est et nichil ei deest; sed cupiditas inexpleta, que iudicat tantum sibi deesse quantum cupit; cupit autem omnia, et optando supervacua fecit necessaria. Ita egestatem minimam cuique perfacile succurri poterat, irremediabilem atque immensam fecit.

4 Rursus enim et illud est verum, quod philosophis placet: avaro tam quod habet deesse, quam quod non habet; nisi quod michi quidem magis videtur avaro deesse quod habet, quam quod non habet. Ex illo enim nil preter solicitudinem perpetuam et veros metus, ex hoc nonnunquam breve falsum gaudium capit, dum sibi arridet et optatum bonum spe fallente preoccupat. Ira nonnunquam satiatur fera quadam, ut aiunt, et inhumana dulcedine; avaritia vero nunquam, nam et successibus inardescit, et satyricum illud verum est:

Crescit amor nummi, quantum ipsa pecunia crescit,

5 et minus hunc optat qui non habet. Cuius rei causam unam, nam plures excogitari queunt, in epystola quadam ponit Anneus Seneca. 'Neminem' inquit, 'pecunia divitem facit; imo contra nulli non maiorem sui cupidinem incussit'; et sequitur: 'Queris que sit
6 rei huius causa? plus incipit habere posse qui plus habet.' Que ratio eo spectat, quod ea que haberi nequeunt, nec optantur temere nec sperantur quidem, et est difficultas rerum ingens impossibilitati proxima. Nemo alas ad volatum nisi amens optat, nemo nisi insanus sperat; at ad iter equum aut vehiculum aut navim multi, ac

clearly, as Seneca says, "it is not the man who possesses too little who is poor, but he who desires more than he has."[6] From this we infer that it is not a shortage of possessions that makes a man impoverished, since nature is content with a little, and if a man has duly met her demands he is rich and lacks nothing; but desire is insatiable, since it judges that it is lacking anything it desires; but it desires everything and by longing has turned superfluities into necessities.[7] So it has made the slightest lack, which could easily have been remedied, beyond cure and beyond measure.

Again the judgment of the philosophers is true, that when a 4
man is greedy he lacks what he possesses just as much as what he does not possess,[8] except that it seems to me the greedy man lacks what he possesses even more than what he does not, because he has from his possessions nothing but unceasing anxiety and real fears, but from his desire he feels at times a brief, false joy while he is pleasing himself and anticipating the longed-for gain with fraudulent hope. Anger is quite often sated with a kind of savage, as they say, and inhuman sweetness,[9] but greed is never sated since it is inflamed by its successes; and the comment of the satirist is true,

> The love of cash increases as much as the money itself
> increases,[10]

and the man without cash feels less longing for it. And Seneca sets 5
down one cause of this (several can be imagined) in one of his letters: "Money never made anyone rich; on the contrary there is no one whom it did not strike with a greater desire." And he adds: "You ask the origin of this pattern? The man who possesses more
approaches the power to have still more."[11] The gist of this argu- 6
ment is that what cannot be acquired is neither casually desired nor hoped for, and the huge difficulty comes close to being an impossibility. No one wants wings to fly unless he is deranged, no one hopes for them unless he is mad, but for a journey many desire

pedum crurumque incolumitatem omnes cupiunt, que tamen ipsa si forte irreparabiliter amissa sit, et sperari desinit et optari.

7 Ad hanc Senece rationem ego alteram addere soleo; ea vero est huiusmodi. Pauper agros aut pecuniam nonnisi in naturales necessitates appetit, que pauce quidem et exigue sunt, inque eos usus in quos inventa est, de quibus ait Flaccus:

Nescis quo valeat nummus? quem prebeat usum?
Panis ematur, olus, vini sextarius, adde
Quis humana sibi doleat natura negatis.

8 His igitur tam angustis in finibus humana cupiditas inclusa restringitur; dives autem necessariis usque ad fastidium abundans, voluptuosa et supervacua, que infinita sunt, insatiabili pervagatur animo, et rura latissima, non ut agros indigentie subventuros sed ut regna suffectura superbie, et, nummorum cumulos ingentes solitus mirari, non iam pecuniam ut pecuniam sed ut auri montes cogitat; in quibus haud dubie latissimum avaritie regnum patet.
9 Neque enim ullus est optandi, cum nullus sit crescendi modus; non si fines usque ad terminum regionis mercando et rapiendo porrexerit, non si montibus aurum exequaverit, ut Satyricus alter ait, conquiescet. Optare enim restat donec agrorum finibus maria montesque transiverit, donec auri mole alpes excesserit et vertice sidera tangat, Cesare eousque potentior ut non tantum imperium occeano terminet, sed trans occeanum extendat, Mida demum eousque sit ditior, ut non modo quicquid tetigerit, sed et quicquid aspexerit aurum fiat.

10 Multos vidimus, cum querendo pervenissent quo nunquam cogitassent spesque suas et cupiditates primas omnes a tergo relictas magno spatio superassent, cupiditates novas atque alias spes ordiri

a horse or cart or boat, and everyone desires healthy feet and legs; yet if that is lost beyond recovery, hope and desire come to an end.

I usually add another argument to this point of Seneca's; it is as 7
follows. A poor man seeks land or money only for the needs of nature, which are few and small, and for the uses for which they were devised; as Horace says:

> You don't know the power of cash, the use it gives?
> It buys bread, greens, a pint of wine, and add to these
> Whatever our nature suffers if denied.[12]

So human desire, confined within such narrow bounds, is under 8
control; but the wealthy man, overflowing with necessities to the point of excess, surveys in his insatiable mind the infinite range of luxurious and superfluous things and the widest estates, not to have lands to assist his poverty but kingdoms to satisfy his pride; accustomed to marvel at huge heaps of cash, he no longer thinks of money as money but as mountains of gold; beyond doubt this
opens up the widest dominion for greed. Indeed, there is no limit 9
to desire, just as there is no limit to increase; not if a man extends his territory by dealing and stealing to the outer limits of the region, not if he brings his gold to the height of mountains, as another satirist says, will he take rest.[13] So what remains is longing, until he has leaped over seas and mountain ranges with the boundaries of his estates, until he has outstripped the Alps in the mass of his gold, and "strikes the stars with his head."[14] So much more powerful than Caesar that he does not just limit his empire by the Ocean, but stretches it out beyond the Ocean, until finally he is so far wealthier than Midas,[15] that not only everything he touches but everything he looks on turns to gold.

We have seen many people, when they had gained a level of 10
wealth they had never imagined, and then, leaving all their original hopes and desires behind them, exceeded them a hundredfold, embark on new desires and other hopes as if they were going mad

et velut ex integro insanire; quibus si ad memoriam antiqua reduxeris, irascantur, et quasi vel plebeium quiddam sit modestia, vel ipsi quo avariores eo et meliores effecti sint creveritque cum pecunia et cupiditate licentia, humilium pudeat votorum. Quem his igitur vel sperandi vel optandi finem speres, nisi ut nichil usquam supersit optabile? nam dum aliquid supererit quod optetur, simul et sperabitur et queretur, et cum proximas spes attigerint, alie ap-
11 parebunt atque inde alie; ita nullus erit finis nisi mors sola. Quod non ita contingeret, si non semper res querendas, sed aliquotiens et se ipsos et quesita respicerent; sed illa optantibus pretiosa, adeptis vilia evanuerunt, unde fit ut concupiscentia infinita sit, quia fundum non habet quo parta serventur, impleturque non cupiditas quidem unquam, sed propheticum illud Aggei: 'Qui merce-
12 des congregavit, misit eas in sacculum pertusum.' Venio ad reliquas pestes, et eius quidem quam accidiam nostri vocant, eadem ratio est que invidie fuit; gula autem ac libido sepe suis fruuntur delitiis, quibus exultant et gaudia fugitiva percipiunt; avaritia nulla re fruitur, nisi curis amarissimis: dum enim querendis inhiat, et illa non habet et quesita non videt, nisi ad supplicium; hinc trepida, inde solicita. Que cum ita sint, iure avaritia sororum omnium pestilentissima dici potest, quam radicem malorum omnium vocat Apostolus.

13 Nec sum nescius te mirari quid hodie tecum hac, ut aiunt, importuna philosophia preter solitum uti velim. Ego autem non te magis quam mortales fere omnes et precipue tuum genus alloquor, inter quos maxime et solium posuisse et vexillum fixisse victrix

all over again. If you restored their old circumstances to their memory, they would be angry and feel shame at their old humble desires, as if moderation were vulgar or they had become as far superior as they were more greedy, and their license had increased with money and desire. So what end either of hoping or desiring would you expect for such men except that there should be nothing left for them to desire? For while anything is left to be desired, it will at once be longed for and sought out, and when they have achieved their most recent hopes, others will manifest themselves
and others still; so there will be no end save only death. And this 11
would not happen as it does if men did not always have an eye to acquiring things, but sometimes looked back at themselves and their acquisitions; but those things precious to men who longed for them faded away as worthless, once possessed; hence their lust is unlimited because it has no bottom where acquisitions may be kept safe, and desire is never filled; but the prophetic saying of Haggai is fulfilled: "He who has gathered together his profits is
dropping them into a leaking sack."[16] Coming now to the other 12
plagues, the nature of what we call "sloth"[17] is the same as that of envy, whereas gluttony and lust often enjoy their pleasures and delight in them, taking their fleeting joys. But greed enjoys nothing except the most bitter cares, since while it gapes at things to be acquired, it not only does not have them but does not see what it has acquired, except as a form of punishment: on this side it is fearful, on the other harassed. In the circumstances, greed can be called the most plaguing of the sister vices, the one the Apostle calls the root of all evil.[18]

I know you must be wondering why I am employing this un- 13
welcome philosophy, as they call it, in addressing you today, beyond my usual practice. But I am not addressing you more than virtually all mortal men, and especially your own class. It is especially among them that desire seems to triumph and command, having set its throne and planted its banner; this I wonder at with

michi videtur et imperiosa cupiditas; quod eo indignantius miror,
14 quo minor vobis cupidinum causa est. Cui enim hos auri cumulos acervatis? legitima quidem vobis negata posteritas. Vos parcus et exiguus cultus decet; reliqua pauperum Cristi sunt, quos fraudare predarique non timetis, domino illorum spectante desuper et minitante vindictam. Et nescitis cui vestrum crimen utile sit futurum, quod vobis interim laboriosum pestiferumque et funestum est. Multi se propter filios excusant, et vitio animi velum pietatis obtenditur; sic leena, sic tigris fit, enixa, ferocior, et animalia man-
15 sueta nove prolis amor exasperat. Vobis excusatio nulla, velamen vitii nullum est; ante totius orbis oculos nudi estis digitoque monstramini populorum omnium cum exprobratione mordaci. 'Ecce virtutis' inquiunt, 'precones, qui cum de vita eterna deque animi libertate multa magnifice loquantur, sine causa tamen et tempora-
16 libus addicti et avaritie servi sunt.' Re enim vera, etsi de omnibus dicat, nonne de vobis tantum sensisse videtur David, ubi ait: 'Universa vanitas, omnis homo vivens; veruntamen in imagine pertransit homo, sed et frustra conturbatur'; et ut rabiem pontificalis avaritie tot post seculis futuram notaret, expressius: 'Thesaurizat' inquit, 'et ignorat cui congregabit ea'?

17 Hec utique vobis ante alios, avari pontifices, dicta sunt; parentes quidem thesaurizantes filiis et legimus et videmus, quamvis sepe, fortuna paternis votis obstante, quod aliis partum erat ad alios devolvatur; parentum tamen intentio nota est. Vestra intentio quenam, queso? quid agitis? cui thesaurizatis, nisi dyabolo et angelis eius, qui solicite vos observant, numerant dies et hereditatem vestram avidissime prestolantur, gratissima trophea vestris

even greater indignation, because you and your peers have less cause for desires. For whom are you heaping up these piles of 14
gold? You are not permitted lawful heirs.[19] A sparing and modest style of life is appropriate for you; the rest belongs to the poor of Christ, whom you are not afraid to cheat and plunder, while their Lord watches from above and threatens his vengeance. You do not know whom your crime will benefit, although meanwhile it brings you toil, ruin and death. Many men excuse themselves on account of their children, and the cloak of family duty is spread over this spiritual vice. This is why a lioness or tiger becomes more savage after giving birth and love for newborn offspring arouses tame creatures. You, however, have no excuse, no cloak for your vice; 15
you are naked before the eyes of the whole world and are pointed to with the finger of all nations with biting rebuke. They say: "See these preachers of virtue, who when they say grandiose things about eternal life and freedom of the spirit are still addicted without reason to earthly things and slaves of greed!" In truth, was not 16
David, even if he is speaking about all men, thinking only of you when he said:[20] "Every thing and every living man is nothing but vanity: truly man passes through his life in a state of illusion, yet troubles himself in vain." And to brand the rage of papal greed that would come to pass after so many generations he said more explicitly: "He builds up treasure and does not know for whom he is gathering up those things."

These things were undoubtedly said to you before all others, 17
greedy prelates; we read and see parents building up treasure for their sons, although often when fortune obstructs the father's wishes, what had been won for one set of heirs passes on to another; still the purpose of parents is well known. But what is your purpose, I ask? What are you aiming for? For whom are you building up treasure, except for the devil and his minions, who watch you attentively, count your days and most greedily await your inheritance, planning to set up most grateful trophies

inscripta nominibus in limine Tartari de manubiis spoliatorum
18 pauperum erecturi? Sed admirans percontabere: 'Cur hodie potius ista quam alias? an vel hactenus nos non avaros, vel avaritiam vitium non fuisse? vel te nunc primum oculos aperuisse crediderim, qui prius ista non videris'? Respondebo admirationi tue. Et sciebam vos avaros, et avaritiam vitium esse, nemo usquam est qui
19 nesciat, et in utrunque non nunc primum oculos aperio; sed cum forte nudiustertiano die venissem ad te, altaria tua, imo vero altaria domini virtutum, argento atque auro et gemmis honusta conspexi, atque insanis fulgoribus percussus obstupui, et dixi mecum: 'Ecce nova avaritie arma, novum pereundi genus; avaritia nobis nostra non sufficit, nisi avarum quoque Cristum facimus et

divos, ipsumque vocamus
In partem predamque Iovem,

ut Virgilius ait.' Vos quidem divitias male partas iustificasse videmini, si prede rapinarumque vestrarum pauperem Cristum cogitis esse participem et auro obsidetis invitum. Non hic placandi numi-
20 nis modus. Annon legistis apud Senecam deos tunc propitios fuisse, cum fictiles fuerunt? atqui deos nunquam propitios fuisse nec esse potuisse certum est; quomodo enim propitius aliis esse potest, qui miserrimus est sibi? Placet igitur non hec Senece sen-
21 tentia, sed verba, que feliciori materie licet inserere. Profecto Cristus semper propitius humano generi; sed tunc presentior fuit cum fictilis fuit. Nunc aureus atque gemmatus irascitur et preces nostras iustissima indignatione non audit. Non aurum odit ille sed cupidos, quibus optandi querendique nullus est finis. Primi hominum quod erant, aperte profitebantur: querebant divitias ut abundarent; vos queritis ut ornetis Cristum: pium opus, si spoliis Ille

inscribed with your names on the threshold of Tartarus from the
spoils of the poor you have plundered? But you will ask in wonder: 18
"Why say all that today rather than on other occasions? Is it that
up to now we have not been greedy, or greed was not a vice? Or
am I to believe that you have only now opened your eyes, and you
did not see this before?" I will answer your surprise. I knew you
were greedy and greed was a vice, since there is no man anywhere
who does not know this, and I am not opening my eyes to either
vice now for the first time. But when I happened the other day to 19
come to you I saw your altars, or rather the altars to the Lord of
the virtues, loaded with silver and gold and jewels, and I was dazed,
struck by their mad glitter, and said to myself: "See the new weapons of greed, a new path to ruin; our own greed is not enough for
us, unless we make Christ too a man of greed and as Vergil says:

> We call the gods
> and Jove himself to their share and the spoils."[21]

But you seem to be justifying your ill-gotten wealth if you compel
the poverty of Christ to share in your spoils and thefts, and be-
siege him with gold against his will. This is not the way to appease
the Godhead. Have you not read in Seneca that the gods were 20
propitious when they were made of earthenware?[22] But it is certain that those gods were never propitious, nor could they have
been, for how can a being be propitious to others who is most
wretched in himself? So what I approve is not Seneca's comment
but the words which we may insert into a fitter context. Surely 21
Christ is always propitious to the human race, but he was closer to
us when he was made of earthenware. Now he is made of gold and
jewels and is angered and with most justified indignation will not
heed our prayers. He does not hate gold, but greedy men who
know no end of longing and acquiring. The first men first openly
confessed what they were: they sought wealth to be well supplied,
but you seek it to adorn Christ; this would be a devout act if he

miserorum et non potius virtutibus ac devotione fidelium vellet ornari, et si non fictioni iuncta cupiditas odiosior Deo esset.

22 Animadverti olim tale aliquid in principibus dominisque terrarum, qui omni studio libros querunt petunt rapiunt mercantur, non literarum amore quas ignorant, sed avaritia inducti, nec animi sed thalami querentes ornatum, nec scientiam sed nomen, neque librorum sententias sed pretia cogitantes. Verum his colorata excusatio, licet falsa, non deerit; dicent enim sobolem se ac posteros cogitare; et verbo quidem nondum natis aut quod vite genus eligant prorsus incertis, vere autem avaritie proprie atque ignorantie ingens bibliotheca congeritur.

23 Vobis congerendarum opum quis est color? respondebitis ut Cristi templa farciatis auro. Sed quid Persio dicitis exclamanti:

> O curve in terris anime et celestium inanes,
> Quid iuvat hoc, templis *vestros* immittere mores?

Neve hoc aliis dictum crederetis, audite ut statim vestro nomine vos appellat:

> Dicite, pontifices, in sancto quid facit aurum?

Respondete, pontifices; vobis enim loquitur. Respondete tot senes
24 uni iuveni, tot theologi uni poete, tot cristiani uni pagano. Quid dicitis? in sancto quid facit aurum? si respondere negligitis poete, annon saltem respondebitis prophete, qui non aurum, sed alia quedam a vobis ornamenta templorum exigit? Apud Malachiam legitis: 'Filius honorat patrem, et servus dominum suum timebit; si ergo pater ego sum, ubi est honor meus? et si dominus ego sum,

wanted to be adorned with the spoils of the wretched, and not the virtue and devotion of believers instead, and if desire was not more hateful to God when combined with a false excuse.

I noticed such behavior long since in the princes and lords of 22
the earth, who acquire and seek out and steal books with all passion, not led on by love of literature, which they do not know, nor seeking an adornment for their mind but for their bedroom, thinking not of knowledge but repute, not the wise thoughts of books but their price.[23] But they will not lack a plausible excuse, even if false: they will say they are thinking of their children and descendants; according to them they are accumulating a vast library for their children—who are not even born yet and in any case it is quite uncertain what life they will choose—whereas in reality they are accumulating it for their own greed and ignorance.

What is your excuse for heaping up wealth? You will answer 23
that it is in order to stuff the temple of Christ with gold. But what have you to say to Persius when he cries out:[24]

> You souls bent on earth, empty of heavenly value,
> What avails this, to impose your morals on the temples?

And so that you don't believe this was aimed at other men, hear how he immediately calls you by your name:

> Tell me, priests, what business has gold in a holy place?

Answer him, priests, for it is you he is talking to. All you many old men, answer one young one, so many theologians answer one
poet, so many Christians one pagan. What have you to say? What 24
business has gold in a holy place? If you don't care to answer the poet, will you not at least answer the prophet who is demanding not gold but different adornment of the temples from you? You read in the book of Malachi: "The son honors his father, and the slave will be afraid of his master; so if I am father, where is my honor? And if I am Lord, where is the fear due to me? So speaks

ubi est timor meus? dicit dominus exercituum'; et ut noscatis quia
vobis dicit, sequitur: 'ad vos, o sacerdotes, qui despicitis nomen
25 meum.' Nisi forte quisquam est qui putet ulla unquam etate dignius hoc quesitum, quam nunc queritur. Video quidem, ut dixi,
vulgus avaritia ardere, et fateor, nichil excusat: nulla est enim excusatio peccati, nam si excusatio iusta est, peccatum utique non est;
sed natorum caritas multiplexque necessitas et vulgaris ignorantia
crimen levant. Vos vero, pontifices, dicite, oro: quid sibi vult hec
rabies habendi inter divitias tam certas, in tanta rerum divinarum
humanarumque notitia, in vita solitaria et celibe et de crastino
cogitare prohibita?

26 Illud michi forte notissimum ingeretis: 'Aurum habet Ecclesia.' Bene si habet, pessime si habetur; placere possunt divitie virorum, viri divitiarum penitus non placent, qui cum somnum suum dormierint, in manibus suis nichil invenient. Verior igitur illa responsio quam percontationi proprie Persius ipse subiecit; cum enim secundo quesisset: 'In sancto quid facit aurum?,' intulit:

> Nempe hoc, quod Veneri donate a virgine pupe.

27 Facessat, oro, iantandem aurum templis inutile, et in alia templa
Dei, hoc est in usus hominum egentium, conferatur; sit Cristi caritas, que seculi pompa est; nec semper, sub obtentu devotionis,
ydolatrie serviatur. Nescitis quod avaritia est ydolorum servitus?
nulla tot ydolis gens abundat, nulli convenientius dicitur: 'cavete a
simulacris.' Credite michi, pontifices, aurum potuit Cristus habere
sed noluit; dives esse potuit dum inter homines agebat, pauperta-
28 tem maluit; Chorintiis vasis uti potuit, fictilibus usus est. Nolite,
pontifices, excusationes frivolas aucupari, aut sub Cristi nomine

the Lord of hosts." And so you may know that he is speaking to
you this follows: "To you, priests who despise my name."[25] Unless 25
perhaps there is someone who thinks this question was more properly asked in any other age than now. Indeed I see, as I mentioned, the common mob burning with greed and I admit nothing excuses this; for there is no excusing a sin, since if the excuse is just, that was certainly not a sin; but affection for children and manifold necessity and common ignorance dilute the charge. But you prelates, tell me, please, what is the meaning of this madness to possess amid such sure wealth, in such knowledge of human and divine affairs, in a solitary and celibate life forbidden to think about the morrow?

Perhaps you will thrust upon me that most hackneyed saying: 26
"The Church possesses the gold." Good if it possesses gold, but bad if it is possessed by it; the wealth of men can be approved, but men of wealth are utterly excluded from approval; when these have slept through their sleep they will find nothing in their hands.[26] That answer which Persius himself gave to his own question is nearer to the truth; for when he had asked for the second time "what business has gold in a holy place?" he commented:

> The same, I suppose, as dolls given by a virgin to Venus.[27]

Away, please, with gold, so long useless to the temples, and let it 27
be bestowed in a different temple of God, that is, the service of needy men; let what is the display of the world become the charity of Christ and not always be enslaved to idolatry under the pretext of devoutness. Don't you know that greed is enslavement to idols? No nation is overflowing with so many idols, and to none can one say more fittingly "beware of images."[28] Believe me, priests, Christ could have had gold but he rejected it; he could have been rich while he lived among men, but he preferred poverty; he could have
used Corinthian bronze vessels[29] but he used earthenware. Don't 28
hunt for hollow excuses, prelates, or gather the food for greed and

avaritie pabulum et vestris alimenta furoribus aggregare: Cristus vestro auro non eget, nec vestris superstitionibus delectatur; puri ac nudi cordis est appetens, piorum actuum, honestarum cogita-
29 tionum et humilium voluntatum. Quis inter hec auro locus? nolite, miseri, curare quam superbe sacrificetis, quam ornate, quam splendide, sed quam pie quam humiliter quam caste quam sobrie; sacrificate quod diruptis vinculis suis liberatori suo rex propheta sacrificat, hostiam scilicet laudis, et nomen domini invocate; sacrificate, inquam, sacrificium laudis, sacrificate sacrificium iustitie et
30 sperate non in auro sed in domino. Audite Psalmistam, surdi, diebus ac noctibus clamantem: 'Sacrificium Deo, spiritus contribulatus.' Quid hic opus est auro? spiritu opus est, eoque nonnisi contribulato; opus est corde, sed contrito et humiliato. Hoc est sacrificium Deo gratum, atque homini sine terrarum effossione parabile; submisso et immaculato opus est animo, contra nec terso nec rudi auro opus est.

31 Nescio quid amplius dicam et vereor verba iactare; sed si post prophetam, ipsum quoque Persium poetam audire non piget, videte quid ibidem paganus homo pontificibus suis dicat:

> Quin damus id superis, de magna quod dare lance
> Non possit magni Messale lippa propago?

Et ne dubium foret quid est hoc superis offerendum, quod genere atque opibus superbi, ceci divitum filii, non possunt, subsecutus expressit:

> Compositum ius fasque animi sanctosque recessus
> Mentis et incoctum generoso pectus honesto.

Preclarum verbum, dignumque quod de Cristo dictum esset. Tu vale et equam fidelibus convitiis aurem prebe.

fuel for your crazes in the name of Christ: Christ doesn't need your gold, and is not pleased by your superstitions; he is eager for a pure and naked heart, pious behavior, honorable thoughts
and humble wills. What room is there among these for gold? 29
You wretches, do not care how grandly you sacrifice, with what adornment and what splendor, but how piously and humbly and chastely and soberly; sacrifice what the prophet king sacrificed to his liberator when he burst apart his chains, that is the offering of praise, and called on the name of the Lord;[30] I say sacrifice the sacrifice of praise, the sacrifice of justice and put your hopes not in
gold but in God.[31] Listen to the Psalmist, you deaf men, as he 30
cries out night and day: "The sacrifice belonging to God is a contrite spirit."[32] What need is there for gold? We need the spirit, and that only if it is contrite; we need the heart, but mortified and humiliated. This is the sacrifice welcome to God and can be provided for man without excavating the earth; we need a submissive and unsullied spirit, and to the contrary we need neither polished nor raw gold.

I don't know what more I can say and I am afraid to waste 31
words, but if you do not mind listening to the poet Persius after the prophet, see what that pagan man says to the priests of his time:

> Why don't we give to the gods what the bleary child
> of great Messala cannot spill from a great dish?[33]

And not to leave in doubt what this is that should be offered to the gods, as if men proud in family and wealth, the blind children of the rich, cannot give, he continues by specifying:

> Justice and right set firm in the spirit, and holy shrines
> of the mind, and a breast imbued in noble honor.

A glorious saying and worthy to have been said about Christ! As for you, farewell, and offer an impartial ear to my loyal scolding.

: 2 :

*Ad Gerardum, germanum suum, monachum cartusiensem, de felicitate status illius et miseriis seculi cum exhortatione ad propositi perseverantiam.*

1 Subit animum, luce michi carior germane, longevo silentio finem ponere, quodsi forsan obliviosi animi indicium arbitraris, falleris; non prius te quam memet ipsum obliviscar. Timui hactenus tyrocinii tui quietem interrumpere; fugere te strepitum, amare silentium sciebam; me vero si semel inciperem, haud facile desiturum; is amor tui est, ea rerum tuarum admiratio. E duobus igitur extremis non quod michi gratius, sed quod tibi tranquillius eligebam; nunc ut verum fatear, non tam tibi quam michi consulturus ad
2 scribendum venio. Quid enim tu sermunculis meis eges, qui celeste iter ingressus angelicis assidue colloquiis recrearis? felix animi fortunatusque propositi, qui mundum tum maxime blandientem medio etatis flore sic spernere potuisti interque Sirenum voces
3 obstructa tutus aure transire. Dum ergo te alloquor, ipse res meas ago, si forte vel sic sacro ardori tuo ad motum torpens et longo gelatum situ pectusculum meum incalesceret; tibi autem clamor meus ut minime utilis, sic minime importunus esse debebit. Neque enim tyro ut olim, sed Cristi iam miles es longa militia probatus, gratias Illi qui tanto te honore dignatus est et ut sepe alias, ex agmine medio adversarum partium insignem transfugam ad sua
4 signa convertit. Prius ergo verebar intempestivas tibi voces ingerere; deinceps securum te securus ipse compello. Incipientibus

: 2 :

*To his brother Gherardo, the Carthusian monk, about the happiness of his circumstances and miseries of the world, with an exhortation to perseverance in his intent.*

The urge takes me, brother dearer to me than light, to put an end 1
to long silence, and if you happen to think this a mark of a forgetful heart, you are misled; I should sooner forget myself than you. I was afraid of disturbing the repose of your novitiate. I knew you shunned disturbance and loved silence, while for my part if once I had started writing I would have found it hard to stop: such is my love for you and such my admiration for your life. So out of two extremes I chose not what was more pleasing to me but what was more peaceful for you; now, to tell the truth, I come to write with
more consideration for myself than for you. In fact, what do you 2
need my chatter for, since you have embarked on the heavenly journey and are constantly refreshed by angelic conversation? You are blessed in your spirit and fortunate in your resolve to have been able to scorn the world at its most beguiling in your prime and pass the voices of the sirens safely by blocking your hearing.[1]
So while I am addressing you, I am pursuing my own interests if 3
my poor breast, sluggish and frozen with long neglect, may be warmed by contact with the heat of your holy passion. My cry, though it be scarcely useful, ought to be as little disturbing as possible. For you are no apprentice as you once were, but an established soldier of Christ, tested by long service, thanks to Him Who has thought you worthy of so great an honor and, as often on other occasions, has won over to His standards a distinguished
deserter from the heart of opposing forces. Previously I was afraid 4
to burden you with inopportune cries; subsequently, knowing you free of trouble, I myself will call on you now I am free of trouble.

formidolosa sunt omnia; multa que timuimus pueri, adolescentes
risimus; militem inexpertum strepitus omnis exanimat, duratus
bellis nullo fragore concutitur; rudis nauta primo ventorum murmure terretur, gubernator antiquus qui totiens fatiscentem et exar-
matam puppim perduxit in portum, ex alto despicit iratum mare.
5 Spero autem in Illo qui te ab utero matris tue ad hoc laboriosum
certe sed gloriosum iter assumpsit, ut per varias difficultates tutus
in patriam pervenires, quod nulla te amplius rerum facies movebit,
non luctus non cure non morbi non senectus non metus non
fames non egestas,

> Terribiles visu forme, lethumque laborque,

postremo non ingens

> ianitor Orci
> Ossa super recubans antro semesa cruento,

et quicquid aliud ad exterrendum corda mortalium poetarum inge-
6 niis cogitatum est. Neque plus constantie tribuerit adversus omne
terrificum Herculi suo Iupiter adulterio pater, quam tibi natus
virgine pater omnium eternus, qui rectas in se sperantium respicit
7 et adiuvat voluntates. Que cum ita sint, sine metu iam tuorum
voces audire et, siquid vacui temporis inter occupationes optimas
affulserit, et respondere breve aliquid potes. Patere autem me secularibus tecum uti testimoniis, quibus non solum Ambrosius et
Augustinus noster ac Ieronimus abundant, sed et apostolus Paulus
uti interdum non erubuit, neque cellule tue aditu prohibeas que et
ore meo digna sunt et tuis auribus non indigna.

8 Pithagoras peracuti vir ingenii fuit, sed cuius acumen longe relicta veritate, sepe usque ad aniles ineptias penetraret. Hinc illa

Everything is fearful to men beginning a task; we laughed as young men at many thing we feared as boys; every noise panics an inexperienced soldier, whereas a hardened veteran is not shattered by any of the din of war; the raw sailor is terrified by the first sound of the winds, whereas the ancient pilot who has so often brought into harbor his leaky ship, shorn of its rigging, holds the angry sea
in contempt when he is on the deep. Now my hope is in that God 5
who brought you from your mother's womb to this toilsome but glorious journey, that you may reach your native country safely through various difficulties, since no appearance of circumstances will alarm you, not grief nor anxiety nor disease nor old age nor fear nor hunger nor poverty nor

> shapes dreadful to behold, death and toil,[2]

finally not the huge

> janitor of Hell
> resting on bones half-eaten in his bloody cave,[3]

and whatever else has been thought up by the talents of poets to
intimidate the hearts of mortals. Nor did Jupiter, his adulterous 6
father, give Hercules more courage to face every dreadful thing than did the Eternal Father of us all, born of the Virgin,[4] Who looks on and assists the correct desires of those who hope in Him.
In these circumstances you can now fearlessly listen to the cries of 7
your kin and if any time of leisure shines on you between your virtuous activities, you can give me some brief answer. So let me use worldly witnesses, with which not only Ambrose and our Augustine and Jerome are well supplied, but which even the Apostle Paul did not blush to use, and you will not exclude from entry to your cell words worthy of my eloquence and not unworthy of your ears.

Pythagoras was a man of keen wits but his shrewdness, leaving 8
truth far behind, often stretched to the follies of old women.

ridicula per multa et varia corpora volutatio animarum et renas-
cens de bellatore philosophus yliaci belli testis Euphorbius; denique famosa illa METEMΨIKOCIC, quam miror sequi vel Platonem vel Aristotilem potuisse; sed magis miror Origenem, qui
eandem complecti visus insaniam, ab ipso miratore suo et lauda-
tore Ieronimo et a reliquis veri sectatoribus meruit in fine dam-
9 nari. Verum, ne Pithagore occursus me deviare coegerit, vir ille
cuiuscunque ingenii, morum illa etate gravissimorum fuit claris-
simeque modestie; unde et viventi summus honor impensus et
ipse post mortem deorum concilio ascriptus est; domus eius apud
posteros pro templo habita. Huius ergo prima institutio quenam
10 fuit? nempe ut discipuli sui quinquennio silerent. Preclare. Stultum est enim prius loqui velle quam discas. Ceterum ad amoven-
dum ori, non dico custodiam, que amovenda nunquam est, sed
repagulum, quinque tempus annorum sufficiens extimavit; tu vero,
si rite computo, in servitio Iesu Cristi et in scola eius iam septimum annum siles. Tempus est ut loqui posse aliquid incipias, vel
si pre omnibus silentium dulce est, michi vel in silentio respondeas.

11 Meministi, frater, qualis olim rerum nostrarum status erat et
animos nostros quam laboriosa dulcedo et quantis amaritudinibus
aspersa torquebat; meministi, puto, ut nunc et libertati tue congau-
deas et fraterne condoleas servituti, que me adhuc solitis compedibus arctatum tenens, iam cultrum lateri iam laqueum collo parat,
peregissetque iampridem ni liberatoris tui dextera, que te servitio
exemit, me ab interitu defendisset. Orabis, frater, ut me quoque
iantandem libertati restituat et uno ventre progressos pari fine feli-
12 citet, et si preire debueram, non pudebit sequi. Meministi, inquam, quis ille et quam supervacuus exquisitissime vestis nitor, qui
me hactenus, fateor, sed in dies solito minus, attonitum habet;

Hence that ridiculous rotation of souls between many different
bodies, and Euphorbius, reborn as the philosopher himself after
being a warrior and witness of the Trojan war, and in short that
notorious "metempsychosis" which I am surprised that either Plato
or Aristotle could have accepted; but I am more amazed at Origen, who by apparently embracing the same folly deserved to be
damned in the end by his own admirer and panegyrist Jerome and
the other votaries of truth.[5] But not to let the contact with Py- 9
thagoras lead me astray, despite his intellect, he was a man of the
most serious character at that time and glorious modesty; hence
great honor was paid to him living, and he himself after death was
enrolled in the council of the gods; his house was treated as a
temple by posterity. So what was his first rule? That his pupils
should be silent for five years.[6] Splendid. It is stupid to want to 10
talk before you learn; at any rate he thought five years enough to
remove, I won't say guardianship of one's mouth, which is never to
be removed, but its bolt. And if I calculate rightly it is now the
seventh year that you have been silent in the service of Jesus Christ
and his school. It is time for you to begin to speak a bit or, if silence is sweet beyond all else, to answer me even by your silence.

Do you remember, brother, what our condition once was, and 11
what toilsome sweetness seasoned by what bitterness tormented
us? I think you remember, so that you now rejoice in your liberation and grieve for your brother's enslavement, which still holds
me confined by the usual shackles, preparing now a knife for my
breast and a noose for my neck, and would have finished me off
long ago if the right hand of your Liberator which released you
from slavery had not defended me from destruction. You will pray,
brother, that He restore me too at last to liberty and bless with a
like ending those who emerged from the same womb, and even if
I was obliged to go before you, I will not be ashamed to follow.
You remember, I say, the empty glamour of the most exquisite 12
clothing, which still holds me spellbound, I confess, but each day

quod illud induendi exuendique fastidium et mane ac vesperi repetitus labor: quis ille metus ne dato ordine capillus efflueret, ne complacitos comarum globos levis aura confunderet; que illa contra retroque venientium fuga quadrupedum, nequid adventitie sordis redolens ac fulgida toga susciperet neu impressas rugas collisa
13 remitteret. O vere inanes hominum sed precipue adolescentium curas! quorsum enim ea mentis anxietas? ut placeremus scilicet oculis alienis. Et quorum oculis, queso? profecto multorum qui nostris oculis displicebant. Seneca in quadam ad Lucilium epystola 'Quis eam' inquit, 'quam nulli ostenderet, induit purpuram?' Mira quidem dementia statum nostrum non animi ratione sed vulgi furore moderari et in consilium vite nostre illos admittere
14 quorum nobis vita contemptui est. Nemo cicatricosum tergo ducem, nemo gubernatorem naufragiis insignem eligit; illos legimus quos miramur, illis solemus nostra committere quos rerum suarum administratio claros facit. Itaque vulgus insanum, cuius mores rideas, cuius omnem opinionem vitamque despicias, in moribus
15 tuis sequi, plusquam vulgariter insanientis est. Ut enim inceptum sequar, cesset ambitio et vulgus procul exulet; quanto utilior atque ad omnes oportunitates aptior, quantoque tractabilior est vestis plebeia quam regia! Nobis tamen eo tempore longe aliter videbatur quorum studii laborisque precium erat conspici et, ut ait ille,

digito monstrarier: hic est.

16 Quintus Hortensius orator fuit clarus, sed delicatior quam deceat virum, et forme non minus quam eloquentie studiosus, nunquam speculo inconsulto in publicum processit; in illo se comere, in illo se mirari, in illo vultum togamque componere consueverat. Multa sunt eius viri muliebria, sed illud in primis, collegam suum, quod

a little less; our fastidiousness in putting it on and taking it off and how the effort was repeated each morning and evening; how great our fear that our hair would lose its coiffure if the slightest breeze should disturb the curls we fancied; the way we recoiled from passing animals in case our fragrant and gleaming toga should smell of accumulated dirt, or be crushed and lose its pressed
pleats. How truly foolish are the concerns of men but especially 13
young men! For what was the purpose of that anxiety? To please the gaze of others. And whose gaze, I ask you? Surely that of the many, who were displeasing in our own eyes. In a letter to Lucilius Seneca says: "Whoever put on purple without intending to show it?"[7] It is really amazing folly to regulate our condition, not by reason but by the madness of the crowd, and to take counsel about our life from men whose life is an object of our contempt.
No one chooses a commander with scars on his back nor a pilot 14
famous for shipwrecks; we choose the men we admire and usually commit to men whose administration of their own affairs makes them distinguished. So it is more than ordinary madness to follow in your behavior the crazy crowd whose behavior you mock,
whose every opinion and life you despise. To continue what I be- 15
gan to say, let ambition flag and the crowd be exiled far away; how much more useful and fit for all occasions, how much easier to handle is plebeian dress than a royal robe! But at that time it seemed very different to us, since it was the prize of our effort and toil to be noticed, as that famous poet says:

> To be pointed out: This is the man![8]

Q. Hortensius was a famous orator but more refined than befitted 16
a man, and no less dedicated to his appearance than to his eloquence; he never went out in public without consulting a mirror; he used to comb himself before it or admire himself and compose his features and toga in front of it. This man had many feminine characteristics, but the principle instance was how he took it upon

is casu obvius arcto quodam loco in eum impegisset et artificiosum ex humero toge sinum turbasset collisione fortuita, iniuriarum accusare sustinuit prorsus feminea vanitate, quasi capitale crimen esset tam compositi habitus qualisqualis offensio.

17 Nos, frater, etsi nulli diem diximus ob eiusmodi iniuriam, animo tamen haud absimiles fuimus; sed te de tantis errorum tenebris eduxit repentina mutatio dextere Excelsi; ego sensim multisque laboribus assurgo, credo ut intelligi detur nullum hic adminiculum literarum, nullum opus ingenii, sed totum Dei munus esse, qui forte et michi manum porriget imbecillitatem meam ingenue confitenti. Id sane, si ratio non persuaserit, senectus coget, quam magis magisque in dies adventare et iam finibus meis ob-
18 equitare sentio. Quid de calceis loquar? pedes quos protegere videbantur, quam gravi et quam continuo premebant bello! meos, fateor, inutiles reddidissent, nisi extremis necessitatibus admonitus offendere paululum aliorum lumina quam nervos et articulos meos
19 conterere maluissem. Quid de calamistris et come studio dixerim? quotiens somnum quem labor ille distulerat, dolor abrupit! quis pyraticus tortor crudelius nos arctasset quam propriis ipsi manibus arctabamur? quos mane nocturnos sulcos in speculo vidimus rubenti fronte transversos, ut qui capillum ostentare volebamus,
20 faciem tegere cogeremur! Dulcia sunt hec patientibus, passis vel memoratu horrida, incredibilia inexpertis. Quantum vero te nunc illa preterita memorantem, presentia ista delectant! calceus laxus pedis non vinculum sed munimen; coma alte resecta et capillorum sepes non iam auribus importuna nec oculis; toga simplicior et

himself to accuse his own colleague of committing a tort because he had by chance brushed against him in a confined space and disturbed the artistic drapery of his toga by this accidental collision. It was surely a mark of womanish vanity to treat any kind of damage to his carefully ordered grooming as though it were a capital offense.[9]

As for us, brother, if we did not lodge a suit against anyone for 17
that kind of wrong, we were not so different in attitude, but a sudden transformation made by the right hand of the Most High led
you from such darkness of error; I am rising gradually and with
much effort, I think, so that men can understand that this illumi-
nation is not owed to letters or to talent, but entirely the gift of
God, who may perhaps extend his hand to me as well if I openly
confess my weakness. Certainly if reason has not persuaded me,
old age will compel me, as I feel it approaching day by day and
now cantering around my boundaries. Need I mention shoes? 18
They seemed to protect our feet, but with what painful and unceasing warfare they oppressed them! They would have made my
feet useless if I had not been advised by extreme need to prefer
giving slight offense to other men's eyes rather than wearing away
my sinews and joints. What should I say about hair-curlers and 19
devotion to styling our locks? How often pain broke off the sleep
which that toil had postponed! What pirate torturer would have
confined us more cruelly than we were constricted by our own
hands? What nightly furrows we saw in the morning slashing
across our reddened brow, so that we who wanted to display our
hair were forced to cover our face! These things are sweet to those 20
who endure them but after the experience they are horrid even to
recall and unbelievable to those who have not tried them. Yet how
much even now, as you recall those past actions, your present circumstances delight you! The loose shoe, not squeezing but reinforcing the foot; hair cut back on top and the hedgerow of hair
neither troubling the ears nor the eyes; a simple toga easy to

quesitu et custodia facilis nec egressu laboriosior quam ingressu,
tamque animum ab insania defendens quam corpus a frigore. O te
felicem, qui ut hec dulcius saperent, illas amaritudines pregustasti!

21 Et ut hec leviora preteream, recordare etiam, quo promptius e
tanta Caribdi liberatus dignas Deo gratias agas, quanta nobis fuerat cura quanteque vigilie ut furor noster late notus et nos multorum essemus populorum fabula. Quotiens sillabas contorsimus,
quotiens verba transtulimus, denique quid non fecimus ut amor
ille, quem si extinguere non erat, at saltem tegi verecundia iubebat,
22 plausibiliter caneretur? Laudabamur in studiis nostris et capita
delirantum peccatoris oleum impinguabat; sed ineffabilis Dei pietas gressus tuos interea pedetentim revocabat ad rectum iter et sa-
tietate rerum pereuntium preceps illud desiderium castigabat, ut
scilicet diversis etatibus utrobique incola, quid interesset inter Ba-
23 bilonem atque Ierusalem expertus agnosceres. O misericors Deus,
quam tacite consulis, quam occulte subvenis, quam insensibiliter
mederis! quid enim tantis laboribus, bone Iesu, quid aliud nisi
amorem mortalem imo vero mortiferum petebamus, cuius nos
fallacem et multis sentibus obsitam suavitatem attingere summote-
nus permisisti, ne grande aliquid inexpertis videretur, et ne tanta
esset ut opprimeret, misericorditer providisti, delitiis nostris e
medio sublatis, cum quibus dextera tua spes nostras e terra pene
24 radicitus extirpavit? Iuvenili etate revocasti eas morte quidem, ut
spero, illis utili, nobis necessaria, et abstulisti a nobis animarum
nostrarum vincula; et tamen, o ceca mens mortalium, quotiens
questi sumus quasi ante tempus accidisset quod cum summo vite
nostre discrimine trahebatur, aut quasi salutare aliquid intempestivum sit! Quot suspiria quot lamenta quot lacrimas in ventos

obtain and maintain and no more troublesome in going out than coming in, defending the mind as much from madness as the body from cold. O happy man who sampled those bitter things in advance so that these would taste the more sweet!

To pass over these trivialities, remember, so that you will thank 21
God more worthily once freed from this Charybdis,[10] how much
toil there was for us and how much vigilance was needed to make
our lovesick folly broadly known and ourselves the gossip of many
peoples. How often we twisted syllables and reversed words, and
after all that, what did we not do so that our love, which modesty
ordered us at least to conceal if we could not quench it, might be
sung to earn praise! We were praised in our studies and "the un- 22
guent of the sinner made our heads gleam"[11] in our craziness. But
all this time piety toward the God who surpasses language was
gradually calling back your feet to the right path and from surfeit
of transient goods it chastened that headlong desire, so that at different ages, by becoming a dweller in each place, you recognized
the difference between Babylon and Jerusalem by experience.[12] O 23
merciful God, how silently You advise, how secretly You aid us,
how imperceptibly You heal! For what were we seeking, dear Jesus,
with such efforts except mortal, that is deadly, love, whose decep-
tive sweetness, choked by many thorns, You allowed us to taste
only superficially, so that it would not seem something great to our
lack of experience, and in mercy You took precautions that its
sweetness would not be so great as to overwhelm us when You removed the sources of our pleasure from life, and your right hand
uprooted our hopes along with them, almost root and branch
from the earth? In our youth You recalled them by death which 24
was, I hope, useful to them and necessary for us, and You took
away from us the bonds of our souls;[13] and yet—how blind the
heart of mortals!—how often we complained as if what was being
prolonged at great risk to our life had happened prematurely, or as
if anything that brought health was ill-timed! How many sighs

effudimus, et more freneticorum medico nostro insultantes, manum tuam repulimus, lenimen optimum nostris vulneribus ad-
25 hibentem! Nunc ergo, dic michi, vir Deo ex hoste familiaris ex
adversario civis, dic michi, quoniam et ista pertractas et illa re-
tractas, quid simile habent cantiuncule inanes falsis et obscenis
muliercularum laudibus referte, turpi et aperta cum confessione
libidinis, quid simile habent divinis laudibus et sacris excubiis, in
quibus modo per menia et propugnacula civitatis Dei mira ordina-
tione dispositi, Cristi vigiles adversus antiqui hostis insidias inten-
tissime pernoctatis? felix et invidiosa militia magnusque, fateor, et
durus labor, sed brevis et eterno pensandus premio.

26 Michi autem adhuc restat de quo tecum, si pateris, Deus meus,
disceptare velim. Quid est enim, responde michi, quod cum ego et
frater meus gemino laqueo teneremur, utrunque contrivit manus
tua, sed non ambo pariter liberati sumus? ille quidem evolavit, ego
nullo iam laqueo tentus sed visco consuetudinis pessime delinitus,
alas explicare nequeo et ubi vinctus fueram, solutus hereo. Quid
cause est nisi quod contritis pari conditione laqueis, nequaquam
quod sequitur par fuit, 'adiutorium nostrum in nomine Domini'?
27 Cur autem hanc daviticam cantilenam tanto concentu ceptam tam
dissona voce complevimus? Nulla Dei voluntas sine causa est,
quippe cum omnes inde dependeant et illa sit omnium fons causarum. Frater ergo rite cecinit erecto ad celum animo, ego terrena
cogitans et curvatus in terram; et forte liberatricem dexteram non
agnovi, forte de propriis viribus speravi; aut hoc aut aliud cause est
cur effracto laqueo non sim liber. Misereberis, Domine, ut dignus
sim cui amplius miserearis; sine gratuita enim misericordia tua
nullatenus potest humana miseria misericordiam promereri.

and laments and tears we poured out to the winds and, insulting
our doctors like lunatics, we pushed away your hand as it was offering the best soothing cure for our wounds! So now tell me, as a 25
man grown friendly with God having been an enemy, made a citizen having been an adversary, since you are repenting of that past
and meditating on the present, what do our empty little songs,
crammed with false and obscene praises of women along with a
shameful and open confession of lust, have in common with divine
praises and sacred vigils, in which, around the walls and bastions
of the City of God, wondrously arranged, you spend your nights
as Christ's watchmen against the treachery of the old enemy? This
is a blessed and enviable service and a great and harsh toil, I admit,
but short and to be paid by an eternal reward.

I still have something to dispute with You, my God, if You al- 26
low it. For why is it, answer me, that when I and my brother were
held by a twin noose, your hand ground down both of us, but we
are not both equally freed? He at least has flown away but I, held
by no noose but enticed by the birdlime of the worst habits, cannot unfold my wings and although released, am still held fast
where I had been bound? What is the reason except that when
"the nooses were worn away" in the same fashion, "our help in the
name of the Lord"[14] that followed was hardly equal? Why have we 27
brought to an end with such dissonant voices our Davidic psalm
that had its origin in such harmony? No act of God's will is without cause since every man depends on it and it is the source of all
causes. So my brother sang with due ceremony, raising his spirit to
heaven, but I was thinking of earthly things and bent toward
earth. Perhaps I did not recognize the liberating hand, perhaps I
hoped for it from my own strength; either from this or some other
cause, although my noose is broken, I still am not free. You will
pity me, Lord, so that I become worthy for You to pity me further,
since without the mercy of your grace human misery cannot to
any degree earn mercy.

28 Nunc ad te, frater, redeo et sensim ad graviora conscendo, ut gradatim te tibi felicissimum ostendam. Recordare quis ille concursus hominum, quenam prelia salutantium, quanta concursantium offensio; quantum ve sudoris ac laborum, ut compti et elaborati nunc hic nunc illic in publico cerneremur. Et, Deus optime, qui cecos illuminas, claudos erigis, mortuos suscitas, qualis illa iactatio est! postquam enim omnibus vicis omnibusque porticibus noti erimus, omnibus scenis circumacti, restat iter patrum nostrorum agere et formidatum sepulcri limen irredituro pede transcendere.
29 Adde nunc conviviorum gloriosa fastidia, que sine magno, ut aiunt, fame discrimine non vitantur, et epularum variam procellam concusso stomaculo fluctuantem. Que si ab amicis patimur incommoda, quid expectes ab hostibus? quorum multa sunt genera: domestici externi, horumque alii clandestini alii ex professo inimicitias agunt, et rursum alii lingua alii fraudibus alii gladio decertant; brevius loquor omne genus experto.

30 Ad hec quid, queso, non iniuriarum a servis contumeliarumque
perpetimur? Excusat eos Seneca multis quidem verbis et omnem
culpam reflectit in dominos, Luciliumque suum laudat servis familiariter conviventem. Quid dicam? vereor tanti viri vellicare senten-
31 tiam; et tamen quid prohibet? longe michi aliter videtur. Potuit
illis forte vel prudentia ut bonos servos facerent, vel fortuna ut in-
venirent, prestitisse; michi, fateor, hactenus neutrum fuit, cum
utriusque studium semper fuerit. Itaque de se alii viderint, ego
quod nescio laudare non possum; apud me et iniquissimum est
servorum genus et proverbium illud vetus a Seneca reprehensum
32 veri locum habet: 'totidem hostes esse quot servos.' At de bonis
servis epystola illa est, mali enim eodem auctore a dominorum

Now I return to you, dear brother, and gradually rise to more 28
serious matters, to show you by degrees how you are most blessed. Recall to mind the crowding together of men: the battles to pay one's respects to patrons, the clash of competing individuals, the enormous sweat and effort to groom ourselves so as to be seen in public, hither and yon. And, Best of Gods, who throws light on the blind and raises up the lame, and rouses the dead, what a buffeting that is! For after we shall be known in all streets and porticoes, dragged around every stage, we have still to follow the path of our fathers and cross the dread threshold of death with a step
that will not return. Add to this the boastful bother of banquets 29
which cannot be avoided, as they say, without great risk to reputation, and the assorted storms of feasting, seething in a bloated stomach. And if we suffer these discomforts from friends, what would you expect from enemies? There are many varieties of them, domestic and foreign, and of these some are hidden, while others openly pursue feuds, and again some fight with their tongue, some with cheating, and some with the sword; I speak more briefly as to someone who has experienced all kinds of enemy.

In addition, what do we not suffer in wrongs and insults from 30
our servants? Seneca excuses them with many words and turns around all blame onto the masters. He praises Lucilius for living intimately with his servants.[15] What am I to say? I am afraid to criticize the views of such a great man, yet what stops me? Things
seem very different to me. Perhaps their prudence had the power 31
to make their servants good, or fortune helped them find good servants. So far I have had neither, though my desire for both has always persisted. So let other men examine their own case, I cannot praise what I do not know, but in my case the tribe of servants has been utterly wicked, and the old proverb criticized by Seneca contains the truth that "you have as many enemies as you have
servants."[16] And yet that letter is about good servants, since on the 32
same authority the bad ones are kept away from associating with

consortio excluduntur. Credo; sic enim sonant verba et bonorum
exempla de libris non pauca colligimus; nec id quidem ignoro neque scriptoribus fidem nego, sed sive temporum mutatio sive sors
sive impatientia mea est, ego bonum servum nunquam vidi; quero
tamen, et si forte obvius fuerit, velut occursu bicipitis hominis
33 obstupescam. At nequis hoc vel sevitie vel desidie mee imputet,
omnia tentavi, neque minus ego quam Lucilius familiariter cum
servis meis vixi et ad consilium et ad confabulationes et ad cenam
illos admisi, meque ipsum et res meas illorum fidei commisi fide-
lesque ut facerem credidi; nec credendo profeci, quin potius ars
34 omnis in contrarium versa est. Servorum enim a colloquio meo
nemo non procacior discessit, nemo non contumacior surrexit a
cena, et ut familiaritas insolentes, sic fidutia fures esse docuit; ut
ergo Senece de suis, sic michi de meis et amicorum servis—omnes
enim fere nescio quomodo pares sunt—vera loqui liceat; ego qui-
35 dem, fateor, servili pervicacia nil molestius patior in vita. Cetera
enim bella indutias habent, cum domesticis hostibus sine intermis-
sione pugnamus; quamvis non sim nescius equo animo ferendum
esse quod maximis viris accidisse video. Nempe et Ulixem illa
prima etate quam heroicam vocant, inter multos quos sustinuit
labores, servorum et ancillarum quoque contumeliis affectum
clarissimi loquuntur auctores; et hoc recentiori evo Fridericus
romanus imperator de servorum iniuriis, ut fama fert, vivens mo-
riensque conquestus est. Ceterum hec servorum incidens querela
hoc agit ut te felicem scias, qui servili tyrannide liberatus, levissimo ac suavissimo Cristi iugo colla subieceris.

36 Quid de aliis dicam? quod illud adulationis latens inter dulcia
venenum coram arridentium retroque mordentium? que illa de

their master. I believe him, for that is the effect of his words, and we have collected quite a few examples of good servants from books; I am not unaware of this nor do I deny credit to the writers, but whether it is a change of times or chance or my impatience, I never saw a good servant; but I keep looking and if by chance one came my way I would gape as if I met a two-headed
man. But to prevent anyone blaming this on my cruelty or laziness 33
I have tried everything and have lived intimately with my servants no less than Lucilius, and I have invited them into deliberation and conversation and dinner, and have entrusted myself and my affairs to their trust and hoped to make them trustworthy. But I have achieved nothing by trust—on the contrary all my effort has
turned into its opposite. None of my servants left my conversation 34
without becoming more pert, no one got up from dinner without being more insulting, and as intimacy taught them to be insolent, so confidence taught them to be thieves; for as Seneca speaks about his own servants, so may I be allowed to tell the truth about mine and those of my friends—for somehow they are all the same: I confess I suffer nothing more tiresome in my life than the
perversity of servants. Other wars have truces but we fight without 35
any break against our enemies in the household, although I well know that we must endure calmly what I see has happened to great men. For in that first age which they call heroic the most distinguished authors say Ulysses suffered the abuse of servants and maids among the many hardships he endured.[17] And in our recent age Frederick the Roman emperor complained while alive and on his deathbed, as rumor has it, about the wrongs done by his servants.[18] However, this intrusive lament about servants has the purpose of making you know you are blessed, being freed from the tyranny of the servile while submitting your neck to the light and pleasant yoke of Christ.

What should I say about other troubles? What about the poi- 36
son of flattery lurking among sweet comments of those who smile

transverso fame vulnera incertis auctoribus et e media vulgi acie clam iaculata convitia? que illa avaritie rabies animos efferantis omnisque divini et humani iuris oblivionem pestiferam afferentis? Hec de curatoribus predones efficit. Extremum autem mali genus est dum remediis aconita miscentur: eligis hominem cuius fide inter hominum fallacias sis tutus, ille te primum fallit. Quid hic consilii capias? et ut Satyricus ait,

> quis custodiet ipsos
> Custodes!

37 Hec nos pestis ab infantia prosequitur; seu fortuna seu simplicitas nostra est, adolescentes soli incuriosi et apti iniurie visi sumus. Tritum assiduitate proverbium est: 'occasio furem facit.' Hec nos, frater, ut semel expediam, de divitibus inopes fecit; imo certe, quod divini muneris fuisse recognoscimus, de occupatissimis otio-
38 sos et de impeditissimis expeditos. Accessit quod omnes qui se spoliis nostris honeraverant, brevi quidem ipsius Fortune manibus excussos et vel gravi morte consumptos vel inopia extrema et misera senectute languentes vidimus; nec parvum iniurie solamen ultio est, Deo presertim auctore contingens.

39 Quid dicam de fori ac litium tempestate, que michi non curiam modo sed terrarum orbem odiosum facere potens est? quid de aliis, que preter mortem gravissima iudicantur, captivitatis insidiarumque periculis, qualia multa olim terra pelagoque pertulimus,
40 quorum commemoratio stuporem michi renovat et horrorem? Sed evasimus. Non id nostre nature privilegio accidit sed divina

to your face but criticize you behind your back? What about the glancing wounds to our reputation from unknown sources and abuse secretly hurled from the midst of the massed crowd? What about the frenzy of miserliness which makes men's spirits savage, bringing deadly forgetfulness of all divine and human right? This turns guardians into plunderers. But it is the extreme form of evil when aconite poison is mixed in with remedies: you choose a man whose good faith should keep you safe amid the cheating of men, and you are the first one he cheats. What plan can you adopt? As the satirist says:

> Who will guard
> the guardians themselves?[19]

This plague followed us from infancy; whether it is our fortune or simplicity we seemed to be unprotected young men, thoughtless and fit to be wronged.[20] The proverb is hackneyed from constant use: "It is the opportunity that makes the thief." It is this, brother, to dispatch it once and for all, which has turned us from wealthy men into paupers; in fact—something we recognize as a divine gift—it has made us leisured, not busy men, and ready for battle, 37
not encumbered with gear. In addition to this we have seen all the men who have loaded themselves with our spoils soon stricken by the hands of Fortune and either destroyed by a grim death or wasting away in extreme poverty and wretched old age; and retribution is no small comfort for being wronged, especially when it is God who is responsible for taking vengeance. 38

What shall I say about the storm of public business and lawsuits, able to make not just the courts but the whole globe of earth loathsome to me? What about the other misfortunes that are thought the worst, next to death, the risks of captivity and treachery, such as we have endured abundantly by land and sea, so that 39
recalling them renews my paralysis and panic? But we survived. 40
This did not happen through the privilege of our nature but by

clementia. Evasimus; sed perire potuimus et certe debuimus, nisi nos misericors Pater vivificis oculis aspexisset. Evasimus; sed eisdem periculorum generibus noti et sotii periere: incendio gladio carcere naufragio aliisque innumerabilibus modis, quorum propter duros et recentes amicorum casus tristis et acerba narratio est. Inter hos laqueos ambulavimus atque inter hos scopulos navigavimus, frater.

41 Quid loquor, quasi equa conditio sit amborum? ego miser inter eosdem versor assidue; tu iam Deo gratias portum tenes; felix hora qua natus es, felix omne periculum quod te per multa experimenta
42 formidabilium rerum ad amorem securitatis adduxit. Confer, oro, nunc ista cum illis: cum turbulentis opibus quietissimam paupertatem, cum amaris negotiis dulce otium, cum iniquis hostibus optimos fratres, denique cum litibus silentium, cum turbis solitudinem, cum urbibus silvas, cum comessationibus ieiunia, cum diurnis choreis nocturnos choros, postremo cum Avenione Cartusiam, cum terrenis periculis celestem pacem, cum servitute dyaboli amicitiam Dei, cum morte perpetua sempiternam vitam; necesse
43 erit te felicissimum fateare. 'Urge propositum' ut ait Seneca, 'preme quod cepisti'; non te labor terreat, non frangat asperitas. Flacci verbum est:

nil sine magno
Vita labore dedit mortalibus.

Quodsi in hac vita de qua ille loquebatur, minima etiam magno constant, quod totiens incassum anhelando probavimus, quis labor magnus videri debet quo ad eternam beatitudinem pervenitur?
44 Absit segnities, languor abscedat; dum matutino tempore excitaris, ad divinum te colloquium evocari credito. Et heu, quotiens nos mortalis domini iussus excivit, quotiens periculis ac laboribus

divine mercy. We survived, but we could have perished and certainly deserved to, if the merciful Father had not looked on us with eyes that gave us life. We survived, but men known to us and our companions perished in dangers of the same kind, by fire, the sword, prison, shipwreck and countless other ways which it is grim and bitter to tell because of the harsh and recent misfortunes of our friends. We walked among those snares and sailed between those reefs, dear brother!

Why do I speak as though both of us experienced equal cir- 41
cumstances? I, poor fool, am constantly moving among the same difficulties, whereas, God be thanked, you now have made it to harbor. Happy the hour you were born, happy each danger which led you to the love of safety through many tests and terrifying
events. Now compare your life with those: your utterly calm pov- 42
erty with troubled wealth, your sweet leisure with the bitter world of affairs, your excellent brothers with cruel enemies, and finally silence with quarreling, solitude with riots, the woods with cities, fasting with banquets, daily hymns with nocturnal dances; in short the Charterhouse with Avignon, heavenly peace with earthly perils, the friendship of God with enslavement to the Devil, eternal life with lasting death—then you will have to confess that you
are most blessed. "Drive toward your goal," as Seneca says, "press 43
on with what you have begun";[21] do not let toil deter you nor harshness break you. This is Horace's saying:

> Life gave nothing
> to mortals without great toil.[22]

And if in the kind of life he was discussing even small things cost a great deal, as we have so often proved by vain, breathless striving, what labor ought to seem great which leads to eternal blessedness?
Let sloth be far from us and weariness depart. When you wake up 44
in the morning, believe you are being summoned to a divine colloquy. Alas, how often the order of a mortal master roused us,

obiecit! et quis, oro te, fructus? nempe nonnisi amicitia humana
anceps periculosa difficilis; tibi amicitia divina proponitur, certa
45 secura parabilis. Crede michi; cadet ex animo tedium, somnus ex
oculis cum tibi proposueris vocantem Deum, et optime tecum agi
senties quod vigilare, vulgo circum stertente, iubearis. Mos impe-
ratorum est probatis militibus difficilia committere; dum coqui
pistoresque et, ut horatiano sermone utar, ambubaiarum collegia
circa forum cupidinarium oberrant, illi inter gladios ac tela versan-
tur et periculum ingens tenui gloria consolantur. Cum autem
orando colloqui ceperis, gaudium cum reverentia certabit, ut in-
46 somnem te atque impigrum sub tanto prebeas spectatore. Audisti
ex historiis Marci Catonis milites illo presente et sitim et pulverem
et estum et serpentum morsus tolerare solitos et sub illo teste sine
gemitu ac lamentis occumbere. Audisti Scevam, illum fortem potius quam iustum virum, sub oculis sui ducis non modo pugnare
47 sed mori etiam exoptantem. Quodsi mortalis domini veneratio
prestare potuit, quid Cristi presentia posse debet? Is equidem non
expectandus ut veniat, sicut Cesarem suum infelix ille bellator ex-
pectat, sed suscipiendus colendusque; omnibus locis omnibusque
temporibus presens est, videt actus nostros, cogitationes introspi-
cit, ingens calcar animo nisi funeste consuetudinis torpor obsistat.
48 Epycuri doctrina est imaginarium vite testem querere; amico scribens, 'Sic' inquit, 'fac omnia tanquam spectet Epycurus.' Seneca
vero, ut illustrioris viri presentia Lucilii sui vitam formet, monet ut
Catonem eligat Scipionem Lelium vel alium quemlibet spectate
fame virum. Non potest non placere sententia a magnis viris laudata; nam et Marco Tullio placuisse eam video, quam Quinto
49 Cioeroni fratri suo scribens licet aliis verbis inseruit. Placet ergo

how often it exposed us to dangers and toil! And with what reward, I ask you? Nothing but human friendship, dubious, dangerous and difficult; whereas you are being offered divine friendship,
sure, free of care and accessible. Believe me, the weariness will fall 45
away from your heart and sleep from your eyes when you imagine God calling you, and you will believe you are being excellently treated because you are ordered to keep vigil while the common crowd snores. It is the practice of generals to entrust difficult enterprises to tested soldiers: while cooks and bakers and, to use Horace's phrase, the "guilds of belly dancers"[23] wander around the pleasure market, the soldiers move among swords and spears and find comfort from immense danger in slender glory. So when you begin to converse in prayer, joy will compete with reverence to make you prove yourself sleepless and tireless with such a Spectator. You have heard in the histories how Cato's soldiers in his pres- 46
ence endured thirst and dust and heat and snake bites, and died without groaning and lamentation with him as witness. You have heard how Scaeva, that man more brave than just, longed not only
to fight but to die beneath the gaze of his leader.[24] And if rever- 47
ence for a human master could do this, what ought the presence of Christ to achieve? We should not wait for Him to come, as that unlucky warrior Scaeva waited for Caesar, but take up his cause and worship Him; He is present in every place and at every time, He sees our deeds, He penetrates our thoughts, an immense spur to the spirit if the inertia of deadly habit does not obstruct it.
There is a teaching of Epicurus to look for an imaginary witness to 48
our life. He writes to his friend: "Do everything as though Epicurus is watching";[25] and Seneca, in order to shape the life of his Lucilius by the presence of a more distinguished man, warns him to choose Cato or Scipio or Laelius or any other man of tested repute.[26] A pronouncement approved by great men cannot fail to please; for I see that it pleased Cicero, and writing to his brother
Quintus he inserted it, albeit in other words.[27] So Epicurus' rec- 49

Epycuri consilium inter illos a quibus scriptum atque probatum est. Nobis hac arte nil est opus; testem fictum non querimus cum vivum ac verum presentemque semper Cristum habeamus. Nam 'et si ascendero in celum, illic *est*, et si descendero in infernum, *adest*.' Omnia igitur coram Illo non quasi spectante sed vere spectante faciamus; pudebit non modo actuum sed archanarum etiam voluntatum, quas non tantum fictus sed etiam vere presens epycureus testis non posset agnoscere; novit autem eas Ille cuius oculis nichil est impervium.

50 Putemus Illum ante oculos nostros positum clamare: 'Quid agitis, ceci et ingrati? ego pro vobis mortem sponte sustinui, vos
michi laborem exiguum negatis; hec vestra pietas, hec accepti be-
51 neficii memoria est! Qui nutu celum terrasque et maria guberno,
qui fulmina de nubibus iacio, qui alternis vicibus tempestates ac
serenum reveho, qui diem noctemque suis luminibus exorno et
vario horarum numero tenebras lucemque demetior, qui perpetuum solis obsequium duodeno stellarum ordine ad quaternas
temporum varietates adhibeo et fastidio consulens grata rerum et
incessabili novitate anni circulum circumvolvo, qui non modo cal-
cabilem terram labilem aquam atque auram spirabilem sed innu-
merabilium rerum vobis presidia et oblectationes et ornamenta
52 congessi, denique qui ad imaginem meam—quamvis stulti obstre-
pant—de nichilo vos creavi et quo me queri vellem iter vobis
ostendi, ipse ego, inquam, ut post tot beneficia rebellantes ac de-
vios revocarem, inter vos ex alto sub servili habitu dissimulata
maiestate descendens, pro salute vestra paupertatem labores insidias convitia contumelias carcerem verbera flagella mortem cru-
cemque non timui. Vos michi quid redditis, non dico par tantis
meritis, quod nec cogitare sufficitis; sed quod omnino signum
ostenditis animi non ingrati?'

ommendation pleases those by whom it is written and approved.
We have no need of this device; we are not looking for an imaginary witness since we have Christ alive and real and ever present.
For "if I ascend to heaven He is there and if I descend to hell He
is present."[28] So let us do everything not just as if He is looking
on, but because He is looking on: we shall feel shame not only for
our deeds but even our secret wishes, which no imaginary nor
even actual Epicurean witness could identify; God on the contrary,
to whose eyes nothing is impenetrable, knows these wishes.

Let us think He is set before our eyes crying out: "What are 50
you doing, blind and ungrateful men? I voluntarily accepted death
for you and you are denying me a little toil! This is your piety, this
your remembrance of the kindness you have received! I Who gov- 51
ern heaven, earth, and seas with my nod, Who hurl thunderbolts
from the clouds, Who bring storms and calm weather in alternating sequence, Who adorn day and night with their lights and measure darkness and light with the differently numbered hour, Who
apply the unending service of the sun with its twelvefold order of
constellations to the four varieties of the seasons, and with thought
for your satiety turn around the circle of the year in welcome and
unyielding novelty, I Who not only have made the earth for you to
tread and water for you to glide through and air to breath, but
have heaped up for you the protection and pleasures and ornaments of countless things; in short, though fools may heckle, I 52
have made you from nothing into something after my own image
and shown you the way by which I want you to seek Me—I myself, I say, to recall you from rebelling and straying after so many
kindnesses, came down from on high to dwell among you, conceal-
ing my majesty under a slave's clothing, and did not fear poverty,
toils, treachery, abuse, insults, prison, blows, lashings, death and
the cross for your salvation. And what do you give Me back, I
don't mean matching such services, which you are not even able to
imagine, but what sign do you show of a grateful spirit?"

53 Quid ad hec, frater, responsuri sumus? an hic quicquam ambigui est? profecto si hec intus in anima loquentem Dominum audire voluerimus, surgemus nocte alacres — hoc enim agere ceperam — ut eo tempore devotius Cristo laudes canamus, quo Illum pro nobis opprobria et iniurias passum esse meminerimus.

54 Sed quia diu iam te, frater, ab altitudine contemplationum tuarum distraxisse vereor, hec summa est. Cristus tibi totius vite testis semper assistit; Illum igitur intuere, si vis nullo labore nullis omnino vigiliis fatigari. Ad hoc enim inaccessibili et inenarrabili Trinitatis consilio effectum est ut eternus et immortalis et omnipotens Dei filius vestem nostre mortalitatis indueret, ut scilicet, quoniam inter Deum atque hominem nulla proportio erat, ipse Dei et hominum mediator utranque perfectissime in se uniens naturam, et ad Deum homines attolleret et Deum ad homines inclinaret possetque mortalis acies in Deum figi mortali carne vesti-
55 tum. Quodsi immortalitate recepta in gloriam sue divinitatis ascendentem sequi oculis et mente difficile est, et puri hominis testimonio delectaris, elige tibi aliquos de professionis tue ducibus: Iohannem Baptistam, Antonium, Macharium vel, si rigidiores hi videntur, elige Benedictum, elige ab erroribus seculi redeuntes Augustinum et Arsenium, quos multum semper placuisse tibi scio. Habes Patrum vitas; illas perlege, ut facis; ibi amicum invenies, quem testem secretis consiliis non recuses, quo conscio te ipsum vitamque modereris tuam, sine quo denique nichil agas nichil co-
56 gites. Lege Gregorii dyalogum, Augustini soliloquia et scatentes lacrimis confessionum libros, de quibus quidam ridiculi homines ridere solent; tu in eis solamen ac refrigerium non mediocre reperies. De Psalterio enim non dubito te Ieronimi consilium sequi, ut e manibus tuis nunquam excidat; de quo more meo poeticum

What shall we reply to these reproaches, brother? Is there anything unclear in this? Surely if we are willing to hear God speaking like this in our soul, we shall rise up eagerly by night—for this is what I began—to sing Christ's praises more loyally at that hour when we remember that He suffered abuse and injury on our behalf.[29] 53

But since I fear I have distracted you too long from the loftiness of your thoughts, this is the outcome. Christ is always present as witness to your whole life; so gaze on Him if you wish to be wearied by no toil or wakefulness. To this purpose in fact, it has come to pass by the inaccessible and ineffable design of the Trinity that the eternal and immortal and almighty Son of God put on the clothing of our mortality, so that, since there was no common measure between God and man, He might as mediator between God and men, combining both natures perfectly in himself, raise men up to God and bend God toward men, and mortal sight could be fixed on God clothed in the flesh. If it is difficult to fol- 55 low God with eyes and mind when He has recovered immortality and ascends to the glory of his divinity, and you take pleasure in the witness of a pure man, choose some leaders of your vocation: John the Baptist, Anthony, Macarius; or if these seem too unbending, choose Benedict or Augustine and Arsenius, turning away from the errors of our world, whom I know always greatly pleased you.[30] You have the *Lives of the Fathers:* read them through as you do and there you will find a friend whom you would not reject as witness to your secret designs, with whom as witness you would steer yourself and your life, without whom, in short, you would not do or think anything. Read the *Dialogues* of Gregory, 56 the *Soliloquies* of Augustine and his books of *Confessions* pouring fountains of tears, about which some frivolous men usually laugh; you will find no ordinary consolation and refreshment in them.[31] I do not doubt that you are following Jerome's advice about the Psalter, never to let it drop from your hands;[32] on this in my 54

nescio quid pridem scripsi, quod quoniam placere tibi animad-
57 verti, ne modo gravareris, secuturo reservatum nuntio accipies. Tu vero, ut finem faciam, vitam omnem inter contemplationem ac psalmodiam et orationem lectionemque partire. Corpori tuo, tanquam rebellaturo si possit et contumaci mancipio, nichil tribuas nisi quod negare non potes; in vinculis habe; serviliter tractari debet ut intelligat unde sit. Suspectam pacem facit hostis infidus; nosti quorum insidias in seculo pertuleris; ab his in perpetuum
58 cave; cum fidefragis inimicis non tuto reditur in gratiam. Hec inter gaude spera suspira serviens Domino in timore et exultans ei cum tremore, ac gratias agens quod tibi pennas dedit tanquam columbe ut volares et requiesceres, quibus non segniter usus es, sed elongasti fugiens ut in solitudine constitutus innumerabilia mundi mala de cetero non sentires, que ego miser sentio et quibus ob-
59 sideor ac circumspiciens contremisco. Nec ideo dum adhuc de Babilone patet exitus, effugio; noli tamen desperare, obsecro te; ora potius ut aliquando consurgam. Multum est, fateor, peccati mei pondus, sed finitum tamen, ac Eius unde auxilium expecto, infinita clementia est. Hec tibi, germane unice, non meo sed peregrino stilo ac prope monastico dictavi, te potius quam me ipsum cogitans; leges dum ex commodo licebit et si hinc perfectioni tue nichil accesserit, scito me michi saltem profuisse dum scriberem, quoniam mea me pericula meditantem status tui felix interim torsit invidia. Vale, mei memor.

*VII Kal. Octobris, ex oppido Carpensi.*

fashion I long ago composed something in verse, and since I notice it pleased you, I have reserved it for the next messengers, so you
would not be overburdened.[33] And to bring this to an end, you 57
should now divide your whole life between contemplation and psalmody and prayer and reading. Grant nothing to your body except what you cannot deny, as if to a disrespectful servant who would rebel if he could—keep it in fetters. It should be handled like a slave that it may know its origin. An untrustworthy enemy makes peace suspect; you know whose treachery you endured in the world; beware of them forever; there is no safe reconciliation
with oath-breaking enemies. Amid all this, rejoice, hope, sigh, 58
serving God in your fear and exulting for him with trembling, and giving thanks that he gave you "wings like a dove to fly and take rest."[34] You have not used them slackly but extended them in flight, so that set up in solitude you might not feel the countless evils of the world, which I, poor wretch, feel, and by which I am
beset and tremble as I look around me. Nor am I fleeing Babylon 59
because the way out is still open;[35] do not despair I beg you; rather pray that I may rise at some future time. The weight of my sin is great, I admit, but it is finite and the mercy of Him from Whom I expect aid is infinite. I have dictated this for you, my only brother, not in my style but in an alien, almost monastic style, thinking of you rather than myself; you will read it while you may at your convenience and if nothing is added from it to your perfection, know that I at least did myself good as I wrote it, since a happy envy of your blessed condition tormented me as I meditated upon my own dangers. Farewell, keep me in your heart.

*September 25, from the town of Carpi.*

## : 3 :

## *Ad amicum, in fide catholica hesitantem.*

1 Mitto alia de quibus colloqui dabitur, ut spero; unum periculi maioris et quod moram respuit, scribam. Suspitiones tuas de summa salutis egre fero, quod sepe tibi presens dixi, sed ut video, non tam sepe quam debui et quantum duro pectori necessarium
2 erat ut frangeretur. Quid vero nunc aliud rear inter ambages rerum et fallacias dyaboli animum cogitantis involvere, nisi id quod negari non potest, non esse dignum genus humanum cui hec celitus fierent que facta credidimus, eo quod hic fur, ille periurus, ille sit adulter et talibus plena sit omnis terra quales induxisse legimus Creatorem ut diceret: Penitet me fecisse hominem? Quomodo
3 ergo talia Tantus tam indignis? Hec forte nunc tecum dicis. Animadvertere autem oportet, non hec ad incredulitatem sed ad humilitatem et gratitudinem debere conferre; pauci benificiis Dei digni, fateor, imo nullus omnino, nisi quem Ille dignum fecerit: tanto maior illa benignitas, liberalitas clarior insigniorque clementia.

4 Illud forte etiam tuas suspitiones exaggerat, quod ante Cristi adventum tot vel ingenio vel moralibus virtutibus excellentes viros fuisse nemo dubitat; nobis autem hodie funditus virtutes et ingenium deesse utinam minus evidens foret! nutat hic animus et quod cur fieret non videt, factum esse non credit. Sed et hoc eodem spectat et tale est quod devotionem augere atque dilectionem

## : 3 :

## *To a friend wavering about the Catholic faith.*

I leave aside other topics which I hope we will have a chance to 1
discuss. I shall write about one matter, involving a greater peril, which brooks no delay. I am distressed by your doubts about our ultimate salvation, as I have often said to you in person, but, as I see, not as often as I should nor as much as was needed to break a
hard heart. What else would I think between the confusions of life 2
and the trickery of the Devil, always contriving ways to entangle one's mind, except a fact that cannot be denied, that the human race does not deserve those benefits which we believe have been conferred on them by the heavens, given that one man is a thief, another a perjurer, another an adulterer, and the whole earth is full of such fellows as led the Creator (so we read) to say: "I wish I had never created man"?[1] So how is it that so great a Being does such
things for such unworthy men? Perhaps you are saying this to 3
yourself now. Now one should note that these divine actions should not contribute to incredulity but to humility and gratitude. Few men, I admit, or rather no man at all, is worthy of God's kindnesses except one whom He has made worthy. So much the greater, then, is his kindness, so much more glorious his generosity, and more conspicuous his pity.

Perhaps this fact increases your uncertainties: that no one 4
doubts there were so many men excelling either in intellect or in moral virtues before the coming of Christ, whereas I only wish it were less obvious that virtues and intellect are completely lacking in us today! At this the mind wavers, and since it does not see why this should have happened, does not believe it has happened. But this too tends in the same direction and is such that it should have increased our devotion and produced love, not incredulity, so that

non incredulitatem parere debuisset, ut quo indigniores nos agnos-
cimus, eo maiorem Illius erga nos munificentiam agnoscamus et
5 miremur, sed non usqueadeo miremur ut negemus. Quis enim,
nisi pessimus, a domino suo valde sine meritis honestatus, aut domino rebellat aut accepti benificii obliviscitur, et non potius dicit:
'gratis me amasti, indignum melioribus pretulisti, habeo gratiam,
agnosco pium dominum, agnosco fortunam optimam quam tu
michi fecisti, virtuosorum premia sine virtute percipio, felix ultro
factus sum, hoc ipsum non meo labore sed tua benivolentia quesi-
6 tum, non michi non alteri sed tibi uni debeo'? Quid autem in
omni doctrina que de Cristo traditur ab his qui Veritatem ipsam,
qui Cristus est, diligunt, quid, inquam, vel impossibile Deo est vel
nobis incredibile nisi quod tanta Dei humilitas, tanta misericordia
et erga hominem pietas ostenditur, ut eam vix capere possit mens
humana? et per omnia verum est quod ait Augustinus in Psalmo
CXLVII°: quoniam 'etsi certa sunt, que multum leta sunt vix cre-
7 duntur.' Habes ergo, mortalis homuncio, unde incredulitate depo-
sita gratiarum suscipias actionem; felicior factus es quam credere
potuisses. Crede quod factum est. 'Ipsa Dei sapientia, unicus
consubstantialis et coeternus Patri Filius' ad te liberandum venit;
poterat et de maiestatis sue solio iubere et necesse erat areri in celo
et in terra; efficacius agere voluit et humilius; 'totum hominem
suscipere dignatus est' ut ait Augustinus, 'et Verbum caro factum
8 est et habitavit in nobis.' Et sequitur ratio: 'Ita enim' inquit, 'demon-
stravit carnalibus et non valentibus intueri mente veritatem corpo-
reisque sensibus deditis, quam excelsum locum inter creaturas habeat humana natura, quod non solum visibiliter — nam id poterat

the more we recognize and marvel at our unworthiness, the more
we should recognize and marvel at his greater lavishness, but not
marvel to the extent of denying it. Indeed who, except the worst of 5
men, having been greatly honored by his Lord without deserving
it, either revolts from his Lord or forgets the kindness received,
and doesn't say instead: "You have loved me without reward and
preferred me, unworthy as I am, to better men; I am thankful and
acknowledge You as a pious Lord, I acknowledge the great fortune
that You have created for me; I am receiving the rewards of virtuous men without possessing virtue, and have been spontaneously
blessed; this itself has been obtained not by my toil but by your
kindness; I owe it not to myself or another but to You alone"?
Now what is there in all the doctrine transmitted about Christ by 6
those who love the truth itself, that is Christ—what, I ask, is either impossible for God or incredible for us except that such great
humility on God's part, such mercy and such piety is shown toward men that the human mind can barely conceive it? And what
Augustine says in his commentary on *Psalm* 147 is true in all respects, since "even if they are assured, things of great joy are
scarcely believed."[2] So you have reason, mortal creature, to discard 7
your incredulity and perform the act of thanks; you have been
made happier than you could have believed. Believe what has been
done. "The very wisdom of God, the one Son consubstantial and
coeternal with the Father,"[3] has come to set you free; He could
have ordered it from the throne of his majesty and it would inevitably have been obeyed on heaven and earth. But He wanted to act
more powerfully and more humbly and so "He deigned to take on
the whole nature of man," as Augustine says, "and the Word was
made flesh and dwelt among us."[4] And the reason follows: "For in 8
this way," he says, "He showed to fleshly creatures, abandoned to
bodily senses, without the strength to understand the truth with
their mind, how lofty a place human nature has among creation,
because He not only appeared in our sight, which would also have

et in aliquo ethereo corpore ad nostri aspectus tolerantiam tempe-
rato — sed etiam hominibus in vero homine apparuit.' Cuius quoque dicti ratio subsequitur: 'Ipsa enim' ait, 'natura suscipienda erat
que liberanda.' Hactenus Augustinus.

9 Sic ergo, amice, cum te periclitantem Deus cerneret, perire non
est passus, cumque prostratum verbo posset, manu maluit attollere, et qui ardenter amantium mos, se se in terram inclinavit ubi
tu iacebas atque ulnis amplexus sustulit et quo gravissime preme-
baris pondus subiit transtulitque peccatum tuum. Impletum est
illud daviticum: 'Quantum distat ortus ab occidente, longe fecit a
10 nobis iniquitates nostras.' Poterat, ut dixi, verbo facere, sanguine
suo fecit, et, ut ait quidam,

hoc tecum percussum est sanguine fedus;

noli tu illud frangere; Ipse enim servantissimus promissorum est;
si potuisse Illum te liberare certus es, voluisse quid dubitas? quid
credere hesitas quod et necessarium tibi est et facile largienti et sua
dignissimum maiestate? quid times quod valde desideras in animum admittere, nisi quia, ut dixi, et magnum gaudium mens an-
11 gusta non recipit et te tanto munere sentis indignum? Gaude
iam toto animo: habes unde; tantaque gaudendi materia est ut
eam vix apprehendas. Hinc nempe magis consolari, non minus
credere convenit. Tu indignus Ille benignus, tu peccator Ille misericors; agnosce benificium, amplectere gratiam, pelle suspitiones.
Longo sine fine supplicio dignus eras: gloria tibi, nisi renuis, eterna
proponitur; severum iudicem metuebas, pium patrem invenisti:
12 'Quomodo miseretur pater filiorum, misertus est Dominus timen-

been possible in the form of some heavenly body adapted to being sustained by our gaze, but even appeared to men as a true man." And the reason follows for this claim also: "He needed to assume the same nature that He needed to save." This is Augustine's comment.

So dear friend, when God saw you at risk, He did not allow 9
you to be ruined, and although He could have raised you from your prostration by a word, He preferred to raise you by his hand, and in the fashion of men passionately loving, He stooped down to earth where you lay and embracing you in his arms lifted you and took on the burden that pressed you down most heavily and took on your sin. That saying of David was fulfilled: "As far as the sunrise is distant from the sunset, so far away did He send our
offenses."[5] As I said, He could have done this by a word, but He 10
did it with his blood, and as someone says:

This treaty with you is struck with my blood.[6]

So do not break it; for God himself is most observant of his promises and if you are sure that He could have freed you, why do you doubt that He wished to do so? Why do you hesitate to believe what is both necessary for you and easy for Him in his generosity and is most worthy of his majesty? Why do you fear to admit what you passionately long for in your spirit, unless because, as I said, a narrow mind cannot hold great joy, and you feel yourself unworthy of so great a gift? Rejoice now with all your spirit; 11
you have reason to, and the matter for rejoicing is so great that you can scarcely comprehend it. For this reason it is right to be more consoled, not to believe less firmly. You are unworthy but He is kind, you are a sinner but He is merciful; acknowledge his kindness, welcome his grace, drive away suspicions. You deserved a long punishment without end; but eternal glory is offered to you unless you demur. You feared a severe judge, but found a pious
father. "As a father shows mercy to his sons, the Lord has shown 12

tibus se,' non quia id nostra peccata mererentur, sed quia 'Ipse co-
gnovit figmentum nostrum *et* recordatus est quoniam pulvis sumus'; non ergo tam peccatis nostris irascitur quam fragilitati
13 compatitur et indigentibus opem fert. Tanta res est ut non facile
credenda videatur, pro malo bonum, pro offensa gratiam referri ab
Eo presertim quem offendisse tam indignum sit et qui se tam facile possit ulcisci; credenda tamen hauddubie est, et agnoscenda
misericordia Redemptoris, quoniam, ut in eo libro quem profun-
dissime *De vera religione* fundatum edidit, pater ait Augustinus,
14 'non iam illa hominis sacrosancta susceptio et Virginis partus et
mors Filii Dei pro nobis et resurrectio a mortuis et in celum ascen-
sio et consessus ad dexteram Patris et peccatorum abolitio et iudicii dies et corporum resuscitatio, cognita eternitate Trinitatis et
mutabilitate creature, creduntur tantum et non etiam iudicantur
ad summi Dei misericordiam, quam generi humano exhibet, pertinere.'

15 Pro quibus omnibus, amice, admiratio nobis ingens, fateor,
stuporque salubris et pavor devotus amplectendus atque tenendus
est, quoniam vere 'mirabilis in altis Dominus,' vere 'magnus et terribilis super omnes qui in circuitu eius sunt,' vere 'terribilis in consiliis super filios hominum'; idem tamen 'suavis et mitis et multe
misericordie omnibus invocantibus eum'; idem 'miserator et misericors Dominus, longanimis et multum misericors' ac 'patiens et
multe misericordie et verax'; idem 'dulcis et rectus Dominus *et qui*
legem *dat* delinquentibus in via,' hanc legem scilicet ut ad eum re-
16 deant et salventur. Quid multa? profecto ut nemo terribilior, sic
nemo misericordior, nemo tranquillior; multos laborare cogit ne
lasciviant, periclitari aliquos sinit ut corrigat, neminem vult perire

mercy to those fearing him,"[7] not because our sins deserved it, but
because "He himself has recognized our composition and has recalled that we are dust." So He is not as angered with our sins as
He is sympathetic toward our frailty and brings help to us in our
need. This fact is so great that it does not seem easy to believe, 13
that good should be returned for evil and grace for an offense, especially by Him Whom it is so outrageous to have offended and
Who could so easily take his revenge; but it must undoubtedly be
believed and the mercy of the Redeemer must be acknowledged, as
Father Augustine declared in the book *On True Religion*, which he
established on such deep foundations: "That holy incarnation and 14
the birth pangs of the Virgin and the death of the Son of God for
our sake and his resurrection from the dead and ascension into
heaven and sitting at the right hand of God the Father and the
abolition of sins and the day of judgment and resurrection of the
body recognized by the eternal nature of the Trinity and mutabil-
ity of creation—all these are not simply believed, but judged to be
objects of the highest Mercy of God which He extends to the human race."[8]

For all these reasons, my friend, we must embrace and hold fast 15
to immense wonder, I admit, and salutary amazement and devout
awe since God is truly "marvelous in the heights,"[9] truly "great and
terrible beyond all who are in his presence," truly "terrible in the
counsels about the sons of men"; yet the Same is "gentle and mild
and of great mercy toward all who call upon Him"; He is "our
Lord, merciful and showing mercy, patient and most merciful" and
"patient and showing much mercy and truthful," and He is "a
sweet and upright Lord who gives the law to those who deviate
from the path," that is, the law that they should return to Him
and be saved. In short, just as no one, surely, is more terrible, so 16
no one is more merciful, no one more calm; He makes many men
toil so that they do not indulge in mischief, and allows others to
be at risk so as to correct them; He wants no one to be lost and

atque omnia facit ne pereamus. Itaque pellenda procul desperatio, abicienda durities, exuenda impietas, incredulitas relinquenda; quod enim nemo sanus ignorat, nichil impossibile imo nec difficile aliquid est Deo; quodque nemo pius diffidit, nichil Illi arduum
17 videtur quod ad salutem sue pertineat creature. Perversi ingenii est suspicari aliud, et misereri ac peccata diluere vel nolle Deum vel non posse; hinc enim, non de fonte alio, desperatio nasci solet; quorum altero 'bonus,' altero negatur 'omnipotens,' utraque blasphemia est in Spiritum Sanctum, que neque in hoc neque in futuro seculo dimittitur, dum summe potenti summeque bono vel
18 impotentia ulla vel invidia nostre salutis obicitur. In quod malum incidisse creditur Cain ubi ait: 'Maior est iniquitas mea quam ut veniam merear,' neque enim maior esse poterat creature miseria quam misericordia creatoris. In hoc ipsum Iudas infelix incidit quando proiectis argenteis in templo, abiens laqueo se suspendit; qui etsi multo amplius peccasset quam Cain, desperatio tamen illi etiam sola obstitit ne misericordiam inveniret, quam si a Cristo
19 petiisset, invenisset, ut Ambrosio placet. Nunc neque misericordiam petiit et apud illos se peccasse confessus est, qui de peccato eius gaudebant, de supplicio non curabant; postremo magis, ut Ieronimo videtur, desperatione Cristum lesit quam proditione: memorandum valde.

20 Quid ergo potest Deus? omne quod vult; vult autem omne quod nobis salutiferum novit: hoc firma fide constantique fidutia tenendum est. Cessent inanes et pavide coniecture, et religiose aures susurris demonum obstruantur; magnum fuerit propter nos Deum suo quodam mirabili more nasci; maius, inter necessitates miseriasque nostras vivere; maximum, plusquam nostro comuni,

does everything so that we may not be lost. So we must drive despair far away, cast away our hardness of heart, shed our impiety,
abandon our incredulity: as no sane man is unaware, nothing is
impossible, nor even difficult for God: and as no pious man may
doubt, nothing seems hard to Him that concerns the salvation of
his creation. It is the mark of a perverse nature to suspect anything 17
else, that God either is unwilling to show mercy and wash away
our sins, or unable. For despair is usually born of these errors, not
some other source: one of which denies God is good, the other
that he is all-powerful. Each statement is blasphemy against the
Holy Spirit, which is not allowed in either this or any other age, as
long as no impotence or envy of our salvation is made a reproach
against Him Who is supremely powerful and supremely good.
Cain is thought to have slipped into this evil when he said: "My 18
wickedness is too great for me to earn pardon,"[10] since the wretchedness of creation could not be greater than the mercy of the
Creator. The unhappy Judas fell into this very error when he cast
away the pieces of silver in the temple and went away and hanged
himself with a noose.[11] And even if he had sinned far worse than
Cain, only his despair blocked him from finding mercy: if he had
sought it from Christ he would have found it, as Ambrose believes.[12] Instead, he did not seek mercy and he confessed that he 19
had sinned to men who rejoiced in his sin and were indifferent to
his punishment; finally, as Jerome sees it, he harmed Christ more
from despair than by his treachery:[13] it is most important to recall
this.

What then can God do? Whatever he wishes; and he wishes 20
everything that He knows to pertain to our salvation; this must be
kept in mind with firm faith and unyielding confidence. Let there
be an end to empty and timorous conjectures, and may devout
ears be blocked against the whispering of demons. It will be a
great marvel that God was born in his own wondrous fashion for
our sake, greater that He lived amid our need and misery, greatest

suo quodam ad nos misericordi, in se autem miserabili more mori.
21 Mira hec et ineffabilia quedam divini amoris signa, quis neget? sed an ideo nos ingratos faciet benificii magnitudo? Absit a mentibus piis hic furor! Sentiamus nos benificiis tantis indignos, et nos ad persolvendas meritas grates verbo etiam longe impares agnoscamus; victam fragilitatem nostram immensa Dei clementia fateamur; animo tamen quantum possumus grati simus et obsequentes et creduli et fideles, neque quia res magna, nos indigni, ideo nobis Illum consulere nequivisse vel noluisse propter inaccessibilem sue potentie ac pietatis excellentiam, desperemus. Vale.

*IV Kal. Aprilis.*

## : 4 :

## *Ad Gerardum cartusiensem monachum, quenam vera philosophia, quenam vera lex, quis ambarum optimus magister.*

1 Religiosi cuiusdam viri manibus religiosior michi libellus tuus allatus est. Aperui lecturus eum in crastinum; erat enim pars diei ultima. Ipse michi blanditus est, ut ait Seneca; itaque non ante deposui quam totum in silentio perlegissem; ita cena corporis in noctem dilata, splendide interim cenatus animus cibis suis suavi-
2 terque refectus est. Delectatus sum, germane unice, plusquam dici potest, intelligens non modo propositi sancti constantiam speratam semper ex te aut contemptum rerum fugacium ab olim michi

of all that He died in a way beyond our common death, by his own death merciful toward us, but in his own case most wretched. Who would deny that these are marvelous and inexpressible signs 21
of divine love? But will the greatness of this benevolence make us ungrateful? Keep this madness far from pious minds! Let us feel that we are unworthy of such great kindnesses, and acknowledge that we are by far too weak to pay due thanks even in speech; let us admit that our frailty is overwhelmed by God's immense compassion; yet let us be as grateful in heart as we can be and obedient and trusting and faithful. Just because the marvel is great and we are unworthy, we should not believe in our despair that He was unable or unwilling to take thought for us because of the unapproachable excellence of his power and piety. Farewell.

*March 29.*

## : 4 :

*To Gherardo the Carthusian monk: what is the true philosophy and what the true law, and who is the best instructor in them both.*

I received from the hands of a man of religion your pamphlet, 1
even more concerned with religion. I opened it, intending to read it the next day, since it was already the last part of daylight. But it charmed me personally, as Seneca says, and so I did not put it down before I had read the whole text in silence;[1] thus postponing the bodily dinner until nightfall, my spirit dined splendidly on its own nourishment, enjoying sweet refreshment. I was delighted, 2
my dear and only brother, more than can be expressed, recognizing not only the constancy of your holy purpose, always expected from you, or your contempt of fleeting goods, long since very well

notissimum, sed insperatam et inopinam hanc copiam literarum, quarum expers religionem illam Deo gratissimam ac pene nudus
3 intrasti. Quamvis enim in literis non sit salus, est tamen fuitque iam multis ad salutem via; signum preterea excellentis et facile in altum evasuri animi, posse rem tantam sine preceptore percipere; licet, ut verum fatear, non tu hec sine preceptore perceperis, sed cum habueris preceptorem, qui non tantum colere possit ingenium sed largiri, sub quo te brevi tempore profecisse adeo non miror;
4 cum sepe dicto citius summam Ille virtutem ac sapientiam multis infuderit, multos ex imis tenebris ad supremam lucem nutu miserante subvexerit, te quoque nunc, frater, aspiciendo et miserando doctum ex indocto et de naufrago salvum fecit. Illi laudes et gratias non tibi, nequid forte me tibi hodie adulatum putes; quod si nunquam feci, non est huius etatis ut incipiam.

5 Solebant equidem prisci viri studiorum causa cecropias Athenas petere, presertim antequam ut militie atque imperii sic literarum quoque Roma fons esset; nostra secula Parisius aut Bononiam petunt, quam nos—meministi enim—prima etate petivimus, frustra quidem, quod sepe amicorum cupiditas questa est, nos autem
6 semper non in ultima divinorum munerum parte posuimus. Ita peregrinationes sumptuosas atque difficiles avide subit humana durities nullumque respuit laborem, quo ventose pars una philosophie aut legum insidiosa loquacitas queratur ac singulis hauriendis exhauriatur etas tota, nulla parte temporis curis melioribus depu-
7 tata. Tu veram philosophiam veramque legem vixdum pleno decennio didicisti; nolo enim opineris hanc esse philosophiam quam in una urbe mille nunc homines profitentur; non adeo vulgare bonum est ut multi credunt. Hec quam prostitutam vulgo cernimus,

known to me, but also the sudden unexpected abundance of literary culture lacking and almost naked of which you entered upon
your religious life, a life most welcome to God. Although salvation 3
does not come from literature, it has still been the path to salvation for many; and it was moreover a sign that your excellent spirit was easily going to rise to the heights that you could grasp so much without an instructor—although, to admit the truth, you did not grasp literary knowledge without an instructor, but, since you were given an instructor who could not only develop understanding but bestow it, I am not surprised that under him you
quickly achieved progress. Since God often spreads with amazing 4
speed supreme virtue and wisdom to many, and has brought many from the deepest darkness into supreme light by His merciful approval, so, dear brother, by gazing on you too and showing mercy He made you learned from your ignorance and saved you from shipwreck. So I give praise and thanks to Him, and not to you, for fear you should think I am flattering you today: if I have never done this, it does not fit my age to start now.

The ancients used to make for Cecropian[2] Athens for the sake 5
of their studies, especially before Rome became the source of culture as it was of warfare and empire; our generation makes for Paris or Bologna, as we (you remember it) made for this last university in our first youth—in vain, as the greed of our friends often complained, while we did not always put [wealth] among the
last of divine gifts.[3] So human hardihood eagerly enters on ex- 6
travagant and difficult travels and rejects no toil by which one part alone of windy philosophy or the deceitful loquacity of the laws is won, and our whole youth is drained in imbibing matters of detail,
delegating no part of its time to superior concerns. But you have 7
learned true philosophy and true law after barely completing the tenth year. I don't want you to think this is the kind of philosophy that a thousand persons now claim to practice in a single city. It is not such a common asset as many men believe. What is the pur-

quid intendit nisi solicite atque anxie circa questiunculas et verba versari, quorum ignorantia sepe non minus tuta, forte etiam tutior
8 quam scientia est? Ita penitus oblivioni veritas datur, negliguntur mores boni, res ipse spernuntur in quibus philosophia illa nobilis est que neminem fallit, inanibus tantum verbis intenditur; quod ita esse philosophorum vita testatur, nichil implens omnium que
9 predicat. 'Quotus enim quisque philosophorum invenitur' ut in Tusculano suo Tullius ait, 'qui sit ita moratus, ita vita et moribus institutus ut ratio postulat, qui disciplinam suam non ostentationem scientie sed legem vite putet, qui obtemperet ipse sibi et decretis suis pareat? Videre licet alios tanta levitate et iactatione ut eis fuerit non didicisse melius; alios pecunie cupidos, glorie nonnullos, multos libidinum servos, ut cum eorum vita mirabiliter
10 pugnet oratio, quod quidem michi videtur esse turpissimum. Ut enim si grammaticum se professus quispiam barbare loquatur, aut si absurde canat is qui se musicum velit haberi, hoc turpior sit quod in eo ipso peccet cuius profitetur scientiam, sic philosophus in vite ratione peccans hoc turpior est quod in officio cuius magister esse vult, labitur artemque vite professus delinquit in vita.' In quibus Tullii verbis illud inter multa notabile, quod philosophiam non verborum artem dicit esse sed vite.

11 Vis, amantissime frater, nosse, si forte non nosti, quenam philosophia vera sit, ut intelligens quantum in ea brevi tempore profeceris, alacrior pergas ad reliqua? vis omnibus qui falso philosophie nomine tumescunt negatas aures michi prebere meque unum hic

pose of this activity we see commonly prostituted if not to bother
anxiously and fretfully about petty problems and wording? Yet ignorance of such things is often no less safe, perhaps even safer
than knowledge. So truth is often utterly consigned to forgetful- 8
ness; we neglect good behavior and spurn the very matters which
ennoble that philosophy which deceives no man; their aim is only
empty language, as the life of philosophers shows to be the case, as
it practices nothing of what it preaches. "How rarely do we find 9
the man among philosophers," as Cicero says in his *Tusculan Disputations*, "who has such morals and is so trained in life and moral
behavior as reason demands, who thinks his training not a display
of learning but a law for living, who heeds himself and obeys his
principles? We may see that some people have such frivolity and
boastfulness that it would have been better for them not to have
learned anything; others are greedy for money, quite a few eager
for glory, many slaves of their lusts, so that their talk is astonish-
ingly in conflict with their lives, which certainly seems to me most
disgraceful. For just as if someone claiming to be a grammarian 10
speaks barbarously, or a man sings ridiculously who wants to be
thought a musician, this would be all the more disgraceful because
the man is blundering in the very expertise which he claims to
know; just so a philosopher blundering in his way of life is all the
more disgraceful because he slips up in the activity which he
wishes to teach, and having claimed to practice the art of living,
fails in his life."[4] And among these many comments of Cicero the
noteworthy thing is that he calls philosophy not the art of speech
but the art of life.

Dear loving brother, do you want to know, if by chance you 11
don't already know, what is the true philosophy, so that once you
realize how far you have advanced in it in a short time, you may
move on more keenly to what remains? Do you want to offer me
your ears which you have refused to all those puffed up with pride
in the name of false philosophy, and listen to me alone now, or

audire, imo non me sed philosophorum principem Platonem et
Cristi philosophum Augustinum libro superne civitatis VIII?
12 'Nunc' inquit,

> satis sit commemorare Platonem determinasse finem boni
> esse secundum virtutem vivere, idque ei soli evenire posse
> qui notitiam Dei habet et imitationem, nec esse aliam ob
> causam beatum. Ideoque non dubitat hoc esse philosophari,
> amare Deum, cuius natura sit incorporalis; unde utique col-
> ligitur tunc fore beatum studiosum sapientie, id enim est
> 13 philosophum, cum frui Deo ceperit. Quamvis enim non con-
> tinuo beatus sit qui eo fruitur quod amat — multi enim
> amando ea que amanda non sunt, miseri sunt et miseriores
> cum fruuntur — nemo tamen beatus est qui eo quod amat
> 14 non fruitur. Nam et ipsi qui res non amandas amant, non se
> beatos putant amando sed fruendo; quisquis ergo fruitur eo
> quod amat verumque et summum bonum amat, quis eum
> beatum nisi miserrimus negat? Ipsum autem verum et sum-
> mum bonum Plato dicit Deum, unde vult esse philosophum
> amatorem Dei, ut quoniam philosophia ad beatam vitam
> tendit, fruens Deo sit beatus qui Deum amaverit.

15 Hec apud Augustinum sententia Platonis ad verbum relata est, qui
unus ex omni philosophorum cetu propinquior accessit ad veram
fidem, quem in hoc ut in aliis multis complexus Augustinus, eodem libro: philosophie 'ipsum nomen' inquit, 'si latine interprete-
mur, amorem sapientie profitetur: porro si sapientia Deus est, per
quem facta sunt omnia, sicut divina autoritas veritasque monstra-
16 vit, verus philosophus est amator Dei.' Quibus illud incuntanter

rather not to me but to Plato, chief of philosophers, and Augustine, philosopher of Christ in Book 8 of his work on the Heavenly City? "Now," he says, 12

> let it be enough to recall that Plato defined the aim of the good as living according to virtue, which could only happen to the man who possessed the knowledge and power to imitate God, and he was blessed for no other reason. So he does not doubt that philosophizing is loving God, whose nature is not bodily; from this it is inferred that the devotee of wisdom, that is the philosopher, will be blessed when he begins
> to enjoy God. Yet the man who enjoys what he loves is 13
> not immediately blessed—since many are wretched in loving what should not be loved, and all the more wretched when they enjoy it—yet no man is blessed who does not enjoy
> what he loves. For the men who love what should not be 14
> loved do not think themselves blessed in loving but in enjoying it; so who except the most deluded wretch would deny that the man is blessed who enjoys what he loves and loves the one, true, highest good? Now Plato says the true and highest good is God and so he wants the philosopher to be the lover of God, so that since philosophy aims for the blessed life, whoever will have loved God may enjoy God and be blessed.[5]

This is the opinion of Plato in Augustine, reproduced word for 15
word: he who alone of the entire crowd of philosophers came closest to true faith, whom Augustine has embraced in this as in many other beliefs. He says in the same book: "If we translate the name of philosophy in Latin, it proclaims 'love of wisdom'; furthermore, if it is the wisdom of God by whom all things were made, as divine authority and truth has demonstrated, the true philosopher is
the lover of God."[6] I would unhesitatingly add to these words that 16

addiderim, apud nos qui quotidie fatemur Cristum Deum nostrum, consequenter veraciterque concludi verum philosophum nonnisi verum esse cristianum. Quid vero michi tribuo? nichil est additum a me preter Cristi nomen; quid enim aliud sentiebat Augustinus ipse ubi ait:

17 Si sapientia Deus est per quem facta sunt omnia, hic enim proculdubio est Cristus; etsi enim unaqueque persona Trinitatis Deus sit, quod fateri, ut ait Athanasius, cristiana veritate compellimur, atque ita sit summa potentia summa sapientia summa bonitas, proprie tamen Cristus sapientia Patris est per quem omnia facta sunt, quod et ex evangelio Ioannis et ex simbolo fidelis assidue cantat Ecclesia?

18 Et Augustinus idem *Vere religionis* libro de operibus Trinitatis agens: 'Non aliam' inquit, 'partem totius creature fecisse intelligatur Pater, aliam Filius, aliam Spiritus Sanctus, sed simul omnia et unamquanque creaturam Patrem fecisse per Filium in dono Spiritus Sancti.' Hoc est quod idem et sepe alias et in eiusdem libri fine repetiit: 'Unum Deum, a quo sumus, per quem sumus, in quo sumus'; et rursus: 'Unum Deum, a quo omnia, per quem omnia,
19 in quo omnia.' Idem XI *De civitate Dei:*

> Cum in unaquaque creatura, inquit, requiritur quis eam fecerit, per quid fecerit, quare fecerit, respondeatur: Deus, per Verbum, quia bona est, ut cum altitudine mystica nobis ipsa Trinitas intimetur, hoc est Pater et Filius et Spiritus Sanctus;

et post pauca:

among us who daily confess Christ to be our God the true conclusion must follow that the true philosopher cannot be anything but a true Christian. But what am I crediting to myself? I have added nothing except the name of Christ; since what else did Augustine believe when he added:[7]

> If Wisdom is God by whom all things were made, this God 17
> is undoubtedly Christ; for even if each and every person of the Trinity is God, which, as Athanasius says, we are compelled in Christian truth to confess,[8] and so is the highest power, the highest wisdom, the highest goodness, nevertheless Christ is really the Wisdom of the Father by whom all things were made, as we learn from the Gospel of John[9] and as the Church faithfully proclaims according to its Creed?

Again in the book *On True Religion,* discussing the works of the 18
Trinity, he says: "Let the Father not be understood to have made one part of all creation and Christ another, and the Holy Spirit yet another, but the Father made everything together and every individual creature through his Son by the gift of the Holy Spirit."[10] This is what Augustine also said often elsewhere and repeated at the end of the same book: "One God from whom we exist, through whom we exist, in whom we exist."[11] And again: "One
God from whom, by whom, and in whom all things are." And 19
Augustine says the same in the eleventh book of *The City of God:*

> When the question is asked about every single creature who was its creator, by what means he created it and why He created it, let our answer be: God, through the Word, because this creation is good, so that the Trinity may be made known to us with a mystic loftiness, that is the Father and Son and Holy Spirit;[12]

then a little later he says:

> Credimus, inquit, et tenemus et fideliter predicamus quod Pater genuerit Verbum, hoc est sapientiam, per quam facta sunt omnia, unigenitum Filium, vivus vivum, eternus coeternum, summe bonus equaliter bonum.

20 Non expedit que sequuntur inserere, cum omnis scriptura de Cristo loquens omnia per ipsum facta confirmet. Si hec igitur sapientia est Deus idemque Cristus Dei Filius, philosophia autem sapientie amor est, ex ipsis etiam Augustini verbis sine dubietate concluditur verum philosophum nisi Dei amatorem verumque
21 cristicolam esse non posse. Hanc tu ergo philosophiam, germane optime, non Athenis aut Rome, non Parisius, sed devoto in monte ac religioso in nemore feliciter apprehendisti, multo illis verior securiorque philosophus, qui, ut Augustinus idem ait, 'siquando ad disputationem venitur, platonico nomine ora crepantia quam pec-
22 tus vero plenum magis habere gestiunt.' Quod si de Platonicis etiam verum est, qui ex omni philosophorum acie preferuntur a nostris, quanto de illis est verius de quibus Apostolus loquens ait: '*Cavete* nequis vos decipiat per philosophiam et inanem *seductionem* secundum elementa mundi,' qui scilicet alias atque alias, quas nunc enumerare non oportet, innumerabiles sectas ex infinitis erroribus extruxerunt!

23 Quid nunc de legibus me dicturum putas? Multos legum inventores diversis in gentibus fuisse novimus; sed ut obscuriora preteream, clari sunt legibus inventis apud Argos Phoroneus, apud Lacedemonios Lycurgus, apud Athenienses Solon, cuius leges ad Romanos inde transvecte multum ornatus atque amplitudinis ac-
24 ceperunt. Hinc et lex duodecim tabularum legesque alie et senatusconsulta et plebiscita et honorarium ius pretorum, postremo

> We believe and hold firm and faithfully declare that the Father begat the Word, that is Wisdom, through which all things were made, his only begotten Son: the living God begat a living God, the eternal God one coeternal with Him, one supremely good begetting one equally good.

It is not helpful to include what follows here, since Scripture 20
in speaking of Christ confirms that everything has been made through Him. So if this wisdom is God and also Christ, the Son of God, and furthermore philosophy is love of wisdom, it can be concluded without doubt from Augustine's words too that there cannot be a true philosopher except he be a lover of God and a
true worshipper of Christ. This is the philosophy which you, dear 21
brother, learned not at Athens, Rome, or Paris but most happily took possession of on the devout hillside and religious woodland, becoming a much truer and more sure philosopher than they who, as Augustine says, "if ever it comes to a disputation, are more keen to have their mouths uttering the name of Plato than to have a
heart full of truth."[13] And if this is true of Platonists, who are 22
preferred from all the ranks of philosophers by our own teachers, how much more true is it of those about whom the Apostle speaks: "Beware that anyone deceive you through philosophy and a hollow seduction according to the elements of the world."[14] Surely these men have constructed other sects and yet others whom we should not list, making countless sects out of their unending errors!

Now what do you think I am going to say about the laws? We 23
know that there were many legislators among different peoples, but to pass over the more obscure, Phoroneus was distinguished in Argos for his invention of laws, Lycurgus among the Spartans and in Athens Solon, whose laws were imported among the Romans
and received much embellishment and elaboration.[15] This was the 24
source of the law of the Twelve Tables and other laws and the

dictatorum ac principum edicta; he autem leges omnes et sique
alie sunt, sicut humanitus adinvente sic humanitus immutate, pro
varietate temporum mutatis affectibus et voluntatibus hominum in
quibus ille fundate erant; comune est enim ut una lex aliam corri-
25 gat. Vis eternam legem esse? eternum illi subicias fundamentum.
Lex populo israelitico per Moysen Deo dictante data est; illa quidem stabilior; sed nunquid eterna? certe per Moysen lex, per Iesum Cristum gratia implens legem; Ille non evacuans sed im-
plendo, non quidem legem ipsam at multa legis sacramenta finivit;
26 unde in Psalmo CXLIII Augustinus:

> Meministi, inquit, quanta in veteri lege et legamus et non observemus, sed tamen aliqua significatione premissa et posita intelligamus, non ut abiciamus legem Dei, sed ut sacramenta promittentia, impleta promissione, non celebremus; quod enim promittebant venit; gratia enim Novi Testamenti in Lege velabatur, in Evangelio revelatur; velum removimus, quod velabatur agnovimus; agnovimus autem in gratia Domini nostri Iesu Cristi, capitis et salvatoris nostri, qui pro nobis crucifixus est, quo crucifixo etiam velum templi conscissum est.

27 Quod Augustini testimonium precipue propter hoc ultimum inserui, ut liquido animadvertas scissuram veli, quam in Evangelio legimus, ingentis cuiusdam ineffabilisque mysterii fuisse, signantem velo veteri, quo usque in illud diem legis archana tegebantur, Cristi passione conscisso, revelata omnia populo humili ac novo, que

decrees of the senate and the laws of the people, and the law code
of the praetors and finally the edicts of dictators and emperors;[16]
all these laws and any others were changed, just as they had been
discovered, by human decision, when the attitudes and wills of
men changed with the change of times after the laws were laid
down; for it is common practice that one law corrects another. Do 25
you want a law to be eternal? Then give it an eternal foundation. The law was given to the Israelites by Moses at God's dicta-
tion;[17] so that is more stable; but is it really eternal? Certainly the
law comes through Moses but the grace fulfilling the law came
through Jesus Christ: he acted not by emptying but filling, and did
not limit the law itself but many of its sanctions. Hence com- 26
menting on *Psalm* 143 Augustine said:

> You remember how many things in the old law we read and do not observe; yet we understand them as having been placed first and laid down as a sort of introduction, and it is not that we discard the law of God, but we simply do not observe sacraments which made promises, once these promises have already been fulfilled; since the grace of the New Testament was veiled in the Old Law but unveiled in the Gospel; we have removed the veil and recognize what was veiled. Now we acknowledge it in the grace of our Lord Jesus Christ, our source[18] and savior who was crucified for our sake, and at whose crucifixion the veil of the temple was rent.[19]

I especially inserted this testimony of Augustine on account of this 27
last saying, so that you could clearly note that the rending of the veil which we read of in the Gospel[20] was a matter of vast and inexpressible mystery marking that, when the old veil, by which the secrets of the law were concealed up to that day, was rent at the passion of Christ, all things were revealed to a humble and new nation, which the proud and more ancient people had not seen

superbus antiquior tumidis et caligantibus oculis non vidisset.
28 'Iudei enim, quamvis uni omnipotenti Deo supplicent' ut alio quodam loco Augustinus idem ait, 'sola tamen temporalia et visibilia bona de Illo expectantes, rudimenta novi populi ab humilitate surgentia in ipsis suis scripturis nimia securitate noluerunt advertere atque ita in veteri homine remanserunt.' 'Vetera autem' ut alibi ait idem, 'quamvis priora sint tempore, nova tamen anteponenda sunt dignitate, quoniam illa vetera preconia sunt novorum.'

29 Itaque ut ad propositum revertar, lex ipsa mosaica, quamvis humanarum legum omnium sanctissima, ipsa tamen ut vides in multis gratie cessit, que per Iesum Cristum facta est. Huius autem solius est lex illa immobilis et eterna, nulli unquam cessura sed cui vel cessure sunt omnes vel cesserunt; hec est illa 'suscipienda lex Dei' de qua Lactantius Cecilius Formianus non otiose agit in quodam loco,

> que nos ad *sapientie* iter *dirigit,* illa sancta, illa celestis, quam Marcus Tullius in libro *De republica* III pene divina voce de-
> 30 pinxit, cuius ego, ne plura dicerem, verba subieci: 'Est quidem' *inquit Cicero,* 'vera lex, recta ratio, nature congruens, diffusa in omnes, constans, sempiterna, que vocet ad officium iubendo, vetando a fraude deterreat, que tamen frustra neque probos iubet aut vetat nec improbos vetando aut iubendo movet. Huic legi nec abrogari fas est, neque derogari aliquid ex hac licet, neque tota abrogari potest; nec vero aut per senatum aut per populum solvi hac lege possumus,
> 31 neque est querendus explanator aut interpres eius; nec erit alia lex Rome, alia Athenis, alia nunc, alia posthac, sed et omnes gentes et omni tempore una lex et sempiterna et

with its befogged and swollen eyes. For "although the Jews pray to 28
the single and almighty God," as Augustine again says in another passage, "they expected only earthly and passing goods from Him, and, relying too much on the Scriptures, were unwilling to take notice that the rough beginnings of a new people were arising from humble origin, and so they remained in the mode of old mankind."[21] And as he says in another passage: "Although the old things were earlier in time, the new should be put before them in dignity, since those old sayings were heralding the new."[22]

So to return to my theme, the Mosaic law itself, although most 29
sacred of all human laws, yielded nonetheless, as you see, to Grace in many instances, since Grace was created by Jesus Christ. For to Him alone belongs the old immovable and eternal law that will never yield to any, but to which all others either have yielded or shall yield. This is the "law of God we must take up," of which Lactantius speaks purposefully in a certain passage,

> which directs us to the path of wisdom, that sacred and heavenly law which Cicero depicted in the third book *On the Republic* in almost divine terms, and so as not to speak more
> in person I have added its words: "The true law," says Cicero, 30
> "is right reasoning, harmonious with nature and spread among all men, unchanging, eternal, that summons us to duty by ordering and deters from deceit by forbidding, that never either orders or forbids upright men in vain, nor can rouse the wicked either by ordering or forbidding. It is neither right for this law to be abolished nor for anything to be amended from it, nor can it be totally abolished; indeed we cannot be exempted by the senate or the people from this law, nor should we seek for an expositor or interpreter of it.
> Nor shall there be one law at Rome and another at Athens, 31
> one now and another subsequently, but one law everlasting and unchangeable shall bind all nations and at all times; and

> immutabilis continebit; uniuscuiusque erit comunis quasi magister et imperator omnium Deus, ille legis huius inventor disceptator sator, cui qui non parebit, ipse se fugiet et naturam hominis aspernatus, hoc ipso luet maximas penas, etiamsi cetera que putantur supplicia effugerit.'

32 Hec est ergo, mi frater, ciceroniana lex Dei, quam vir ille, non dicam quod Lactantius ait, 'longe a veritatis notitia remotus,' sed qui veritatem hanc, Cristo quem non noverat revelante, cognosceret, adeo significanter expressit ut significantius nemo posset aut brevius, eorum quoque qui vere fidei sacramentis initiati sunt, quod sine dubio — in hoc enim a Lactantio non discordo — divino
33 aliquo spiritu instigatus fecisse credendus est. Scis autem cur immobilis divina lex est? quia ab Illo lata est qui semper idem ipse est, et 'anni sui non deficient,' et de rebus est non transeuntibus neque mutabilibus, sed eternis; etsi nonnunquam de transitoriis loquatur, in ipsa tamen mente legislatoris omnia ad eternam illam referuntur vitam ultra quam nichil est; ita legem ab infinito et immutabili et de immutabilibus atque impossibilibus aliter se habere editam, in eterna republica interminabilem quoque et immutabilem esse necesse est.

34 Huius auctor legis est Cristus et hec est illa 'lex Domini immaculata convertens animas,' de qua loquitur Psalmista, illudque 'testimonium Domini fidele sapientiam prestans parvulis.' Hanc tu legem, germane carissime, non inter scolasticorum greges in strepitu, sed solus in silentio didicisti, quod utique non fecisses si
35 parvulus non fuisses; pro parvulis enim humiles accipi, locus ille testatur ubi scriptum est: 'Sinite parvulos venire ad me, talium est

> God shall be the common master and commander of every single man, God the inventor, explainer and creator of this law. Whoever shall not obey it shall shun his own self and, scorning the nature of man, by this very condition pay the greatest penalty, even if he escapes the other so-called punishments."[23]

This then, dear brother, is the Ciceronian law of God, which 32
that man—I shall not quote Lactantius' comment, "a man far removed from the knowledge of truth,"[24] yet a man who would have known this truth in the revelation of Christ whom he did not know—that man Cicero expressed so vividly that no one could have spoken more vividly or shortly, even those initiated into the sacraments of the true faith, and which undoubtedly—and here I do not dissent from Lactantius—we must believe he composed
under the inspiration of some divine spirit. Now do you know 33
why the divine law is immovable? Because it was given by Him Who is always the same and "Whose years shall not fail,"[25] and it concerns not transient or changeable things, but eternal matters; even if it sometimes speaks of transient things, everything is related in the mind of the legislator to that eternal life beyond which there is nothing; so that law, which is issued by an unending and immutable Being and concerns things unchangeable that cannot be otherwise, must also be without end and unchangeable in that eternal Republic.

The author of this law is Christ and this is that "immaculate 34
law of the Lord converting souls," which the Psalmist names,[26] and that "faithful witness of the Lord offering wisdom to the little ones." Dearest brother, you have learned this law not among the scholastic herds with their din, but alone in silence, which you surely would not have done had you not been a humble person.
That humble men are those meant by "little ones" is confirmed by 35
the passage where it is written: "Allow the little ones to come unto

enim regnum *celorum*,' et ille: 'Abscondisti hec a sapientibus et prudentibus et revelasti ea parvulis,' sed in primis ille a te non pretermissus, ubi cum dixisset: 'Custodiens parvulos Dominus,' ut aperte monstraret qui sint isti parvuli, mox adiecit 'Humiliatus sum et liberavit me,' tanquam si diceret: 'Cum custodiat Dominus parvulos, ut me quoque custodiat, humilitate parvulus factus sum.'
36 Ceterum huic tante docilitati ydoneus preceptor accessit, non in philosophicis Aristotiles, non Pithagoras aut Plato, non in lege Papinianus, non Ulpianus aut Scevola, sed Cristus; utrobique sub tanto magistro facile devotum et humile fructificavit ingenium; Illum ama, Illum cole, Illi, quia nichil aliud Illo dignum habes, multo dignius quam Eschines Socrati, da te ipsum; meliorem reddet ille te tibi; quod discipulo suo Socrates pollicetur, Iste pre-
37 stabit. Age illi gratias semper cum pro multis tum pro eo nominatim, quod hunc tibi animum dedit, quem antequam daret non habebas; neque hic verearis ne sis nimius neve gratias agendo, laudando et amando illius benificentiam excedas, quam equare nunquam poteris cogitando. Hoc unum est quo illud Terrentii trahi nequit: 'nequid nimis,' de quo illud potius vere dicitur: 'nunquam satis.'

38 Ac ne forte tam efficax Cristi magisterium mireris, quod sub illo tantum brevi tempore profeceris quantum nec in academia Platonis, nec in omnium philosophorum aut iurisconsultorum scolis toto tempore profecisses, cogita quantalibet hominis magnitudo, Deo comparata, quam sit nichil omnino. Plato magnus vir, magnus Pithagoras, magnus Aristotiles, magnus Varro; ita dico:
39 magnus horum quilibet si per se consideres. Non magne stature fuisse fertur Augustus Cesar, verum adeo elegantis ut facile corporis brevitatem venustate redimeret; id vero non amplius quam dum

Me, for of such is the Kingdom of Heaven,"[27] and that saying: "You have concealed these things from the wise and clever and revealed them to the little ones,"[28] but above all the passage you have not passed over where he had said: "The Lord guarding the little ones"[29] to show explicitly who these little ones are; then he quickly added: "I was humbled and he freed me," as if he were saying: "Since the Lord watches over the little ones, I have by humility become a little one, in order that he may watch over me too."
But a fitting teacher adds support to this great docility, not Aris- 36
totle in his philosophical works, nor Pythagoras nor Plato, nor Papinianus in law nor Ulpian nor Scaevola,[30] but Christ; and in both respects, under this great teacher your devout and humble intellect bore fruit. Love Him, worship Him, give to Him—since you have nothing else worthy to give—yourself, a gift far more worthy than Aeschines gave to Socrates.[31] He will restore you to yourself a better man, He will guarantee what Socrates promises
to his pupil. Always thank Him for many things but explicitly for 37
this, that He gave you this soul which you did not have before He gave it; and in this do not be afraid of being excessive nor outdoing His generosity in thanking Him, praising Him and loving Him, since you can never match Him in reflection. This is the one thing to which that famous saying of Terence cannot be applied: "don't overdo it."[32] Rather one should say: "never enough."

And in case you should marvel that Christ's ministry is so pow- 38
erful that you have advanced under him in so short a time as you would never have advanced in Plato's Academy or in all the schools of philosophers and legal experts, think how the greatness of any man, compared with God, is utterly nothing. Plato was great, and Pythagoras was great, Aristotle was great, and Varro great,[33] but I call any man like these "great" when considered in
their own terms. Augustus Caesar is said to have been of modest 39
stature, but so shapely that he easily compensated for his shortness of body with beauty: but even that only until someone of greater

quisquam procerior accessisset: tunc ingenio dissimulata brevitas
40 apparebat. Vis tu et horum qui maximi videntur magnitudinem
veram nosse? unumquemlibet ex illis vel potius omnes simul et
quotcunque precesserunt aut secuti sunt aut usque in finem seculi
sequentur, confer uni Cristo; videbis elata forte sed inania nomina
41 et quod valde suspexeras, cognita veritate despicies; subito splendor ille cessabit ubi sol iustitie Cristus illuxerit, ad quod credendum, quamvis non sis exhortandus, ut tamen securius maiori cre-
das, velim tibi cogitanti de hac re ad memoriam redeat ille Psalmi
locus: 'Absorpti sunt iuncti petre iudices eorum,' sive, ut translatio
vetus habet, 'Absorpti sunt iuxta petram iudices eorum'; petra
42 autem, ut novimus, Cristus est. Itaque locum illum exponens Augustinus:

> Tota terra, inquit, a solis ortu usque ad occasum, laudate
> nomen Domini. Quid faciunt pauci aliter disputantes? iu-
> dices sunt impiorum. Sed quid ad te? vide quod sequitur.
> 'Absorpti sunt iuxta petram iudices eorum.' Quid est 'ab-
> sorpti sunt iuxta petram'? 'Petra' autem erat Cristus; 'absorpti
> sunt iuxta petram,' 'iuxta,' idest comparati; 'iudices' magni
> potentes docti. Ipsi dicuntur 'iudices eorum' tanquam iudi-
> 43 cantes de moribus et sententiam proferentes. Dixit hoc Aris-
> totiles: adiunge illum petre, et absorptus est; quis est Aristo-
> tiles? Audiant dixit Cristus et apud Inferos contremiscit.
> Dixit hoc Pithagoras, dixit hoc Plato: adiunge illos petre,
> compara autoritatem illorum autoritati evangelice, compara
> inflatos crucifixo; dicamus eis: 'Vos literas vestras conscrip-
> sistis in cordibus superborum; Ille crucem suam fixit in
> frontibus regum; postremo mortuus est et resurrexit; mortui

height approached.[34] Then it was obvious that his shortness had
been concealed by his skill. Do you want to know the true great- 40
ness of those who seem very great? Compare any one of these or
all taken together and however many came before them or followed them or shall follow until the end of time, with Christ
alone; you will see their names are exalted but hollow and you will
contemn what you strongly respected once you grasp the truth.
That splendor will suddenly fail when the sun of Christ's justice 41
rises. To believe this, although you do not need exhorting, anyway
to believe your elders more easily, I would like that passage in the
Psalms to come to you as you meditate on this matter: "Their
judges have been overthrown, bound to the rock" or, as the old
translation has it, "their judges have been overthrown beside the
rock";[35] for the rock is Christ, as men say. So Augustine explaining 42
that passage says:

> In the whole earth from the sunrise to the sunset, praise ye
> the name of the Lord. What are the few doing who argue
> otherwise? They are the judges of the impious. But how
> does it concern you? See what follows: "their judges have
> been overthrown beside the rock." Now the rock was Christ
> and "overthrown besides the rock" means in comparison to
> the rock; the judges are the mighty, powerful and learned.
> These men are called "their judges" as if they are judging
> morals and putting forward their verdict. "Aristotle said it": 43
> put him close to the rock and he is overthrown; who is Aris-
> totle? Let them hear: "Christ said it," and Aristotle trembles
> in the underworld. "Pythagoras said it," "Plato said it": set
> them close to the rock and compare their authority with the
> authority of the Gospel; compare these exalted beings with
> the crucifix; let us say to them: "You have written your writ-
> ings in the hearts of the proud. He impressed his cross on
> the foreheads of kings; finally He died and was resurrected,

estis et nolo querere quemadmodum resurgatis.' Ergo absorpti sunt iuxta petram iudices eorum; tandiu videntur aliquid dicere donec comparentur petre.

44 Hec ad literam Augustinus. Multa quidem hodie, ut vides, de alieno supra morem meum interserui, quanquam, ut a doctis viris accepimus, quicquid ab ullo bene dictum est nostrum sit vel utendo certe nostrum fieri possit; est enim ut rerum sic verborum usucapio. Feci autem ut plus fidei dictis meis esset apud te, tantorum hominum testimonio probatis, apud quem tamen, fateor, ut magna michi semper autoritas fuerit sine ullis externis adminiculis, non meritum quidem meum sed tua vere utique germana caritas fecit.

45 Et hactenus quidem, frater, letissimo stupori meo, qui ex insperata literarum tuarum ubertate oritur, responsum sit. Nichil modo prorsus ad reliqua, nisi quod quecunque libellus ille tuus continet, que sunt multa, magno plausu complector et laudo supplicibusque votis postulo ne minus adiuvent animum quam delectant. Vale, decus meum.

*Modoetie, VII Idus Novembris.*

## : 5 :

## *Ad Iohannem de Certaldo, de vaticinio morientium.*

1 Magnis me monstris implevit, frater, epistola tua, quam dum legerem stupor ingens cum ingenti merore certabat. Uterque abiit dum legissem. Quibus enim oculis nisi humentibus tuarum lacrimarum

> but you are dead and I don't want to ask how you will be resurrected." So their judges have been overthrown beside the rock—they seemed to be saying something significant only until they were measured against the rock.[36]

This is what Augustine said word for word. As you see I have introduced many borrowed quotations today, contrary to my habit, although as we have heard from learned men, whatever has been well said by any man should be ours or could become ours by usage:[37] for there is possession by right of usage of words as of property. So I have done this to give you more faith in my arguments, tested by the witness of so many men, although I admit that I always had authority over you without any extraneous props: it is not my deserts but your own brotherly love that has achieved this. 44

This is enough, then! Let this be my reply to my own most happy amazement arising from the unexpected richness of your letter. I really have nothing to say just now about the rest, except that whatever your pamphlet contains, and it contains a great deal, I embrace and praise with mighty applause and ask with suppliant vows that its contents may help me as much as they delight me. Farewell, my pride and joy. 45

*Monza, November 7.*

## : 5 :

## *To Giovanni [Boccaccio] of Certaldo, on the prophetic activity of the dying.*

Your letter, dear brother, filled me with portentous alarms because 1
a vast shock competed with huge grief as I read it. But both emo- 2
tions faded once I had read it. How could I read without moist- 3

tuique tam vicini obitus mentionem legere potui, rerum nescius
4 omnino solisque inhians verbis? Ubi demum in rem ipsam inter-
nos flexi oculos defixique, mutatus illico animi status et stuporem
seposuit et merorem. [§§5–13 *omissis*]

14 Scribis nescio quem Petrum, senensem patria, religione insigni
et miraculis insuper clarum virum, nuper obeuntem multa de multis, inter quos de utroque nostrum aliqua predixisse idque tibi per
quendam, cui hoc ille commiserat, nuntiatum, ex quo exactius
dum quereres quemadmodum sanctus ille vir nobis incognitus nos
15 novisset, sic responsum: fuisse illi propositum, ut intelligi datur,
pium aliquid agere, quod cum implere denuntiata sibi, auguror,
morte non posset, orasse Deum efficaci et ad celum perventura
prece rebus ydoneos vicarios designaret, quibus negatum sibi cepti
16 seu destinati operis exitum divinitas largiretur, cumque familiaritate illa que Deum inter iustique animam est se intelligeret
exauditum, ne quid in re dubii foret, Cristum ipsum habuisse
presentem, cuius in vultu omnia cognovisset

que sunt, que fuerunt, que mox ventura trahantur,

non ut apud Maronem Protheus, sed plenius multoque perfectius
17 ac clarius; nam quid, oro, non videat illum videns 'per quem omnia
18 facta sunt'? Illum oculis vidisse mortalibus magna res, fateor, si
vera; usitatum enim et vetustum est plerunque mendaciis fictisque
sermonibus velum religionis sanctimonieque pretendere, ut huma-
19 nam fraudem tegat divinitatis opinio. De quo in presens nil pronuntio. Cum ad me defuncti nuntius ille pervenerit — quem ad te

ened eyes the mention of your tears and your approaching death,
knowing nothing and gazing only at your words? But when I fi- 4
nally focused my mind's eyes and held them there, my state of
mind changed immediately and it set aside both bewilderment and
grief.[1] [§§5–13 *omitted*]

You write that some man called Peter, a Sienese,[2] a man re- 14
markable for his devotion and famous for miracles, recently uttered many prophecies as he was dying about many men, including
some predictions about each of us, and that this had been reported to you by some person to whom he had entrusted the information, and when you questioned this messenger more precisely how this holy man, unknown to us, had knowledge of us,
the answer was that his intention, as the messenger had been given 15
to understand, had been to perform a pious action, which, as I
surmise, he realized he could not fulfill in the face of his coming
death; hence he prayed to God, with a prayer that would successfully reach heaven, to indicate suitable delegates for his business,
so that divinity would bestow on them the completion of the work
he had begun but had been unable to carry out: With that inti- 16
macy which exists between God and a just soul he understood
that his request had been granted, and to leave no doubt of the
matter, he had Christ himself present, from whose expression he
had learned everything

> that is, that was and will soon be brought into being,

not like Proteus in Vergil but more fully and much more perfectly
and clearly.[3] Indeed, I ask you, is there anything a man would not 17
see when he sees the divine Being "through Whom all things were
made"?[4] To have seen him with mortal eyes is a great achievement, 18
if it is true; for it is routine and longstanding among many to hold
up the veil of religion and sanctity in front of lies and false tales so
that the belief in divinity conceals human deceit. I make no judg- 19
ment on that for now, but when the messenger from the dead man

primum, quod esses forte vicinior, expositisque mandatis mox
Neapolim, inde mari in Gallias atque in Britanniam perrexisse
significas, novissime me visurum et michi virilem mandatorum
partem ex ordine prolaturum—, tum demum quantum apud me
20 sit fidei reperturus videro. Etas hominis, frons, oculi, mores, habitus, motus, incessus, sessio voxque ipsa et oratio et super omnia
conclusionis effectus ac loquentis intentio ad consilium vocabun-
21 tur. Nunc, quantum ex tibi dictis elicio nos duos aliosque nonnullos ex hac vita discedens ille vir sanctus vidit ad quos quedam
secretiora committeret huic sue huiusmodi ultime voluntatis
22 executori industrio, ut tu extimas, ac fideli. Hec, ni fallor, historie
summa est.

23 Ceterum quid ex hoc alii audierint in dubio est; tu, quod ad
statum tuum attinet, duo hec—nam cetera supprimis—audisti:
vite tue terminum instare paucorumque tibi iam tempus annorum
superesse—hoc primum—; tibi preterea poetice studium inter-
24 dici—hoc secundum ultimumque. Hinc illa consternatio me-
rorque ille tuus, quem legendo meum feci meditandoque deposui
et tu, si michi aurem, imo si tibi, si rationi insite animum prestas,
25 abicies et videbis inde te doluisse unde potius sit gaudendum. Non
extenuo vaticinii pondus: quicquid a Cristo dicitur verum est. Fieri
26 nequit ut Veritas mentiatur. At id queritur, Cristusne rei huius
auctor sit an alter quispiam ad commenti fidem, quod sepe vidi-
27 mus, Cristi nomen assumpserit. Esto autem, inter ignaros huius
nominis res agatur: si poetis, si philosophis gentilium fides est,
multa vaticinari solitos morientes et Grecorum litere loquuntur et
28 nostre. Vides ut Hector homericus mortem vaticinetur Achilli,

reaches me—the man you refer to came to you first because you
were nearer, and after carrying out his instructions soon went to
Naples and from there continued his journey by sea to the Gauls
and Britain, intending to visit me last and produce the part of his
instructions owed to me in due order—then and only then shall I
see how much credit he will find with me. The man's age, face, 20
eyes, behavior, deportment, movement, pace, way of sitting and
actual voice and speech and above all the impact of his argument
and purpose of his speech will be called in to advise me. Now as 21
far as I can divine from your words, that holy man saw us two and
a few others as he was departing life, to whom he wanted this in-
dustrious (as you consider him) and loyal implementer of his last
wish to pass on some more secret information. This is the gist of 22
the story, unless I am mistaken.

But what other men have heard from this person is in doubt; 23
whereas you, as far as concerns your case, have heard these two
statements—for you have suppressed the rest—that the end of
your life is imminent and only a few years' time is left—this is the
first prophecy—and that the pursuit of poetry is forbidden to
you—this is the second and last. Hence your panic and grief, 24
which I have made mine by reading it and I have cast off by reflection upon it; and you too, if you lend me your ear or yourself,
or rather your innate intelligence and reason, will cast it away, seeing that you are suffering grief over something that should rather
be a source of rejoicing. I am not diluting the weight of his proph- 25
ecy: whatever is said by Christ is true. And the Truth cannot lie.
But the issue is whether Christ is the source of this matter or 26
someone else has adopted the name of Christ to give credibility to
his invention, something we often see. So be it; let the matter be 27
discussed among men ignorant of this name; if the poets and philosophers of the pagans are to be credited, the dying were accustomed to utter many prophecies, as both Greek literature and our
own Latin works attest. You see how the Homeric Hector foretells 28

virgilianus Horodes Mezentio, ciceronianus Theramenes Critie,
Calanus Alexandro et, quod est his similius que te premunt, apud
Possidonium philosophum sua etate clarissimum Rhodius quidam
moriens brevi post se morituros sex ex coequevis suis nominat et,
29 quod plus est, ordinem adicit moriendi. De quarum rerum vel
veritate vel causa disputandi non est locus.

30 Sed ut hec et que similia traduntur ab aliis, postremo que terri-
ficator hic tuus nuntiat vera sint, quid est tamen quod te usque
31 adeo permoveat? Vulgaria et nota contemnimus; inopina nos qua-
32 tiunt ac perturbant. An tu, queso, modicum vite esse quod superest, si iste tibi non diceret, ignorabas, quod nec hodie natus infans,
33 si ratione uti possit, ignoret? Omnium vita mortalium brevis est
senumque brevissima, etsi sepe preter opiniones spesque hominum, quod quotidie querimur ac lugemus, nascendi ordinem mors
34 pervertat, ut ex vita qui huc ultimi venere primi abeant. Profecto
fumus, umbra, somnium, prestigium, nichil denique nisi luctus et
35 laboris area vita est que hic agitur. Quod unum boni habet, ad
aliam vitam via est; alioquin non contemptibilis modo, sed odiosa
prorsus ac misera et de qua considerantissime dictum sit 'Longe
36 optimum non nasci, proximum quam primum mori.' Ne ve
suspecta sit pagani hominis precisa sententia, Hebreorum sapien-
tissimus illi accedit, imo vero, quod et Ambrosius fratris obitum
deflens suo more vestigat et sic esse discussa temporum ratione
deprehenditur, non ille philosophos, sed illum philosophi sequun-
37 tur. Cuius ego sensum tibi de Ambrosio potius quam Salomone
38 descripserim, ut dicto uni duplex esset autoritas. Sic ergo ait:

the death of Achilles, how the Vergilian Orodes forecasts to Mezentius, how Theramenes in Cicero foretells death to Critias,
Calanus to Alexander, and something closer to the warnings that
oppress you, how a certain Rhodian on the point of death named
to Posidonius, the most distinguished philosopher of his age, six
of his peers who would die shortly after, and more strikingly,
added the order of their dying.[5] This is not the place to discuss the 29
truth or reason for argument about these matters.

But suppose these anecdotes and others like them passed on by 30
others and the announcements of your intimidator are true, what
is there to disturb you so much? We despise common and well- 31
known tales, whereas the unexpected shatters and disturbs us.
Were you unaware, pray, of the small amount of life that remains, 32
if he had not told you, something that any infant born this day, if
he could use his reason, would know? The life of all mortals is 33
short and that of old men shortest, even if death often reverses the
sequence of birth, contrary to the opinions and hopes of men,
something we protest each day and mourn over, when those who
came last into this life are first to depart from it. For sure the life 34
we lead here is smoke, shadow, dreaming, a conjurer's trick, nothing but a site of mourning and suffering. The one good thing it 35
contains is the path to a different life; otherwise it is not just contemptible but loathsome and wretched and such that it has most
rightfully been said: "Far the best is not to be born, next best to
die as soon as possible."[6] And to avoid casting suspicion on this 36
concise statement by a pagan, the wisest of the Jews agrees with
him, or rather—as Ambrose, in a lament for his brother's death,
explores in his own fashion and as it is proved to be right when we
clarify the chronological sequence—this wise Hebrew is not following the philosophers but the philosophers are following him. I 37
would define his meaning to you based on Ambrose rather than
Solomon, to give double authority to the single statement. Thus 38
Ambrose says:

> Non nasci longe optimum secundum sancti Salomonis sen-
> tentiam. Ipsum enim etiam hi qui sibi visi sunt in philoso-
> 39 phia excellere secuti sunt. Nam ipse illis anterior, nostris
> 40 posterior in *Ecclesiasten* locutus est: 'Et laudavi ego omnes
> mortuos qui iam defuncti sunt magis quam viventes quicun-
> que vivunt usque adhuc et optimus supra hos duos qui non-
> dum natus est, qui non vidit opus malum quod factum est
> sub sole.'

41 Nec ita multo post: 'Et hoc,' inquit 'quis dixit nisi ille qui sapien-
42 tiam poposcit et impetravit?' Et mox paucis de sapientia illius in-
terpositis: 'Quem igitur' ait 'non latuerunt celestia quemadmodum
laterent mortalia?' Et:

> 43 De sue conditione nature, quam in se expertus est, errare aut
> mentiri potest, sed non solus hoc sensit, etsi solus expressit.
> 44 Legerat sanctum dixisse Iob: 'Pereat dies illa qua natus sum';
> cognoverat nasci malorum omnium esse principium et ideo
> diem qua natus est perire optavit, ut tolleretur origo incom-
> modorum.

45 Post hec David ac Ieremie testimonio adhibito sic concludit:

> 46 Si igitur, inquit, sancti viri vitam fugiunt, quorum vita etsi
> nobis utilis, sibi tamen inutilis extimatur, quid nos facere
> oportet qui nec aliis prodesse possumus et nobis vitam hanc
> quasi fenebrem pecuniam usurario quodam cumulo graves-
> cente onerari in dies peccatorum ere sentimus?

47 Que si dixit Ambrosius, si tales ante eum viri dixerant, quid miser
ego dicturus sum, cuius vita non solum peccatis obnoxia atque
48 oppressa, sed tota nil nisi temptatio ac peccatum est? Verum etsi

> It is far better never being born according to holy Solomon.
> For even those who thought themselves to excel in philoso-
> phy followed him. He in fact spoke in *Ecclesiastes* before them 39
> but after our writers: "And I praised all the dead who are 40
> now departed, rather than the living, whoever lives up to
> now, and he is best beyond these two who is not yet born,
> who has not seen the evil that is done under the sun."[7]

And soon after Ambrose says: "And who spoke these words except 41
he who demanded and obtained wisdom?" And soon, after a few 42
comments on his wisdom: "How could mortal matters remain
hidden from one to whom the things of heaven did not remain
hidden?" and:

> He may be mistaken or lie about the condition of his nature 43
> that he has experienced in himself, but he was not alone in
> realizing this, even if he alone expressed it. He had read that 44
> holy Job said: "Cursed be the day I was born"[8] and realized
> that being born was the beginning of all evils and so desired
> the day he was born to vanish, so that the source of misfor-
> tunes might be eliminated.

After this, producing the witness of David and Jeremiah,[9] he con- 45
cludes:

> If holy men flee from life, whose life, even if it is useful to us, 46
> is thought useless to themselves, what ought we to do, who
> cannot benefit others and feel our life being burdened each
> day with the coin of sinners, like money at usury, as the ac-
> cumulation of debt grows more heavy?

And if Ambrose said this, if other such men said it before him, 47
what am I to say, a wretched man whose life is not only open to
sins and weighed down by them, but is entirely nothing but temp-
tation and sinning? But if many things are said by others on this 48

multa hic et dicantur ab aliis et a nobis etiam dici possint, quos
malorum experientia doctos fecit, tibi tamen vel ista superfluunt.
49 Neque enim docendus michi, sed excitandus es, ut memineris
quid divini homines, quid tu ipse hac de re senseris antequam tibi
repens stupor tui memoriam extorqueret.

50 Ex quo tamen huc loquendo pervenimus, insistam paululum.
51 Quamvis igitur hec, ut dixi, ab ingentibus viris disputata atque
firmata sint, sic ut non tantum rationibus sed autoritate etiam
premant sua, non alienum fuerit fortasse quid de his ipsis alii
52 senserint audire. Sunt autem duo hec: unum, quod hec nostra
que dicitur vita mors est. Hoc iuvenis Cicero VI *Reipublice* libro
scripsit; idem senex *Tusculanarum questionum* prima luce repetiit.
53 Alterum eodem *Tusculani* libro primo posuit: 'Non nasci homini
54 longe optimum, proximum quam primum mori.' Utrunque fortas-
55 sis et Cicero ipse alibi et multi alii dixerunt. Et primum quidem,
tametsi innumerabilibus vite malis non verum modo, sed verissimum videatur, simpliciter tamen vitam mortem dici animosum
56 potius arbitror quam usquequaque verum aut libratum satis. Quid
vero? Placet gregoriana illa moderatio e sermone illo quotidiano:
'Temporalis' inquit 'vita eterne vite comparata mors est potius di-
57 cenda quam vita.' Hoc et tutius et salubrius dici puto. De secundo
autem et de utroque, quamvis, ut vides maximi sint auctores, quid
tamen vir doctus et eloquens Lactantius Formianus hinc senserit
non alienum videtur inserere, qui libro *Institutionum* non recordor
quoto impatientiam arguens humanam

> Quid dicemus ergo, ait, nisi errare illos qui aut mortem appetunt tanquam bonum aut vitam fugiunt tanquam malum,

topic and could be said by us too, who have learned from evil experience, still, even these thoughts are superfluous for you. For I 49
have not to teach you but rouse you to action, to remember what
divine men, what you yourself thought before this sudden bewilderment destroyed your memory of yourself.

Yet I would linger a little on the passage which was our point of 50
departure. Although these arguments have been disputed and con- 51
firmed by men of great importance, so that they urge you not only
by their arguments but by their own authority, it would not perhaps be inappropriate to hear what yet others felt about these issues. These are two statements: one is that what is called our life 52
is death. This is what Cicero wrote as a young man in the sixth
book of his *On the Republic,* and he wrote the same sentiment as an
old man on the first day of the *Tusculan Investigations.* The other 53
statement he set down in this same first book of the *Tusculans:* "It
is far the best for a man not to be born, next best to die as soon as
possible."[10] Perhaps Cicero himself and many others made both 54
claims elsewhere. And even if the first claim, given the countless 55
woes in life, seems not just true but extremely true, I think simply
calling life death is vigorous rather than a completely true or well-
balanced statement. What then? I choose the moderation of Greg- 56
ory in his daily sermon; he says: "Worldly life compared to eternal
life should be called death rather than life."[11] I think this is expressed more cautiously and beneficially. But about the second 57
saying, and indeed both of them, although as you see the sources
are of the greatest authority, it does not seem inappropriate to insert here what that wise and eloquent man Lactantius felt. When
he reproached human impatience in a book (I don't recall which
one) of his *Institutes,* he said:

> What then shall we say except that men are misguided when
> they seek out death as a blessing or shun life as an evil, ex-

nisi quod sunt iniquissimi qui pauciora mala non pensant
58 bonis pluribus? Nam, cum vitam omnem per exquisitas et varias traducant voluptates, mori cupiunt siquid forte his amaritudinis supervenit, et sic habent, tanquam illis nun-
59 quam fuerit bene si aliquando fuerit male. Damnant igitur vitam omnem plenamque nichil aliud quam malis opinantur.
60 Hinc nata est inepta illa sententia, hanc esse mortem quam nos vitam putemus, illam vitam quam nos pro morte timeamus; ita primum bonum esse non nasci, secundum citius mori.

[*§§61–78 omissis*]

79 Mitto alia et hec ipsa si plura sunt quam voluisses ignoscito; eo enim pergunt ac te retrahunt unde te meror abduxerat, ut nec valde vitam diligas neque vite finem oderis aut metuas neque propinquum iam provecte stupeas etati qui nunquam pueritie vel in-
80 fantie longe erat, etsi longissime fingeretur. Illud potius mirare, contigisse tibi quod nescio an cuiquam alteri preter Ezechiam regem omnibus seculis acciderit, ut scilicet tui vatis elogio certus sis aliquot annos vite tibi nunc etiam restare; neque enim tam pauci
81 esse possunt quin saltem duo sint. Sic, ubi nemo mortalium diei unius, nemo vel hore integre, tu annorum teneas sponsionem, nisi forte proximam nuntianti mortem creditur, non sic vite spatium
82 exprimenti. Et est hoc sane in his vanitatibus importunum, ut ex malis nuntiis timor dolorque certus oriatur, ex bonis inane gaudium, spes incerta.

83 Utcunque res casura est, an non virgiliani carminis meminisse oportuit:

cept that those men are most wicked who do not weigh the
smaller number of evils against so many blessings? Indeed 58
when they have passed their whole life in many kinds of refined pleasures, they want to die if any bitter experience follows them, and behave as though they never enjoyed good
things if at some time they had a bad experience. Therefore 59
they condemn life entirely and they deem it full of nothing
else but evils. Hence that silly opinion arises calling "death" 60
what we consider life, and life what we fear as death; thus the very best thing is never being born, the second best is dying as soon as possible.[12]

[*§§61–78 omitted*]

I drop the rest, and you should pardon me if this discussion is 79
more than you wanted, for these arguments proceed and draw you back to the point from which your grief distracted you, so that you neither love life too much nor hate or fear its end, nor go into a daze as it approaches you in your advanced age: the end was never far from you in boyhood or infancy, even if it was imagined
as extremely remote. Instead, be amazed that something has hap- 80
pened to you which happened to no one else except King Hezekiah in all the ages,[13] that you should be sure from your prophet's funeral speech that a specific number of years are still left to you,
nor can they be so few that they are not at least two years. So 81
when no mortal holds a guarantee of a single day, or even a complete hour, you could have a guarantee of years, unless perhaps you believe it when one announces that death is close, and you don't
when he announces the duration of your life. And this is the dis- 82
turbing thing in these frivolities, that sure fear and pain arises from bad news, but from good news an empty rejoicing and unsure hope.

However the matter turns out, shouldn't we have recalled the 83
Vergilian poem:

stat sua cuique dies, breve et irreparabile tempus
omnibus est vite, sed famam extendere factis
hoc virtutis opus?

84 Factis, inquam, non tenuem fame sonum aucupantibus, sed
85 virtutem ipsam, que necessario e se vere glorie umbram iacit. Dicerem salutare diceremque unicum in hac rerum perplexitate consilium, ni poeticum sciens auribus tuis parcerem ab hac omni
consideratione prohibitis; qui multum michi maior priore stupor
86 incidit. Nam si id seni, ut aiunt, elementario diceretur, equo
animo pati possem. 'Senuisti, iam vicina mors est, age res anime.
87 Intempestivum senibus amarumque negotium literarum, si novum
88 atque insolitum proponatur; sin una senuerint, nil dulcius. Seram
hanc igitur curam linque. Sine Musas eliconias fontemque casta-
89 lium. Multa puerum decuerant que dedeceant senem. Frustra niteris: torpet ingenium, memoria labascit, oculi caligant omnesque
90 corporei sensus hebent novoque iam fragiles sunt labori. Memento
virium et metire quod aggrederis, ne irritis conatibus mors irrum-
91 pat. Fac potius quod semper bene fit quodque, cum omni etati sit
92 honestum, necessarium est extreme.' Hec horumque similia in-
choanti seni quid ni graviter ac magnifice dicerentur? Docto autem
93 suumque iam habenti cur dicantur nescio. 'Ecce iam morti proximus linque seculares curas, pelle reliquias voluptatum, malas fuge
consuetudines, reforma animum ac mores in Deo placitam novitatem et renascentia vitia, que hactenus abscindebas, radicitus nunc
extirpa, in primis avaritie studium, quod senibus cur annexum

Each man's day is fixed, and the time of life is short
and irreplaceable for all, but spreading glory by our deeds:
this is the task of virtue?[14]

Deeds, I say, not those that chase the insubstantial sound of 84
fame, but those that pursue virtue itself, which inevitably casts
from itself a shadow of true glory. I would call it beneficial and the 85
only good advice in this confusion of life, if I did not, knowing
this was a poet's verse, spare your ears, barred from every consideration of this kind; a dazed condition affecting me far worse than
the former bewilderment. For if this comment were made to an 86
old man beginning his schooling, as they say,[15] I could accept it
calmly: "You have grown old; death is nearby, concern yourself
with matters of the soul. The business of letters is untimely for old 87
men and bitter if set before them as something new and unfamiliar, but if they have grown old together nothing is sweeter. So 88
abandon this belated concern. Leave the Heliconian Muses and
Castalian Spring.[16] Many things were suited to a boy which dis- 89
credit an old man. You are striving in vain: your mind is dulled,
your memory fails, your eyes are dim and all your physical senses
blunted and too brittle for a new task. Remember your strength 90
and measure what you are attempting for fear that death should
burst in on futile attempts. Rather do what is always done well 91
and what, while it is honorable at every age, is essential to the final
phase." How could these reproaches and others like them not be 92
uttered with superb weight to the old man who is just beginning?
However, I do not know why they are said to a learned man who
already has his education. "See, now you are near to death, leave 93
your worldly cares, drive away the remains of pleasures, shun bad
practices, reform your spirit and behavior into a new shape pleasing to God and now uproot outright the regrowth of vices which
until now you were cutting away, above all the devotion to greed,
something I am amazed to find associated with and peculiar to old

ac peculiare sit miror. Hoc unum stude et hoc cogita, ut paratus,
ut securus ad extremum venias.' Optime, inquam, prudenterque.
94 'Linque literas,' seu poeticas seu quascunque alias, in quibus non
iam tyro sis, sed emeritus veteranus, in quibus quid tenendum,
quid respuendum tibi sit noveris, in quibus denique non iam labor,
sed oblectatio vite sit iocunditasque reposita: hoc certe quid sit
aliud non video, nisi auferre solatium ac presidium senectuti.

95 Quid vero siquid tale Lactantio dictum esset? Quid si dictum
96 et creditum Augustino? Dicam quod in animo est: neque ille tam
valide peregrinarum superstitionum fundamenta convelleret neque
iste civitatis Dei muros tanta arte construeret aliquantoque ieiu-
nius Iuliano atque aliis pari impietate latrantibus responderet.
97 Quid tandem si Ieronimo, quamvis id ipse dictum memoret et,
quod credi vult, etiam vigilanti? Quid vero si poeticis, si philoso-
98 phicis, si oratoriis, si historicis semper literis abstineret? Nunquam ille Ioviniani et hereticorum calumnias reliquorum tanta
persuadendi facilitate contunderet, nunquam Nepotianum sic vel
vivum doceret vel defunctum fleret, nunquam denique epistolas ac
99 libellos suos tanta orationis luce perfunderet. Ut enim a veritate
verum, sic artificiosum atque ornatum dicendi genus unde, oro,
100 nisi ab eloquentia requirendum est? Quam poetarum atque oratorum propriam esse nec Ieronimus ipse negaverit et est notius
101 quam ut probari egeat. Non discurro per singulos, sed ad summam non intelligo quid his studiis non dico senem imbui — nichil
enim bene fit quod non et tempore suo fit —, sed puero haustis uti
sobrie vel in senectute prohibeatur, scientem dico quid ex his ad

men. Study only this and think about this, to approach the end ready and free of care." This is excellently said and prudent, I say.
But "abandon letters," whether poetic or any others, in which you 94
are not a beginner but a seasoned veteran, in which you know what should be kept and what rejected, in which not toil but enjoyment of life and pleasantness are situated—I simply do not see what else this is except to take away the consolation and defense of old age.

Indeed what would happen if something of this kind had been 95
said to Lactantius? What if it had been said and believed by Augustine? I will tell you what is in my mind, that neither would the 96
former have been so vigorous in uprooting the foundations of foreign superstitions, nor the latter have constructed the fortifications of his City of God with such art, and he would have replied with rather less vigor to Julian and other enemies barking with equal impiety.[17] What then if this were said to Jerome, though he 97
himself recalls it being said, and said, as he claims, to him even while awake?[18] What if he had refrained from the writings of poetry, philosophy, oratory and history? He would never have 98
crushed the slander of Jovinian and the other heretics with such fluency in persuasion, he would never have taught Nepotianus while he lived or lamented his death, he would never, in short, have bathed his letters and pamphlets in such a great light of eloquence.[19] For as the true comes from truth, where, I ask is the 99
artistic and adorned style of speaking to be sought except from eloquence? Jerome himself did not deny that the high style was 100
peculiar to poets and orators, and it is too well known to need proving. I am not going to run through individuals, but in the end 101
I do not understand why an old man should be forbidden—I will not say to be dipped in these studies, since nothing is done well if not done at the right time—but to use soberly in his old age what he has drunk in as a boy—an old man, that is, who knows which of these precepts can be applied to knowledge, to morality, to elo-

rerum notitiam, quid ad mores, quid ad eloquentiam, quid postremo ad religionis nostre patrocinium trahi possit, quod fecisse illos maxime videas quos proxime memoravi. [*§§102–21 omissis*]

122 preter hec igitur et que sunt id genus innumerabilia, nonne et nostri omnes, quos imitari optamus, vitam omnem in literis consumpserunt, in literis senuerunt, in literis obierunt, ita ut eorum quosdam legentes aut scribentes ultimus dies invenerit neque ulli unquam, quod audierim, preter unum quem dixi Ieronimum noxe fuit disciplinis secularibus floruisse, cum multis fuerit glorie,
123 nominatim sibi? Nec me fallit laudatum a Gregorio Benedictum quod inceptum studium solitudinis et propositi rigidioris amore
124 deseruit. At non ille poeticas, sed omnes omnino literas neglexerat. An vero laudator suus idem si tunc faceret laudaretur? Minime
125 arbitror. Aliud est enim didicisse quam discere aliterque puer spem quam senior rem, ille impedimentum, hic ornamentum, ille laborem et querendi studium anceps, hic laboris fructum certum, delectabilem et quesitum studio preciosum thesaurum literarum abicit.

126 Quid expectas? Scio multos ad sanctitatem eximiam sine literis pervenisse, nullum literis hinc exclusum scio, etsi audiam Paulo apostolo quesitam literis insaniam exprobrari; quam iuste autem
127 mundo notum. Quin potius, si de proprio loqui licet, ita sentio: planum forsitan, sed ignavum iter per ignorantiam ad virtutem.
128 Unus est finis omnium bonorum, multiplices autem vie eodemque
129 tendentium multa varietas. Ille tardius, hic ocius, ille obscurius,

quence, and finally to the protection of our religion, something you see those men I have just mentioned did most fully.[20] [*§§102–21 omitted*]

So besides these and other countless examples of this kind, 122
didn't all our ancients whom we desire to imitate spend all their life in literary studies? Didn't they grow old with them and die with them, so much so that the last day found some of them reading or writing, and, as I have heard, it was no detriment for any of them, except for Jerome only, whom I mentioned above,[21] to have been successful in secular fields—rather it was actually a source of glory to many, and to him in particular? I am well aware that 123
Gregory praised Benedict for abandoning the studies he had begun from love of solitude and a more severe goal.[22] But he 124
had been indifferent not only to poetry but to absolutely every kind of literature. Or do you think that the man who praised him would have won praise if he did the same thing? Not at all.
For having already learned something is not the same as learning 125
it, and it is different for a child to abandon hope and an older man achievement: the former leaves an obstacle, the latter an adornment; the one casts away toil and a perilous dedication to seeking knowledge, the other the sure fruit of his toil, the precious, delightful treasure of literature that he has sought out and found through his dedication.

What do you expect me to say? I know that many have reached 126
exceptional holiness without culture, and I know that none of them has been severed from it by literary study, even if I hear it said that the Apostle Paul was reproached for having become mad
from study;[23] yet the world knows with what justice. Rather, if I 127
may speak in my own case, this is my view: that the path to virtue through ignorance may be level but it is an ignoble and spiritless
one. All good things share one end, but there are many separate 128
roads of all kinds making for the same goal. One man gets there 129
more slowly, the other faster; one is more unnoticed, the other

130 hic clarius, ille depressius incedit, hic altius. Quorum quidem omnium peregrinatio est beata, sed ea certe gloriosior que clarior, que
altior: unde fit ut literate devotioni comparabilis non sit quamvis
131 devota rusticitas. Nec tu michi tam sanctum aliquem ex illo grege
literarum inopum dabis cui non ex hoc altero sanctiorem numero
obiciam.

132 De his autem cogente materia quoniam sepe michi necesse fuit
133 ut loquerer, te amplius hodie non morabor. Qui si cepto heres, ut
studia hec, que pridem post tergum liquimus, literasque omnes,
quantum innuis, ac distractis libris ipsa etiam velis literarum instrumenta proicere atque ita undique persuasum tibi est, gratum
hercle habeo me librorum avidum, ut tu ais, ego non inficior, ne
si negem scriptis ipse meis arguar, in hac emptione omnibus tuo
134 iudicio prelatum. Et quamvis ipse rem meam videar empturus,
nolim tamen tanti viri libros huc illuc effundi aut profanis, ut fit,
135 manibus contrectari. Sicut igitur nos, seiuncti licet corporibus,
unum animo fuimus, sic studiorum hec supellex nostra post nos, si
votum meum Deus adiuverit, ad aliquem nostri perpetuo me-
136 morem pium ac devotum locum simul indecerpta perveniat. Sic
enim statui ex quo ille obiit quem studiorum meorum speraveram
137 successorem. Libris autem precia statuere, quod tua michi prebet
indulgentia, non possum, quorum nec nomina certe nec numerum
138 noverim nec valorem. Tu michi per literas rem digere, ea lege ut, si
quando tibi forsan in animum venerit mecum has quantulascun-
que temporum reliquias agere, quod et ego semper optavi et tu
aliquando pollicitus videbare, et eos ipsos et hos non minus tuos,
quos modo convexi, sic simul invenias ut detractum nichil, sed
nonnichil tibi sentias accessisse.

more conspicuous; one proceeds more humbly, the other more
loftily. While all men's journeying is blessed, the path is surely 130
more glorious which is more conspicuous and lofty; hence illiter-
acy, however pious, is not comparable to lettered piety. You will 131
not name anyone so saintly from that flock without literary skills
against whom I cannot match a more saintly man from this other
group.

Since I have often needed to talk of these matters when the 132
subject compelled me, I will not detain you longer today. If you 133
insist on your undertaking to cast away these studies which we
began so long ago, and all literature, as you hint, and you want to
sell off your books and cast away even the tools of literature—
if you are convinced of this in all respects, since I am, as you
say, greedy for books (and I don't deny it, for fear that if I denied
it my books would refute me), I am really grateful for being preferred to all others, in your judgment, in this matter of purchase.
And although I may seem to be buying in my own interest, I 134
wouldn't want the books of so important a man to be scattered on
all sides and soiled, as often happens, by the hands of the profane.
Then just as we have been united in spirit though separated in 135
body, so, if God grants my wish, may this equipment of our studies reach together and unscathed some place of piety and devotion
that will always preserve our memory. This indeed is what I de- 136
cided after the death of the man whom I hoped to see as successor
to my studies.[24] But I cannot set prices on books, as your indul- 137
gence offers me, since I do not know either their names or quantity or value. Break it down for me in writing, on condition that if 138
ever it comes into your head to spend this scanty remainder of our
time with me, as I always desired and you at times seems to have
promised, you may find these books—and those too, just as much
yours, which I recently brought together—in such a state that you
feel nothing has been subtracted but quite a little has been added.

139 Extremum sit ut, quod te multis, inter quos michi, pecunie de-
bitorem facis, pro me negem mirerque quisnam hic supervacuus,
140 ne ineptus dicam, conscientie tue scrupulus. Possum tibi terentia-
141 num illud obicere: 'nodum in scirpo queris.' Nil michi debes nisi
amorem. Sed nec illum debes, quem pridem, fateor, bona fide in-
tegerrime persolvisti, nisi forte ideo quia quod semper accipis
semper debes; sed et quod solvis continue nunquam debes.

142 Nam ad id quod, ut sepe olim, de inopia quereris, nolo tibi
consolationes, nolo pauperum illustrium nunc exempla congerere:
143 nota sunt tibi. Quid ergo? Clara equidem semperque una voce re-
144 spondeo. Laudo quod me magnas, licet seras, tibi divitias pro-
curante libertatem animi quietamque pretuleris egestatem: quod
145 amicum totiens te vocantem spreveris non laudo. Non sum qui
ditare te hinc possim; quod si essem, non verbo, non calamo, sed
146 re ipsa tecum loquerer. Sum vero cui uni tantum suppetit quantum abunde sufficiat duobus unum cor habentibus atque unam
147 domum. Iniuriosus es michi si fastidis, iniuriosior si diffidis. Vale.

*Patavi, V Kal. Iunias.*

## : 6 :

### *Ad Urbanum quintum Romanum pontificem, de dilato nimis nec iam amplius differendo Ecclesie reditu in suam sedem.*

1 Aliquandiu, pater beatissime, an aliquid tibi seu quid scriberem
dubius fui. Hinc vulgari fama, hinc literis amicorum de te multa et

Finally when you call yourself a financial debtor to many in- 139
cluding me, it is left to me to deny this, amazed at this unnecessary, if not even foolish, scruple of your conscience. I could re- 140
proach you with Terence's phrase "you are looking for a knot in a
reed."[25] You owe me nothing but affection. But you don't even owe 141
that, since you long since paid up in full good faith, unless you
mean that, because you are always receiving something, you always
owe it; but neither do you owe what you are constantly repaying.

Concerning the complaint of poverty which you make, as often 142
before, I don't want to heap up consolations now or examples of
distinguished poor men; you know them all. What then? I am al- 143
ways answering you loudly and clearly. I applaud the fact that as I 144
was obtaining great, if delayed, wealth for you, you have preferred
freedom of spirit and a calm poverty;[26] but I don't applaud your
spurning a friend who so often has called you to himself. I am 145
not the man to enrich you from this place; if I were I would be
talking to you, not with words or penmanship but with deeds.
But I am a man with sufficient means to be abundant for two who 146
share the same heart and home. You do me wrong if you disdain 147
it, and greater wrong if you mistrust me. Farewell.

*Padua, May 28.*

## : 6 :

*To Urban V, pope of Rome, about the return of the Church to its seat, too long delayed and now to be delayed no longer.*

Most blessed father, for some time I was in doubt whether, or in- 1
deed what, I should write to you. I was roused from this condition
by common report, by the letters of friends who told me many
fine things about you, and before all others by that friend who has

preclara narrantium excitabar, illius ante alios qui de tam multis michi pene unicum vite solatium remansit, diu oculis ereptum animo presens semper, Philippi patriarche Ierosolimitani; qui, ne veterum studiosum nova sineret ignorare simulque ut scribendi materiam gloriosam atque uberem stilo offerret, sepe per hoc tempus de tuis rebus mirisque morum laudibus tuorum deque apostolici propositi sanctitate gravissimas ad me nec minus ferventissimas scripsit epistolas, quibus, fateor, iam defessum tepentemque
2 animum vehementer accenderat. Aderat hortatrix alia, vetus scilicet et prescripta iam consuetudo mea scribendi non tantum pari fiducia parvis ac magnis, sed eo semper alacrius quo maioribus sim scripturus, a quibus et bene dictorum ampliorem gratiam et erro-
3 rum promptiorem veniam sperem. Nempe, ut lividi deiectique animi non solum alienis erroribus implacabiliter irascuntur sed alienis quoque laudibus hostiliter obstrepunt, sic sereni erectique
4 et laudibus gratulantur et miserentur erroribus. Ita vero michi persuaseram, neque opinione dimoveor, ei qui bona fide loqueretur errorem imputari posse, non scelus et reprehensione fortassis,
5 non supplicio neque odio dignum esse. Hec me opinio et hec spes impulit ut predecessoribus tuis duobus ante proximum Romanis Pontificibus, quin et Romano Imperatori ac principibus et regibus terre, sepe etiam ignotis, scriberem, nec sum veritus ne parvitatem meam illorum opprimeret magnitudo; non enim me maioribus conferebam neque equabam verbis, quos natura parens aut fortuna tanto secreverat intervallo, sed ad obsequium veritatis uti spiritu
6 libertatis non licitum modo sed debitum arbitrabar. Neque ipse michi quodammodo videbar loqui; mea fides, mea devotio, meus amor rei publice loquebatur. Itaque et ad Benedictum duodeci-

survived as almost my only comfort out of so many, long ago
snatched from my sight but ever present in my heart, Philip, patriarch of Jerusalem;[1] he would not let me, devoted to antiquity
though I am, remain ignorant of modern events, and in order at
the same time to provide a glorious and fertile theme for his pen,
has often in this period written the most impressive and no less
enthusiastic letters to me about your achievements, as well as marvelous praise for your character and the holiness of your apostolic
intention; in these he passionately inflamed my—I admit—weary
and failing spirit. He was aided by a second source of encourage- 2
ment, my old and predetermined practice of writing, not only with
equal confidence to humble and important persons, but always
with greater alacrity the more eminent the persons addressed,
from whom I hoped for a more generous thanks for what I had
spoken well, and a more ready forgiveness for my blunders. For as 3
envious and low minds are not only angered beyond appeasement
by other men's blunders, but also cavil maliciously at other men's
praises, so calm and upright men offer thanks for praise and pity
for blunders. So indeed I had convinced myself, and I have not 4
changed my opinion, that the man who spoke in good faith could
be charged with error but not with criminal intent, and was worthy perhaps of rebuke but not punishment and hatred. This belief, 5
and this hope drove me to write to two of your predecessors, those
just before the most recent, and even to the Roman emperor and
the princes and kings of this earth,[2] often unknown to me, and I
did not fear that their greatness would crush my humble status,
since I was not comparing myself with greater men or matching in
words those whom mother nature or fortune had separated from
me by so great a distance, but thought I was using out of obedience to truth a spirit of liberty not just permitted but obligatory.
Indeed in a way I did not seem to be myself addressing them; it 6
was my loyalty, my devotion, and my love of the state that was
speaking. So as a youth I wrote to Benedict XII and in the prime

mum adolescens adhuc scripsi et ad Clementem sextum medio
7 iuvente; cur non tibi iam senex scriberem? Maior est, fateor,
iuventutis fervor et audacia, sed maior autoritas ac gravitas senectutis, maior quoque animus — quod mirum forsitan quis dixerit —
maiorque securitas; unde est responsum illud famosissimum Solo-
nis, quem cum Pisistratus Atheniensium tyrannus interrogaret
8 qua fiducia sibi tam constanter obsisteret, 'Senectute' inquit; et illud Marci Castricii, verbo aliud, idem sensu, cui cum iratus Carbo,
consul nomine, re tyrannus, inter minas diceret multos se gladios
9 habere, respondit: 'Et ego annos.' Quam sententiose, quam breviter gladiis annos opposuit, quasi annoso homini noceri ne gladiis
10 quidem possit! Et re vera quid metuat is qui vitam ipsam pro qua
omnia hic timentur a tergo habet? Aut quid eripi potest illi qui
11 suum recepit et in tuto posuit? Nec tempestas naute portum iam
tenenti nec grando implenti horrea nocet agricole. Intrepidi fines
rerum, meticulosa principia esse solent et omnino vite satietas se-
12 curitas animi magna est. Michi autem apud te, summum culmen
Ecclesie, non de mea etate sed de tua humanitate fiducia nascitur;
audio enim te libenter audire que vera sunt, etsi acria sint; falsa
13 autem, quamvis dulcia, aspernari. Neque id mirum: veritatis vive
vicarius es in terris. Si Dominum tuum amas, que illius que ve ab
illo sunt amare omnia est necesse; omne autem verum a veritate
verum esse ait Augustinus. [§§14–55 *omissis*]

56 Hec cogitans toto te triennio expectavi iamque, ut vides, quartus annus circumvolvitur dum dies transeunt et fit nichil, eorum
dico que ut maxima atque optima sic et prima esse debuerant.
57 Dicebam mecum et cum aliis dicebam: 'Pastor noster illius exemplo cuius gregem pascit omnia bene fecit; unum, et id quidem

of my young manhood to Clement VI; why should I not write to
you, now that I am already old? I admit the passion and boldness 7
of youth is very great, but the authority and dignity of old age is
greater still, as is its courage—which some might perhaps call
strange—and its confidence. Hence that famous retort of Solon,
when Pisistratus as tyrant of Athens asked him what gave him the
confidence to resist him so persistently, he said: "Old age";[3] and 8
that reply of Marcus Castricius, using different words but having
the same meaning. When Carbo, nominally consul but in fact a
tyrant, angrily said that he had many swords, Castricius replied:
"And I have many years."[4] How meaningfully and succinctly he 9
matched years with swords, as if no harm could be done to an
aged man even by swords! And truly what should a man fear who 10
has life itself, on behalf of which we fear all things, behind him?
Or what can be snatched from the man who has taken back his
property and put it away safely? The storm does not harm the 11
sailor when he is already in harbor, nor does hail harm the farmer
filling his granaries. The ends of actions are usually fearless,
whereas their beginnings are fearful, and complete satiety with life
gives great freedom of spirit. But my confidence speaking before 12
you, highest summit of the church, is born not from my age but
from your humanity: indeed I hear that you hear gladly whatever
is true, even if it is bitter, but reject what is false, however sweet.
This is not strange, for you are the representative of living truth on 13
earth. If you love your Lord, it is necessary to love all things that
are his or come from Him; for Augustine says that any true thing
is true by coming from the truth.[5] [§§14–55 *omitted*]

Allowing for these considerations I have been waiting for you 56
for three whole years, and now, as you see, the fourth year is coming round while the days pass and nothing is done—nothing, I
mean of those acts which ought to have been first, just as they
were greatest and best. I said to myself and to others: "Our shep- 57
herd has done everything well, following the example of Him

summum ac precipuum, differt, gregem ipsum ad suum proprium
58 et antiquum ovile reducere. Neque id sponte sed coactus ipsa magnitudine rerum facit. Assuevit grex externis pascuis herbisque pa-
lustribus hisque iam tanta cum voluptate fruitur ut salubrium im-
59 memor sit herbarum. Habet consuetudo longior viscum tenax et
perplexos laqueos, quos abrumpere dubium, absolvere operosum
sit. His illa nunc sacra mens curis exercita nondum executione in-
60 cipit quod iam intentione perfecit. Cito exigui cogitatus prodeunt
in actum, at magnarum rerum apparatus magni etiam sint oportet;
inter deliberationem enim et rem ipsam magnus quidam mons, ut
dici solet, est medius, cui exuperando et intentione animi et labore
61 est opus et tempore.' Hec dicebam, sic credebam, sic diffidentibus
respondebam, qui nunc a me promissi mei fidem exigunt nec qui-
62 bus hanc viis expediam invenio. Itaque, quando michi spem qua
desiderium leniebam non tu quidem sed res eripit, nec me amplius
nec alios fallere neque sanctitati tue subtrahere aliquid est animus
63 eorum omnium que ad aurem cordis michi loquitur fides mea. Ita
vero, eaque cum reverentia qua illum cuius inter homines locum
tenes, te nunc alloquor tibique prenuntio ut iam hinc ad patientiam inclines animum et aures potentium more blanditiis assuetas
reprehensionibus iustis, ut puto, licet iniusto peccatoris ab ore ve-
64 nientibus parumper accomodes. Totus pene orbis, summe patrum,
65 qua cristianus est, uno tibi nunc ore blanditur. Si tua illa vera est
que fertur integritas, eventurum spero ut inter tot adulatores non
patienter modo sed lete unum audias reprehensorem et, si forte
aliquid plus minus ve quam deceat audieris, fidem laudes, ignorantiam excuses. Hac spe fretus incipio.

whose flock he is feeding; he is postponing one thing only and that
is the greatest and most important, to lead back the flock to its
own fold. And he is not doing this of his own accord but is com- 58
pelled by the enormous scale of the issues at stake. The flock
has become accustomed to foreign pasture and marsh plants and
now enjoys them with such pleasure that it has forgotten healthy
grasses. Too long a habit produces sticky birdlime and entangling 59
snares, which it is uncertain how to break and laborious to untie.
Now his holy mind is beset with these anxieties and has not
yet begun implementing what he has completed in his planning.
Small designs soon reach execution, but the preparations for great 60
enterprises must also be great, since there is a mighty mountain, as
people say, between deliberation and the act itself—to overcome it
requires concentration of purpose and toil and time." I kept saying 61
this and believing it, and this was my reply to mistrustful people
who are now demanding from me the fulfillment of my promise;
and I cannot find ways to bring this about. So since not you, but 62
events snatched from me the hope with which I soothed my longing, I no longer have the will to disappoint myself or others, nor to
hold back from your Holiness any of those things which my loyalty speaks to the ear of my heart. So truly with the same respect 63
with which I address Him whose place you occupy among men, I
am addressing you and announcing to you that you should now
incline your spirit to patience and accommodate the ears, accustomed like all potentates to flattery, to my justified rebukes, even if
these come from the unjust mouth of a sinner. Almost the entire 64
Christian world, Highest of Fathers, now appeals to you with one
voice. If the integrity attributed to you is true, I hope it will come 65
to pass that among so many flatterers you will pay not just patient
but glad attention to one reprimand, and if by chance you hear
anything more or less than is fitting, you may praise my loyalty
and excuse my ignorance. Relying on this hope I shall begin.

66 Cunta quidem apud Avinionem prospere, magno cunta consilio
67 geruntur. Dixi iam: laudo. Sic te decet ut ubicunque fueris bene ac
feliciter universa succedant et presentiam tuam virtus ac prosperi-
68 tas comitentur. Sed dic, oro: quid agit interim sponsa tua? quo
consule regitur? quo duce defenditur? quibus comitibus consola-
69 tur? Respondebis, imo non tu quidem, qui interrogationem meam,
non dubito, placatus atque equanimis accipis, sed aliquis unus
70 minor et impatientior respondebit: 'Tu Romano Pontifici legem
ponis aut unam illi sponsam tribuis cui sponsa est non ea sola
quam intelligis, sed universalis Ecclesia? Ubicunque ille sibi mo-
71 ram eligit, illic sponsa, illic sedes propria sua est.' Non infitior,
pater beatissime, neque angusto tibi sedem tuam, quam libenter
extenderem, si in me esset, occeanique litoribus undique termina-
rem; utinamque tam late hodie coleretur Cristi nomen quam late
olim cultum fuisse multis quidem sed in primis hinc Ambrosio
hinc Augustino teste cognovimus, qui iisdem pene verbis latiores
72 cristiane religionis quam romani imperii fines locant. Quod si ut
sonat nec devote magis quam historice dictum credimus, mutatio-
73 nem rerum maximam ac flebilem quis non videt? Certe enim, id si
nunc quoque verum foret, sedes ac possessio tua esset 'mare et
74 plenitudo eius orbis terrarum et universi qui habitant in eo.' Sed
non ita est. Cristus enim, ut celi sic maris terreque dominus et
creator, 'idem ipse est' et uno semper tenore dives permanet: nos
peccatis promerentibus 'pauperes facti sumus nimis' et ad hunc
angulum occidentis arctati, quem ipsum infidelium insultus hinc
75 atque hinc quatiunt et infestant. Adhuc tamen ubicunque rite co-
litur Cristi nomen illic sedem tuam esse nec nego nec dubito. Illud
michi non negetur, quod inter omnes alias singulare tecum aliquid,

Everything in Avignon goes well and everything is done with 66
great forethought. I have already said that I praise this. It is fit and 67
right that wherever you are everything should proceed well and
successfully, and virtue and prosperity accompany your presence.
But tell me, pray, what is happening to your betrothed in the 68
meanwhile?[6] By what consul is she ruled? By what leader defended? By what companions is she comforted? You will reply— 69
no, not you yourself, who accept my questioning, I don't doubt,
calmly and impartially—but some other lesser but more impatient
fellow will reply: "Are you are laying down the law for the Roman 70
pope, or assigning him a single betrothed, when not just she
whom you have in mind but the entire church is betrothed to
him? Wherever he chooses to make his stay, there is his betrothed
and there his true residence."[7] Most blessed Father, I don't deny it 71
nor am I narrowing down your residence which I would gladly
stretch out if I had the power, and limit only by the shores of
Ocean on all sides; if only the name of Christ was today so
broadly worshipped as it was widely worshipped formerly according to many witnesses but especially Ambrose and Augustine, who
in almost the same words place the boundaries of the Christian
faith further apart than those of the Roman Empire.[8] If we believe 72
this was said literally and not more devoutly than historically, who
does not see this enormous and lamentable change in the world?
Surely if this were still true today, your residence and estate would 73
be "the sea and the abundance of his world and all those who dwell
in it."[9] But it is not so, because if Christ, Lord and Creator of 74
earth and sea as of heaven, "is himself unchanged"[10] and remains
always evenly wealthy, we on the other hand with our guilty sins
"have been made too poor"[11] and cramped into this corner of the
West, which the assaults of the unbelievers are shaking and harassing on either side. Still, I do not deny or doubt that your resi- 75
dence is wherever the name of Christ is duly worshipped. But let
no one deny this to me, that Rome uniquely has a claim, in fact

76 imo quam plurimum habet urbs Roma. Cetere enim omnes suos
habent sponsos, tibi quidem uni subditos sed suis ecclesiis presi-
dentes, illa vero nullum habet nisi te. Itaque summus in reliquis, in
romana urbe solus es pontifex, solus sponsus.

77 De illa tua igitur nec alterius sponsa nexu coniugii spiritalis te
78 interrogo: quid nunc agit? quo in statu est qua ve in spe? Si tu
taces, ipse michi respondeo: egra, inops, vidua, miserabilis, sola est
et vestem viduitatis induta diebus ac noctibus flens propheticum
79 illud canit: 'Quomodo sedet sola civitas plena populo, facta est
quasi vidua domina gentium, princeps provinciarum facta est sub
tributo?' totumque per ordinem a principio in finem flebile illud
carmen ingeminat, illic vero mestius fracta voce singultibus fessa
80 subsistit ubi scriptum est: 'Non est qui consoletur eam ex omnibus
caris eius; omnes amici eius spreverunt eam et facti sunt ei ini-
81 mici'; et iterum: 'Idcirco ego plorans et oculus meus deducens
aquam, quia longe factus est a me consolator convertens animam
82 meam.' Hic, inquam, illa profundius suspirat te significans. Nam
quis alius consolator? Quis convertere animam suam potens nisi
tu, cui et prompta remedia et sponse necessitates ac miserie note
83 omnes? Et si quid forte notitie defuerit, scito quoniam te absente
abest requies, pax exulat, bella adsunt et civilia et externa, iacent
domus, labant menia, templa ruunt, sacra pereunt, calcantur leges,
iustitia vim patitur, luget atque ululat plebs infelix tuumque no-
84 men altis vocibus invocat. Neque tu illam audis neque malorum
piget miseretque tantorum neque venerabilis sponse pias lacrimas
vides teque illi debitum restituis, qui, ut aliis minus dignis ac
minus egentibus suos redderes curiam tuam providentissime
85 vacuasti? Ita popellus quilibet suum habet epyscopum, populus

the greatest claim upon you among all other cities. For all other 76
cities have their bridegrooms, subject to you alone but presiding
over their churches, but only Rome has no groom except you.[12] So
in other cities you are the highest, but in Rome you are the only
pope, the only bridegroom.

This is why I am asking you about your betrothed, betrothed to 77
no other in the spiritual bond of marriage. How is she faring?
What is her condition or expectation? If you keep silent I shall 78
answer myself: she is ailing, penniless, widowed, pitiable, alone
and clad in widow's weeds, weeping night and day and singing that
song of the prophet: "How does a city full of people sit alone, how 79
did the mistress of nations become like a widow and how was the
mistress of provinces laid under tribute?"[13] and she redoubles that
weeping lament in sequence from beginning to end; indeed she
has paused more mournfully with broken voice and wearied by
sobbing, where it is written: "There is no one to console her out of 80
all her loved ones; all her friends have scorned her and have become her enemies." And again: "For this reason I am weeping and 81
this eye is shedding water because my consoler to change my soul
has been taken far from me." Here, I say, she sobs more deeply,
having you in mind. Indeed what other comforter has she? Who is 82
able to change her soul except you, who know swift cures and all
the needs and wretchedness of your betrothed? And if perhaps 83
you lack some news, know that in your absence repose is absent,
peace is exiled, wars both civil and foreign are close at hand, the
houses are laid low, the walls tottering, the temples collapsing, the
rites failing, the laws are trampled down, justice is violated, and
the unhappy common people mourn and groan, calling on your
name with raised voices. But you do not hear her, nor regret and 84
pity such great woes nor see the devoted tears of your revered
bride nor bring yourself back to her, you who have most wisely
emptied your own court so as to restore their own attendants to
others less worthy and less in need. Shall every little community 85

romanus suum pontificem non habebit? et parve urbes suorum in amplexibus requiescent, regina urbium semper vidua erit? quodque viduitate peius dixerim, sponsum suum semper cum aliis habitantem captumque peregrinis amoribus audiet nec tenere illum poterit nec videre, qui sui presentia se et illam gloriosos faceret ac felices?

86 Sed quo animo — da, queso, misericors pater, temerarie devotioni mee veniam —, quo, inquam, animo tu ad ripam Rodani sub auratis tectorum laquearibus somnum capis et Lateranum humi iacet et ecclesiarum mater omnium tecto carens ventis patet ac pluviis et Petri et Pauli sanctissime domus tremunt et apostolorum que nunc edes fuerat iam ruina est informisque lapidum acervus lapideis quoque pectoribus suspiria extorquens? [*§§87–105 omissis*]

106 Sepe enim divina sapientia ad sue voluntatis effectum humanis actibus utitur: successione, electione, donatione, acquisitione et si qui alii sunt modi quibus homines ad aliquam potestatem perveniunt, ubi humanorum actuum vestigia atque effectus apparent, voluntas ac dispositio Dei latet, doctis tamen ac fidelibus non ignota. Et hoc calle ad papatum ante te nostra memoria perve-
107 nerunt omnes. Est ubi ipsa Dei voluntas tam evidenter emineat ut lippis quoque cecisque etiam nota sit; sic se Deus per se ipsum sine medio velle aliquid ostendit, ut nulle ibi partes hominum videantur quorum linguis aut manibus pro organo quodam instrumentoque utitur illis ipsis quid per eos fiat ignorantibus factumque mirantibus ac fortasse dolentibus. Hoc tu nostra etate
108 solus tramite conscendisti. Nemo te fallat, pater prudentissime, nemo tibi persuadeat esse aliquem tuorum cardinalium qui vel

have its bishop, and the people of Rome not have its pope? Shall little cities rest in the embrace of their protectors, and the Queen of Cities be a perpetual widow and, experiencing something I would call worse than widowhood, shall she always fear that her groom, living with others, will be beguiled by foreign loves, and that she will neither be able to keep him nor see him, although by his presence he would make himself and her glorious and blessed?

But in what spirit, I ask—O merciful father, forgive my rash 86
devotion—with what state of mind, I say, will you take your repose under the gilded ceilings of your residence on the banks of the Rhône when the Lateran lies fallen to the ground and the mother of all churches is stripped of a roof and open to the winds and rains, and the most holy dwellings of Peter and Paul totter, and what was recently a shrine of the Apostles is now a ruin and a shapeless heap of stones, that would extort sighs even from stony breasts?[14] [*§§87–105 omitted*]

For often Divine Wisdom uses human actions for the fulfill- 106
ment of his will: succession, election, presentation, or acquisition, and any other ways in which men reach some power of office, where the traces and consequences of human actions are manifest but the will and intention of God is hidden, albeit not unknown to learned and faithful worshippers. And within our memory all
men before you reached the papacy by this path. It can happen 107
that God's own will presents itself so manifestly that it is known even to impaired or blind men; in this way God shows through Himself without an intermediary that He wills some event, so that no participation can be seen by men whose tongues or hands He uses like some tool or instrument, while the men themselves do not know what is taking place, and are amazed and perhaps regretful at its occurrence. Within our age you alone ascended the
throne by this path. Let no man deceive you, most thoughtful fa- 108
ther, let no one persuade you that there is anyone among your cardinals who thought even once about, I will not say promoting

semel unquam cogitaverit te ad papatum non dicam promovere,
109 sed poscere. Siquis forte tibi aliud insusurrat, verba dat: te sibi
110 mendacio obligatum cupit. Deus te profecto, Deus, inquam, solus
et nemo mortalium elegit, linguis licet illorum, ut dixi, usus, quas
ad aliud dispositas ad suum vertit obsequium; quodque ipse vole-
111 bat, dictu mirabile, per nolentes fecit. Hoc tibi acutissimo hominum quomodo rear incognitum, quod nemo fere vulgarium igno-
112 ravit? Sed si nunc etiam notius fieri vis quorum electus es vocibus,
113 mores atque animos tibi notissimos contemplare. Pone ante oculos
fastum illum: nusquam tanta rerum suarum extimatio parque con-
114 temptus alienarum. Alto loco assueti omnes ad summum singuli
aspirant, quo vix est qui alium quam se unum dignum censeat.
115 Sed quoniam nominare alios est necesse, quisque se cogitans alium
116 nominat vicissim ab aliis nominandus. Ita neque se quisquam nominare potest neque alium vult nisi ex eodem numero unde tanti
117 beneficii vicem speret. Quando ergo illi hoc iudicio et his moribus,
quamvis vita conspicuum et literis excellentem, humilis abbatem
118 cenobii nominassent aut tante rei ydoneum iudicassent? Aut quomodo illis in animum venisset quod sibi quisque vel suis optabat
exteris dare seu quem ex alto despicerent supra se cernere seu quo
119 ministro usi essent dominum habere? Audacter forsan, sed, ni
fallor, vere dixerim: nunquam, quo sunt animo, tale aliquid sponte
120 pati, ne dicam facere, potuissent. Non refert autem quid homines
velint, sed quid Deus. Is te vero, non alium volebat consiliumque
suum ultro non consensuris occultabat, quibus scrutinia profunda

you, but asking for your promotion to the papacy. If anyone hap- 109
pens to whisper another account to you, he is playing tricks on
you: he wants you to be obliged to him for his lie. Indeed God, 110
God and no other, I say, and no mortal chose you, certainly using
the tongues of those cardinals, as I said, which were inclined toward another choice when He turned them to obey Him; and,
strange to relate, He effected what He wanted through these unwilling men. How could I believe this was unknown to you, most 111
shrewd of men, something practically none of the common crowd
failed to know? But if you now want to know even better by 112
whose votes you were elected, consider their characters and behavior, so well known to you. Put before your eyes their arrogance; 113
nowhere else is there such great self esteem for their own condition and contempt for that of others. They are accustomed to a 114
lofty status, and each of them individually aspires to the highest
rank, so that hardly any one holds another man worthy of it rather
than himself. But since they are obliged to name others, each man 115
thinks of himself while he nominates another from whom he
expects to be nominated. So no man can either name himself nor 116
is he willing to name another except from the same group from
whom he can expect the return of this great favor. So when would 117
these men with this opinion and this character have nominated
the abbot of a humble monastery, however admirable in his life
and preeminent in his learning, or judged him fit for such a
power? Or how would it enter their heads to give to outsiders 118
what each wanted for himself or for his own kin, or to see someone they despised set above them, or accept as master the man
they had used as a servant? I would say, perhaps boldly but, unless 119
I am mistaken, truthfully that never with their attitude could they
have allowed, still less enacted, such a choice of their own free will.
It is not what men want but what God wills that matters. Truly 120
He wanted you, not another, and deliberately hid his intention
from men who would not agree; as they turned over their deep

versantibus sic clanculum tuum nomen inseruit ut ex tot nominibus romano cardine fulgidis cum solus abbas Massilie sonuisset, dolor et timor malos, gaudium et spes bonos, admiratio ac stupor omnes arriperet, omnes tamen una voce, variis licet affectibus, in laudem Dei, 'qui facit mirabilia magna solus,' stupentia ora resolverent. [§§*121–36 omissis*]

137 Fuerunt in hoc numero quos perpendi et Italiam extra orbem esse et equor innavigabile et Alpes impervias opinari, cum et
138 utrunque iter amenissimum et Italia iuxta sit. Quibusdam sensi aerem, aquas, vina, cibos esse suspectos; que suspitio cessaret, si aut his unquam usi essent aut italicam celi temperiem ac suavitatem et que timent omnia apud probatissimos auctorum, non magis italos quam externos, laudata semper atque omnibus prelata didicissent.

139 Hoc loco aliqua michi ad memoriam redeunt, parva quidem in
140 se, sed ad probandum quod loquor non inefficacia. Cum enim Benedicto duodecimo Vulsini lacus anguille mire magnitudinis et saporis insoliti misse essent et ipse admirans eas inter cardinales dividi iussisset exigua sibi parte servata, non multis post diebus, dum ad eum ex more convenissent, earundem mentione orta, ut erat iocosus in sermone, 'si pregustassem' inquit 'scivissemque quales erant, non fuissem tam largus distributor; sed nunquam
141 credidi tale aliquid nasci posse in Italia.' Quo dicto Iohannes de Columna cardinalis, semper michi reverenti suspirio memorandus, sub quo illis in locis adolescentiam totam egi, vultu motus atque animo — erat enim colere nobilis et que nichil vel visu fedum vel auditu absonum pati posset —, subito sic exarsit ut diceret mirari se quid ita vir doctus, qui tam multa legisset, excellentem cuntis in rebus Italiam ignoraret. [§§*142–53 omissis*]

scrutinies he inserted your name so secretly that, when only the name of the abbot of Marseilles rang out from among so many glittering names in the Roman college of cardinals, pain and fear struck the wicked, joy and hope the good, but wonder and amazement seized hold of all, and all with one accord—though with various emotions—opened their gaping mouths to the praise of God "who alone achieves mighty marvels."[15] [*§§121–36 omitted*]

There were men in this group whom I understood to say that Italy was outside the world, they thought its sea unnavigable and the Alps impenetrable, although each route is most pleasant and Italy neighbors on France. I realized that to some the air, water, wine and food were suspect—a suspicion which would lapse if they had ever enjoyed them, or learned that the moderate climate of Italy or its sweetness and all the things they fear were always praised and preferred to all else by the best authors, and by foreigners no less than Italians.[16] 137 138

Here some details come into my mind, small in themselves but not ineffective in proving my case. For when Benedict XII was sent eels of amazing size and unique flavor from the Volsinian lake, and he marveled at them and ordered them shared out among his cardinals, saving only a tiny portion for himself, after a few days when the guests came as usual to his dwelling and the eels were mentioned, being a jester in conversation he said: "If I had had a sample in advance and known how good they were I would not have shared them out so generously, but I never thought anything of such quality could be bred in Italy." At this Cardinal Giovanni Colonna, whom I will always recall with a respectful sigh and in whose service I spent all my youth in that region, was moved in expression and mood (for he had the temper of a noble, and could endure neither to see anything disgusting nor hear anything dissonant)—he suddenly flared up to say he was amazed that such an educated man who had read so much, was ignorant that Italy excelled in all things. [*§§142–53 omitted*] 139 140 141

154 Dabo tamen, si expediat, testes magnos, quibus non credere
pudor ipse prohibeat. Sed quid apud te opus est testibus, quem
155 unum testem ego negantibus sim daturus? Addam tamen alium
testem, vivum quoque et alienigenam et preclarum, Guidonem
Portuensem, quem memini et ipse etiam, puto, meminerit, anno
iubileo ab illa sua gloriosa legatione redeuntem, dum iter suum
innata michi ad illum devotione prosequerer et ad Benacum Venetie lacum nobilissimum venissemus atque ipse non suorum modo
sed italicorum procerum atque equitum turba ingenti circumsep-
tus supra quendam herbose telluris tumulum constitisset, ut est
ingenio agilis et eloquio facilis ac iocundus, Alpes ad dexteram
nivosas estate media et profundissimi lacus estum equoreo parem,
ante retroque colles exiguos, ad levam vero uberem latamque
planitiem diu oculis metientem, ad postremum me nominatim
evocasse ac dixisse cuntis audientibus: 'Plane fateor vos pulcriorem
156 multoque meliorem quam nos patriam habere'; dumque me confessione tam clara letum cerneret eamque non nutu solum sed
verbis et plausibus approbantem, addidisse: 'At nos tranquilliorem
157 vobis statum habemus regimurque quietius'; dumque hoc dicto
quasi victor abscederet, vinci nolens hac illum voce detinui, imo
non ego sed veritas; dixi enim: 'Vestrum nos confestim, ut velle
ceperimus, statum habere quis prohibet? Nam vos talem terram
158 habere prohibet natura.' Tacuit ille subridens, ut qui me vera locutum intelligeret nec michi cedere nec obniti vero vellet. Ita inde
discessum est.

159 Transeo autem ad errorum species alias. Sunt qui in Italia nichil
preter incolarum mores metuant, quibus se odio atque contemptui
160 futuros putant. Qui si Ecclesiam meminissent in Italia, non alibi,
ab humillimis radicibus in hanc altitudinem excrevisse, si preterea
cogitarent pene omnem quantacunque est, que utique magna est,
potentiam eius temporalem intra Italie fines esse, suspitionem

I will add another witness, still living and foreign and distinguished, that is Guy de Boulogne, bishop of Porto, whom I re- 154
member, and he too remembers me, I think.[17] When he was returning from his brilliant visit as legate in the year of the Jubilee I was escorting his journey out of my natural devotion to him and we came to Lake Garda, the most noble lake of the Veneto. He was surrounded by a vast throng, not only of his own retinue, but of Italian nobles and knights. He took position on a grassy mound and being quick of intellect and fluent and agreeable in speech he scanned with his gaze the Alps to our right covered with snow in midsummer, and the currents of the great lake equal to the sea tides, and the small hills in front and behind with the broad and fertile plain opening up on the left; finally he called me out by name and said in the hearing of all: "I openly admit you have a 155
country much more beautiful and finer than ours." Seeing me 156
overjoyed at so open an admission and approving his saying, not just with a nod but in words and applause, he added: "But we are in a more peaceful condition than yours and are ruled more calmly." And as he moved away as if victorious, not wanting to ad- 157
mit defeat, I—or rather the truth itself—answered him with this remark: "What prevents us from instantly enjoying your peaceful state, if we wish? On the contrary Nature forbids you from possessing such a land." He fell silent and smiled as if he recognized 158
that I spoke the truth but did not wish either to yield or oppose me. And so we departed.

I pass on now to other misunderstandings. There are men who 159
fear nothing in Italy except the behavior of the natives, who they think will regard them with loathing and contempt. But if they 160
remembered that the Church had grown up in Italy and nowhere else, from the most humble roots to this lofty grandeur, moreover if they thought that almost all the Church's temporal power, such as it is, and it is surely great, lay within the boundaries of Italy, they would perhaps cast away their false, unnecessary and unwor-

161 falsam, supervacuam atque indignam fortasse deponerent. Repeto
etiam hunc sermonem michi fuisse cum quodam habentium nomen a cardine, viro nobili originis transalpine, quantum noscere
poteram mitissimo purissimoque hominum, presente tunc Tala-
rando Albanensi, qui lucidum nuper Ecclesie sidus fuit, et sepe
simplicitatem illius meumque, ut ipse vocabat, astum lepidissimis
162 iocis interpellante. Cum ille me percontaretur an fieri posset ut
Romanus Pontifex sacrumque collegium Rome tuti agerent, ego
autem non solum tutos ibi, sed nusquam tutos alibi nusquamque
dicerem honoratos, modo, quod maxime eos decet, iuste atque
honeste vivere in animum inducerent, id si fecissent, non colendos
tantum, sed paulo minus adorandos, dicebat ille persuasum sibi
quod, si forte servorum aliquis suorum supplicio dignum aliquid
163 egisset, in caput domini periculum redundaret. Respondebam,
dummodo non ipse iudicium impediret, alienum scelus non sibi
periculo neque infamie sed glorie futurum, quo amicus iustitie
164 probaretur; cumque inter verba, ut fit, incidisset mentio Bonifacii
octavi velut efficacissimum argumentum ad deterrendos hinc
animos, respondebam ego Bonifacium non Rome sed in sua,
Rome tunc prelata, patria neque a Romanis — non tamen adde-
165 bam 'sed a Gallis' — captum; quin ut tutus liberque esset, illico, ut
abeundi facultas fuit, Romam, hoc est arcem cristiane fidei, pe-
166 tiisse. Que ille audiens et singula secum volvens, dixit quidem
multa que sileo, sed in finem suspirans et vix lacrimas tenens
Cristum cuntosque celicolas clara voce testatus est optare se totis
167 precordiis Rome vivere, Rome mori. Tunc Albanensis, vir oculatis-
simus, puritatem hominis admirans, ad aurem michi iocundissimo
murmure 'Habes' inquit 'quod volebas. Exhausisti hunc hominem:
168 vis ne aliquid amplius audire?' Quod idcirco memoravi ut appareat

thy suspicion. I recall I had this discussion with one of the cardi- 161
nals, a nobleman born north of the Alps, the mildest and purest of
men as far as I could tell, when Élie de Talleyrand, cardinal of
Alba, so recently a brilliant star of the Church, was present;[18] he
often challenged that man's simplicity and what he was pleased to
call my own shrewdness, with delightful jokes. When he asked me 162
whether the Roman pope and sacred college could live safely at
Rome, I said that not only would they be safe there but they
would not be safe nor honored anywhere else—provided that, as
was most fitting for them, they made up their minds to live justly
and honorably: if they did that they would not only be respected
but little short of adored. He said he was convinced that if perhaps one of his servants committed a capital crime, the effect
would rebound on his master's head. I answered that so long as he 163
did not personally obstruct the trial, another man's crime would
not endanger him nor bring him discredit but rather glory, since
he would be proved the friend of justice. And when the mention 164
of Boniface VIII arose in our talk, as if it were the most effective
argument to deter men's minds from that course, I answered that
Boniface was taken prisoner not at Rome but in his own country,
which at that time he preferred to Rome, and not by Romans—
and I did not add "but by Frenchmen."[19] Indeed to be safe and 165
free, he had instantly, once he had the chance to escape, made for
Rome, that is the citadel of the Christian faith. Hearing this 166
and turning it over in his mind, he said many things which I pass
over, but finally sighing and scarcely containing his tears he called
Christ and all the saints to witness in a loud voice that he wholeheartedly wanted to live in Rome and die in Rome. Then the car- 167
dinal of Alba, a very shrewd man, admiring the man's purity, said
in my ear with a most charming whisper "You have got what you
wanted. You have exhausted him. Do you want to hear anything
more?" I mentioned this to make it clear that I had formed this 168

hanc me atque alias illius ordinis suspitiones ex ipsorum quoque non fictis sermonibus concepisse. [§§*169–222 omissis*]

223 Persuade cardinalibus tuis — illos enim hac in re maxime vereor — Italiam non esse qualem ipsi putant, sed esse nullo scripto-
rum illustrium discordante optimam atque clarissimam et famosissimam mundi partem, esse, ut ipsi testantur et attestatur veritas,
unam ex omnibus cui pene nichil mali adsit, nichil absit boni,
224 modo pax una non desit, que deesse te presente non poterit. Doce
illos esse hic urbes nobilissimas atque pulcerrimas, quibus visis
225 fetida vilescat Avinio pudeatque non antea viluisse. Esse aerem
saluberrimum atque inter frigus estumque eximie temperatum,
quam causam scriptores quidam romani atque universalis imperii
posuere, quod sic ex contrariis mixtum esset ut et australes astu-
tias vigore corporeo et virtutibus animi arthoam contunderet feri-
tatem atque ita necessarium fuisse ut de utrisque participanti
226 medio extrema succumberent. Esse hic lacus piscosissimos, quot
quales ve nulla regio tam parvo habet in spatio; esse et flumina
opportunissimis flexibus nature consilio sic diversis locis errantia
ut Italie magna pars, Liguria et Venetia et Emilia atque Flaminia,
vix insignem locum habeant qui non a quiescente aquis obsequen-
227 tibus adeatur. Esse in circuitu geminum mare crebris portubus et
nobilium urbium corona et in utrunque decurrentium fluviorum
faucibus insigne, ita ut undis hinc salsis hinc dulcibus Italia ferme
228 omnis sine labore permeabilis atque amena sit. Esse ubi desunt
maria Alpes aerias barbarico oppositas furori, esse per medium
colles virentissimos et apricas valles et campos uberrimos et qui
Italiam quam longa est silvosis iugis intersecat patrem montium

and other suspicions about his order from their own unfeigned conversation.[20] [*§§169–222 omitted*]

Persuade your cardinals—for it is they whom I must fear in 223
this matter—that Italy is not what they themselves imagine, but as all the great writers agree without exception, the best and most glorious and famous part of the world; that it is, as they themselves bear witness and the truth confirms, the one land of all which has almost no evil and lacks nothing good, just so long as
there is peace, which is present when you are present. Teach them 224
that here there are most noble and handsome cities, the sight of which will cheapen stinking Avignon and shame them that it was
not already cheap in their eyes. The climate is most healthy and 225
marvelously blended between chill and heat, which is the reason adduced by certain writers for the origin of Rome and her empire over the world, because it was so blended from opposites that it countered the trickery of the South with physical vigor, and suppressed the savagery of the North with its moral virtues, so that it was inevitable that the extremities would surrender to the mean,
which shared in both their natures.[21] Here there are lakes full of 226
fish, such as no other region has in so small a space; there are rivers curving by the design of nature into most convenient bends in scattered places, so that a great part of Italy, Liguria and Venetia and Emilia and the Flaminian region scarcely have a distinguished place that is not accessible to a man calmly traveling along delightful waters.[22] There are twin seas surrounding it, remarkable for 227
their frequent harbors, and a garland of noble cities and the estuaries of rivers flowing down on both sides, so that almost all Italy is accessible without effort and agreeable, now by salt water and
now by fresh. Where seas are lacking there are the soaring Alps, 228
placed to oppose barbarian frenzy; there are most verdant hills in the center and sunny valleys and most fertile plains and the Apennine range, father of mountains, which cuts into the whole length of Italy with wooded hills, pregnant with gleaming waters on this

Apenninum, nitidis hinc illinc amnibus gravidum, et laticum varietate salubri fontes gelidos tepentesque, sanis delectabiles, egris utiles, sitientibus oportunos; simul et metallorum venas omnium et bellantium armentorum acies et navigiorum species his nostris iam cuntis equoribus imperantes, ita ut hoc totum quod Mediterraneum vocant mare, si Italici nolint, nisi occulto latrocinio nulla
229 gens naviget. Esse hic frumenti, vini et olei, esse arborum et fructuum et pomorum que vester orbis ignorat, esse silvarum et quadrupedum et ferarum et piscium et volucrum et ciborum omnis generis infinitam copiam, ne fortassis fame mori metuant, non tu quidem, qui et hec nosti et ab annis teneris in religione optima enutritus carnis inedia impinguare spiritum didicisti sacroque ieiunio assuefactus esuriem amas, crapulam execraris; sed qui avinionensibus delitiis assuevere nichil preter Rodanum cogitare queunt nec, si queant, volunt; tam dulcis est enim error consuetudine saporatus et conditus annis, ut palato animi veri gustus amarior fiat; quo profecto spirituali egritudine laborantibus nichil est funestius. [§§*230–63 omissis*]

264 Unum silui sive ad extremum distuli quod primum esse potuerat. Nosti quo in statu cristiani tui sint per orientem; quin et
265 propinquius malum est. Non audisti ut inermes Asie populi, quos nostra desidia fortes facit, atque in primis olim Friges, Turchi hodie, miseram Greciam sine fine diripiunt et Egeo sparsas Cycladas populantur? Que etsi longis erroribus obstinate pervicacie iustas penas dent, inde tamen ad nos verosque catholicos est transitus.
266 Iam Cyprus, Creta, Rhodus, Euboea viciniorque nobis tentatur Achaia et Epyrus, iam calabrum litus flentis Grecie mestissimas

side and the other; there are, with a healthy variety of streams, both cool and warm springs, delightful to the healthy and useful to the sick and convenient for those thirsty; at the same time there are veins of all the metals and herds of war horses and varieties of ships which now command all our waters, so that no race could sail the whole Mediterranean Sea, as they call it, except in stealthy
brigandage, if the Italians were to forbid it.[23] Here there is an un- 229
limited supply of grain, oil and wine, and trees and fruits and apples that your world does not know; here there are woods and animals and wild beasts and fishes and birds and every kind of foodstuffs — in case the cardinals are afraid they might die of hunger. This doesn't apply to you, who know all these things and have learned how to enrich your spirit by starving your flesh, as you were brought up in the best religion from your tender youth, and became accustomed to holy fasting, you who love hunger and abhor hangovers. But those men are who so accustomed to the luxuries of Avignon can think of nothing but the Rhône, and would not want to if they could; so sweet is a delusion flavored by custom and seasoned by the years that the taste of truth is too bitter for their mind's palate; and surely nothing is more deadly to those suffering from sickness of the spirit.[24] [*§§230–63 omitted*]

I have kept silent on one topic, or rather postponed it, which 264
could have come first, to the end. You know the condition of your
Christians in the East; but the evil is nearer than that. Have you 265
not heard how the unarmed peoples of Asia, whom our apathy has made brave, and especially the Phrygians, now Turks,[25] are plundering wretched Greece without cease and stripping the Cyclades scattered over the Aegean? And although the Greeks are paying the just penalty for their longstanding errors and impertinent obstinacy,[26] yet from there it is an easy move for the Turks to
attack us, the true Catholics. Now Cyprus, Crete, Rhodes, Eu- 266
boea, and nearer to us Achaia and Epirus are being assailed; now the Calabrian shore listens with anxious ears to the broken-

267 voces trepidis auribus accipit. Sic nunc itaque fides Cristi, ut vides,
ad orientem periclitatur: tu ad occidentem sedes adhuc, o maxime
268 dux nostrarum et pontifex animarum? Qui ut tuum munus im-
pleres, nisi fallor, pridem surrexisse debueras teque vel solum difficultatibus obvium ferens non Romam modo sed Constantinopo-
269 lim perrexisse; quanquam solus esse non potes: Cristus ipse, cuius
res agitur, tecum erit et Cristi acies quocunque ieris te sequetur.
270 Non est boni ducis se periculo subtrahere, multo minus autem labori, sed illuc properare quo eum plurimus bellantium clamor
271 vocat. Potuit Cristus crucem fugere, si nos deserere voluisset: nullis nostris meritis obstrictus pro salute nostra mori voluit. Nos
beneficio preventi pro illius gloria non solum mortem fugimus sed
272 laborem. Iam dudum debuit omnis status, omnis etas arma corri-
pere et in illo spei anchoram figere qui nullum unquam in se
sperantium fefellit, qui Theodosio cum paucis contra immensos
exercitus barbarorum prelianti miram incredibilemque victoriam
273 dedit et pro eo fecit elementa pugnare. In quo quidem eleganter
conterraneus meus, quamvis Cristum nesciens, Deo tamen vero-
que testimonium perhibuit his versibus:

Te propter gelidis Aquilo de monte procellis
obruit adversas acies revolutaque tela
vertit in actores et turbine repulit hastas.
O nimium dilecte Deo, cui fundit ab antris
Eolus armatas hiemes, cui militat ether
et coniurati veniunt ad classica venti.

274 Et nos dilecti Deo essemus, si eum qua tenemur mente diligere-
mus; nunquam nempe se diligentibus abfuit, ut qui interdum se
275 persequentibus affuit. Et nobis ab antris Cristus, non Eolus, arma-

hearted cries of weeping Greece. So now the faith of Christ, it 267
seems, is in danger toward the East; yet you still sit unmoving in
the West, great leader and priest of our souls? To meet your task, 268
unless I am mistaken, you should have arisen long since and
advanced not just to Rome but to Constantinople to confront
these challenges, even without allies; and yet you cannot be alone: 269
Christ Himself, whose dominion is at issue, will be with you, and
his fighting force will follow you wherever you go. It is not the ac- 270
tion of a good leader to withdraw from danger, still less from toil,
but to hasten where the fiercest shouting of warriors summons
him. Christ could have shunned the cross if He had wanted to 271
desert us: He was bound by no services of ours but He was willing
to die for our salvation. We have been anticipated by his gift and
yet we do not simply flee from death but even from labor for his
glory. Every rank and every age should long since have seized their 272
arms and planted the anchor of hope in Him who never yet has
deceived anyone, putting hope in Him: He gave a wondrous and
unbelievable victory to Theodosius when He was battling with a
small force against vast armies of barbarians and made the elements
themselves fight for Him.[27] On this theme my compatriot, al- 273
though he did not know Christ, bore elegant witness to God and
truth in these verses:

> For you the North Wind with chill mountain storms
> crushed the opposing ranks and turned their weapons back
> against the force that wielded them, fending off their spears
> with whirlwind power. O greatly loved by God, for whom
> Aeolus
> pours armored tempests from his caves, for whom the air
> now fights, and winds conspiring gather to his trumpets.[28]

We too would be loved by God if we loved Him with the resolution 274
that sustains us; for God was never far from those who loved Him,
just as He at times supported those who persecuted Him. And for 275

tas hiemes funderet, nobis ether et auxiliares ad classica venientes
276 militarent venti. Sed quis ingratis militet? Quis sopitis atque tor-
277 pentibus opem ferat? Non sopiti tantum sed exanimes et peccato
mortui longeva iamque in naturam versa voluptate marcuimus.
Iam moribus malis obruti sepultique et ob hoc ipsum celestibus
auxiliis destituti sumus.

278 Ad te autem redeo. Ubique, fateor, utilis, ubique sancta et venerabilis presentia tua est, sed quid, queso, quid Rodanus, quid
279 Sorgia et Ruentia tui egent? Quis ibi tuorum protegendus? Quis
hostium comprimendus? Egent tui Ionium et Egeum et Helles-
280 pontus et Propontis et Bosphorus. Quid hic igitur monstri est?
Non possum satis hoc querere. In oriente pugnatur: tu quid agis
281 in occidente, spiritualium dux bellorum? Est hic quidem dominorum error publicus, qui profecto tuus esse non potest, ut se
suis voluptatibus dominos fieri putent cum necessitatibus alienis
282 fiant. Tu si nominis, si officii, si Domini meministi qui suis in
pascuis te pastorem fecit, non illic herebis ubi umbra fortassis aut
fons gratior, sed ubi predo seu lupus infestior, ubi necessitas domi-
283 nici gregis maior, memor illius evangelice sententie: 'Bonus pastor
animam suam dat pro ovibus suis, mercenarius autem et qui non
est pastor, cuius non sunt oves proprie, videt lupum venientem et
284 dimittit oves et fugit.' Tu es pastor; tue sunt oves que Domini tui
sunt. Omnia tibi commisit, omnem tibi gregis curam, omne ius
285 contulit. Lupus ad ovilis ostium fremit et tu cessas? Si non mercenarius sed verus es pastor, offer te preclaro pioque discrimini,
quod sicut temere optare non est prudentis, sic molliter declinare
non est viri fortis ac magnanimi.

us too Christ, not Aeolus, would pour armed storms, for us the
sky and winds would fight as auxiliaries, answering the trumpet
call.[29] But who would fight for the ungrateful? Who would bring 276
aid to men drugged and paralyzed? Not only drugged but lifeless 277
and dead from sin, we have withered away as hedonism has under-
mined our character. We are now crushed and buried in evil ways
and abandoned by our heavenly support for this very reason.

Now I return to you. Your presence is beneficial, holy and wor- 278
shipful everywhere, but I ask you, what does the Rhone or Sorgue
or Durance need from you?[30] Who among your people needs 279
protecting? What enemies need to be crushed? It is the Ionian and
Aegean and Hellespont and Propontis and Bosphorus that need
you. So what is this unnatural situation? I cannot ask this enough. 280
There is fighting in the East: what are you doing in the West,
leader of our spiritual wars? This is indeed a common error of 281
masters—but cannot be yours—that they think they are masters
by means of their pleasures whereas they are masters through
other men's needs. If you are mindful of your name, your duty and 282
your Lord who has made you shepherd over his pastures, you will
not linger here, where perhaps the shade or spring is more pleasing, but go where the brigand or wolf is more aggressive, where the
need of your Lord's flock is greater, keeping in mind the saying of
his Gospel: "The good shepherd gives his life for his sheep, but 283
the hired man who is not their shepherd, to whom the sheep do
not belong, when he sees the wolf approaching, abandons the
sheep and runs."[31] You are their shepherd, the sheep who belong 284
to your Lord are your sheep. He has entrusted everything to you,
and conferred on you all the care of the sheep and a right over
them. The wolf is growling at the door of the pen and you are
hanging back? If you are not the hired man but their true shep- 285
herd, submit yourself to this pious and glorious danger; since just
as it is not the nature of a prudent man to want it rashly, so it is
not the behavior of a brave and noble man to shirk it.[32]

286 Mitte oculos in longinqua non locorum modo sed temporum:
videbis quanta ibi calamitas presens sit quantumque periculum
287 futuri. Nam, ut ait Comicus,

> Istud est sapere, non quod ante pedes modo est
> videre, sed etiam illa que futura sunt
> prospicere.

288 Certe nisi iam hinc prospicis, nisi occurris, actum est: pudendam
nobis cristiani nominis illis in partibus ruinam et prorsus indignam ac miserabilem audiemus, que, ut dixi, non Cristi, qui est
iniurie inaccessus, sed nostra iactura est, nostra secordia, noster
pudor, qui iam tantus ibi est ut an maior esse possit in dubio sim.
289 Nescio enim an peius sit amisisse Ierusalem an ita Bizantion possidere: ibi enim non agnoscitur Cristus, hic leditur, dum sic coli-
tur; illi hostes, hi scismatici, peiores hostibus; illi aperte nostrum
imperium detrectant, hi verbo Romanam Ecclesiam matrem
dicunt, cui quam devoti filii sint, quam humiliter Romani Pontifi-
290 cis iussa suscipiant, tuus a te illis datus patriarcha testabitur. Illi
minus nos oderunt quia minus metuunt; isti autem totis nos visceribus et metuunt et oderunt. Constat quia nos canes iudicant et, si
291 loquendi libertas affuerit, canes vocant. Interfui ego solemni die
dum romano ritu missa celebraretur: Grecus quidam, homo non
illiteratus sed multo maxime stultus atque arrogans, exclamavit et
'Non possum pati' inquit 'Latinorum nugas.' Quod verbum intel-
292 lectum si fuisset a populo, non impune, ut auguror, tulisset. Sed
sic est, sic de nobis sentiunt; et basilicas suas siquis ex nostris in-
troierit, quasi humano sanguine aut fedo facinore violatas recon-
ciliant et expurgant.

Direct your gaze not only to distant places but to ancient times. 286
You will see how great a disaster is at hand and how much danger
is to come. For as the comic dramatist says: 287

> That is true sense, to see not only things
> before your feet, but even look ahead
> to things to come.[33]

For surely unless you look ahead, unless you confront trouble, all 288
is lost; we shall hear of a shameful collapse of the name of Christ
in those regions, one utterly undeserved and wretched. This, as I
said, is not Christ's loss, for He is beyond being wronged, but
ours; it is our apathy, our shame, which I doubt could be any
greater there than it now is. For I don't know whether it is worse 289
to have lost Jerusalem or to possess Byzantium on the present
terms;[34] for Christ is not recognized in the former, while he is
harmed in the latter, so long as he is worshipped in the Orthodox
Greek fashion; the Turks are enemies, but the Greeks are heretics,
worse than enemies: enemies openly abuse our empire, but heretics
call the Roman Church their mother in name only. Your patriarch
whom you gave to them will bear witness how devout they are as
sons, and how humbly they obey the orders of the Roman pope.[35]
The enemy hates us less because they fear us less; but those here- 290
tics both fear and hate us with all their heart. It is a fact that they
judge us to be dogs, and when they have the freedom to talk they
call us dogs. I was present on a holy day when the Mass was being 291
celebrated according to the Roman rite. Some Greek, not an uneducated man but very stupid and arrogant, cried out: "I can't bear
the nonsense of the Latins." If this remark had been understood
by the people, he would not have got away with it, as I reckon. But 292
that is how it is. That is their opinion of us, and if any of us enters
their basilicas, they atone and purify them as if they had been violated by blood or a vile offense.

293 Et hec quidem Romana Ecclesia diu novit et passa est. Quod
an dici torpor an patientia mereatur, cum tam facile dilui possit
294 hoc dedecus, iudicandum linquo aliis. Certe nos nostrosque hostes, a quibus nunc Ierosolima detinetur, magnum equor interiacet. Itaque cum illis, ut res nostre et illorum sunt, non parvus est
labor. Unde fit ut dilationem nostram impotentia fortassis excuset,
quamvis impotentie non nisi ex nostris dissensionibus exorte excu-
295 satio nulla sit. Inter nos autem et hos Greculos nichil est medium,
nisi noster sopor ac nostra segnities, quibus ut odii plurimum, sic
296 nichil est virium nilque ibi volentibus negotii est. Duobus Italie
populis sponsor sim, si tu bene velle ceperis, brevi eos, non iunctos
modo sed unumquenque per se, vel imbelle illud imperium eversu-
ros vel ad iugum matris Ecclesie deducturos. Quo magis magisque
conniventiam hanc stupeo nec satis intelligo quid ita res maxime
297 negliguntur cum minimarum tanta solicitudo sit hominibus. Et
licet hic omnium cristianorum publicus pudor sit, tamen in omni
exercitu male rem gerente ducum pudor est maximus. Sepe
quidem sub uno duce periere qui sub alio salvi essent, sepe culpa
ducis qui dispositi erant ad victoriam victi sunt, sepe etiam et fere
298 semper militum culpam vulgi opinio reflectit in duces. Quamobrem vobis, qui omnium duces estis, tibi dico romanoque principi,
quo studio assurgendum sit ut non solum vestre sed comunis
etiam molem vitetis infamie, ipsi cognoscitis. Nec cognoscere satis
est: plus aliquid, imo plus multum exigitur a vobis, ne putetis hanc
299 vos gratis magnitudinem consecutos. Per difficultates medias itur
ad gloriam. Nunquam quiescet quem virtutis calcar attigerit. Ex

This too the Roman church has long known and endured; 293
whether this deserves to be called torpidity or patience, given that this shame could so easily be washed away, I leave others to judge.
Admittedly a great sea lies between us and our enemies, who now 294
occupy Jerusalem. Hence the effort to come to grips with them, in our and their present circumstances, is by no means small. This is why incapacity may perhaps excuse our delay, although there is no excuse for an incapacity that only arises from our own conflicts.
Further, there is nothing between us and these Greeklings except 295
our own sleepiness and sloth, since although they feel a great resentment, they are powerless and it is no great business to go there
for those who wish to do so. I guarantee that with two Italian cit- 296
ies,[36] if you start to show goodwill, they will quickly, not just as allies but each individually, either overthrow that unwarlike empire or bring it back under the yoke of the Church. This makes me marvel even more at our acquiescence, and I do not know why these most urgent matters are being neglected while men feel such
anxiety over trivial things. Even if this is a public disgrace to all 297
Christians, still, in every army that fails, the greatest disgrace accrues to the leaders. Often in fact men have died under one leader though they would have survived under another; often through their commander's fault men prepared for victory have been defeated; often—or almost always—the opinion of the masses turns
the blame from the soldiers onto their leaders. For this reason you, 298
who are the leaders of us all, I mean you and the Roman emperor,[37] personally recognize how zealously you must rise up to escape the deadweight of not only your personal but also the general shame. And it is not enough to recognize this: something, indeed a great deal more is expected from you, to prevent you
thinking that you have achieved this greatness at no cost. The path 299
to glory runs through the midst of great challenges; the man pricked by the spur of virtue will never rest. His unwearying endurance will march from one challenge to the next and, as it were,

una in aliam indefessa constantia gradietur et ceu totidem altioris
fame iuga conscendet eritque sibi is labor omni dulcior quiete, imo
quidem ea sola requies animo in altum suspiranti, cui ab egregiis
actibus feriari, is demum mestus est labor miserumque otium.
300 Legisti ut Iulius Cesar bella sibi deesse damnum vocet fugamque
hostium turbatus aspiciat, ut Titus Vespasiani diem perdidisse se
doleat quo nichil suo more magnifice liberaliterque gessisset, ut
Alexander Macedo adolescens primum inter coetaneos lamentetur
quod Philippus pater crebris victoriis hostes sibi vincendos atque
omnem bellice laudis occasionem materiamque preripiat, vir deinde ne hostes fuga dilabantur solicitus atque intentus vigilet
eoque metu dempto iam securus dormiat, quasi nichil nisi securi-
301 tatem metuens et laborum finem; utque aliquid de literis sacris
immisceam, israelitici dux populi Iosue, dum post illam de tot regibus victoriam nox instaret et posset parta gloria contentus re-
quiescere et diurnum laborem nocturno sopore diluere, et laborem
ipsum et cum illo gloriam augere cupiens, ut consisteret soli iussit;
302 et paruit. Sic est ergo: generosi animi pabulum ac delitie sunt labores non propter se quidem, sed propter id quo non aliter quam
per illos ascenditur.

303 Hec duobus vobis ante alios semper habenda sub oculis semperque animis agitanda proposui non fervide tantum sed etiam
304 importune, ut qui cunta michi deesse maluerim quam fidem. Meo
quidem vel forsitan alieno officio functus sum; vera utique et ab
alio melius dicenda cui maior esset auctoritas, sed vel nulli cogitata
vel omnibus formidata disserui, a posteritate certe gratiam, a tua
autem sanctitate et illius alterius maiestate veniam saltem sperans.
305 Que si ab illo, ut dixi, in optimam semper partem sunt accepta, eo

climb as many ridges of loftier glory, and this toil will be sweeter
to him than any repose, indeed that will be the only repose for his
spirit aspiring to the heights; for such a man, being on holiday
from deeds of distinction is in the end but sad toil and wretched
leisure. You have read how Julius Caesar called it an occasion of 300
loss to be without wars and looked with anxiety on the rout of his
enemy, how Titus son of Vespasian grieved that he had wasted the
day on which he had done nothing grand and generous in his
usual style, how Alexander of Macedon first lamented as a youth
among his peers that his father Philip had snatched from him by
his frequent victories the enemies for him to conquer and every
chance and scope for glory in warfare, then as a man kept watch in
urgent anxiety lest the enemy might slip away in flight, and only
when relieved of this fear slept without care, as if he was not afraid
of anything except being carefree and at an end of his struggles.[38]
And to add in something from the Scriptures, Joshua, leader of 301
the Israelites, when the night after that victory over so many kings
was approaching, when he could rest content with the victory he
had won and ease his daily struggle with sleep by night, wanting
to increase both his struggle and his glory along with it, ordered
the sun to stand still, and it obeyed.[39] That is so; struggles are the 302
fuel and delight of a noble spirit not on their own account, but
because of what can be achieved only through them.

I have set out for both of you beyond all other men these ideals 303
that must always be kept before your eyes and I did so not only
with zeal but with insistence, being a man who would rather lose
everything than abandon my loyalty. I have performed my office— 304
or perhaps another's; in any case I have certainly spoken the truth,
and perhaps it would have been better said by someone of greater
authority, but I have set out things that either no one thought to
say or everyone feared to say, hoping that by doing so I would earn
the thanks of posterity and from Your Holiness and His Imperial
Majesty at least pardon. And if they have always been taken in 305

nunc a te mitius accipienda confido quo successor Petri mitior
306 debet esse quam Cesaris. Et cum illo quidem, ut materia incidit,
sepe olim, tecum hodie primum michi sermo iste susceptus est,
seu verius, quoniam crebro michi hec tecum in silentio lis fuit,
307 nunc noviter productus ad calamum. Qui quoniam, etsi pro desiderio meo brevis, pro tua tamen multiplici occupatione longissi-
mus evasit, aliquo tandem fine claudendus est. [*§§308–34 omissis*]

335 Hec ego, pater clementissime, fide pura stilo humili dictaverim
fisus tibi amariusculam veritatem quam melliculas blanditias ca-
336 riorem. Si erravi aut si sanctitatem tuam mea libertas offendit,
337 flexis anime poplitibus veniam peto. Tu vero nunc reiectis consultoribus vanis tecum cogita tecumque delibera an quod superest
temporis in ceno avinionensi agere malis an Rome, que tota caro et
sanguis est martirum; an in saxo illo et in illa ventorum patria
quam nunc colis, an in Vaticano potius sepeliri eligas, locorum
omnium nostri orbis sine ulla comparatione sanctissimo; ad
extremum in die ultimi iudicii an resurgere ames inter avinioni-
cos peccatores, famosissimos nunc omnium qui sub celo sunt, an
inter Petrum et Paulum, Stephanum et Laurentium, Silvestrum et
Gregorium et Ieronimum et Agnetem et Ceciliam et tot milia
sanctorum vel in Cristi confessione feliciter quiescentium vel pro
338 Cristi fide felicius peremptorum. Denique, quicquid elegeris,
unum Roma suo iure flebiliter poscit, ut si tu illam deseris — quod
quam iustum sit nemo te melius novit — sponsum saltem sibi alterum suum, Cesarem restituas, quem Innocentius sextus, ut perhibent, is qui te proximus antecessit, ab amplexu eius iurisiurandi
339 religione prohibuit. O divortium, si vera loqui licet, indignum ne-

best part by him, as I said, I am confident that they must be welcomed more mildly by you, inasmuch as Peter's successor should
be milder than Caesar's heir. And I have often in the past urged 306
him as the need occurred, but today is the first time I have attempted to raise this topic with you, or more truly, since I often
had this disagreement with you in silence, I have now brought it
freshly forth on my pen. And since, though shorter than I desired, 307
it has proved extremely long in view of your manifold occupations,
it must be brought to some kind of end.[40] [*§§308–34 omitted*]

I have dictated these words, most indulgent father, with pure 335
good faith but in humble style, confident that to you a rather bitter truth would be dearer than honeyed flattery. If I have blun- 336
dered, or my frankness has offended Your Holiness, I seek your
pardon, bending the knees of my spirit. So now, casting away 337
hollow advisors, reflect and deliberate with yourself whether you
wish to spend what remains of your time in the midden of Avignon or at Rome, which is entirely the flesh and blood of the
martyrs; or whether you would prefer to be buried on that crag in
that land of winds which you now inhabit, or on the Vatican Hill,
incomparably most sacred of all places in our world; or you wish
at the day of Last Judgment to be resurrected among the sinners
of Avignon, now the most infamous of all men under the sky, or
with Peter and Paul, Stephen and Laurence, Silvester and Gregory, and Jerome and Agnes and Cecilia and so many thousands of
saints, who either rest calmly in Christ or were more blessedly
martyred for Christ's faith.[41] Finally, whatever you choose, Rome, 338
weeping, asks you one favor in her own right, that if you desert
her — and no one knows better than you how just that may be —
you will at least restore to her Caesar, as her second groom, whom
Innocent VI, as they say, the pope who immediately preceded you,
prevented by the bond of an oath from approaching her embrace.[42]
O, what an undeserved divorce, if one may speak truly, and 339
doomed to harm both the espoused couple and the whole region

340 que sponsis tantum sed toti vicinie nociturum! Tu, patrum optime
et boni comunis amantissime, obicem hunc, qui solus potes, amove
et Cesarem Rome esse non solum permitte sed precipe, ne nolle te
341 ibi esse crudelitas, nolle alium invidia videatur. Et hoc tibi vel, si
respuis, hoc sibi presens ac ventura plebs cristiana per os meum
quamvis insulsum et parviloquum et indoctum, ab illo tamen dictum credat qui mentiri nescit quique dum vult non peccatores atque ignaros tantum sed bruta quoque animalia loqui facit, quia
dum Roma sponsis suis vidua suisque luminibus orba erit, neque
res humane unquam bene ibunt neque cristiani fines conquiescent.
342 Si alterum receperit, bene erit, at si ambos, optime gloriose feliciter.

343 Cristus omnipotens dies tuos proroget in longum evum aperiat-
que cor tuum consiliis non blandis nec fortasse delectabilibus sed
sanis ac fidelibus, utque arbitror, Deo gratis.

*Venetiis, III Kal. Iulias.*

## : 7 :

## *Ad Urbanum quintum Romanum Pontificem, gratulatio pro reducta in suas sedes Ecclesia et exhortatio ad perseverantiam.*

1 'In exitu Israel de Egipto, domus Iacob de populo barbaro facta est'
in celis gratulatio angelorum atque in terris hominum piorum.
Ecce, pater beatissime, beasti, quod in te est, cristianum populum.
2 Iam non ultra vagabitur aut Dominum aut vicarium Domini sui

around her! Best of fathers and most devoted to our common 340
good, remove this obstacle, you who alone have power to do so, and do not simply permit Caesar to stay in Rome but instruct him to do so, for fear your reluctance to be present should seem cruelty and your unwillingness to permit another's presence seem outright
envy. And may the present and future Christian people believe 341
that this letter, addressed to you—or if you reject it, to them—was delivered through my lips, however foolish, meager and uneducated, but it was said by Him who does not know how to lie, and Who makes not only sinners and ignorant fellows but even brutish animals speak at His will. In fact, while Rome is widowed of both the husbands pledged to her and bereaved of her glories, human affairs will never go well nor the territories of Christianity
find repose. If she recovers either of the two it will be good, if 342
both it will be excellent, glorious, and blessed.

May Christ Almighty prolong your days for long years and 343
open up your heart to advice that is not, perhaps, flattering or even pleasurable, but beneficial and loyal and, as I hope, welcome to God.

*Venice, June 29.*

## : 7 :

## *To Urban V, Roman pontiff, congratulating him for having led the Church back to its own seat and urging him to persevere.*

"When Israel went out of Egypt, when the house of Jacob went 1
out from a barbarous people,"[1] there was rejoicing of the angels in heaven and of pious men on earth. See, most blessed father, you have given a blessing, as is in your power, to the Christian people.
Now it will stray no further seeking either the Lord or his Vicar, 2

querens, sed illum in celo sursum et in anima sua intus, quoniam
utraque sedes Dei est, hunc in terra et in propria sua sede reperiet,
illa, inquam, sede quam Dominus preelegit, in qua et vivens vica-
3 rius primus sedit et moriens resedit. Orbem nostrum serenasti et
quasi sol oriens longe noctis algorem simul ac tenebras effugasti.
4 O felicem te conscientia tam preclari operis! Fecisti quod iam impossibile homini videbatur, sed Deus proculdubio tecum fuit, is
5 qui ait apostolis: 'Sine me nichil potestis facere.' Hoc in te rarum
et eximium, quod, cum Deus ipse amator et conditor humani generis multis imo omnibus se offerat, ab omnibus fere repellitur;
mundus, caro, demonia, superbia, voluptas ac nequitia oppressere
animos ut assurgere porrigenti manum Deo nequeant; tu, imbecillitatis conscius humane, non modo non repulisti Domini celestis
auxilium neque tibi ad aurem cordis salubria inspirantem consilia
spiritum extinxisti, sed invocasti eum, scio, piis precibus lacri-
6 misque potentibus celum flectere. Quas cum ille qui nullum in se
sperantem despicit auribus atque oculis percepisset et poscenti
opem laturus advenisset, existi ei obviam et manu prehensum
Dominum tuum intimo in talamo fidelis anime devotione humili
suscepisti, idque secretius, ne comperto adventu regis glorie sui et
tui hostes obstreperent et, ut soliti sunt, pium sanctumque princi-
7 pium impedirent. Inde, ubi secum in silentio deliberans que
agenda essent in illo tuo nobili et glorioso proposito confirmatus
es, in apertum exiens illo duce magnum opus aggressus supra om-
8 nium spem magnificentissime consummasti. O iterum te felicem,
o felicem diem qui te matris ex utero in lucem edidit et ceu

but will find Him in heaven above and his own soul within, since
each is the seat of the Lord; it will find his Vicar on earth and in
his own proper dwelling, I mean that dwelling which the Lord
predetermined, in which his first vicar was seated while living, and
reposed when dying.[2] You have given calm to our world and "like 3
the rising sun,"[3] have put to flight the cold and darkness of the
long night. Happy man, to be conscious of so glorious an achieve- 4
ment! You have done what now seemed impossible to man; but
undoubtedly God was with you, God who said to the apostles:
"You can do nothing without me."[4] This quality in you is exceptional and unique. In fact God, lover and founder of the human 5
race, offers Himself to many, indeed to all, but He is driven away
by almost all: the world, the flesh, the mass of demons, pride,
pleasure and moral worthlessness have overwhelmed their minds
so that they cannot rise up to God who is offering his hand. You
on the contrary, conscious of human weakness, not only did not
reject the aid of our heavenly Lord, and did not quench the spirit
breathing beneficial advice into the ear of your heart, but called
upon Him, I know, with pious prayers and tears able to sway the
heavens. When He, who scorns no one who puts their hope in 6
Him, perceived them with his ears and eyes and approached to
bring help to you when you were seeking it, you went forth to
meet Him and taking your Lord by the hand led Him with humble devotion into the innermost chamber of your faithful soul,
doing so more secretly for fear that when they discovered the coming of the King of Glory, his and your enemies might raise protests and, as is their wont, obstruct your loyal and holy beginning.
Then, silently deliberating with Him what should be done, you 7
were strengthened in your noble and glorious plan; hence going
out in the open, you tackled a mighty enterprise under his guidance and completed it most magnificently beyond all men's expectations. O twice happy man, and happy the day that brought you 8
forth from your mother's womb and gave you to the world like

9 benignum sidus aliquod mundo dedit! Nunc verus michi, vere
summus ac romanus es pontifex, vere Urbanus, verus Petri succes-
10 sor, verus vicarius Iesu Cristi. Eras et ante, non inficior, potestate,
dignitate atque officio; nunc, quod est optimum, voluntate, pietate
11 atque exercitio. Neque enim aut voluntas sanctior aut purior pietas esse potest homini quam tibi est semperque fuit, ut puto, sed
nunc ita rebus ipsis eminuit ut iam nemini esse possit occulta;
neque a quoquam promptius posset aut cautius in actum deduci,
12 sine quo quidem sterilis est voluntas. Quinque pontificum, statu
parium non animis, et sexaginta vel eo amplius annorum negligen-
13 tias unus tu diebus paucissimis emendasti. Permitte michi, oro te,
qui preter tuam benedictionem nichil ex te cupio, nichil peto, sine
adulationis suspicione pleno ore laudare quod plena dignum laude
censeo, memor quanta cum libertate arguam quod reprehensione
14 dignum iudico. Parvus vermis non modo terrarum dominos sed
duo illa mundi luminaria duosque illos gladios iustitie sepe olim et
te ipsum nuper, horum alterum, ita pupugi ut aut multa esset fides
15 aut multa dementia. Huius ultimi iudicium aliorum sit: ego michi
16 fidei sum conscius. Opto ut bene eant res humane, ut, quas in
statu pessimo vivens vidi, in optimo moriens relinquam, siquo fieri
potest modo; quod certe post Deum nisi per te atque illum alterum temporalia moderantem nullo modo fieri posse video aut
17 spero. Profecto autem, si pungere audeo, cur ungere metuam?
Utrunque enim medice manus est proprium, utrunque ego pari
fide facio, etsi neutro forsan ydoneus.

18 Equidem, licet pauca didicerim, multa legi, multa etiam in hoc
vite stadio decurrenti visa michi vel audita commemini et Cristum
testor, veri Deum, nichil me vidisse unquam vel audisse nostro

some benevolent star! Now you are for me the true pope, truly 9
supreme and Roman pope, the true Urban, the true successor of
Peter, the true Vicar of Jesus Christ. You were so before, I don't 10
deny it, in power, rank and function, but now, as is best of all, in
your will, piety and practice. For no will can be more holy or no 11
piety more chaste in any person than it is for you and always has
been, as I think; but now it has so shone forth from events that it
can no longer be hidden from any man, nor could it have been
brought into action more swiftly or cautiously—and without action the will is barren. You alone have corrected the neglect of five 12
popes, equal to you in standing but not in courage, and of sixty or
more years, alone and in a very few days.[5] Permit me, I beg, want- 13
ing nothing, seeking nothing from you except your blessing, to
praise in full voice without any suspicion of flattery what I believe
worthy of full praise, keeping in mind the frankness with which I
accuse what I find worthy of blame. Although I am a humble 14
worm, I have stung not only the lords of the earth but those two
brilliant lights of the world and those two swords of justice often
in the past, and more recently one of them, you yourself, in such a
way that I had to possess either the greatest loyalty or the greatest
folly.[6] Leave to others the judgment of this last; I am confident in 15
my own loyalty. I desire that human affairs should go well so that 16
I may leave as I die circumstances restored to the best condition,
which I saw in the worst condition while living, if this can in any
way be achieved; and I see and hope that this can in no way be
possible except by the act of God, and after him through you and
that other governor of temporal matters. Now surely if I dare to 17
prick you, why should I fear to anoint you?[7] For both acts are
proper to a doctor's hand, and I am applying both with equal loyalty, even if I am perhaps unsuited to either.[8]

Though I have learned little, I have read much and remember 18
witnessing and hearing many things in this race of life: I call to
witness Christ, the God of truth, that I have never seen or heard

gestum evo, nescio an et nichil etiam legisse, quod his tuis excel-
lentissimis actibus comparari queat vel intentione vel consilio vel
19 effectu. Magna pars principum et, quod mestus dico, magna quoque pars presulum nil preter se ipsos et utilitates suas ac proprias
20 voluptates cogitant. Tu contemptis magno animo atque oblitis affectibus, qui ut hominem alio forsitan te trahebant, solus omnium
pontificum nostre etatis bonum publicum cogitasti. [§§21–76 *omissis*]

77 O consuetudo cuntis in rebus potentissima, de patria exilium,
78 de exilio patriam fecisti! Que omnia libentius, ut par esset, his
scripsissem quos hec tangunt, nisi et numerus capitum et olim
michi notissima elatio animorum, respuens indignanter quicquid
79 auribus delicatis infertur asperius, obstitissent. Illi igitur scripsi ad
quem culpe omnis expertem pertinet sola correctio quique non
stili asperitatem sed rei veritatem neque conditionem sed intentio-
nem scribentis examinat.

80 Procedo autem et hos transeo quos tuo iure compescere poteras
vel, si cepto hererent, tuo itidem iure contemnere; ut tamen tua
modestia nota esset omnibus hominibus, adversus hos quoque et
perversas horum opiniones inflexibilesque sententias multum te
81 laboris ac molestie pertulisse non dubitem. Illud notissimum ac
maximum, quod reges ac principes, quibus te pro Ecclesie decore
morigerum prebes, his consentientes, a te autem tota mente discordes, suaviter graviterque ut iniqua vota deponerent admonendi
erant, ante alios inclitus rex Francorum, Ecclesie filius, qui devoto
quidem sed iuvenili amore matrem cupiens propinquam nec consi-
derans quanto honestius ac melius abfutura esset, ad te abitum

anything accomplished in our age, indeed I doubt I have even read anything such in intention or planning or implementation that could be compared with these actions of yours. The majority of 19
princes, and as I say regretfully, the majority of bishops, think of nothing but themselves and their own advantages and personal pleasures. But you, despising and discarding with lofty spirit the 20
emotions which might perhaps have drawn you, being a mortal, in another direction, you alone of all popes in our age have taken thought for the public good.[9] [*§§21–76 omitted*]

O habit, strongest human failing in all matters, you have made 77
an exile out of your own country and a country of your exile. And 78
I would prefer to write this, as would be proper, to those who have incurred these reproaches, if the number of persons and their arrogance of spirit, long known to me, did not oppose me, rejecting with indignation whatever is inflicted on their delicate ears too harshly. So I have written to the one man innocent of all guilt 79
whose business is only to correct others, a man who does not examine the roughness of style but the truth of the matter, and not the social rank of the writer but his intention.

I move on, then, passing over those whom you could control in 80
your own right or, if they persisted in their undertakings, could disregard in your own right; but, to make your modesty known to all mankind, I would not doubt that you have endured a great deal of toil and trouble from these men too and their perverse opinions and inflexible views. But the best known and most important issue 81
is that the kings and princes to whom you show yourself properly attentive on behalf of the church's dignity, who were agreeing with these fellows and completely in conflict with you, had to be warned with eloquence and gravity to put aside their unjust desires. Above all, the famous king of the French, the son of the Church, who with loyal but childish love wants his mother near him, not considering how much better and more honorable it would be to keep her distant, has aimed all the snares he could

meditantem quos potuit laqueos direxit, quibus sacros pedes apostolicos ad omne pium sanctumque opus paratissimos implicaret, doctum scilicet ac disertum, ut perhibent, quendam virum, qui, coram te ac fratribus tuis cupide nimis audientibus verba faciens, in eo partem maximam sue orationis absumpsit ut celotenus suam Galliam attolleret Italiamque deprimeret. Magnum opus atque arduum nec sibi tantum sed cuicunque difficile, ne dicam impossibile; nequit enim sermo hominum res mutare, etsi sepe mendacio
82 verum velet. Et o utinam presens te mandante dignus fuerim qui, licet impar eloquio et inferior statu, veritatis auxilio fretus illi calumnie responderem! Ostendissem illi forsitan te iudice rem se
83 aliter habere quam diceret. Et nunc, si cause sue fidit deque hoc ipso literatum inire certamen est animus, quamvis semper occupa-
84 tus et iam fessus, offero me duello pro veritate, pro patria. Scribat igitur vel que dixit vel que potest: ego illi Gallo Italorum ultimus respondebo et erit utilior disputatio scriptis commissa quam verbis; verba enim fugiunt, scripta manent; illa ad paucos, hec ad multos, illa ad presentes tantum, hec etiam ad absentes
85 posterosque perveniunt. Spero iudicem Cristum habens et te convitiatori illi, viro alioquin docto et insigni sed in loquendo calore atque impetu animi prolapso quo non decuit, facile probaturum me falsa esse que minime, ut auguror, sibi mandata de capite
86 suo dixit. Nosse michi videor regis adolescentis canum et senilem animum ac precipuam quandam urbanitatem lingueque modestiam magnis michi olim in rebus expertam: iniunxisse illi crediderim ut te oraret, ut Galliam laudaret; iurare pene ausim, ut vitupe-
87 raret Italiam non iniunxit. Sed hic nuntiorum mos quorundam est, ut, nisi de suo aliquid addiderint, nil egisse videantur. Profecto

think of against your attempt to leave:[10] in order to entangle your
sacred apostolic feet, most ready for all pious and holy tasks, he
has suborned a learned and eloquent man, as they claim, who
orating in front of you and your brothers, who listen only too eagerly, made it the chief purpose of his speech to raise his Gaul as
high as the heavens and weigh down on Italy.[11] This is a mighty
undertaking, difficult not just for him, but for anyone, if not impossible: for men's talk cannot change the facts even if it often
covers the truth with lying. And if only I had been present and 82
worthy of acting on your instruction so as to be able, if unequal in
eloquence and lower in status, to rely on the truth and reply to
that slander! I would perhaps have shown him, with you as my
judge, that things were not as he said. And now, if he trusts his 83
argument and has the spirit to enter on a learned contest[12] on this
very matter, although I am always busy and now weary, I offer
myself in single combat for the sake of truth and for my country.
So let him write what he said or what he can; I as humblest of the 84
Italians shall reply to that Gaul,[13] and my disputation will be more
useful committed to writing than to speech. Spoken words fade
away, but writing remains,[14] the former are addressed to a few, the
latter to many, the former reach only those present, the latter reach
men who are absent and posterity. I hope that with Christ and 85
you as my judge, I shall easily prove to that abusive fellow, a man
otherwise learned and distinguished, but carried away by heat and
impulse to a point he should not have reached, the falsehood of
those statements which were not at all, as I suppose, the message
entrusted to him by the king, but conjured from his own ideas. I 86
think I know the sage and mature spirit of the royal youth and his
special refinement and moderation of speech, which I once experienced in important business.[15] I would think he had given the
man orders to implore you and to praise Gaul; I would almost
dare to swear he did not instruct him to abuse Italy. But that is the 87
way of some messengers, that unless they have added something

autem multi sunt qui non credant sua posse laudari nisi aliena vi-
tuperent.

88 Proinde, ut breviter summa perstringam, de rebus ac gloria Italorum et Gallorum quid ve inter utrosque intersit adeo notum est
ut dubitari nequeat ab homine cui historiarum notitia ulla sit.
89 Nam de ingeniis disceptare ridiculum: libri extant veri testes.
Quid, queso, de liberalibus artibus, quid de rerum cognitione seu
naturalium seu gestarum, quid de sapientia, quid de eloquentia,
quid ve de moribus et de omni parte philosophie habet lingua la-
90 tina quod non ferme totum ab Italis sit inventum? Siquid enim
externi de his rebus feliciter ausi sunt, vel Italos imitati sunt vel in
91 Italia scripserunt, in Italia didicerunt. E quattuor Ecclesie doctori-
bus duo sunt itali ac romani, duorum reliquorum alter iuxta et
prope intra Italie fines ortus, certe intra Italiam doctus ac nutritus,
alter in Italia conversus et conversatus; omnes in Italia sunt sepulti.
92 Nullus est gallicus, nullus doctus in Gallia. Ius utrunque quo uti-
mur Itali condidere conditumque Itali exposuere, ita ut horum
nichil aut perexiguum exteris cedat; et in altero quidem longe
93 Grecos Itali superant, de altero nemo est qui litiget. Oratores et
poete extra Italiam non querantur, de latinis loquor: vel hinc orti
94 omnes vel hic docti. Sed quid ago? Aut quid rem certissimam
verbis traho? Radix artium nostrarum et omnis scientie fundamentum latine hic reperte sunt litere et latinus sermo et latinitatis
nomen quo ipsi Gallici gloriantur. Omnia, inquam, hic exorta, non
95 alibi, atque hic aucta sunt. Possem singulatim de his agere, sed

of their own, they feel they have achieved nothing. Indeed there are many who do not think their own possessions can be praised unless they abuse those of others.

So to skim briefly over the chief points, concerning the circum- 88
stances and glory of Italians and Gauls, the difference between them is so well known that it cannot be questioned by a man who
has any knowledge of the histories. For it is ridiculous to dispute 89
about intellectual gifts: books survive as records and witnesses of the truth. What, I ask you, does the Latin language report concerning the liberal arts, what about the investigation of either natural or historical matters, what about philosophy, about eloquence, about morals and every part of philosophy—which of
these was not almost entirely invented by the Italians? If foreigners 90
have made some successful ventures in these fields they either imitated the Italians or wrote in Italy and learned them in Italy. Of 91
the four Doctors of the Church, two are Italian and Roman, while one of the other two was born nearby and almost within Italy's boundaries—certainly he was taught and reared in Italy, while the other was converted in Italy and associated with Italians; and all the fathers are buried in Italy.[16] None of them was a Gaul, and
none of them was educated in Gaul. The Italians created the two 92
codes of law that we use, and Italians wrote the commentaries on them, so that nothing or precious little is left to outsiders, and in one kind of law the Italians far surpass the Greeks, while no one
would dispute about the other.[17] Orators and poets, I mean the 93 
Latin ones, are not to be sought outside Italy, and all such men
either came from here or were educated here. But what am I argu- 94 
ing, or why am I lingering over a most obvious fact? Latin letters, root of our arts and foundation of all knowledge, was discovered here, and so were Latin speech and the name of Latinity of which the Gauls themselves boast. I repeat, everything grew here, not
elsewhere, and reached its full development here. I could argue 95 
about these points one by one, but enough has been said to those

96 intelligentibus satis, reliquis nimis est dictum. Et quid, oro, tot
tantarum rerum studiis quod obiciant habent? Nisi forte, ut est
gens sibi placens et laudatrix sui, unus his omnibus fragosus Stra-
97 minum vicus obicitur. Ad hec et omnis hic floruit politia et siqua
98 usquam superest aliqua in parte Italie floret adhuc. Duo mundi
99 vertices hic sunt, papatus et imperium. Iam de armis, de victoriis,
de triumphis, de disciplina militie, de iugo denique gentium omnium ac tributis annuis loqui nolim, ne perturbem gallicum inge-
100 nium. De moribus vulgaribus fateor Gallos et facetos homines et
gestuum et verborum lenium, qui libenter ludant, lete canant,
101 crebro bibant, avide conviventur. Vera autem gravitas ac realis mo-
ralitas apud Italos semper fuit et, licet, quod flebile damnum est,
virtus toto orbe decreverit, sique tamen eius sunt reliquie, in Italia,
102 nisi fallor, sunt; siquid est perversi moris, inter ipsos est. Nusquam advene tanto sunt in honore et—de quo nemo, ne convitia-
tor ille quidem dubitet—nusquam tanta est Ecclesia, seu potentiam illius seu devotionem non italici tantum sed totius credentis
in Cristum populi metiare, ut que hic orta, hic adulta, hic ad
summum glorie culmen evecta est, hic Deo volente teque agente,
103 ut spero, in perpetuum permansura. Est, fateor, gallicana pars Ecclesie opulenta et nobilis, sed Ecclesie caput, ut imperii, in Italia
104 esse nemo sani capitis neget. Siquis horum est incredulus, romanum patrio titulum permutet: tunc quid fuerit sentiet et quid sit,
interque supremum caput imaque membra quid intersit intelliget.
105 Durum valde grande aliquid debere cui nolis. Si romani adeo nominis pudet, romanas abiciant dignitates et res suas ac patriam ut
106 verbis sic electionibus preferant. Ego vero sat insanus sim qui sua-

who understand, and too much for the rest. And what do they 96
have to oppose to so many studies in such great disciplines? Unless perhaps, as the race is self-satisfied and prone to its own
praise, one rough-surfaced Street of Straw is set against all these.[18]
Add the fact that every kind of constitutional state flourished here 97
and if any still survives it is flourishing in some part of Italy. The 98
two summits of the world are here, the papacy and the empire. I 99
would not want to talk now about battles and victories, triumphs
and military discipline, or indeed the yoke set upon all races and
annual taxes, so as not to upset his Gallic intellect.[19] In terms of 100
common behavior I admit the Gauls are witty fellows of elegant
gesture and speech, who gladly sport, cheerfully sing, often drink
and hungrily party together. But true seriousness and real morality 101
was always to be found among the Italians, and although—a lamentable loss—virtue has shrunk all over the world, if there are any
remains of it they are in Italy, unless I am mistaken. And yet, if
there is any warped behavior it is among themselves. Nowhere are 102
newcomers so honored and—something no one, not even that
abuser, would doubt—the Church is greater here than anywhere
else, whether you measure her power or her devotion, not only
among Italians but among every faithful people adhering to Christ,
so that the Church, born, grown and carried to the height of its
glory with God's goodwill and your activity, as I hope, will last
forever. I admit the French part of the Church is rich and noble, 103
but no sane man would deny that the head of the Church, as of
the Empire, is in Italy. If anyone is doubtful of these facts let him 104
exchange his Roman title for his native region;[20] then he will realize what he has been and is, and understand the difference between the head in high authority and its lowest members. It is 105
hard to owe anything truly important to anyone against your will,
but if they are so ashamed of the Roman name, let them cast away
their Roman ranks and property and prefer their native land, not
just in words but in their choices. It would be quite foolish of me 106

deam italicas ecclesiasticas dignitates suas abicere, quibus solis magni clarique sunt, his qui non suas italicas civitates ambiant atque usurpent inaudita tirannide stupente Petro, Cristo autem mirante etiam ac minante; et nisi ille de celo, tu de terris occurritis, quandoquidem incertum quo germine hausto Itali consopiti sunt, actum est de rebus nostris, servam mox Italiam et perproprie, quod dici solet, Ecclesiam militantem, imo et armatam videbimus et pugnantem de imperio, non de fide, denique etiam triumphantem priusquam ad celum arcusque sidereos sit perventum et singulos clericos singulis urbibus triumphaliter presindetes, donec experrectis qui nunc dormiunt omnia deformentur et reformentur mutatione terribili. [§§*107–49 omissis*]

150 His itaque, qui scientes contra verum litigant, nil omnino—
frustra enim surdo canitur; hebetavit iudicium voluntas—, reliquis, siqui sunt qui ignorantia labi possent, hoc modo responsum
151 sit. Italie caput Romam, nec Italie tantum sed totius orbis, multis
bellis ac cladibus interque alias longa suorum pontificum ac principum absentia extenuatam et attritam ac pene consumptam do-
lens fateor, cuius vastitas quantum non soli Italie sed membris
omnibus, hoc est mundo, noceat, et in primis cristiano generi,
152 vident omnes, nisi quorum livor tumorque oculos premit. Hec tamen ipsa urbs tot vastantium e manibus tibi celitus reservata, ni
respuis, et divine gratie tueque virtutis adminiculo restauranda felicitatem tibi in celis eternam atque in terris immortalem gloriam
153 allatura est. Potest haud impudenter optare nobilis opifex ut aliquid rebus desit quo suum ingenium, sua ars, sua virtus appareat.
154 De reliqua autem Italia quid dicam nisi sententiam illam meam
155 veterem et, ni fallor, veram? Non dico equidem quam nunc est
memor universalis pestilentie illius, cui nulla etas parem habuit, a

to persuade them to throw away their Italian ecclesiastical dignities, the only source of their greatness and fame, with which they canvass Italian communities which are not theirs and dominate them in unheard-of tyranny, while Peter gapes and Christ marvels and threatens them. And if He does not oppose them from heaven and you on earth, since the Italians have been lulled into inaction by some mysterious drug, our affairs will be ruined. Soon we shall see Italy enslaved and, in the very apt phrase, the Church on the march, nay armed and fighting for her authority, not her faith; in short, triumphant before it reaches heaven and the starry cycles, and individual churchmen oppressing in triumph individual cities, until those who now sleep are aroused and everything is dismantled and remade in a terrifying revolution. [*§§107–49 omitted*]

To those who knowingly quarrel with the truth, I have nothing 150
to say, since it is folly to sing to the deaf: wishful thinking has blunted their understanding. To the others, if there are any who have slipped through their own ignorance, let this be the reply.
Rome, the capital of Italy, and not just of Italy but of the whole 151
world, is weakened and frayed and almost worn out by many wars and disasters, among them the prolonged absence of its popes and emperors. I am pained to admit it, and all men, unless their eyes are closed by envy and arrogance, see how her devastation harms not just Italy, that is the head, but all the limbs, that is the world
and above all the Christian community. However, this very city, 152
preserved by heaven for you from the hands of so many plunderers (unless you reject it), and destined for restoration with the support of divine grace and your vigor, will bring you eternal blessedness in
heaven and immortal glory on earth. A noble craftsman can with- 153
out shame look for something to be lacking in the situation so that
his talent and art and vigor can be made manifest. What shall I 154
say about the rest of Italy except my old judgment, a true one if I
am not deceived? I do not mention how bitterly it remembers that 155
universal plague, unequaled in any generation, experienced now

qua vigesimus nunc annus agitur, que postea alternatim exhaustum discerptumque orbem quodam velut anniversario malorum torrente repetiit, sed non minus Galliam quam Italiam laceravit; imo ad impetum pestis aerie terrestris hominum rabies et longissimi belli furor accessit tamque atrociter illis terris incubuit ut, dum male fida pace rebus reddita per ea loca ad regem missus iter agerem, cunta undique ferro atque igni eversa conspiciens lacrimas non tenerem; non enim sumus qui, ut isti, cetera omnia nostri
156 amore orbis oderimus. Sed indubie ac fidenter affirmem hanc ipsam Italiam nunquam viris atque opibus et presertim maris imperio potentiorem fuisse quam nostra fuit etate, nunquam, si concordes animi utque olim bene validum caput esset, recipiendo orbis imperio nec ferendis infidelium tot mollibus atque indignis impe-
157 riis aptiorem. Non sequor animum calamumque, ne beatitudinem tuam hac in parte amplius fatigem, maxime cum de hoc ipso multa alibi questus sim, non ignarus tamen his obstare Tarentum, Ca-
158 puam, Ravennam aliasque magnas olim urbes, nunc non ita. Sed opponam illis omnibus vel hanc unam unde tibi hec scribo, Venetorum urbem maximam, imo regnum ingens, cui magna olim regna subiecta sunt, urbem longe dissimilem ceteris utque ego dicere soleo, orbem alterum, que tunc nichil aut minimum fuit, quamvis et Veneti ducis et Venetie non urbis sed provincie nomen antiquissimum sit; urbis enim nomen, quod meminerim, supra Vespasianum principem non legi, sed constat eam non multis ante
159 hoc tempus seculis in hanc magnitudinem excrevisse. Sunt tamen et alie quas opponam: Ianua olim oppidum obscurum, civitas nunc preclara; patria quoque mea, urbs, quod verbum sonat, florentissima, nondum tamen romana re publica iam florente fundata.

twenty years ago: thereafter the plague sought the world, drained and ravaged turn and turn about with a kind of annual cataract of woes; but it ravaged Gaul no less cruelly than Italy. Indeed, over there the madness of men on earth and the frenzy of a prolonged war was added to the onslaught of the plague coming from the sky. It assailed the lands so cruelly that while I was traveling in those regions, as envoy to the king after an untrustworthy peace was restored, I saw everything on all sides overthrown by sword and fire, and could not hold back my tears.[21] For we are not men like them, who hate everything else in the world from love of our own region.
But I would declare confidently and without doubt that Italy itself 156
was never more powerful in men and resources, and especially command of the sea, than in our generation, and never, if men's spirits were in harmony and the capital was healthy as once it was, was Italy more fit to recover its command over the world and resist
so many decadent and unworthy empires of the infidels. I will not 157
extend my mind and pen for fear I weary Your Beatitude further on this topic, especially since I have greatly lamented this situation elsewhere, well aware that on this theme cities once great but now no longer, like Tarentum, Capua and Ravenna[22] would resist these
claims. But I will set against all these this single city from which I 158
am writing, the mighty city of the Venetians,[23] indeed their huge dominion, to which great kingdoms submitted long since. It is a city far different from the rest and, as I usually say, another world, but in antiquity it was very small or nothing, although the name of the leader Venetus and Venetia, not as a city but a province, is most ancient. For I have not read the city's name, as far as I recall, in texts before Vespasian's time, but it is agreed that Venice had grown to this present greatness not many generations before this
time.[24] There are other cities for me to compare: Genoa, once an 159
unknown town, is now a splendid city; my own homeland too, a most flourishing city as its name indicates, had not yet been founded when the Roman state was already in a flourishing condi-

160 Quid Bononiam tuam loquar? Quam supradicti principis etate
felicissimam dictam invenio quamque ego, siqua in terris est felicitas, vere felicissimam puer vidi, deinde, ut retrograde res mortalium sunt, lapsu temporis felicem, post et miseram, ad extremum
per hos annos proximos miserrimam videmus, nunc te auspice fe-
161 licitati sue redditam videmus. Certe hec et alie in eodem tractu
non antique admodum bello punico secundo per Italiam tonante a
Romanis condite sive insigniter aucte sunt ceperuntque esse quod
non fuerant nec multo post tempore quasi ad nichilum redacte
162 sese maiores denuo surrexere. Quarum in epistola ad Faustinum
mesto stilo ac pio meminit pater Ambrosius, nominatim Bononiam ipsam Mutinamque et Regium et Placentiam aliasque tunc
semirutas urbes deflens, quibus hodie, etsi non omnibus plena
tranquillitas, decor tamen et sua manet integritas gaudendumque
quod hac una in re viri sapientissimi atque sanctissimi fefellit au-
163 gurium, quo illas in perpetuum prostratas dixit ac dirutas. Et ad
summam tota hec Italie pars que candidas Alpes ac viridem Ap-
penninum interiacet multo his temporibus est dicior frequen-
tiorque quam antiquitus; partes alie humani morem status varie-
164 tate testantur. Ceterum opinentur ut libet; nichil est enim opinione
liberius. Ad multa alia vi coguntur multi, ad credendum nullus.
165 Credant ergo, si videtur, Italiam nichil esse quam totus sepe orbis
166 sensit esse aliquid. An non saltem illud intelligunt, in hoc nichilo
totam fere illam suam excellentiam esse inclusam nec referre quam
sit vilis arcula que plena thesauri sit ingentis? [*§§167–80 omissis*]

181 Multi sunt et pene omnes qui preclarum nichil incipiunt nec
infames sunt, quippe nec cogniti. At qui se glorioso principio

tion.[25] Need I speak of your beloved Bologna, which I find was 160
called most happy in the generation of the emperor I just mentioned, and which I saw as a boy truly happy, if there is any happiness on earth? Then as human affairs slip backward, in the passage of time it was first happy, then wretched, and finally in these recent years I found it most wretched, but now under your protection it has been restored to its original happiness.[26] Surely this city 161
and others of not too ancient origin were founded or largely expanded by the Romans in the same region when the Second Punic War was raging in Italy, and began to be important as they had not been, but in a short time, after being reduced as if to nothing, arose again greater still. Father Ambrose mentions these cities in 162
pious and melancholy fashion in his letter to Faustinus, lamenting by name Bologna, Modena, Reggio and Piacenza and "other cities then half-demolished" which have retained nowadays their elegance and intact nature, if not perfect tranquility. We must rejoice that in this one matter that wise and holy man's prophecy was mistaken, in which he called them "laid low forever" and "demolished."[27] In short, all this part of Italy which lies between the 163
snowy Alps and green Apennines is much wealthier and more populous nowadays than in ancient times. Other regions show by their differences the shifting pattern of human conditions. But let 164
men think as they choose, since nothing is more free than opinion: many men are coerced into many other actions, but no one is coerced into belief. So if they see it that way, let them believe that 165
Italy is insignificant, although the whole world often felt that it was of some importance. At least, don't they realize that almost all 166
their own preeminence is included in this "insignificant" place, and it does not matter how cheap the strongbox if it is full of a vast treasure?[28] [*§§167–80 omitted*]

There are many persons, indeed almost all, who do not begin 181
any work of distinction but are not in ill-repute, because they go unrecognized; but the man who makes himself known by a glori-

182 notum fecit, si id sponte destituat, infamiam non evadet. Tu non
solum cepisti, sed magna ex parte peregisti. Vide ne tuis manibus
tuum opus, et tale opus, evertas; id enim non modo quam non
183 cepisse sed quam ceptum omisisse multo fedius. Solet namque
actibus mediis quidam torpor irrepere specie difficultatis obiecta;
profecto autem consummata bona atque ad exitum perducta res-
184 cindere invidia est. Cepto igitur nusquam calle deflexeris: nullus
185 est rectior ad salutem. Nusquam substiteris: tempus breve, lon-
186 gum iter, lenit laborem operis spes mercedis. Nusquam denique in
terga respexeris; nosti enim quod 'nemo mittens manum suam in
aratrum et aspiciens retro aptus est regno Dei' nec ignoras ut vel
apud scriptores gentium Orpheus retro versus eductam ab inferis
suam perdit Euridicen vel apud nostros Loth e Sodomis exeunti ut
'salvet animam suam neque post tergum respiciat' imperatur; quod
vel oblita vel despiciens 'uxor eius respiciensque post se in statuam
salis versa' exemplum atque utile condimentum posteris liquit, quo
in similibus salliantur, ne insipido rerum gustu ad ea que bene
187 dimiserint animo aut oculis se convertant. Quibus ita se habentibus fama et vulgus suo more veris falsa permisceant: meam michi
188 nullus opinionem verbis eripiet. Si te abeuntem audiam, nisi videam, non credam et, si videam, vix credam. Sunt que vix oculis
189 credantur. Magnam de te tuisque de rebus, magnam tua de sanctitate, de magnitudine animi, de constantia, de fide, de ingenio spem
190 concepi. Credo ego te forsitan blanda egros animos spe solari et id
agere, ut inter honeste more tedium et inhonesti spem reditus

ous beginning will not escape disgrace if he abandons it of his own
accord. You have not just begun but largely completed this under- 182
taking; see that you do not overturn your achievement, and so fine
an achievement, by your own actions: that would be not only
more vile than failing to begin it, but even more vile than dropping
it once begun. Indeed a certain lethargy overtakes actions in mid- 183
course, when opposed by apparent difficulty. But surely to reverse
meritorious plans completed and brought to their outcome is odi-
ous. So never turn aside from the path you have begun—for no 184
other path to salvation is more direct. And do not pause, since 185
time is short, the journey long, and the hope of reward softens
toil. Finally, never look back, since you know how "no man who 186
has put his hand to the plow and looks back is fit for the kingdom
of God."[29] And you know well how even in the pagan writers, Orpheus lost his dear Eurydice when he was leading her out of the underworld, or how in our Scriptures Lot when he left Sodom was ordered "to save his soul" and "not to look behind him"; and either forgetting or scorning this, "his wife behind him looked back and was turned into a statue of salt," leaving a useful example and condiment for posterity with which to season in comparable situations, for fear that when the savor of food was tasteless they would turn back their mind or eyes to what they had done well to
leave behind.[30] In such circumstances, let rumor and the common 187
crowd mix falsehoods with truth as it does: no man's speech shall
rob me of my opinion. If I hear that you are departing I shall not 188
believe it unless I see it, and even if I see it shall scarcely believe it:
there are matters on which we scarcely believe our eyes. I have 189
formed a great hope in you and your actions, a great esteem for
your holiness, your nobility of mind, your constancy, integrity and
intellect. I believe that you may perhaps comfort their discon- 190
tented minds with an appealing prospect and follow a policy to
make the days slip by through the weariness of honorable delay

elabantur dies utque assolet, tempore contractum et tempore desiderium evanescat.

191 Perge oro, beatissime, et ita fac (fac, si potes; potes autem omnia supra hominem omnipotentis Domini vicarius): fac in titulis suis edificent qui tam diu tamque avide in non suis edificarunt; honesti lapides, honeste trabes, honesta calx fuerit, denique hones-
192 tus labor honesteque cure et honesti sumptus in propriis; qui alienis in finibus quam honesti fuerint, quam decorum quamque conveniens quod ruente Roma, pulcerrima rerum, ut Virgilius ait, qua nil maius sol vidit, ne sit irrita Horatii vatis oratio, parva et turpis Avinio super astra se tolleret et que vix competens cauda
193 est, fieret mundi caput, diffinire non est meum: eorum conscientie relinquatur, qui prostrata metropoli urbium omnium que sub celo sunt, qui labentibus tectis apostolorum et suis, imo sanctorum domibus, quarum edituos sunt professi, sparsis ac laceris, domos illic aureas erexerunt inspectante universorum domino ac iudice,
194 nescio an etiam approbante. Fac incipiant, pater providentissime, fac incipiant tantum: voluptas una aliam trudit; actum erit, mox domorum veterum ut ceperint oblivisci et lutum avinionicum non
195 mirari. Longis erroribus infecti animi subito convalescere nequeunt; tempore lesi, ut dixi, tempore etiam curabuntur, sed non solo: tua mens, tua frons, tua vox et indeficiens cura, tua illos vigi-
196 lantia, tua virtus, tua franget autoritas. Interim dies ibunt: mentes verioribus sententiis, oculi melioribus spectaculis assuescent. Cum gustare ceperint quid est Roma, imo verius quid est fides, quid debitum, quid honestas, siquis homo vel casus eos cogeret unde

and the hope of a dishonorable return, so that, as usually happens, longing incurred over time may melt away over time.

So I beg of you, most blessed pope, persevere and do this, do it 191
if you can—and being Almighty God's vicar over mankind you can do anything: make them build on their titular sites, these men who have built on others' sites with such prolonged greed. Let the stones, the beams, and the cement be honorable in purpose, in short the toil will be honorable and the concern and expenses on
their own property. It is not my role to describe how honorably 192
they have behaved on land not their own, or how creditable and fitting it is that when Rome, "most handsome of cities" as Vergil says, is collapsing, Rome, "the greatest that the Sun has seen," not to waste Horace's phrase,[31] little, shameful Avignon should rear itself above the stars, and a place scarcely adequate as a tail shall
become the world's head and capital. Let it be left to the con- 193
science of those who have built themselves golden houses in that city[32] when the mother of all cities beneath the heaven has been laid low, when the dwellings of the apostles and homes of the saints—which these men have claimed to serve as sacristans—are disintegrating and scattered in ruins, under the scrutiny of the
Lord and judge of all men, but doubtless without his approval. Let 194
them get started, most prudent Father, just get them started. One pleasure drives out another. Soon it will come to pass that they forget their old homes and no longer marvel at the mud of Avignon. Their spirits, contaminated by prolonged diversions, cannot 195
suddenly regain strength. Damaged by time, as I said, they will be cured by time, but not only by time. Your mind, your expression, your voice and unceasing care, your vigilance, your virtue and your
authority will break them in. Meanwhile the days will pass and 196
their minds become used to better judgments and their eyes to better sights. Once they have begun to savor what Rome is, or better, what Faith is, what is their obligation, what is honor, if any man or mischance compelled them to return to the place which

tam tristes modo veniunt reverti, crederent vel ad mortem vel ad
miserum exilium se compelli.

197 Adhuc tamen et tua sublimis sanctitas et mea fidelis humilitas,
198 scio et sentio, contradictoribus patent. Sunt qui dicant—plane
enim illos hinc audio—romanum aerem insalubrem esse; quibus
190 iam ex parte responsum est. Nulla enim non civitas tantum augus-
tissima sed angusta domus tam salubris fuerit quam non suspectam faciant ruine. Quamlibet purus aer, si inclusus esse ceperit, fit
200 infamis. Hec romanam urbem eiusque temperiem atque aeris puritatem vel concutiunt vel accusant. Accedit et solitudo longior et
201 menium squalor ac raritas incolarum. Que omnia quid aliud,
queso, quam illa de qua supra questus sum romanorum pontificum ac principum invexit absentia? Quid ve aliud quam eorundem
202 possit expurgare presentia? Vetus est proverbium, cuius Aristotiles
meminit: nulla melius equum re quam domini sui oculo pingues-
203 cere. Urbem tuam a suis pastoribus derelictam providentie ac pie-
204 tatis tue oculus impinguabit ac reficiet. Illam tu, quod a Cristo
Iesu poscitur, et labentem respicies et videndo corriges; nam cor-
205 rigi quidem illa, ni deseritur, curarique potest. Non te ergo deter-
reat brevis labor, quo eternum premium meriturus sis. Redde illi
206 te, imo redditum conserva. Redde illi, inquam, suum caput: statim
et membra reddideris et vigorem, etsi non pristinum, at magnum;
illum enim redintegrare non potest nisi is 'qui facit mirabilia magna
solus.' [§§207–39 *omissis*]

they recently left with such regret, they would think they were being driven to death or a wretched exile.

Up to now your lofty holiness and my faithful humility, as I 197
know and feel, are vulnerable to our antagonists. Some say—I 198
hear them clearly from here—that the climate of Rome is unhealthy, and I have already given them an answer in part. For not 199
only a most august community but even a cramped house will not be so healthy that ruin does not make it suspect; air however pure,
if it becomes confined, earns ill-repute. Such arguments either 200
undermine or accuse this city of Rome and its climate and the purity of its air. An additional factor is the prolonged emptiness of abandonment, the disrepair of the walls and scarcity of inhabitants; but what else brought this on, if not the absence of Roman 201
popes and princes of which I am complaining? And what else besides their presence can purge these ills? There is an old proverb 202
recorded by Aristotle: "Nothing succeeds in making a horse grow
fat as well as his master's eye."[33] The eye of your forethought and 203
piety will fatten your city, abandoned by its shepherds, and restore
it. As Christ demands, you will look to it in its collapse and by 204
watching correct it: surely it can be set right and taken care of
provided it is not deserted. So do not be discouraged by the brief 205
time of effort through which you will earn an everlasting reward; give yourself to it, or rather preserve what has been given back to
you. Give it back its head, I say, and you will immediately have 206
given back its limbs and strength—a great strength, even if it is not that original might. For no one can renew that except Him "who alone performs great marvels."[34] [*§§207–39 omitted*]

# [PART VIII]

: 1 :

## *Ad Pulicem Vicentinum poetam, de materia et causa sequentium epystolarum Ciceroni ac Senece et reliquis inscriptarum.*

1 In suburbano vicentino per noctem hospitatus novam scribendi materiam inveni. Ita enim accidit ut sub meridiem Patavo digressus, patrie tue limen attingerem vergente iam ad occasum sole. Ibi ne igitur pernoctandum an ulterius procedendum, quod et festinabam et longissime lucis pars bona supererat, deliberabundus herebam, dum ecce — quis se celet amantibus? — tuus et magnorum aliquot virorum, quos abunde parva illa civitas tulit, gratissimus
2 interventus dubium omne dimovit. Ita enim fluctuantem animum alligastis varii et iocundi fune sermonis, ut ire cogitans staret et non prius labi diem quam noctem adesse perpenderet. Et illo die et sepe alias expertus sum nulla re alia magis tempus non sentientibus eripi, quam colloquiis amicorum; magni fures temporis sunt amici, etsi nullum tempus minus ereptum, minus perditum videri
3 debeat, quam quod post Deum amicis impenditur. Illic ergo, ne infinita recenseam, meministi ut forte Ciceronis mentio nobis oborta est, que crebra admodum doctis hominibus esse solet. Ille tandem vario colloquio finem fecit; in unum versi omnes; nichil inde aliud quam de Cicerone tractatum est; simbolum confecimus

# PART VIII

## LETTERS TO THE ANCIENTS

: I :

### *To Pulice, poet of Vicenza, on the subject and origin of the following letters addressed to Cicero and Seneca and the others.*

1 While I was staying in the suburbs of Vicenza overnight I found new material for writing. It happened that after leaving Padua around noon I reached the entrance to your city when the sun was already setting.[1] So, undecided whether to spend the night or keep going, since I was in a hurry and the best part of the light was now over, I was dithering in deliberation when suddenly—who could conceal himself from his devotees?—your most welcome appearance, together with several of the important men whom that little community has produced in quantity, removed all my doubts. You 2 so bound my wavering spirit with the braid of your pleasant and variegated conversation that even as I planned to leave, I stayed put, and did not notice the day's disappearance before night was at hand. Both on this day and often at other times I have felt that time is never more stolen from us unawares than by the conversation of our friends. Friends are great time stealers, although no time should seem less stolen or wasted than what is spent on a friend, after time spent on God. There, not to repeat endless de- 3 tails, you remember how the mention of Cicero arose, as it quite often does among educated men. But his name put an end to our assorted discussion; everyone turned to the one topic; after that nothing was discussed except about Cicero; we assembled our

et palinodiam sibi, seu pangericum dici placet, alternando cecini-
4 mus. Sed quoniam in rebus mortalium nichil constat esse perfec-
tum, nullusque hominum est in quo non aliquid quod merito
carpi queat, modestus etiam reprehensor inveniat, contigit ut dum
in Cicerone, velut in homine michi super omnes amicissimo et
colendissimo, prope omnia placerent, dumque auream illam eloquentiam et celeste ingenium admirarer, morum levitatem multisque michi deprehensam indiciis inconstantiam non laudarem.
5 Ubi cum omnes qui aderant sed ante alios senem illum, cuius
michi nomen excidit non imago, conterraneum tuum annis veren-
dum literisque, attonitos viderem novitate sententie, res poscere
visa est ut codex epystolarum mearum ex archula promeretur.

6 Prolatus in medium addidit alimenta sermonibus; inter multas
enim ad coetaneos meos scriptas, pauce ibi varietatis studio et
ameno quodam laborum diverticulo antiquis illustrioribus inscri-
buntur, que lectorem non premonitum in stuporem ducant, dum
7 tam clara et tam vetusta nomina novis permixta compererit. Harum due ad ipsum Ciceronem sunt: altera mores notat, altera laudat ingenium. Has tu intentis omnibus cum legisses, mox amica
lis verbis incaluit, quibusdam scripta nostra laudantibus et iure
reprehensum fatentibus Ciceronem, uno autem illo sene obstina-
tius obluctante, qui et claritate nominis et amore captus auctoris,
erranti quoque plaudere et amici vitia cum virtutibus amplecti
mallet quam discernere, nequid omnino damnare videretur homi-
8 nis tam laudati. Itaque nichil aliud vel michi vel aliis quod responderet habebat, nisi ut adversus omne quod diceretur, splen-
dorem nominis obiectaret, et rationis locum teneret autoritas.

tributes and offered him a palinode, or if you prefer to call it a panegyric, taking turns in our homage. But since in mortal matters 4
it is agreed that nothing is perfect and there is no man without some flaw that can be rightly be criticized, so that even a moderate critic can find fault, it happened that while everything delighted me in talking about Cicero, whom, I hold, deserves love and worship above all others, while I was expressing admiration for his golden eloquence and heavenly intellect, I could not praise his volatility of behavior and instability, which I had detected from many incidents.[2] Then, when I saw that all present, but in partic- 5
ular an old man whose name I forget but not his appearance, your fellow citizen, entitled to respect for his age and literary attainments,[3] were astonished by the novelty of my opinion, the situation seemed to demand my book of letters to be brought out from its chest.

When it was presented to the group it fed fuel to our talk, for 6
among many letters written to my peers there were a few addressed, in pursuit of variety and as a pleasant digression from my toil, to the more famous ancients, which would lead the unwary reader to confusion when he found such glorious and ancient names mixed in with the others. Two of these letters are to Cicero 7
himself: the first censures his behavior, the second praises his intellect. When you had read these aloud with attentive listeners a friendly disagreement flared up, with some present praising our writings and declaring that Cicero deserved reproach, but this one old fellow put up an obstinate resistance: he was beguiled by the glory of Cicero's reputation and his love for the writer, and preferred to praise Cicero even when he was misguided and to embrace his friend's faults along with his virtues, rather than distinguish between them, in case he might seem to condemn anything in a man so admired. So he had no other answer to me or the 8
others, but simply opposed every statement by putting forward the glory of Cicero's reputation, and authority usurped the place of

9 Succlamabat identidem pretenta manu: 'Parcius, oro, parcius de Cicerone meo'; dumque ab eo quereretur an errasse unquam ulla in re Ciceronem opinari posset, claudebat oculos et quasi verbo percussus avertebat frontem ingeminans: 'Heu michi, ergo Cicero meus arguitur?,' quasi non de homine sed de deo quodam agere-tur. Quesivi igitur an deum fuisse Tullium opinaretur an hominem; incuntanter 'deum' ille respondit, et quid dixisset intelligens,
10 'deum' inquit, 'eloquii.' 'Recte,' inquam, 'nam si deus est, errasse non potuit; illum tamen deum dici nondum audieram; sed si Platonem Cicero suum deum vocat, cur non tu deum tuum Ciceronem voces? nisi quia deos pro arbitrio sibi fingere non est nostre religionis.' 'Ludo' inquit ille; 'hominem, sed divino ingenio fuisse Tullium scio.' 'Hoc' inquam, 'utique rectius; nam celestem Quintilianus in dicendo virum dixit; sed si homo fuit, et errasse profecto potuit et erravit.'

11 Hec dum dicerem, cohorrebat et quasi non in famam alterius sed in suum caput dicerentur, aversabatur. Ego vero quid dicerem,
12 ciceroniani nominis et ipse mirator maximus? Senili ardori et tanto studio gratulabar, quiddam licet pithagoreum redolenti; tantam unius ingenii reverentiam esse tantamque religionem, ut humane imbecillitatis in eo aliquid suspicari sacrilegio proximum haberetur gaudebam, mirabarque invenisse hominem qui plus me
13 illum diligeret, quem ego semper pre omnibus dilexissem, quique quam michi puero fuisse memineram, eam de illo senex opinionem gereret altissime radicatam, nec cogitare quidem posset ea etate: si homo fuit Cicero, consequens esse ut in quibusdam, ne
14 dicam multis, erraverit. Quod ego certe iam partim cogito, partim scio, etsi adhuc nullius eque delecter eloquio; nec ipse de quo

reasoning. He repeatedly protested, extending his hand in appeal: 9
"Speak with more restraint, I beg you, about my Cicero." And when he was asked whether he could believe that Cicero was never mistaken in any matter he shut his eyes and turned away his gaze as if the phrase had struck him, and repeated: "Alas! So is someone accusing my Cicero?" as if this were a matter not of a man but some deity. So I asked him whether he believed Cicero had been a god or a man, and he answered without hesitation: "A god"; then realizing what he had said, he added: "The god of eloquence."
"You are right," I said, "for if he is a god he could not have been 10
mistaken, but I had never heard him called a god. But if Cicero calls Plato his god,[4] why can't you call Cicero yours? Except that it goes against our religion to fashion gods according to our whim." "I am joking," he said, "I know Cicero was a man, but one of divine intellect." "That is more like it," I said, "for Quintilian calls Cicero heavenly in his speaking,[5] but if he was a man, he certainly could be and was mistaken."

When I was saying this, he shuddered and flinched as if these 11
words were uttered not against the other man's reputation but his own life. What could I say, being myself the greatest admirer of
Cicero's renown? I congratulated him on his old man's enthusiasm 12
and loyalty, though it savored of some Pythagorean tribute.[6] I was delighted that there should be such great reverence and awe for one man's mind that to suspect him of human frailty was almost sacrilege; I rejoiced and marveled that I had found someone who loved more than I did the man whom I had always delighted in
more than any other. And I rejoiced that he bore as an old man 13
the deeply rooted opinion which I remembered holding as a boy: at this age he could not work out that if Cicero was a mortal it followed that he would be mistaken in some, indeed many, matters. Certainly I both think and know this, even if to this day no 14
man's eloquence thrills me more; and Cicero himself, whom we are discussing, is not unaware of and often lament his own mistakes;

loquimur, Tullius, ignorat, sepe de propriis graviter questus erroribus; quem nisi sic de se sensisse fateamur, laudandi libidine et notitiam sui ipsius et magnam illi partem philosophice laudis eripimus, modestiam.

15 Ceterum nos die illo post longum sermonem, hora demum interpellante, surreximus atque inde integra lite discessum est; sed
exegisti ultimum ut, quod tunc brevitas temporis non sinebat, ubi
primum constitissem, exemplum tibi epystole utriusque transmit-
terem, quo re acrius excussa, vel sequester pacis inter partes vel
16 siquo modo posses, tulliane constantie propugnator fieres. Laudo
animum ac postulata transmitto; dictu mirabile, vincere metuens,
vinci volens, ut unum noveris: si hic vincis, plus tibi negotii superesse quam putas. Pari etenim duello Anneus Seneca te poscit ath-
letam, quem proxima scilicet carpit epystola. Lusi ego cum his
magnis ingeniis, temerarie forsitan sed amanter sed dolenter sed ut
17 reor vere; aliquanto, inquam, verius quam vellem. Multa me in illis
delectabant, pauca turbabant; de his fuit impetus ut scriberem, qui
hodie forte non esset; quamvis enim hec propter dissimilitudinem
materie ad extrema reiecerim, ante longum tamen tempus excude-
ram. Adhuc quidem virorum talium fortunam doleo sed non minus culpam, nec illud te pretereat non me Senece vitam aut Cic-
18 eronis erga rempublicam damnare propositum. Neve duas lites
misceas, de Cicerone nunc agitur, quem vigilantissimum atque
optimum et salutarem consulem ac semper amantissimum patrie
civem novi. Quid ergo? Varium in amicitiis animum, et ex levibus
causis alienationes gravissimas atque pestiferas sibi et nulli rei
utiles, in discernendo insuper suo ac publico statu iudicium reli-
quo illi suo impar acumini, ad postremum sine fructu iuvenile al-
19 tercandi studium in sene philosopho non laudo. Quorum scito

indeed if we did not admit, in our lust for praising him, that he
could be critical of himself, we would deny him self-knowledge
and modesty, a great part of his glory as a philosopher.

So on that day when the hour made us break off after a long 15
conversation, we got up and left with the dispute unresolved. But
you demanded a last service which the shortness of time did not
allow, that wherever I first stopped my journey I should send you
a copy of each letter, so that after examining the matter more thoroughly you should be either an umpire establishing peace between
the sides, or if you could, become the defender of Cicero's consistency. I praise your spirit and pass on what you demanded, afraid 16
of winning the argument and eager to be defeated (strange to say),
in order to let you know that if you win you have more trouble
ahead than you think. For Seneca wants you as a champion in an
equal contest, since my next letter scolds him. I have been sporting
with these great intellects rashly perhaps, but with love and sorrow
and, as I think, justly—certainly more justly than I would like.
Many aspects of these lofty intellects delighted me, but a few dis- 17
turbed me; my urge was to write about these, although perhaps I
no longer feel it. I have postponed these issues to the last because
of the discrepancy in their content, but I had worked them into
shape a long time since.[7] I still grieve for the misfortune of such
men but equally over their responsibility for it; do not fail to notice that I am not condemning Seneca's life or Cicero's political
policy. Do not confuse the two quarrels: my present subject is Cic- 18
ero, the most vigilant and best and most beneficial consul and a
citizen always devoted to his country. What then? I cannot praise
his shifting attitude to his friendships and his estrangements from
trivial causes that were most harmful and destructive to himself
and good for nothing, his judgment about his own and political
circumstances, inferior to his sharpness of wit in other matters,
and finally his unrewarding relish for bandying charges, a childish
feature of a mature philosopher.[8] Know that neither you nor any 19

neque te neque alium quemlibet equum iudicem fieri posse, nisi omnibus Ciceronis epystolis, unde ea lis oritur, non a transcurrente perlectis. Vale.

*III Idus Maias, ex itinere.*

: 2 :

## *Ad Marcum Tullium Ciceronem.*

1 Franciscus Ciceroni suo salutem. Epystolas tuas diu multumque perquisitas atque ubi minime rebar inventas, avidissime perlegi. Audivi multa te dicentem, multa deplorantem, multa variantem, Marce Tulli, et qui iampridem qualis preceptor aliis fuisses noveram, nunc tandem quis tu tibi esses agnovi. Unum hoc vicissim a vera caritate profectum non iam consilium sed lamentum audi, ubicunque es, quod unus posterorum, tui nominis amantissimus,
2 non sine lacrimis fundit. O inquiete semper atque anxie, vel ut verba tua recognoscas, o preceps et calamitose senex, quid tibi tot contentionibus et prorsum nichil profuturis simultatibus voluisti? Ubi et etati et professioni et fortune tue conveniens otium reliquisti? Quis te falsus glorie splendor senem adolescentium bellis implicuit et per omnes iactatum casus ad indignam philosopho
3 mortem rapuit? Heu et fraterni consilii immemor et tuorum tot salubrium preceptorum, ceu nocturnus viator lumen in tenebris gestans, ostendisti secuturis callem, in quo ipse satis miserabiliter
4 lapsus es. Omitto Dyonisium, omitto fratrem tuum ac nepotem, omitto, si placet, ipsum etiam Dolabellam, quos nunc laudibus ad celum effers, nunc repentinis malidictis laceras: fuerint hec tolera-

other man can be a fair judge unless he has read thoroughly all Cicero's letters, which are the source of this dispute, and not skimmed them. Farewell.

*May 13, while traveling.*

: 2 :

## *To Marcus Tullius Cicero.*

1 Francesco sends greetings to his Cicero. I have been reading most greedily your letters which I searched for long and hard[1] and found where I least expected. I listened to you saying and lamenting and shifting your judgment on many topics, Marcus Tullius, and although I had long since discovered what kind of teacher you once were for others, I finally recognized how you taught yourself. Now hear in return this one piece, not of advice but of grievance, wherever you are, a complaint that one of your successors, and
2 most devoted to your renown, pours out with real tears. Troubled and anxious as you are or, to confront you with your own words, "you precipitate and disastrous old man,"[2] what business of yours were all these disputes and profitless quarrels? Where did you abandon the leisure fitted to your age and career and position? What false glitter of glory involved you, an old man, in the warfare of young fellows and swept you, buffeted by every misfortune, to a
3 death unworthy of a philosopher?[3] Alas, heedless of your brother's advice[4] and so many wise recommendations of your own, like a traveler by night carrying a lantern in the dark, you showed your
4 followers the path on which you yourself stumbled pitiably. I pass over Dionysius, I pass over your brother and nephew, I pass over, so please you, even Dolabella, men you at times exalt to heaven with praises and at times savage with curses: these mistakes would

bilia fortassis. Iulium quoque Cesarem pretervehor, cuius spectata
clementia ipsa lacessentibus portus erat; Magnum preterea Pompeium sileo, cum quo iure quodam familiaritatis quidlibet posse
5 videbare. Sed quis te furor in Antonium impegit? Amor credo
reipublice, quam funditus iam corruisse fatebaris. Quodsi pura
fides, si libertas te trahebat, quid tibi tam familiare cum Augusto?
Quid enim Bruto tuo responsurus es? 'Siquidem' inquit, 'Octavius
tibi placet, non dominum fugisse sed amiciorem dominum que-
6 sisse videberis.' Hoc restabat, infelix, et hoc erat extremum, Cicero, ut huic ipsi tam laudato malidiceres, qui tibi non dicam
malifaceret, sed malifacientibus non obstaret. Doleo vicem tuam,
amice, et errorum pudet ac miseret, iamque cum eodem Bruto 'his
artibus nichil tribuo, quibus *te* instructissimum *fuisse* scio.' Nimirum quid enim iuvat alios docere, quid ornatissimis verbis semper
7 de virtutibus loqui prodest, si te interim ipse non audias? Ah
quanto satius fuerat philosopho presertim in tranquillo rure se-
nuisse, de perpetua illa, ut ipse quodam scribis loco, non de hac
iam exigua vita cogitantem, nullos habuisse fasces, nullis triumphis inhiasse, nullos inflasse tibi animum Catilinas. Sed hec quidem frustra. Eternum vale, mi Cicero.

*Apud superos, ad dexteram Athesis ripam,*
*in civitate Verona Transpadane Italie,*
*XVI Kalendas Quintiles, anno ab ortu Dei illius*
*quem tu non noveras, MCCCXLV.*

perhaps have been forgivable.[5] I also pass beyond Julius Caesar
whose undisputed clemency was itself a harbor for those who assailed him;[6] I am silent too about Pompey the Great, with whom
it seemed you could have exercised any power by right of friendship.[7] But what madness drove you against Antony? Your patriot- 5
ism, I suppose, for the republic which, you admitted, had already
collapsed utterly. If pure integrity and freedom drew you on, why
did you have such intimacy with Augustus? What can you reply to
your friend Brutus? He says: "If you give your approval to Octavius, you will seem not to be shunning a master, but seeking a
more well-disposed master."[8] This was left for you, poor man, and 6
the worst outcome, that you should curse this man you praised so
much, who did not, shall I say, wrong you, but offered no resistance to those who did. I grieve for your fate, dear friend, and I
feel shame and pity for your mistakes and, like Brutus himself, "I
give no credit to the skills in which I know you were expertly
trained."[9] Indeed what is the point of teaching others, what the
advantage of speaking in most elegant words about the virtues, if
you don't listen to yourself? How much better it would have been, 7
especially for a philosopher, to have grown old in a calm country
setting, thinking about that everlasting life (as you yourself write
somewhere)[10] not about this petty life of ours, to have held no
symbols of power, to have thirsted after no triumphs, for no Cati-
lines to have puffed up your spirit. But these complaints are futile.
Farewell for ever, dear Cicero.

*From the world above on the right bank of the Adige*
*in the city of Verona in Transpadane Italy,*
*on the 16th of June in the 1345th year*
*after the birth of the God you never knew.*

## : 3 :

## *Ad eundem.*

1 Franciscus Ciceroni suo salutem. Si te superior offendit epystola (verum est enim, ut ipse soles dicere, quod ait familiaris tuus in *Andria:*

> Obsequium amicos, veritas odium parit),

accipe quod offensum animum ex parte mulceat, ne semper odiosa sit veritas; quoniam veris reprehensionibus irascimur, veris laudi-
2 bus delectamur. Tu quidem, Cicero, quod pace tua dixerim, ut homo vixisti, ut orator dixisti, ut philosophus scripsisti; vitam ego tuam carpsi, non ingenium non linguam, ut qui illud mirer, hanc stupeam; neque tamen in vita tua quicquam preter constantiam requiro, et philosophice professioni debitum quietis studium et a civilibus bellis fugam, extincta libertate ac sepulta iam et complo-
3 rata republica. Vide ut aliter tecum ago ac tu cum Epycuro multis in locis sed expressius in libro *De finibus* agebas; cuius enim ubilibet vitam probas, rides ingenium. Ego nichil in te rideo, vite tan-
4 tum compatior, ut dixi; ingenio gratulor eloquio ve. O romani eloquii summe parens, nec solus ego sed omnes tibi gratias agimus, quicunque latine lingue floribus ornamur; tuis enim prata de fontibus irrigamus, tuo ducatu directos, tuis suffragiis adiutos, tuo nos lumine illustratos ingenue profitemur; tuis denique, ut ita dicam, auspiciis ad hanc, quantulacunque est, scribendi facultatem
5 ac propositum pervenisse. Accessit et alter poetice vie dux; ita enim necessitas poscebat, ut esset et quem solutis et quem frenatis

: 3 :

## *To the same.*

Francesco greets his Cicero. If my earlier letter offended you (for, as you yourself often say, and your friend Terence said in the *Andrian Girl:* 1

Flattery produces friends, but truth hostility),[1]

hear what will partly sooth your offended spirit, so that the truth will not always be offensive, since we get angry at true criticism
but delight in true praise. With your leave, I shall say, Cicero, that 2
you lived like a man, spoke like an orator and wrote like a philosopher; it was your life I criticized, not your intellect or speech, as one who marvels at the former, and am struck dumb by the latter; and I find missing from your life nothing except consistency, the devotion to repose owed to the profession of philosopher and the flight from civil wars, once liberty was quenched and the republic
already buried and lamented. See how I am treating you differ- 3
ently from the way you treated Epicurus in many places, but most explicitly in *On Moral Ends,* in which you approve his life everywhere but mock his intellect.[2] I am not laughing at any aspect of you, only sympathizing with your life. As I said, I congratulate
you on your intellect and eloquence. Great father of Roman elo- 4
quence, not only I, but we all give you thanks, whoever among us is adorned with the ornaments of the Latin language: we water our meadows with your springs, we acknowledge freely that we are guided by your leadership, aided by your support and illuminated by your light; in sum it is under your auspices, so to speak, that we
have reached this ability and purpose, such as it is, in writing. And 5
another guide joined you, in his case to the road of poetry; for necessity demanded this, that we should have someone to follow

gressibus preeuntem sequeremur, quem loquentem, quem canentem miraremur, quoniam cum bona venia amborum, neuter ad utrunque satis erat, ille tuis equoribus, tu illius impar angustiis.
6 Non ego primus hoc dicerem fortasse, quamvis plane sentirem; dixit hoc ante me, seu ab aliis dictum scripsit, magnus quidam vir Anneus Seneca Cordubensis, cui te, ut idem ipse conqueritur, non etas quidem sed bellorum civilium furor eripuit; videre te potuit, sed non vidit; magnus tamen operum tuorum atque illius alterius laudator; apud hunc ergo quisque suis eloquentie finibus circum-
7 scriptus collega suo cedere iubetur in reliquis. Verum expectatione torqueo; quisnam dux ille sit, queris. Nosti hominem, si modo nominis meministi: Publius Virgilius Maro est, mantuanus civis, de quo egregie vaticinatus es. Cum enim, ut scriptum legimus, iuvenile quoddam eius opusculum miratus, quesivisses auctorem eumque iuvenem iam senior vidisses, delectatus es, et de inexhausto eloquentie tue fonte, cum propria quidem laude permixtum, verum tamen preclarumque ac magnificum illi testimonium
8 reddidisti. Dixisti enim:

Magne spes altera Rome.

Quod dictum ex ore tuo auditum, adeo sibi placuit inseditque memorie, ut illud post annos viginti, te pridem rebus humanis exempto, divino operi suo eisdem penitus verbis insereret, quod opus si tibi videre licuisset, letatus esses de primevo flore tam certum te venturi fructus presagium concepisse; necnon et latinis gratulatus musis, quod insolentibus graiis vel reliquissent ambi-
9 guam vel certam victoriam abstulissent. Utriusque enim sententie auctores sunt; te, si ex libris animum tuum novi, quem nosse michi non aliter quam si tecum vixissem videor, ultime assertorem

in the ease of prose and a different guide when reined in by verse, one man for us to admire in speech and another in song, since, with both men's leave, neither was enough for both skills: he could not match your broad expanses nor you his compression. Perhaps 6
I would not be the first to say this, though I clearly thought it, but it was said by others and written by that great man Seneca of Cordova, whom the frenzy of civil war, not his age, robbed you of seeing him, as he himself complains.[3] He could have seen you; yet he did not, but he was a mighty admirer of your work and that other genius; according to him each man restricted in the bounds of his own eloquence is ordered to yield to his colleague in the rest. But I torment you with suspense; you want to know who that 7
guide may be. You know the man, if you just recall his name: it is Publius Virgilius Maro, citizen of Mantua about whom you, Cicero, uttered wonderful prophecies. For as we read[4] you marveled at a youthful work of his and asked who was the writer and when in your old age you saw this young man you were thrilled, and from your unquenchable spring of eloquence you paid him a tribute, mixed to be sure with your own self-praise, yet true and glorious and magnificent. You called him: 8

Second hope of mighty Rome.

Overhearing this saying of yours so pleased him and so sank into his memory that twenty years after, when you were long since removed from human life, he inserted it in exactly the same words into his divine poem. And if you had been allowed to see this epic, you would have rejoiced to have conceived so sure a prophecy of the future harvest to come from his early flowering, and would have congratulated the Latin Muses for either leaving the victory over the arrogant Greek Muses in dispute or achieving a sure victory. There are sources to support each opinion,[5] but if I know 9
your nature from your books—you whom I seem to know as if I lived with you—I do not doubt that you would have supported

futurum, ut que in oratoria dedisti sic in poetica palmam Latio
daturum, atque ut *Eneydi* cederet *Ylias* iussurum fuisse non dubito,
quod iam ab initio virgiliani laboris Propertius asseverare non ti-
10 muit. Ubi enim pyerii operis fundamenta contemplatus est, quid
de illis sentiret et quid speraret aperte pronuntiavit his versibus:

Cedite romani scriptores, cedite graii;
Nescio quid maius nascitur Yliade.

Hec de altero latine duce facundie magneque Rome spe altera;
nunc ad te revertor.

11 Quid de vita, quid de ingenio tuo sentiam, audisti. Expectas
audire de libris tuis, quenam illos exceperit fortuna, quam seu
vulgo seu doctioribus probentur? Extant equidem preclara volu-
mina, que ne dicam perlegere, sed nec enumerare sufficimus. Fama
rerum tuarum celeberrima atque ingens et sonorum nomen; perrari autem studiosi, seu temporum adversitas seu ingeniorum he-
betudo ac segnities seu, quod magis arbitror, alio cogens animos
12 cupiditas causa est. Itaque librorum aliqui, nescio quidem an irreparabiliter, nobis tamen qui nunc vivimus, nisi fallor, periere:
magnus dolor meus, magnus seculi nostri pudor, magna posteritatis iniuria. Neque enim satis infame visum est ingenia nostra
negligere nequid inde fructuosum perciperet sequens etas, nisi laboris etiam vestri fructum crudeli prorsus et intoleranda corrupis-
semus incuria; profecto namque quod in tuis conqueror, et in
13 multis virorum illustrium libris accidit. Tuorum sane, quia de his
michi nunc sermo erat, quorum insignior iactura est, hec sunt nomina: reipublice, rei familiaris, rei militaris, de laude philosophie,

the latter hypothesis, giving to Latium the palm of victory in poetry which you bestowed in oratory, and you would have ordered the *Iliad* to give way to the *Aeneid*[6] — something Propertius
was already not afraid to declare when Vergil first began this task.
For when he considered the foundations of the Pierian work, he 10
openly declared what he believed and hoped about them in these
verses:

> Give way, you Roman writers, Greeks give way:
> A greater work than the *Iliad* is coming to birth.[7]

This is my verdict about the other guide in Latin eloquence and the "second hope of mighty Rome," but now I come back to you, Cicero.

You have heard what I feel about your life and your intellect. 11
Are you waiting to hear about your books and what fortune befell
them, how they are approved by either the common crowd or
more learned folk? Certainly glorious volumes have survived, ones
we are barely equal to listing, let alone reading thoroughly. The
fame of your deeds is most renowned and your name is mighty
and resonant: but real scholars are very rare. Either the hostility of
the age is the reason, or the dullness and sloth of intellects, or, as
I think more likely, greed that drives men in other directions. So 12
some of your books, perhaps irretrievably, have been lost for us
who are living now, if I am not deceived: it is a great grief to me, a
shame to our age, and a wrong done to posterity. Nor have we
thought it enough shame to neglect our intellects so that the following age may derive no profit from them, but by our cruel and
intolerable indifference we have even corrupted the product of
your labor; this I lament in the case of your work but it has happened to many books of distinguished men. However, those of 13
your works, since these are my present subject, whose loss has
been more conspicuous, include: *On the Republic, On Household
Matters, On Warfare, On the Praise of Philosophy, On Consolation, On*

de consolatione, de gloria, quamvis de his ultimis spes michi magis
14 dubia, quam desperatio certa sit. Quin et superstitum librorum magnas partes amisimus, ut velut ingenti prelio oblivionis et ignavie superatis, duces nostros non extinctos modo sed truncos quoque vel perditos sit lugere. Hoc enim et in aliis multis, sed in tuis maxime oratoriis atque achademicorum et legum libris patimur, qui ita truncati fedatique evaserunt, ut prope melius fuerit periisse.

15 Reliquum est ut urbis Rome ac romane reipublice statum audire velis, que patrie facies, que civium concordia, ad quos rerum summa pervenerit, quibus manibus quantoque consilio frena tractentur imperii; Hister ne et Ganges, Hiberus, Nilus et Tanais limites nostri sint, an vero quisquam surrexerit

Imperium Occeano, famam qui terminet astris,

aut

super et Garamantas et Indos
Proferat imperium,

16 ut amicus ille tuus mantuanus ait. Hec et his similia cupidissime auditurum te auguror; id michi pietas tua suggerit et amor erga patriam usque in tuam pernitiem notissimus. Verum enimvero tacere melius fuerit; crede enim michi, Cicero, si quo in statu res nostre sint audieris, excident tibi lacrime, quamlibet vel celi vel erebi partem tenes. Eternum vale.

*Apud superos,*
*ad sinistram Rodani ripam Transalpine Gallie,*
*eodem anno, XIV Kalendas Ianuarias.*

*Glory*, though about these last works I nurture uncertain hopes rather than outright despair.[8] Indeed, we have lost large portions 14
of the surviving works, so that like those overwhelmed in a great battle of forgetfulness and sloth, we have to mourn our leaders as not only deceased but mutilated or missing. We suffer this loss in many other cases but especially in your books on oratory and the *Academica* and *Laws* which have emerged so mutilated and disfigured that it would almost have been better for them to be lost.[9]

What is left is that you want to hear about the state of the city 15
of Rome and the Roman republic, the condition of your country, the harmony among your citizens, the men upon whom leadership has fallen, and by what hands and with what policy the reins of empire are being handled, and whether the Danube and Ganges, Ebro, Nile and Don are our boundaries,[10] or whether some man has arisen

> to bound our empire by the Ocean and our glory by the stars,

or

> beyond the Garamantes and the Indians
> extend our empire's sway,

as your Mantuan friend puts it. I am sure you will listen most ea- 16
gerly to these and other such details; your loyalty suggests this to me and your love for your country, so famous it almost brought your own ruin. But surely it would be better to keep silent, for believe me, Cicero, if you hear the condition of our affairs you will shed floods of tears, whatever part of heaven or the underworld[11] you occupy. Farewell for ever.

*In the world above*
*on the left bank of the Rhône in Transalpine Gaul,*[12]
*December 19th in the same year.*

## : 4 :

## *Ad Anneum Senecam.*

1 Franciscus Anneo Senece salutem. Petitam a tanto viro impetratamque veniam velim, siquid asperius dixero quam aut professionis tue reverentiam deceat aut quieti sit debitum sepulcri. Qui enim me Marco Ciceroni, quem latine eloquentie lumen ac fontem, teste te, dixerim, non pepercisse legerit, si reliquis itidem vera loquens
2 non pepercero, indignationis iuste materiam non habebit. Iuvat vobiscum colloqui, viri illustres, qualium omnis etas penuriam passa est, nostra vero ignorantiam et extremum patitur defectum. Certe ego quotidie vos loquentes attentius quam credi possit audio; forte non improbe ut ipse a vobis semel audiar optaverim. Inter omnis quidem evi clara nomina tuum nomen annumerandum esse non sum nescius, idque si aliunde nescirem, magno quo-
3 dam et externo teste cognovi. Plutarchus siquidem grecus homo et Traiani principis magister, suos claros viros nostris conferens, cum Platoni et Aristotili — quorum primum divinum, secundum demonium Graii vocant — Marcum Varronem, Homero Virgilium, Demostheni Marcum Tullium obiecisset, ausus est ad postremum et ducum controversiam movere, nec eum tanti saltem discipuli veneratio continuit. In uno sane suorum ingenia prorsus imparia non erubuit confiteri, quod quem tibi ex equo in moralibus preceptis obicerent non haberent; laus ingens ex ore presertim hominis animosi et qui nostro Iulio Cesari suum Alexandrum Macedonem comparasset.

## : 4 :

## *To Annaeus Seneca.*

1 Francesco sends greetings to Seneca. I would like to seek and obtain pardon from a great man such as you if I say anything more critical than befits my respect for your standing or is due to the repose of your tomb. Whoever reads that I did not spare Cicero, that light and fountain of Latin eloquence (on your own witness),[1] will not have cause for just indignation if I speak equally unsparing truth about other men.
2 It is my delight to talk with you, O famous men, of whom every age has suffered a scarcity, while our own age suffers from ignorance and a total lack of them. Certainly I listen to you talking each day with more attention than you can imagine, so it is perhaps not wrong for me to wish to be heard once at least by you. I know that your name, Seneca, should be counted among all the glorious names of every age, and if I did not know it from some other source, I have learned it from a great and independent witness.
3 The Greek Plutarch actually, tutor of the emperor Trajan,[2] who compared his distinguished fellow Greeks with our Romans, matched Varro with Plato and Aristotle (the first of whom is called divine by the Greeks, the second daimonic[3]) and Vergil with Homer, and Cicero with Demosthenes, and even dared in the end to raise a dispute about military leadership, nor did his reverence for his mighty pupil hold him back from making these comparisons. But in one respect alone did Plutarch not blush to acknowledge that the minds of his fellow Greeks were completely inferior: the fact they had no one to oppose to you on equal terms in moral instruction. This is high praise, especially from the lips of a spirited man who had compared his Macedonian Alexander with our Julius Caesar.[4]

4 Sed nescio quomodo sicut corporum sic animorum egregias
formas aliqua sepe gravis iniuria nature variantis insequitur, sive
quod omnium parens perfectionem mortalibus invidet, eoque magis quo ad illam propius videntur accedere, sive quod inter tam
multa decora deformitas omnis apparet, et quod in obscura facie
facilis nevus esset, in preclara cicatrix feda est: tanta lux in rebus
5 contrariorum vicinitate oritur. Tu vero, venerande vir et morum, si
Plutarcho credimus, incomparabilis preceptor, errorem vite tue, si
non molestum est, mecum recognosce. In omnium seculorum cru-
delissimum principem incidisti et tranquillus nauta preciosis mer-
cibus honustam navim ad infamem et procellosum scopulum ap-
6 pulisti. Cur autem illic hesisti, queso te? an ut in tempestate
aspera magisterium approbares? sed hoc nemo nisi amens eligit,
neque enim ut fortis est perpeti, sic prudentis est optare periculum; quin etiam si libera prudentie reliquatur electio, otiosa semper erit fortitudo: nichil enim incidet, adversus quod illius auxilium implorandum sit; modestia potius suis utens partibus et
7 letitiam frenabit et votiva moderabitur. Sed quoniam innumerabiles casus eveniunt et multa fert vita hominum quibus consilia
nostra vincuntur, idcirco virtus invicta furenti opponitur fortune,
non quidem secundum electionem, ut dixi, sed secundum necessi-
tatis inevitabiles ac ferreas leges.

8 At ego nunquid satis sanus videar si diutius cum magistro virtutis de virtute disputem, et probare nitar id cuius contrarii proba-
tio impossibilis sit—vincam profecto vel te iudice vel quolibet qui
inter huius vite fluctus mediocriter navigare didicerit—, non fuisse
9 consilium Syrtibus herere? Quodsi laudem ex difficultate captabas,
id ipsum summe laudis erat, emergere et in portum aliquem salva
puppe confugere: impendentem iugiter cervicibus tuis gladium
videbas, nec timebas, nec tam ancipitis rei exitum providebas,

But somehow, some severe harm of inconsistent nature persecutes minds of exceptional beauty, just like bodies, either because the Father of us all begrudges men perfection, and all the more as they seem to come nearer to it, or because ugliness is displayed in full among so many handsome aspects, and a wart that would be acceptable in an ordinary fellow is a disgusting scar in a glorious appearance; so great is the light that is shed on things when op- 4
posites are juxtaposed. But as for you, revered and incomparable 5
moral teacher, if we believe Plutarch, please review with me now the misdirection taken by your life, if it is not troublesome to you. You fell into the hands of the most cruel emperor of all ages, and as a peaceful sailor you wrecked your ship, loaded with precious
goods, on a shameful and stormy reef. So why did you cling to it, 6
I ask?[5] To win approval for your captaincy in a savage storm? But only a madman chooses this course, and it is not a prudent act to choose danger as it is a brave act to endure it. Indeed, if prudence is left a free choice, courage will always be superfluous, since nothing will happen against which you need implore the latter's help. Rather modest restraint, playing its role, will rein in joy and moderate men's wishes. But since countless mischances occur and men's 7
life brings many crises which overcome our deliberations, so virtue is set undefeated against raging fortune, not as a matter of choice, as I said, but according to the inevitable and iron laws of necessity.

But surely I would not seem sane to dispute about virtue with 8
a teacher of virtue, trying to prove something when its opposite cannot be proved (I would win my case with you as my judge or any man who has learned to steer at least adequately among the breakers of our life) — that it was not a wise counsel to founder in
the Syrtes.[6] If you were seeking to win glory from difficulty, that in 9
itself would deserve great credit, to emerge and take refuge in some harbor with your ship unharmed. You saw the sword continually hanging over your head[7] without fearing or foreseeing the outcome of this two-edged business, especially when — and this is

presertim quando—quod moriendi miserrimum genus est—intelligere poteras mortem tuam et fructu quolibet et gloria carituram.
10 Veneras, o miserabilis senex, in hominis manus qui quicquid
vellet posset, nil nisi pessimum velle posset. Somnio iam a prima
eius familiaritate deterritus, vigilans deinde multiplicibus argu-
mentis fidem turbide quietis acceperas; quid igitur tibi cum his
laribus tandiu, quid cum inhumano cruentoque discipulo, quid
11 cum dissimillimo comitatu? Respondebis: 'Effugere volui, sed ne-
quivi,' et illum Cleantis versiculum pretendes, quo in latinum
verso uti soles:

Ducunt volentem fata, nolentem trahunt;

illud insuper proclamabis voluisse te opibus tuis renuntiare, ut vel
sic laqueum libertatis abrumperes, teque in tutum ex tanto naufragio vel nudus eriperes: rem et veteribus historicis notam, et michi
ipsi illorum vestigiis incedenti haudquaquam silentio pretermis-
12 sam. Verum ibi palam loquens secretiora continui; nunc autem,
quando ad te unum michi sermo est, putas ne, silebo quod indignatio veritasque suggesserint? Ades modo et accede propius,
nequa externa auris interveniat, sentiens non nobis etatem rerum
tuarum notitiam abstulisse; testem nempe certissimum habemus
et qui de summis viris agens nec metu flectitur nec gratia, Sueto-
13 nium Tranquillum. Is ergo quid ait? Avertisse te Neronem a 'cognitione veterum oratorum,' quo scilicet in tui illum admiratione
diutius detineres: illi igitur pectori carus esse studuisti, cui ut
fieres vilis et missione dignus habereris vel simulato certe vel etiam
accersito lingue vitio curare debueras: prima hec miseriarum tua-
14 rum radix ab animi levitate ne dicam vanitate profecta. Inanem
studiorum gloriam, dure senex, nimis molliter, ne rursus dicam
pueriliter, concupisti. Ipsum quod ad immitis fere magisterium

the worst kind of dying—you could have understood that your
death would be without any benefit or glory.

You came, pitiable old man, into the hands of a person who 10
could do whatever he chose, and could choose only the worst.
When you were deterred by a dream from your first intimacy with
him, you discovered on awaking the trustworthiness of your troubled rest from manifold proofs.[8] So why did you associate with
this house for so long, why stay with your inhuman and bloody
pupil and with such an abhorrent retinue? You will answer "I 11
wanted to escape but I could not," and excuse yourself with this
line of Cleanthes, which you use to quote in a Latin version:

The fates lead on the willing but drag the reluctant man.[9]

Furthermore you will proclaim that you wanted to renounce your
wealth so as to snap the noose of freedom and snatch yourself to
safety from so great a shipwreck, even stripped of all possessions.
This was known to the ancient historians[10] and I did not pass it
over as I walked in their tracks. But then while speaking openly I 12
held back the more private elements; now since my conversation is
with you alone, do you think I shall suppress in silence what indignation and truth have put into my mind? Only come to me and
draw near so that no foreign ear intercepts us, believing that time
has not taken away the knowledge of your career: for we have a
most reliable witness, a man who is not swayed by fear or favor in
dealing with great men, Suetonius. So what does he say? That you 13
turned Nero away from getting to know the ancient orators in order to prolong his admiration of you.[11] You wanted to be dear to
that breast, when you should have taken care to be thought cheap
and worthy of dismissal either by simulating or even by acquiring
a deliberate weakness of speech. This first root of your misfortunes arose from the triviality if not the vanity of your spirit. Ob- 14
stinate old man, you lusted too self-indulgently and too like a child
for the empty glory of learning. The fact that you had embarked

accesseras, fuerit vel iudicii vel erroris vel fati cuiuspiam, quando
excusationes studiosius aucupamur et culpas nostras in fata reflec-
timus; votum hoc utique iudicii tui fuit; non potes accusare fortunam: quod optaveras invenisti.

15 Sed quo pergis, ah miser? Postquam in admirationem tui vesa-
num iuvenem eousque perduxeras ut nulla libertatis aut commea-
tus occasio superesset, nunquid non equanimius pati poteras iugum quod sponte subieras, et hoc saltem prestare ne domini tui
16 nomen immortalibus maculis insignires? Non equidem ignorabas
tragediam omne genus scripti gravitate vincere, ut ait Naso; hanc
tu quam mordaciter, quam venenose, quam acriter in illum scrip-
seris notum est, et ut est animus veri impatiens, eo iniuriosius quo
verius; nisi illa forsan opinio est vera, que tragediarum non te illa-
17 rum, sed tui nominis alterum vult auctorem. Nam et duos Senecas
Cordubam habuisse hispani etiam testes sunt; et *Octavie* — id enim
tragedie illi est nomen — locus aliquis hanc suspitionem recipit,
quam si sequimur, quod ad rem attinet, expers tu culpe huius;
quod ad stilum, nichil ille te inferior, quisquis est, evo licet secundus ac nomine; ita quantum morum demitur infamie, tantundem
ingenii fame detrahi oportet; alioquin excusatio, nisi fallor, famosi
18 carminis nulla est. Non quod ego nullam vel ingenii vel sermonis
acrimoniam nefandis actibus equari posse hominis rear illius, si
modo hominis nomine tam trux inhumanitas digna est; vide tamen num te deceret id scribere, de imperatore subiectum, de domino familiarem, de discipulo preceptorem, postremo de illo cui
tam multa blandiri, ne dicam blandiendo mentiri, solitus eras.
19 Relege libros quos ad eum ipsum de clementia, relege quem ad

on the teaching of a ruthless beast could have arisen either by your judgment or an error or some fate, since we hanker too eagerly for excuses and divert our guilt onto the fates; this wish however was the product of your judgment, and you cannot accuse fortune: you found what you had desired.

Poor wretched man, what are you aiming at? After you had 15
seduced this mad young fellow into such admiration of you that no opportunity was left you of freedom or movement, could you not have endured more calmly the yoke you had freely put on and at least ensured that you would not mark your master's name with ineradicable stains? You were well aware that tragedy surpassed 16
every genre of writing in weightiness, as Ovid says.[12] Yet it is well known how bitingly and poisonously and savagely you wrote one against Nero, and given the impatience of your mind with truth, what you wrote was all the more harmful, because it was true.[13] Unless perhaps the opinion is correct that claims not you, but another man of your name was author of the tragedies.[14] For even 17
the Spaniards claim that two Senecas lived at Cordova, and a passage in the *Octavia* (for this is the name of that tragedy) admits this suspicion. If we subscribe to this belief, as concerns the theme, you were guiltless of this offense; as concerns the style, whoever composed it was in no way inferior to you, although second in age and repute, so that whatever shame is subtracted from your character ought to be subtracted from the fame of your intellect. Otherwise, unless I am mistaken, there is no excuse for this scandalous poem. Not that I think any bitter abuse of either 18
character or language can be matched by the man's abominable actions, if such brutal inhumanity deserves the name of man; but consider whether it was proper for you to write this, as a subject about your emperor,[15] as a member of his household about your master, as a teacher about your pupil, finally about a man to whom you habitually paid so many flatteries, not to mention lying flatteries. Read over again the books you wrote to him *On Clem-* 19

Polibium de consolatione dictasti; si vel libros vel librorum memoriam lethei gurgitis unda non obruit, pudebit, credo, laudati discipuli; qua enim fronte de tali talia scripsisse potueris, ignoro; certe
ego illa sine pudore non relego.

20 Sed hic rursus occurres, et adolescentiam principis atque indo-
lem multum spei melioris preferentem obiciens, errorem tuum repentina morum eius mutatione tutabere, quasi hec nobis ignota
sint. Verum ipse considera quam sit excusabile, paucula personati
principatus opuscula vel simulate pietatis voculas obliquasse animum ac iudicium tibi tali viro, tali etate, tanta rerum experientia
21 ac doctrina. Quid enim, oro, tibi placuit ex illius actis, que ab
historicis, ut eorum verbis utar, 'partim nulla reprehensione, partim non mediocri laude digna' memorantur, prius scilicet quam se
totum in scelera et probra demergeret an aurigandi potius an ci-
tharizandi studium, quibus tam curiose deditum accepimus, ut
secretius primo, coram servis ac plebe sordida, deinde etiam in
publico, universo populo spectante, princeps auriga decurreret, et
quasi numen aliquod oblatam sibi citharam adoraret, egregius ci-
22 tharista? quibus tandem successibus evectus et velut italicis non
contentus ingeniis Achaiam petiit, et grecorum musicorum adula-
tionibus inflatus, solos Grecos studiis suis dignos asseruit, ridicu-
23 lum monstrum, ferox belua. An illud omen certius magni simul ac
religiosi principis habuisti, quod barbe primitias et illas inhumani
oris exuvias in Capitolio consecravit?

24 Hi certe sunt actus Neronis tui, Seneca. Ea etate qua historici
adhuc eum inter homines numerant, tu eum inter deos nec lau-
dante nec laudato dignis preconiis conaris inserere et — cuius an te
pudeat nescio sed me pudet — optimo principum divo Augusto

*ency*, the book to Polybius on *Consolation*: if the water of the stream of Lethe has not buried these books or their memory, you will feel shame, I believe, at the praise of your pupil.[16] For I don't know with what effrontery you could write such things about such a man; at any rate I do not reread them without shame.

But here again you will counter me, and claiming the emperor's 20
youth and promise of acquiring better prospects, you will defend your mistake by supposing a sudden transformation of his character, as if I did not know these things. But consider: how excusable is it for a few minor literary works by the playacting emperor or a few utterances of feigned piety to have skewed the mind and judgment of such a man as you, at your age and with your experience
of the world and education? What pleased you, I ask, among his 21
deeds mentioned by historians, to use their words, as "worthy in part of no reproach, in part of moderate praise,"[17] before in fact he soaked himself in crimes and scandals or the passion for chariot driving and lyre playing, activities we understood he was so excessively devoted to that while emperor he raced as a charioteer, more privately at first before slaves and the common mob, then even in public with the whole nation watching,[18] and being a fine lyre player, worshipped his lyre as if it were some god offered to him?[19]
Finally, carried away by these successes, as if not content with Ital- 22
ian talents, he made for Achaea and, swollen by the adoration of Greek musicians, he said that only the Greeks were worthy of his
expertise, that absurd monster and savage beast.[20] Or did you take 23
this as a surer omen of a great and devout emperor that he dedicated the first shavings of his beard and the spoils of his inhuman face on the Capitol?[21]

These are the acts of your Nero, Seneca. In an age when the 24
historians still count him among men, you dared to intrude him among the gods with a proclamation worthy neither of you who praised him nor of the man you praised, and—I don't know if it shames you, but it shames me—did not hesitate to put him before

preferre non dubitas, nisi forte illud maiori gloria dignum putas,
quod cristianos, hominum genus revera sanctum et innocuum, verum ut sibi videbatur et Suetonio referenti, 'superstitionis nove ac
malifice,' suppliciis affecit, omnis pietatis persecutor atque hostis
25 crudelissimus. Ego quidem de te ista non suspicor, eoque magis
propositum tuum miror; nam et superiora illa frivola nimis ac
vana sunt, et ultimum hoc nefarium etiam et immane; et ita tibi
visum, una quidem epystolarum tuarum ad apostolum Paulum
26 non modo innuit sed fatetur. Neque tibi videri potuisse aliter certus sum, illis tam sacris ac celestibus monitis aurem non neganti,
oblatamque divinitus amicitiam complexo; quam utinam arctius
tenuisses nec divellereris in finem, ut cum illo precone veritatis pro
veritate ipsa et pro eterni premii promissione tantique promissoris
pro nomine morereris. Sed progressus sum longius dicendi impetu, et intelligo me ad hec exaranda serius processisse, quam ut
ulla tempestive frugis spes appareat. Eternum vale.

*Apud superos,*
*in Gallia Cisalpina ad dexteram Padi ripam,*
*Kalendis Sextilibus anno ab ortu Eius*
*quem an tu rite noveris incertum habeo, MCCCXLVIII.*

: 5 :

## *Ad Marcum Varronem.*

1 Franciscus Marco Varroni salutem. Ut te amem ac venerer tua me singularis virtus et industria, tuum me clarissimum nomen cogit. Sunt quos benificiis ac meritis amamus; qui scilicet, ceteris con-

Augustus, the best of emperors.[22] Unless perhaps you think it an act worthy of greater glory that he imposed the death penalty on the Christians, a truly holy and innocent body of men, but, as they seemed to him and to Suetonius who records it, "men of a new and dangerous superstition"[23]—Nero, that most cruel persecutor and enemy of all piety. For my part I do not suspect you of 25
such an attitude, and so I am all the more amazed at your intention, for those earlier matters are too trivial and vain, but this last detail is wicked and monstrous. And one of the letters that you wrote to the Apostle Paul not only hints but openly says that this
was how you saw it.[24] And I am sure you cannot have thought 26
otherwise, since you did not refuse your ear to such holy and heavenly warnings and embraced the friendship divinely offered to you; if only you had clasped it more closely and not been severed at the end, so that with that herald of truth you would have died for the truth itself and the guarantee of an eternal reward and in the name of so mighty a guarantor. But I have gone too far in the urge to speak and I realize I have moved to scratch out these thoughts too late for any hope of timely benefit to arise. Farewell for ever.

*From the world above,*
*in Cisalpine Gaul on the right bank of the Po*
*on the first day of August in the thirteen hundred and forty-eighth year*
*from the birth of Him whom I am uncertain you knew properly.*

## : 5 :

## *To Marcus Varro.*

Francesco greets Marcus Varro. Your unique virtue and diligence 1
and your glorious reputation compel me to love and revere you. There are men we love for their kindnesses and services, men who

spectu et odore graviter offendentibus, ipsi doctrinis instruunt
exemplisque delectant, quique licet hinc abierint 'in comunem lo-
2 cum,' ut ait Plautus, tamen absentes prosunt presentibus. Tu nichil aut modicum prodes, non tua quidem sed omnia corrumpentis
evi culpa. Etas nostra libros tuos perdidit: quidni autem, unius
numorum custodie studiosa? quis usquam invise rei custos bonus
fuit? Tu notitie rerum supra fidem deditus, non ideo actuose vite
semitam declinasti, utroque calle conspicuus, et illis summis viris
3 Magno Pompeio ac Iulio Cesari merito tuo carus. Itaque sub altero militasti, ad alterum scripsisti libros mirabiles omnisque discipline refertissimos, inter bellorum et publicorum munerum diver-
sissimas curas. Magna laus non ingenii modo sed propositi, in actu
perpetuo corpus simul atque animum habere, et posse et velle non
4 etati tue tantum sed omnibus seculis prodesse. Hi tanto studio
elaborati libri digni non sunt habiti qui per manus nostras ad posteros pervenirent; ardorem tuum nostra vicit ignavia; nemo tam
parcus pater unquam fuit, cuius non longevam parsimoniam brevi
tempore luxuriosus filius posset evertere. Quid nunc libros perditos enumerem? quot librorum tuorum nomina, totidem fame
nostre sunt vulnera; prestat igitur siluisse, nam et contrectatione
vulnus recrudescit et sopitus dolor damni memoria excitatur.

5 Sed, o incredibilis fame vis, vivit nomen sepultis operibus,
et cum de Varrone prope nichil appareat, doctorum tamen omnium consensu doctissimus Varro est, quod 'sine ulla dubitatione'
Marcus icero his ipsis in libris in quibus nichil affirmandum disputat, affirmare non timuit, ut quodammodo luce tui nominis

while seriously offending the rest because of their appearance and smell, personally instruct us in learning and delight us with examples; although these men have departed to "the common place of death," as Plautus says,[1] even in their absence they are still useful to our present generation. Unfortunately, you can hardly be 2
useful to us, or just moderately so, not through your fault but through the fault of time which reduces everything to decay. Our age has lost your books: how could it not, given that its one passion is keeping its money safe? Who was ever a good guardian of something he despised? You were dedicated beyond belief to scholarship, but did not reject the way of active life for that reason, conspicuous in both ways of life, and dear through your own excellence to those great men Pompey and Caesar. So you cam- 3
paigned under the former and wrote to the other marvelous books packed with every kind of expertise, among the widely different concerns of warfare and public office.[2] This does great credit not only to your intellect but to your purpose, to keep both your body and mind in constant activity, to have the ability and will to benefit not only your own age but all generations. These books you 4
toiled over with such enthusiasm were not thought worthy of passing through our hands to posterity; our laziness defeated your passion; indeed no father was ever so thrifty that an extravagant son could not rapidly overthrow his father's patient economy. Why should I list the lost books? The many names of your lost works are so many wounds to our reputation, so it is better to keep quiet, since handling the wound reopens it and dulled pain is aggravated by the memory of loss.[3]

But so unbelievable is the power of fame that your name lives 5
although your works are buried, and although almost nothing is visible of Varro, Varro is decreed the most learned by the unanimous agreement of all learned men, as Cicero attests without any hesitation: in those very books in which he argues that nothing can be asserted, he was not afraid to assert this, so that, as the light of

prestringente oculos, videatur interim dum de te loquitur, suum
6 principale propositum non vidisse. Quod Ciceronis testimonium quidam latinitatis angustiis includunt, apud quos Romanorum doctissimi nomen habes, alii ad Grecorum metas extendunt, precipueque Lactantius, vir ex nostris eloquentia et religione clarissimus, qui nullum Varrone doctiorem ne apud Grecos quidem
7 vixisse non dubitat. Sed inter innumerabiles precones tuos famosissimi duo sunt: primus est ille cuius supra mentionem feci, coetaneus et concivis et condiscipulus tuus, Cicero, qui multa tibi et cui tu multa, servata ex Catonis precepto ratione otii, scripsisti, cuius ut vivaciora sint opera, stili forsitan dulcedo prestitit; secundus vir quidam sanctissimus et divino ingenio, Augustinus, origine afer eloquio romanus, cum quo utinam de libris divina tractantibus deliberare potuisses, magnus nempe theologus futurus, qui eam quam poteras theologiam tam scrupulose tractasti, tam anxie divisisti.

8 Ut vero rerum tuarum nichil ignores, quamvis ita de te scriptum sit, legisse te 'tam multa ut aliquid *tibi* scribere vacasse miremur, tam multa *scripsisse* quam multa vix quenquam legere *potuisse* credamus,' nulle tamen extant seu admodum lacere tuorum operum reliquie, e quibus aliqua pridem vidi, et recordatione torqueor summis, ut aiunt, labiis gustate dulcedinis, et ea ipsa, precipue divinarum et humanarum rerum libros, qui nomen tibi sonantius peperere, adhuc alicubi latitare suspicor; eaque multos iam per annos me fatigat cura, quoniam longa et solicita spe nichil
9 est importunius. Tu vero solare animum, et laboris egregii fructum ex conscientia percipiens, mortalia periisse ne doleas; sciebas peritura dum scriberes: mortali enim ingenio nichil efficitur immortale. Quid autem refert an statim an post centum annorum

your name somehow dazzles the eyes, he seems in talking of you to have overlooked his fundamental axiom.[4] Some confine this evi- 6
dence of Cicero to the narrow world of Latin speakers with whom you hold the title of most learned of the Romans, but others extend this to the limits of the Greeks, especially Lactantius, most eloquent and devout among our Roman people, who does not doubt that no man even among the Greeks was more learned than
Varro.[5] But among your countless heralds there are two very fa- 7
mous men. First, the man I mentioned above, your contemporary and fellow citizen and fellow student Cicero, who wrote many things for you and for whom you wrote much, observing the use of leisure recommended by Cato;[6] Cicero's sweetness of style perhaps excels, so that his works are more lively.[7] The second is that most holy man of divine intellect, Augustine, African in birth but Roman in eloquence. If only you could have deliberated with him about your books that deal with divine matters! You would surely have become a great theologian, since you discussed the theology known to you so scrupulously and you divided its parts so carefully.

But so that you miss nothing that concerns you, although it is 8
written about you that you read "so much that we are amazed you had any leisure for writing, and you wrote as much as scarcely anyone could read,"[8] there are no remains, or only tattered ones, of your works, of which I have seen some in the past and am tormented that I only sampled their sweetness on my lips, as they say. Those actual works, especially the books of human and divine matters which gave you a more resounding name, are still lurking somewhere, I suspect. This preoccupation has wearied me for many years, since nothing is more troublesome than a long and
anxious hope. But console your spirit, and obtaining the fruit of 9
your exceptional labor from your good conscience, do not grieve that your mortal works have perished. You knew they would perish even as you wrote them, since nothing immortal is produced by a mortal intellect. What difference does it make whether some-

millia pereat quod aliquando perire est necesse? Est quidem illustris simili studio flagrantium cohors haudquaquam fortunatior laborum, quibus exemplis utcunque sortem tuam equanimius ferre
10 debes. Ex his nunc aliquos iuvat attingere, quoniam clarorum no-
minum vel sola commemoratio dulcis est. Sunt autem hi: Marcus
Cato Censorius, Publius Nigidius, Antonius Gnipho, Iulius Hyginus, Ateius Capito, Gaius Bassus, Veratius Pontificalis, Octavius
Hersennius, Cornelius Balbus, Massurius Sabinus, Servius Sulpi-
tius, Cloatius Verus, Gaius Flaccus, Pompeius Festus, Cassius
Emina, Fabius Pictor, Statius Tullianus, multique alii quos enumerare longum est, olim clari viri nunc cinis ambiguus et preter
primos duos vix cognita nomina; quos omnes meis verbis tuo ore
11 salutatos velim. Iulium et Augustum Cesares et aliquot alios ex illo
ordine, quamvis studiosissimos atque doctissimos teque nonnullis
horum familiarissimum sciam, equius tamen extimo nostris impe-
ratoribus salutandos linquere, si tamen hos non illorum pudet,
quorum studio ac virtute fundatum imperium everterunt. Eternum vale, vir vigilantissime.

*Apud superos,*
*in capite orbis Roma,*
*que tua fuit et mea patria facta est,*
*Kalendis Novembris anno ab ortu Eius*
*quem utinam novisses, MCCCL.*

thing perishes instantly or after a hundred thousand years, if it
must perish at some time? There is a distinguished crowd burning
with the same scholarly zeal, scarcely more fortunate in the fate of
their works,[9] and on that basis you should endure your lot more
calmly. Now it pleases me to touch on some of these, since even 10
the mention of glorious names is sweet. These are: Cato the Censor, Publius Nigidius, Antonius Gnipho, Julius Hyginus, Ateius
Capito, Gaius Bassus, Veranius Pontificalis, Octavius Hersennius,
Cornelius Balbus, Massurius Sabinus, Servius Sulpicius, Cloatius
Verus, Gaius Flaccus, Pompeius Festus, Cassius Hemina, Fabius
Pictor, Statius Tullianus, and many others whom it would be tedious to list, once glorious men, now unidentified ashes and, besides the first two names, barely known.[10] I would like them all to
be greeted by you as mouthpiece for my words. I know that you 11
were most intimate with Julius and Augustus Caesar and some
others of that rank; but, although they were most devoted and
learned and intimate with you, I think it fairer to leave them to be
greeted by our emperors, if they are not ashamed in front of those
who founded with passion and virtue the empire they have destroyed. Forever farewell, most wakeful of men.

*Written among the living,*
*in Rome, capital of the world,*
*which was your fatherland and became mine,*
*on the first day of November in the year 1350*
*from the birth of Him whom I only wish you had known.*

## : 6 :

## *Ad Quintilianum.*

1 Franciscus Quintiliano salutem. Olim tuum nomen audieram et de tuo aliquid legeram, et mirabar unde tibi nomen acuminis; sero ingenium tuum novi: *Oratoriarum Institutionum* liber, heu, discerptus et lacer, venit ad manus meas. Agnovi etatem vastatricem omnium et dixi mecum: 'Facis ut solita es; nil bona fide custodis, nisi quod perdere lucrum erat. O etas segnis et insolens, tales michi remittis insignes viros cum ignavissimos colas! o sterilis et feda pars temporum tot rebus ediscendis ac scribendis dedita que me-
2 lius nescirentur, opus hoc habere integrum neglexisti.' Ceterum is michi de te veram liber opinionem attulit; diu tuis in rebus erraveram; errori finem advenisse gratulor. Vidi formosi corporis artus effusos; admiratio animum dolorque concussit; et fortasse nunc apud aliquem totus es, et apud talem forsitan qui suum hospitem habet incognitum. Quisquis in te reperiendo fortunatior fuit, sciat se rem magni precii possidere, quamque si noverit, primas inter
3 divitias locet. Tu quidem in his libris, qui quot sint nescio sed hauddubie multi sunt, rem a Cicerone iam sene summo studio tractatam refricare ausus, quod factu impossibile iudicabam, post tanti viri vestigia novam non imitationis sed doctrine proprie preclarique operis gloriam invenisti. Adeo diligenter ab illo instructus

: 6 :

## *To Quintilian.*

Francesco greets Quintilian. I long since heard your name and 1
read some of your work and wondered how you acquired your reputation for shrewdness; it was only lately that I came to know your talent. Alas, your book called *The Institutes of Oratory* came to my hands fragmented and mutilated. I recognized the power of our age to destroy all things and said to it in my heart: "You are doing your usual thing; you do not protect anything in good faith except what it would have been profitable to lose. O what a slothful and arrogant time this is, to hand over distinguished men to me in such damaged condition, while you cherish the most worthless! O sterile and ugly period, devoted to memorizing and writing out so many things that would be better left unknown, while you
have not bothered to keep this masterwork intact!" But that vol- 2
ume brought me a true opinion about you, whereas I had long strayed in approaching your contents; I am thankful that my error has come to an end. I saw the limbs of that handsome body spread out and admiration and grief shattered my spirit; perhaps even now your complete text is in some man's possession, a man so uninformed that he does not recognize his guest. Whoever was more successful in finding you should know that he has an object of great value and, if he comes to know it, he would count it
among his chief riches. In these books, whose number I do not 3
know but they are undoubtedly many,[1] you have dared to revive a matter treated by Cicero as an old man with the greatest enthusiasm,[2] a thing I had judged to be impossible; following in the footsteps of so great a man you have found a new glory, not from imitation but from your own learning and a distinguished piece of work. So truly has the orator, trained by him, been carefully

orator a te comptus ornatusque est, ut multa ab illo vel neglecta vel non animadversa videantur, atque ita singulatim omnia colligis duci tuo elapsa, ut quantum vinci eloquio tantum diligentia vin-
4 cere recto ni fallor iudicio dici possis. Ille enim suum oratorem per ardua causarum ac summos eloquentie vertices agit et iudicialibus bellis ad victoriam format; tu longius repetens, oratorem tuum per omnes longe vie flexus ac latebras ab ipsis incunabulis ad supremam eloquii arcem ducis; placet, delectat et mirari cogit; eo namque aspirantibus nichil utilius. Ciceroniana claritas provectos illuminat et celsum validis iter signat, tua sedulitas ipsos quoque fovet invalidos et optima nutrix ingeniorum, lacte humili teneram pascit infantiam.

5 Sed ne tibi veritas blanda suspecta sit, mutandus est stilus. In te igitur re apparuit verum esse quod Cicero idem ait in *Rethoricis*: 'oratori minimum de arte loqui, multo maximum ex arte dicere'; non tamen ut ille Hermagore de quo agebat, sic ego tibi horum alterum concedo, alterum eripio; utrunque concesserim, sed hoc mediocriter illud eximie, atque adeo excellenter ut vix quicquam
6 adici iam humano posse videatur ingenio. Equidem quantum hoc tuo magnifico opere collato cum eo libro quem de causis edidisti — qui idcirco non periit ut constaret etatem nostram optimarum rerum precipue negligentem, mediocrium non ita —, satis intelligentibus patet multo te melius cotis officio functum esse
7 quam gladii et oratorem formare potentius quam prestare! Id ne ad iniuriam trahas velim sed intelligas in te ipso inque aliis nunquam sic ingenium unum par ad omnia, ut non aliqua in parte se vinceret. Magnus fateor vir fuisti, sed instituendis formandisque

groomed and adorned by you, that it is clear many elements were either neglected or unnoticed by him, and you have collected each and every item that escaped your guide, so that you can be said with good judgment, if I am not mistaken, to have triumphed as much in diligence as he did in eloquence. Cicero drives his orator 4
over the steep slopes of court cases and lofty summits of eloquence and shapes him for victory in judicial conflicts; you go back further and guide your orator through all the twists and turns of a long route from the cradle itself to the high citadel of eloquence;[3] it pleases, delights and compels admiration, since nothing is more helpful for men aspiring to this goal. Cicero's clarity throws light on those who have progressed and marks a lofty path for the strong; your careful attentiveness cherishes even the weak and is the best nurse of intellects, nourishing tender infancy with humble milk.

But to avoid you suspecting my true words of flattery, I must 5
change my style. In you it has been made manifest that what Cicero says in his *Rhetoric* is true: "It befits the orator to say least about art but speak mostly with art," not however, as he said of Hermagoras, that I grant you one of these two but deny you the other;[4] I would grant both, but the former to a moderate degree, the latter exceptionally, and so excellently that it hardly seems anything could be added by human intellect. When I have com- 6
pared this magnificent work of yours with the book you published on court declamations[5]—which escaped being lost to prove that our age was especially indifferent to the best products, but not of mediocre things—it is clear to men of understanding that you performed the role of a whetstone[6] much more successfully than that of a sword, and were more powerful in forming an orator than acting as one. I do not want you to treat this as an injus- 7
tice, but realize that in yourself and others no single intellect is so well matched to all challenges that it does not defeat itself in some respect. I admit you were a great man, but greatest of all in train-

magnis viris maximus et qui si materiam ydoneam nactus esses, te maiorem ex te facile gigneres, doctus nobilium cultor ingeniorum.

8 Fuit autem tibi emulatio non levis magni cuiusdam viri alterius, Anneum Senecam dico; quos etas, quos professio, quos natio iunxerat, seiunxit parium pestis, livor; qua in re nescio an tu modestior videare: siquidem nec tu illum pleno ore laudare potes, et ille de te contemptissime loquitur. Ego si tantas inter partes iudex sim, quanquam iudicari a parvis magis verear quam iudicare de
9 magnis merear, meum iudicium dicam tamen. Ille uberior tu acutior, ille altior tu cautior; et tu quidem ingenium eius et studium et doctrinam laudas, electionem ac iudicium non laudas, stilum vero corruptum et omnibus vitiis fractum dicis; ille autem te inter eos numerat quorum cum ipsis fama sepulta est, cum necdum tua fama sepulta sit, nec tu illo scribente aut sepultus esses aut mor-
10 tuus. Ille etenim sub Nerone obiit, tu post illius et Neronis obitum sub Galba Romam ex Hispania venisti, multosque ibi post annos sororis Domitiani principis nepotum curam ipso mandante suscipiens morumque et studiorum iuvenilium censor factus, utriusque rei eximia spe ostensa, quod in te fuit, credo fidem impleveris; tamen, ut statim post Plutarchus ad Traianum scribit, tuorum adolescentium temeritas in te refunditur. Nichil modo quod scriberem aliud fuit; opto te incolumem videre, et sicubi totus es, oro ne diutius me lateas. Vale.

*Apud superos, inter dextrum Apennini latus*
*et dextram Arni ripam,*
*intra ipsos patrie mee muros,*
*ubi primum michi ceptus es nosci,*

ing and molding great men; if, as learned trainer of noble minds,
you had happened on the right material, you would easily have
begotten a greater man from your own self.

You felt however a severe envy of another great man, Seneca: 8
you two, whom age, profession and nationality had brought together, were separated by envy, the plague of equals, a matter in
which you may seem to be more moderate: for you cannot praise
him with a full throat, but he speaks most contemptuously about
you.[7] Supposing I were to judge between such powerful parties—
although I would be more afraid of being judged by small men
than qualified to pass judgment on great men—I will still voice
my judgment. He was more fertile, you more keen, he more lofty, 9
you more cautious; indeed you praise his talent and enthusiasm
and learning, but do not praise his choice and judgment, declaring
his style altogether corrupt and effeminate with every kind of
fault,[8] whereas he counts you among those whose fame is buried
along with them, despite the fact that your fame was not yet buried, nor would you be buried nor dead during his career.[9] For he 10
died under Nero, but you died after his death and Nero's too,
coming as you did to Rome under Galba's patronage from Spain;[10]
and there, after many years, taking on the education of the great-
nephews of the emperor Domitian by his sister upon his order,[11]
you were made censor of their morals and studies. You brought
out their future excellence in both respects, and within your powers I believe you fulfilled your commitment. But, as Plutarch
writes immediately after to Trajan, the rashness of your young
pupils spilled back over onto you.[12] I have nothing else to write; I
long to see you unharmed, and wherever you exist in whole form I
beg you not to hide from me any longer. Farewell.

*Among the living, on the right slope of the Apennines*
*and the right bank of the Arno*
*within the walls of my native land,*[13]
*where I first began to know you,*

*eoque ipso tempore, VII Idus Decembris,*
*anno Eius quem dominus tuus persequi maluit*
*quam nosse, MCCCL.*

## : 7 :

## *Ad Titum Livium historicum.*

1 Franciscus Tito Livio salutem. Optarem, si ex alto datum esset, vel me in tuam vel te in nostram etatem incidisse, ut vel etas ipsa vel ego per te melior fierem et visitatorum unus ex numero tuorum, profecto non Romam modo te videndi gratia, sed Indiam ex Galliis aut Hispania petiturus. Nunc vero qua datur te in libris tuis video, non equidem totum sed quatenus nondum seculi nostri de-
2 sidia periisti. Centum quadraginta duos rerum romanarum libros edidisse te novimus, heu quanto studio quantisque laboribus! Vix triginta ex omnibus supersunt. O mos pessimus nosmet ipsos de industria fallendi! Triginta dixi quia omnes vulgo id dicunt, ego autem deesse unum his ipsis invenio: novem et viginti sunt, plane tres decades, prima tertia et quarta, cui librorum numerus non
3 constat. In his tam parvis tuis reliquiis exerceor quotiens hec loca vel tempora et hos mores oblivisci volo, et semper acri cum indignatione animi adversus studia hominum nostrorum, quibus nichil in precio est nisi aurum et argentum et voluptas, que si in bonis habenda sunt, multo plenius multoque perfectius non tantum mute pecudis sed immobilis etiam et insensibilis elementi quam rationalis hominis bonum erit.

4 Verum hec et longa et nota materia est; nunc vero tibi potius tempus est ut gratias agam cum pro multis tum pro eo nominatim,

*and on the same day, the seventh of December,*
*in the year 1350 of the age of the One*
*Whom your master preferred to persecute rather than to know.*

: 7 :

## *To the historian Titus Livius.*

Francesco sends greetings to Livy. I would have preferred, if it had 1
been granted from on high, that either I fell in your generation or
you in mine, so that through your agency either the age itself or I
would be improved; and as one of the number of your visitors, I
would have traveled from the Gallic provinces or Spain to see you,
not just to Rome but as far as India.[1] But as it is I see you in your
books, not admittedly whole, but at least in the measure in which
you have not yet been lost by the sloth of our age. We know you 2
published a hundred and forty-two books of Roman history, and
with what enthusiasm and effort! Scarcely thirty of them all have
survived. O what a dreadful practice to deceive ourselves on purpose! I said thirty because everyone commonly says it, but I find
that this is one short; they are twenty-nine, that is three decades:
the first, third, and fourth, in which the number of books is not
agreed.[2] I exercise myself on these scanty remains of yours when- 3
ever I want to forget these places and times and modern behavior,
always with fierce indignation at heart against the passion of our contemporaries who value nothing except gold and silver and pleasure. If these are to be counted as goods, the good of not only a dumb beast but of even an immobile and insensate mineral will be superior to the good of a reasoning man.

But this is both a long and well known theme; now is the time 4
rather to thank you for many reasons but especially for this service,

quod immemorem sepe presentium malorum seculis me feliciori-
bus inseris, ut inter legendum saltem cum Corneliis, Scipionibus
Africanis, Leliis, Fabiis Maximis, Metellis, Brutis, Deciis, Catoni-
bus, Regulis, Cursoribus, Torquatis, Valeriis Corvinis, Salinatori-
bus, Claudiis Marcellis, Neronibus, Emiliis, Fulviis, Flaminiis,
Atiliis, Quintiis ac Camillis, et non cum his extremis furibus, inter
5 quos adverso sidere natus sum, michi videar etatem agere. Et o si
totus michi contingeres, quibus aliis quantisque nominibus et vite
solatium et iniqui temporis oblivio quereretur! Que quoniam simul apud te nequeo, apud alios sparsim lego, presertim in eo libro
ubi te totum sed in angustias sic coactum video ut librorum nu-
6 mero nichil, rebus ipsis infinitum desit. Tu velim de antiquioribus
Polibium et Quintum Claudium et Valerium Antiatem reliquos-
que quorum glorie splendor tuus officit; de novis autem Plinium
Secundum veronensem vicinum tuum, atque emulum quondam
tuum Crispum Salustium salutes, quibus nuntia nichilo feliciores
eorum vigilias fuisse quam tuas. Eternum vale, rerum gestarum
memorie consultor optime.

*Apud superos, in ea parte Italie*
*et in ea urbe in qua natus et sepultus es,*
*in vestibulo Iustine virginis*
*et ante ipsum sepulcri tui lapidem,*
*VIII Kalendas Martias, anno ab Illius ortu*
*quem paulo amplius tibi vivendum erat ut cerneres*
*vel audires natum, MCCCLI.*

that you often involve me in happier generations, forgetful of present woes, so that at least while reading I seem to be passing my life
with the Cornelii, the Scipiones Africani, Laelii, Fabii Massimi,
Metelli, Bruti, Decii, Catos, Reguli, Cursores, Torquati, Valerii
Corvini, Salinatores, Claudii Marcelli, Nerones, Aemilii, Fulvii,
Flaminii, Atilii, Quintii and Camilli,[3] and not with these desperate robbers among whom I was born under a hostile star. And O, 5
if only you had come to me whole, how many other great names I
could have sought out as a comfort in life and as a source of forgetfulness of this evil time! But since I cannot read about them
together in your text, I read them scattered in other writers, especially in the book in which we have you complete but so shrunken
that there is no difference in the number of books but an infinity
in their contents.[4] I would like you to give my greetings to the 6
older historians Polybius and Quintus Claudius Quadrigarius and
Valerius Antias and the rest whose glory your splendor now has
eclipsed for us; of the more recent writers report to Pliny, your
neighbor from Verona, and to your former rival Sallust: tell them
that their wakeful nights have been no more successful than
yours.[5] An everlasting farewell, best of advisers on historical
events.

*From the world above, in the part of Italy*
*and the city in which you were born and buried,*
*in the vestibule of the Virgin Justina and*
*before the actual monument of your tomb,*[6]
*on February 22nd in the year 1351 since the birth of the One*
*Whom you would have to have lived a little longer*
*to know or hear of.*

## : 8 :

## *Ad Asinium Pollionem oratorem.*

1 Franciscus Asinio Pollioni salutem. Dum venisset in animum ut
familiaribus epystolis aliquot procul absentes eloquii duces et rara
quedam lingue itale ornamenta complecterer, silentio tuum nomen
obruere nolui, quod magnorum testimonio supremis quoque
nominibus par videbam; sed quoniam pene nuda rerum ad nos
tuarum fama pervenerat magisque aliorum scriptis adiuta quam
tuis—quod ipsum merito inter evi nostri pudores ac damna quis
2 numeret—, breve fuerit quod tecum loqui habui. Tibi quidem
consulari pariter ac triumphali viro, cum pro summi ingenii flo-
rideque facundie laudibus proque aliis multis corporis atque animi
fortuneque dotibus, tum pro eo expressim gratulor, quod sub optimo et studiorum ac virtutum amantissimo principe senuisti, ex-
3 timatorem rerum nactus ydoneum. O felix qui adhuc incolumi
Augusto iustam vivendi mensuram assecutus, octuagesimo etatis
anno in Tusculano rure preclaram vitam tranquillo claudens exitu,
evasisti cruentas Tiberii manus, in quas Asinius Gallus orator incidit, infausta progenies tua, quem diris ab illo suppliciis enecatum
4 legimus. Bene quod, in tantas miserias vergenti iam fato, peropor-
tuna mors affuit, que oculos tuos saltem tam tristi spectaculo liberaret; paucis expectandum annis erat, ut mestissimus nati comes
aut spectator fieres; cuius eventu, si, ut quibusdam sapientibus visum est, extinctos tangit fortuna superstitum, non parva felicitati
tue portio subtrahitur.

5 Unum tacita dissimulatione transire fidelis amicitie lex vetat,

: 8 :

## *To the orator Asinius Pollio.*

Francesco greets Asinius Pollio. When the idea came to me of including in my *Letters to Friends* a number of long distant leaders of eloquence and some rare adornments of the Italian tongue, I did not wish to bury your name in silence, because I saw that on the evidence of great men you were equal to the highest names; but since the reputation of your deeds had come down to us almost naked, and aided more by other men's writings than by your own — a fact that might itself rightly be counted among the losses and sources of shame of our age — what I had to say to you was short. You were a consul and won a triumph,[1] and I congratulate 1
2 you for the praises due to your consummate intellect and colorful eloquence, and for your many other talents of body, mind and fortune. I also explicitly congratulate you on growing old under an excellent emperor, devoted to studies and accomplishments, having found yourself a proper critic of your deeds. Happy man, to
3 reach the right measure of life when Augustus was still unharmed, ending your distinguished life peacefully on your Tusculan estate in your eightieth year! Thus you escaped the bloody hands of Tiberius into which the orator Asinius Gallus, your unfortunate child, fell, murdered by him, as we read, with dreadful tortures.[2] It
4 is good that when fate was inclining to such wretchedness, a most opportune death came to you, freeing your eyes at least from so grim a spectacle: you would have had to wait only a few years to become most unhappy either as companion of your son's death or as a witness of it. By this outcome, if, as it seemed to certain wise men, the fortune of survivors affects the dead,[3] no small share is subtracted from your blessed lot.

There is one thing which the law of loyal friendship forbids me 5

qua clarorum omnis evi hominum cineri ac fame non aliter ac presentium obstringor; illud ergo tuum michi displicuit quod Marco Tullio, cuius nomen tuo in primis preconio celebrari par
6 fuerat et attolli, censor acerrimus, ne dicam reprehensor asperrimus, esse volueris, quod si tibi iudicii libertas prestitit, ut iudicium non probo sic ipsam tibi non invideo libertatem, sed ea certe parcius utendum fuisse denuntio — serum licet —, etsi eadem adversus ipsum mundi dominum sepe usus, ab aliis veniam facile merearis. Et sane in tanta fortune indulgentia frenare animum ac linguam subdifficile est; sed ex te ut exacta omnia requiram, etatis et doctrine tue gravitas facit, utque te liberius hac in re quam vel filium ipsum tuum, qui patrem secutus idem sensit, vel Calvum cete-
7 rosque participes eiusdem iudicii reprehendam. Neque vero tam mei ipsius oblitus sim, ut tibi in coetaneo tuo negem viso et cognito, quod ego michi post tot secula in homine tam antiquo tantique nominis usurparim; nullus hominum est cui non aliquid desit. Quis te, talem virum, vetet in vicini tui moribus notandum aliquid advertere, cum ego de longinquo in scriptis eius invenerim
8 quod notarem? At quod illius eloquentie famam tentas, quod facundie principatum vis eripere celitus illi datum et totius pene nostri orbis consensu sine litigio permissum, vide ne aperta nimis iniuria sit. Vide, tecumque Calvus videat, ne cum illo viro non equa bella sumpseritis de eloquentie principatu, quod nobis spectantibus vestra certamina facillimum est videre. Itaque pridem corone iudicio victi estis; vos tamen frustra nitimini et obstatis, nec verum cernere interni luminis tumor sinit, magni, fateor, viri si

to pass over in silence, by which I am bound to the ashes and renown of famous men of all ages as I am to those still living; your
words offended me when you chose to be a most fierce critic, not
to mention a rough abuser, of Cicero, whose name should have
been celebrated and exalted by your voice especially. And if the 6
freedom of your judgment gave you this opportunity, I no more
approve it as a judgment than I begrudge you your very freedom,
but I do declare—however late—that you should have used it
with more restraint, even if you often employed the same candor
toward the master of the world,[4] and thus easily deserve pardon
from others. Admittedly, to control one's spirits and tongue amid
such indulgence from fortune is a bit difficult; but the seriousness
of your age and education makes me inquire into everything exactly and reproach you more freely in this matter than even your
son, who followed his father with the same judgment, or Calvus[5]
and the other men who shared this opinion. Nor have I so forgot- 7
ten myself as to deny you the right in criticizing the contemporary
whom you saw and knew, which I myself would claim after so
many ages over so ancient and highly reputed a man:[6] there is no
man who does not lack something. Who would forbid you, the
man that you are, for commenting on something culpable in your
neighbor's behavior when I, writing from so great a distance of
time, find something to criticize in his writings? But for your act 8
in assailing the renown of his eloquence and in wishing to snatch
the supremacy in speaking given to him by heaven and allowed by
the agreement of the whole world without contention, see to it
that this is not too open an injustice. See to it and let Calvus too
see to it, that you do not take up warfare on unequal terms against
such a man over supremacy in eloquence, as it is easy for us, observing your competition, to see. Thus you were long since defeated by the opinion of the bystanders; but you are striving in
vain and resisting, and the conceit of your inner vision does not let
you see the truth: you would, I admit, be a great man if you could

9 maiorem pati possetis. At humana superbia, dum supra id quod
est opinionibus falsis attollitur, infra id quod esse poterat vero iudicio deiecta redigitur; plerique mortalium aliene glorie appetitu
propriam amisere. Quodsi vos huc forte livor impulit, quamvis
utrobique et tumoris et livoris multi sint comites, eo tamen id
egrius in te fero, quo in Calvo aliquam certe nec exiguam non livoris sed odii, in te nullam odii causam scio, et aliquanto michi quidem indignius videtur in tam altum ingenium, humi serpere soli-
10 tam, invidiam ascendisse. Eternum vale, et ex graiis Isocratem
Demosthenem et Eschinem, ex nostris oratoribus Crassum et
Antonium salvere iube, Corvinum quoque Messalam et Horten-
sium, si modo illi memoria, quam biennio antequam hinc migraret
amiserat, carnis fasce deposito restituta, huic alteri non erepta est.

*Apud Mediolanum Insubrium,*
*Kalendis Sextilibus anno etatis ultime MCCCLIII.*

## : 9 :

### *Responsio ad epystolam magnam multaque continentem sub Homeri poete missam nomine et apud Inferos datam.*

1 Franciscus Homero graie muse principi salutem. Dudum te scripto alloqui mens fuerat, et fecissem nisi quia lingue commercium non erat. Nam nec ego grecis literis discendis satis felix, et tu latinas, quibus olim per scriptores nostros adiutus uti solebas, sequentium negligentia dedidicisse videbare; utrinque exclusus conticueram.

bear a greater. But human arrogance, when it is raised up beyond 9
its merits by false opinions, is cast down by true judgment and rejected beneath what it could have been: most of mankind lose their own glory from the greed for another's. If envy drove you to this point, although there are many companions in your arrogance and envy, I take it the worse in you, because in Calvus there was certainly reason for some considerable hatred, rather than envy, toward Cicero,[7] but I know of no motive for hatred in you, and it seems to me rather more discreditable for envy, which usually
creeps along the ground, to rise up in such a lofty intellect. Fare- 10
well for ever, and give my greetings to Isocrates, Demosthenes and Aeschines among the Greeks, and Crassus and Antonius among our orators; greet also Messala Corvinus and Hortensius, provided that Messala's memory, which he lost two years before his death, has been restored after casting off the burden of flesh, and the other has not yet lost his memory.[8]

*In Milan of the Insubrians,*[9]
*on the first of August in the year 1353 of this last age.*

## : 9 :

## *Reply to a long letter containing many topics, sent under the name of Homer and dispatched from the Underworld.*

Francesco sends greetings to Homer, originator of the Greek po- 1
etic muse. I had long intended to address you in writing, and would have done so, except that there was no language for communication between us. Certainly I was not successful enough in learning Greek, and you, though you once used to employ Latin with the aid of our writers, now seemed to have unlearned it through the indifference of their successors;[1] so I fell silent, shut out by both circumstances. One man brought you back in Latin to

Unus vir nostro te latinum seclo revehit; non hercle avidius neque
2 diutius Ulixem tuum sua Penelope expectavit quam te ego. Iamque
michi sensim spes abibat; preter enim aliquot tuorum principia
librorum, in quibus velut exoptati amici supercilium procul ambiguum et raptim vibrans seu fluctuantis come apicem intuebar, latini nichil obtigerat, nichil denique sperabatur ubi te cominus
contemplarer; nam libellus ille vulgo qui tuus fertur, etsi cuius sit
non constet, tibi excerptus tibique inscriptus, tuus utique non est.
Vir iste si vixerit, totum te nobis reddet, et iam cepit, ut non
modo divinorum fructu operum eximio, sed tuarum quoque
3 confabulationum illecebris perfruamur. Quarum unius ad me nuper latinis vasis grecus sapor allatus est, in quo plane sensi validum
et velox ingenium posse omnia. Itaque Ciceronem licet eloquentia
sua in carminibus destitutum et Virgilium oratione soluta illa felicitate ingenii derelictum scribat Anneus Seneca, quorum alter in
multis interpres, alter in pluribus imitator tuus fuit—ambo autem
latini duces eloquii sunt—, utrunque tamen sic accipio ut quisque
secum non cum alio collatus, ipse sibi impar seque inferior habea-
tur; alioquin et Ciceronis versiculos non ineptos et Virgilii epysto-
4 las oratione libera non inamenas legi. Quod in te quoque nunc
experior, cuius etsi carmen proprium atque precipuum opus sit,
etsi Ieronimum, quendam ex nostris linguarum peritia insignem
virum, secutus aliquando scripserim te non modo ad verbum in
nostram linguam versum sed in tuam ipsam resolutum, videri de
poeta eloquentissimo vix loquentem, nunc tamen, quod mirari
5 compulit, et solutus places et latinus. Quod idcirco prefatus sim,
nequem forte moveat quod qui ligatis Virgilium, te solutis verbis
alloquor; illum enim compellabam, tibi vero respondeo, atque ideo

our age;[2] nor by Hercules, did his beloved Penelope wait more eagerly and longer for your Ulysses than I awaited you. And grad- 2
ually hope was fading; besides the beginnings of some of your books, in which I seemed to gaze on at a distance, mysterious like the swiftly flickering brow of a longed-for friend, or the peak of his flowing locks, nothing in Latin came through to me, there was no hope of contemplating you at close hand, since that booklet commonly treated as yours, even if its author is uncertain, excerpted and inscribed in your name, is surely not yours.[3] If that man lives he will soon translate you entire, and he has already begun, so that we may enjoy to the full not only the exceptional fruit
of your divine works, but the charms of your narratives. The 3
Greek taste of one of these narratives has recently been brought to me in Latin containers, and I realized from this that a strong and speedy intellect could achieve everything. So even if, as Seneca writes, Cicero was deserted by his eloquence in his poems and Vergil abandoned by his felicity of intellect in prose speech[4] (one of them was your interpreter in many passages and the other an imitator of you in many respects[5]—but both are leaders of Latin eloquence), yet I take each of them in such a way that each, if compared not with another man's work but with his own, is judged unlike and inferior to himself: still I have read verses of Cicero which are not clumsy, and not unattractive letters of Vergil
in prose.[6] I find this in you too, since even if poetry is your proper 4
and particular work, even if following Jerome, one of our men distinguished for expertise in language, I once wrote that you, if not only translated word for word into our speech but also relaxed into a prose form in your own language, seemed scarcely to be like the most eloquent poet you were—now on the contrary something has happened that has made me marvel: you please me both
in prose and in Latin.[7] I mentioned this in advance in case it 5
should disturb anyone that I, who wrote to Vergil in rhythmic language,[8] am addressing you in prose; but then I was accosting

illic comunem ipsius, hic non tuum illum veterem sed epystole ad
me misse novum quendam et michi quotidianum, tibi ut reor insolitum, stilum sequor. Quanquam quid me utrique vestrum 'loqui' dixerim? 'Strepere' est quicquid ab ullo vobis dicitur: nimis
excellitis supraque hominem estis et toto vertice itis in nubila. Sed
dulce michi velut infanti est cum disertissimis nutritoribus balbu-
tire. Et de stilo quidem hactenus; ad rem venio.

6 Quereris de quibusdam, cum de omnibus prope iure optimo
queri possis; nam quid in rebus, queso, hominum est quod queri-
moniis iustis vacet? Nisi quod querele, ubi inefficaces esse ceperint, quodammodo iuste esse desinunt; carent enim non causa
quidem iustitie sed effectu, qui est ut damnando preterita presentibus consulat futurisque provideat. Quia tamen interdum luctuo-
sam animam exhonerant, non usquequaque supervacue videri de-
7 bent. His tu nunc igitur, summe vir, affluis, ex quibus longam licet
epystolam texueris, ut longior esset tamen optavi; ita nichil omnino longum sentias, nisi tedio adiuncto. Sed ut iam singula qua
visum erit expediam, supra modum supraque fidem delectavit animum sciendi discendique avidum quod scripsisti de preceptoribus
tuis, olim michi ignotis, fateor, ac deinceps tanti merito discipuli
8 verendis; de poetice ortu quam longissime repetito deque vetustis-
simis musarum cultoribus, in quibus, preter notos Eliconis acco-
las, Cadmum Agenoridem et Herculem quendam, nescio an Alci-
dem, locas; de patria demum tua, cuius apud nos opinionum
9 nubes multa erat, nec, ut video, apud vos multa serenitas; de pere-
grinationibus insuper studiosis in Pheniciam atque Egiptum, ubi

him, now only replying to you, so there I used the tongue I share with him, but here not your own ancient speech but a style echoing the new and for me familiar idiom of the letter you sent to me, which I suspect is not your custom. Yet why should I say that I am "speaking" to either of you? Whatever is said to you Greeks by any man is just confused clamor: you excel too greatly and tower above men, with your whole head surging into the clouds. But it is pleasant for me like an infant to stammer with his eloquent nurses. And that is enough about style; I come to the matter in hand.

You complain about some individuals when you could with full 6
justice complain about them all. For I ask you, what part of human affairs is free of just complaint? Except that complaints, when they begin to be without effect, somehow cease to be just: what they lack is not the cause of justice but its outcome, which is that by condemning the past it takes thought for the present and foresees the future. Yet since they sometimes unburden a grieving spirit,
these complaints should not seem utterly hollow. So now, greatest 7
of men, although you have an abundance of such complaints and have woven such a long letter from them; still I desired it to be longer: it is true that one feels nothing is long unless it is also associated with boredom. But to cover the details now as it seems fit, my spirit in its eagerness to know and learn was delighted beyond measure and belief by what you wrote about your teachers, once unknown to me, as I admit, but deserving respect from that time
for the achievements of so great a pupil. You wrote on the origin of 8
poetry, tracing it as far back as possible, and on the most ancient worshippers of the Muses, among whom you count, besides the known residents of Helicon, Cadmus son of Agenor and someone called Hercules, perhaps Alcides himself.[9] Finally there is dispute about your native land, confused by a thick fog of opinions among us, and as I see it, there is not much clarity even among you
Greeks. In addition you wrote about your journeys of inquiry to 9
Phoenicia and Egypt, lands to which illustrious philosophers trav-

post te aliquot seculis peregrinati sunt philosophi illustres et Pithagoras et Plato et Atheniensium legifer idemque Pyeridum serus
cultor, ille doctissimus senex Solon, qui tibi, quem vivens mираba-
tur, puto post obitum familiarissimus factus sit; denique de tuorum numero librorum, quorum magna pars Italis ipsis, vicinis ac
10 proximis tuis, inaudita est. Nam hi barbari quibus utrique contin-
gimur et a quibus non Alpe tantum aeria, sed toto utinam quod
usquam est pelago disiuncti essemus, vix non dicam libros sed
nomen audiverunt tuum, ut intelligas quantula est hec fama mor-
11 talis ad quam tanto anhelitu suspiramus. In his sane tot dulcibus
amarissimum illud de ipsorum librorum interitu miscuisti. Heu
michi ter et amplius, quam multa pereunt, imo quam nichil manet
omnium que sub sole versabili ceca texit industria! O labores curasque hominum, o tempus breve sed perditum, o vanitatem su-
perbiamque de nichilo! quid sumus, quid agimus, quid speramus,
12 quis vero nunc lumini fidat ambiguo? Summus eloquii sol eclipsim
patitur; quis queri audeat perire sibi aliquid aut quis omnino mansurum sibi quicquam spondeat ex omnibus studiis suis? Non
parva ex parte homerice vigilie perierunt, non tam nobis — nemo
enim perdit quod non habuit — quam Graiis, qui nequa nobis in re
cederent, ignaviam quoque nostram in literis supergressi, Homeri
libros multos quidem quasi totidem alterius suorum luminum radios amisere, indigni qui hac tanta cecitate fulgur illud habuisse
glorientur.

13 Movit preterea suspenditque animum legentis quod de tuo fine
memorasti. Quamvis enim etiam apud nostros illa mortis fama
vulgata sit atque ipse ego alibi famam sequens idem scripserim,
sed nota ambiguitatis adhibita, iuvabat tamen et, si sinis, iuvat de
te simul ac Sophocle melius opinari, quam ut turbulentissime

eled some centuries later, Pythagoras and Plato and the Athenian
lawgiver who was also a late developing worshipper of the Pierides,
that most learned old man Solon, who I think became most intimate after his death with you after adoring you in his lifetime,[10]
and finally about the number of your books, of which a great part
had not been heard even by the Italians, your nearest neighbors.
For the barbarians, by which we both are bordered and from 10
whom I only wish we had been separated, not only by the aerial
Alps but by all the seas worldwide, have scarcely heard not just
your books but your name, so that you may understand how small
is this mortal fame which we strive toward with such breathless
longing. Among these many pleasing things you added to the mix- 11
ture that most bitter lament about the loss of your books.[11] Alas,
three times and more, how many things perish; worse, how little
survives of all that our blind industry has woven beneath the re-
volving sun! O for the toils and cares of men, the short but wasted
time, the vanity and arrogance without basis! What are we worth,
what is our purpose, what do we hope for, who could now trust a
wavering light? The highest sun of eloquence suffers eclipse. Who 12
would dare to complain that some work of his is lost, or promise
himself that something would survive out of all his pursuits? The
products of Homer's wakeful nights have largely perished, not so
much for us—for no one loses what he did not possess—as for the
Greeks, who, to avoid yielding to us in any matter, outdo our neglect in literature too: they have lost a great many books of Homer,
like losing the light of one of their eyes, and are unworthy of boasting in their great blindness of the brilliance they once possessed.

I was also excited and held in suspense as I read what you re- 13
corded about your death. For although the legend of your death
was even broadcast among us and I myself, following the tale,
wrote the same thing in another place, but attaching a hint of uncertainty, it gave me pleasure, and if you permit, still pleases me to
have a better opinion of you and Sophocles as well, rather than

passiones, animi meror et gaudium tantum in tam celestibus po-
14 tuisse videantur ingeniis. Nam de Philemonis exitu, si fame credimus, ridiculo, graviora tandem et opinatiora didicimus, non risu illum, ut dicere solebamus, sed vi quadam contemplationis altissime consopitum expirasse. Sed ad te unum sortemque tuam redeo, quam copiose admodum et graviter deplorasti. Solare autem queso animum, faciesque — certus sum — si discussis passionibus ad te redis.

15 Multa de imitatoribus tuis, multa de ingratis, multa de indoctis insultatoribus questus es; iuste quidem in omnibus, si solus hec patereris, neque humana, quin et trita inter homines essent que te premunt; unde fit ut conquiescere debeas, summus in hoc numero, fateor, sed non unus. Iam vero de imitatione quid dicam? Debuisti presagire, dum tam alte alis animi te sublatum cerneres, nunquam tibi defuturos imitatores; gaudendum vero talem te cui multi si-
16 miles fieri velint sed non multi possint. Quidni autem gaudeas tu, primi semper certus loci, cum ego, ultimus hominum, gaudeam, nec gaudere sat est, glorier quoque, tanti me nunc fieri, ut sit aliquis, si tamen est aliquis, qui imitari optet ac fingere? illud magis gavisurus tales imitatores fore qui superent; atque illum non Apollinem tuum sed meum verum ingenii Deum precor, ut siquis me imitatione dignum duxerit, nisu facili quem sequitur consequatur
17 ac transeat. Ego mecum bene gloriose feliciter agi credam, si ex amicis — nemo enim nisi amet imitabitur — multos michi pares, aliquantoque felicius si superiores aspexero, quique ex imitatoribus sint victores. Si enim genitor carnis filium se maiorem cupit, quid
18 optare debeat pater ingenii? Tu qui maiorem victoremque non

thinking that the most violent passions, grief and joy of mind, had
so much power over such heavenly spirits.[12] For if we believe tradi- 14
tion about the absurd death of Philemon, we have learned a more
serious and judicious version, that he did not die of laughter, as we
used to think, but breathed his last in a deep trance of contemplation.[13] But I am returning to you alone and your destiny, which
you have lamented abundantly and earnestly. I beg you, comfort
your spirit, and you will do so, I am sure, if you shake off your
passions and return to your nature.

You have made many complaints about your imitators, about 15
ungrateful men, about uneducated abusers[14]—justly enough in all
cases if you alone suffered this, and the things that oppress you
were not human—whereas they are indeed commonplace among
men; hence you should calm yourself, since you are the greatest
victim in this crowd, but not the only one. Now what am I to say
about imitation? You should have foreseen, when you saw yourself
raised so high aloft on the wings of the spirit, that you would
never lack imitators; but you should rejoice that you are of such
merit that many wish to be like you, but not many succeed. So 16
why should you not rejoice, always sure of holding first place,
when I, last of men, rejoice—no, that is not enough; I even
boast—that I am counted of such value that there is someone (if
there is someone) who desires to imitate and fake my work. And I
would be all the more joyful that there will be imitators who
outdo me, and I beseech God—not your Apollo[15] but my true
God of intellect—that if anyone thinks me worthy of imitation he
will catch up with and surpass the man he follows with an easy bit
of exertion. I would think I was being treated well and gloriously 17
and happily if I see many of my friends matching me—for no one
is imitated without affection—and I would be even more happy if
I see them overtaking me and from being imitators become actual
victors. For if a parent in the flesh wants his son to be greater than
himself, what should a father of the mind desire? You who do not 18

metuis, imitatores equanimis fer; quanquam et de victoria inter te et eum de quo multa quereris Virgilium, in libris *Saturnalium* magna lis pendeat, et quidam preterea nostrorum inter vos dubiam palmam velint, alii certam illi tribuant victoriam; quod non tam ut cuiusquam sententie faveam aut adverser, quam ut noris quid de te posteritas et quam varie sensit, apposui. Ex his autem admoneor ut antequam longius abeam, Virgilium ipsum, cuius anima, ut Flaccus ait, non candidiorem aliam terra tulit, tibi, optime dux
19 noster, excusem. Profecto equidem que de illius imitatione dixisti, non vera modo sed vulgo etiam nota sunt, et multa alia que—verecundia dicam an modestia?—siluisti; que tamen ex ordine ipsis in *Saturnalibus* scripta sunt, quamvis hoc loco ille suus iocus innotuerit; cui cum obiceretur ab emulis quod versus tibi tuos eriperet, magnarum virium esse respondit auferre clavam Herculi; nec sim
20 dubius quin latentem salem ioci huius intelligas. Ne vero, quod multi faciunt, quem excusaturum me profiteor, accusem, fateor plane que dicis omnia, neque ideo querelam tuam totis auribus accipio, quod scilicet nulla usquam tui nominis mentio apud illum sit exuviis honustum et ornatum tuis, cum Lucanus, ut vere memoras, Smyrnei vatis honorum grata narratione meminerit. Adiuvare querimoniam tuam libet: et Flaccus sepe tui meminit semperque magnifice; nam et quodam loco te philosophis ipsis prefert et alio primam tibi inter poetas sedem tribuit; meminit tui Naso et Iuvenalis et Statius. Sed quid memores memorem? nemo fere nostrorum tui immemor fuit.

21 'Quid ergo?' inquies, 'unum illum tam ingratum patior quem omnibus gratiorem merui?.' Antequam tibi respondeam, addam

fear a greater victor bear imitators with good humor, even if the victory between yourself and Vergil, about whom you complain so much, is the subject of a great quarrel in some books of the *Saturnalia,* and some of our Romans want the palm to be in dispute between you, while others credit him with a sure victory[16] — something I have added here, not to support or oppose any man's judgment, but so that you may know what posterity has felt, and how variously, about you. And I am reminded from these considerations that before I move further away, I should excuse Vergil himself to you, our best leader and guide; as Horace says, the earth has produced no fairer spirit than his.[17] Indeed, what you 19
said about his imitation is not only true but commonly known, as well as many other details which — shall I say out of bashfulness or modesty? — you have left in silence. Yet they have been recorded in due sequence in the *Saturnalia,* although it was from this passage that the famous witticism of Vergil's became known: when he was reproached by his rivals for stealing your verses, he replied that it required great strength to make off with Hercules' club, and I have no doubt that you understand the hidden wit of this passage.[18] So not to accuse the man I claim to be excusing, as many 20
do, I openly admit everything you say, but I still don't accept wholeheartedly your complaint that there is no mention of your name in his work, loaded and adorned as he is with your spoils. And yet Lucan, as you rightly recall, has recorded in a grateful narrative the honors of the Smyrnaean poet.[19] I choose to support your lament, and Horace often recalls you, always with great praise; for in one place he puts you before the philosophers and in another offers you the highest throne among the poets.[20] Ovid recalls you and Juvenal and Statius.[21] But why recall those who recall you? Nobody among our Latin speakers has been ungrateful to you.

So you will say: "Am I to endure the ingratitude of this one 21
man whom I deserved to find more grateful than all the others?" Before answering you I will add something to your grievance. So

etiam nunc querele. Nequis enim elatum eque forsitan in omnes putet, et Musei et Lini et Orphei non semel ille quidem meminit quodque humilius fuit, et Hesiodi ascrei et Theocriti siracusii poete, postremo, quod nunquam siquis in illo esset livor sineret,
22 nec Varum Gallumque neque alios coetaneos suos tacet. Quid vero? Num satis auxisse iam videor querelam quam vel minuere vel auferre decreveram? Utique, si nil amplius dixero; sed attendenda rerum ratio, et, quicquid agas, in consilium evocanda presertimque si iudices. Nempe ille Theocritum in *Bucolicis* ducem nactus, in *Georgicis* Hesiodum, quemque suis locis inseruit. 'Et cur' inquies, 'tertium in heroyco carmine ducem habens, nulla eius operis in parte me posuit?.' Posuisset, michi crede, mitissimus verecundissimusque mortalium, quodque de illo scriptum scimus,
23 'omni probatus vita,' nisi mors impia vetuisset. Licet autem alios ubi occurrit atque ubi commodum fuit annotasset, tibi uni, cui multo amplius debebat, non fortuitum sed certum certoque consilio destinatum reservabat locum. Et quem reris, nisi eminentiorem cuntis atque conspectiorem? Finem ergo preclarissimi operis expectabat, ibi te suum ducem tuumque nomen altisonis versibus laturus ad sidera. Ubi enim, queso, dignius quam in fine vie dux laudandus? Multum habes igitur quod de morte festina nimis merito queri possis; habet et italus orbis tecum; de amico nichil.
24 Quod sic esse, vicino et simili conicies ab exemplo: nam ut te ille sic illum imitatus est Statius Pampinius, cuius supra mentio incidit, vir preter ingenii laudem insigni morum urbanitate conspicuus; nec tamen ingenue ducem suum nisi in fine poetici itineris recognovit; licet enim alio quodam loco se stilo inferiorem

that no one think him equally puffed up against them all, he mentions Musaeus and Linus and Orpheus more than once[22] and, more humbly, he mentions Hesiod of Ascra and Syracusan Theocritus as poets;[23] finally—something he would never have let pass if there was any envy in him—he is not silent about Varus and Gallus and other contemporaries.[24] Well then? Do I seem to have 22
increased the grievance which I had resolved to decrease or eliminate? Certainly I do, if I say nothing more. But we must pay attention to the proper scale of things, and whatever your purpose you should take its advice, especially if you are judging. For Vergil took Theocritus as his guide in the *Eclogues* and Hesiod in the *Georgics*, and he included each man in his text.[25] And you will protest: "Why, since he took me as his third guide in the epic, did he not mention me in any part of that work?" He would have included you, believe me, being the mildest and most modest among men and, as we know they wrote about him, "approved in his whole life,"[26] if impious death had not forestalled it. Even if he 23
referred to others where it occurred to him and was convenient, he reserved for you alone, to whom his debt was far greater, no random place but a fixed place marked off by a fixed plan. And what place do you think, if not a position more prominent and noticeable than all the rest? So he waited for the end of his most glorious work, and was going to raise you there as his highest guide to the stars, and mark your name in lofty verses. For I ask you, where should a guide be praised more deservedly than at the end of the journey? So you have many just grievances against his premature death; the Italian world shares them with you; but there is no complaint against our friend. You will guess that this is so from a 24
similar and close example; for as Vergil imitated you, so Statius, whom I mentioned incidentally, imitated him: Statius was conspicuous for the distinguished courtesy of his manners as well as the glory of his intellect; yet he did not openly call Vergil his guide until the end of his poetic journey, even if in another passage he

secretius designasset, illic tamen bona fide totum grati animi debi-
25 tum benemerite persolvit *Eneydi*. Si et hunc mors igitur prevenis-
set, ut te Virgilius sic iste Virgilium siluisset. Hec ita esse ut dico,
tibi persuadeas velim. Certe enim, ni fallor augurio, ita est, et si
forte aliter sit, in dubiis tamen opinio est anteponenda benignior.
Et hec quidem pro excusatione maiorum Virgilii operum dicta
sint; nam si ad eos quos iuveniles ludos vocant, primos scilicet
adolescentie sue libellos, oculum deflectis, scriptum ibi tuum nomen invenies.

26 Reliquum est ut sparsa per totum epystole tue corpus querela-
rum tuarum fragmenta perstringam. Discerptum te ab imitatoribus tuis doles: sic oportuit; nemo in totum tanti ingenii capax erat.
Indignaris illos tuis indutos spoliis insultare: sic est usus; non
potest valde ingratus esse nisi qui magno benificio preventus est.
27 Luges nomen tuum apud priscos iurisconsultos ac medicos gloriosum, successoribus esse contemptui, nec advertis causam: hi quidem omnes dissimillimi sunt illorum; nam si similes essent, similia
colerent atque amarent. Cesset indignatio, cesset dolor, optima
spes assurgat. Sunt primitie virtutis et ingenii displicuisse malis et
indoctis; tam clara frons ingenii tui est ut eam lippe acies ferre non
valeant; idemque tibi accidit quod soli, cuius non infamia sed ex-
cellens laus est quod infirmi oculi et nocturne illum fugiunt aves.
28 Apud antiquos quidem ac modernos, siqui sunt, in quibus scintilla
vel tenuis prisce indolis adhuc vivat, non modo philosophus sacer,
ut ipse ais, sed, ut dixi, philosopho maior atque sublimior haberis,
ut qui pulcerrimam philosophiam ornatissimo ac tenuissimo tegas

described himself more discreetly as inferior in style; nonetheless he paid up in good faith his debt to the meritorious *Aeneid*.[27] So if 25 death had overtaken him, Statius would have been as silent about Vergil as Vergil was about you. I would like you to convince yourself that this is how it happened. Certainly, unless I am deceived in my guess, it is so and if by chance it were different, in cases of doubt the kinder opinion should be preferred. And let these arguments be advanced to excuse Vergil's major works, for if you turn your eyes aside to the works they call his youthful amusements, the first little poems of his youth, you will find your name written there.[28]

It remains for me to touch on the fragments of your com- 26 plaints, scattered through the whole body of your letter. You lament that you have been torn apart by your imitators, but it had to be so, for no one possessed the full capacity of your great intellect. You are indignant that they are prancing around dressed in your spoils: but that is the practice, and a man can't be a real ingrate unless he has first been done a great kindness. You grieve 27 that your reputation, most glorious among the early legal experts and doctors, is an object of contempt for their successors,[29] and do not notice the reason for this. All of these men are quite different from the men of old; for if they were like them, they would respect and love the same models. Let your indignation cease, and your pain; let the best of hopes rise up. It is the first fruits of virtue and talent to offend bad and ignorant men; the gaze of your intellect is so glorious that bleary eyesight cannot bear it, and the same thing has happened to you as to the sun, whose excellent glory, not shame, it is that weak eyes and night birds shun it. Now 28 with the ancients and those moderns, if there are any in whom even a tiny spark of the old intellect still lives, not only are you held to be a sacred philosopher, as you yourself say, but, as I said, you are considered greater and more lofty than a philosopher because you cover most noble philosophy with a most richly adorned

velo. Quisnam apud hec portenta hominum habeare, tua non interest; imo vero quamplurimum, optandumque ne placeas quibus displicere primus ad gloriam gradus est, proximus non agnosci.
29 Pone iam, precor, solicitudinem ac merorem et ad campos Elysios, pristinam illam tuam tibique debitam sedem, redi, unde te talibus ineptiis pulsum dicis. Non decet animum sapientis stultorum contumeliis frangi; alioquin quid fiet aut quis erit huius mali modus, cum verissime dicat hebreus Sapiens quod 'stultorum infinitus est numerus' et nichil verius dici posse, vici atria plateeque omnes consonent?

30 Illud sane iocosum penitusque festivum in auribus meis fuit—quod tu tamen acerrime querebaris, adeo quidem palato ac stomaco amaro dulcia etiam amarescunt; fles unde ridere par fuerat—, quod comunis amicus, quem tu thesalum facis ego bizantinum rebar, te intra florentes patrie mee muros peregrinari, sive ita mavis, exulare coegerit; quod illum summa fide, summoque tui amore et fecisse et facere certum habe, unde omnibus amicis tui nominis, qui perrari licet, adhuc aliqui supersunt, ob hanc preci-
31 pue causam cepit esse carissimus. Vide ergo iure ne succenseas cui nos omnes tui amantes tuo simul ac nostro nomine gratias agimus, quod te nobis ac musis ausoniis ereptum, siqua fors cepto faverit, restituet. Quod autem fesulana vallis et Arni ripe nonnisi tres tibi amicos tulerint, mirari desine; satis est, multum est, plus est quam
32 sperabam in patria lucro dedita tres pyerios spiritus invenisse. Et tamen, ne diffidas, magna frequensque est civitas: quartum si queris, invenies; quintum his adderem et meretur, peneia seu alphea

and refined cloak.[30] Whatever is thought of you among these monsters of men, does not affect you. On the contrary it most greatly affects you and is to be desired that you do not please those whose displeasure is the first step toward glory, while the next best achievement is to go unrecognized. Now, I pray you, cast off your 29
anxiety and mourning and return to the Elysian Fields,[31] your original and proper dwelling, from which you say you were expelled by such follies. It is not proper for the spirit of the wise man to be broken by the insults of fools; otherwise what will happen or what will be the limit of this evil, since the Hebrew wise man most truly says that "the number of fools is countless"[32] and the streets and halls and squares all ring out that nothing truer can be said?

The tale about which you complained most fiercely was obvi- 30
ously a joke and quite amusing in my ears (to such an extent do even sweet things become bitter to a bitter palate and gullet: you are weeping where it would have been fair to smile), that our common friend, whom you make a Thessalian but I thought a Byzantine, compelled you to travel abroad among the flourishing walled cities of my country or, if you prefer, to be sent in exile.[33] You may be sure that he did this in all good faith and with great devotion. Hence he began to be most dear to all the friends of your name, who, albeit few, still survive. So consider whether you are right to 31
be angry with the man whom all of us who love you thanked, both in your name and ours, because he will restore you to us, though formerly stolen from us and the Ausonian Muses,[34] if any chance favors the enterprise. And if the valley of Fiesole and the banks of Arno have only produced three friends for you, do not be surprised: it is enough, it is a lot, it is more than I hoped in a country devoted to profit to have found three Pierian spirits.[35] Yet do not 32
be discouraged: the city is great and populous: if you seek you will find a fourth, and I would add a fifth, and he fully deserves it, with his head bound in the laurel of Peneus and Alpheus; but somehow

redimitus lauro; sed nescio qualiter transalpina Babilon illum nobis eripuit. Parum ne tibi videtur tales quinque viros uno tempore atque in una urbe concurrere? Quere alias. Tua illa Bononia quam suspiras, studiorum licet hospes amplissima, funditus ut excutias, unum habet; Verona duos; Sulmo unum, atque unum Mantua, nisi illum celum terris abduceret; tuis namque desertis ad Ptho-
33 lomei signa transfugit; ipsa rerum caput Roma, mirum quam pene ad unum talibus incolis sit exhausta; Perusia unum tulit, futurum aliquid nisi se ipse negligeret, sed ille non Parnaso tantum, verum Apennino etiam atque Alpibus relictis, lucrosamque calamo papirum sulcans, nunc senior Hispanias pervagatur; tuleruntque alios urbes alie, sed omnes quos ego noveram, in comunem illam et
34 eternam urbem ex hoc mortali domicilio commigrarunt. Proinde quid velim vides, ne scilicet de amico pergas queri, quod te in terram duxit, etsi paucis at pluribus certe quam ulla, hodie amicis ac miratoribus habitatam tuis. An nescis quanta etiam apud vos huius generis raritas semper fuit? Nostra enim etate, nisi fallor,
35 amicus hic noster iam tota in Grecia solus est. Erat alter modo preceptor meus, qui cum iocundissimam me in spem erexisset, in ipso studiorum lacte destituit moriens; quamvis iam ante destituisset, ad epyscopalem curam, me qui deserebar adiuvante plusque illum quam me ipsum cogitante, promotus.

Quibus ita se habentibus, patere raritatem hanc tuorum et ignosce seculo senescenti quod florenti etiam ignovisses. Pauci olim, nunc paucissimi, mox ut auguror nulli erunt, quibus in pre-
36 cio sint honesta studia. Cum his ipsis dum licet, avide versare neque tibi in mentem veniat nostrum amnem maiore alveo permutare; non tu nauta, ne piscator quidem; quin imo, si quam falsam

Transalpine Babylon snatched him from us.[36] Does it seem too
little to you that five such men should come together at one time
and in one town? Go look elsewhere. Your Bologna, which you
long for, though the most generous host of studies, if you search it
thoroughly has just one;[37] Verona two, Sulmona one, and Mantua
one, unless he has risen from earth to heaven; for he has deserted
your standards and joined Ptolemy's constellations.[38] Rome itself, 33
chief head of the world, is strangely drained of such residents almost to a man; Perugia produced one, who would become something great if he did not neglect himself, but he has left behind not
just Mount Parnassus but the Apennines and Alps, scratching
paper profitably with his pen, and now wanders as an old man in
the Spanish provinces.[39] Other cities have produced other men,
but all those I knew have moved from this mortal residence to the
common and eternal city. Accordingly you can see what I want: for 34
you to cease complaining about your friend; in fact he brought you
to a land inhabited by friends and admirers of yours, even if only
a few, yet more than elsewhere. Or don't you realize what a great
scarcity of such men there always was, even among you Greeks? In
our age, unless I am mistaken, our friend is now the only man in
all Greece.[40] There was recently my other teacher, who had roused 35
me into the most pleasant expectation, but deserted me by dying
when our studies were still unweaned, although he had already left
me for a bishop's charge, promoted with my help although I was
being deserted and thinking more of his interests than my own.[41]

Given these circumstances, bear with this scarcity of your devotees and forgive an age in decline what you would have forgiven
even to one in its prime. For there were once a few and now very
few and soon, as I guess, there will be none, who hold honorable
studies in esteem. So while you may, associate eagerly with your 36
friends, and do not let it enter your mind to change our river Arno
for a greater basin. You are not a sailor nor even a fisherman: indeed if the story is true, which I would prefer to be false, you

cupio, vera est fama, non sat faustum ea tibi cum gente colloquium fuit. Parva tibi Castalia placuit, humilisque Elicon; noster tibi Arnus nostrique colles placeant, ubi et nobiles ingeniorum scaturigines erumpunt et dulces nidificant philomene; pauce ille quidem, fateor, sed si, ut dictum est, vicina pariter ac longinqua circumspi-
37 cis, multe sunt. Extra quas quid te in populo reperturum speras nisi fullones textoresque et fabros, ut sileam impostores publicanos fures diversorum generum et mille fraudum species, et que fraudibus nunquam carent, popularia studia et avaritie anxium atque inane negotium totasque olidas mechanicarum feces artium, ubi te quasi aquilam noctuis aut leonem simiis irrisum alto animo ferre debes, et dicere quod tanto inferior Ennius dixit: Nam

volito vivus *docta* per ora virum.

Ora indocta suam ignorantiam insulsosque sermunculos ruminent; quid ad te tuasque res, vel nesciant vel illudant, quorum laus honoratum infamie genus est?

38 Verum, ut ingenio et etate novissimus in extremo sedeam, ad me redeat oratio. In hac quidem tua fortuna meum poscis auxilium: o sors dura et immitis, et o utinam opis aliquid in me esset, quo tanto succursum viro ante omnes partos aut speratos titulos
39 perpetuo gloriarer! Nam — Cristum tibi incognitum Deum testor — preter piam commiserationem ac fidele consilium nichil est penitus quo tibi subveniam. Quid enim prestare potest alteri qui sibi nichil potest? An forte non audisti et sequaces tuos tecum sola tui nominis invidia lacerari haberique pro insanis in conciliis insanorum? Quod si tua etate studiosissima Athenarum in urbe tibi accidit, quid voluptuosis in urbibus nunc aliis eventurum arbitra-

did not have a happy encounter with that tribe.[42] Little Castalia pleased you and humble Helicon; let our Arno and our hills please you, where noble fountains of genius spring up and sweet nightingales build nests;[43] only a few, I admit, but if, as is said, you look around at nearby places as well as distant ones, there are many.
Beyond these, what do you hope to find among the common peo- 37
ple except fullers and weavers and carpenters, not to mention imposters, tax gatherers and thieves of various kinds and a thousand varieties of conmen, and—something never without deceits—popular pursuits and the anxious and hollow business of avarice and all the stinking dregs of the mechanical arts? In all this you need to carry yourself with a lofty spirit like an eagle mocked by an owl, or a lion by these apes. You must say what Ennius, so much inferior, said:

> I hover living on the lips of learned men.[44]

Let ignorant mouths regurgitate their own incompetence and stupid chatter. What bearing does it have on you and your affairs whether they are ignorant or jeering, men whose praise is an honorific kind of disgrace?

But if I am seated last, as the latest in intellect and age, let the 38
argument come back to me. You demand my help in your present condition. O cruel and merciless fate, and O, if only there were some help in me so that I might boast forever of having helped so great a man, a boast to be placed before all my titles won or hoped
for! For I bear witness by Christ, the God unknown to you, be- 39
yond pious sympathy and faithful advice I have absolutely no way of coming to your aid. What can any man provide to another who can do nothing for himself? Or have you not heard that your followers are torn apart along with you from sheer envy of your name, and are treated as madmen in the councils of madmen? And if this happened to you, in the most scholarly city of Athens, in your own age, what do you think will happen to others now in

40 ris? Horum ego unus — miror et nescio quamobrem — vulgo videor
inscio; vere utinam, sed nichil ad rem quam vera sit invidie causa,
si invidia vera est. Refugium meo petis in gremio: o fati vertigo
insolens, cui nulla usquam regia satis ampla satis ve sit fulgida, si
quales fortune gradus altior, tales honores ambiat ingenii altitudo.
Sed non ita est, atque ideo sepe illa turres et aulas spernit indoctas
41 et deserto tugurio delectatur. Quod ad me attinet, etsi tanto hos-
pite non me digner, tamen te vel grecum vel qua licuit latinum
domi habeo, brevi, ut spero, totum habiturus, si thesalus tuus
cepta peregerit; et ut secretiore adito te locandum scias, anime medio receptaculum tibi avidissime prorsus ac reverentissime prepa-
ravi. Ad summam amor ad te meus sole clarior ferventiorque est,
42 extimatio ingens ut nullius maior. Hec tibi, dux paterque, quia
potui et prestiti; liberare te vulgari ludibrio, preterquamquod tue
singularis atque unice laudis imminutio futura sit, non meum
certe nec alterius est, nisi qui possit vulgi furoribus finem dare;
quod quanquam possibile Deo sit, nec fecit tamen hactenus, puto
nec faciet. Multa dixi quasi ad presentem; sed iam ab illa vehementissima imaginatione rediens, quam longe absis intelligo, vereorque
ne tam multa in tenebris egre legas, nisi quia multa ibi etiam scrip-
43 sisse te video. Eternum vale, Orpheaque et Linum et Euripidem ac
reliquos comites, cum in tuam sedem veneris, salvere iube.

*Apud superos,*
*medio amnium clarissimorum Padi Ticini Ardue*
*aliorumque, unde quidam Mediolanum dici volunt,*
*VII Idus Octobris anno etatis ultime MCCCLX.*

our pleasure-loving cities? I seem one of these followers of yours 40
to the unlettered crowd; I wonder and don't know why—if only
this were true, but the cause of envy is irrelevant if the envy is real.
You are looking for a refuge in my arms. O absurd giddiness of
fate! For you no palace would ever be great or gleaming enough, if
the loftiness of your intellect could aim at such honors, as the
highest degree of Fortune does. But it is not like that, and so a
lofty intellect often disdains uneducated fortresses and courts and
takes delight in an abandoned hut. As for me, even though I do 41
not think myself worthy of so great a guest, yet I have you in
Greek or as far as possible in Latin at home, and soon, as I hope,
will have you entire, if your Thessalian friend completes his undertaking.[45] I want you to know that you are to be placed in a secret
shrine, and I have most eagerly and reverently prepared in my
heart a treasure chest for you. In short my love for you is more
brilliant and burning than the sun, and my respect so vast that no
man can surpass it. This is what I have been able to do for you, 42
guide and father, to guarantee you freedom from common mockery; besides the fact that it would be a reduction of your singular
and unique glory, it is neither in my power nor any other man's,
unless he can put an end to the frenzies of the mob; and although
that is in God's power, He has not achieved it so far, and I think
He will not. I have said a great deal as if you were here before me,
but now returning from that most passionate imagining, I realize
how far away you are, and I am afraid you may be reading so long
a screed with difficulty in the darkness, except that I see you have
written a long letter even from there. An everlasting farewell. Bid 43
greetings to Orpheus and Linus and Euripides and your other
companions when you reach your dwelling.[46]

*Written among the living*
*in the midst of the most glorious rivers Po, Ticinus and Adda*
*and others from which some want Milan to have taken its name,*[47]
*on October 9th in the year 1360 of the last age.*

# [PART IX]

## : 1 :

## *Ad Guidonem Septem archiepyscopum ianuensem, de mutatione temporum.*

1 Scio iam hinc michi obstare illam Flacci sententiam ubi de moribus senis agens difficilem illum dixit et querulum seque puero acti
2 temporis laudatorem. Non nego id quidem ita esse, sed licet id
michi sepe alibi fortassis, huic nunc tamen epistole non adversum
3 dico. Quamvis enim ego querulus et laudator veterum, hec tamen
4 seu veterum laus seu querela presentium vera erit. Sepe per os
mentiri solitum veritas sonat, cui etsi auctor fidem deroget, ipsa
5 sibi fidem facit. Dico ego teque fassurum spero, dico et queror et,
si virum decet, lugeo: quid ita peioribus annis senectutem agimus
6 quam pueritia acta est? Nisi quod auguror ut arboris sic hominis
etatem esse, ut sicut illa celi minas atque aerias tempestates, ita hec
mundi difficultates et procellas rerum durior ferat quas tenerior
7 non tulisset. Sed hec consolatio nobis accommoda est, aliis non
ita; nam innumerabiles nobis et senescentibus pubescunt et pubes-
centibus senescebant fierique potest ut et hos tranquilla maneat
8 senectus et illis pueritia inquieta transiverit. Quamobrem omissis
aliis ad rem nostram venio.

# PART IX

## MEMORY

: I :

### *To Guido Sette, archbishop of Genoa, on the changes in the times.*

I know that I have against me the famous saying of Horace, when 1
he is discussing the character of the aging man, and calls him ir-
ritable and complaining and an encomiast of the time past when
he was a boy.[1] And I don't deny it is true, but although this may 2
perhaps be often true on other occasions, I declare it cannot be
held against this letter: although I am a plaintive encomiast of the 3
past, this praise of the past or complaint about the present circumstances will be true. Often truth resounds through a mouth 4
accustomed to lie, and even if the source diminishes credit, the
truth itself imposes belief. I say this and hope you will acknowl- 5
edge it: I declare it and complain and, if mourning befits a man, I
am mourning: why is it that we are spending our old age in worse
years than we experienced in our boyhood? Unless, as I guess, the 6
age of a man is like that of a tree, and just as the tree bears the
threats of heaven and tempests in the sky, so old age bears with
more hardihood the difficulties of the world and the storms of life
which it could not have borne when it was younger. But this con- 7
solation fits us, while it is less fitting to others. For countless men
come to manhood as we grow old and were becoming old when we
were growing up, and it is possible that a calm old age awaits one
generation while the boyhood of others passed in disturbance. So 8
leaving other considerations aside, I come to our own business.

9 Profecto enim, ut vivendo ad malorum tolerantiam duriores simus, ad multa fragiliores facti sumus et, quod nemo neget, in-
dignantiores ad omnia; nichil est enim indignantius senectute.
10 Motus hec animi etsi placare norit ac tegere, sentit tamen sic ut
11 etas nulla profundius, fessa iam et vite confecta fastidiis. Hec sententia mea est quam non audiendo nec legendo sed experiendo
didici, quamque an tu probes nescio: certe quod de etatis mutatione in peius ac ruina dicere institui approbare ipsa te sole clarior
12 veritas coget. Nec iniocundum, puto, nec inutile fuerit aliquantu-
13 lum nunc etiam preteriti temporis meminisse. Quam longissime
igitur potes retro mecum verte oculos.

14 Et primam quidem illam vite partem tu domi tue, ego in exilio
15 meo egi. Neque vero magna hinc elicias argumenta ubi tam exi-
16 guum lumen sit rationis animique. In ipso sane infantie pueritie-
que confinio forte in Galliam Transalpinam, eam scilicet que provincia Provincie nunc dicitur, olim Arelatensis provincia dicebatur,
uno prope tempore transvecti ambo confestimque qualem etas illa
patitur amicitia iuncti usque ad exitum duratura unum vite iter
17 arripuimus. Atque hic ego tuam Ianuam sileo, unde tunc nobis
transitus fuit, cuius tu ortus in finibus, nunc pontificatus in vertice
constitutus nosti omnia et ego quidem de his latius duci urbis illius et consilio scripsi olim epistolamque illam tibi cognitam et
18 probatam scio. Meta puerilis nostre peregrinationis illa fuit que
19 ab antiquis Avennio, a modernis Avinio dicta est. Inde quoniam
Romano Pontifici et Ecclesie secum ibi tunc noviter peregrinanti
neque in suam sedem usque post annum sexagesimum reversure

Surely as in life we become more hardened to endure misfor- 9
tunes, so we have become more brittle in many situations, and, as
no one would deny, more prone to indignation about them all. For
nothing is more indignant than old age: even if this time of life 10
knows how to appease and conceal the mind's emotions, it suffers
more deeply as no other age does, wearied as it now is and exhausted by the distasteful aspects of life. This is my judgment, 11
which I have formed, not from listening or reading but from experience at first hand, and I do not know whether it has your approval. Surely truth itself, more brilliant than the sun, will compel
you to approve what I set out to say about the change of the times
for the worse and its collapse. As I think, it will not be unpleasant 12
or harmful to recall now a little of the past time: so cast your eyes 13
back with me as far as you can see.

You spent the first part of your life at home, but I passed it in 14
exile:[2] but one may not elicit large conclusions from this period 15
when the light of reason and the spirit is so faint. At the border 16
between infancy and boyhood we happened to be carried at almost
the same time to Transalpine Gaul, to the province which is now
called Provence, but was once called the province of Arelate,[3] and
we immediately joined in the kind of friendship which that age
allows, one that would last until our end, and seized on the same
path of life. Here I do not mention your Genoa, through which I 17
passed at that time and in whose territory you were born and
where you are now placed at the summit of its priesthood: you
know it all, and I once wrote about all these facts more fully
to the leader and council of that city and know that the letter
was brought to your attention and approved some time ago.[4] The 18
goal of our boyhood travels was the place called by the ancients
Avennio and by moderns Avignon. Then, since the place was too 19
cramped for the Roman pope and his Church which had but recently traveled abroad with him, and was destined not to return to
its own abode until after the sixtieth year, and since there was a

locus angustus erat, domorum ea tempestate inops incolarumque
colluvie exundans, consilium nostrorum senum fuit ut mulieres
20 cum pueris ad locum proximum se transferrent. In qua transmigra-
tione et nos duo, iam pueri necdum puberes, cum reliquis simul,
21 sed ad aliud, hoc est ad scolas grammatice missi fuimus. Carpentoras loco nomen, urbs parva quidem sed provincie parve caput.
22 Tenes memoria tempus illud quadriennii, quanta ibi iocunditas,
quanta securitas, que domi quies que ve in publico libertas, que
23 per agros ocia quod ve silentium. Tu credo idem sentias: certe ego
adhuc illi tempori imo vero omnium temporum auctori gratiam
habeo qui id michi spatium tam tranquillum dedit ut absque ullo
rerum turbine pro ingenii imbecillitate doctrine puerilis tenerum
24 lac haurirem quo ad cibi solidioris alimentum convalescerem. Sed
mutati sumus, dicat aliquis; hinc est ut mutata simul nobis omnia
videantur; sic oculo sic palato alia quidem sano, egro alia eadem
25 res videtur. Mutatos fateor: quis enim non dicam carneus sed fer-
26 reus aut saxeus tanto non mutetur in tempore? Enee atque mar-
moree evo cedunt statue, urbes manu aggeste et que iuga montium
premunt arces, quodque est durius, solide ipsis ex montibus rupes
ruunt: quid facturum rear hominem, mortale animal fragilibus
27 membris et cute tenui compactum? Sed an mutatio tanta est ut
28 manente anima iudicium aut sensus abstulerit? Satis extimo, si
nobis quales hodie sumus que tunc fuit etas illa redeat, non omnino talem visum iri qualis eo tempore visa est, ne nichil penitus
29 annis actum dicam: alia certe videbitur. Nunquid tamen non longe
30 melior multoque tranquillior quam que nunc agitur? An quia fortassis minutissimum illud opus Mirmichidis quadrige, quam tege-
bat, ut perhibent, alis musca, rotarum radios non discernunt oculi

shortage of housing at that time and Avignon overflowed with a
stream of population, it was our fathers' decision that the wives
and children should transfer themselves to a nearby place. In this 20
removal, the two of us, still boys and not yet grown to youth, were
sent with the others but to another destination, that is, grammar
school. The place was called Carpentras, a little town but head of 21
its little province.[5] Do you remember that period of four years,[6] 22
what fun we had, what freedom from care, what calm at home,
what liberty in public, what peace in the countryside, what silence?
I believe you feel the same; certainly to this day I give thanks to 23
that time and indeed to the divine Creator of all times, who gave
me such a peaceful interlude so that, untroubled by the disturbances of life, I might drink up the gentle milk of boyish studies,
fitting an intellect that was still weak to gain strength for the di-
gestion of more solid food. But we have changed, someone would 24
say; this is the reason why everything seems to have changed with
us:[7] so things seem different to a healthy eye and palate than they
seem to a sick one. I admit we too have changed; for who doesn't 25
change over time, even supposing they were made of iron or rock
rather than flesh? Bronze and marble statues collapse with age, 26
cities built up by hand and citadels weighing down on mountain
ridges and, something harder still, solid boulders from the actual
mountains collapse: what would I expect from man, a mortal creature constructed with frail limbs and thin skin? But is that change 27
so great that it has taken away our judgment or sense while the
spirit survives? I am quite convinced that if that age, as it was 28
then, returned to us as we now are, it would not seem at all like
what it seemed at that time, and I don't mean to say that nothing
at all happened with the passing of the years: things will surely
seem different. Yet won't it also seem far better and much more 29
peaceful than what is happening now? Or perhaps, just because 30
our eyes cannot distinguish the spokes of the wheels in that miniature work of art, the chariot of Murmex, which as they say a fly

seu Calcitratis non dinumerant formicarum pedes partesque alias
humani aciem obtuitus tenuitate frustrantes neque *Yliadem* illam,
quam subtiliter adeo fuisse descriptam ut tota unius testa nucis
includeretur, ait Cicero, clare expediteque perlegunt, idcirco sic
caligant ut urbes vicosque urbium cives mores habitus domos templa non videant? Sic mens hebet ut mutata et deformata omnia
31 non agnoscat? An non sepe postea civitatulam illam revidimus a se
ipsa usqueadeo diversam ut alienati magis animi videri possit tantam tamque enormem mutationem rerum omnium non videre?
32 Non multis annis ex quo inde discessimus totius, quod ante non
fuerat, provincie litigiorum sedes, dicam rectius domus demonum
facta est: cessit otium, cessit gaudium cessitque tranquillitas; cunta
33 illico iudiciariis tumultibus atque clamoribus plena erant. Quid
nobis obicitur mutatio, qui translati alio et locis mutatis et acce-
34 dente evo mutari utique poteramus et hauddubie mutabamur? Ipsi
iam cives vix suam patriam agnoscebant, quod crebra notorum la-
35 mentatione didicimus. Sed hec mutatio pro iustitia fuit, dixerit
36 quispiam, que raro sine clamoribus exerceri potest. Ego autem de
37 mutatione ipsa, non de causa disputo. Nunquid vero illud etiam
iustitie fuit, quod post annos ea ipsa urbs et circumfusa regio, que
securissima et apostolice cui subest sedis reverentia pene armis
exempta et inaccessibilis videbatur Marti, predonum exercitu non
vexata tantum sed vastata atque ad extrema miseriarum redacta
38 est? Hec nobis pueris siquis illic unquam eventura vaticinaretur,
39 nonne invisus pariter atque insanus haberetur vates? Sed teneo
ordinem et, quanquam de maioribus possem, ut memoria tamen
tua nostre astipuletur assertioni, de his que simul ambo vidimus

covered with its wings, or cannot count the feet of ants by Callicrates and other parts which by their delicacy frustrate the keenness of human gaze, or again because men cannot read clearly and
quickly that text of the *Iliad* so minutely copied that it was entirely
included in the shell of a nut, as Cicero says,[8] does it follow that
our eyes are so clouded over that they do not see cities and city
districts, citizens, human manners and behavior, houses and temples? Is the mind so blunted that it does not recognize that everything is changed and disfigured? Surely we have seen that little 31
community often since then, so different from itself that it might
seem the mark of a disturbed mind not to see such a great and
unnatural change in things? It is not many years since we left 32
there, and it has become the seat of lawsuits in all the province
(which it was not before), indeed I might more correctly say a
house of demons;[9] leisure and joy and peace have retreated: everything was instantly full of the tumult and shouting of the courts.
Why is that change held against us, since we were removed else- 33
where with a change of places and the onset of age, and so could
be, and without doubt were, changing? The citizens themselves 34
barely recognized their homeland, as we learn from the frequent
laments of those we know. But this change was in the interest of 35
justice, someone will say, which can seldom be imposed without
uproar. However, my dispute is about the change itself, not its 36
motivation. Was it in the name of justice that years later the very 37
city and region surrounding it, which seemed perfectly secure and
almost exempt from arms and inaccessible to warfare out of respect for the nearby Apostolic See, was not just harassed but ruined and reduced to extreme misery by an army of brigands?[10]
Surely if anyone had prophesied when we were boys that this 38
would happen, he would have been thought a mad and hateful
prophet? But I will maintain the order of my argument. And al- 39
though I could speak about greater changes, I am more eager to
talk to you about what we both saw together, so that your memory

40 cupidius tecum loquor. Inde igitur simul quoque—nam quid divi-
sim magna etatis parte gessimus?—vicina iam pubertate ad Montem Pessulanum, florentissimum tunc oppidum, iurisque ad studium delati aliud ibi quadriennium exegimus; cuius tunc potestas
penes Maioris Balearice regem erat, exiguum preter loci angulum
Francorum regi subditum, qui, ut semper prepotentium impor-
41 tuna vicinia est, brevi totius oppidi dominium ad se traxit. Quenam vero tunc ibi quoque tranquillitas, que pax, que divitie merca-
42 torum, que scolarium turba, que copia magistrorum! Quanta ibi
nunc horum omnium penuria publicarumque et privatarum rerum
quanta mutatio, et nos scimus et cives, qui utrumque viderunt
tempus, sentiunt.

43 Inde Bononiam perreximus, qua nil puto iocundius nilque libe-
44 rius toto esset orbe terrarum. Meministi plane qui studiosorum
conventus, quis ordo, que vigilantia, que maiestas preceptorum.
45 Iurisconsultos veteres redivivos crederes; quorum hodie prope nullus est ibi, sed pro tam multis et tam magnis ingeniis una urbem
illam invasit ignorantia, hostis utinam et non hospes! vel, si hospes,
at non civis seu, quod multum vereor, regina! sic michi omnes vi-
46 dentur abiectis armis manum tollere. Quenam ibi preterea tunc
ubertas rerum omnium que ve fertilitas, ut iam prescripto cogno-
47 mine per omnes terras pinguis Bononia diceretur! Incipit illa,
fateor quidem, huius Pontificis Maximi qui nunc rebus presidet
consilio ac pietate revirescere atque pinguescere, verum hactenus,
ut illius urbis non modo precordia sed medullas rimareris, nichil
48 macrius, nichil aridius invenisses. Facete, ut in malis iocari solitus
erat, ille vir optimus ad illius regimen legatus de latere, ut ipsi vocant, missus novissime; ad quem visendum anno retro tertio cum

may vouch for my assertion. So we moved again, leaving there to- 40
gether—and did we ever act independently of each other for the
better part of our youth?—and at the approach of puberty were
sent to Montpellier, a most flourishing city at that time, for the
study of law, and spent another four-year period there. At that
time it was under the control of the king of Majorca, apart from a
small corner of land subject to the king of France. Since being
neighbors to an overwhelming power is always threatening, the
latter soon established lordship over the whole town.[11] But what 41
calm there was, even there in those days, what peace, what rich
merchants, what a crowd of students, what an abundance of
teachers! But now we know what an impoverishment there has 42
been, what a change in all these public and private affairs, as the
citizens realize who witnessed both times.

Then we went on to Bologna,[12] which I think the most pleasant 43
and free of cities in the whole wide world. You certainly remember 44
the gatherings of students, the order, the vigilance, the dignity of
our teachers. You would think the ancient jurisconsults were res- 45
urrected! But now there is barely one of them there: instead of so
many great intellects, one universal Ignorance has invaded the
city—and would that that Ignorance were regarded as an enemy
and not a guest, or merely as a guest and not as a citizen or, I very
much fear, a queen! For it seems to me they all have thrown away
their arms and are raising their hands in surrender. But what 46
abundance there was of everything there at that time, what fertility, so that the nickname of "Fat Bologna" was applied in every
country![13] It is beginning, I admit, to revive and grow fat again by 47
the design and piety of this Roman pope, who now presides over
its government[14]—but only up to a point; if you were to probe not
just the belly but the bone, you would find nothing leaner or dryer.
The excellent man who was most recently sent to the city govern- 48
ment as "legate from the side," as it's called, made the following
witty comment, as was his habit in misfortune. When I went

venissem, post parvi hospitis letos et nimis honorificos amplexus sermonem varium exorsi sumus; querentique michi publico de statu 'Hec,' inquit 'amice, Bononia olim fuit, nunc autem Macerata est': Piceni nomen oppidi traxit in iocum.

49 Sentis, puto, ut dulci quadam cum amaritudine inter hec mala
50 et bonarum memoriam rerum versor. Heret memorie mee, credo
et tue, indelebile fixumque vestigium illius temporis quo studioso-
51 rum unus ibi agebam. Venerat iam etas ardentior, iam adolescen-
52 tiam ingressus et debito et solito plus audebam. Ibam cum equevis
meis, dies festos vagabamur longius, sic ut sepe nos in campis lux
desereret, et profunda nocte revertebamur et patentes erant porte.
53 Siquo casu clause essent, nullus erat urbi murus, vallum fragile
iam disiectum senio urbem cingebat intrepidam; nam quid muro
54 seu quid vallo tanta opus erat in pace? Sic pro uno multi erant
aditus; quisque commodiorem sibi carpebat ingressum; nil diffi-
55 cile, nil suspectum erat. Ut muro, ut turribus, ut propugnaculis, ut
armatis custodibus, ut nocturnis excubiis opus esset interne primum venena tyrannidis, post externorum fecere hostium insidie
56 atque insultus. Quid notissima ruminans circa Bononiam demo-
rari stilum cogo, nisi quia tam recens illius michi veteris Bononie
memoria est ut quotiens hanc videre contingit somniare credide-
57 rim neque oculis ipse meis fiderem? Sic multos iam per annos paci
bellum, libertati servitus, copie inopia, ludis meror, cantibus querele, choreis virginum predonum cunei successere, ut preter turres
atque ecclesias adhuc stantes miseramque urbem altis verticibus
despectantes hec que Bononia dicebatur diu quidvis potius quam
Bononia videretur.

there three years ago to see him, after he greeted his humble guest
with joyful and excessively honorable embraces, we began to talk
of this and that, and when I asked about the city's condition, he
said: "My friend, this was once Bologna, but now it's Macerata,"
making a pun on the name of the Picentine town.[15]

I think you can feel how I am shifting in bittersweet mood be- 49
tween these misfortunes and the memory of good times. There 50
sticks in my memory, and I think yours too, the fixed and indelible
mark of that time when I lived there as a student. A more passion- 51
ate phase had already set in, I was already embarked on youth and
dared more than was due or customary. I used to go around with 52
my peers and we wandered further afield on holidays, so that the
light often deserted us in the countryside and we used to come
back at dead of night and the gates would be standing open; if 53
they happened to be closed, no matter: the city had no walls; a
frail rampart dilapidated with old age surrounded the fearless city;
for why would we need a wall or rampart in such great peace?
Hence there were many ways in instead of one, and each of us 54
picked the best way in for himself: nothing was difficult or a cause
for suspicion. It was, first, the internal poison of the tyranny, then 55
the treachery and assaults of external enemies which made it need
a wall and towers and bastions, armed guards and night watches.[16]
Why does my pen linger, mulling over the well-known stories 56
about Bologna, unless the memory of the old Bologna is so fresh
that whenever I happen to see it, I would believe I was dreaming
and not trust my own eyes? So for many years now war has fol- 57
lowed peace, enslavement liberty, poverty abundance, mourning
play, laments songs, and squadrons of brigands bands of dancing
maidens, so that apart from the towers and churches still standing
and looking down on the wretched city from their high summits,
this city once called Bologna has long since come to seem anything
but Bologna.

58 Sed ut iam Bononia discedamus, acto ibi triennio domum redii,
illam dico quam pro Arni domo perdita mea michi sors—bona
59 utinam!—reddiderat Rodani turbidam ad ripam; qui locus, a
principio in finem etsi uno semper tenore iudicii non tam propter
se quam propter concursantes et coactas ibi concretasque totius
orbis sordes ac nequitias multis atque ante alios michi pessimus
omnium visus sit, tanto tamen sese peior factus est ut, quod nemo
nisi prorsus impudenti mendacio negare audeat, sibi ipse collatus
60 fuisse olim optimus videri possit. Nam, ne singulis immorer,
quanquam nulla ibi unquam fides, nulla caritas et, quod de Hani-
bale dicitur, 'nichil veri, nichil sancti, nullus Dei metus, nullum
iusiurandum, nulla religio,' ubi non quidem propter se sed propter
presidentis electionem summa vere religionis arx esse debuerat,
erant ibi tamen, quantum oculis apparebat, multa securitas ac libertas, que ita funditus periere ut cum ceteris et publicanorum
inaudito ibi hactenus et ignoto deprimatur iugo et metu gravi hostium sine fine circumsonantium necesse fuerit novis urbem menibus circumplecti et ubi noctibus totis aperta omnia fuerant luce
61 media portarum aditus armis obstruere. Neque id valuit quin male
tuta ferro ac menibus redimenda auro et precibus salus esset; idque ego Dei nutu gestum seu permissum reor ut vel sic vicarius
suus quique illi assident neglecte diu nimis sponse in memoriam
ac desiderium traherentur, quod sive hac causa sive insita virtute
iam in pontifice factum vides; reliquos duriores aut Deus molliat
62 aut mors, quod cepisse iam visa est. Ceterum mala hec si capiti
acciderunt, patientius ferant membra nec miretur quisquam si

But to leave Bologna behind, after three years there I came back 58
home, to the home, I mean, which my unhappy lot—if only it had
been good—substituted on the turbulent bank of the Rhône for
my lost home on the Arno:[17] a place from beginning to end incur- 59
ring the same criticism, not so much on its own account as because of the squalor and debaucheries of the whole world which
were crowded, compressed and encrusted there: it seemed to many
and to me before the others the worst place of all; yet it had become so much worse than itself that (something no one would
dare to deny except in an utterly shameless lie) in comparison, it
seemed to have once been excellent. For, not to linger over details, 60
although there was nowhere any good faith, nor affection and, as
is said about Hannibal, "nothing true or sacred, no fear of God, no
oath, no scruple"[18] in the place which should have been religion's
highest citadel—not on its own account, but by the choice of its
chief representative—yet there was, in appearance at least, much
freedom from anxiety and much liberty. This has so utterly perished that, along with the rest, it is now trampled down under the
previously unheard-of and unknown yoke of tax collectors and,
from fear of the enemy echoing ceaselessly all around, it became
necessary to enclose the city in new walls, and where all approaches had been open through the night, they blocked access to
the gates with men under arms in broad daylight.[19] Nor was this 61
enough to avoid the misfortune that their survival, ill secured by
steel and fortifications, had to be ransomed with gold and supplications.[20] I think this occurred or was authorized by God's decision, so his vicar and his counselors might be drawn into desire and longing for their spouse, neglected for too long.[21] This
is what, you see, has already happened to the pope, either from
this motive or through his innate virtue. May either God or
death soften the harsh opposition, as seems to have already set
in.[22] Now the limbs ought to endure such blows more patiently if 62
they happened to the head; and no man should be surprised if

quos a limine proprio presens Romanus Pontifex ipse non arcuit eiusdem absentis reverentia non coercet; ne qua enim vetus mali consuetudo recens bonum interpellet vellicansque nondum stabiles animos redeundi forte ingerat appetitum, plagam illam latrociniis maxime nunc infestam scimus.

63 Unum hic, antequam longius eam, quod me premit dicam ni-
tarque hodie, quod verum nolim, tecum loquendo iuvenescere.
64 Nosti ut in illo surgentis vite flore cuius ante memini, quem grammaticorum in stramine velut in delitiis egimus, cum semel parens meus patruusque simul tuus, qui ea ferme tunc etate erant qua nunc sumus, ad carpentoratensem quam modo dicebam civitatulam de more venissent, patruum ipsum quasi advenam voluntas cepit, ex vicinitate, credo, et novitate rei orta, preclarissimum illum fontem Sorgie videndi; qui per se olim notus — si parva de re gloriari cum amico, idest secum, licet — meo longo postmodum inco-
65 latu meisque carminibus aliquanto notior factus est. Re audita puerilis et nos cupiditas excivit ut duceremur; et quoniam non sat tuto committi equis videbamur, singuli nobis famuli dati sunt qui
66 equos ipsos nosque, ut fit, a tergo complexi regerent. Atque ita, matre illa omnium optima quas quidem viderim, que carne mea, amore autem comunis michi tecum fuit, vix tandem exorata sed multa pavente ac monente, profecti sumus cum illo viro cuius vel sola recordatio leta est cuiusque tu nomen et cognomen retines,
67 doctrine autem et fame plurimum addidisti. Cum ad fontem ventum esset — recolo enim non aliter quam si hodie fuisset — insueta tactus specie locorum pueriles inter illos cogitatus meos dixi ut potui: 'En nature mee locus aptissimus quemque, si dabitur, ali-
68 quando magnis urbibus prelaturus sim!.' Hec tunc ego mecum tacitus, que mox postea, ut virilem etatem attigi, quantum non otio

reverence for the pope in his absence had no control over the bands he could not drive from his threshold even when he was in his home. So to ensure that the old familiarity with evil does not interrupt the recent good and, by plucking at their still unstable spirits, build up their appetite to return, we know that this region is now utterly exposed to the hostile attacks of robbers.

Let me say one thing that troubles me here before I go further, 63
and let me attempt today something I would not really wish, to
regain my youth with you as we talk. You know how in that flower 64
of growing life which I mentioned before, which we spent in the straw bedding of grammarians as if in luxury, when once my father and your uncle, who were then about the age we are now, came as was their custom to the little town of Carpentras which I just mentioned, your uncle was seized like a tourist by a whim, arising from the nearness of the Sorgue and the novelty of the occasion, to see that most glorious source, once known on its own account, but now somewhat better known from my long residence and my songs—if I can boast about a small matter to a friend, like
talking to myself.[23] When we heard about it, a boyish desire 65
roused us to be taken there, and since it seemed we could not be safely entrusted to horses, individual servants were assigned to us to ride the horses while clutching us from behind, as one does.
And so when that best of all mothers that I have ever seen,[24] who 66
was mine in the flesh but shared by me and you in love, was finally persuaded, though still very anxious and full of warnings, we set out with that man, whose memory alone is itself pure joy, whose first and last name you have kept, while adding greatly to his
learning and fame.[25] When we reached the source (and I remem- 67
ber it just as if it were today) I was moved in my boyish thoughts by the unfamiliar aspect of the landscape and I said as best I could express it: "Here is the place best fitted to my nature and which I
shall prefer to mighty cities, if it is ever granted me!" This is what 68
I said to myself silently then; and soon after, when I reached

meo mundus invidit, late claris indiciis nota feci; multos illic enim
annos sed avocantibus me sepe negotiis rerumque difficultatibus
interruptos egi, tanta tamen in requie tantaque dulcedine ut, ex
quo quid vita hominum esset agnovi, illud ferme solum tempus
69 vita michi fuerit, reliquum omne supplicium. Iam tunc indivisi-
biles animis distracti studiis eramus: tu litigium et rostra, ego
ocium sectabar et nemora, tu calle politico divitias honestas quesi-
visti, que me, mirum dictu, solitarium contemptorem profugum in
70 medias silvas usque ad invidiam insecute sunt. Quid vero tibi nunc
ego illud agreste silentium, illud nitidissimi amnis assiduum murmur, illum boum sonoris in vallibus mugitum, illos volucrum in
71 ramis non diurnos modo concentus sed nocturnos explicem? Scis
omnia, etsi me hac in parte non penitus sequi ausus, quotiens tamen urbanis tumultibus te furari posses — quod perrarum erat —
72 cupide illuc ut e procellis in portum fugere solitus. Quotiens autem reris me nox atra solum procul in campis invenerit? Quotiens
per estatem media nocte surrexerim et nocturnis Cristo laudibus
persolutis unus ego, ne somno pressos famulos inquietarem, nunc
73 in agros, presertim sublustri luna, nunc in montes exierim? Quotiens hora illa, nullo comite, non sine voluptate horrida immane
illud fontis specus intraverim quo vel comitatum luce ingredi hor-
74 ror est? Unde autem ea tanta fiducia si queritur, nempe umbras
larvasque non metuo, lupus nunquam in ea valle visus erat, homi-
75 num pavor nullus. Bubulci in pratis, piscatores in fluvio pervigiles,
illi quidem canebant, hi silebant, utrique certatim me colebant seque ad omnimodum obsequium horis omnibus offerebant, quippe

manhood, whenever the world did not begrudge me my leisure, I
made it known far and wide with famous memorials. I spent many
years there, although they were often interrupted by life's difficulties and duties calling me away, but I spent them in such repose
and sweetness that, since the time I recognized what men's life was
like, this time almost alone was life for me, and all the rest torment.[26] So we were inseparable in heart but torn apart at that time 69
by our pursuits; you pursued the law courts and the speakers'
platform, I pursued leisure and the woods;[27] you sought honorable
wealth by the political pathway, and this wealth, amazingly, pursued me, its solitary despiser, who had taken refuge in the midst of
the forest to the point of envy. Why should I outline for you that 70
rustic silence, that constant murmur of the gleaming river, the
lowing of the cattle in the echoing valleys, the songs of birds in the
branches not only by day but by night? You know it all, even if 71
you did not dare to follow me utterly in this matter, yet whenever
you could steal yourself away from urban troubles, which was very
seldom, you came there eagerly like one accustomed to escape
from storms into harbor. How often do you think black night 72
found me alone far in the fields? How often in the summer I got
up in the dead of night, and once I had paid my due praise and
thanks to Christ, I went alone, in order not to disturb the sleeping
servants, at times into the field especially when the moon was
glimmering, at times into the hills? How often in those days I 73
went with no companion and not without a certain shuddering
pleasure, into the huge cavern of that source, which one enters
with a shudder even accompanied and by daylight? If you ask the 74
reason for such confidence, I am certainly not afraid of shadows
and ghosts, no wolf was ever seen in that valley—and there was
no fear of men. Both the cowherds in the meadows and the fisher- 75
men in the stream were awake, the one group singing, the others
silent and they competed in honoring me and offered themselves
for every kind of service at all hours, since they knew that their

cum suum locique dominum scirent non amicum michi tantum
76 esse, sed fratrem optimum, sed parentem. Sic ubique benivoli, hostes nusquam. Itaque cuncta deliberans sic michi te favente atque
idem sentiente persuaseram: si totus orbis bello quateretur, illum
77 immobilem ac pacificum locum fore. Quod ut crederem et Romane respectus Ecclesie, de quo dixi, et multo maxime vicinitas
faciebat, super omnia autem paupertas, securissima rerum et con-
temptrix avaritie atque armorum.

78 Quid deinde? Mirari posses ni rem nosses. Adhuc me ibi agente
lupi advene usque in oppiduli domos cathervatim ruere ceperant et
facta gregum cede attonitos trepidosque ipsos loci incolas habere
nec damnum modo sed augurium esse et luporum, credo, qui ven-
79 turi erant presagium armatorum. Siquidem, non multo postquam
inde discesseram, parva quedam fedaque et infamis manus furum
sed ignavie accolarum fidens omnibus circum pererratis ac direptis
ad extremum, prorsus ut sacri fures essent ac de furto suo Laverne,
furum dee, rite sacrificarent, ipso dominico natali die incautum rus
aggressi ablatis que auferri poterant reliqua flammis exusserunt
inque illud hospitiolum, ex quo Cresi regiam spernebam, ignis
80 immissus est. Testudo vetus incendio restitit; properabant enim
81 fures impii. Libellos aliquot, quos illic abiens dimiseram, villici
mei filius, iam id ante presagiens futurum, in arcem contulerat,
quam predones, inexpugnabilem ut est rati, sed ut erat indefensam
82 ac vacuam ignorantes, abiere. Sic diris e faucibus preter spem ser-
vati libri providente Deo ne tam turpes ad manus preda tam nobi-
83 lis perveniret. I nunc et illius Clause Vallis opacis in receptaculis
spem habeto! Nil clausum nilque altum, fuscum nichil est furibus

own master and that of the place was not just my friend but a
brother, and a father to me.[28] So there were well wishers ev- 76
erywhere and enemies nowhere. Hence, considering it all, I had persuaded myself with your support and agreement that if the whole world were shattered by war, that place would be still and a
source of peace. Both the respect for the Roman Church about 77
which I spoke,[29] and especially its nearness led me to believe this, as did above all my poverty, the most carefree of conditions, contemptuous of greed and warfare.

What next? You might be surprised if you did not know what 78
happened. While I was still living there, strange wolves began to rush in packs right into the houses of the little town and they slaughtered the flocks and kept the natives of the place stricken and trembling, and I believe this was not just a loss but an omen
and a presage of the armed human wolves who were to come. In- 79
deed not long after I left, a small and vile and shameful band of thieves, relying on the inertia of the villagers, after wandering around and plundering everything, finally on Christmas Day itself—so that they could become accursed thieves and duly pay sacrifice to Laverna, the goddess of thieves—they attacked the unsuspecting countryside and, taking away what they could carry, set fire to the rest; flames entered into that little shelter from
which I had scorned the palace of Croesus.[30] The old roof resisted 80
the fire, since the impious thieves were in a hurry! The son of my 81
overseer, anticipating this future trouble, had removed some books that I had left there on my departure and collected them in the castle, which the brigands thought impossible to storm, as it is, so they went off, not knowing it was then empty and undefended.
This is how the books were saved unexpectedly from their dread- 82
ful jaws through the providence of God to ensure that such noble
booty did not come into such vile hands. So go now[31] and put 83
your hope in the hidden shelters of that Enclosed Valley![32] Nothing is closed or out of reach, nothing hidden from thieves and

atque predonibus: omnia penetrant, omnia provident ac rimantur.
84 Nullus tam munitus tamque excelsus est locus in quem non scan-
85 dat armata cupiditas et soluta legum vinclis avaritia. Sed ita me
Deus amet ut presentem loci statum cogitans memorque preteriti
vix opinari possum esse illum ubi in montibus noctu solus ac secu-
86 rus erraverim. Verum ego non ruris illius ignobilitate sed solitudinis mee suavitate pensata plura forsitan quam pro re dixerim. Ut
antiqua equidem novis iungerem, ex quibus rerum mutatio nota
esset, ordinem deserui: sed revertor.

87 Quarto igitur postquam Bononia redieram anno, cum illo viro,
sepe michi et multum, nunquam vero quantum meruit, laudato,
Tholosam Garumneque alveum et Pireneos colles adii celo sepe
88 turbido sed serenissimo comitatu. Et quid de his dicam nisi quod
de aliis? Eadem Tholosa eademque Vasconia, Aquitania eadem
nomine, re omnes prorsus alie sibique ipsis preter unam soli super-
ficiem omni ex parte dissimiles.

89 Inde autem reversus quarto item anno iuvenili ardore videndique cupidine Pariseorum urbem petii; in quo quidem itinere ac
reditu — sic iuvente calcar urgebat — extremos regni angulos Flan-
driamque et Brabantiam atque Anoniam et inferiorem Germa-
90 niam circumivi. Quo cum nuper ex negotio rediissem, vix aliquid
omnium recognovi, opulentissimum in cineres versum regnum
videns et nullam pene domum stantem nisi urbium aut arcium
91 menibus cincta esset. De quo tunc ad venerabilem senem Petrum
Pictavensem scripsi latius ac dixi, qui post obiit, ante non multum
92 tempus felicius obiturus. Ubi est enim illa Pariseos, que licet
semper fama inferior et multa suorum mendaciis debens, magna

brigands: they penetrate everything, they anticipate and scrutinize everything. No place is so well fortified and lofty that armed greed 84
and avarice, free from the bonds of the laws, cannot climb there
But so may God love me, considering the present condition of the 85
place and remembering its past, I can scarcely imagine it is the place where I wandered in the hills, safe and carefree by night!
Indeed, reckoning not with the humble nature of that countryside 86
but rather with the pleasantness of my solitude, I have perhaps said too much for the topic. I deserted my sequence of thought to heap the old upon the new, to make the change known, but now I am returning to it.

So in the fourth year after I returned from Bologna, I went 87
with the man I praised much and often, but never as much as he deserved, to Toulouse and the basin of the Garonne and the Pyrenaean mountains, often in turbulent weather, but with the most
sunny companionship.[33] And what am I to say about these regions 88
except what I said about the other places? It is still the same Toulouse, the same Gascony, and Aquitania has the same name but in fact all these places are utterly changed and in every respect different from themselves except for the mere contours of the land.

Next after my return from there, likewise in the fourth year, 89
with a young man's passion and desire to see the world, I made for the city of Paris, and in the journey and my return from it (so the spur of youth drove me on) I saw the remotest corners of the kingdom, Flanders and Brabant and Hainaut and lower Germany.[34] But when I recently went back on diplomatic business I 90
scarcely recognized anything, seeing this most wealthy kingdom in ashes and hardly any house standing unless it was enclosed by the
walls of cities or castles.[35] In fact I wrote and spoke about this at 91
length to that venerable old man Peter of Poitiers who died soon after, though he would have been happier to die a short time before.[36] For where is that city of Paris which, although always infe- 92
rior to its fame and owing much to the fictions of its residents,

93 tamen haud dubie res fuit? Ubi scolasticorum agmina, ubi Studii
94 fervor, ubi civium divitie, ubi cuntorum gaudia? Non disputan-
tium ibi nunc auditur sed bellantium fragor, non librorum sed
armorum cumuli cernuntur, non sillogismi non sermones sed
95 excubie atque arietes muris impacti resonant. Cessat clamor ac
sedulitas venatorum: strepunt menia, silent silve, vixque ipsis in
urbibus tuti sunt; cessit enim penitusque abiit que illic templum
nacta tranquillitas videbatur. Nusquam tam nulla securitas, nus-
96 quam tam multa pericula. Quis hoc unquam queso divinasset,
quod Francorum rex, quamvis quod ad se unum attinet invictissi-
mus hominum, vinceretur et in carcerem duceretur et ingenti pre-
97 cio redimeretur? Tolerabilius tamen hoc efficit auctor mali: rex a
98 rege, licet impari, victus est. Illud prorsus miserum pudendumque
reditu in patriam prohibitos et regem ipsum et filium, qui nunc
regnat, coactosque cum predonibus pacisci ut tutum per suas ter-
99 ras iter agerent. Quis hoc, inquam, illo in regno felicissimo non
100 dicam cogitasset, sed, autumo, etiam somniasset? Quando vero
credent hoc posteri si, ut sunt volubiles res humane, regnum ipsum quandocunque suo statui restitutum fuerit? Nos enim non
credimus, sed videmus.

101 Inde autem, hoc est a prima gallicana peregrinatione reversus,
quarto itidem post anno primum Romam adii, que etsi iam tunc
multoque prius nichil aliud quasi quam illius Rome veteris argumentum atque imago quedam esset ruinisque presentibus preteri-
tam magnitudinem testaretur, erant tamen adhuc cinere in illo
102 generose alique faville; nunc extinctus et iam gelidus cinis est. Erat
ex cineribus veterum renatus phenix unicus, senex ille gloriosissimus Stephanus Columnensis, eius quem supra memoravi mei

was undoubtedly once a great place? Where are the hordes of 93
students, the excitement of its university, the riches of citizens, the
amusements of them all? It is not the clash of argument that is 94
heard there but of warfare; you see heaps not of books but of
weapons, no syllogisms, no disputations, but night watches and
battering rams that echo as they are driven against the walls. The 95
shouting and enthusiasm of hunters is suspended; the walls are
full of bustle, the woods are silent, and men are scarcely safe in the
cities themselves; the calm which seemed to have found a sanctu-
ary in that place has given way and utterly departed; nowhere is
there so little freedom from anxiety, nowhere so many dangers. I 96
ask you, who would have imagined this, that the king of France,
though the most unconquered of men in person, should be defeated and taken to prison and be ransomed for a huge price?[37] Yet 97
the author of this evil makes it more bearable: a king has been
defeated by a king, although an inferior. What is utterly wretched 98
and shameful is that the king and his son, who is ruling now, were
barred from return to their native land and forced to bargain with
brigands for safe-conduct through their own country.[38] I am tell- 99
ing you: who would have, I won't say thought it, but even, as I
think, dreamed it? But how will future generations believe this 100
if—as human affairs are volatile—their kingdom at some remote
time is restored to its condition? Indeed we don't believe it although we are seeing it.

Likewise, four years later, that is, since returning from my first 101
travels through Gaul, I came to Rome for the first time, and even
if Rome was already, and for a long time before that, nothing but
an outline or shadow of the glorious ancient Rome, and bore witness by its present ruins to its past greatness, yet there were in
those ashes still some noble sparks; but now those ashes are extinct and long since cold.[39] There was only one phoenix reborn 102
among the ashes of the ancients, that glorious old man Stefano
Colonna, the father of that leader of mine mentioned above and of

ducis magneque et illustris sed caduce nimium genitor familie, vir
103 cum suis sepe michi dictus dicendusque. Erant alii quibus ruine
ille saltem patrie care essent, quorum nullus aut ibi nunc aut humanis in rebus iam superstes est.

104 Quarto rursus anno Neapolim perrexi; et licet sepe post id
tempus Romam Neapolimque redierim, prime tamen impres-
105 siones herent animo. Erat ibi tunc Robertus, Sicilie, imo Italie,
106 imo regum rex, cuius vita felicitas, mors exitium regni fuit. Ipse
quidem me digresso non diutius supervixit. Et plane, si celo
obstante vetabatur ingruentibus malis occurrere ut solebat, vix
cuiquam tempestivius mori contigit, ut michi plane ad eximiam
107 vite felicitatem talis mors accessisse videatur. Ego autem anno demum quarto — sic tunc vitam quaternario partiebar — illuc rediens,
nunquam rediturus nisi me Clementis tunc Romani Pontificis
iussus urgeret, muros quidem et plateas et mare et portum et cir-
cumfusos colles vitiferosque eminus hinc Phalernum hinc Vese-
vum vidi, Capreas quoque et Inarimen et Prochitam ictas fluctibus
insulas et fumantes hibernis mensibus Baias: notam michi Neapo-
108 lim non inveni; semina vero cladium multarum atque impendentis
signa miserie clara perspexi, cuius me tam certum fuisse vatem
109 doleo. At quid inde sentirem non verbo solum sed et literis, tonante iam fortuna, nondum tamen fulminante, testatus sum; que
ita post illicet impleta sunt omnia et multa insuper addita, ut vati-
cinium ipsum meum quamvis horribile infinita malorum serie
vinceretur, que deflere quam enumerare facilius multo sit.

that great and glorious but too mortal family, a man whom I have
often mentioned and must continue to mention along with his
kin.[40] There were others too who held dear at least those ruins of 103
our country, none of whom is now surviving either there or in our
mortal world.

After four more years I went on to Naples, and although I often 104
returned to Rome and Naples after that, those first impressions
are fixed in my mind.[41] Robert, king of Sicily—indeed king of It- 105
aly, indeed king over kings—was there: as his life was the blessing
of that kingdom, so his death was its destruction. In fact he did 106
not live much longer after I left Naples and, if he was prohibited
from confronting the coming evils as he had usually done before,
because Heaven prevented it, death had scarcely come more opportunely to any man, so that such a death seemed to me to have
been added to his exceptional fortune in life.[42] But returning 107
there finally after four years (for that is how I then divided my life,
into quadrennia) and intending never to return if the order of
Clement, the Roman pope at that time, had not driven me to
it,[43] I saw the walls and squares and sea and harbor and hills
spread around and at a distance the vine-laden area of Falernus on
one side and on the other that of Vesuvius; I saw Capri too and
Ischia and Procida, those wave-beaten islands, and Baiae, steaming
in the winter months, but I did not find the Naples that I knew.[44]
Indeed I saw the seeds of many disasters and clear signs of immi- 108
nent wretchedness, and I grieve now that I was so sure a prophet
of these woes. But I have already borne witness to what I felt 109
there, not just in speech but in writing, when Fortune was thun-
dering but not yet sending her lightning bolts: after that everything was fulfilled with many other woes added on, so even
my prophecy, awful as it was, was outdone by the unending sequence of evils, which it would be far easier to lament than to
enumerate.[45]

110 Non multo ante id tempus in has terras, in quibus adolescens studiosus fueram, otiosus et iam vir reversus amicitia trahente illius cuius adhuc memorie multum debeo, Cisalpinam hanc Galliam, quam tantummodo prius attigeram, totam vidi non ut advena sed ut accola urbium multarum, Verone in primis et mox Parme ac Ferrarie, demum Patavi, quo me illa, quam discutere nescio, cathena eadem traxit amicitie, sed alterius viri optimi,
111 cuius casum nunquam sine dolore meminero. Qui cum undique maximus clarissimusque vir esset, peregrini parvique hominis et solo nomine cogniti nec unquam, ut ipse aiebat, nisi semel visi, idque in transitu, familiaritatem diu sic ambivit quasi per hoc magnum aliquid sibi sueque reipublice quesiturus. Et eius quidem urbis incolatus, illo superstite continuus michi, sicut auguror, futurus, eodem rebus exempto perpetuus tamen fuit, licet interruptus
112 ex causis. Proinde urbs hec quo primum tempore ad eam veni sic recenti peste illa terribili attrita erat, ut dehinc primogeniti illius providentia ac studio et usque ad hoc tempus inconcussa pace fateri oporteat unam hanc ex omnibus erectam potius quam deiectam, ad id vero quod anno antequam illuc venirem, hoc est ante pestis initium fuerat, imparem sibi ac dissimilem prorsus ut reliquas.

113 Mediolanum serius ac Ticinum novi: et quid vis dicam? Nulla omnium est que fuit non dico ante multa secula, sed nuper nostra
114 memoria; visa enim, non lecta loquor vel audita. Ipsa urbs Mediolanum, quam ante mille quingentos annos florentissimam lego et que, ut puto, nunquam magis quam nostra floruit etate, nunc non floret ut solita est, quamvis adhuc magnitudine et potentia
115 atque, ut dicitur, pondere suo stet. Cives suos interroga: fatebun-
116 tur hec ita esse tristiusque aliquid de suo addent. Quid nunc Pisas, ubi vite septimum annum egi, seu quid Senas loquar? Quid

Not much before, after returning to those lands where I had 110
been a studious youth, now a man and at leisure, drawn by the
friendship of that man to whose memory I owe so much, I saw all
of the Cisalpine part of Gaul which I had only touched on before,
not as a mere visitor but as a resident of many cities, especially
Verona, then Parma and Ferrara, finally Padua, where that same
bond of friendship, which I cannot shed, drew me of another excellent man, whose death I shall never recall without grief.[46] Al- 111
though he was the greatest and most glorious leader all around, he
so courted the friendship of an unimportant foreigner, known to
him only by name and, as he said, seen only once in passing, as if
he were winning some great gain for himself and his community.
While he lived, my residence in that city would, as I imagine, have
been lasting; but when he was taken from our world it still contin-
ued, although interrupted by special circumstances.[47] So this city, 112 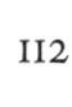
when I first came to it, was exhausted by the recent dreadful
plague,[48] but to the extent that subsequently, through the prudence and diligence of his son and heir, it has enjoyed undisturbed
peace up to this time, I must admit that this city alone has been
restored rather than ruined. Yet compared with what it was in the
year before I came there, that is before the onset of the plague, it
is weaker and unlike itself, just like the others.[49]

I came to know Milan and Pavia relatively late.[50] And what am 113 
I to say? None of all these cities is what it had been, I don't mean
many generations before, but recently, within our memory; for I
am speaking of what I saw, not what I read or heard. Milan itself, 114 
which I read was "most flourishing" fifteen hundred years ago[51]
and which, I think, never flourished so greatly as in our age, does
not flourish now as it was wont, although it still stands firm
thanks to its size and power and, as one says, sheer weight.[52] Ask 115 
her citizens: they will admit it is so and add some sadder details
from their own experience. What am I to say of Pisa, where I 116
passed the seventh year of my life, or about Siena? What about

dilectum michi primi exilii atque originis mee locum Aretium vici-
117 numque illi Perusium quid ve alias dicam? Una omnium conditio
est. Non sunt hodie quod heri, ut, cum sit mira varietas rerum,
tum incredibilis ac stupenda celeritas.

118 Possem te modo per Italiam totam, imo et per omnem Europam passim circumducere, nova ubilibet ad inceptum argumenta
reperturus, sed vereor ne me ipsum teque et alios, siqui hoc nostrum colloquium audituri lecturique sunt, fatigem, si te per omnes
terras stilo ducam quarum recens simul et misera et aperta muta-
119 tio est. Delectatus tamen sum . . . — nescio an sat proprie hoc
dixerim, nisi sit quedam in merore delectatio —, sed profecto libuit
michi tecum hactenus fando peregrinari per transactos annos ac
loca distantia, eaque maxime in quibus aliquando tecum fui, et
quod iter pedibus aut navibus mensi sumus calamo remetiri.

120 Nullo autem pacto harum rerum per memoriam indicta patria
transire possum. Illa vero quid est aliud quam varietatis infauste
121 argumentum evidens? Que nudiustertius convenientissimum nacta
vocabulum inter alias non italicas modo sed cristianas urbes rebus
omnibus usque ad invidiam florebat, mox deinde crebris malis extra, incendiis ac bellis intersectis ac pestibus, usque ad misericordiam deformata, omnes certe mortales, ante alios quidem suos
cives admonet, quanta sit in rebus pereuntibus spes habenda.

122 Hic michi contentiosus forte aliquis obviet. Est enim genus
hominum, quibus quoniam virium nichil est ad veritatem de-
fendendam et quiescere nesciunt, fallaciis hanc oppugnant idque
123 sibi artificium fecere. Quod negari igitur nequit in his quas dixi

my beloved Arezzo, the place of my birth and early exile, or about its neighbor Perugia and other cities?[53] They all suffer the same 117
condition; they are not today what they were yesterday, so that there is both an amazing variety as well as an incredible and dizzying speed in the change of circumstances.

I could lead you around all of Italy, rather through all Europe, 118
and everywhere find new evidence for the argument I have been advancing, but I am afraid of wearying myself and you and others (if there is anybody who is going to listen or read this conversation of ours), if I guide you with my pen through all these lands which have recently undergone this wretched and obvious transformation. Yet I have found pleasure—perhaps I am not expressing this 119
rightly, except that there is a kind of pleasure in grief—, but certainly I enjoyed traveling this far with you in words over the past years and remote places, especially those in which I was from time to time with you, and to retrace with the pen the path we followed on foot or shipboard.

But there is no way I can travel in my memory of these events 120
without mentioning my native land.[54] What else, if not the obvious proof of this ill-omened changeability, is that city, which only 121
the other day, possessing that most fitting name of Florence, flourished enough to provoke envy among all other cities, and not just Italian ones, but all Christian cities? Then shortly after, disfigured with the intrusion from outside of a rapid succession of woes, besides fires and wars and plagues, to the point of rousing men's pity, she warns all mortal men, and her own citizens in particular, how little hope one should put in perishable things.

At this point some argumentative fellow will oppose me. For 122
there is a kind of person, who, lacking any strength to defend the truth and unable to keep quiet, attacks the truth with false quibbles; they make this their profession. What cannot be denied he 123
will admit to be true in the cities I mentioned, but perhaps not in

urbibus, verum hoc esse fatebitur, in aliis forsitan non ita atque hoc respectu mutationem universi nullam esse, quod quantum uni
124 decreverit accrescit alteri. Cui ego respondeo: ostendat michi in
125 occidente aut in artho vel in una urbe contrarium et vicerit. Certe enim hec ipsa, unde tibi nunc scribo et cuius ad ultimum incola factus sum non tam oblectationem quam securitatem et quietem querens, Venetorum urbs, quamvis et consilio civium et locorum situ inter omnes alias nostri orbis prospero ac tranquillo sit in statu, fuit tamen aliquando prosperiore, tunc scilicet cum visendi gratia cum preceptore meo huc primum e Bononia adolescens veni; et hoc quoque sic esse non negantes cives audias, etsi—quod nec ipse negaverim—aliquid imo quamplurimum edificiis accesse-
126 rit. Sin me longius cavillator traxerit, fatebor me quod apud Seres Indosque agitur nescire, sed Egyptum Syriamque et Armeniam totamque Asiam Minorem non alio rerum incremento nec meliori
127 uti sorte quam nos. Nam Grecie calamitas vetus est, sed Scitharum recens, ut, unde nuper ingens annua vis frumenti navibus in hanc urbem invehi solebat, inde nunc servis onuste naves veniant quos urgente fame miseri venditant parentes iamque insolita et inextimabilis turba servorum utriusque sexus hanc pulcerrimam urbem scithicis vultibus et informi colluvie velut amnem nitidissi-
128 mum torrens turbidus inficit; que si suis emptoribus non esset acceptior quam michi et non amplius illorum oculos delectaret quam delectat meos, neque feda hec pubes hos angustos coartaret vicos neque melioribus assuetos formis inameno advenas contristaret occursu, sed intra suam Scithiam cum Fame arida ac pallenti lapidoso in agro, ubi Naso illam statuit, raras herbas dentibus velleret atque unguibus. Et hec quidem hactenus.

others, and he will say that in this respect there is no universal change, because whatever has been lost by one city will be gained
by another. My answer to him is: let him show me the opposite in 124
the West or North in even a single city, and he will have won.
Certainly this city of the Veneti from which I am writing now and 125
of which I have become a resident most lately, in search not so much of amusement as of safety and repose, is now, through the planning of its citizens and fortunate position, in a prosperous and calm condition among all other cities in this part of the world, but it was at one time more prosperous, to wit when I came here first as a youth from Bologna with my tutor for a visit.[55] And you would hear its citizens admitting that this is true, even if, as I myself would not deny, it has expanded somewhat with a quantity,
in fact a very great quantity, of buildings. But if this carping critic 126
draws me on further, I will admit I don't know what is going on among the Chinese and Indians,[56] but that Egypt and Syria and Armenia and all Asia Minor are not enjoying any improvement in
their conditions or a better fortune than us. Indeed the ruin of 127
Greece is an old story, but that of the Scythians is new:[57] while once a vast quantity of corn each year was imported to this city by ship, the ships now come loaded with slaves, whom their wretched parents are selling, being overwhelmed by starvation; and now an unfamiliar and uncountable crowd of slaves of both sexes pollutes this most beautiful city with Scythian features and ugly sewage, as
a stream swollen by storm water spoils the most shining river. If it 128
was not more welcome to its purchasers' eyes than to me and did not delight their eyes more warmly than it does mine, this loathsome young brood would not crowd the streets nor sadden those used to handsomer figures with unpleasant encounters, but would have stayed in Scythia with dried and pallid hunger "in that stony ground" where Ovid set her, and "pulled out scanty grasses with her teeth and nails."[58] But enough of this.

129 Sed instabitur et varietatem queri dicar immerito, quasi huius
130 tantummodo sit etatis cum sit omnium. Ego autem nichil queror,
sciens ab initio rerum volvi omnia, nichil stare. Nec dico: 'Quid
putas cause est quod priora tempora meliora fuere quam nunc
sunt?'; 'stulta est enim,' ut ait Salomon, 'huiuscemodi interrogatio.'
131 Multe quidem possunt esse cause, Deo note et quedam fortassis
132 hominibus. Non queror ergo mutata tempora nec causas quero,
sed mutationem astruo contra opinionem iuvenum nostrorum, qui
hec inter mala geniti, quia aliud nil viderunt, nil aliud fuisse con-
tendunt, inscii atque increduli, et mutationem temporum, mani-
festam prorsus ac flebilem, mutatis studiis nostris atque animis
133 imputant. Quos mutatos fateor et gaudeo, sed mutatio hec nichil
ad alteram; neque enim minus rapido acta impetu rota ingens vol-
vitur quod formica interim per illam segnis incedit.

134 Illud denique in litem veniet, mutationem hanc non rerum esse
nec temporum, ac nec mundi quidem, sed solorum hominum;
quod ipse etiam in parte non negem, sciens mundi appellatione
sepe homines accipi, quibus hauddubie factus est et quorum usui
mundus obsequitur; et sane mutationum huiuscemodi multe ipsis
in hominibus cause sunt et, siquis altius fodiat, fortasse omnes,
135 sed alie apparent, latent alie. Certe quod pietas, quod veritas, quod
fides, quod pax exulet, quod impietas, quod mendacium, quod
perfidia, quod discordia et bellum regnet et toto seviat orbe terrarum, quod predonum manus impie quasi iuste acies pro libito va-
gentur et vastent ac diripiant quicquid est obvium neque his urbes

But the critic will persist, and I shall be blamed for unjustly 129
complaining about diversity, as though what is common to all ages
were peculiar to this age. Now I am not complaining, knowing 130
that everything is subject to vicissitudes from the beginning and
nothing stands still. Nor am I saying: "What do you think is the
reason that earlier times were better than they are now?" For, as
Solomon says, "this kind of question is foolish,"[59] since there can 131
be many reasons known to God and some perhaps to mankind.
Therefore I am not complaining at the change of the times nor 132
looking for explanations, but I am setting out this change against
the opinion of our young fellows, who because they were born
amid these misfortunes and have seen nothing else, argue that
there has not been anything else, being ignorant and incredulous.
So they assign the obvious and lamentable change of circumstances to the change in our studies and attitudes. I admit these 133
have changed, and I am glad; but this change is not relevant to
that other one, and a vast wheel does not roll on any the less,
driven by its swift momentum, because a sluggish ant is walking
on top of it.

Finally the claim will be entered in the dispute that this change 134
is not one of things or times and not even of the world but only
among men. Even I would not deny that claim in part, since I
know that the phrase "the world" often refers to human society,
men by whom it was indeed shaped and whose convenience the
world obeys. Clearly many explanations of this change lie in men
themselves and, if anyone probes more deeply, perhaps all its
causes lie in mankind, but some are manifest and others not. Cer- 135
tainly, since piety and truth and loyalty and peace are in exile,
while impiety, falsehood, treachery, discord and warfare are ruling
and raging over the whole earth, and since impious bands of brigands wander as they choose like proper armies and lay waste and
plunder whatever is in their path, and neither cities nor kings have
the strength to resist them, or again, since morals are polluted,

obstare valeant neque reges, quod infecti mores, depravata studia, deformati habitus, palam est nonnisi in hominibus radicem mali totam esse, quamvis ego, ut iam dixi, non de causis nunc sed de rebus tantum disputem, que profecto nobis pueris adolescentibusque non erant.

136 Rara bella inter regna vel populos de finibus aut de iniuriis ge-
rebantur: societas contra omne genus humanum nulla usquam
137 nostro evo fuerat. Erant societates mercatorum, quas ipsi vidimus,
quibus ante omnes patria diu floruit mea, per quas quante com-
moditates afferrentur hominibus difficile est dictu, difficilius cre-
ditu; per has enim totus fere noster orbis regebatur, reges ac prin-
138 cipes universi harum ope et consilio fulti erant. Alterius generis
societates peregrinorum magno agmine devota loca Ierosolimam
139 Romamque petentium cernebantur. Fures ibant singulatim, noctu,
pavidi; nulle furum diurne acies campis explicabantur, nulli armati
societatum duces famam sibi gentium cladibus et propria feritate
140 quesierant. Quintus et vigesimus annus est ex quo auribus pri-
141 mum nostris horrisonum hoc nomen intonuit. Quod malum brevi
quantum creverit quorsum ve processerit videmus at miseri cives
et agricole imo et reges et pontifices usque ad summum maxi-
mumque omnium experti sunt, qui, ut supra attigi, ad Rodanum,
unde nuper abiit, semiobsessus ab illis atque ad indignam redemp-
tionem extitit coactus; quod nec ipse tunc tacitus tulit, sed inter
suos merito quidem graviter questus est, nec ego ad eum scribens
142 silui. Quis terribilem igitur et infandam hanc mutationem temporum non agnoscit aut quis negat? Consequens enim est ut aut
143 sensu careat aut pudore. Dissimulari nequit sese oculis ingerens
pessimarum ac novarum rerum fulgor horrificus ac lugubris

studies are perverted and manners disfigured, it is obvious that the evil is completely and exclusively rooted in human beings; although I am not now discussing causes, as I said,[60] but only events which certainly did not occur when we were boys and young men.

Then too there were occasional wars between kingdoms and 136
peoples about territorial boundaries and material injury, but never in the time of our youth was there an association against the
whole human race.[61] There were associations of merchants which 137
we have seen in person, the guilds through which my country long flourished beyond all others; it is hard to report and harder to believe what great advantages they brought to men.[62] In fact almost all of our earth was controlled through these associations,
and all kings and princes had relied on their aid and advice. As- 138
sociations of pilgrims of a different kind were seen marching in a mighty host for the sacred places of Jerusalem and Rome.[63]
Thieves moved around one at a time, by night and frightened; no 139
armies of thieves were drawn up on the plains by day, no armed leaders of these "companies" had won their fame by the defeats of
nations and innate savagery. It is now the twenty-fifth year since 140
this terrifying name first thundered in our ears,[64] and we see how 141
swiftly this evil has developed and to what point it has advanced, but the wretched townsfolk and peasants, and indeed kings and priests too, up to the highest and greatest priest of all, have suffered this. As I have already said, the pope is more or less besieged by them on the Rhône, which he just recently left, and is known to have been compelled to an outrageous ransom; he too did not endure this silently, but rightly complained grievously among his
own court, and I did not keep silent when I wrote to him.[65] So 142
who does not recognize, or who denies this terrible and unspeakable transformation of the times? For it would follow that he
lacked sense or shame. That horrendous and funereal flash of the 143
worst and most unprecedented affairs cannot be concealed, thrust-

quando ea nunc quotidie mundus infelix patitur que nuper hominum nullus audierat.

144 Quid de aliis? Nomen pestis auditum erat et in libris lectum,
145 pestis universalis exhausura orbem visa non erat nec audita. Hec
per annos iam viginti ita omnes terras proterit ut intermissa quidem alicubi forsitan aut lentescens, extincta utique nusquam sit
adhuc, ita in dies dum visa est abiisse revertitur brevique gaudio
circumventos aggreditur; et hec ipsa divine, nisi fallor, ire testis ac
scelerum humanorum, que si aliquando finirentur aut decrescerent
146 celestes quoque mitescerent ultiones. Terremotus preterea auditum
lectumque erat nomen, at rem ipsam ab historicis, rei causam a
philosophis querebamus et motiunculas nocturnas forte aliquas,
raras quidem et ambiguas somnioque simillimas, curiosi sibi homines fingebant; terremotum verum nostro evo nullus senserat.
147 Vigesimus annus est nunc — unum enim mali utriusque principium fuit — ex quo Alpes nostre, quarum motus insolitos ait Maro,
VIII Kal. Februarias tremuere inclinata iam parumper ad occasum
die Italieque simul ac Germanie pars magna contremuit tam vehementer ut adesse mundi finem inexperti quidam crederent, quibus
148 insueta prorsus et nunquam cogitata res erat. Verone tunc in bibliotheca mea solus sedens, quanquam non in totum rei nescius,
repentina tamen et nova re perculsus solo tremente sub pedibus et
undique concursantibus ac ruentibus libellis obstupui et egressus
thalamo familiam moxque populum trepidissime fluctuantem vidi.
149 Omnium in ore funereus pallor erat. Qui hunc proxime secutus
est anno Roma tremuit usque ad ruinam turrium ac templorum;
simul et partes Etrurie tremuerunt; de quo tunc sollicitus ad
150 Socratem nostrum scripsi. Anno inde septimo tremuit inferior

ing itself before our eyes, given that the unhappy world suffers every day what until recently no man had heard of.

What about other matters? The name of the plague had been 144
heard and read about in books,[66] but that universal plague that
would empty out the world had not been seen or heard of. For 145
twenty years this has trampled so fiercely on all lands that although it is suspended or retarded in some places, it certainly has not been extinguished anywhere yet; so often it comes back days after it seemed to have departed and assails men tricked into a brief rejoicing.[67] And this itself is, unless I deceive myself, evidence of divine anger and human crimes, whereas if they at some time should end or diminish, acts of celestial vengeance would also
grow mild. Besides this, the word "earthquake" was heard or read, 146
but we looked to the historians for the actual event and the natural scientists for its explanation.[68] Inquiring men imagined tremors by night, but rare and uncertain and like mere dreams; no man
had felt a real earthquake in our age. It is now the twentieth year 147
(for both evils had the same beginning) since our Alps, whose disturbances are called unusual by Vergil, trembled on the 25th of January, when the day was gradually sinking toward sunset, and a large part of Italy and Germany trembled at the same time so violently that ignorant men thought the end of the world was at hand, since this phenomenon was unfamiliar and unimaginable.[69]
At that time I was sitting alone in my library at Verona, and 148
though not completely ignorant of the occurrence, I was shattered by the sudden new event, as the ground trembled under my feet and my books fell down and hit each other on all sides; I was dazed and left my chamber to see my household and then the common people roiled by the utmost panic. There was a deadly
pallor on everyone's face. In the following year Rome was shaken 149
so badly it caused the collapse of towers and churches; at the same time areas of Tuscany were shaken and I wrote in anxiety about
this to our dear Socrates.[70] Seven years later lower Germany and 150

Germania totaque Rheni vallis, quo tremore Basilea concidit, non
tam magna urbs quam pulchra et ut videbatur stabilis; sed contra
151 nature impetum nichil est stabile. Inde ego paucis ante diebus
abieram Cesare ibi hoc nostro, bono quidem mitique principe sed
ad omnia lento, per mensem expectato; qui michi tandem in ex-
152 trema barbarie querendus fuit. De quo motu ad Iohannem, urbis
illius venerandum presulem, scribere animus fuit, quod ab illo satis honorifice visum me non obliviscerer, et an scripserim non
153 memini; apud me autem exemplum epistole non extat. Ceterum
die illo in ipsius Rheni ripis hinc atque hinc octoginta vel eo am-
154 plius castella solo equata referuntur. Futurum nostra illa prima
etate portentum memorabile si pastoris leve tugurium tremuisset;
155 at malorum usus metum ac stuporem mortalibus excutit. Et in his
quidem mutatio de qua loquor eminet causis latentibus, ut dicebam, nisi quod credendum est, ut alia, sic et hec culpis hominum
156 provenire, quarum nullus est modus aut numerus; interesse autem
quod illa homines faciunt, hec natura permittente quidem aut
iubente Deo propter humana flagitia; que si quando desinerent,
desinerent et flagella.

157 Postremo, quecunque sit malorum causa, quisquis agens, hec
158 veritas est. En, pater, ut die uno annos nostros omnes tibi ante
oculos congessi, merito quidem longe impares, numero autem
pares, quem ego nuper ad amicum scribens bona fide sum profes-
159 sus. Tu an idem facias an adhuc, quod nonnulli senum solent,
iuventam respiciens aliquid etiam nunc occultes, nescio. Vive felix
et vale, nostri memor.

the entire Rhine valley were shaken with an earthquake which brought down Basel, a city not so great as it was beautiful and firmly established—as it seemed; but nothing is stable against the
onslaught of nature.[71] I had left there a few days before, after wait- 151
ing a month for our Caesar, a good and mild prince but one slow to act in any business. From there I had to seek him out in the
remotest barbarian region.[72] I meant to write about this earth- 152
quake to Johannes, the reverend bishop of that city, because I did not forget that I had been welcomed by him with generous treatment, but I do not remember whether I wrote; at any rate I have
no copy of the letter.[73] However, on that day it was reported that 153
eighty or more castles on both banks of the Rhine were leveled to
the ground. In our first youth it would have been a memorable 154
portent if a shepherd's flimsy hut had shaken; but being accustomed to misfortunes has driven fear and amazement out of mortals. And the change I am talking about is conspicuous in those 155
events, though the reasons are hidden, as I said,[74] except that we must believe that these evils, like others, happen through the sins
of men, which have no limit or number; the difference is that men 156
commit the sins but nature causes the evils, with God's permission or even command, because of human wickedness, and if this ever were to cease, then its scourging would also cease.

In short, whatever is the cause of these evils, whoever inflicts 157
them, this is the truth. See, Father, how I have heaped all our 158
years up in front of you within one day, and though they are far different in importance, they are the same in number, as I sincerely
declared when writing recently to my friend.[75] Whether you are 159
doing the same or, as a number of old men do, while looking back to your youth, are still suppressing something even now, I don't know. Live happily and fare well, keeping me in your heart.

: 2 :

## *Posteritati.*

1 Fuerit tibi forsan de me aliquid auditum; quanquam et hoc dubium sit, an exiguum et obscurum longe nomen seu locorum seu temporum perventurum sit. Et illud forsitan optabis nosse: quid hominis fuerim aut quis operum exitus meorum, eorum maxime quorum ad te fama pervenerit vel quorum vel tenue nomen audieris. Et de primo quidem varie erunt hominum voces; ita enim ferme quisque loquitur, ut impellit non veritas sed voluptas: nec laudis nec infamie modus est. Fui autem vestro de grege unus, mortalis homuncio, nec magne admodum nec vilis originis, familia, ut de se ait Augustus Cesar, antiqua, natura quidem non iniquo neque inverecundo animo, nisi ei consuetudo contagiosa no-
2 cuisset. Adolescentia me fefellit, iuventa corripuit, senecta autem correxit, experimentoque perdocuit verum illud quod diu ante perlegeram, quoniam adolescentia et voluptas vana sunt; imo etatum temporumque omnium Conditor, qui miseros mortales de nichilo tumidos aberrare sinit interdum, ut peccatorum suorum,
3 vel sero, memores sese agnoscant. Corpus iuveni non magnarum virium sed multe dexteritatis obtigerat; forma non glorior excellenti, sed que placere viridioribus annis posset: colore vivido inter candidum et subnigrum, vivacibus oculis et visu per longum tempus acerrimo, qui preter spem supra sexagesimum etatis annum me destituit, ut indignanti michi ad ocularium confugiendum esset auxilium. Tota etate sanissimum corpus senectus invasit, et solita morborum acie circumvenit.

: 2 :

## *To Posterity.*

Perhaps you will have heard something of me, though even this is 1
questionable, whether my humble and obscure name will have traveled over the distance, whether of place or time. And maybe you will desire to know what sort of man I was, or about the success of my works: most of all of the works whose fame has reached you, or of whose reputation you have faintly heard. In fact men's judgments about the first question will be different, since that is how each man speaks, not driven by the truth, but as his pleasure inclines him; there is no limit to glory nor infamy. Now I was one of your own tribe, a mortal fellow of neither great nor humble origin, from an ancient family, as Augustus says of himself,[1] by nature of no mean or immodest spirit, except when infectious
company had caused it harm. My boyhood misled me, my young 2
manhood carried me off, but old age corrected me and taught me by experience the truth that I had read diligently long before, that youth and pleasure are hollow;[2] rather it was the Creator of all ages who taught me, who sometimes lets wretched mortals, who are arrogant without any grounds, go astray, so that they may be mindful of their sins, however late, and come to know themselves.[3] As a young man my body was not one of great strength 3
but quite agile; I do not boast a handsome appearance but one that was able to please in my greener years; my complexion was fresh, somewhere between fair and dark, my eyes were lively and for a long time I enjoyed very keen eyesight, which suddenly abandoned me after my sixtieth year, so that I reluctantly resorted to the aid of spectacles.[4] Old age assailed my body, which had been perfectly healthy all my life, and surrounded me with the usual battalions of disease.

4 Divitiarum contemptor eximius: non quod divitias non optarem, sed labores curasque oderam, opum comites inseparabiles. Non michi, ut ista cura esset, lautarum facultas epularum: ego autem tenui victu et cibis vulgaribus vitam egi letius, quam cum exquisitissimis dapibus omnes Apicii successores. Convivia que dicuntur, cum sint comessationes modestie et bonis moribus inimice, semper michi displicuerunt. Laboriosum et inutile ratus sum ad hunc finem vocare alios, nec minus ab aliis vocari; convivere autem cum amicis adeo iocundum ut eorum superventu nil gratius
5 habuerim, nec unquam volens sine sotio cibum sumpserim. Nichil michi magis quam pompa displicuit, non solum quia mala et humilitati contraria, sed quia difficilis et quieti adversa est. Amore acerrimo sed unico et honesto in adolescentia laboravi, et diutius laborassem, nisi iam tepescentem ignem mors acerba sed utilis extinxisset. Libidinum me prorsus expertem dicere posse optarem quidem, sed si dicam mentiar. Hoc secure dixerim: me quanquam fervore etatis et complexionis ad id raptum, vilitatem illam tamen
6 semper animo execratum. Mox vero ad quadragesimum etatis annum appropinquans, dum adhuc et caloris satis esset et virium, non solum factum illud obscenum, sed eius memoriam omnem sic abieci, quasi nunquam feminam aspexissem. Quod inter primas felicitates meas numero, Deo gratias agens, qui me adhuc integrum et vigentem tam vili et michi semper odioso servitio liberavit. Sed ad alia procedo.

7 Sensi superbiam in aliis non in me; et cum parvus fuerim, semper minor iudicio meo fui. Ira mea michi persepe nocuit, aliis nunquam. Intrepide glorior, quia scio me verum loqui, indignantissimi

I was exceptional in my scorn for wealth, not because I did not desire riches, but because I shunned the toils and anxieties that are inseparable companions of wealth. I did not have the resources for elegant dinners to cause me that trouble; instead I spent my life more happily with a plain diet and ordinary foods than all of Apicius' successors with their immensely refined banquets.[5] Dinner parties, as they are called, always offended me, since feasts are the enemies of moderation and good behavior. I thought it toilsome and harmful to invite others for this purpose, and no less to be invited by them, whereas spending time with my friends was so enjoyable that I found nothing more welcome than their visits, and 4
never willingly took a meal without a companion. Nothing of- 5
fended me more than display, not only because it is bad and opposed to humility, but because it is inconvenient and hostile to calmness. I suffered in my youth from a most passionate but single-minded and honorable love, and would have suffered longer, if a bitter but beneficial death had not put an end to my now fading passion.[6] I would have liked to be able to say I was quite innocent of lust, but if I said so I would be lying. This I could say without doubt, that although I was swept into it by the heat of youth and my constitution, I always cursed that vileness in my
heart. But soon, approaching my fortieth year, when I still had 6
heat and strength enough, I cast away not only that obscene activity but its entire memory, as though I had never looked upon a woman.[7] This is something I count among my first good fortunes, thanking God that he had freed me of such a low and always loathsome enslavement while I was still healthy and vigorous. But I move on to other things.

I felt pride in others but not in myself, and when I was little I 7
always appeared inferior to my own judgment. My anger very often harmed me, but never others. I make this boast without fear because I know I am telling the truth. My spirit was prone to

animi, sed offensarum obliviosissimi, beneficiorum vero permemo-
ris. Amicitiarum appetentissimus honestarum et fidelissimus cultor fui, sed hoc est supplicium senescentium: ut suorum sepissime
8 mortes fleant. Principum ac regum familiaritatibus et nobilium
amicitiis usque ad invidiam fortunatus fui. Multos tamen, eorum
quos valde amabam, effugi: tantus fuit michi insitus amor libertatis, ut cuius vel nomen ipsum illi esse contrarium videretur, omni
9 studio declinarem. Maximi regum mee etatis et amarunt et co-
luerunt me; cur autem nescio: ipsi viderint. Et ita cum quibusdam
fui ut ipsi quodammodo mecum essent; et eminentia eorum nul-
10 lum tedium, commoda multa perceperim. Ingenio fui equo potius
quam acuto, ad omne bonum et salubre studium apto, sed ad
moralem precipue philosophiam et ad poeticam prono; quam ipsam processu temporis neglexi, sacris literis delectatus, in quibus
sensi dulcedinem abditam, quam aliquando contempseram, poeti-
11 cis literis non nisi ad ornatum reservatis. Incubui unice inter multa
ad notitiam vetustatis, quoniam michi semper etas ista displicuit;
ut nisi me amor carorum in diversum traheret, alia qualibet etate
natus esse semper optaverim et hanc oblivisci, nisus animo me aliis
semper inserere. Historicis itaque delectatus sum; non minus tamen offensus eorum discordia, secutus in dubio quo me vel veri
12 similitudo rerum vel scribentium traxit auctoritas. Eloquio, ut
quidam dixerunt, claro ac potenti; ut michi visum est, fragili et
obscuro. Neque vero in comuni sermone cum amicis aut cum
familiaribus eloquentie unquam cura me attigit; mirorque eam
curam Augustum Cesarem suscepisse. Ubi autem res ipsa vel locus
vel auditor aliter poscere visus est, paulo annisus sum; idque quam
efficaciter, nescio: eorum sit iudicium coram quibus dixi. Ego,

indignation but also to forgetting wrongs, while I keenly recalled kindnesses. I was most eager for honorable friendships and most faithful in tending them, but here is the punishment of those who grow old, that they are often in tears at the deaths of those they
love. I was enviably blessed by the intimacy of princes and kings 8
and by the friendship of noble men. But I avoided many of them, even those I greatly loved; so great was my innate love of liberty that I shunned intently anyone whose very name seemed hostile to
it. The greatest kings of my generation loved and paid court to me, 9
why I don't know; but that is their business.[8] And I spent time with some of them in such a way that they were spending time on my terms, and experienced no boredom from their distinction, but
many advantages. I was even-tempered rather than sharp-witted, 10
well fitted to every good and healthy pursuit, but particular inclined to moral philosophy and to poetry; yet I neglected this too with the advance of time, taking delight in sacred writings, in which I felt a hidden sweetness which I had once despised,
keeping poetic composition only for adornment.[9] Amongst many 11
choices I devoted myself uniquely to the knowledge of antiquity, since the current age always offended me, so that if the love of those dear to me had not pulled me in the opposite direction I would always have longed to be born in another age and to forget this one, striving to insert myself in spirit into other periods. So I took pleasure in historians, yet was alienated by their disagreement, following the interpretation, in matters of doubt, to which
either probability or the authority of the writers attracted me. As 12
some said, I was gifted with a brilliant and powerful eloquence, but as it seemed to me it was frail and dim. Attentiveness to eloquence did not interest me either in general conversation with friends or with acquaintances; I am amazed that Augustus took such pains over it.[10] But when the occasion or the place or audience seemed to require something special, I put in additional effort, though I don't know how effective it was; let my audience be

modo bene vixissem, qualiter dixissem parvifacerem: ventosa gloria est de solo verborum splendore famam querere.

13 Honestis parentibus florentinis origine—fortuna mediocri, et, ut verum fatear, ad inopiam vergente—sed patria pulsis, Aretii in exilio natus sum, anno huius etatis ultime que a Cristo incipit
14 MCCCIV, die lune ad auroram XIII kalendas Augusti. Tempus meum sic vel fortuna vel voluntas mea nunc usque partita est. Primum illum vite annum neque integrum Aretii egi, ubi in lucem me natura protulerat; sex sequentes Ancise, paterno in rure supra Florentiam quattuordecim passuum milibus, revocata ab exilio genetrice; octavum Pisis, nonum ac deinceps in Gallia Transalpina, ad levam Rodani ripam—Avinio urbi nomen—ubi romanus pontifex turpi in exilio Cristi tenet Ecclesiam et tenuit diu, licet ante paucos annos Urbanus quintus eam reduxisse videretur in suam
15 sedem. Sed res, ut patet, in nichilum rediit, ipso—quod gravius fero—tunc etiam superstite et quasi boni operis penitente. Qui si modicum plus vixisset, hauddubie sensisset quid michi de eius abitu videretur. Iam calamus erat in manibus, sed ipse confestim gloriosum principium, ipsum et vita destituit. Infelix! Quam feliciter ante Petri aram mori et in domo propria potuisset! Sive enim successores eius in sua sede mansissent, et ipse boni operis auctor erat; sive abiissent, et tanto ipsius clarior virtus, quanto illorum culpa conspectior. Sed hec longior atque incidens est querela: redeo ad ordinem.

16 Ibi igitur, ventosissimi amnis ad ripam, pueritiam sub parentibus, ac deinde sub vanitatibus meis adolescentiam totam egi. Non

the judges. So long as I lived rightly I would not care much how I spoke: it is a windy kind of glory to seek fame just from the splendor of one's words.

My origin was from honorable Florentine parents (perhaps only 13
middle in rank and to speak truly, approaching poverty), but exiled from their native land, and I was born at Arezzo in exile in the one thousand three hundred and fourth year of this last age that began with Christ, on a Monday at dawn, on the 20th of
July.[11] This is how either fortune or my own will divided my life. I 14
spent that first year of life, not quite complete, at Arezzo, where nature had brought me to birth, then the next six years at Incisa, on my father's estate fourteen miles from Florence, when my mother was restored from exile; I spent the eighth year at Pisa, and my ninth and subsequent years in Transalpine Gaul on the left bank of the Rhône (the city is called Avignon),[12] where the Roman pope keeps and has long kept the Church of Christ in shameful exile, although a few years ago Urban V seemed to have
restored it to its proper place. But as it appears, the attempt came 15
to nothing even while—something I mind more deeply—he himself was still alive and apparently regretting his honorable enterprise. If he had lived just a little longer I don't doubt he would have realized what I felt about his withdrawal. The pen was already in my hands but he rapidly deserted his glorious beginning, as life deserted him. Unhappy man! How happily he could have died before the altar of Peter and in his real home! If his successors had stayed in their proper place he too would have had the credit for a good undertaking, or if they had deserted, his own virtue would have been as much more glorious as their guilt was more conspicuous. But this is too long a complaint, and intrusive. I return to my narrative.

So I spent my boyhood on the bank of that most windy river[13] 16
under my parents' control, and then spent my entire youth at the whim of my own frivolities. But my stay there was not without

tamen sine magnis digressionibus: namque hoc tempore Carpentoras, civitas parva et illi ad orientem proxima, quadriennio integro me habuit; inque his duabus aliquantulum grammatice dyaletice ac rethorice, quantum etas potuit, didici; quantum scilicet in scolis
17 disci solet, quod quantulum sit, carissime lector, intelligis. Inde ad Montem Pessulanum legum ad studium profectus, quadriennium ibi alterum, inde Bononiam, et ibi triennium expendi et totum iuris civilis corpus audivi: futurus magni proventus adolescens, ut multi opinabantur, si cepto insisterem. Ego vero studium illud omne destitui, mox ut me parentum cura destituit, non quia legum michi non placeret auctoritas, que absque dubio magna est et romane antiquitatis plena, qua delector, sed quia earum usus nequitia hominum depravatur. Itaque piguit perdiscere quo inhoneste uti nollem, et honeste vix possem, et, si vellem, puritas inscitie tribuenda esset.

18 Itaque secundum et vigesimum annum agens domum redii. Domum voco avinionense illud exilium ubi ab infantie mee fine fueram: habet enim consuetudo proximam vim nature. Ibi ergo iam nosci ego et familiaritas mea a magnis viris expeti ceperat; cur autem nescire nunc me fateor et mirari, tunc equidem non mirabar, ut qui michi, more etatis, omni honore dignissimus viderer.
19 Ante alios expetitus fui a Columnensium clara et generosa familia, que tunc romanam curiam frequentabat, dicam melius: illustrabat. A quibus accitus, et michi nescio an et nunc, sed tunc certe indebito in honore habitus, ab illustri et incomparabili viro Iacobo de Columna, lomberiensi tunc epyscopo, cui nescio an parem seu viderim seu visurus sim, in Vasconiam ductus, sub collibus Pireneis estatem prope celestem multa et domini et comitum iocunditate

great detours, for at this time Carpentras, a little city near to Avignon on the East, kept me for a full four years,[14] and between the two cities I learned a certain amount of grammar, dialectic and rhetoric, as far as my youth was able; as much in fact as is usually learned in schools, and you know, dear reader, just how little that is. From there I set out to Montpellier to study the law and spent 17
another four-year period there, and from there to Bologna, where I spent three years and attended lectures on the entire corpus of civil law and was judged, as many thought, to be a young man of great promise, if I would stick to my undertaking.[15] But in fact I soon abandoned the whole discipline when deprived of parental guidance, not because I disliked the authority of the laws, which is undoubtedly great and full of Roman antiquity,[16] which delights me, but because their application is perverted by the wickedness of men. So I was not satisfied to learn thoroughly what I was unwilling to use dishonestly, and could scarcely use honorably, and if I wished, my purity would be attributed to ignorance.[17]

So during my twenty-second year I returned home. I call "home" 18
that exile in Avignon where I had lived since the end of my infancy, since familiarity has a power near to that of nature. There I began to be known and great men sought my friendship. But I admit I don't know now and I wonder why they did so, but then I did not wonder, since because of my youth I thought myself most worthy of every honor. I was courted by the famous and 19
noble family of Colonna before all others; at that time they attended the Roman Curia, or better, gave the Curia brilliance. Summoned by them and treated with honor beyond my deserts (I won't say whether it is still undeserved, but certainly it was at that time), I was taken to Gascony by that brilliant and incomparable man Giacomo Colonna, then bishop of Lombez—and I don't know whether I have ever seen or will ever see his like. I spent an almost heavenly summer enjoying the pleasant company of my master and companions under the Pyrenaean hills, so that I shall

20 transegi, ut semper tempus illud memorando suspirem. Inde rediens sub fratre eius Iohanne de Columna cardinali, multos per
annos non quasi sub domino sed sub patre, imo ne id quidem, sed
cum fratre amantissimo, imo mecum et propria mea in domo fui.
Quo tempore iuvenilis me impulit appetitus ut et Gallias et Germaniam peragrarem. Et licet alie cause fingerentur ut profectionem meam meis maioribus approbarem, vera tamen causa erat
21 multa videndi ardor ac studium. In qua peregrinatione Parisius
primum vidi, et delectatus sum inquirere quid verum quidve fabu-
losum de illa urbe narraretur. Inde reversus Romam adii, cuius
vidende desiderio ab infantia ardebam; et huius familie magnani-
mum genitorem Stephanum de Columna, virum cuilibet antiquorum parem, ita colui atque ita sibi acceptus fui, ut inter me et
quemlibet filiorum nil diceres interesse. Qui viri excellentis amor
et affectus usque ad vite eius extremum uno erga me semper tenore permansit; et in me nunc etiam vivit, neque unquam desinet
22 nisi ego ante desiero. Inde etiam reversus, cum omnium sed in
primis illius tediosissime urbis fastidium atque odium, naturaliter
animo meo insitum, ferre non possem, diverticulum aliquod quasi
portum querens, repperi vallem perexiguam sed solitariam atque
amenam, que Clausa dicitur, quindecim passuum milibus ab Avinione distantem, ubi fontium rex omnium Sorgia oritur. Captus
loci dulcedine, libellos meos et meipsum illuc transtuli. Longa erit
historia si pergam exequi quid ibi multos ac multos egerim per
23 annos. Hec summa est: quod quicquid fere opusculorum michi
excidit, ibi vel actum vel ceptum vel conceptum est; que tam multa
fuerunt ut usque ad hanc etatem me exerceant ac fatigent. Fuit
enim michi ut corpus sic ingenium: magis pollens dexteritate
quam viribus; itaque multa michi facilia cogitatu, que executione
24 difficilia pretermisi. Hic michi ipsa locorum facies suggessit ut Bucolicum carmen, silvestre opus, aggrederer, et Vite solitarie libros

always sigh for that unforgettable time.[18] On my return I worked 20
for his brother, Cardinal Giovanni, for many years, not serving
him as a master but as a father—no, not even that, but as though
he were a most loving brother. In fact it was like being with my
own self and in my own home. At that time my young man's in-
quisitiveness sent me to travel across the Gauls and through Germany.[19] And though I invented other reasons to win approval for
my journey from my superiors, the real motive was my passion
and enthusiasm to see many sights. On this journey I saw Paris 21
for the first time and was delighted to investigate which tales told
about that city were true and which were fanciful. After my return
from Paris, I went to Rome which I had been passionate to see
from my infancy. And I paid such respect to Stefano Colonna, the
greathearted progenitor of that family, a man equal to any of the
ancients, and was so welcome to him that you would say there was
no distinction between me and any of his sons. The love and affection of that excellent man endured consistently to the very end of
his life, and still lives in me, nor will it ever cease unless I myself
have ceased to be.[20] When I returned to Avignon, since I could 22
not bear the distaste and loathing of everything but especially of
that most distasteful city, which was innate in me, I sought out a
place apart like some haven, and found a tiny valley, lonely and
pleasing, called "The Enclosed Valley," fifteen miles from Avignon,
where the Sorgue surfaces as king of all springs. Enchanted by the
sweetness of this place, I moved my books and myself there. It will
be a long tale if I try to follow in detail what I did there for many,
many years. In sum, however, almost any work I ever happened to 23
write was either completed or begun or conceived there; and these
were so many that up to my present age they still harry and weary
me. For my intellect was like my body, more effective in agility
than strength: so I left aside many works as easy to conceive, but
difficult to execute. Here the actual aspect of the place prompted 24
me to attempt the *Bucolic Poem*, a pastoral work, and two books *On*

duos ad Philippum, magnum semper virum sed parvum tunc
epyscopum cavallicensem, nunc magnum sabinensem epyscopum
cardinalem; qui michi iam solus omnium veterum superstes, non
me epyscopaliter, ut Ambrosius Augustinum, sed fraterne dilexit
25 ac diligit. Illis in montibus vaganti, sexta quadam feria maioris
hebdomade, cogitatio incidit, et valida, ut de Scipione Africano
illo primo, cuius nomen mirum inde a prima michi etate carum
fuit, poeticum aliquid heroico carmine scriberem (sed, subiecti de
nomine, Africe nomen libro dedi, operi, nescio qua vel sua vel mea
fortuna, dilecto multis antequam cognito), quod tunc magno ceptum impetu, variis mox distractus curis intermisi.

26 Illis in locis moram trahenti — dictu mirabile! — uno die et ab
urbe Roma senatus, et de Parisius cancellarii Studii ad me litere
pervenerunt, certatim me ille Romam, ille Parisius ad percipien-
dam lauream poeticam evocantes. Quibus ego iuveniliter glori-
abundus et me dignum iudicans quo me dignum tanti viri iudica-
rent, nec meritum meum sed aliorum librans testimonia, parumper
tamen hesitavi cui potius aurem darem. Super quo consilium Io-
hannis de Columna cardinalis supra nominati per literas expetii.
27 Erat enim adeo vicinus ut, cum sibi sero scripsissem, die altero
ante horam tertiam responsum eius acciperem. Cuius consilium
secutus, romane urbis auctoritatem omnibus preferendam statui;
et de petitione et de approbatione consilii eius mea duplex ad illum extat epystola. Ivi ergo; et quamvis ego, more iuvenum, rerum
mearum benignissimus iudex essem, erubui tamen de me ipso
testimonium meum sequi, vel eorum a quibus evocabar; quod proculdubio non fecissent, nisi me dignum oblato honore iudicassent.

*Solitary Life* dedicated to Philippe, always a great man but at that time a modest bishop of Cavaillon, and now the mighty cardinal bishop of Sabina;[21] he is now the only survivor of all the old friends, a man who has always loved me and still loves me not like a bishop, as Ambrose loved Augustine,[22] but like a brother. As I 25
wandered in those hills on the sixth holy day of the Easter week, the idea came to me, and it was a powerful one, of writing some poem in epic verse on the first Scipio Africanus, whose marvelous name had been dear to me from my earliest years; but I gave to the book the name *Africa* based on its theme—a work, I am not sure whether by its good fortune or mine, that was loved by many even before it was known. But though it was begun with great enthusiasm at the time, I soon suspended work on it, distracted by various anxieties.[23]

When I was lingering in those places—wondrous to relate—I 26
received on the same day letters both from the senate of the city of Rome and from the chancellor of the University of Paris, who competed in summoning me, the former to Rome and the latter to Paris, to receive the laurel of poetry. In youthful pride, judging myself worthy because such great men thought me worthy, weighing up not my deserts but other men's recommendations, I still hesitated a little while as to whom I should obey, and I asked advice from Cardinal Giovanni Colonna, whom I mentioned above, by letter.[24] But actually he was so near that although I wrote to 27
him late in the day I received his reply the next day before the third hour. Following his advice I decided the authority of the city of Rome should be preferred to all others; and my two letters to him are still extant in which I requested his advice and approved it once received. So I went, and although like most young men I was a most generous assessor of my own abilities, I blushed to follow my own self-commendation, or that of the men who had summoned me; but beyond doubt they would not have done so if they had not thought me worthy of the honor they offered.

28 Unde Neapolim primum petere institui; et veni ad illum summum et regem et philosophum Robertum, non regno quam literis
clariorem, quem unicum regem et scientie amicum et virtutis nostra etas habuit, ut ipse de me quod sibi visum esset censeret. A
quo qualiter visus et cui quam acceptus fuerim, et ipse nunc miror
et tu, si noveris, lector puto mirabere. Sed longa nimis historia est.
29 Audita autem adventus mei causa, mirum in modum exhilaratus
est, et iuvenilem cogitans fidutiam et forsitan cogitans honorem,
quem peterem, sua gloria non vacare, quod ego eum solum iudicem ydoneum e cuntis mortalibus elegissem. Quid multa? Post
innumeras verborum collationes variis de rebus, ostensamque sibi
Africam illam meam, qua usqueadeo delectatus est ut eam sibi
inscribi magno pro munere posceret — quod negare nec potui certe
nec volui —, super eo tandem pro quo veneram certum michi de-
putavit diem, et a meridie ad vesperam me tenuit. Et quoniam,
crescente materia, breve tempus apparuit, duobus proximis diebus
idem fecit. Sic triduo excussa ignorantia mea, die tertio me dignum laurea iudicavit. Eam michi Neapoli offerebat et, ut assenti-
rer, precibus etiam multis urgebat; vicit amor Rome venerandam
30 tanti regis instantiam. Itaque, inflexibile propositum meum cer-
nens, literas michi et nuntios ad senatum romanum dedit, quibus
de me iudicium suum magno favore professus est. Quod quidem
tunc iudicium regium et multorum et meo in primis iudicio consonum fuit; hodie et ipsius et meum et omnium idem sentientium
iudicium non probo: plus enim in eum valuit amor et etatis favor
quam veri studium. Veni tamen; et quamlibet indignus, tanto tamen fretus fisusque iudicio, summo cum gaudio Romanorum, qui
illi solemnitati interesse potuerunt, lauream poeticam adhuc
scolasticus rudis adeptus sum. De quibus etiam et carmine et soluta oratione epystole mee sunt. Hec michi laurea scientie nichil,

From there I began first to make for Naples and I came to Rob- 28
ert, that supreme philosopher and king, distinguished greatly for
his monarchy but even more in literature, the only king whom our
age possessed as a friend to both knowledge and virtue, so that he
would pass judgment in person of how I seemed to him.[25] And I
marvel now how he looked upon me and how welcome I was to
him, and you, reader, would marvel too, I think, if you knew. But
the story is too long. Now when he heard the reason for my com- 29
ing he was marvelously cheered, both thinking of my youthful
confidence and perhaps that the honor which I was seeking did
not lack glory for him, inasmuch as I had chosen him as the only
adequate judge among all mortal men. In short, after countless
verbal exchanges on various topics and after I had shown him my
*Africa*, which so delighted him that he asked as a great tribute that
I should dedicate it to him (which I neither could nor wanted to
deny him), he appointed a fixed day for the hearing I had come to
seek, and kept me from noon to the evening. And as the material
increased and the time seemed too short, he did the same thing on
the next two days. When he had explored my ignorance over three
days he judged me worthy of the laurel on the third. He offered
the laurel to me at Naples and even urged me with many supplications to consent; but the love of Rome overcame the urgency of so
great a king. So seeing my intention was inflexible, he gave me a 30
letter and dispatches to the Roman senate in which he declared his
judgment on me with great favor. This judgment of the king
matched that of many and indeed my own, but today I do not approve of his verdict or mine or of all those who shared this opinion; for his affection and favor to my youth was stronger than his
devotion to the truth. Still I came, and unworthy as I was, relying
and trusting on so great a verdict, with the great rejoicing of the
Romans who were able to take part in this ceremony, I obtained
the laurel of poetry while still a raw student. And there are letters
of mine in both verse and prose about this.[26] This laurel won me

plurimum vero quesivit invidie; sed hec quoque historia longior est quam poscat hic locus.

31 Inde ergo digressus Parmam veni et cum illis de Corrigia viris in me liberalissimis atque optimis, sed inter se male concordibus, qui tunc urbem illam tali regimine gubernabant, quale nec ante in memoria hominum habuerat civitas illa, nec etate hac, ut auguror,
32 habitura est, aliquantulum tempus exegi. Et suscepti memor honoris, solicitusque ne indigno collatus videretur, cum die quodam in montana conscendens forte trans Entiam amnem reginis in finibus silvam que Plana dicitur adiissem, subito loci specie percussus, ad intermissam Africam stilum verti, et fervore animi qui sopitus videbatur excitato, scripsi aliquantulum die illo; post continuis diebus quotidie aliquid, donec Parmam rediens et repostam ac tranquillam nactus domum (que postea empta nunc etiam mea est) tanto ardore opus illud non magno in tempore ad exitum deduxi, ut ipse quoque nunc stupeam. Inde reversus, ad fontem Sorgie et ad solitudinem transalpinam redii. [. . .] Et intra breve tempus extincta illa Columnensium gloriosa, sed, heu, nimium caduca familia, iterum ad Italiam redii, cum iam quartum et quadragesimum etatis annum post terga relinquerem diuque et Parme et Verone versatus, et ubique, Deo gratias, carus habitus multo amplius quam valerem.

33 Longum post tempus, viri optimi et cuius nescio an e numero dominorum quisquam similis sua etate vir fuerit (imo vero scio quod nullus), Iacobi de Carraria iunioris, fame preconio benivolentiam adeptus, nuntiisque et literis usque trans Alpes quando ibi eram, et per Italiam ubicunque fui, multos per annos tantis precibus fatigatus sum et in suam solicitatus amicitiam, ut, quamvis de

no knowledge but a great deal of ill will; but this story too is longer than this letter requires.

So departing from Rome I came to Parma and spent some small time with the family of da Correggio, who were excellent men and generous to me but in conflict with each other; they were ruling the city at that time with a kind of government which that city-state had not had in previous memory, nor will it have, as I reckon, in this generation.[27] Keeping the honor received in my mind and anxious that it would not seem conferred on someone unworthy, one day when I was climbing the hills I happened to come to the wood called Selvapiana, after crossing the river Enza in the territory of Reggio: immediately struck by the beauty of the place I set my pen to work on the interrupted *Africa,* and once the passion was roused which had seemed drugged, I wrote something on that day. Afterward on successive days I wrote a passage every day until I returned to Parma and acquired a calm and secluded house (which I subsequently bought, and it is still mine)[28] and in no great time I brought that work to its end with such passion that I myself am amazed even now.[29] When I left I returned to the source of the Sorgue and my Transalpine solitude. [. . .][30] And within a short time that glorious but alas too mortal family of the Colonnas was extinct,[31] and I returned to Italy when I had already left behind me my forty-fourth year and had passed a long period both at Verona and Parma, thanks be to God, held far more dear everywhere than I deserved.[32] 31 32

After a long while I won from the publicity given to my fame the generosity of the younger Giacomo of Carrara, that most excellent man; I don't know whether any prince was his equal in his generation — or rather I do know there was none.[33] Through messengers and letters sent far beyond the Alps when I was there, and wherever I was across Italy, he wearied me with such powerful prayers over many years, urging me to friendship with him, that although I expected nothing from wealthy and successful men I 33

felicibus nil sperarem, decreverim tandem ipsum adire et videre
34 quid sibi hec magni et ignoti viri tanta vellet instantia. Itaque, sero
quidem, Patavum veni, ubi ab illo clarissime memorie viro non
humane tantum sed sicut in celum felices anime recipiuntur acceptus sum, tanto cum gaudio tamque inextimabili caritate ac pietate,
ut, quia equare eam verbis posse non spero, silentio opprimenda
35 sit. Inter multa, sciens me clericalem vitam a pueritia tenuisse, ut
me non sibi solum sed etiam patrie arctius astringeret, me canoni-
cum Padue fieri fecit. Et ad summam, si vita sibi longior fuisset,
michi et errorum et itinerum omnium finis erat. Sed—heu!—nichil inter mortales diuturnum, et siquid dulce se obtulerit amaro
mox fine concluditur. Biennio non integro eum michi et patrie et
mundo cum dimisisset, Deus abstulit, quo nec ego nec patria nec
36 mundus—non me fallit amor—digni eramus. Et licet sibi filius
successerit, prudentissimus et clarissimus vir, et qui me per pa-
terna vestigia carum semper atque honoratum habuit, ego tamen,
illo amisso cum quo magis michi presertim de etate convenerat,
redii rursus in Gallias, stare nescius, non tam desiderio visa milies
revidendi quam studio, more egrorum, loci mutatione tediis con-
sulendi.

decided to approach him at last and find out what the great urgency of so important a man toward an unknown implied. So, al- 34
beit late, I came to Padua, where I was welcomed by that man of glorious memory, not just with human courtesy but as the blessed souls are given welcome in Heaven, with such delight and such inestimable affection and piety that, since I cannot hope to match it in words, it must be buried in silence. Among many other fa- 35
vors, knowing I had observed the discipline of a cleric from my boyhood, he had me made a canon of Padua to bind me more closely not only to himself but to his country.[34] In effect, if his life had been longer, this would have been the end of all my wandering and traveling. But — alas — nothing is lasting among mortals and if anything sweet is offered, it soon ends bitterly. Within less than two years God, who had given him to me and his country and the world, took him away, a man of whom — love does not deceive me — neither I nor his country nor the world was worthy. And 36
though he was succeeded by his son, a most prudent and distinguished man, who always followed in his father's footsteps, keeping me dear and well honored, still, having lost the friend whom I matched especially in age, I returned to the Gauls, not knowing how to stay still, and not so much from the longing to see again what I had seen a thousand times, as from the desire, like that of sick men, to heal my boredom by a change of place.[35]

# APPENDIX I

## *Chronology of Events in Petrarca's Life**

1304–26 *Childhood, Adolescence, and Education*

1304 Petrarca is born on July 20, at Arezzo, from Eletta Canigiani and ser Pietro (called Petracco or Petraccolo) di Parenzo, who was in exile from Florence since 1302.

1305 In the early months of 1305, Petrarca moves with his mother to a family estate at Incisa, near Florence.

1310 In summer 1310, Petrarca's family (now including also Petrarca's brother, Gherardo, born 1307) moves to Pisa, probably thanks to the great expectations raised by the emperor Henry VII's descent to Italy; it may be during this stay at Pisa that Petrarca sees Dante.

1311 By the summer 1311 Petrarca's family moves to Avignon, where the papal Curia had resided since 1309.

1312 Petrarca's family moves from Avignon to the more quiet nearby town of Carpentras; here he meets Guido Sette, the same age as himself and with whom he ends up spending the entire course of his education.

1312–16 At Carpentras Petrarca receives his primary education under the grammarian Convenevole da Prato.

1316–20 Petrarca advances to higher education and moves to Montpellier, where he starts studying law. Petrarca's

* *Sources:* Wilkins, *Life of Petrarch*; Dotti, *Vita di Petrarca*; and, above all, Rico and Morozzi, "Petrarca, Francesco."

mother dies around 1318, an event commemorated in *Metrical Epistle* 1.7.

1320–26 Petrarca continues his legal studies at Bologna, though with several interruptions. At Bologna he meets the Roman nobleman Giacomo Colonna, who becoms a great friend and his first patron.

1326–37 *Residence at Avignon and Early Journeys*

1326 Upon his father's death, Petrarca quits the study of law and returns to Avignon, where soon after he takes minor orders as a cleric.

1327 Petrarca records that he met Laura, the *fin amour* of his *Canzoniere*, for the first time on Good Friday (April 6th).

1330 In the summer, along with Ludwig van Kempen (Socrates) and Angelo Tosetti (Laelius), Petrarca accompanies Giacomo Colonna to his new bishopric in Lombez (Gascony). In the fall, back in Avignon, he officially enters the service of Cardinal Giovanni Colonna, thanks to an introduction by Giovanni's brother Giacomo.

1333 During the spring and summer months of 1333, Petrarca obtains leave from his patron Cardinal Colonna to visit northern Europe. The trip takes him to Paris and the Low Countries — Ghent, Liège, Flanders, and Brabant — as well as to Charlemagne's capital of Aachen. He then continues on to Cologne and Lyons. In Liège he discovers a copy of Cicero's oration *In Defense of Archias*. His passion for the ancient world also leads him to produce an edition of Livy's *History of Rome* during these years (above all in 1328–29).

1337 In the first half of 1337, Petrarca visits Rome for the first time, hosted by the Colonna family. On his return, he moves from Avignon to the small village Vaucluse, west of Avignon, where he had bought a small country estate. In the same year, his son, Giovanni, is born of an unknown woman at Avignon.

1337–53 *Residence at Vaucluse Alternating with Trips to Italy*

1337–41 *First stay at Vaucluse.* Petrarca begins composing *On Famous Men* and the *Africa;* he also works on his Italian love poetry, continuing a practice that probably began in his early youth. In September 1340 he receives two simultaneous offers to be crowned with the laurel for his work as a poet and a historian, one from the University of Paris, the other from the Senate of Rome; he decides to accept the latter.

1341–42 *Poetic coronation and trip to Italy (Naples, Rome, and Parma).* Before receiving the laurel crown in April 1341, Petrarca is examined for the honor by the learned king Robert of Naples (February 1341), for whom Petrarca retains a lifelong admiration. After his coronation, Petrarca moves to Parma at the invitation of its ruler, Azzo da Correggio, and remains there until early 1342, when he returns to Vaucluse. During his time in Parma he resumes composition of the *Africa*.

1342–43 *Second residence at Vaucluse.* Petrarca finishes the first book of *On Famous Men* and begins composing *On Things Worth Remembering* and perhaps assembles a first collection of his Italian love poetry. In 1343 Petrarca's brother Gherardo enters the Carthusian order and around the same period Petrarca's daughter, Francesca, is born of an unknown woman.

1343–45 *Second period of residence in Italy (Naples, Parma, and Verona).* After King Robert's death, Petrarca is sent to Naples by Cardinal Giovanni Colonna on a diplomatic mission (September–November 1343). Thereafter, he returns to Parma, again invited by Azzo da Correggio, but when the city is placed under siege as a result of dynastic conflicts, Petrarca abruptly escapes, taking refuge in Verona at the end of February 1345. Here he remains until the end of 1345. During this period he discovers Cicero's *Letters to Atticus, To Brutus,* and *To Quintus* in the Biblioteca Capitolare of Verona's Cathedral. It is reading Cicero's letters that inspires him to collect his own correspondence. This new project seems to lead him to interrupt his work on *Things Worth Remembering.*

1345–47 *Third stay at Vaucluse.* Once back in Provence at the end of 1345, Petrarca turns down an offer to become an apostolic secretary to the pope. He starts composing *On the Life of Solitude* (1346) as well as the *Bucolic Poem* and *On Religious Retirement* (1347), inspired by his brother Gherardo's monastic profession. In 1347 he probably also begins devising the *Secret Book.* He also composes around this time, anonymously, a series of epistolary invectives, later collected under the title *Book Without a Name.* His initial support for Cola di Rienzo's uprising against the feudal rule of noble families in Rome, including the Colonna, leads to a rupture with his patron, Cardinal Giovanni Colonna, in 1347.

1347–51 *Third period of residence in Italy (principally Parma and Padua).* In November 1347 Petrarca leaves Provence to go to Verona on a diplomatic mission for Pope Clement VI. His initial intention of moving on to Rome to join Cola di Rienzo is soon abandoned, owing to the sudden failure of Cola's revolution. Petrarca instead returns to Parma, where through the intercession of Azzo da Correggio he obtains a canonry and later, in the year 1348, is made archdeacon of the Parma cathedral, a much richer benefice. In the spring of 1349 he obtains another rich benefice, a canonry at Padua, thanks to his great admirer Giacomo II da Carrara, ruler of the city. Petrarca spends the following two years alternating periods of residence in these two cities, with visits to numerous other locations in northern Italy, including Verona, Treviso, Venice, Ferrara, and Mantua. In the fall of 1350, on the way to Rome for the jubilee, he stops in Florence, where he meets Boccaccio and other Florentine literati, who in the spring of the following year obtain for him the offer of a chair at the city's university and the restitution of his father's confiscated properties. Around the same time, Petrarca is summoned back to Avignon by Pope Clement VI. Given the political instability of Italy at the time, he declines the Florentine offer and moves back to Provence. Between the years 1348 and 1351, he is greatly afflicted by the loss of many loved ones in the Great Plague, including Cardinal Giovanni Colonna and Laura, both of whom died in 1348. In December 1350 his patron and great admirer Giacomo da Carrara is assassinated. During these years Petrarca composes the *Penitential Psalms,* continues work on his *Secret Book,* and starts assembling his collection of *Familiares* as well as his *Metrical Epistles*. He also begins to shape his vernacular poems into the collection that will become the *Canzoniere*.

1351–53 *Fourth stay at Vaucluse*. Petrarca moves back to Provence in June 1351, where he is again offered a position as apostolic secretary by Pope Clement VI and again refuses. He divides his time between Vaucluse and Avignon, principally with the aim of finding a benefice for his son, Giovanni, who in the end obtains a canonry at Verona. The first design for what will become the *Triumphs* probably belong to this period, as does the second book of *On Famous Men* and the *Invective against a Physician*. Work continues as well on the *Secret Book*. Petrarca's disgust with the corruption of Avignon is captured in an invective he writes in this period, the *Invective Against a Physician*, as well as in further anonymous letters that go into the collection *Book Without a Name*. In May 1353 Petrarca finally leaves Avignon and Vaucluse for good and moves to Italy.

1353–61 *Period of Residence in Milan*

Once in Italy, Petrarca accepts, at the end of June, Archbishop Giovanni Visconti's invitation and moves to Milan to work in his service. The decision disappoints Boccaccio and Petrarca's other Florentine friends, for whom the Visconti were tyrants and enemies of Florence. Petrarca later defends his decision, with an invective against Cardinal Jean de Caraman, one of his detractors (the 1355 *Invective Against a Man of High Rank with no Knowledge or Virtue*). The years spent in Milan are the high point of Petrarca's career as a diplomat. He is sent on several important diplomatic missions: to Venice in the fall of 1353 (to negotiate peace with Genoa, then under Milanese control); to Basel and Prague in 1356 (to seek an alliance with Emperor Charles IV); to Paris in 1360–61 (to congratulate King John the Good on his liberation after the Treaty of Brétigny and to strengthen his alliance with the Visconti). In 1354–55 Petrarca praises Charles IV's descent to Italy to be crowned as king of Italy in Milan and later Holy Roman emperor in Rome. In this period Petrarca composes *On the Remedies for Fortune Fair and Foul,* continues work on the *Familiares* and his Italian poetry, and composes the short but erudite *Itinerary from Genoa to Jerusalem and the Holy Land* (1358). He also completes the *Book Without a Name* (1361).

1361–74 *Residence in Padua, Venice, and Arquà*

1361–62 *Residence in Padua.* In the early summer of 1361, a new outbreak of plague forces Petrarca to abandon Milan; in June he moves to Padua and remains there until the following summer, when the plague arrives and he flees again. In the summer of 1361 Petrarca loses to the plague his ill-behaved son, Giovanni, as well as his greatest friend, the dedicatee of the *Familiares,* Ludwig van Kempen (Socrates).

1362–68 *Residence in Venice.* Petrarca's services as diplomat and secretary are in less demand in the Venetian Republic, but he obtains a house from the government in exchange for the pledge to bequeath his rich library to the city (a promise that in the end remains unfulfilled). Petrarca resides in Venice from summer 1362 to the spring of 1368, interrupted by short visits to other cities, especially Pavia, where he spends almost every summer as the guest of its ruler, Galeazzo II

Visconti. In this period Petrarca is again stricken by the loss of many of his dearest friends: in 1363 he loses both Angelo Tosetti (Laelius) and Francesco Nelli (Simonides), the dedicatee of the *Seniles*. In Venice he also brings to completion the collection of *Metrical Epistles* (1364), the *Familiares*, the *Bucolic Poem* and *Remedies for Fortune Fair and Foul* (the last three all in 1366), thanks to the valuable help of his young secretary, Giovanni Malpaghini, who remains at Petrarca's service from 1364 to 1368. From 1366 to 1367 Malpaghini also begins copying the final redaction of the *Canzoniere* (in what is now manuscript Vaticanus Latinus 3195), which Petrarca himselfcompletes after Malpaghini's departure; he continues work on the *Triumphs*. Petrarca also composes the philosophical invective *On His Own Ignorance and that of Many Others* (1367). During his Venetian years, Petrarca repeatedly turns down offers by Urban V to join him, first in Avignon and then in Rome, where in 1367 he had succeeded in moving the Curia; Petrarca alleges that the infirmities of old age prevent him from travel.

1368–70 *Residence in Padua*. In the spring of 1368, Petrarca moves to Padua, where its ruler, Francesco da Carrara, presents him with an estate near the village of Arquà in the Euganean Hills. While having his house built there, Petrarca mostly resides in Padua. In this period he works chiefly on his biographical compendium, *On Famous Men*, at the request of Francesco da Carrara, who becomes its dedicatee, and who wishes to use it as a basis for a cycle of frescos in his palace at Padua. In this period Petrarca also serves his patron on a few political matters, and in late spring 1368, he is sent to Udine on a diplomatic mission, seeking the emperor Charles IV's support during a period of tensions with the Visconti.

1370–74 *Residence at Arquà.* In March 1370 Petrarca moves to Arquà, later joined by his daughter (Francesca) and her husband (Francescuolo da Brossano). In April 1370 he sets out to meet Pope Urban V in Rome, in a last attempt to persuade him to remain there, but illness forces him to give up his plan. Urban, yielding in the end to pressure from the French cardinals, leaves Rome in September of that year and dies at Avignon only three months later. In 1373 Petrarca again writes to advocate the Curia's return to Rome, in a fierce invective against the French theologian Jean de Hesdin (*Against a Detractor of Italy*). In the fall of the same year, he is employed in his last diplomatic mission, going to Venice to negotiate peace on behalf of the Carrara dynasty. In his last years, he continues to add to the *Seniles* and to revise *On Famous Men*, the *Canzoniere*, and the *Triumphs*.

1374 Petrarca dies on July 19, 1374, on the eve of his seventieth birthday, allegedly while still working at his books.

# APPENDIX II

## *Petrarca's Literary Works*

The following overview of Petrarca's works aims to provide basic information on each of his known writings, excluding only legal documents (i.e., Petrarca's two pleas to Pope Clement VI or the official document in which he declared his intention to bequeath his library to the Venetian Republic; see Feo 2003, 455 and 519), or various kinds of notes (such as, for example, the notes on his personal copy of Vergil, which include brief obituaries of his friends on its flyleaf, or the literary notes in his copy of Cassiodorus' *De Anima,* which include a list of about fifty favorite books; see Feo 2003, 458–518). For an exhaustive survey of the chronology and manuscript tradition of the entire *corpus,* see Feo 2003. The reference editions to each of the following works are cited in the Bibliography; secondary literature referred to here may also be found in the same place.

### I. WORKS IN LATIN

#### A. LETTER COLLECTIONS

1. *Rerum familiarium libri* (*Familiar Letters* or *Letters to Friends*): 24 books, containing 350 letters of varying length (all in prose, except *F.* 24.10 to Horace, in Asclepiadic meter, and *F.* 24.11 to Vergil, in hexameters). Most letters preserve a real correspondence, as revised for publication, but a number are fictitious (as in the series of letters to the ancients in Part VIII). Letters are organized in roughly chronological order and are meant to illustrate Petrarca's concerns in various phases of his life. The first four books include many letters that appear to be fictitious and form a kind of episto-

lary autobiography of his early years. See the Introduction in Volume 1 for further details concerning its composition.

2. *Rerum senilium libri* (*Letters of Old Age*): 18 books, including 128 letters of varying length. Like the *Familiares,* the *Seniles* are organized in roughly chronological order and include both real letters, revised for publication, and fictitious ones. The collection, dedicated to Francesco Nelli, was started in 1361 as a continuation of the *Familiares* and continued to the end of his life.

3. *Epystole metrice* (*Metrical Epistles*): three books, containing sixty-six epistles in hexameters, dedicated to Barbato da Sulmona. Among these are Petrarca's earliest attested writings (for example 1.7, lamenting his mother's death, which occurred around 1318). They were organized into a collection around 1350 and were finally published in 1364, shortly before Barbato's death. Petrarca continued to retouch them after publication (see Feo 2003, 293–94). The collection is inspired by the ancient genre of the poetic epistle (above all Horace's *Epistles*).

4. *Liber sine nomine* (*Book Without a Name*): a collection of nineteen letters, organized in roughly chronological order and introduced by a preface. Petrarca composed them between 1342 and 1361. The first thirteen letters were written while still in Provence, while the last six, along with the preface, were written and put in order during Petrarca's last years in Milan; the collection was finished by 1361 (see Cascio, *Liber sine nomine,* 8–12). The title reflects the fact that the addressees' names are concealed to protect them from unhappy consequences, as the letters contain fierce political invectives against the corruption of the papal curia at Avignon.

5. Uncollected letters: letters (all in Latin prose, except Letter 49 in Italian) that have been preserved in various manuscripts, though they were excluded from Petrarca's collections. The reference edition for the entire known *corpus* of these letters is presently Pancheri (*Lettere disperse*), which includes seventy-six letters, presented in chronological order from 1338 to 1372.

## B. Poetical Works

1. *Philologia Philostrati* (*Philostratus' Philology*): a juvenile work that has not survived but is mentioned in *F.* 2.7.5 and *F.* 7.16.6 as well as in one of Petrarca's uncollected letters (Letter 5 in Pancheri, *Lettere disperse*) and in Boccaccio's *Life of Petrarca* 30. It was a comedy in verse (employing a form of the iambic senary; see Mariotti, "La Philologia del Petrarca," 193–203), probably inspired by Terence, and dedicated to Cardinal Giovanni Colonna.

2. *Africa*: an epic poem in hexameters, comprising nine books and originally dedicated to King Robert of Naples. It draws on the epic model of Vergil's *Aeneid* and on Livy for its historical matter and is centered around the figure of Scipio Africanus the Elder, the hero of the Second Punic War. The poem follows his political ascent up until his decisive victory over Hannibal at Zama in 202 BCE, followed by his triumph. Petrarca begun the *Africa* in 1338–39, and parts of it were circulated, contributing to his crowning with the laurel in 1341. He resumed working on it at Parma in 1341–42, but, despite what he claims at IX.2.32, the work remained unfinished (see Vincenzo Fera's article in Feo 2003, 254).

3. *Bucolicum carmen* (*Bucolic Poem*): a collection of twelve eclogues in hexameters, discussing in an allegorized pastoral setting various themes, from Petrarca's poetics and personal experiences to contemporary politics. Petrarca composed all the eclogues between 1346 and 1349, but revised the collection in 1357, and, after further revision, in 1361 sent a copy to Jan ze Středa, chancellor of Emperor Charles IV. He nevertheless kept retouching his work for a few more years, before it reached its final form in 1366 (see Nicholas Mann in Feo 2003, 278).

4. *Psalmi Penitentiales* (*Penitential Psalms*): a collection of seven prayers written in rhythmic prose and inspired by the biblical book of Psalms. They were probably composed around 1347–48, after having been drafted all in one day, as Petrarca claims at *S.* 10.1.133, a letter written around 1367; the letter accompanied the

gift of a copy of the *Psalms* to Sagremor de Pommiers (see Coppini, *Psalmi penitentiales; Orationes,* 11–12).

5. Uncollected Latin poems: various kinds of occasional poems and fragments written in Latin and preserved in manuscripts, though excluded by Petrarca from any of his collections intended for publication. No comprehensive modern edition of this material exists, but an overview of the corpus is offered by Feo 2003, 308–13.

### C. Works of History, Biography, and Erudition

1. *Vita Terrentii* (*Life of Terence*): a short biography of Terence, the second-century BCE Latin playwright, active in the so called Scipionic Circle. Its date of composition remains uncertain; Petrarca may have drafted it around 1340, as a complement to his editorial activity on Terence's comedies (and perhaps at the same time as he was also writing the lost Terentian comedy *Philostratus' Philology*), and may have been revising it as late as the 1350s (see Arzálluz, *La Vita Terrentii de Petrarca,* ix and 101–2).

2. *De viris illustribus* (*On Famous Men*): a collection of biographies of ancient figures, consisting of several series composed by Petrarca at different times, from 1338 to the very end of his life (on the chronology, see Ferrone, *De viris illustribus,* ix–x, and Feo 2003, 363–67). The collection is divided in two books, the first containing twenty-three biographies of ancient leaders (all Romans, with the exception of Alexander the Great, Pyrrhus, and Hannibal), in chronological order (from Romulus to Cato the Elder); it was composed between 1338 and 1343, beginning with Scipio Africanus, Petrarca's great hero. The second book, composed around 1351–53, contains twelve biographies of non-Roman figures: eight Biblical characters (ordered chronologically from Adam to Moses), to which the Assyrian Ninus and Semiramis (the only woman) are added, as well as the Greeks Jason and Hercules. In the late 1360s Petrarca revised the work again, at Francesco da Carrara's request:

a new preface was added at that time. The *Quorundam illustrium virorum et clarissimorum heroum epithoma* (*Epitome on some famous men and most famous heroes*) was planned in accordance with da Carrara's wishes: the *Epithoma* was to contain the twenty-three biographies of the first book plus thirteen new biographies of Roman leaders, a total of thirty-six lives, from Romulus to Trajan. Despite this ambitious plan, Petrarca was able to complete only the long biography of Caesar, which he had composed separately, under the title *De gestis Cesaris* (*On Caesar's Deeds*); the remaining twelve biographies were completed posthumously by Petrarca's last secretary, Lombardo della Seta. Da Carrara had also asked for a shortened version of the thirty-six ancient biographies: this became the *Compendium* (*Abridgment*), which Petrarca left unfinished at his death; this work too was finished posthumously by Lombardo della Seta.

3. *Collatio inter Scipionem, Alexandrum, Hanibalem et Pyrrum* (*Comparison between Scipio, Alexander, Hannibal and Pyrrhus*): this short work is tightly linked to the *De viris illustribus* and was perhaps originally intended as part of the *Life of Scipio*. It compares the four famous ancient leaders, building on an anecdote about a supposed conversation between Scipio Africanus and Hannibal after the end of the Second Punic War. It was perhaps first drafted around 1357, or more probably in earlier years while still working on the *Africa*; see Enrico Fenzi, "Da Annibale ad Alessandro: per la redefinizione di un percorso petrarchesco," *Quaderni Petrarcheschi* 11 (2004): 89–117.

4. *Itinerarium breve de Ianua usque ad Ierusalem et Terram Sanctam* (*Short Itinerary from Genoa to Jerusalem and the Holy Land*): this work, better known under the title of *Itinerarium Syriacum* (*Syrian Itinerary*), is an erudite description of a possible itinerary from Genoa to the Middle East, cast in the form of a letter addressed to Giovanni Mandelli, a relation of the Visconti. In spring 1358 Mandelli was in fact planning a pilgrimage to the Holy Land and had invited Petrarca to join him: Petrarca declined the offer and sent

the *Itinerary* instead (cf. Lo Monaco, *Itinerario in Terra Santa,* 15–16 and 32–34, and Cachey, *Petrarch's Guide to the Holy Land*).

## D. Works of Moral Philosophy

1. *Rerum memorandarum libri* (*Things Worth Remembering*): a collection of exemplary anecdotes meant to illustrate the four cardinal virtues. Between 1343 and 1345 Petrarca composed what was to have been the first four books, devoted to the virtue of prudence, but then abandoned the dauntingly large project (see Petoletti, *Rerum Memorandarum Libri,* 7–11). The collection, inspired to Valerius Maximus' *Memorable Deeds and Sayings,* organizes the anecdotes thematically, further subdividing them into three categories according to the origin of their protagonist: ancient Romans, ancient "foreigners" (that is, Greeks or other ethnicities), and contemporaries (including, for example, King Robert of Naples and Dante).

2. *De vita solitaria* (*On the Life of Solitude*): a treatise, divided in two books, exploring the advantages of living away from the crowds and spending one's time in honorable studies and devotional practices. Petrarca began it in 1346, during a period of retirement at Vaucluse, and continued to revise it until 1366, when he sent a finished copy to its dedicatee, Philippe de Cabassoles. Yet he was still making further additions in 1372 (see Enenkel, *De Vita Solitaria. Buch 1,* 8).

3. *De otio religioso* (*On Religious Retirement*): a treatise in two books, praising monastic life and condemning the enticements of the world. It was begun in 1347 after Petrarca's visit to his brother, Gherardo, at Montrieux and was dedicated to his Carthusian community. Petrarca kept revising it until after 1357 (see Goletti, *De otio religioso,* 7).

4. *De secreto conflictu curarum mearum* (*On the Secret Conflict of My Anxieties,* also known as *My Secret Book* or *The Secret*): a dialogue in three books modeled on Boethius' *Consolation of Philosophy,* consist-

ing of an imaginary conversation between Petrarca and Saint Augustine, held in the presence of a female figure representing Truth. In the dialogue Petrarca questions the value of his worldly loves for Laura and for glory, measuring them by the standard of the love of God. Its dramatic date is 1342 (sixteen years after his first encounter with Laura), but it was probably composed a few years later, perhaps between 1347 and 1353. It was never circulated in Petrarca's lifetime (see Feo 2003, 378–79, and the introduction to Mann's translation in this I Tatti series).

5. *De remediis utriusque fortune* (*On the Remedies for Fortune Fair and Foul*): this work consists of a series of 253 short dialogues, divided in two books. It draws on classical sources, with the aim of providing a guide to moral behavior in all situations of life. It was composed in the period 1354/60 and dedicated to Azzo da Correggio, Petrarca's host in Parma, a man who had himself undergone striking shifts of fortune during his life. The work, however, reached its final form only in 1366, after Azzo's death (see Perucchi, *Petrarca e le arti figurative*, 87–92). This was Petrarca's most famous Latin work during the Renaissance itself, both in Italy and beyond the Alps (see Hankins, "Petrarch and the Canon of Neo-Latin Literature").

## E. Invectives

1. *Invective contra medicum* (*Invectives Against a Physician*): an extended invective in four books directed against contemporary medicine and physicians. Written in 1352–53, the work originated in a dispute with an unnamed doctor assisting Pope Clement VI. Petrarca revised and extended the text in 1355 or 1357 before sending a copy to Boccaccio (see Bausi, *Invective contra medicum*, 12 and 15).

2. *Invectiva contra quendam magni status hominem sed nullius scientie aut virtutis* (*Invective against a Man of High Rank with No Knowledge or Virtue*): this invective was addressed in 1355 to Cardinal Jean de

Caraman (who is never named in the text); Petrarca defends himself against the accusation of being in the service of tyrants, the Visconti (see Feo 2003, 425).

3. *De sui ipsius et multorum ignorantia* (*On His Own Ignorance and That of Many Others*): Petrarca's most ambitious philosophical essay, written in 1367 as a polemical response to an accusation made by four scholastic philosophers that he lacked wisdom because his knowledge of Aristotle was inadequate. The text was later enlarged and in 1371 was sent, in its final version, to its dedicatee, Donato Albanzani (see Fenzi, *De ignorantia*, 107–8, and for its layers of revision, the I Tatti Renaissance Library edition by David Marsh).

4. *Contra eum qui maledixit Italie* (*Against a Detractor of Italy*): an invective responding to a pamphlet by the French theologian Jean de Hesdin (never named in the text) and attacking a group of French cardinals who strongly opposed the return of the Curia to Rome. Petrarca's response was composed in Padua in early 1373, after he was sent de Hesdin's pamphlet by Uguccione da Thiene. De Hesdin's pamphlet had been composed a few years earlier, around 1369–70, in response to Petrarca's own challenge in VII.7.83 (cf. Berté, *Jean de Hesdin e Francesco Petrarca*, 24–26).

### F. Speeches

1. *Collatio laureationis* (*Coronation Speech*): the speech pronounced by Petrarca on the occasion of his poetic coronation, celebrated on the Capitoline Hill in Rome at the beginning of April 1341. (Sources attest to various dates between April 8 and 17; see Rico and Morozzi, "Petrarca, Francesco.") It is handed down with the official document ratifying Petrarca's coronation, which was also recited during the ceremony, and is believed to have been written, at least in part, by Petrarca himself; it is preserved under the title of *Privilegium laureationis* (*Coronation Privilege*).

2. *Arenga facta Veneciis super pace tractanda* (*Speech pronounced in Venice on negotiating peace*): a speech given in the presence of Doge Andrea Dandolo in Venice on November 8, 1353 (see Feo 2003, 435), on the occasion of Petrarca's diplomatic mission on behalf of the Visconti to negotiate peace between Venice and Genoa, the latter city being under Milanese control at the time.

3. *Arringa facta Mediolani de morte domini archiepiscopi Mediolanensis* (*Speech pronounced in Milan upon the death of Milan's Archbishop*): this speech, transmitted indirectly through an anonymous Italian translation, was delivered at the funeral of Archbishop Giovanni Visconti in Milan on October 7, 1354 (see Feo 2003, 435).

4. *Arenga facta in civitate Novarie* (*Speech pronounced in the city of Novara*): a speech delivered on June 19, 1358 (see Rawski, "Petrarch's Oration in Novara," 149), on the occasion of Galeazzo Visconti's triumphal entrance into Novara after he had wrested the city from the Marquess of Montferrat.

5. *Collatio coram domino Iohanne Francorum rege* (*Speech before King John of France*): an address given in Paris before the king of France, John the Good, on January 13, 1361, on the occasion of a diplomatic mission on behalf of the Visconti, who sought to strengthen their alliance with the French crown (see Feo 2003, 442).

6. *Speech for the second embassy to Venice:* this speech, transmitted indirectly through an Italian summary by a contemporary chronicler identified as Nicoletto d'Alessio, was pronounced on October 2, 1373, in Venice (see Feo 2003, 442), in the course of a legation to negotiate peace with Venice on behalf of the Carrara.

## Other Works

1. Uncollected prayers: ten prose prayers of varying length, preserved either in Petrarca's own books or attributed to him in later manuscripts, composed at various times in Petrarca's life. See the edition of Coppini, *Psalmi penitentiales; Orationes.*

2. *Testamentum* (*Will*): a document signed on April 4, 1370, probably in view of Petrarca's proposed trip to see Pope Urban V in Rome (cf. Mommsen, *Petrarch's Testament,* 3). This official document, in which he named his devoted son-in-law, Francescuolo da Brossano, as primary heir, offered Petrarca another occasion to sketch a portrait of his own life.

## II. WORKS IN ITALIAN

1. *Rerum Vulgarium Fragmenta* (*Fragments on Vernacular Matters*): Petrarca gave this Latin title to his collection of Italian poems, which later became his most famous work, better known under its Italian title of *Canzoniere* (i.e., *Songbook*) or *Rime sparse* (i.e., *Scattered Verses*), from the collection's opening line. The *Canzoniere* includes 366 lyrics in different forms and meters, touching on different aspects of Petrarca's life, from politics to poetics and friendship, but its central theme is his forbidden love for Laura and his troubled aspiration to worldly glory, symbolized by the laurel crown. While the first manuscript evidence for Petrarca's Italian poetry dates to the years 1336–38, he must have started composing poems in Italian quite early in his youth, even before the date on which he claimed first to have met Laura, April 6, 1327, Good Friday. The project of a poetic collection organized around his love for Laura is thought to date from after Laura's death (allegedly on April 6, 1348). Petrarca continued to polish the collection to the end of his life. On the *Canzoniere*'s composition history, see Santagata, *Canzoniere,* lxiv–lxvii and ccv–ccxii).

2. *Triumphi* (*Triumphs*): as in the case of the *Rerum vulgarium fragmenta,* Petrarca also gave a Latin name to his other major collection of Italian verse. The *Triumphs* are a linked series of six allegoric poems in tercets with interlocking rhymes (the meter used in Dante's *Divine Comedy*), which picture a sequence of visions that appeared to Petrarca upon falling asleep at Vaucluse on the anni-

versary of his first encounter with Laura: in the *Triumphus Cupidinis* (*Triumph of Love*), Petrarca sees Love's triumphal parade and finds himself ensnared too; in the *Triumphus Pudicitie* (*Triumph of Chastity*), Love encounters Laura, but she resists and prevails over him. In the midst of Laura's triumph, the sequence moves on to the *Triumphus Mortis* (*Triumph of Death*), in which Death suddenly comes forth and kills her, although she soon reappears to the poet as a blessed soul. In the *Triumphus Fame* (*Triumph of Fame*), Death is overcome by Fame, who then leads her own parade of glorious men and women from the past; but in the *Triumphus Temporis* (*Triumph of Time*), yet another vision shows the vanity of worldly glory and Time's triumph over Fame. The final vision, in the *Triumphus Eternitatis* (*Triumph of Eternity*), opens a different perspective and reveals the world of eternity beyond time, where the just will enjoy true glory and where the poet will see Laura again, in her true splendor. The chronology of the *Triumphs'* composition is debated, but the currently prevailing view is that Petrarca devised the actual project of this long allegorical poem only after Laura's death, in the early 1350s. He then (as usual) kept adding to it and revising it until just a few months before his death (in particular, the last two *Triumphs* belong to the years 1370–74). The text, however, never reached a final state. The most recent synthesis on the question of the work's composition history and textual transmission is Feo 2003, 171–76, with the contribution of Emilio Pasquini on 170.

3. Uncollected Italian poems: these include a series of thirty-three poems and poetic fragments (according to Vecchi Galli, "Voci della dispersione," 23–24), composed at various times in his life but excluded from Petrarca's final redaction of the *Canzoniere*; they are preserved in various manuscripts and are referred to as *Rime estravaganti* or *Rime disperse* (i.e., uncollected verses).

# APPENDIX III

## *Biographical Notes on Petrarca's Correspondents*

The following appendix provides basic biographical information on the addressees of the letters included in the present volumes. They are ordered alphabetically by family name (or patronymic); individuals whose given name is further specified only by toponymics are listed by their given names, while emperors, kings, and popes are listed by their ruling name. Each name is followed by a list of those letters addressed to the individual that are included in these volumes.

ACCIAIUOLI, NICCOLA (1310–1365). V.5, IV.6. Born in Montegufoni near Florence from an illegitimate branch of the Acciauoli family, the eminent Florentine bankers. He was sent to Naples at the age of twenty-one to take care of the family business but soon managed to find favor with King Robert and above all with his sister in law, the Latin empress of Constantinople, Catherine II of Valois, probably becoming her lover. After King Robert's death, he succeeded in placing Catherine's young son Luigi of Taranto on the throne, reserving for himself the role of grand seneschal of the kingdom and in practice maintaining his rule over the country until his death. Petrarca sent a few letters to Acciaiuoli from the beginning of the 1350s, but he first met him in person only in 1360, when Acciaiuoli visited his house at Milan (see *F.* 22.6). One letter by Acciaiuoli to Petrarca is still extant and is published in Dotti 2012, 653–57.

AGHINOLFI, GIOVANNI (CA. 1290–CA. 1358). IV.13, IV.16. Born in Arezzo. He became chancellor of Mantua under the Gonzaga and probably met Petrarca during one of his diplomatic missions at Avignon back in the late 1320s. The two always remained good friends, and Petrarca addressed several letters to him. In his last years, Aghinolfi moved back to Arezzo.

Baiardi, Giberto. V.3. Nothing is known about this school teacher from Parma aside from what can be inferred from Petrarca's letter (V.3), addressed to him. Petrarca sent his son, Giovanni, to study at his school in 1351.

Barbato da Sulmona (ca. 1300–1364). III.6, VI.3. Born in Sulmona, the birthplace of Ovid. After studying law at Naples, he soon started working at the court and in 1342 was appointed royal secretary of King Robert of Anjou. He died back in his native Sulmona, where he had spent his last years. Petrarca met him during his first trip to Naples in 1341: Barbato became a strong supporter of Petrarca's poetic *laurea,* and their friendship was maintained for the rest of their lives. Petrarca addressed to him numerous letters and, above all, dedicated his collection of *Metrical Epistles* to him. Four letters by Barbato to Petrarca are preserved (published in Dotti 2012, 375–401). Barbato was among the most active promoters of Petrarca's letters and other works in the Kingdom of Naples; see Billanovich, *Petrarca letterato,* passim.

Barrili, Giovanni (d. 1355). IV.6. Born at an uncertain date from a family of the Neapolitan high nobility. He became one of King Robert's most trusted counselors and held important offices in the administration of the kingdom, but he seems to have lost influence after the king's death. Petrarca met him during his first visit at Naples in 1341, and their relationship remained strong through the following years, as is attested by the letters Petrarca addressed to him.

Bartolomei, Niccolosio (1311–1388). IV.5. Born in Venice, a cultivated member of an eminent merchant family in Lucca. He befriended Petrarca, who also addressed to him *Variae* 5 (= 15 ed. Pancheri, *Lettere disperse*), as well as Boccaccio and Coluccio Salutati.

Bersuire, Pierre (ca. 1290–1362). IV.14. Born in Saint-Pierre-du-Chemin, a town in the region of Poitou. He became first a Franciscan, then a Benedictine monk, and attended the University of Paris around 1350; there he was accused of heresy but later absolved. Under the patronage of John II of France, he was promoted to be abbot of Saint Éloi on the Île de la Cité in Paris, where he lived until his death in 1362.

Bersuire was author of two encyclopedic works, the *Repertorium Morale* and the *Reductorium Morale;* the fifteenth book of the latter was a commentary *moralisé* on Ovid's *Metamorphosis*. He also made a popular translation of Livy into French. He first met Petrarca at Avignon around 1338, and the two remained good friends. Petrarca also addressed *F.* 22.13 to Bersuire.

Boccaccio, Giovanni (1313–1375). II.5, II.7, II.17, III.16, III.18–22, VII.5. Author of the famous *Decameron* and of numerous other writings both in Italian and Latin. He was born in Certaldo near Florence, as the illegitimate son of an agent of the banking company owned by the Florentine Bardi family. In 1327 he moved to Naples, where his father worked for the Bardi, but in 1341 he had to move back to Florence as a result of an international financial crisis, where he lived in more straitened circumstances. In the following years he sought patronage at Forlì and Ravenna, but in the end he remained in Florence, where he was employed by the city's government for diplomatic missions and held a variety of civic offices. It was in Florence that he composed, between 1349 and 1351, his masterpiece, the *Decameron*. In 1361, following a coup that involved several of his friends, he retreated to his native Certaldo, where he mostly resided until his death. He became a great admirer of Petrarca after the latter won his poetic *laurea* in 1341, which led Boccaccio to compose a short, adulatory biography of his hero (see IX.2). Yet the two met for the first time only in 1350, when Petrarca stopped in Florence on his way to Rome for the jubilee. Boccaccio was delegated to be Petrarca's host, and later to be the city's spokesman when it offered him the chair of rhetoric at the Florentine university. Boccaccio also advocated the restoration of Petrarca's family properties, confiscated when his father was exiled. Yet the failure of these negotiations in 1351, and, above all Petrarca's decision in the summer of 1353 to accept an invitation from Archbishop Giovanni Visconti (Florence's chief enemy at the time) to move to Milan provoked a crisis in their relationship. Boccaccio sent Petrarca a furious letter (Dotti 2012, 236–51) reproaching him with greed and political dishonesty in preferring the patronage of tyrants to the freedom of the Florentine commune. The negative rhetoric of this reproach, obliquely cast as a bucolic allegory, seemed irrevocable, and the two were probably not reconciled until 1355. Their renewed friendship is attested both in Petrarca's numerous letters to Boccaccio after that date, and by Boccaccio's own letters, which were exchanged until the very end of their lives. Petrarca's influence is also surely the chief reason for Boccaccio's shift, in the mid-1350s, from composing vernacular poetry and novels to compiling moral and antiquarian treatises in Latin. The five extant letters by Boccaccio to Petrarca are published in Dotti 2012, 223–87.

Bruni, Francesco (ca. 1315–1385). IV.12. Born in Florence. He taught rhetoric at the University of Florence until 1361, afterward becoming an apostolic secretary in the papal Curia. In this role he contributed to the goal of bringing the Curia back to Rome under Pope Urban V. He maintained his role in the Curia until 1382, when he moved back to Florence. There he was chosen Standard-Bearer of Justice in 1383–84 (the ceremonial head of the Florentine state) and died the following year. Petrarca probably never met Bruni in person, but he valued his relationship with him and addressed him numerous letters. (It may be noted that Bruni was no relation to the great fifteenth-century humanist, Leonardo Bruni.)

Bussolari, Giacomo (ca. 1300–1380). VI.13. Born in Pavia of humble origins and soon entered the Augustinian order. Thanks to his extraordinary gift for eloquence, he managed to become a leading political figure in Pavia starting in 1355. He successfully commanded the city's resistance to a siege by the Visconti in 1356, and shortly afterward his powerful preaching established his supremacy at Pavia, driving out the Beccaria family, who took refuge with the Visconti. Yet two years later the Visconti mounted a new campaign; Bussolari tried to rally a last resistance but had to negotiate surrender in November 1359. Galeazzo II Visconti then became lord of the city, and Bussolari was imprisoned in the Augustinian convent of Vercelli by January 1360. He was freed only in 1373, when the Visconti lost Vercelli, and the following year was rehabilitated by Pope Gregory XI at Avignon. After serving on a few diplomatic missions for the pope, he finally retired to the island of Ischia, where his brother Bartolomeo was bishop and where he died. In addition to VI.13, Petrarca addressed to him a second letter, written in the name of Bernabò Visconti (*Miscellaneae* 7 = 39 ed. Pancheri, *Lettere disperse*).

Caetani da Ceccano, Annibaldo (d. 1350). VII.1. Born at an uncertain date, descended from the noble family of the counts of Ceccano (a town near Frosinone). He became an eminent theologian at the University of Paris. In 1326–27 he was appointed archbishop and cardinal at Naples by Pope John XXII and continued his successful ecclesiastical career under the following pope, accumulating a large number of benefices. He became famous, or notorious, for his luxury and extravagance, which he displayed in his palace at Avignon; there he hosted a particularly luxurious reception in 1343 that drew criticism from Petrarca. He died (perhaps assassinated) at Naples.

Caloiro, Tommaso (ca. 1302–1341). V.1. Very little is known about him beside the information derived from Petrarca's writings. He was born at Messina and studied law at Bologna, where he met Petrarca, and like him wrote poetry. Petrarca addressed several letters to him and seems to have referred to him in a couple of his Italian poems. At his death, Petrarca composed an epitaph for him (included within *F.* 4.10, a letter of condolences to one of his brothers).

Casini, Bruno. See headnote on IV.1.

Charles IV (1316–1378). (Holy Roman emperor) VI.9–10, VI.12. Born in Prague, he was the son of John the Blind of Luxembourg, king of Bohemia. He was elected as king of the Romans in 1346, and then in 1347, after his father was killed fighting for the French in the Battle of Crécy, he succeeded him on the throne of Bohemia. In January 1355 he received the Iron Crown of Lombardy in Milan and in April of the same year was crowned Holy Roman emperor at Rome. He cooperated with successive popes; thus when Cola di Rienzo appealed to him to intervene in Italy, he kept Cola as hostage until he could surrender him to the curia at Avignon (1350–52), and on the occasion of his imperial coronation in 1355, he kept faith with the commitment he had given Pope Clement VI to renounce all inherited claims against the Papal States and to leave Rome immediately after his formal coronation. The disturbed state of both Rome and Italy discouraged Charles from pursuing an expansionist policy south of the Alps, and even after his imperial coronation he continued to neglect Italian affairs in favor of protecting his inherited transalpine domains and strengthening the administration of the empire. In 1356 he issued the famous Golden Bull, which regulated imperial elections and, more importantly, excluded the pope from the selection process. Charles was also a great patron of the arts and founded Prague University in 1348. Only once more, in 1368, did he try to intervene in the Italian situation, but again without success. In his last years he mostly focused on securing the kingdom of Bohemia. He died at Prague. Petrarca cherished great but unrealistic hopes for Charles IV to unify Italy under his imperial crown and bring it back to its ancient splendor; even after his disillusionment at Charles' quick departure from Rome after his coronation in 1355, Petrarca kept urging him to return to Italy (see headnote on VI.9). The two met three times: the first time at Mantua in 1355, as Charles was on his way to Rome (see VI.11, to Angelo Tosetti); the second in Prague in 1356, while Petrarca was on a diplomatic mission for the Visconti (see II.17.20); and the third in Udine in 1368, where Petrarca was representing Francesco da Carrara. Two of Charles' letters to Petrarca survive and are published in Dotti 2012, 583–95.

Cicero (106–43 BCE). (Marcus Tullius Cicero) VIII.2–3. Famous Roman politician, orator, and philosopher born at Arpinum. In the early stage of his career, he became famous for prosecuting the governor of Sicily Verres for his corrupt administration. During his consulate in 63, he exposed Catiline's conspiracy, but he was charged with sentencing the conspirators to death without a trial and thus was sent into exile by his political opponents in 58. The following year he was rehabilitated and came back to Rome, resuming his activity as advocate and politician. At the outbreak of the civil war in 49, he sided with Pompey the Great. After Caesar's victory he received a pardon, followed by a period of relative retirement from the political scene, during which he devoted himself to his philosophical and rhetorical works. Caesar's death brought him back as a political leader, and he engaged in a prolonged oratorical campaign (preserved in the *Philippic Orations*) against Caesar's political successor, Marc Antony, who eventually had him killed. Cicero was, with Vergil, Petrarca's most beloved literary model, and he hunted for copies of Cicero's works throughout his entire life; in particular, Petrarca rediscovered Cicero's oration *Pro Archia* and, above all, his *Letters to Atticus, To*

*Brutus*, and *To Quintus*, a find that inspired Petrarca's own epistolary collections.

Colonna, Giacomo (ca. 1301–1341). III.4. Born in Rome, fourth son of Stefano Colonna the Elder. He studied at Bologna, where he met Petrarca and soon became one of his dearest friends. In 1328 he was appointed bishop of Lombez in Gascony, and in spring 1330 he took residence there, accompanied by Petrarca, Ludwig van Kempen, and Angelo Tosetti, a trip that remained one of Petrarca's most treasured memories until the end of his life. In the same year, Giacomo had introduced Petrarca to his powerful brother, Cardinal Giovanni, who became his patron. In 1333 Giacomo left Lombez to visit his brother in Avignon and was then recalled to Rome to deal with the feuding supporters of the Colonnas and Orsini. It was there, in 1337, that he met Petrarca for the last time. In late 1340 he moved back to Lombez, where he died a few months later. Petrarca expressed deep sadness at his death in IV.15 and frequently recalls him in his letters. Giacomo's premature death may explain why he is the addressee of only three letters in Petrarca's epistolary collections (*F.* 1.6, *F.* 2.9, and III.4 in this collection).

Colonna, Giovanni, Cardinal (ca. 1295–1348). III.2–3, IV.15. Second son of Stefano Colonna the Elder, born in Rome. In 1327 he was appointed cardinal deacon of the titular church of Sant' Angelo in Pescheria. In 1330 he became Petrarca's patron after his brother, Giacomo Colonna, introduced them. Petrarca addressed numerous letters to him and, while in his service, was sent on several diplomatic missions, which gave him unusual opportunities to travel to Italy and northern Europe. But their relation grew colder as a consequence of Petrarca's support for Cola di Rienzo, who was fiercely opposed by the Colonna family, and in the end Petrarca broke away from Cardinal Giovanni in 1347. Petrarca composed an eclogue, *The Divorce* (i.e., *Bucolic Poem* 8), justifying his estrangement. Giovanni died of plague only a year later.

Colonna, Giovanni (ca. 1298–1343/44). (Dominican friar) II.2, V.2. Belonged to a branch of the Colonna family that came from the town of Gallicano, while his namesake, the cardinal, belonged to the Palestrina branch. After completing his studies in France, he entered the

Order of Preachers (i.e., the Dominican order) in 1320. As we know from Petrarca's letters to him, he traveled extensively, residing for several years in Cyprus, before moving back to Rome and Avignon. Petrarca probably met him at Avignon through Cardinal Giovanni and addressed a few letters to him, beginning in 1336.

COLONNA, STEFANO (D. 1378). II.13. Grandson of Giacomo Sciarra Colonna, hence the great nephew of Stefano Colonna the Elder (Giacomo's and Cardinal Giovanni's father). (Stefano Colonna the Younger, il Giovane, called Stefanuccio, who died in 1347 fighting against Cola di Rienzo, was the elder son of Stefano Colonna il Vecchio.) Our Stefano Colonna, on the contrary, was the son of Pietro Colonna, called Sciaretta, who in turn was the son of Giacomo Sciarra Colonna and, therefore, the brother of Stefano Colonna il Vecchio. The son was provost of the cathedral in the town of Saint Omer in northern France and a diplomat; he later advanced in his ecclesiastical career, reaching cardinalship just before his death. Petrarca must have met him through either Giacomo or Cardinal Giovanni Colonna and addressed a few letters to him. See Claude Cochin, "Recherches sur Stefano Colonna prévot du chapitre de Saint-Omer, cardinal d'Urbain VI et correspondant de Pètrarque," *Revue d'histoire et de littérature religieuses* 10 (1905): 352–83 and 554–78, esp. 355–56.

CRISTIANI, LUCA. (alias Olympius) IV.11. From Ferentino near Frosinone. He was about the same age as Petrarca, and the two met at Bologna during their years of study; their friendship continued as they both entered at the service of Cardinal Giovanni Colonna. Petrarca addressed *F.* 8.2–5 and *F.* 11.12 to him and gave him the literary name "Olympius" (although the explanation for the nickname is obscure). The date and circumstances of his death are unknown, but he was still alive in 1353.

CROTUS. See de Apibus, Jacopo Domenico.

DANDOLO, ANDREA (1306–1354). VI.8. Elected doge of Venice in 1343 and remained in office until his death. He guided the city through the plague of 1348 and through famine and wars, of which the most devastating, with Venice's old trading rival, Genoa, broke out in August 1350;

it ended in a ruinous defeat for the Venetians at the Battle of Portolungo (or Sapienza) in November 1354, less than two months after his death. He was a great patron of the arts and a learned man in his own right, writing a respected work on the history of Venice. Petrarca met him in late fall 1353, during a diplomatic mission on behalf of the Visconti to negotiate peace between Venice and Genoa. He had already addressed him in VI.8 (1351) to the same purpose, and would write again, *F.* 18.16, a few months after their meeting. (In 1352 he had sent him *F.* 15.4 on a more personal matter.) Two letters by Dandolo in response to Petrarca's letters are still extant and are published in Dotti 2012, 635–51.

D'ANDREA, GIOVANNI (1270–1348). III.7–8. Famous professor of canon and civil law at Bologna, among the finest legal minds of the Trecento. Petrarca had been one of his students and addressed him in two letters that criticize his limited knowledge of pagan authors, and more subtly, assert the dignity of his own, literary field of expertise, long subordinated in the medieval schools to legal or theological studies.

DE APIBUS, JACOPO DOMENICO (B. CA. 1300). (alias Crotus) III.13. Born at Bergamo from a noble family. He was a learned man and was his father's successor as professor of logic and rhetoric at the school he had founded in their hometown. The meaning of "Crotus," the nickname he chose for himself, is unclear. Petrarca did not know Crotus in person when he first wrote to him, in *F.* 18.13–14, inquiring about certain works of Cicero that Crotus owned.

DE CABASSOLES, PHILIPPE (1305–1372). II.8–11. Famous papal diplomat, born at Cavaillon from a noble family. In 1334 he was appointed bishop of his home city. He became chancellor of Naples after the death of Robert of Anjou; in 1361 he received the title of Latin Patriarch of Jerusalem and on April 11, 1367, was named vicar general and governor of Avignon in Urban V's absence. A cardinal since 1368, in 1370 he became cardinal-bishop of Sabina, a diocese in Lazio. He died at Perugia during a diplomatic mission on behalf of Pope Gregory XI. As bishop of Cavaillon, Philippe became Petrarca's spiritual and feudal lord when the latter moved to Vaucluse, a twenty-minute walk from Philippe's castle. Their relation soon grew deeper: Philippe became one of Petrarca's most intimate friends and is the addressee of numerous letters and the dedicatee of the treatise *On Solitary Life*. His death is included among those recorded by Petrarca on the flyleaf of his private copy of Vergil.

DELLA SETA, LOMBARDO (D. 1390). IV.8. From Padua. He met Petrarca in 1368 and soon became his favorite disciple and last secretary: after Petrarca's death, he played an important role in the posthumous publication of his works, finishing the *Epithoma* and the *Compendium* of his *On Illustrious Men*. Petrarca also addressed him, in *S.* 11.10–11; two letters by Lombardo to Petrarca are preserved and are published in Dotti 2012, 503–27.

DE' ROBERTI, DIONIGI (LATE 13TH C.–1342). II.1, VI.1. Born at Borgo Sansepolcro. He was trained as an Augustinian at Paris, and transferred to Avignon in 1328, where he continued his teaching in theology and philosophy. There he met Petrarca, probably through Cardinal Giovanni Colonna, and the two became great friends. Around 1338 Dionigi moved to Naples and the court of King Robert and was later appointed bishop of Monopoli in Puglia. He was one of the organizers of Petrarca's poetic coronation in 1341 (see VI.1) and was the addressee of Petrarca's famous account of his ascent of Mt. Ventoux (II.1). Petrarca also addressed him in one of his poetic letters (*Metrical Epistle* 1.4) and lamented his death in a second (1.13). Dionigi composed a well-known commentary on Valerius Maximus, and probably on Seneca's tragedies and other authors as well.

DI RIENZO, COLA (1313–1354). (shortened dialectal form of Nicola di Lorenzo) VI.4. Born from a humble Roman family. Yet he was able to become notary public, and despite being self-educated he acquired exceptional expertise in eloquence and knowledge of antiquity, soon rising to political prominence in Rome. In 1342 he was sent as a delegate to Pope Clement VI in Avignon, where he first met Petrarca. After coming back to Rome, he started working toward his political project of reviving Rome's past greatness against the decadence and injustices of the time, which he blamed on the feudal rule of the noble Roman families. This led to a revolt in May 1347, which ended with his being proclaimed tribune of a restored Roman Republic. This provoked fierce opposition from the Roman nobility, above all the Colonna, resulting in Cola's victory in the battle of Porta San Lorenzo in November 1347, in which three Colonnas were killed. Yet Cola was unable to maintain political control over the city, and less than a month later he fled Rome, finding refuge in Naples, during the invasion of his ally Louis I of Hungary, then in Abruzzo. Finally, he fled to Prague, in the hope of finding support from the emperor Charles IV. But instead Charles kept Cola as a hostage and eventually surrendered him to the papal curia at Avignon in 1352 (see VI.5). Pope Clement VI put Cola on trial, but with the accession of Pope Innocent VI in December 1352, Cola was exonerated by the cardinals appointed to try him, then sent to Rome with the status of senator in the retinue of Cardinal Albornoz (1353–54). At Rome, however, he again alienated the citizens and was killed in a street conflict. Cola's extraordinary political rise and his effort to revive the ancient greatness of Rome raised Petrarca's sincere enthusiasm at first, but he was soon disillusioned by Cola's subsequent failure and, above all, by his support for the king of Hungary's invasion of Naples. In addition to VI.4, Petrarca sent Cola two letters included in the *Book Without a Name* (2 and 3) and a few more that he did not include in his published collections (*Variae* 38, 40, 42, and 48 = 8–11 ed. Pancheri, *Lettere disperse*). One letter by Cola to Petrarca is preserved and published in Dotti 2012, 629–33.

Federico d'Arezzo. See headnote on III.23.

Fedolfi, Giovanni (b. ca. 1300). IV.2. A jurist from Parma. He is the probable addressee of IV.2 (addressed anonymously "to a friend"). He is the explicit addressee of Petrarca's *Variae* 50 and 61 (= 30–31 ed. Pancheri, *Lettere disperse*).

Francesco I da Carrara (1325–1393). (ruler of Padua) V.6. Son of Giacomo II da Carrara, lord of Padua, who was also a great admirer of Petrarca. After his father's assassination in 1350, Francesco overcame a number of internal rivals to become sole ruler of Padua from 1355. He followed an expansionist policy, which alarmed Venice and led to war in 1372. Francesco suffered repeated defeats by the Venetians, and in 1388 left rule of the city to his son, Francesco II (also called Francesco Novello), but in the same year Padua was briefly conquered by the Visconti, and Francesco I died their prisoner. Francesco I, following in his father's footsteps, had a good relationship with Petrarca and in 1368 presented him with an estate at Arquà near Padua, where Petrarca built himself a country house and spent the last years of his life. In addition to V.6 and *S.* 14.2, Petrarca also dedicated his *On Illustrious Men* to him and demonstrated his sincere gratitude for his patronage by bequeathing his valuable library to him.

Giovanni dell'Incisa. See headnote on III.1.

Guido I Gonzaga (ca. 1290–1369). (ruler of Mantua) IV.4. Son of Ludovico I, who established the family dynasty in Mantua. He participated in his father's efforts to secure their family's political supremacy over the city and Mantua's independence from neighboring states. Yet after Ludovico's death in 1360, he accepted the protection of the Visconti, remaining commander in chief of the city until his own death. He was interested in the arts and literature and admired Petrarca, whom he repeatedly invited to Mantua. In addition to IV.4, Petrarca addressed to him a verse letter (*Metrical Epistle* 3.30), which accompanied the gift of a copy of the *Roman de la Rose*.

Homer. See headnote on VIII.9.

Laelius. See Tosetti, Angelo.

Lapo da Castiglionchio (ca. 1300–1381). (alias Giacomo da Firenze) III.9. Born in the Florentine noble family native to the territory of Castiglionchio (southeast of Florence). Lapo (a diminutive of Giacomo) became professor of canon law and shared Petrarca's profound interest in the classics and their rediscovery. He met Petrarca at Florence in 1350 and, along with Boccaccio and other Florentine intellectuals, joined a group of his admirers. Petrarca addressed several letters to him. He died at Rome.

Livy (59 BCE–17 CE). (Titus Livius) VIII.7. Born at Padua. He did not embark in a political career, but pursued philosophical and historical studies under the patronage of Augustus. From around the year 25 BCE, he began composing his major work, a history of Rome from its foundation to his own day (*Ab Urbe condita libri*), that was perhaps left unfinished at his death. Livy's histories eventually comprised 142 books and came down to his own lifetime (perhaps out of an original project in 150 books meant to come down to the death of Augustus in 14 CE), but fewer than 40 books have survived: the extant books are 1–10 (i.e., the "first decade" of books) and 21–45 (i.e., the third and fourth decades, and half of the fifth one), covering the years from Rome's origin to 293 BCE and from 218 to 167 BCE, respectively. Petrarca knew even less than that: the manuscripts in his possession included only Books 1–10 and 21–40, with the fourth decade lacking Book 33 and the end of 40. (The last five books were discovered only in the sixteenth century.) Around 1328–29 Petrarca produced a careful edition of this text, which became one of his treasured possessions, Livy being the best guide to the monarchy and early and middle Republic, which Petrarca like most humanists saw as the most glorious period in Roman history. Petrarca also knew the main sources for the content of Livy's lost books: the so-called *Periochae* (very short summaries of all the books, except 136–37, composed in the third or fourth century CE) as well as the work of the imperial historian Anneus Florus, the *Epitoma de Tito Livio bellorum omnium annorum DCC* (Epitome, based on Livy, on all wars over seven hundred years), which, as the title declares, used Livy as its main source.

LUCA DA PENNE (CA. 1320–CA. 1390). II.6. Born in the town of Penne near Pescara. II.6 was the only letter Petrarca addressed to his younger friend, about whom not much is known. He studied law at Naples, becoming a jurist. He wrote a respected commentary on a part of the *Corpus iuris civilis* and was a prominent legal expert in the papal Curia.

LUDWIG VAN KEMPEN (1304–1361). (alias Socrates) I.1, I.3, II.3, IV.3, IV.9, IV.10. Born in 1304 at Beringen, in the Flemish region of Campine: hence the names by which he is commonly known, Ludwig van Kempen or Louis de Beringen. (His original Flemish name was Lodewijk Heyligen, latinized as Ludovicus Sanctus.) Petrarca gave him the nickname "Socrates," citing the combination of seriousness and wit in his character (see *F.* 9.2.8). He was a highly trained musician and musical theorist and worked at the papal court in Avignon; in particular, he was cantor and master of music, as well as secretary, to Cardinal Giovanni Colonna. He was an extremely learned man and shared Petrarca's thirst for the revival of all things ancient. He traveled with Petrarca to Lombez in Gascony in 1330, accompanying Giacomo Colonna to his new bishopric, and Petrarca always considered him as one of his very best friends: Ludwig was one of Petrarca's most frequent and beloved correspondents and the addressee of the collection of *Familiares*. See the Introduction in volume 1 for further comments on their relationship.

MORANDO, NERI. III.15. Born at Forlì at an uncertain date. He was secretary to Doge Andrea Dandolo in Venice until Dandolo's death in 1354 and afterward was in the service of the Holy Roman emperor Charles IV. Petrarca probably met Neri at Venice in 1353 and addressed several letters to him after their meeting. Neri was still alive in 1365, as in that year he was one of the recipients of an addition to Petrarca's *Bucolic Poem*.

NELLI, FRANCESCO (D. 1363). (alias Simonides) I.2, I.4, II.12, III.10, III.17, VI.5. Born in Florence of a wealthy and eminent family (the date is uncertain, but he seems to have been roughly the same age as Petrarca). He became prior of the Church of the Holy Apostles in Florence and later, in 1361, moved to Naples in the service of Florentine Niccola Acciaiuoli. There he died of plague. He was a man of exceptional culture, and his friendship and correspondence with Petrarca flourished from their first meeting, in 1350. In particular, Petrarca dedicated the *Seniles* to Nelli, under the name of the Greek poet "Simonides" (a name perhaps chosen to honor his exceptional piety; see the note on I.4.9). Thirty of Nelli's letters to Petrarca are preserved and published in Dotti 2012, 21–221.

OLYMPIUS. See Cristiani, Luca.

PAGANINO DA BIZZOZZERO (CA. 1300–1349). V.4. Born in the Milanese noble family of the lords of Bizzozzero (a town near Varese). He was podestà of several cities under Milanese influence and a brilliant diplomat for the Visconti. His last office was as podestà of Parma from 1346 to 1349, where he died of the plague. Petrarca, who had met Paganino in 1347 in Parma, held him dear and lamented his death, both in *F.* 8.8, to Ludwig van Kempen, and on the flyleaf of his private copy of Vergil. Three of Petrarca's letters are addressed to him, V.4 in this collection and *F.* 3.16–17.

Pandolfo II Malatesta (1325–1373). (ruler of Pesaro) II.16, IV.7. Descended from the Malatesta family, the lords of Rimini. He was a famous condottiere and in 1343 became the ruler of Pesaro, when the territories controlled by the Malatesta were divided among various members of the family. He was also a man of letters and a great admirer of Petrarca, whom he met in 1356, when both were in Milan in the service of the Visconti. Petrarca also addressed to him *S.* 13.11 and *Variae* 18 (= 63 ed. Pancheri, *Lettere disperse*).

Petracco, Gherardo di ser. (Petrarca's brother) II.4, VII.2, VII.4. On him, see the Introduction, vol. 1, xxx–xxxviii.

Petrarca, Giovanni di Francesco (1337–1361). (Petrarca's son) II.15. Born at Avignon in 1337 from a woman whose name has remained unknown. It is not clear at what age Petrarca took on responsibility for his illegitimate son, but he took him along on some of his journeys and provided for his education (see *F.* 19.5.5). Petrarca clearly expected too much from the boy both intellectually and in terms of plain living and industry; he procured a canonry at Verona for him, but the boy became involved in disputes and lost it. On the difficulties of their relationship, see II.15 (and on Giovanni's earlier education, see V.3 to Giberto Baiardi). Also *F.* 17.2 is clearly addressed to him, but neither this letter nor II.15 in this collection ever address him by name. Giovanni died of the plague in Milan, away from his father (then in Padua). On the flyleaf of his copy of Vergil, Petrarca recorded his son's death, referring to him as, "My Giovanni, a man born to weary and hurt me, who strained me with burdensome and endless preoccupations during his lifetime and wounded me with sharp pain at his death" (*Iohannes noster, homo natus ad laborem ad dolorem meum, et vivens gravibus atque perpetuis me curis exercuit, et acri dolore moriens vulneravit*).

Pierre d'Auvergne (d. 1365). III.11. Abbot of the Benedictine monastery of Saint Bénigne near Dijon and a member of Cardinal Guy de Boulogne's entourage. (He was no relation to the scholastic philosopher of the same name.) Petrarca met him in Padua in 1349–50 and also addressed him in *F.* 15.5–6. See also IV.3, a letter of recommendation for him addressed to Ludwig van Kempen.

Pollio. See headnote on VIII.1.

Portonario, Marco. See headnote on III.14.

Pulice, Enrico. VIII.1. From Costozza (near Vicenza). Very little is known of him. He worked as a notary public and was a poet and a member of the Vicentine circle of intellectuals that welcomed Petrarca during his visits. VIII.1 is the only letter Petrarca addressed to him.

Quintilian. See headnote on VIII.6.

Robert of Anjou (1278–1343). (king of Naples and Sicily) III.5, VI.2. In 1309, at his father Charles II's death, became king of Naples. According to the conditions established by the 1302 Peace of Caltabellotta, he was also to receive back the crown of Sicily at the death of Frederick III of Aragon, but, when Frederick died in 1313, his son Peter II refused to give up the succession, thus leaving Robert only nominally "king of Sicily." In the continuous fight over the control of the Italian peninsula, Robert, as an ally of the papacy (especially under Pope John XXII) and of the Italian Guelfs, strenuously opposed the Ghibelline powers, who instead were bound to the Holy Roman emperor (first Henry VII, exalted by Dante, and then Louis IV the Bavarian). He also always strove to regain rule over Sicily, but without success. The kingdom of Naples flourished under Robert's administration, earning him the epithet of "the Wise," and, as a man of high learning himself, Robert was always a generous patron of learning in all its branches. He first met Petrarca at Naples in 1341, when he examined him for his poetic coronation: Robert was deeply impressed by him and offered to crown him with laurel at Naples, but when Petrarca insisted on receiving the *laurea* at Rome, the king sent representatives to accompany the poet there. He would live for less than two years after Petrarca's visit, and his death threw the kingdom into disarray. Petrarca addressed only the two letters in this selection to him, but he recalled him often with admiration and nostalgia in many of his writings.

Seneca (4 bce–65 ce). (Lucius Annaeus Seneca; Seneca the Younger) VIII.4. Born at Cordoba to a wealthy family. His nephew was the poet Lucan; his father was the rhetor and historian Seneca the Elder (55 bce — 40 ce), author of a selection of model speeches and excerpts (the *Suasoriae* and the *Controversiae*), the only surviving part of a large rhetorical opus entitled *Oratorum et rhetorum sententiae, divisiones, colores* (Phrases, Divisions and Colors of Orators and Rhetors). In the Middle Ages the distinction between the two Senecas had been lost and also these rhetorical works were assigned to the Younger Seneca. Seneca the son moved to Rome and received his education there. In 41 he was suspected of involvement in a palace plot and was relegated to Corsica by the emperor Claudius, but in 49 he was recalled through the intervention of the emperor's wife, Agrippina, who then had him tutor her young son, Nero. After Nero's accession to the throne in 54, Seneca, along with the praetorian prefect Afranius Burrus, influenced his politics for a few years, until Nero progressively shook off all controls, by killing his mother and Burrus and forcing Seneca to retire and eventually to commit suicide, on the pretext of being involved in a conspiracy against him. Petrarca was familiar with all the texts of Seneca known to us (philosophical dialogues, treatises and tragedies), which were commonly available in late Middle Ages, but he also shared the medieval confusion about the rhetorical works of Seneca's father attributed to his son.

Sette, Guido (1304–1367). II.14, IX.1. Born at Luni, at the time under Genoese control, in the same year as Petrarca, and both their families moved to Avignon in 1311, where the boys met and shared their schooling, first at Carpentras, then at the universities of Montpellier and Bologna. Guido advanced quickly in the Church, becoming archbishop of his native Genoa. He died at the monastery of Cervara, which he had founded, near Portofino. Petrarca addressed numerous letters to him throughout his life and in particular the important IX.1, with its famous autobiographical retrospective.

Sigeros, Nicolas (ca. 1300–ca. 1357). III.12. Learned Byzantine scholar. He acted as the legate of the Byzantine emperor John VI Cantacuzenos. Petrarca met him at Verona in 1348, when Sigeros was on a mission to negotiate with Clement VI over the reunification of the Eastern and Western Churches. Petrarca asked and obtained from him a copy of Homer's *Iliad,* and III.12, which is the only letter addressed to Sigeros in Petrarca's letter collections, thanks him for the precious gift.

Simonides. See Nelli, Francesco.

Socrates. See Ludwig van Kempen.

Tosetti, Angelo (d. 1363). (alias Laelius) VI.7, VI.11. Born in Rome at an uncertain date from a family strongly connected to the Colonnas. Thus, like Petrarca, he worked first in the service of Giacomo Colonna, then of his brother, Cardinal Giovanni. After the death of Giovanni in 1348, he moved back to Rome, where he married and had children and remained (with the exception of a period back in Avignon during the years 1355–59) until his death. Petrarca had met him in 1330 while accompanying Giacomo Colonna on his first visit to Lombez. They remained great friends from then on: Petrarca addressed Angelo numerous letters, naming him "Laelius," which perhaps echoed the Italian nickname "Lello" for "Angelo," but above all recalled, as Petrarca explained at *F.* 19.4.9, the name of Scipio Aemilianus' exemplary friend, the wise and loyal Gaius Laelius. His death is lamented along with that of Francesco Nelli in II.5 to Boccaccio.

Urban V, Pope (1310–1370). (Guillaume de Grimoard) VII.6–7. Born from a noble family of the Languedoc. In 1327 he entered the Benedictine order. Guillaume had spent most of his life away from the exercise of power, in study at his monastery (first at Saint Victor in Marseille and then at Saint Germain at Auxerre) and teaching at the University of Montpellier, and later perhaps in Paris and Avignon, only interrupted by occasional diplomatic missions carried out for both Popes Clement VI and Innocent VI. Yet in 1362, the college of cardinals unexpectedly could not agree on a candidate for the papacy and turned to him as a compromise candidate. Urban V's austere and idealistic attitudes were reflected in his central goals of mounting a crusade against the Turks and, above all, of moving the Curia back to Rome, which he in fact did, among endless difficulties, in 1367. Yet the disorders still persisting both in Rome and in the surrounding territories and the unyielding opposition of the French cardinals ended up forcing Urban to withdraw from Italy in September 1370. He died three months later at Avignon. Petrarca had always been strongly in favor of a return of the papacy to its traditional seat in Rome and kept writing to Urban V, urging him to realize his plan and to persevere in it — even until a few days before Urban's final departure from Rome (see the interrupted letter preserved as *Variae* 3 = 71 ed. Pancheri, *Lettere disperse*). On the political issues of his papacy, see J. N. D. Kelly, *The Oxford Dictionary of the Popes* (Oxford, 1986), 223–25.

VARRO. See headnote on VIII.5.

# *Note on the Text and Notes*

The text of the *Familiares* provided here follows that of Vittorio Rossi and Umberto Bosco's edition for the Edizione Nazionale delle Opere di Francesco Petrarca (1933–42). For the *Seniles*, the text prepared under the auspices of the Commissione per l'Edizione Nazionale delle Opere di Francesco Petrarca by Silvia Rizzo, with the collaboration of Monica Berté, has been followed, whenever available: that is, for Books 1 to 12 (2006–14) at the time of this writing; for Books 13 to 18 the text established by Elvira Nota in Ugo Dotti's edition for Les Belles Lettres (Paris, 2002–13) has been adopted instead. I regret that Laura Refe's fine new edition and study of the letter *Ad Posteritatem* (2014) did not come to me in time for it to be employed in these volumes.

The notes accompanying Silvia Rizzo's edition of *Seniles* and those supplied by Dotti in his editions of both *Familiares* and *Seniles* for Les Belles Lettres, as well as in his editions for Aragno, are an invaluable source of information on Petrarca's historical context, his contemporaries, and his literary sources. The Notes to the Translation in the present volume, which aim to provide basic guidance for students and general readers, are greatly indebted to these scholarly studies and rely on them especially for the chronology of the letters and other historical and biographical details.

The three Appendices and the Bibliography in these volumes were compiled by Dr. Ornella Rossi, Assistant Editor of the I Tatti Renaissance Library. The Notes to the Translation were compiled by Elaine Fantham and Ornella Rossi with the assistance of the series editor, James Hankins. The proofs were read by James Hankins.

# *Notes to the Translation*

## ABBREVIATIONS

| | |
|---|---|
| *DBI* | *Dizionario biografico degli italiani* (Rome, 1960–) |
| Dotti 2002–5 | *Pétrarque: Lettres Familières*, ed. with notes by Ugo Dotti; French trans. by André Longpré, 5 vols. (Paris, 2002–5) |
| Dotti 2002–13 | *Pétrarque: Lettres de la vieillesse*, ed. Elvira Nota, with introduction and notes by Ugo Dotti, 5 vols. (Paris, 2002–13) |
| Dotti 2004–9 | *Petrarca: Le Familiari*, ed. with Italian trans. and notes by Ugo Dotti, 5 vols. (Turin: 2004–9) |
| Dotti 2004–10 | *Petrarca: Le Senili*, ed. Elvira Nota, with an Italian trans. and notes by Ugo Dotti, 3 vols. (Turin, 2004–10) |
| Dotti 2012 | *Lettere a Petrarca*, ed. with trans. and notes by Ugo Dotti (Turin, 2012) |
| Feo 2003 | *Petrarca nel tempo: Tradizioni, lettori e immagini delle opere*, ed. Michele Feo (Pontedera, 2003) |
| Rizzo 2006–14 | *Francesco Petrarca: Res Seniles*, ed. Silvia Rizzo with the collaboration of Monica Berté, 2 vols. to date (Florence, 2006–14) |
| Rossi 1933–42 | *Francesco Petrarca: Le Familiari*, ed. Vittorio Rossi and Umberto Bosco, 4 vols. (Florence, 1933–42) |
| *SHA* | *Scriptores Historiae Augustae* (Writers of Imperial History) |

Full citations to these and other works cited in the notes in short form may be found in the Bibliography.

## PART V

### V.1 To Tommaso of Messina

This letter closes a group of three letters on similar themes addressed to Tommaso Caloiro of Messina (*F.* 1.7–9, followed by two more letters, also addressed to Tommaso) and composed around 1350–51. On him see Appendix III. While Tommaso was a real friend of Petrarca, the letters were fictitious in the sense that they were not written as replies to correspondence or related to any specific time or occasion: *F.* 1.7, "Against old professors of dialectic," and *F.* 1.8, "On invention and intellect," are longer than *F.* 1.9 [= V.1] but seem designed to lead up to its theme, defending formal rhetoric as a necessary complement of philosophy.

1. See Vergil, *Georgics* 3.8–9, lines composed to recall Ennius' epitaph, known to Petrarca from his reading of Cicero, *Tusculan Disputations* 1.34.

2. Juvenal, *Satires* 8.24.

3. The introduction to Cicero's *On Invention*, Book 1, illustrated the great power of rhetoric along with its necessary intertwining with *sapientia*, that is, moral philosophy. Orpheus and Amphion were both poets with semimagical powers. According to the myth, Amphion helped construct the walls of Thebes by drawing rocks from Mount Cithairon through the power of his songs. The allegorical interpretation of these myths is drawn from Macrobius' commentary on Cicero's *Dream of Scipio* 2.3.

### V.2. To Giovanni Colonna of the Order of Preachers (*F.* 6.4)

This is the last of a group of three letters addressed to the Dominican friar Giovanni Colonna: II.2, on the sights of Rome; the extended *F.* 6.3, aimed to console Giovanni for an attack of self-pity; and the present letter, on the usefulness of reinforcing argument by examples. It is dated to September 25, and is probably from 1342. It is phrased as a response to criticism.

1. This is Juvenal's justification for taking up satire (*Satires* 1.30).

2. Cicero reports Marius' courage in his discussion of enduring pain at *Tusculan Disputations* 2.53. Both Cicero and Marius came from Arpinum.

3. Livy describes how the Decii performed the rite of self-sacrifice (*devotio*) to guarantee Roman success in battle: as commander at the battle of Veseris against the Samnites in 340 BCE, Publius Decius Mus vowed his life to the gods of the dead (*Manes*) in return for the victory of his legions (Livy 8.8–9); in the next generation this man's son, Decius, repeated the rite at Sentinum in 295 BCE (see Livy 10.28) and his grandson against Pyrrhus in the battle of Asculum of 279 BCE. The last episode is not extant in Livy, but see Cicero, *On Moral Ends* 2.61.

4. In Cicero, *Tusculan Disputations* 4.44, Themistocles is said to have been spurred to glory by the desire of emulating Miltiades.

5. Suetonius (*Life of Julius Caesar* 7) reports that when Caesar went to Gades (Cadiz), the western limit of Europe associated with the pillars of Hercules, he was overcome by envy of Alexander, who had traveled to the eastern limit of known Asia.

6. This saying, shared by Fabius Maximus Cunctator and Scipio Africanus, is reported by Sallust, *War against Jugurtha* 4.5.

7. It was Cicero's ambition to match Demosthenes, the great Athenian orator, as Vergil too emulated Homer. Petrarca knew Quintilian's comparisons of the two orators in *Institutes of Oratory* 10.105–12 and of the two great epic poets at 10.85–86.

8. Petrarca mentions the three models of conversion quoted by Augustine immediately before reporting his own conversion, but not in Augustine's sequence: see *Confessions* 8.6.14 and 12.29 for Saint Anthony of Egypt; *Confessions* 8.2.3 and 5.10 for the longer story of Augustine's predecessor, the pagan rhetorician and Platonic philosopher Marius Victorinus; and *Confessions* 8.6.15 for the men of affairs at Trier. The direct quotation is *Confessions* 8.5.10, which actually describes Augustine's reaction to the story of Victorinus' conversion reported by Simplicianus, whereas Ponticianus (here spelled "Pontianus") was his only source for the other two stories.

### V.3. To Giberto (*F.* 7.17)

This letter, addressed to Giberto Baiardi (on whom see Appendix III), was sent from Padua in 1351. Its double title, adding the moral training of boys to their professional schooling (*institutio scholastica*), like Giberto's own professional designation as *grammaticus*, implies his expertise on teaching composition and literary criticism through the *praelectio*, but it also evokes the kind of moral training that preoccupied Petrarca. Petrarca's son, Giovanni, fourteen at the time of this letter, had previously been sent to Moggio Moggi of Parma, then to Rinaldo Cavalchini of Villafranca (near Verona) from 1345 to 1348, before Petrarca approached Baiardi. Petrarca does not seem to have been an understanding father: see II.15 for the breakdown of the relationship with his son. The present letter exploits the occasion to present Petrarca's views on educating boys, which reflect some of the humane precepts of Quintilian in Book 2 of *Institutes of Oratory*: but like most fathers and would-be psychologists, he was more convincing at the general than the particular level.

1. Servius, in a famous passage of his commentary to Vergil (on *Aeneid* 6.136), quotes a theory attributed to Pythagoras according to which the path of human life can be compared to the shape of the letter "Y," because childhood is undetermined, since it has not yet given itself to vices or virtues. But the crossroad of letter "Y" begins in youth, when men follow either vices (the left fork) or virtues (the right fork).

2. Matthew 7:13–14.

3. The expression *iter ferratum* (or *via ferrata*) seems to indicate a paved road, originally built to provide easy movement for the army (hence corresponding to what ancient historians called *via militaris*): see Rossi 1933–42, *ad loc.*

4. The principle of "cure by opposites" (*contraria contrariis curantur*) goes back to the founder of Greek medicine, Hippocrates (e.g., in the Hippocratic *corpus*, *De Flatibus* 6.92.10–11), and is a fundamental principle of ancient and medieval medicine, also echoed, for example, in Seneca, *On Anger* 2.20.4.

5. Petrarca leaves the New Testament for a chain of Old Testament sayings in support of his argument: first, Proverbs 2:13, followed by Psalm 34:6, then more excerpts from Proverbs (4:19, 3:17, 15:19, and 4:27).

6. Jeremiah 21:8, addressed to the Jewish nation.

7. The famous motto *sic itur ad astra* is from *Aeneid* 9.641, but Petrarca follows the wording *hac itur ad astra* found in Seneca, *Epistulae morales* 10.73.15.

8. Petrarca quotes Apollo's praise of the young boy Ascanius (Vergil, *Aeneid* 9.641), followed by *Aeneid* 6.542–43, where the Sibyl shows Aeneas the parting of the ways between the good and the damned in Hades.

9. The sentence is attributed to Solomon in Ecclesiasticus (or Wisdom of Sirach) 21:11.

### V.4. To Paganino of Milan (*F.* 3.7)

The date and addressee of this letter are disputed. In one group of manuscripts it is addressed to a "royal advisor," which gave rise to the notion it was to Dionigi de' Roberti, as adviser of King Robert of Naples. But the king of this text is clearly a very different character from Robert, and according to the definitive edition of Rossi, it addresses Paganino da Bizzozzero, whom Petrarca came to know at Parma at the end of 1347 and who is the addressee of *F.* 3.16–17. Paganino acted as adviser to Luchino Visconti and died on May 23, 1349 (see Appendix III). If the latter theory is correct, the phrase "I would prefer no king other than our own" most likely refers to the condottiere and lord of Milan Luchino Visconti, famous for his cruelty, who was poisoned to death on January 24, 1349; this was four years before Petrarca took up residence in Milan. The phrase is much less likely to refer to Giovanni Visconti, the archbishop of Milan, who took power in the city after Luchino's death. In theoretical terms, the letter's interest lies in its dichotomy between government by the many (understood by Petrarca not as an aristocracy but as the *popolo*, or middle classes, who ruled Florence and other republican cities) and by a single ruler.

1. Petrarca starts with examples of Greek kings, mostly drawn from Valerius Maximus: the humanity of third-century BCE Pyrrhus, king of Epirus, is mentioned at 5.1.ext.3; the good fortune of Alexander of Macedon is proverbial; finally, Zaleucus of Locri was a legendary lawgiver of the

seventh century BCE, mentioned for his justice at ibid. 6.5.ext.3. Then Petrarca moves on to attribute some virtue to each of the first six kings of Rome (while obviously excluding the seventh and last king, the infamous Tarquin the Proud), following above all Livy's accounts in Book 1 of his history: Romulus' courage allowed him to lay Rome's foundations and establish the first community against the threat of the neighboring peoples; Numa Pompilius, known for his piety, was credited with the creation of important religious insitutions, as well as of entertaining a relationship with the nymph Egeria; the warrior king Tullus Hostilius was able to expand the Roman territory by conquering Alba Longa and defeating other populations of the area; Ancus Marcius' lavishness refers to the great expansion of the city of Rome he is said to have fostered; for Tarquinius Priscus' demeanor, see Livy 1.34.11; as Dotti 2002–5, *ad loc.*, rightly points out, Servius Tullius' "foresight" may here allude both to the far-seeing constitutional reform with which he is credited (i.e., the creation of the *comitia centuriata*, extending voting rights to commoners), and to the *omina* that accompanied his ascent to the throne.

2. Phalaris of Akragas, Dionysius I of Syracuse, and Agathocles, also of Syracuse, were all Sicilian leaders who rose to tyrannical power in classical or Hellenistic Greece. Gaius (Caligula) and Nero were the two worst Julio-Claudian emperors, while Petrarca knew Heliogabalus' madness (early in the third century CE) from the *SHA*.

3. Every five years at Rome, censors were elected to count the citizens and record their property, and then to review the army, ending with a hymn asking the gods that the Roman republic increase in size and greatness. Scipio Aemilianus (alias Scipio Africanus the Younger), censor in 142 BCE, declared that it was enough to ask the gods that Rome be great and good and preserved unharmed forever. The anecdote is reported by Valerius Maximus 4.1.10.

4. Dotti (2002–5, *ad loc.*) refers this allusion to Luchino Visconti's planned inroads into Piedmont and possibly the attack on Genoa planned in 1348, both a source of alarm to Pope Clement VI.

5. This is the famous saying of Manius Curius Dentatus when he refused a Samnite bribe of gold, quoted by Cicero in *On Old Age* 55.

## V.5. To Niccola Acciaiuoli (*F.* 12.2)

In February 1352 (the same month as this letter), Pope Clement VI confirmed Louis of Taranto as King Louis I of Naples. Louis was the nephew of Robert of Anjou, the king of Naples who had awarded Petrarca the laurel crown. Already under King Robert the powerful Florentine banker Niccola Acciaiuoli had made his way at the court and had become counselor to Louis' mother, Catherine II of Valois. The tenor of Petrarca's first letter to Niccola, *F.* 11.13, in August 1351, suggests that Niccola had approached Petrarca to write some substantial and encomiastic work related to the recent successes of the monarchy under Niccola's guidance. The years 1351 to 1353 were a very active period of political involvement for Petrarca, and as he wrote this second letter of advice to Niccola, he was also composing his own appeals to the Holy Roman emperor Charles IV. Petrarca would surely have seized the opportunity to compose his own "mirror" for the new ruler, a *speculum principis* (see the image of King Robert as *nitidissimum speculum* in §35). Niccola certainly did not need Petrarca's advice, and we must conclude that Petrarca composed this letter to seal and demonstrate his good relations with Acciaiuoli. The letter's language is conspicuously high-flown, and the translation tries to reflect this. It should be emphasized that Niccola was not a formal regent for an underage prince, but seneschal (chancellor) to a youthful king. The bulk of Petrarca's recommendations from §10 onward are appropriate to the young man's personal behavior at court: his choice of friends and treatment of flatterers, his deportment and self-discipline. He would not be expected to deal with the finances of the state or its relations with its neighbors; rather, this kind of business was Niccola's to decide, and he would not welcome public comments on these topics. Niccola later visited Petrarca in Milan (*F.* 22.6) and they remained friends: see *F.* 23.18 and *S.* 3.3. This letter was translated early into Italian and was widely circulated in that language.

1. See Psalm 23:10.

2. See Psalm 111:10.

3. Latium is here extended by metonymy to southern Italy.

4. Julius Caesar was famed for his swiftness of action on the battlefield and in politics, also for his insatiable ambition; see Suetonius, *Life of Julius Caesar* 7.

5. Livy recounts that Hannibal and his troops were softened by wintering in luxurious Capua after his victory at Cannae (see Livy 23.45.4) and by their time spent at the resort of Baiae on the gulf of Naples, despite his earlier victory at the Trebia (see Florus 1.22).

6. See Juvenal 6.292–93.

7. Petrarca is confusing (following Augustine, *City of God* 1.30) the Elder Publius Cornelius Scipio Nasica, judged the best noble by the senate as a young man in 205 BCE and consul in 191 (see Livy 29.14.8), with his son of the same name, who opposed the destruction of Carthage a generation later in opposition to Cato. The quotation is drawn from Florus 1.31.4–5.

8. Petrarca adapts the famous opening words of Cato the Younger in the senate debate of Sallust, *Catiline's Conspiracy* 52.

9. Petrarca's metaphor is chosen to evoke Aeneas "buffeted on land and sea" on his way to glorious kingship (Vergil, *Aeneid* 1.3).

10. This is Manius Curius Dentatus, who refused a bribe of gold from the Samnites, according to Cicero, *On Old Age* 55; the saying is also quoted in V.4.6, above.

11. On the province in the kingdom of Naples called *Terra Laboris* (land of toil), see note 8 on II.13.9: the region had been ravaged by recent turmoil and military invasions.

12. Compare Sallust, *War against Jugurtha* 10.4 and 6.

13. In the early conflicts of the Roman Republic, Menenius Agrippa ended civil strife between patrician and plebeians with his parable of the cooperation needed between human limbs and the belly: see Livy 2.32, and Valerius Maximus 4.4.2.

14. See Seneca, *Moral Letters* 3.2.

15. The proverb was known to Petrarca from Cicero, *On Friendship* 76.

16. The emperor is Domitian, in Suetonius, *Life of Domitian* 9.3.

17. For this tale about Alexander the Great, see Valerius Maximus 3.8.ext.6; Justin, *Epitome of Trogus' Histories* 11.8.5–8; and Curtius Rufus, *History of Alexander the Great* 3.6.

18. Suetonius, *Life of Augustus* 51.3.

19. All three leaders (Pisistratus, the sixth-century BCE Athenian tyrant; Pyrrhus, the third-century BCE king of Epirus, who invaded Italy; and Pompey, Caesar's opponent in the civil war of 49 BCE) are quoted for their tolerance by Valerius Maximus 5.1.9–10 and ext.2 and 3.

20. For Scipio Africanus' act inviting Hannibal's scout to come and see whatever they wanted in his camp, see Valerius Maximus 3.7.1, and Livy 30.29. Caesar's *Civil War* reports the surrender of the republican Domitius Ahenobarbus and the crude confidence of Labienus, who had served him but subsequently deserted to join Pompey in Thessaly. Petrarca would also have read both episodes in Lucan's *Pharsalia* 2.512–21 (Domitius), and 5.345–47 (Labienus). The reference to Caesar's habit of not reading his enemies' correspondence may be drawn from Seneca, *On Anger* 2.23.4: after his victory over Pompey, Caesar is said to have burned a chest full of his correspondence that could have been extremely compromising for those who had sided with him, especially those who had done so in secret.

21. Seneca, *Thyestes* 612.

22. The quotation is from Livy 28.27.7, reporting Scipio Africanus' speech after a mutiny of soldiers.

23. As pointed out by Dotti (2002–5, ad loc.), this may be a reference to Stoic philosophers derived from Augustine, *City of God* 9.5.

24. Vergil, *Aeneid* 6.852–53.

25. This is Scipio Aemilianus, who went on from his conquest of Carthage to defeat the Spanish rebels at Numantia more than a decade later; see Livy, *Periochae* 57, but Petrarca is probably recalling Valerius Maximus 2.7.1.

26. Compare V.2 and Cicero's *In Defense of Archias* on the inspiration to noble deeds derived from heroic examples and heroic poetry written in their honor.

27. This list of mythical parallels mixes teachers like the centaur Chiron, who was Achilles' instructor, with friends of like age: Philoctetes, the devoted follower of Hercules; and Laelius, the friend of Scipio Aemilianus. It is slightly odd to find the loyal helmsman of Aeneas, Palinurus, included with them.

28. Vergil, *Eclogues* 10.69.

29. The end of this letter echoes the closing of Cicero's *Dream of Scipio* (= *On the Republic* 6.29), with his picture of an ideal ascetic ruler.

V.6. To Francesco da Carrara (*S.* 14.1, abridged)
This late letter was sent from Arquà, the estate that Francesco da Carrara had presented to Petrarca to build himself a country house: it is dated November 28, most probably from 1373, soon after the defeat of Padua by Venice, which forced Francesco to accept a humiliating peace in September of that year (on him see also Appendix III). Petrarca's only other letter to the lord of Padua (*S.* 14.2) was written months later, after at least one internal conspiracy against him. Like V.5, the present letter ostensibly answers a request from his friend (§1) for a treatise on government, but it was probably deliberately composed to comfort him in his defeat. Petrarca has culled his moral recommendations systematically from Cicero's *On Duties* and Seneca's *On Clemency.* This full-scale epistolary treatise is also rich in examples of model leaders, drawn not only from Cicero but from Suetonius' *Lives of the Twelve Caesars* (notably of Julius Caesar in §§22 and 101, and Augustus in §§39, 52, 55–56, and 105), and from the less trustworthy *SHA*, especially from the *Life of Alexander Severus*. But he also cites moral precepts from Aristotle's *Politics* (accessible to Petrarca in Latin translation) and from Cicero's reports of Plato's political principles. Given its length, the letter has here been excerpted, including only the proem 1–10, after which Petrarca's precepts begin unfolding (see §11, "So I shall describe what almost all men know though they conceal it, what sort of character a man should have who has been trusted with the administration of his country"), and five other topics: §§15–28, on ruling through love, not fear; §§36–48, on specific issues local to Padua (unusual traffic problems, reconstructing roads, and draining the surrounding swamps); §§51–58, on economic measures on behalf

of the populace ("bread but not circuses"); §§68–71, 74–75, 79, on the hazards of governing through courtiers; and, finally, §§98–105, on the prince's role and reflected glory as host to distinguished foreign intellectuals.

1. Petrarca had already been a protégé of Francesco's father, Giacomo da Carrara, and lamented his death in IV.13.

2. Petrarca is misled by his hero worship of Caesar (whose writings he knew) and by his blindness to the change of circumstances between, on the one hand, Cicero's *Letters to Quintus* (Books 2 and 3), written when Quintus was Caesar's legate in Gaul (and Caesar was reading over Quintus' shoulder), or the "Caesarean" speeches, addressed to Caesar in 46 and 45 BCE on behalf of Pompey's old supporters (Marcus Claudius Marcellus, Quintus Ligarius, and King Deiotarus of Galatia), when Caesar was all powerful, and, on the other hand, Cicero's correspondence to Atticus, meant to be completely confidential, and, finally, his open condemnation of Caesar in *On Duties* and in the *Philippics* against Mark Antony, both written after Caesar's death.

3. Cicero at first expressed positive comments on young Octavian (see, for example, *Letters to Atticus* 15.12.2) but soon changed his mind. Petrarca here refers to the invectives of the pseudo-Ciceronian *Letter to Octavian*, which he believed authentic.

4. Compare the proverbial formula *amicus Plato, sed magis amica veritas*, on which see on III.3.1.

5. That is, Francesco da Carrara.

6. In *Civil War* 3.91, Caesar quotes the loyal cry of the centurion Crastinus, who did in fact hurl the first javelin and fell a casualty.

7. Francesco da Carrara was only twenty-five when his father Giacomo was assassinated in 1350; until 1355 rule of the city was in the hands of his uncle Giacomino.

8. Of the three daughters of Francesco da Carrara, Caterina married Stefano Frangipane, the Venetian count of Segna and Veglia (in Croatia); Carrarese married Frederick von Öttingen; and Gigliola married Wenceslas I, duke of Saxe-Wittemberg and later Ermanno, count of Cilla.

9. Padua had been a Guelf city until 1318, after which it was almost continuosly ruled by the da Carrara family.

10. The unnamed antagonist is the Devil, as enemy of peace, who is held responsible for provoking Venice to launch an attack on Padua in September 1372.

11. Petrarca is alluding to the war against Padua initiated by Venice in 1372 and brought to an end at Padua's expense in September 1373. Dotti 2002–13, *ad loc.*, identifies the allies who failed da Carrara as Hungary and Genoa, as well as closer allies, such as the patriarch of Aquileia and the d'Este family.

12. "Guide" translates the word *rector* used by Cicero to stress the moral direction or guidance he wanted from the ideal prince of *On the Republic*.

13. Romans 13:4.

14. The Thracian emperor Maximin (r. 235–238 CE) is the first of several examples drawn from the *SHA*: here, *Life of the Two Maximins* 8.8.

15. The following two quotations come from Cicero, *On Duties* 2.23.

16. Cicero, *Philippics* 1.33.

17. According to the report of Macrobius, *Saturnalia* 2.7.2–4, Caesar compelled the knight Laberius to perform on stage in one of his mimes, which disqualified Laberius from his rank as a knight. Laberius took revenge in a speech from which this quotation comes; see also the note on IV.16.6.

18. The following two quotations are still from Cicero's *On Duties* (2.23–24), which in turn quoted a verse of the archaic poet Ennius (fr. 182 Jocelyn).

19. Atreus, mythical king of Mycenae and father of Agamemnon and Menelaus, was the villain of Accius' tragedy *Atreus*: this line (*Atreus*, fr. 10 Dangel) was famously quoted by the emperor (Gaius) Caligula (see Suetonius, *Life of Gaius* 30). The line is quoted also in Cicero, *On Duties* 1.97, and repeatedly by Seneca (*On Clemency* 1.12.4 and 2.2.2, and *On Anger* 1.20.4). The attribution of the quotation to Euripides may be Petrarca's hypothesis, as Accius is not explicitly mentioned in these sources.

20. See for example Suetonius, *Life of Julius Caesar* 35.

21. See Cicero, *In Defense of Ligarius* 35.

22. Again, Petrarca takes from Suetonius' narrative (*Life of Julius Caesar* 84.2) a tragic verse from Pacuvius' lost tragedy *Armorum Iudicium* (The Award of Achilles' Armor, fr. 13 D'Anna).

23. Seneca, *Moral Letters* 9.6.

24. Augustus regarded this title as so exalted that he would not accept it from the Senate until 2 BCE, twenty-five years after he took the name Augustus.

25. Matthew 22:39.

26. Cicero, *Philippics* 2.112, commenting on the dead Caesar.

27. Quoted (with a slight change) from Macrobius, *Saturnalia* 2.4.18.

28. The quotation is from Cicero's *Dream of Scipio* (= *On the Republic* 6.16). The "good father" is Aemilius Paulus, natural father of the younger Africanus (who was hence also named Scipio Aemilianus) and addresses the latter. In the younger Africanus' vision, imagined by Cicero in his *Dream of Scipio*, both the young hero's birth father and his adoptive grandfather, Scipio Africanus the Elder, appeared to him and advised him on his duties to his country and the glory that would be his posthumous reward.

29. The following sequence starts from the traditional definition of justice (to give each man his due), formalized in the *Code of Justinian* (*Digest* 1.1.10, and *Institutions* 1.1), but moves on to develop Seneca's thoughts on mercy (*clementia*) in *On Clemency*.

30. See Ambrose, *On the Death of Theodosius* 26.

31. In the passage of Seneca that is Petrarca's model (*On Clemency* 2.4.4–5), Seneca distinguishes "clemency" (*clementia*), a judicious easing of the due penalty, from "pity" (*misericordia*), which Stoics thought a weakness with potential bad consequences but which Christians would value positively as divinely-inspired compassion. Petrarca, who uses the word "clemency" (*clementia*) at §21 above, here changes the vocabulary but keeps the distinction between judicious indulgence and letting the guilty go free.

32. Livy 4.20.7, and Suetonius, *Life of Augustus* 28.3.

33. According to *SHA: Life of Aurelian* (attributed to Flavius Vopiscus) 21.9 and 39, the emperor Aurelian, who ruled from 270 to 275 CE, began the new walls in 271, which were finished after his death. They actually were only about twelve miles, not fifty, in perimeter.

34. Erichthonius (here spelled "Erithonius") was a mythical Athenian king who first taught his people to yoke horses to pull carts.

35. Petrarca contrasts Francesco da Carrara, who rode on horseback through his city, with most princes, who would have traveled behind the curtains of a carriage.

36. Epaminondas was Thebes' greatest general and won the supremacy over Greece after defeating Sparta at the Battle of Leuctra in 371 BCE, but less than ten years later lost it again, along with his life, at Mantinea.

37. Justin, *Epitome of Trogus' Histories* 6.8.3.

38. Petrarca draws this anecdote and the quotation from Valerius Maximus 3.7.ext.5.

39. Padua, already a prosperous city under Augustus, became prominent in the thirteenth century, when the university was founded (in 1222) and the shrine to Saint Antony of Padua was built (between 1232 and 1307). According to tradition, Saint Prosdocimus as patron of the city appeared to drive out the forces of Cangrande della Scala, lord of Verona, in 1324. The local church of Saint Justina also had a magnificent shrine in Padua. Vergil (*Aeneid* 1.242–49) reports the legend of Padua's foundation by the Trojan hero Antenor.

40. The metonymies "Minerva . . . Bacchus . . . Ceres" are used in the fashion of Roman poets to indicate the crops these ancient gods patronized: oil, wine, and grain.

41. See Aristotle, *Politics* 5.11.1314b1–18, known to Petrarca through the Latin translation of William of Moerbeke.

42. The *SHA* quotes this saying in *Life of Hadrian* 8.3, attributed to Aelius Spartianus.

43. Reported by Suetonius, *Life of Augustus* 28.1.

44. See Cicero, *On Duties* 1.101.

45. Suetonius, *Life of Tiberius* 28.

46. Anecdote and quotation are from Suetonius' *Life of Vespasian* 18.

47. *SHA: Life of Aurelianus* 47.4.

48. Lucan, *Pharsalia* 3.58.

49. As Dotti 2002–13, *ad loc.*, observes, this may be an allusion to the 1353 popular uprising in Rome due to a period of famine.

50. See, for example, Suetonius, *Life of Caesar* 26.3 and 38.1; the grain mostly came from Sicily, Africa (Tunisia), and Egypt.

51. The episode and Augustus' retort (mentioned in the following paragraph), referring the crowd to the water provided by the new aqueducts of Agrippa, are reported by Suetonius, *Life of Augustus* 41–42.

52. Allusion to the recent war between Padua and Venice.

53. The episode and the two following quotations are taken from *SHA: Life of Alexander Severus* 65.4 and 66.2, attributed to Aelius Lampridius and here referring back to the lost work of the historian Marius Maximus (ca. 150–ca. 230 CE).

54. Diocletian launched a persecution against the Christians in 303–4; once again, Petrarca is quoting the *SHA*, in this case the *Life of Aurelian* 43.2 and 3–4.

55. The eunuch Posides is known only from Suetonius, *Life of Claudius* 28; on the contrary, the more famous Felix, Narcissus, and Pallas also appear more than once in Tacitus, as powerful and active under both Claudius and Nero. Tacitus' works were, however, not known to Petrarca. The following quotation is drawn from Suetonius, *Life of Claudius* 29.1.

56. "Practice . . . learning . . . nature"; Petrarca articulates the trilogy (first found in Plato's *Phaedrus*), instilled by Cicero and other teachers of rhetoric, that the student must have talent by nature, learn the theory, and master it by practice.

57. In *On Duties* 1.74, Cicero introduces a list of paired famous men, of whom one obtained glory in warfare, the other in civilian politics. Solon was a lawgiver at Athens in the early sixth century BCE, Themistocles (a

century later) founded the Athenian navy and defeated the Persians at Salamis in 480 BCE; Lysander and Lycurgus are both Spartans: the first was victor in the Peloponnesian War, the other was a mythical early king, credited with the Spartan constitution. Among the Romans listed, Marius, the famous general, began his career in the same generation as the politician Marcus Aemilius Scaurus (during the decade from 120 to 110 BCE), who was an opponent of his and, as censor, built the Via Aemilia. The general Pompey the Great was a contemporary of the younger Quintus Lutatius Catulus (consul in 78 BCE), who tried to oppose his rise to power. The younger Scipio Africanus (Aemilianus), responsible for the destruction of Carthage and then of Numantia, was a contemporary of Scipio Nasica, who was responsible for the elimination of Tiberius Gracchus and his followers in 133 BCE. Cicero ends the list at *On Duties* 1.77 with himself and his civil achievement in defeating Catiline's conspiracy. Then Petrarca here compares him with Antonius Hybrida (uncle of Mark Antony), nominal commander at the battle of Pistoia, in which Catiline perished.

58. Cicero, *Philippics* 9.5.10. His own experience as a student at Bologna brought him many friends among the teachers of jurisprudence.

59. As in III.14.18–20, Petrarca provides a list of jurisconsults associated as advisers with several emperors, as he found them identified in the imperial lives of the *SHA*. Joventius Celsus is called here Julius Celsus, according to an erroneous reading that Petrarca found in his manuscript of the *SHA* (*Life of Hadrian* 1.18). Petrarca's "Emperor Antoninus" is known today as Marcus Aurelius (his full name was Marcus Aurelius Antoninus Augustus), under whose rule the jurisconsult Q. Cervidius Scaevola flourished (see *Life of Marcus Aurelius* 11.10). For the jurists active under Septimius Severus and Alexander Severus, see *Life of Septimius Severus* 21.8, and *Life of Alexander Severus* 68.1: the more famous Papinian, Ulpian and Julius Paulus are extensively quoted in Justinian's *Corpus iuris civilis,* while Fabius Sabinus is a more obscure figure.

60. The University of Padua was considered at the time the best university in Italy, especially for the sciences and medicine; in legal studies it was second only to the University of Bologna.

61. *SHA: Life of Alexander Severus* 34.6.

62. See Suetonius, *Life of Julius Caesar* 42.1.

63. Acts 22:28.

64. Petrarca here generically mentions famous writers who happened to be active during Augustus' lifetime, mixing those who actually belonged to the circle of Maecenas and were more directly under Augustus' influence (like Vergil or Horace) with others who were on much less intimate terms with him, such as Cicero or the erudite Varro. Among the famous orators listed here, Asinius Pollio (on whom see VIII.8) founded the first public library in Rome, and Valerius Messalla created a literary circle apart from that of Maecenas; Parius Geminus is a misreading for the declaimer Varius Geminus, praised and cited repeatedly by Seneca the Elder and also by Jerome (*Against Jovinian* 1.28); the latter is probably Petrarca's source here.

65. Augustus' correspondence with Horace and Vergil is mentioned in Suetonius' *Life of Horace*, and Donatus, *Life of Vergil* 31, respectively.

66. Quintilius Varus from Cremona was a poet and a literary critic, member of the circle of Maecenas: his death in 23 BCE was lamented by Horace in a consolatory poem (*Odes* 1.24) addressed to Vergil, as the three of them were good friends. Petrarca here probably mistakes Varus for Varius Rufus, also a poet and a friend of Horace and Vergil, who along with Plotius Tucca served as posthumous editor of the *Aeneid* (see Donatus' reports in his *Life of Vergil* 37–42, derived from Suetonius). On similar confusions in Petrarca, see Francesco Petrarca, *Le postille al Virgilio Ambrosiano*, 2: 525.

67. Ovid reports in his poetry of exile that Augustus himself summoned the poet and condemned him (in 8 CE) to be relegated to the remote military outpost of Tomis (Constanta). He claims he was being punished for his poem (*carmen*, usually taken to mean *The Art of Love*) and for a blunder (*error*) which he cannot explain: his exile is generally associated with the exile and condemnation of Augustus' granddaughter Julia in the same year.

68. For Varro and Livy, see VIII.5 and VIII.7, respectively.

69. Roman citizens were grouped in "tribes" for administrative purposes: tribes reached the number of thirty-five by the end of the Republic. On the number of legions allegedly under Augustus' command, see Orosius, *Histories* 6.18.33 and 20.6.

70. On Augustus' relations with Greek intellectuals, see Suetonius, *Life of Augustus* 89.1.

## PART VI

### VI.1. Dionigi da Borgo Sansepolcro (*F.* 4.2)

This letter, addressed to Dionigi de' Roberti, probably belongs to 1339 or 1340, after Dionigi moved to Naples upon King Robert's invitation in 1338. The bulk of the letter reads as though Petrarca conceived a double audience, hoping Dionigi would convey his thoughts on kingship to Robert himself, but the original version (preserved) of the letter lacks §15, which must have been added later, at the time of preparing it for the collection. This closing paragraph contains Petrarca's earliest reference to his laurel crown in the *Familiares*.

1. Petrarca bases his introductory remarks on the theme of "the vanity of human wishes," developed by Seneca's *Moral Letter* 60, Persius' *Satire* 2, and Juvenal's *Satire* 10, which contrast the moral values of philosophers with the naive wishes of ignorant womenfolk for their newborn children to enjoy material benefits, like long life, health, strength, beauty, eloquence, and power.

2. Juvenal, *Satires* 10.114.

3. Both Cicero and Demosthenes incurred violent death on the orders of men whom they had fiercely attacked: respectively, Mark Antony and the kings of Macedon.

4. Although Petrarca's *beata vita* echoes the title of Seneca's dialogue *De vita beata* (*On the Blessed Life*), there is no coincidence of argument with the Senecan dialogue, which is chiefly concerned with opposing the Epicurean ideal of pleasure.

5. Cicero, *Dream of Scipio* (= *On the Republic* 6.16).

6. Cicero, *On Friendship* 42. Themistocles, by persuading the Athenians to build their navy and abandon the defense of the city itself on land, brought his country to victory over Xerxes at Salamis.

7. Robert of Anjou ruled over the kingdom of Naples as well as Provence.

8. Petrarca says "your" Seneca because Dionigi used Seneca in his teaching and is thought to have composed a commentary on Seneca's tragedies (see Appendix III). The first and second excerpt come from the same choral ode of Seneca, *Thyestes* (vv. 344–49 and 380–88).

9. In the ancient world, Parthian cavalry were famous for their capacity of shooting arrows backward while retreating at full gallop; this became known as "a Parthian shot."

10. The aftermath of the War of Lucca (1338) had made Florence seem unsafe for Dionigi.

VI.2. To Robert, renowned king of Sicily (*F.* 4.3)

The letter is dated Vaucluse, December 26, but its occasion and function have been variously explained: either as a fiction composed in 1352 or 1353, or as a genuine reply to a letter from King Robert of Anjou, composed in 1338 or 1339. Petrarca lavishes praise upon Robert's niece, the dead queen of France (Clemence of Anjou, who entered a convent after a brief marriage to Louis X, and died in 1328). Robert had composed a eulogy for her, which he apparently sent to Petrarca for his approval, or perhaps as an encouragement for him to compose something more panegyrical. Petrarca writes again to King Robert (III.5, from Pisa, April 30 1341) after his return from being examined by the king at Naples and earning his *laurea*. On King Robert, see Appendix III.

1. See 1 Corinthians 15:53–54.

2. Pherecydes, from the island of Syros (not "from Syria" as Petrarca interprets), survives only in quotations. Cicero, *Tusculan Disputations* 1.38, talks of him in connection with Pythagoras of Samos (the sixth-century philosopher and mathematician) as the first one to have hypothesized the immortality of the soul. The pre-Socratics, like Socrates himself, were

only indirectly known to Petrarca. In particular, Seneca, *Moral Letters* 24.6, is the probable source for the anecdote about the Roman Stoic Cato the Younger: previous to committing suicide at Utica, he strengthened his resolve by reading Plato's *Phaedo,* in which Socrates argues for the immortality of the soul, before accepting his sentence of death. Petrarca possessed a copy of the *Phaedo* in the medieval translation of Henricus Aristippus. Other sources for the anecdote include Florus 2.13.71, and Lactantius, *Divine Institutes* 3.18.8–12.

3. The Ciceronian references are *Tusculan Disputations,* Book 1; *On the Republic* 6.24–26; *On Friendship* 13–14; *On Old Age* 78–84.

4. This allusion surely is to the award of the laurel crown to Petrarca by the king.

5. Clemence was born in Provence and married in France.

6. The report that Alexander the Great publicly envied Achilles for his celebration by Homer in the *Iliad* comes from Cicero, *In Defense of Archias* 24.

## VI.3. To Barbato da Sulmona (*F.* 5.1)

Petrarca had written to Barbato (III.6), who served as secretary at the court of King Robert, to report his successful coronation in 1341. King Robert died in January 1343, but it is unlikely that Petrarca only received notice of his death four months later, and at §4 he alludes to the death of Giacomo Colonna (1341) as having occurred within the last year: hence Wilkins, *Studies,* 216–18, thought the letter might be a response to a false death notice received in 1342; but, as Dotti 2002–5, *ad loc.,* argues, the letter must have been edited later, with a view to publication, to work as an announcement of the king's actual death within the collection of the *Familiares.*

1. The younger queen is Robert's granddaughter Joanna I, only sixteen years old at the time, heir to the crown of Anjou and married to Andrew of Hungary, of about the same age. The elder queen is Sancha of Majorca, King Robert's last wife, who after his death retired to a monastery.

2. See John of Salisbury, *Policraticus* 7.6, also applied to King Robert's death in II.13.10.

3. Petrarca's other intellectual guide alluded to here is Giacomo Colonna, who died in Sepetmber 1341. He grieved for that loss in *F.* 4.13, addressed to Angelo Tosetti (Laelius), written from Parma in January 1342; see also IV.15, addressed to Giacomo's brother, Cardinal Giovanni.

4. At Vaucluse, by the Rhône.

### VI.4. To Nicola, tribune of Rome (*F.* 7.7)

Petrarca's first personal political crisis came with the extraordinary revolution of an even more extraordinary man, Cola di Rienzo (on whom see Appendix III). In May 1347 Cola proclaimed himself tribune of Rome and launched a violent revolution, battling against the nobles, including Petrarca's patrons the Colonnas: this ended in his notorious victory in a street battle on November 20, 1347—and the deaths of three Colonnas. At first this letter seems to rejoice with Cola over his victory, but then there is an allusion to a sudden and shocking, but unidentified, reversal. We know from *F.* 7.5.6, to Angelo Tosetti at Rome, that Tosetti had sent Petrarca the text of some radical new letter from Cola. Soon after, Petrarca needed the present letter (composed on November 29, 1347) to explain to a wider readership both his original enthusiasm for Cola's revolution and his disillusionment.

1. This quotation is reported by the younger Scipio Africanus (Aemilianus) in the narrative of his dream at Cicero, *Dream of Scipio* (= *On the Republic* 6.18).

2. This is the letter to Cola of June 1347 found at *Variae* 48 (= 8 ed. Pancheri, *Lettere disperse*), exhorting him to action.

3. Vergil, *Aeneid* 6.126: the Sibyl warns Aeneas before he enters the underworld.

4. The verse is Petrarca's own, *Metrical Epistles* 2.14.273, which he later reused also in his epic *Africa* 7.292.

5. Petrarca's friend who denounced Cola is Angelo Tosetti (Laelius): see headnote.

6. Cicero, *Letters to Brutus* 11.6.1.

7. An allusion to the prophecy of Anchises at *Aeneid* 6.794; the ancient North-African tribe of Garamantes would be known to Petrarca from this passage.

8. Angelo Tosetti may have been biased by his affection for the Colonnas, his patrons and Cola's greatest opponents.

9. Terence, *The Eunuch* 56, advising a young man against a rash love affair.

10. On August 1, 1347, Cola had proclaimed himself "Soldier and candidate of the Holy Spirit, Nicola both severe and merciful, liberator of the city and lover of Italy, the tribune Augustus."

### VI.5. Francesco of the Holy Apostles (*F.* 13.6)

The title and framework of this letter, addressed to Francesco Nelli and written in 1352, the day after III.10 (also to Nelli, but on a very different topic), profess concern with the status of poets, but the letter is really a thin disguise for Petrarca's attempt to redefine or cover up his former commitment to Cola di Rienzo, which he had already come to regret (see VI.4.7). By late 1347, Cola's strong initial support had alarmed the papacy. Losing popular and local support, he sought out foreign allies, disgusting Petrarca by negotiating with the king of Hungary, who was planning to invade Italy with a mercenary force. As these plans failed him, Cola fled to the court of Charles IV at Prague. But Charles too failed to satisfy his hopes and kept him virtually imprisoned by various vassals in northern Europe before handing him over to the papacy in 1352. Pope Clement VI put Cola to trial under a jury composed by the three cardinals, Bertrand de Déaulx, Guy de Boulogne, and Élie de Talleyrand. Petrarca was not a witness of the events that he reports, and he focuses here on the fact that Cola's best hope of pardon was said to be the — mistaken — public belief that this visionary was also a poet. But in the event, the accession of Pope Innocent VI, who succeeded Clement VI in December 1352 — perhaps also thanks to Petrarca's indirect support (through Guy de Boulogne and Élie de Talleyrand) — Cola managed to be discharged and was later sent to Rome with the status of senator in the retinue of cardinal Albornoz (1353–54). At Rome, however, he again alienated the populace and was killed by the mob while trying to escape in 1354.

1. The "most recent letter" is III.10, describing to Nelli how Petrarca had succeeded in avoiding appointment as papal secretary without causing offense.

2. Petrarca was staying near Avignon, at Vaucluse. For the name Babylon applied to Avignon, see the note on II.7.5.

3. Vergil, *Georgics* 1.312.

4. Avignon is by the Rhône.

5. Emperor Charles IV was Bohemian, and Pope Clement VI was a native of Maumont in the region of Limoges.

6. This may refer to some of the letters known as *Variae* (namely 38, 40, 42, 48 = 8–11 ed. Pancheri), or *Sine nomine* 2 and 3, or other letters that were later suppressed by Petrarca.

7. This phrase opens an antiphon sung at the Vespers of the Circumcision and refers to the exchange by Christ of divine for human flesh (see Dotti 2002–5, *ad loc.*).

8. Petrarca borrows Cicero's famous outcry in his denunciation of Catiline (*Against Catiline* 1.2).

9. A reference to the enhanced title claimed by Cola (see on VI.4.13).

10. This letter was not preserved.

11. This refers to VI.4.

12. Petrarca had first met Cola in Avignon back in 1343.

13. Cicero's arguments in his *In Defense of Archias* relied chiefly on the value of poets and poetry in providing models of heroic and patriotic behavior to the Roman elite.

14. Horace, *Satires* 1.4.40–42.

15. During the Middle Ages Vergil was seen as a sage and as a prophet of Christ, even as a wizard, according to a widespread popular belief.

16. The friend is probably Cardinal Élie de Talleyrand; for Avignon as Babylon, see on II.7.5. Petrarca here may refer to Cicero, *Tusculan Dispu-*

*tations* 1.86, and the friendly terms used by Pliny the Elder in addressing the emperor Vespasian in the preface of his *Natural History.* The "Romulean College" he belongs to, mentioned in the following paragraph, here denotes the Roman College of Cardinals, alluding perhaps to Augustus' reconstitution of the college of *Fratres Arvales,* allegedly first founded by Romulus.

17. Sallust, *Catiline's Conspiracy* 51.3.

18. Cicero, *On the Orator* 1.11 (but note Cicero is arguing that true orators are even more rare than poets).

19. For Barbato da Sulmona, see Appendix III; Zanobi da Strada was one of Petrarca's Florentine friends, who was working for the court of Naples at this time. For the name Parthenope to indicate Naples, see on III.4.6.6.

## VI.6. To the four cardinals (*F.* 11.16)

After Cola di Rienzo's failed revolution, public disorder in Rome grew even worse, as rival gangs supporting the Orsini and Colonna families terrorized the streets and slaughtered citizens indiscriminately. In November 1351 Clement VI set up a commission of four cardinals to investigate and recommend a new form of administration for the city: Petrarca's friend Guy de Boulogne as well as Bertrand de Déaulx, Guillaume Court (or maybe Bertrand du Pouget), and a cardinal of Roman birth, Niccolò Capocci. Petrarca's two letters, VI.6 [*F.* 11.16], written on November 18, 1351, and the supplementary *F.* 11.17, written six days later, are the product of his discussions with Capocci. Petrarca backs his main recommendation against including members of either the Orsini or the Colonna families in the government by citing the history of the struggle between plebeians and patricians at Rome in the first two centuries of the republic. He calls for the inclusion of native and popular elements in the city government. Petrarca also wrote separately to Capocci on the same subject, in *Sine nomine* 7.

1. Petrarca had received Rome's honorary citizenship in occasion of the award of his laurel crown in 1341.

2. Petrarca alludes to the saying of Solomon at Ecclesiasticus 3:22.

3. Not necessarily what moderns call "the Roman Republic," that is, the period of consular and senatorial government from the death of Tarquin the Proud in 509 BCE to the Battle of Actium in 31 BCE. The *respublica* in Petrarca's time refers more commonly to the Roman state in general, including the period of the early kings and the emperors; see J. Hankins, "Exclusivist Republicanism and the Non-Monarchical Republic," *Political Theory* 38.4 (2010): 452–82. (Elsewhere in this collection the word *respublica* has usually been translated as "state.")

4. Guy de Boulogne, Bertrand de Déaulx, and Guillaume Court (as well as Bertrand du Pouget) had all had diplomatic or political experiences in Rome in earlier years; the Roman Niccolò Capocci was linked by Petrarca to the *gens Cornelia,* one of the oldest and most important families in ancient Rome: the Scipiones as well as the Gracchi, the most famous tribunes of the people, were descended from it.

5. The Cimbrians were a Gallic tribe conquered by the Romans at the end of the second century BCE.

6. The two families are the Orsini and the Colonna, Petrarca's patrons.

7. The Orsini were said to have come from the hilly area around Spoleto in Umbria, and the Colonna even to have had a German origin.

8. Lucan, *Pharsalia* 8.355–56.

9. The Capitol and its fortress were supposed to have resisted occupation during the capture of Rome by the Gallic tribe of Senones in 390 BCE. The Capitoline temple of Jupiter was the destination of triumphal parades, as well as a place to receive foreign delegations, and traitors were thrown from the Tarpeian Rock at the southern end of the Capitoline Hill.

10. The appeal to Christ marks the emotional climax of the letter but also the issue that drives Petrarca's protests: the rights of the Roman people (§§11, 35). Note also Petrarca's invocation of Christ in §17.

11. Petrarca bases his account of events in early Republican Rome on Livy, but he was well aware that the title and function of senator had

changed radically from the time of the Roman Republic to his own. Before Cola's attempted revolution, Rome was governed by two senators in consultation with an informal council of nobles. In 1351, after Cola's expulsion, Bertoldo Orsini and Giordano Colonna had been appointed not just as senators but as the only senators, and their arbitrary decisions would actually bind the people of Rome, who seem to have had no right of assembly. The rule of these senators, like the power exercised by these two "foreign" noble families (see above on §9), is compared to that of the last king of Rome, the tyrannical (and foreign) Tarquin the Proud.

12. Not Aulus but Titus Manlius Torquatus took this stand against the Latins in Livy 8.5.7.

13. See above on §9. This reference, and the general tenor of the discussion, shows that Petrarca fears that the board of cardinals will appoint as senators prelates in the Avignonese church, perhaps even themselves—rich foreigners who will not have the true interests of Rome at heart and who will feel no compassion for Rome's poorer citizens.

14. This phrase is modeled on Livy 8.5.3.

15. Rome's most powerful and resilient enemies in the third and second centuries BCE.

16. A series of *exempla* of frugality from Roman political and military history of the early Republic is offered here: although all these early statesmen are recorded in Livy, Petrarca is drawing most of his examples (many of which he had recently developed in his own *On Illustrious Men*) from Book 4 of Valerius Maximus: 4.4.1 for Valerius Publicola, 4.4.2 for Menenius Agrippa, 4.4.7 for Quinctius Cincinnatus, 4.3.5–6 for the generals Manius Curius Dentatus and Fabricius Luscinus, and 4.4.6 for Atilius Regulus. Valerius Publicola and Lucius Junius Brutus were Rome's first consuls after the expulsion of Tarquin the Proud in 509 BCE; in the following years Publicola defeated the Etruscans of King Porsenna in their attempt to restore the Tarquins in Rome and then, during his fourth consulate (according to Livy 2.16), he defeated the Sabines; he received public funerals in appreciation for his thriftiness, which brought him to raze his house and rebuild it on lower ground to avoid offending

the people. Menenius Agrippa settled the first secession of the plebs in 494 BCE with his parable comparing the people to a human body, which properly functions only if all its parts work together in harmony. In 458 BCE L. Quinctius Cincinnatus was called from the plow and summoned to dictatorship at a critical moment in the war against the Aequians, as the Roman army had been trapped by the ennemy. Manius Curius Dentatus refused a Samnite bribe of gold, and Gaius Fabricius Luscinus did the same also with King Pyrrhus. Atilius Regulus was the hero of the First Punic War, the captured commander who nobly kept his promise to return to Carthage, torture, and death. Finally, Appius Claudius Caecus (i.e., "The Blind"), the censor of 312 BCE, lived to a great age and saved Rome from a dishonorable treaty with King Pyrrhus in 279 BCE by his denunciation in the senate; see Cicero, *On Old Age* 16 and 37.

17. Sallust, *War against Jugurtha* 64.

18. Petrarca describes the so-called Conflict (or Struggle) of the Orders, a political struggle between patricians and plebs that lasted from 494 to 287 BCE. See Livy's narrative for the secession of the plebs in 494 BCE (2.32) and for the creation of the tribuneship in 472 (2.33).

19. This is not Appius Claudius Caecus (see on §22 above) but Appius Claudius Irregillensis, a much earlier, fifth-century, ancestor. On the *lex Publilia*, creating the tribunes of the plebs elected by the assembly of the people (*comitia tributa*), see Livy 2.56–57.

20. This was the *Lex Canuleia* of 445 BCE.

21. Gnaeus Flavius was elected aedile in 304 BCE; Petrarca follows the account of Livy 9.46 in §§29–30.

22. On the creation of a magistracy of two senators ruling Rome after Cola's fall, see on §12 above. Petrarca notes that these two senators actually resembled ancient consuls, who were also two and had a temporary mandate. In ancient Rome, in fact, consuls held office only for a year, but once a senator, a man remained so for life.

23. In republican Rome, military tribunes were staff officers who commanded a legion. Starting in the mid-fifth century BCE, special military

tribunes with consular powers could be appointed instead of consuls, until in 367 BCE the *leges Liciniae Sextiae* finally authorized one of the two annual consuls to be plebeian.

24. Petrarca echoes Anchises' famous address to the Romans in *Aeneid* 6.853.

25. See Aristotle, *Nicomachean Ethics* 2.9.1109b7.

## VI.7. To Laelius (*F.* 15.9)

This undated letter seems to be a postscript to *F.* 15.8, also to Angelo Tosetti (Laelius), and to judge from the reference to Rome's recent earthquake at §§23 and 25, it belongs to 1353. (On Tosetti see Appendix III.) To Petrarca's hints about his wish to move to Rome itself, continuing a topic of *F.* 15.8, this letter adds two themes: the injustice of calling Rome the new Babylon, and the related beliefs that God had struck the city's great hills out of anger. Petrarca maintains a half-scientific skepticism. See also the earlier letter to Ludwig van Kempen (Socrates), *F.* 11.7, in which Petrarca seems much more overawed by the widespread earthquakes in Italy and the Alpine regions and the earthquake of September 1349 at Rome. The present letter offers a different perspective on the condition of Rome shortly after the attempted revolution of Cola di Rienzo; some of these ecclesiastical ruins would still be unattended to when Urban V came to Rome in 1367.

1. The excerpt comes from Ovid's account of the long letter of the infatuated Byblis to her brother at *Metamorphoses* 9.565.

2. Petrarca is probably echoing the civil wars of Marius and Sulla, of Pompey and Caesar, and of Mark Antony and Octavian, which destroyed the ancient Roman Republic, but he must also have in mind the wars he himself had witnessed and the urban conflicts in Rome that Cola di Rienzo had tried to resolve.

3. Scipio Africanus withdrew from Rome when he and his brother were attacked by political enemies in 187 BCE, and he went to a remote, unfashionable coastal villa at Liternum in Campania, whose simplicity is described in detail by Seneca, *Moral Letters* 86. Baiae, also on the Campa-

nian coast, was, by contrast, the most fashionable of Rome's seaside resorts.

4. Augustine, *City of God* 16.17: Petrarca sees this, and other references by Augustine that follow, as the origin of the reproaches against Rome as Babylon. To him, Avignon, having displaced Rome as seat of the papacy, was the real Babylon, and he repeatedly alludes to it by this name.

5. This and the excerpts at §§7 and 8 are taken from Augustine, *City of God* 18.22. According to the legend, Aeneas' son Ascanius founded the city of Alba Longa and the line of kings from whom Romulus, founder of Rome, descended.

6. Augustine, *City of God* 18.21.

7. Orosius, a disciple of Augustine, wrote a world history, entitled *Histories against the Pagans*, characterized by antipagan polemics: he discusses the parallels between Babylon and Rome at 2.1–3.

8. Jerome, *Letters* 46.11, compares Bethlehem with the city of Rome, to its detriment.

9. King Tullus Hostilius was struck by lightning in his home on the Caelian Hill: see Livy 1.31.

10. This is a paraphrase of Sallust, *Catiline's Conspiracy* 8.5.

11. The quotation is drawn from the ninth-century pope Leo IV, *Sermons* 82.1.

12. See Juvenal, *Satires* 13.225–26, slightly altered.

13. Pliny, *Natural History* 2.136, on the frequency of thunderstorms in Italy, caused by the "mobility" of the atmosphere — not "nobility" as Petrarca writes, following an error in his manuscript of Pliny (see Dotti 2002–5, *ad loc.*).

14. Vergil, *Aeneid* 2.649 (Anchises' reference to his own crippling by Jupiter's thunder).

15. The *Aedes Laterani*, predecessor of San Giovanni Laterano, had been the papal seat until the flight to Avignon; it had been severely damaged by fire in 1308 and was destroyed again in the earthquake of September 9 and 10, 1349.

16. The earthquake of September 9 and 10, 1349, heavily damaged the Basilica of Saint Paul Outside the Walls as well as Santa Maria in Aracoeli, close to the Tarpeian Rock (see *F.* 11.7).

17. The campanile of Old Saint Peter's basilica collapsed when it was struck by lightning on December 11, 1352, and its bells (including the one of Pope Boniface VIII mentioned here by Petrarca) were melted by the heat.

18. Publius Valerius Publicola, first consul with Brutus in 509 BCE, moved from his original house on the Velia to a lower site to avoid public resentment: see Livy 2.7.6, and note 16, above.

19. Petrarca refers to the Capitol, where he was crowned with the laurel of poetry in 1341.

VI.8. To Andrea Dandolo, doge of Venice (*F.* 11.8)

In 1351 Andrea Dandolo had been doge of Venice for eight years (see Appendix III). He had guided the city through the plague of 1348 as well as through famine and wars, of which the most recent, with Venice's old trading rival, Genoa, broke out in August 1350. Petrarca writes, as he says, as an Italian, and treats this war between the important trading cities as a civil war, invoking echoes of Anchises' protest to the future shades of Pompey and Caesar, and echoing Lucan's rebuke to his fellow citizens against civil war. Petrarca's letter, dated March 18, 1351, was answered by Doge Dandolo only two months later, on May 22 (published in Dotti 2012, 635–43). In this reply, Petrarca's lofty patriotic ideals are challenged by a clear explanation of the economic reasons that made a war between Venice and Genoa unavoidable.

1. Ausonia was the name by which ancient Greeks originally indicated Italy: the Lower Sea was an ancient name of the Tyrrhenian Sea, while the Upper Sea indicated the Adriatic. Petrarca's thought seems to be that the regional hegemonies of Genoa and Venice have kept alive belief in the Italians as a sovereign people.

2. Petrarca deliberately echoes phrasing from the opening protest of Lucan's *Pharsalia* 1.2–3.

3. This and the following quotation come from Hannibal's speech before his final defeat at Zama, in Livy 30.30.11 and 20. Petrarca will return to Hannibal's wisdom as leitmotif below.

4. A commission of twenty-five nobles was appointed to manage the war.

5. "Enrolled Fathers" (*patres conscripti*) was the title by which Roman senators were by custom addressed, as originally having been the heads of all noble families.

6. From the same speech (Livy 30.30.19) quoted above at §7.

7. This comes from Numanus Remulus' claim in Vergil, *Aeneid* 9.612, that Italians live harsh lives as peasants and warriors.

8. Petrarca is perhaps calling for Venice and Genoa to direct their military energies into crusades against Turks and Arabs, whose vast empires may be alluded to by invoking the names of famous ancient sites and peoples located in their territories. To be sure, some of these had fallen into decline in Petrarca's time or no longer existed: this was the case with Susa (once capital of the kingdom of Elam but razed by the Mongols in the thirteenth century) and Memphis (once capital of Lower Egypt, but in steep decline during the Byzantine period). Smyrna, a key port on the western coast of Anatolia, and Damascus, capital of Syria, had survived periodic sackings by foreign powers. Thrace and Illyria were proverbially barbaric regions in the ancient world: the former had fallen under the control of the Ottoman Empire in the fourteenth century; the latter was still under Byzantine influence at the time Petrarca was writing.

9. According to the myth, Thebes was torn apart by civil war between the sons of Oedipus: Polynices, the exiled brother, and the ruling king, Eteocles. Petrarca is remembering Statius' great civil war epic, the *Thebaid*.

10. Petrarca was writing from Padua, close to Venice.

11. Both Carthage and Numantia in Spain were destroyed by Scipio Aemilianus in the second century BCE.

12. Juvenal, *Satires* 10.198–99.

13. Scipio Africanus the Elder, hero of the Second Punic War and Petrarca's most cherished model, went through a lightning career and

reached the consulship at thirty-one (nine years under the legal age). Papirius Praetextatus as a boy was honored by the Roman senate for keeping its agenda secret with a clever lie; see Gellius, *Attic Nights* 1.23. As Valerius Maximus reports (3.1.2), Cato the Younger while still a boy told his pedagogue he wanted to kill the tyrant Sulla. In the same chapter (3.1.ext.1), Valerius also reports that Alcibiades as a boy advised Pericles not to give account of his expenses to the people.

14. See Cicero, *Tusculan Disputations* 2.62.

15. Cicero, *Dream of Scipio* (= *On the Republic* 6.29).

16. Again from Hannibal's speech before Zama (Livy 30.30.29).

17. See Servius' commentary to *Aeneid* 1.243, where he mentions a certain king Henetus from Illyria, who first colonized the Venetian region, giving his name to it, *Henetia*, later called *Venetia* in Latin (see also Servius' comments on *Aeneid* 1.292 and 6.359).

18. Petrarca found this excerpt from Ennius' praise of Fabius Maximus Cunctator (fr. 364 Skutsch, from the twelfth book of the *Annales*), who used delaying tactics to ward off engagement with Hannibal, in Cicero, *On Duties* 1.84 and *On Old Age* 10.

19. Venice had requested support from King Peter IV of Aragon in early 1351. It is noteworthy that Petrarca regards the Spanish, a part of the Roman Empire for many centuries, as barbarians. Is this because he saw the Aragonese as descendants of the Visigoths, or because, for him, Italy was the homeland of civilization and all other nations *eo ipso* barbarian?

20. Dotti 2002–5, *ad loc.*, tentatively explains the reference to eastern tyrants by the attempts of the Genoese doge to form an alliance with Anna of Savoy, empress of the Byzantine Empire.

21. These tribal names are a mixture of the enemies of ancient Rome and medieval Italy.

22. In Vergil's first *Eclogue* (vv. 70–72) the Italian shepherd laments that his land has been confiscated as a result of civil war and handed over to a barbarian soldier: the passage is apt for Petrarca's protest against the use of mercenaries.

23. Petrarca learned about Sparta's sparing of Athens at the end of the Peloponnesian Wars in 403 BCE from Justin, *Epitome of Trogus' Histories* 5.8.3–5.

24. See Cicero, *On Duties* 1.64.

25. The echo of Vergil's Anchises (*Aeneid* 6.832–35) is unmistakable. To Petrarca, this war between Italian cities is abominable, because he felt it as a civil war between members of one people.

26. The letter is closed by a long geographical list picturing the potential extension of a combined Venetian and Genoese rule: once again Petrarca resorts to indicating foreign or exotic lands through ancient famous names. The Black Sea (called Euxine by the Greeks), the Ocean, Britain, Africa, and Scythia (a wide region east of the Black Sea into central Asia) were at the outskirts of civilized world in ancient times. The list goes on with great ancient sea powers, particularly those that challenged the Romans: Egypt, conquered by Augustus after defeating Mark Antony and Cleopatra; the Phoenician city of Tyre; the kingdom of Armenia, extending to the Middle Eastern shore before being conquered by Pompey the Great; the pirates from Cilicia on southern Anatolia, also routed by Pompey; and Rhodes, once a key harbor, also made famous by the "Colossus," a gigantic statue of the Sun god Helios. Most of the regions corresponding to these ancient sites were under Islamic rule in Petrarca's time. His list then moves to the western Mediterranean, through Sicily (with a reference to the mythical sea monsters Scylla and Charybdis on the Strait of Messina), and the Balearic islands, famous as pirates' dens both in ancient and in medieval times. The survey is closed by legendary islands at the boundaries of the known ancient world: the Fortunate Isles (or Isles of the Blessed) in the Atlantic Ocean, the Orkney Islands in the North Sea, and the almost mythical Thule (perhaps Iceland); finally, the Hyperborean region indicated the extreme north of the world, while the Antipodean is its southern counterpart.

## VI.9. To Charles IV (*F.* 10.1)

This letter of February 24, 1351, was written to Charles IV, son of John of Luxembourg, elected king of the Romans in 1346 and king of Bohemia in 1347 (on whom see Appendix III). Petrarca's idealistic appeal to Charles passes over the disturbed state of both Rome and Italy, troubled by quarrels both within her cities and among them and also exposed to ravaging mercenary companies. If Charles had wanted to go to Rome and claim his title of emperor, he must have realized the enormous risk of failure. As it is, he did come in 1354–55, but felt bound by the commitment he had given Pope Clement VI to renounce all inherited claims against the papal states and not to linger in Rome after his formal coronation. Even after he was crowned, Charles continued to neglect the troubled land of Italy in favor of protecting his inherited transalpine domains. This letter is the first of a series of appeals preserved by Petrarca: next in sequence are *F.* 12.1 and *F.* 18.1—assigned the important opening position in both books—as is the case of VI.10 [*F.* 19.1], which hails the onset of Charles' Italian expedition of 1354–55. The expedition's evident failure generated fierce rebukes on Petrarca's part (see VI.12), which nevertheless was followed, in later years, by two more appeals (*F.* 23.15 and 21), as Charles seemed to be planning a second expedition. Ironically Charles' formal reply to the present letter (published in Dotti 2012, 584–91) was composed by Cola di Rienzo, when still in favor with the emperor.

1. Charles was thirty-five at the time.

2. Charles was born in Prague, and after 1331 he followed his father, king John of Luxembourg, in his Italian campaigns as imperial vicar; according to the tradition, the imperial crown was awarded in Rome by the pope.

3. Charles is seen as a reincarnation of Augustus, the first and most illustrious of Roman emperors.

4. The name "Caesar" had been an imperial title since the first century CE.

5. Julius Caesar was famed for his swiftness of decision and action: see Suetonius, *Life of Julius Caesar* 57.

6. Cicero, *In Support of Marcellus* 25.

7. Romans had contributed to civilization by their code of laws, the calendar that was still used in Petrarca's time (in the form modified by Julius Caesar), and the art of warfare. The mother-city's harangue sweeps through all the republican history of Rome, which Petrarca knew so well

from Livy and Florus, but lingers specifically on the heroes of Petrarca's own *On Illustrious Men*.

8. See Florus, *Epitome* 1.18.1; Rome's expansion was confined to the Italian peninsula from its traditional origin, in mid-eighth century BCE, until mid-third century BCE, when with the Punic Wars it started extending its power over the Mediterranean; by the end of the republic, in the first century BCE, Rome practically controlled all of it and most of Europe.

9. Petrarca's celebration of Roman republican history begins with a long series of Roman heroes, most of them subjects of chapters in his *On Illustrious Men*. L. Junius Brutus (*On Illustrious Men* 5) expelled the Tarquins and founded the Roman Republic; he executed his sons for having plotted with the exiled Etruscan king and died in single combat against Arruns, the son of Tarquin the Proud. Horatius Cocles (*On Illustrious Men* 6) stood alone to stop Porsenna's Etruscan army while the Romans destroyed the bridge through which Rome could be invaded; then he jumped into the Tiber in full armor and swam across it. The Roman prisoner Cloelia escaped Porsenna's camp by swimming across the Tiber. M. Furius Camillus (*On Illustrious Men* 8) had been exiled after his victory over Veii, but he was later summoned back and rescued Rome after the siege by the Galli Senones in 390 BCE. Papirius Cursor (*On Illustrious Men* 12) triumphed in the second Samnite War. Manius Curius Dentatus (*On Illustrious Men* 13), victor over Pyrrhus at Beneventum, was famous for his extreme frugality, as was Fabricius Luscinus (*On Illustrious Men* 14), who proved incorruptible to the Samnites as well as to Pyrrhus, and Valerius Publicola (see note on VI.6.22), who lived in great poverty but received public funeral for his merits. Cincinnatus (*On Illustrious Men* 7), consul and twice dictator, would always go back to farming his field when not serving his country. Marcus Curtius leaped into a chasm in the Forum (hence called *Lacus Curtius*) in sacrifice to the gods of the underworld. Atilius Regulus was the hero of the First Punic War, the captured commander who nobly kept his promise to return to Carthage, torture, and death. Three generations of the Decii family supposedly devoted themselves to the gods of the underworld to secure victory for the Roman army (*On Illustrious Men* 11): the first defeated the Latins at Veseris in 340 BCE, his son defeated the Samnites at Sentinum in 295 BCE, and

the grandson is said by some sources to have devoted himself before the battle of Asculum against Pyrrhus in 279 BCE. The fourth-century M. Valerius Corvus or Corvinus (*On Illustrious Men* 10) was aided by a crow (*corvus*) when he fought a giant Gaul in single combat. T. Manlius Torquatus (*On Illustrious Men* 9), who had loyally defended his own father against accusations, condemned his son to death for rushing ahead of the battle line. The whole family of Fabii went out to defend their territory and were ambushed at the river Cremera in 477 BCE. The Etruscan king Porsenna could have been mentioned above in the context of Cocles and Cloelia, who led Roman resistance to his siege in the first year of the republic, but Petrarca has reserved him as witness to the heroism of Mucius Scaevola, who failed to assassinate Porsenna but showed defiance by thrusting his right hand into a fiery brazier.

10. Here Petrarca changes tactics, now listing Rome's enemies: the Gallic Senones, who sacked the city in 390 BCE; Pyrrhus, the noble king of Epirus, who invaded southern Italy in the third century BCE; Antiochus III, the wealthy ruler of Syria defeated by Scipio Africanus' brother, Scipio Asiaticus, in 190 BCE; the prolonged resistance of Mithridates VI, who ruled Pontus from 120 to his death in 63 BCE; the treachery of Numidian Syphax in Scipio's African campaign during the Second Punic War; the Ligurians, in the northwest of the Italian peninsula, repeatedly coming to battle with the Romans in the third and second centuries BCE; the Samnites in the Apennine highlands, who repeatedly fought against the Romans in the fourth century BCE; the Cimbrians, who were defeated by Marius in 101 BCE after invading northern Italy; then the second-century Macedonian challenges and the Punic Wars against "deceitful Carthaginians" (a standard accusation: see Florus 1.22.36).

11. Now "Rome" varies her boasts by listing major battles and regions that had been theaters of dangerous wars: Carrhae, where triumvir M. Licinius Crassus was defeated by the Parthians in 53 BCE; Egypt, ruled by Cleopatra and the scene of the crucial last phases of the Roman civil wars; Persis, controlled by the Parthians; and the Arabian peninsula, never completely reduced to Roman control; Pontus, ruled by King Mithridates, and Lesser Armenia, ruled by King Tigranes, both reduced to Roman control in the first century BCE; and Greater Armenia, control

of which was always contended with the Parthians and only briefly conquered by Emperor Trajan; Galatia and Cappadocia in central Anatolia and Thrace come under Roman influence during the second and first BCE century conflicts with the Hellenistic rulers; the African coast, from the west, with Mauretania, ruled by King Bocchus during the Jugurthine War, to the northeast, here indicated by Ethiopia; the Libyan and Spanish coasts, theater of the Second and Third Punic Wars. The list is concluded by a series of famous battlefields: Aquae Sextiae, where the Teutons were defeated by Marius in 102 BCE, then the chain of Hannibalic victories from 218 to 216 BCE at Ticinum, Trebia, Trasimene, and Cannae; and finally the Roman victory over Antiochus III of Syria at Thermopylae (191 BCE), at the site of Leonidas' famous stand against the invading Persians in 480 BCE.

12. Next Petrarca brings in new regions, especially in the East, that came late under Roman control. Conquered regions were often symbolized by geographical landmarks. First, we find a long series of rivers: the Danube and Rhine, flowing through the provinces of north and central Europe; the Rhône, through Transalpine Gaul, and the Ebro, through Spain; the Euphrates and Tigris, through Mesopotamia, Assyria, and Armenia; the Nile, through Egypt; the Hebrus (i.e., Maritsa), through Thrace; the Araxes (i.e., Aras), through Armenia. On the contrary, the Indus, Hydaspes, and Ganges (i.e., Jhelum) in India and the Tanais (i.e., Don) were never included within Roman borders. A list of mountains and mountain ranges follows: Taurus, in Turkey; Olympus, in Greece; Atlas, in the northwest of Africa; and Caucasus, in the Asian hinterland (which was never actually conquered by the Romans). Finally, a list of seas is added, which mixes the Mediterranean seas (the Ionian, Adriatic, Tyrrhenian, and Aegean), the Carpathian Sea (northeast of Crete), the Euboean straits and Hellespontine gulf (the Dardanelles) with the more remote Scythian Sea, probably to be identified with the Caspian, never reached by Roman domination. This long geographical enumeration culminates in the Ocean, the outer limit of the world in the ancient view, which Rome perhaps believed she had tamed with her exploration of the Baltic under Augustus, or her invasion and occupation of Britain in the first century CE.

13. Pope Clement VI had sponsored Charles' election as emperor in 1346 but, in fact, strongly resisted Charles' plan of an armed descent to Rome, fearing it might turn into a conquest. He granted permission to the emperor to come only for the coronation ceremony and without an army in his train.

14. Petrarca is recalling Scipio's campaign in Africa from 204 to 202 BCE, a command Scipio won despite the opposition of Fabius Maximus, and concluded by his victory at Zama.

15. This is Charles' grandfather Henry VII of Luxembourg, who had been cherished by Dante and Dino Compagni and had raised great expectations throughout Italy; he was crowned emperor at Rome in 1312 but died a year later at Buonconvento, near Siena.

## VI.10. To Charles IV (*F.* 19.1)

This letter was probably composed in October 1354, after Charles had finally undertaken his expedition to Italy in order to be crowned emperor in Rome. Petrarca was in Milan at the time.

1. This recalls the previous letters VI.9, *F.* 12.1, and *F.* 18.1.

2. Psalm 15:10.

3. This greeting to Aeneas from his father, Anchises, in the underworld (Vergil, *Aeneid* 6.687–88) is a favorite quotation with Petrarca and is here reused, taking "parent" (*parenti*) to refer to "Mother Rome."

4. Charles IV was born in Prague, the city he would make his capital, but he had spent several years in Italy during his youth (see note on VI.9.7).

## VI.11. To his dear Laelius (*F.* 19.3)

Charles IV had entered Italy, but with only a token force, as promised to the previous pope, and he was headed to Rome, where he would obtain the imperial crown. After sending his congratulations (VI.10), and encouraged by Charles' invitation, Petrarca went from Milan to Mantua (in midwinter) to meet him. This letter, written on February 25, 1355 (see the date of its attachment, *F.* 19.4), to his intimate friend Laelius (Angelo Tosetti), records the significant parts of Petrarca's private conversation with the emperor. The expedition, however, was cut short right after Charles' Roman coronation, and *F.* 19.12 (conjecturally dated to June 1355, four months after this letter) reflects Petrarca's disillusionment and indignation at Charles' retreat.

1. Ovid, *Metamorphoses* 7.826, also *Heroides* 6.21; the sentiment, at times differently worded, is common in Roman elegy.

2. When Hercules in agony chose to die by being burned alive on Mount Oeta, he gave his bow, which was fated to accomplish the fall of Troy, to his beloved friend Philoctetes; Petrarca makes the parallel between this mythical heroic friendship and that of Scipio Aemilianus with Laelius.

3. This alludes to the Elder Laelius (consul in 190 BCE) as friend of the Elder Scipio Africanus, the hero of the Second Punic War, but our sources tell us little of that friendship. The friendship of the younger Laelius (consul in 140 BCE) with Scipio's adoptive grandson Aemilianus, who destroyed Carthage in the Third Punic War, was celebrated by Cicero in his *On Friendship*, one of Petrarca's favorite dialogues. But Petrarca's Laelius (Angelo Tosetti) was exceptional among his friends in being a native of Rome itself.

4. Petrarca addresses Emperor Charles IV with the title "Caesar," by custom due to Roman emperors.

5. Petrarca is echoing the language of Cicero's quotation from Ennius' *Medea* (fr. 353–54 Jocelyn) in *Tusculan Disputations* 1.45, a quotation he could also have read in the *Rhetoric for Herennius* 2.34. Ennius' lost tragedy narrated the adventures of Jason and the Argonauts in their quest for the golden fleece and, in particular, the line in question etymologized the name of the mythical ship "Argo," as derived form "Argives" (inhabitants of the Greek city of Argos).

6. Jason was helped to steal the golden fleece and escape from Colchis by the king's daughter, Medea, who had fallen in love with him, but who secured their escape by murdering her own brother; Euripides and Seneca in their plays called *Medea* depict her as a fatal and destructive prize, later revenging her desertion by Jason with the murders of his bride and his father- in-law, and of her own children.

7. This was Sagrémor de Pommiers, an officer who became Petrarca's friend and a Benedictine monk.

8. See Augustine, *Confessions* 9.6.4, contrasting Italy with the home in North Africa to which he was returning.

9. That is, the gods of war, not those of peace and intellectual leisure.

10. Juvenal, *Satires* 2.8, slightly misquoted.

11. Although Petrarca had begun his *On Illustrious Men* more than ten years previously, he would never recognize it as complete. The implication here is that he might have continued beyond the heroes of republican Rome into his own time, to include the emperor.

12. Chrysippus was the third-century BCE head of the Stoic school and the elaborator of Stoic logic; he was known to Petrarca above all through Cicero.

13. Petrarca refers to his *On Solitary Life*, which he had composed in 1346 with later re-elaborations.

14. Almost certainly Petrarca had Florence in mind. Note also the "Tuscan" soldier whose bon mot is quoted at §24 below.

15. Pliny, *Natural History* 7.110, describes Plato's visit to Dionysius II, tyrant of Syracuse in 366 BCE.

16. On the comparison between Plato and Aristotle, see, for example, Cicero, *Tusculan Disputations* 1.22, and Augustine, *City of God* 8.4.

17. Laelius planned to travel by sea from Avignon to Pisa: *F.* 19.4 is Petrarca's recommendation of Laelius to the emperor.

## VI.12. To Our Caesar (*F.* 23.2, abridged)

Dated March 21, and written in 1361, this is one of several exhortations to Charles IV, urging him to come to Italy (see headnotes to VI.9 and VI.10). It refers in §7 to Petrarca's diplomatic mission to Paris in January of the same year (see *F.* 22.13) and notes in §10 that this is the eleventh year since Petrarca's first appeal to Charles (VI.9), in February 1351. Once returned to Milan, Petrarca received a letter from Charles, which has not survived. The present letter is Petrarca's response to it and lets us gather that Charles had reported the birth of his son Wenceslas and had asked

Petrarca's expert opinion on a delicate matter (on the authenticity of certain allegedly ancient documents produced by Rudolf IV, duke of Austria, in order to prove his independence from the imperial crown). Charles' letter also reiterated his invitation for Petrarca to join him at Prague, and Petrarca's renewed efforts to rally him with pressing invitations occupy much of Book 23 (*F.* 23.8–9, to Charles; and 23.10 and 14, to Charles' chancellor Jan ze Středa). This time, however, Petrarca decided to split his response to Charles' letter: he provides a proper answer to it, with what is now *S.* 16.5, while he devotes the present letter to a vehement exhortation to take real action in Italy at last. In fact, within a frame of courtesy (the initial *captatio benevolentiae* at §§1–8 and the final exhortation and conclusive remarks at 39–43), the letter unleashes a harsh rebuke of Charles, urging him to avoid any further procrastination (§§9–22), timorous indecision (§§23–26), or the alleging of excuses and greater priorities (§§27–38). This selection excerpts most of the letter's first half (§§1–25) and a short later section revealing the pressure put upon Charles by his new situation (§§31–36).

1. This is a sideswipe at the claims of astrologers, comparing their reliance on the stars with his own reliance on God, who made and controlled the stars: see III.20.

2. This allusion to Augustus' known familiarity with Vergil and Horace (on which see V.6.103) flatters Charles by presenting him as Augustus and prepares the ground for Petrarca's persuasive citations of Vergil and Horace in §§11–12 below.

3. Petrarca had just returned from a diplomatic mission for the Visconti at the court of King John the Good of France, who as husband of Charles' sister Bonne of Bohemia was a kinsman of the emperor.

4. That is in VI.9, dated to February 24, 1351.

5. The anecdote in which Trajan is rebuked by an old woman perhaps originated in a passage about Hadrian in Cassius Dio's *Roman History* 69.6.3, and was later elaborated into a legend picturing this famously just emperor as miraculously resuscitated by Pope Gregory the Great, in order to become Christian and be saved. The story enjoyed popularity in the Middle Ages, and it also appears in Dante's *Purgatorio* 10.73–93. Ac-

cording to the tale, as an old widow was insistently asking the emperor Trajan for justice, he replied that he did not have time for her at the moment, but anyway if not he, somebody else would eventually take care of her requests: the woman replied that even if somebody else did her justice, this would not exempt Trajan from the guilt of not having solved the problem himself. Hence the emperor was convinced to deal with her requests at once.

6. Petrarca offers a typical "catena," or cluster, of classical citations to make his point, veiling delicate allusions to coming death in a series of quotations, beginning with Horace, *Odes*.4.7.21–24.

7. The first Vergilian quotation is from *Georgics* 3.66–67, on the swift flight of youth (also much quoted by Seneca), the second from *Aeneid* 10.467–69, in which Jupiter comforts Hercules for the death in battle of young Pallas, his protégé.

8. This rebuke comes from Horace, *Odes* 2.15.15–19.

9. Two quotations from Lucan, *Pharsalia* 6.806–7 and 9.582–84, openly remind Charles of inevitable death in battle.

10. Petrarca turns to Statius, quoting twice from the same address by the prophet-god Apollo to his doomed prophet, King Amphiaraus, at *Thebaid* 7.772 and 774–75.

11. Two citations from Juvenal, *Satires* 9.126–29 and 4.96–97, stress the risk of death before old age, especially for the eminent. Given the (non-military, political) context, the allusion to the rarity of nobles reaching old age warns obliquely against the risk of assassination.

12. See the quotation from Vergil, *Georgics* 3.66–67, at §12 above.

13. Persius, *Satires* 5.66–72, is the rebuke of a teacher to an idle student.

14. Charles had received the imperial crown in 1355.

15. If we count Augustus' "reign" from 42 BCE to his death in 14 CE, we can say he ruled fifty-six years; see Suetonius, *Life of Augustus* 8.3.

16. Charles received the iron crown as king of Italy at Milan in January 1355 and the imperial crown at Rome in April of that year, but by the end of the summer he was already back in Prague.

17. The Scipios may combine here Africanus' triumphant suppression of the Spanish mutiny in 206 BCE (Livy 28.25–29) and the deaths in battle of his father and his uncle in 211 BCE (Livy 25.34–36). Petrarca follows this with Alexander of Macedon's dealings with a mutiny (see, for example, Curtius Rufus, *History of Alexander the Great* 10.2–4) and Julius Caesar's suppression of the mutiny at Piacenza, reported by Suetonius, *Life of Julius Caesar* 69.

18. There seems to be a clever transition here from country as wife (Petrarca often treated Rome as widowed by the loss of emperor and pope) and Charles' new loyalties as husband and father; in the lost letter that Petrarca is responding to, Charles may have pleaded an obligation to his new family and French connections.

19. The allusion of course is to Scipio's expedition to Africa against Carthage in the Second Punic War.

20. See Justin, *Epitome* 12.16.9.

21. Charles began life as king of Bohemia, but now he is father of the newborn crown prince, Wenceslas, and the child can take on his role.

22. See Hebrews 13–14.

23. Charles had promised Pope Clement VI as early as 1346 not to occupy any land belonging to the Church, whether inside or beyond Italy, which Charles took as an obligation not to linger in Rome; hence his almost instant departure after his coronation in 1355. Petrarca wishes that now at last the new pope, Innocent VI, might set Charles free from this obligation.

## VI.13. To Brother Giacomo (*F.* 19.18)

Giacomo Bussolari (on whom see Appendix III) was an Augustinian friar from Pavia (*Ticinum* in Latin), who thanks to his extraordinary gift for eloquence had managed to enter public life there and became a leading political figure starting in 1355. The Visconti wanted to absorb Pavia into their empire, taking over the city by force or intrigue: Petrarca writes from their point of view. Bussolari's powerful preaching established his supremacy there, driving out the Beccaria family, who took refuge with the Visconti. He had successfully led the city's resistance under a first siege by the Visconti in 1356, but after two years the Visconti mounted a new campaign (April 1358, suspended, then resumed more strenuously in March 1359). Bussolari tried to rally a last resistance but had to negotiate surrender in November of that year. Galeazzo Visconti now became lord of the city and Bussolari was imprisoned in the Augustinian convent of Vercelli by January 1360. The present letter was composed in March 1359 and later this year Petrarca addressed a second letter to Bussolari, written in the name of Bernabò Visconti (*Miscellaneae* 7 = 39 ed. Pancheri, *Lettere disperse*).

1. Augustine's *City of God*. The next three quotations come from *City of God* 19.11–12.

2. Cicero, *On Duties* 1.35.

3. This is the first of several quotations from the Psalms: here 33:15.

4. This and the next quotation come from Psalm 121:6.

5. This and the next quotation come from Psalm 121:7.

6. Psalm 71:7.

7. Psalm 36:11.

8. Psalm 4:9.

9. Jeremiah 29:7.

10. Mars and Bellona were pagan war gods.

11. Jeremiah 38:4.

12. Proverbs 16:27–28. The wise man is Solomon.

13. Ecclesiasticus 28:11. The wise man here is Shimon ben Yeshua.

14. Psalm 139:3.

15. Psalm 139:4.

16. This combined praise of Cato the Elder and Scipio Aemilianus comes from Pliny, *Natural History* 7.100, from which the quotation below in this paragraph is drawn.

17. This is Cato the Elder's famous definition of the orator, as reported by Seneca the Elder, *Controversies* 1, preface 9, and Quintilian, *Institutes of Oratory* 12.1.1.

18. In the mythical construction of Thebes, it was Amphion, the lyric poet (not strictly an orator), who built the city and was its first ruler. The epithet "Dircean" echoes Vergil's *Eclogues* 2.24 and alludes to the myth according to which Amphion and his twin brother Zethus killed their aunt Dirce, who had kept their mother, Antiope, imprisoned.

19. Matthew 10:34.

20. John 15:12.

21. Matthew 5:44 and Luke 6:27.

22. Mark 9:49.

23. For example, Mark 5:34.

24. For example, John 20:19.

25. An interesting comment on how the Gospels were read; here, Luke 14:28–31.

26. Hebrews 12:14.

27. Cicero as consul in 63 BCE drove Catiline to leave Rome by the eloquence of his first oration *Against Catiline* (see Sallust, *Catiline's Conspiracy* 32.1), but he was an elected magistrate; Bussolari was a private citizen leading by force of eloquence without elected office.

28. Petrarca's source for Pisistratus, sixth-century BCE tyrant at Athens, and the unexpectedly negative evaluation of Pericles, praised by all Greek historians, follows Valerius Maximus' chapter on the power of eloquence, 8.9., ext. 1 and 2

29. Pavia had been the capital of the Lombard kingdom of Italy in the sixth through the eighth centuries CE.

30. Nothing seems to be known of this exiled giant or about the engagement that Bussolari apparently led at Rocca di Nazzano. Hercules' patronymic Alcides derives from Alcaeus, father of Amphitryon, and so Hercules' putative grandfather.

31. Psalm 44:4–5.

32. Alluding to Judges 6:23–24.

33. Suetonius, *Life of Julius Caesar* 44.1.

34. According to Dotti 2002–5, *ad loc.*, Petrarca may here be referring to those few messages from Caesar attested within Cicero's *Letters to Atticus* and attached to Cicero's own letters.

35. The remains of Augustine were buried in the church of San Pietro in Ciel D'Oro in Pavia, whither they were moved in the eighth century.

36. See Seneca, *Moral Letters* 25.5, also quoted by Petrarca in VII.2.48, to his brother, Gherardo.

## PART VII

### VII.1. To Annibaldo, cardinal bishop of Tusculum (*F.* 6.1)

Annibaldo da Ceccano, from the noble Roman family of Caetani from Ceccano (on whom see Appendix III), was elected bishop of Tusculum in 1327 and, as cardinal, during the papacy of Clement VI constructed for himself a palace of exceptional luxury at Avignon. He was sent to Rome by Clement as papal legate in 1348 after the failure of Cola di Rienzo's attempted revolution (see VI.4) and in preparation for the Jubilee of 1350. He died (perhaps assassinated) at Naples shortly after representing the pope at the Jubilee. The letter (the only one addressed to Annibaldo in Petrarca's collection) cannot be dated but is appropriate to the years after 1343, when Annibaldo displayed his luxury in an extraordinary reception at his palace in Avignon. More likely, given its tone, it was only composed or made public after the cardinal's death.

1. Vergil, *Georgics* 3.37, where envy is trampled beneath the feet of Augustan justice.

2. The story comes from Macrobius, *Saturnalia* 2.2.8.

3. Horace, *Epistles* 1.2.57.

4. Petrarca compares greed unfavorably to all other deadly sins: envy (§§1–2), pride (§2), wrath (§4), sloth, gluttony, and lust (§12).

5. Horace, *Epistles* 1.2.56.

6. Seneca, *Moral Letters* 2.6, the first of several applications of Senecan moralizing in this letter.

7. See Seneca, *Moral Letters* 16.7–8 and 25.4.

8. This is one of the moralizing sayings of the first-century BCE mime writer Publilius Syrus, quoted by Seneca the Elder, *Controversies* 7.3.8. Petrarca, like many others, who knew Publilius only through his one-line maxims, perceived him as a sort of philosopher.

9. Here Petrarca cites Seneca's dialogue *On Anger* about another of the deadly sins: see in particular 2.32.1.

10. Juvenal, *Satires* 14.139.

11. Both quotations come from Seneca, *Moral Letters* 119.9.

12. Horace, *Satires* 1.1.73–75.

13. The other satirist is Juvenal: see his *Satires* 12.129–30.

14. This echoes both Horace, *Odes* 1.1, and Ovid, *Metamorphoses* 7.61. The allusion to limiting his empire by the Ocean in the following sentence is a variation of Jupiter's prophecy about Caesar in Vergil, *Aeneid* 1.287.

15. According to the myth known to Petrarca from Ovid's *Metamorphoses*, among other sources, the ancient Phrygian king Midas gave hospitality to the god Dionysus, who in return granted Midas' wish that everything he touched would be turned to gold: as a result, Midas deprived himself of all nourishment and human contact.

16. This is the first of several citations of the prophets: Haggai 1:6.

17. In *My Secret Book* 2.49, Petrarca pictures Augustine telling him that he is suffering from *accidia*, which is the Christian equivalent of what the Romans called *aegritudo*, a disinclination to work.

18. See 1 Timothy 6:10.

19. The source of most clerical wealth lay in benefices, nonheritable income streams produced by Church properties that reverted to the Church on the death of the holder. Petrarca himself took minor orders so as to be eligible for benefices, and he enjoyed several during his life (see Appendix I).

20. The following two quotations are from Psalm 38:6–7.

21. Vergil, *Aeneid* 3.222–23, where Aeneas' men impiously eat the harpies' cattle.

22. See Seneca, *Moral Letters* 31.11.

23. Petrarca's resentment of wealthy book collectors is based on the belief that he had a better use for books; we may compare Seneca's condemnation, for example, of Calvisius Sabinus in *Moral Letters* 27.

24. The following two quotations are from Persius, *Satires* 2.61–62 and 69.

25. Malachi 16.

26. See Psalm 75:6.

27. Again, Persius, 2.69–70.

28. See Ephesians 5:5 and Colossians 3:5, followed by 1 John 5:21: "protect yourselves from images."

29. "Corinthian bronze" (*aes Corinthium*) was the name given to an alloy of copper, gold, and silver, deemed an object of extreme luxury by ancient Romans.

30. See Psalm 115:16–17.

31. See Psalm 4:6.

32. Psalm 50:19.

33. Petrarca is still citing Persius' second satire: here 2.71–72, followed by 73–74 in the next sentence.

### VII.2. To his brother Gherardo (*F.* 10.3)

This letter, composed in 1349, is the first addressed to Gherardo in this collection and comes after more than six years of epistolary silence with him (see Introduction, vol. 1, xxx–xxxviii): both this letter and VII.4 mention the length of Gherardo's stay at Montrieux, going back to 1343. Foresti, *Aneddoti,* 113, argued that Gherardo entered the monastic order because he had lost a woman he loved in 1340 but spent some time grieving before he resolved to become a Carthusian. Much of the central sections of this letter (§§12–40) are preoccupied with the trials of secular life (one's vain concern for a beautiful appearance, the foolish enticements of love, the empty search for glory, and the treacheries of most human relationships), before Petrarca turns to praising the peace and harmony of Gherardo's monastic world, in terms that he repeats in the treatise *On Religious Leisure*.

1. Petrarca compares his brother to Ulysses, but, in fact, Ulysses did not block his own ears, because he did want to hear the Sirens; instead, he blocked his sailors' ears, so they would not be distracted while he himself was tied to the mast and listened to the sirens' song.

2. This is part paraphrase, part quotation of Vergil, *Aeneid* 6.374–77.

3. Again Vergil, *Aeneid* 6, here 296–97.

4. Petrarca is identifying Christ with God as aspects of the Trinity. Hercules was son of Jupiter and Alcmene, whom Jupiter had seduced under the disguise of her mortal husband, Amphitryon.

5. According to ancient sources, Pythagoras believed in metempsychosis, claiming to have been reincarnated from the Trojan warrior Euphorbus (spelled "Euphorbius" here): see Ovid, *Metamorphoses* 15.1.58–75; Gellius, *Attic Nights* 4.11.14; Lactantius, *Divine Institutes* 3.18.16–17. Petrarca knew of Plato and Aristotle's theories about the soul from medieval sources (for example, Augustine, *City of God* 10.30, on Plato). The hypothesis of metempsychosis had also fascinated the late antique Christian theologian Origen, who was criticized on this and other points of doctrine by Jerome (see, for example, his *Letter* 84).

6. On the honors granted to Pythagoras in his lifetime and after his death, see Justin, *Epitome* 20.4, while the information about the rule imposing five years of silence upon Pythagoras' pupils is drawn from Seneca, *Moral Letters* 52.10.

7. Seneca, *Moral Letters* 94.70.

8. Persius, *Satires* 1.28.

9. This anecdote about the famous first-century BCE orator Quintus Hortensius Hortalus is found in Macrobius, *Saturnalia* 3.13.4–5.

10. Charybdis is the sea monster that, along with Scylla, was believed to produce deadly whirlpools in the Strait of Messina.

11. See Psalm 140:5.

12. Here (and below at §59) Babylon is not specifically—as it is elsewhere—Avignon, conceived as a seat of corruption, but a general worldly city, the antithesis of the Heavenly Jerusalem.

13. Both the woman loved by Gherardo and Petrarca's beloved Laura had died young (the former in 1340, and the latter in 1348)—which might be considered fortunate from a Christian perspective, as this allowed them to reach Heaven sooner.

14. Psalm 123:7–8.

15. See Seneca, *Moral Letters* 47, on the proper treatment of household slaves.

16. Seneca, *Moral Letters* 47.5.

17. Homer's Odysseus disguised himself as a beggar to obtain access to his own palace and was abused at length by Penelope's suitors, as well as by Irus the beggar and Melanthius the cowherd, who, along with numerous other servants and maids (including Melantho, sister of Melanthius), had sided with the suitors. Petrarca's phrasing echoes Cicero, *On Duties* 1.113.

18. The source of this anecdote about Frederick II, Holy Roman emperor, remains unknown.

19. Juvenal, *Satires* 6.347–48.

20. Petrarca seems to have in mind the executors of his father's estate, whom he believed had cheated himself and Gherardo: see II.6.22.

21. Petrarca appears to misquote Seneca: the words cited are not attested in any of his works, but the first part of the quotation echoes not Seneca but Horace, *Satires* 2.7.6–7.

22. Horace, *Satires* 1.9.59–60.

23. This is the opening phrase of Horace, *Satires* 1.2.

24. In Book 9 of Lucan's *Pharsalia,* Cato tests his men by a prolonged march through the Libyan desert, and earlier in the poem the Caesarean centurion Cassius Scaeva performs miracles of valor to honor Caesar,

regretting only that his leader was not present to see his feats (*Pharsalia* 6.140–262; in particular vv. 158–59).

25. Seneca quotes a similar saying of Epicurus in his *Moral Letters:* see for example 11.8–9.

26. See Seneca, *Moral Letters* 25.6.

27. See Cicero, *Letters to Quintus* 1.1.46.

28. Psalm 138:8.

29. Referring to Christ's arrest in the Garden of Gethsemane, when he reproached his disciples for not staying awake to pray with him on his last night before the Crucifixion; see Matthew 26:36–56.

30. John the Baptist withdrew to the wilderness to live a solitary life, which was a model for later Christian hermits. Saint Anthony Abbot (d. 356 CE) was the first Christian hermit to become famous, thanks to a hagiographic life by Athanasius, which was translated into Latin and read by Augustine (see *Confessions* 8.6). Macarius of Alexandria was another, later anchorite particularly revered by Carthusians. Saint Benedict founded the Benedictine Order in the early sixth century. Augustine lived as a monk in his native North Africa soon after his conversion. The senator Arsenius was tutor to the emperor Theodosius' sons but retired to Egypt to become an anchorite.

31. The *Lives of the Fathers* are a collection of hagiographic biographies, mostly of Egyptian hermits, compiled in the sixth century. Gregory the Great's *Dialogues* are a miscellany, mostly including anecdotes and biographical accounts of saints. Finally, both *Soliloquies* and *Confessions* are presented by Augustine as forms of meditation, through an imaginary internal dialogue.

32. See Jerome, *Letters* 52.7.

33. Petrarca's poetic work alluded to here may be the first eclogue of the *Bucolic Poem* (probably composed in 1346), which Petrarca attached to the following letter, *F.* 10.4, and discusses at length at *F.* 10.4.11–33; they might also refer to the *Penitential Psalms;* for both works see Appendix II.

34. Psalm 54:7.

35. Petrarca counters his criticism of secular life by declaring that he is not ready to leave it (Babylon here stands for the secular world, rather than specifically Avignon: see above, on §22).

## VII.3. To a friend (*F.* 16.4)

This letter is tentatively assigned to 1353, but neither the occasion nor the friend are specified, and editors generally believe Petrarca wrote it to disguise his own personal doubts. His main theme is divine Mercy, and the forms "mercy," "merciful," and "showing mercy" have been kept in translation for all Petrarca's deliberate uses of this concept. But there is another, similar word, *pietas*, which Petrarca uses alike for the loving devotion of God's human worshippers and God's own loving kindness. No word in English conveys both the love of the protector and the dependent, and so the terms "pious" and "piety" have been kept.

1. Genesis 6:6.

2. Augustine, *Exposition of the Psalms* 147.17.

3. This and the following excerpts in §§7–8 are from Augustine, *On True Religion* 16.30.

4. Augustine's text here quotes John 1:14.

5. Here Petrarca introduces the first of numerous quotations from the Psalms (here 102:12).

6. The quotation is from Lucan, *Pharsalia* 9.1021, and refers to the pact between Caesar and the king of Egypt sanctioned by the blood of Caesar's dead enemy Pompey the Great; it is quite inappropriate to this highly religious context: hence, perhaps, Petrarca's "someone says."

7. This continues Psalm 102 (see on §9) with verse 13, and in the next sentence verse 14.

8. Augustine, *On True Religion* 8.14.

9. Here begins a long sequence of quotations from the Psalms, going through all of §15; in order, 92:4, 88:8, 65:5, 85:5, 102:8, 85:15, and 24:8.

10. Genesis 4:13.

11. See Matthew 27:5.

12. See Ambrose, *On Repentance* 2.4.27.

13. See Ps.-Jerome, *Breviarium in Psalmos* 108.

## VII.4. To Gherardo (*F.* 17.1)

This letter, dated November 7, belongs most likely to 1353, ten years after Petrarca's brother, Gherardo, entered the order (see §7); it begins with a close echo of Seneca's *Moral Letter* 46 to Lucilius, in which Seneca acknowledged the receipt of a pamphlet or treatise from his addressee. Like Seneca, Petrarca claims to have stayed awake all night until he finished reading the letter and praises the writer's elegant style, but he does not indicate his thesis or arguments, which we can only guess from the contents of Petrarca's response. In fact, Petrarca's praise of Gherardo's literary achievement, seen as inspired by God, leads him to urge his brother on in the pursuit of God's "true philosophy" and "true law," as opposed to human philosophical or legal studies (compare Petrarca's resolve to substitute Christian reading for his beloved secular authors, in III.17). In particular, Petrarca relies heavily on his knowledge of Augustine's works for his exposition.

1. See Seneca, *Moral Letters* 46.1.

2. The epithet derives from Cecrops, the legendary first king of Athens.

3. Paris and Bologna were the most famous universities for philosophical-theological and legal studies, respectively. Petrarca and his brother had been sent by their father to study law at Bologna, but both later abandoned the course.

4. Cicero, *Tusculan Disputations* 2.11–12.

5. Augustine, *City of God* 8.8.

6. Augustine, *City of God* 8.1.

7. The following quotation has not been found in any work of Augustine, nor can it be traced to any other author. The Latin text printed here reproduces that of the authoritative Rossi edition, yet one wonders whether the length of Augustine's quotation has been misrepresented in the manuscripts or misinterpreted by editors. An alternative hypothesis might be that Petrarca is quoting Augustine only at the beginning of the

first sentence: "If Wisdom is God by whom all things were made" (*Si sapientia Deus est per quem facta sunt omnia*), a phrase which in fact comes from *City of God* 8.1, quoted above at §16. What follows that sentence might be taken as Petrarca's own comment, including the end of the sentence "this is undoubtedly Christ" (*hic enim proculdubio est Cristus*), in which Petrarca means to complete Augustine's thought by making it explicit that Christ is part of the Godhead (see §16 introducing this sentence).

8. Athanasius of Alexandria is the fourth-century Christian theologian, a great champion of the Trinitarian doctrine against Arianism, and hence credited with the authorship of the Nicene Creed in 325.

9. John 1:3.

10. Augustine, *On True Religion* 7.13.

11. This and the following quotations are from Augustine, *On True Religion* 55.113.

12. Augustine, *City of God* 11.23, continued in the next sentence by 11.24.

13. Augustine, *On True Religion* 3.5.

14. Colossians 2:8.

15. See the list of lawgivers at Isidore, *Etymologies* 5.1, where we also find the theory deriving Roman legislation from that of Solon. Phoroneus, an ancient king of Argos, is mentioned as a famous legislator also by Augustine, *City of God* 18.3. The mythical Spartan king Lycurgus and the Athenian sixth-century lawgiver Solon were widely known through various indirect traditions.

16. Petrarca enumerates the known sources of Roman law, from the Twelve Tables compiled in 451 BCE to the decrees of the Senate and laws of the people, as well as the supplementary laws issued by praetors in office, then edicts issued by other authorities, such as the republican dictators and later the emperors.

17. For Moses as legislator, see, besides Exodus, John 1:17 and Isidore, *Etymologies* 5.1, cited above.

18. The Latin word *caput,* literally, "head," can mean "fountainhead" and "source," or "chief authority."

19. Augustine, *Exposition of the Psalms* 143.2.

20. The rending of the veil in the temple during the Passion of Christ is recorded by Matthew 27:51, Mark 15:38, and Luke 23:45.

21. Augustine, *On True Religion* 5.9.

22. Augustine, *City of God* 20.4.

23. Lactantius, *Divine Institutes* 6.8.6–9, quoting Cicero, *On the Republic* 3.33. Lactantius' full name was Lucius Caecilius Firmianus Lactantius, wrongly spelled "Formianus" by Petrarca (as though he were a citizen from the Campanian town of Formiae).

24. Lactantius, *Divine Institutes* 6.8.10.

25. Psalm 101:28, possibly mediated by Augustine, *Confessions* 1.6.10.

26. This and the following quotation are from Psalm 18:8.

27. Mark 10:14.

28. Matthew 11:25.

29. This and the following quotations are from Psalm 114:6.

30. Petrarca is recalling, along with the three famous ancient philosophers Aristotle, Plato, and Pythagoras, three famous jurists from the turn of the second and the third centuries CE: Papinian and Ulpian were counselors of Septimius Severus and his dynasty and were authorities cited in the *Digest*; Scaevola, named here, is the second-century CE jurist Cervidius Scaevola, not the famous republican jurist Q. Mucius Scaevola.

31. The exchange between Socrates and his famous pupil, Aeschines of Sphettus, is reported by Seneca, *On Benefits* 1.8: since Aeschines was not wealthy, he claimed he would give his own soul to Socrates in exchange for his teachings; Socrates accepted the offer and responded that he would return it to Aeschines after making it better.

32. Terence, *The Andrian Girl* 61.

33. The great majority of Varro's vast work of erudition had been lost since antiquity, yet the fame of it survived and granted him the title of philosopher and savant: see the note on VIII.7.

34. See Suetonius, *Life of Augustus* 79.2.

35. Psalm 140:6 is also discussed by Petrarca, in *On Religious Leisure* 2.9.10; the first translation comes from Jerome's fourth-century version of the Bible (known as the Vulgate), the second is from a version circulating earlier (generically called "Old Latin" or "Old Italic").

36. Augustine, *Exposition of the Psalms* 140.19.

37. See Seneca, *Moral Letters* 16.7; there is a wordplay here on the Roman legal procedure of *usucapio*.

## VII.5. To Giovanni [Boccaccio] of Certaldo (*S.* 1.5, abridged)

This letter to Giovanni Boccaccio belongs to 1362. The story embedded in it should be seen as an example of Petrarca's wise skepticism about holy men who claimed special insight into the future: Pietro Petroni is a Christian monk, but his prophecies are no more persuasive to Petrarca than those of the astronomers discussed in III.20. Petrarca tended to be expansive in his letters to Boccaccio; this selection offers an abridged version. Petrarca starts out by summarizing the major points in the letter he had received from Boccaccio (§§1–23), then deals first with Boccaccio's fear of his predicted death (§§23–83), and finally with Petroni's second warning, the prohibition of further secular writing (§§84–131). The letter closes with a personal coda (§§132–47), proposing how Boccaccio should act if he is resolved to abandon scholarship and dispose of his books and inviting Boccaccio to pool their libraries and to live with him. Despite his own skepticism, Petrarca treats tactfully both Boccaccio's fears and the dead monk's claims to prophecy, and he draws on the lives of pagan writers and the teaching of Christian authorities to reassure his friend.

1. §§5–13 briefly comments on a secondary topic present in Boccaccio's letter: his questioning of Petrarca's plan to leave Italy and move to Germany at the court of the Holy Roman emperor Charles IV.

2. The Blessed Pietro Petroni, who died May 29, 1361.

3. In Vergil's *Georgics* 4.393 (as in the Homeric model scene in *Odyssey* 4), the omniscient and prophetic sea god Proteus told Aristaeus what he needed to know.

4. Petrarca quotes from the second sentence of Nicene Creed, referring to Christ, "through whom all things were made."

5. All these classical examples, except the last, are of true warnings given by dying men to their antagonist: the dying Hector tells Achilles he too must die, at *Iliad* 22.258, a story known to Petrarca, probably through Cicero's *On Divination* 1.65; the Trojan Orodes warns the Etruscan king Mezentius in Vergil's *Aeneid* 10.739–41; in Cicero, *Tusculan Disputations* 1.96, Theramenes, sentenced to death for being too moderate as one of Athens "Thirty Tyrants," offers a toast to his enemy Critias when forced to drink poison; the Indian sage Calanus warns Alexander the Great before committing suicide in Cicero *On Divination* 1.47. The anecdote about the famous Greek philosopher Posidonius of Apamea also comes from Cicero (*On Divination* 1.64), who had been his student in Rhodes.

6. Cicero, *Tusculan Disputations* 1.114, to which Petrarca returns in §52 below.

7. This and the following quotations in §§41–47 are from Ambrose, *On the Decease of his Brother Satyrus* 2.30; Ambrose's discussion begins by commenting on the words attributed to Solomon in Ecclesiastes 4:2–3.

8. Job 3:3.

9. The text of Ambrose (*On the Decease of his Brother Satyrus* 2.33–34) quotes Psalm 38:5 and Jeremiah 15:10.

10. Petrarca refers to Cicero, *On the Republic* 6.14, *Tusculan Disputations* 1.75 and 114 (from which the quotation is drawn; see also §35 above). Despite Petrarca's remark, Cicero wrote his *On the Republic* around 54–51 BCE, when he was already over fifty; the *Tusculan Disputations*, composed in 44 BCE, is, however, one of his latest works. For the alternative title, *Tusculan Investigations*, see the note on III.1.4.

11. Gregory the Great, *On the Gospels* 2.37.1.

12. The passage comes from Lactantius, *Divine Institutes* 3.19.11–16. On the name *Formianus* attributed to Lactantius, see the note on VII.4.31. In the following sections, omitted here, Petrarca continues to quote Lactantius (§§61–64) and to discuss the relation of life to death and the inter-

pretation of life as an opportunity to prepare for death through meditation (§§64–78).

13. Hezekiah was granted fifteen more years by God, after praying to him while ill: see 2 Kings 20:1–6.

14. Vergil, *Aeneid* 10.467–69 (a consolation for the imminent death of young Pallas).

15. See Seneca, *Moral Letters* 36.4.

16. The Muses supposedly lived on Mount Helicon, while Apollo, god of poetry, was patron of the Castalian spring near Delphi.

17. This is an allusion to Lactantius' *Divine Institutes* and to Augustine's *City of God* and *Against Julian* (attacking Julian of Eclanum, leader of the Pelagian heresy), respectively.

18. Compare Jerome's famous letter to Eustochium (*Letters* 22.30), in which he had a vision of being condemned in the divine court for his love of pagan literature, being "a follower of Cicero, not of Christ."

19. This recalls Jerome's attack on Jovinian (*Against Jovinian*) and his other treatises against the heretics, his letter to young Nepotianus on the duties of priests (*Letter* 52), and his *Epitaph* for Nepotianus.

20. §§102–8 elaborate on the utility of cultivating literary studies for those who are already experts and know very well how to discern good and bad in what they read. This is followed by a long survey, drawn from the classical world, of famous examples of literary activity pursued in old age (§§109–21).

21. Again a reference to Jerome's famous self-accusation of being too attached to secular studies: see on §97 above.

22. Gregory the Great praises Benedict in the prologue to his second book of *Dialogues* for founding his monastic order.

23. In Acts 26:24 the procurator Festus tells Paul, "Much learning hath made thee mad."

24. Rizzo 2006–14, *ad loc.*, identifies this successor as Petrarca's son, Giovanni.

25. Terence, *The Andrian Girl* 941; what we would call nitpicking.

26. Petrarca had recommended to Èlie de Talleyrand both Boccaccio and Nelli to become Zanobi da Strada's successor as apostolic secretary in 1362. Nelli accepted, Boccaccio refused, as Petrarca himself had done.

## VII.6. To Urban V (*S.* 7, abridged)

When Petrarca addressed Pope Urban V in this letter, Avignon had been the seat of the papacy since Clement V (1305–14) had settled the Curia there in 1309. Clement and his papal successors were all French, supported initially by Philip IV of France and appointed by a college of cardinals who were not only French but in many cases related to individual popes as their "nephews," that is, illegitimate offspring. But the election and policies of Urban V (on whom see further Appendix III), alluded to by Petrarca in §§108–20 of this letter, were exceptional in recent papal history. Urban knew Italy well from his diplomatic visits and favored a return of the Curia to Rome. At the same time Avignon itself was increasingly threatened by the Free Companies, bands of mercenary soldiers who had to be bribed to take their attacks elsewhere. The papal territories in Italy were threatened by Bernabò Visconti, with whom Urban had to make peace at last in 1364. Although the pope had announced his desire to return to Rome soon after his accession, the issue only came to the fore when Charles IV arrived in Avignon to promote the move in May 1365. Petrarca himself does not mention this action of the emperor in the present letter, but he does emphasize Charles' parallel role to that of the pope; he uses their Roman titles in an elaborate ring composition starting from the initial *captatio benevolentiae* (§5 and 33–65), where *Romanus imperator* matches Urban as *Romanus pontifex*, and where the emperor is named as the illustrious precedent for Petrarca's daring to correspond with the most powerful religious authority in Christendom. This idea is developed in the course of the letter and in the end closes it with a final invocation addressed to both pope and emperor. It was surely negotiation with the emperor rather than Petrarca's reproaches that prompted Urban's decision to move the Curia back to Rome in 1367. Although Petrarca's letter is dated June 29, 1366, we know that he sent it first to Francesco Bruni, asking him not only to check its content but to refer it to Philippe de Cabassoles and Agapito Colonna for approval before sending it on to the pope himself. Since Petrarca's appeals (VII.6 as well as VII.7) are so extensive, not to say long-winded, and in some respects duplicate each other, only their introductions and several excerpts are offered here. In the present letter, after explaining his patient delay before addressing the pope (§§1–65), Petrarca offers an impassioned account of Rome's Christian shrines now ruined, and the mother-city herself, as the bride neglected by her papal spouse (§§65–89). The letter continues with a discussion of the reasons why Urban V and no other is destined to bring the Curia back to Rome (§§90–129) and a refutation of the arguments advanced by Avignon's advocates, i.e., Rome's lack of good food, beautiful places, safety, and luxury items (§§130–76). The second half of the letter is occupied by an extremely long peroration, within which Petrarca repeats and further expands most of the topics discussed earlier (§§177–263, and the closing exhortation to come back to Rome at §§308–42) and touches on the question of raising another crusade, Urban's own most cherished goal, against both the Ottoman Turks and the Greek Orthodox Church (§§264–307).

1. This is Petrarca's old friend and religious superior at Vaucluse, Philippe de Cabassoles, who at the time held the title of Latin patriarch of Jerusalem, that is, archbishop of Jerusalem, though he did not reside in the inaccessible Holy Land (what would later be styled *in partibus infidelium*) but at Avignon. Petrarca had not seen him since 1353, when Petrarca left Avignon to return to Italy.

2. Petrarca had addressed letters to Pope Benedict XII (*Metrical Epistles* 1.2 and 5) and Clement VI (*Metrical Epistles* 2.5 and *F.* 5.19) but not to Urban's immediate predecessor, Innocent VI, with whom he was on hostile terms (see *Sine nomine* 12); for Petrarca's correspondence with the Holy Roman emperor Charles IV and other rulers, see Part VI.

3. This anecdote on old Solon's attempt to oppose the return of Pisistratus' tyranny in Athens comes from Cicero, *On Old Age* 72.

4. In 84 BCE, during the Social Wars, Marcus Castricius, magistrate at Placentia (Piacenza), refused to give hostages to the consul Gnaeus Papirius Carbo, who was threatening to put the city under siege; the episode comes from Valerius Maximus 6.2.10.

5. See Augustine, *Soliloquies* 1.27. After giving reasons for his daring to write to the pope in the initial paragraphs (§§1–13), Petrarca moves on to explaining why he has not done it earlier: so far Urban had proven his renowned virtue only in minor matters, praiseworthy though they were, and Petrarca was waiting for him to tackle the greater enterprises to which he is destined (§§14–55).

6. The pope was also the bishop of Rome and as such, in the traditional canon-law image, was the city's spouse, responsible for its/her governance.

7. Petrarca alludes to the common proverb "Where the pope is, there is Rome," a favorite of defenders of the Avignon papacy. For the arguments on either side, see Eugenio Dupré Theseider, *I papi di Avignone e la questione romana* (Florence, 1939).

8. The references are to Ps.-Ambrose, *De vocatione omnium gentium* 2.16, and Augustine *Esposition of the Psalms* 95.2. Petrarca had made the same point in *De vita solitaria* 2.4.3.

9. Psalm 97:7.

10. Psalm 101:28.

11. Psalm 78:8.

12. Other cities have bishops to care for them, but the pope is the only bishop of Rome; see note 7 above.

13. Lamentations 1:1, followed by 1:2 and 1:16 in §80.

14. For the holy sites ruined by the earthquake of 1349, see VI.7, which, however, does not name the Church of the Holy Apostles (Basilica dei Santi Apostoli), also completely destroyed by that earthquake. After urging the pope to consider the conditions of Rome, that is, of his own proper see (§§87–89), Petrarca starts to explore the reasons why Urban V and no other is destined to go back to Rome: he chose the name "Urban" (recalling another Latin name for Rome, often simply referred to as the *Urbs*, §§90–102), and he was miraculously elected by God's will, against the will of the corrupt cardinals (§§103–20), evidently because he was destined to fulfill a special mission (§§121–29).

15. Psalm 135:4.

16. After introducing the arguments advanced by Avignon's advocates (§§130–38), Petrarca goes on to challenge them one by one, mostly resorting to personal anecdotes meant to show the falsity of the charges against Rome: that it lacked good food (§§139–41) and beautiful places (§§142–58), or that it was unsafe (§§159–68) and offered no luxuries (§§169–76).

17. Guy de Boulogne was one of Petrarca's trusted friends in the Curia. The reference to the Jubilee dates this episode to 1350.

18. Cardinal Élie de Talleyrand had died in 1364. The identity of the other French cardinal who was a protagonist of this episode is obscure.

19. Pope Boniface VIII was clever, determined, politic, and widely despised. In particular, he quarreled with King Philip IV of France over questions of ecclesiastical taxation and feuded with the Colonna family, Petrarca's patrons. In 1303 he retreated from Rome to his birthplace and seat at Anagni, where he was insulted and seized by Sciarra Colonna and a force commanded by the French king's agent, Guillaume de Nogaret, but subsequently freed by an uprising of Roman citizens.

20. After refuting each of the arguments against Rome, Petrarca goes on with a long section in which he urges the pope, mostly by further expanding on earlier arguments (§§177–263): Urban was created pope in Rome, not Avignon, and even chose a name recalling the ancient city (*Urbs*); Rome is extremely devout and is less dangerous than France, which is threatened by the Free Companies; Italy is safe and beautiful and lacking much less than other places; and, finally, Rome is the very place where the apostles and first martyrs and saints lived.

21. Vitruvius, *On Architecture* 6.1 (in particular §§9–11) is certainly Petrarca's main source for this deterministic theory, claiming that the rise of the Roman Empire was due to the balanced natures of the Italian population, in turn caused by Italy's temperate climate; see also Pliny, *Natural History* 2.189–90, and Claudius Ptolemy, *Tetrabiblos* 2.2. The theory ultimately derives from Aristotle, *Politics* 7.7.3, where it is applied to Greece and the Greeks.

22. Petrarca's encomium springs from the tradition of Vergil's famous *Laudes Italiae* (*Georgics* 2.109–76), itself inspired by Varro's encomium in

his *On Farming* 1.2.3–8. Liguria, Venetia, and Emilia were the regions covering almost all of the north of Italy, including Lombardy, in late antiquity (see the notes on II.13.3–4 and II.5.69); Flaminia was the late antique name of a region roughly corresponding to the contemporary Marche.

23. Petrarca is thinking of the contemporary merchant powers of Venice and Genoa.

24. On the content of §§230–63 omitted here, see on §168 above.

25. Petrarca echoes Vergil's praise of Italy (see above on §226), which speaks not of unarmed but of unwarlike (*imbelles*) Asians (*Georgics* 2.172): the allusion is apparently sarcastic. The Phrygians were an ancient population inhabiting Anatolia.

26. The Greek Orthodox Church, who parted from the Roman Church with the East-West Schism of 1054, is another target against which Urban is urged to take action.

27. Theodosius, Christian general and emperor, defeated the troops of the usurper Eugenius under the command of Arbogast at the river Frigidus in 394 CE, allegedly thanks to a windstorm: see Orosius, *Histories* 7.35.11–21.

28. Claudian, *On the Third Consulship of Honorius* 93–98. Petrarca shares the medieval belief that Claudian was from Florence ("my compatriot"), probably derived from the name "Florentinus," a character addressed within his work *The Rape of Proserpina*. Claudian was pagan, but the Christian interpretation of this passage, as Rizzo 2006–14, *ad loc.*, observes, derives from Augustine, *City of God* 5.26, and Orosius, *Histories* 7.35.21.

29. Claudian's imagery is transferred from the storm of Aeolus in Vergil, *Aeneid* 1.81–91, which is also recalled by Ovid in the flood at *Metamorphoses* 1.74–75, where Neptune summons the rivers as auxiliary troops.

30. These three rivers formed the boundaries of the Comtat Venaissin, the semi-autonomous state around Avignon owned by the pope, though within French territory.

31. John 10:11–12.

32. Petrarca alludes to Aristotle's doctrine of the mean, that the virtuous path lies in the middle between extremes.

33. Terence, *The Brothers* 386–88.

34. Capital city of the Greek Orthodox Church.

35. Paul, bishop of Thebes, was named Latin patriarch of Constantinople by Urban V on April 17, 1366; the Latin patriarch was an office established with the creation of the Latin Empire of Constantinople, after the Fourth Crusade in 1204, and continued to exist even after its fall in 1261, after which the patriarchs resided in Venice.

36. Petrarca is most likely thinking of Italy's two most successful maritime cities, Venice and Genoa, whose fleets would be crucial to any crusade.

37. The Holy Roman emperor Charles IV.

38. Caesar's saying is drawn from Florus 1.45.14–15; that of the emperor Titus from Suetonius, *Life of Titus* 8.1; those by Alexander the Great are drawn from Claudian, *On the Fourth Consulship of Honorius* 374–77 (Alexander as a youth), and Curtius Rufus, *History of Alexander the Great* 4.13.16–24 (as an adult).

39. During the battle of Gibeon, Joshua asked God to stop the sun and the moon, so that he could keep fighting in daylight: see Joshua 10:12–13.

40. Petrarca's peroration spins toward the end by recapitulating, once more, the falsehood of the arguments in favor of Avignon (§§308–17), then rises through a crescendo of reproaches to Urban himself (§§318–34): the pope is accused of being no different than the French cardinals, as he cheats God by having a room called "Rome" in his palace at Avignon, and he is even reminded of his own mortality, which culminates in the image of both God and Saint Peter harshly rebuking him as an ungrateful mortal who has not repaid their sacrifice. From the lofty tone of these protests, Petrarca then finally descends to a more "humble" tone in the closing of the letter, with a wish addressed to both the pope and the Holy Roman emperor to return to their proper seats in Rome (§§335–43).

41. Petrarca lists here a series of saints and martyrs who either died in Rome or whose relics were later transferred to a Roman church. In fact, both Jerome and Stephen died in Palestine, and Jerome's relics were brought to Santa Maria Maggiore in the twelfth century, while several different churches claimed those of Saint Stephen.

42. On the oath pronounced by Charles IV, see the note on VI.12.35.

### VII.7. To Urban V (*S.* 9.1, abridged)

In his determination to restore the papacy to Rome, Urban V had to face opposition from both the French cardinals and the new king of France, Charles V, whose representative, Ancel Choquart, delivered (and circulated) a speech to the Curia at Avignon before Urban's departure that exalted France and denigrated Italy. Nonetheless, in April 1367 Urban did set out for Rome, traveling by sea and reaching Viterbo in June, which the papal commander Cardinal Albornoz had strengthened with a fortress. Urban stayed there four months, because the papal residences at Rome were still in ruins and unfit to house him, but Viterbo too became perilous, when its people rose up against the arrogant behavior of the French cardinals. Despite all these obstacles, Urban actually took up residence at the Vatican on October 16, 1367. But he faced continued obstruction from the cardinals around him in Rome and renewed French vilification of Italy. Although the pope wrote twice from Rome asking Petrarca to come to his aid, the poet excused himself: both the pope (born 1310) and the poet were aging, and Urban was unable to resist the importunities of the French cardinals and perhaps was also influenced by the disorders still persisting in the city. In September 1370 he withdrew from Italy, dying three months later. In this second major appeal, probably written early in 1368, Petrarca presses his argument, blaming the French cardinals and retaliating against the chauvinistic speech of Ancel Choquart, but Petrarca's words will in turn provoke the later pamphlet of Jean d'Hesdin, exalting France and reviling Italy, to which Petrarca will respond with a fully rounded invective, *Against a Detractor of Italy* (*Contra eum qui maledixit Italie*). A text and translation (by David Marsh) of the latter text was published in this I Tatti Renaissance Library (2003).

1. Psalm 113:1–2. Petrarca equates the flight from Avignon with the Israelites' captivity in pagan Egypt, before Moses led their escape.

2. Saint Peter, the first pope, came to Rome and died there.

3. Ecclesiastes 26:21.

4. John 15:5.

5. Petrarca counts sixty years as if from 1305 (from the accession of Pope Clement V, who was in Bordeaux at the time and officially moved the Curia to Avignon only in 1309) to 1365. The five popes are: Clement V (1305–14), John XXII (1316–34), Benedict XII (1334–42), Clement VI (1342–52), and Innocent VI (1352–62).

6. Petrarca treats as parallel rulers the emperor Charles IV (who had visited Avignon to show his interest in Urban's return) and the pope: compare "that other governor of temporal matters" at §16. The allusion is clearly to VII.6, recently sent to the pope.

7. There is a Latin rhyming pun (*pungere/ungere*) here, which Petrarca also uses elsewhere. Both verbs have a physical meaning: to "prick" and to "smear with ointment"; but *ungere* has a second implication, "to anoint a priest or monarch."

8. After the initial warm congratulations for Urban's return to Rome (§§1–17), the letter moves on to a long section (§§18–166) in which the praises for Urban's achievement are intertwined with Petrarca's refutation of most of the arguments against Rome he had already challenged in VII.6: these arguments are now raised not only by the cardinals (§§35–67, Rome lacks good wine and the beauties of the Rhône; §§143–66, Rome and Italy are marginal and powerless) but also by King Charles V's emissary, Ancel Choquart (§§80–142).

9. Urban V came from Castle of Grizac in Languedoc and may therefore be emotionally attached to France.

10. The young king Charles V of Valois, succeeded to his father John the Good in 1364, when he was twenty-six years old. John had been defeated and imprisoned by the English and was only released by the treaty of Brétigny (1360), so the French monarchy had to act vigorously to redeem its prestige.

11. Ancel Choquart, the French envoy sent to persuade the Curia to return to Avignon.

12. The translation "a learned contest" (*literatum certamen*) has here been used for what is perhaps better called a contest of words, which implies a text full of literary and classical allusions.

13. A pun is probably intended on the other sense of *gallus:* a "cockerel" or "rooster."

14. Petrarca's version of the famous proverb *verba volant, scripta manent.*

15. Petrarca had met Charles V during his mission to France on behalf of the Visconti in winter 1360–61.

16. Petrarca starts with the last of the four great Church Fathers, Pope Gregory the Great, born in Rome, and joins his name with the much earlier Ambrose, bishop of Milan, born at Trier around 339 of a Roman family and educated at Rome; then Jerome, born at Stridon in Dalmatia in 347; and Augustine, born at Thagaste in North Africa in 354, who lived and taught at Rome and Milan and experienced his religious conversion there. All of them were buried in Italy: Gregory and Jerome in Rome (Jerome's remains were transferred there, though he had died in Palestine), Ambrose in Milan, and Augustine in Pavia.

17. Petrarca alludes to the civil and canon law, whose foremost authorities were Roman and whose principle medieval expositors were mostly Italian. The ancient Greeks, by contrast, did not produce a significant tradition of jurisprudence.

18. The Rue de Fouarre, the informal seat of higher education in Paris since the twelfth century, the birthplace of scholasticism.

19. This is probably an allusion to France's recent defeat by England, and to the subsequent imposition of taxes and war penalties.

20. Most cardinals had either one of Rome's seven great basilicas as their assigned seat or a diocese in Roman territory. They had the power to tax their titular dioceses and sometimes exploited them like tyrants.

21. France had been ravaged not only by the plague of 1348 but above all by the consequences of the Hundred Years' War. Petrarca had a chance to

witness the effects during his mission to Paris on behalf of the Visconti (see on §86 above).

22. Tarentum and Capua had been powerful cities already in antiquity and had gained new importance under the Normans in the eleventh century, while Ravenna, already a key harbor under the Romans, had seen its moment of greatest splendor under the Byzantines in the sixth century.

23. Petrarca was still living in Venice in early 1368, though about to move to Padua.

24. For the derivation of the name Veneto from a legendary king Henetus, see the note on VI.8.26. The name *Venetia,* as indicating the city itself, originated only in late antiquity, but, as Rizzo 2006–14, *ad loc.*, observes, Petrarca may have been misled by the interpretation of a passage by Pliny the Elder, who lived under the emperor Vespasian, where the name *Venetia* (referring to the region, not the city) is mentioned within a list of city names (see *Natural History* 6.218).

25. The Latin name of Florence, *Florentia,* means "the flowering (or flourishing) city." It was founded only in the first century BCE, when Rome was already a great power.

26. Bologna was the site of Italy's greatest university, especially for the study of canon and civil law, where Urban V had once taught; this is why Petrarca treated the city as particularly dear to the pope. Compare his comments on the recent ruin of Bologna's city walls and its government in IX.1. More recently, Cardinal Albornoz had restored the city to the rule of the Church in 1360. According to Rizzo 2006–14, *ad loc.*, the reason why Petrarca calls Bologna "happiest" (*felicissimam*) under Vespasian probably reflects a misreading of Pliny, *Natural History* 3.115.

27. Saint Ambrose, *Letters* 2.8.3. Among the cities listed in Ambrose's passage, only Piacenza and Modena were founded as Roman settlements around the time of the Second Punic War (218–202 BCE); Bologna and Reggio Emilia (*Regium Lepidi*), on the contrary, were created a few years later, more with a view to protecting Italy from renewed Gallic invasions than from the defeated Carthaginians.

28. A long appeal for Urban to persevere in remaining at Rome occupies the final section of the letter (§§167–239); this is yet again intertwined with Petrarca's retorts to some of the cardinal's arguments against Rome (in particular, its insalubrious air and its ruined and deserted aspect).

29. Luke 9:62.

30. Orpheus' journey to Hades to recover Eurydice was foiled by his own weakness in looking back, contrary to the orders of the gods of the underworld: the versions of this very famous story best known to Petrarca are likely to be Vergil, *Georgics* 4.453–527, and Ovid, *Metamorphoses* 10.1–77. The story of Lot's escape from Sodom with his wife and daughters is told in Genesis 19 (the quotations are from 19:17 and 26).

31. See Vergil, *Georgics* 2.534, and Horace, *Secular Hymn* 9–12.

32. This is surely an allusion to Nero's "Golden House" (*Domus Aurea*), the pleasure palace he built for himself after the great fire of Rome: see Suetonius, *Life of Nero* 38.

33. Aristotle, *Economics* 1.6.1345a.3–4, probably known to Petrarca through the Latin translation of Durandus de Alvernia.

34. Psalm 135:4.

## PART VIII

### VIII.1. To Pulice (*F.* 24.2)

The last book of the *Familiares* contains a series of nine fictitious letters addressed to ancient writers, framed by three letters (*F.* 24.1–2 and the conclusive *F.* 24.13 [= I.3]) addressed to three different friends. *F.* 24.1, to Philippe de Cabassoles, opens the book looking back at the years gone by since the beginning of the epistolary collection and moves to a long meditation on the swift passing of life and the always imminent onset of death. Death certainly casts its shadow on this entire book, since, except for the first two letters, all of Petrarca's correspondents are dead: both his beloved ancient models and his dearest friend Socrates (Ludwig van Kempen), to whom he addresses the closing letter, just shortly after receiving the news of his passing away (see Part I). Yet it is not death that dominates the closing book of the *Familiares*, but rather the human attempt of ultimately defying it through memory: Petrarca feels a very real closeness to those men who lived many centuries before him and whose works he loved so much and in many cases pulled out with his own hands from dusty and forgotten repositories, bringing them back to light—and to life. So in spite of death, he writes letters addressed to them in the underworld, and he addresses the correspondents in frank and intimate terms—really as old friends. In the same way, I.3 addresses Ludwig van Kempen as if he were still alive, and closes the book and the collection with a homage to the man in whose name the collection had been opened. Within this frame, the present letter, addressed to Enrico Pulice from Vicenza (see Appendix III), has the function of providing an explanatory introduction to the novelty of letters to the ancients as a whole, though it names only the first three of them (VIII.2–3 to Cicero and VIII.4 to Seneca); it also recalls Petrarca's original performance/reading of them, explicitly dated to his journey of 1351 from Padua to Mantua through Vicenza and Verona (see II.7).

1. Petrarca left Padua on May 4, 1351: see the note on II.7.1.

2. The key to Petrarca's criticisms, *levitas* and *inconstantia*, recalls what he says at §18, below, in this letter; in general, see the notes on VIII.2–3.

3. According to Dotti 2004–9, *ad loc.*, this old man might be a certain Bartolomeo Popolo, *doctor grammaticae* from the same town as Enrico Pulice.

4. See Cicero's phrase "that god of ours, Plato" in *Letters to Atticus* 4.16.3.

5. See Quintilian, *Institutes of Oratory* 10.2.18.

6. According to Cicero, *On the Nature of Gods* 1.10, Pythagoras' followers believed in anything he said without questioning it; it was enough for them to say, "Ipse dixit (He himself said it)."

7. Petrarca started composing his fictitious letters to the ancients already in 1345, right after discovering in Verona Cicero's epistolary collections to Atticus, Brutus, and Quintus: see the notes on VIII.2.

8. See Petrarca's arguments in VIII.2.

### VIII.2. To Marcus Tullius Cicero (*F.* 24.3)

Both this letter and the next addressed to Cicero are explicitly dated to 1345 (on Cicero see Appendix III). The first one is presented as composed shortly after Petrarca's sensational discovery of Cicero's *Letters to Atticus, Brutus,* and *Quintus* in the Biblioteca Capitolare (Chapter Library) of the Verona Cathedral, and it springs from Petrarca's reaction to reading those texts. The letters exposed Petrarca to an image of Cicero much different from that of the noble statesman and "holy philosopher" that seemed to emerge from his other works. Cicero's letters show him shifting loyalties through difficult political relationships, being trapped by extenuating doubts on what course of action to take, and often being caught by impotent despair. Cicero's letters supply a record of a man who lived through a period of extreme political unrest and through a civil war, and who ultimately died in it. Petrarca himself admits he no longer shared the feelings that initially drove him to "respond" to Cicero's letters and to feel so much disappointment in the character they reveal (see VIII.1.17). Petrarca's criticism above all focuses on Cicero's poor judgment of the political situation and certainly does not take into sufficient account the effect of Caesar's autocracy on senatorial government as Cicero knew it. Given the near-worship of Julius Caesar in Petrarca's generation, it is not surprising that Petrarca should take particular offense at Cicero's condemnation of Caesar, once the dictator's death had restored his freedom of political comment.

1. The phrase echoes Cicero, *In Defense of Sulla* 73.

2. The self-reproach comes from Ps.-Cicero, *Letter to Octavian* 6.

3. Cicero wrote more than once that after his consulship he hoped to enjoy "leisure with prestige" (*otium cum dignitate,* see, for example, *On the Orator* 1.1), but the later course of his life convinced him that this was not an option; after Caesar's victory and the Egyptian assassination of Pompey in 48 BCE, he refrained from political activism until the death of Caesar in 44 BCE. At that point Cicero was over sixty years old, yet he engaged in a fierce contest with Mark Antony, Caesar's political successor, who in the end had Cicero killed by his henchmen while he was trying to flee to Greece.

4. See Cicero, *On the Orator* 3.13, recalling Quintus' advice to look at the downfall of many powerful men and avoid dangerous enmities.

5. Dionysius was a learned slave who taught Cicero's son Marcus in the 50s BCE. Cicero greatly exalted him in his earlier *Letters to Atticus* (Books 4–6; see, for example, 4.11.2), but in equal measure criticized him after their relation grew colder (beginning with Cicero, *Letters to Atticus* 7.7.1 through Books 7–10; see, for example, 9.12.2), and then again welcomed him in his favor (see *Letters to Atticus* 13.2b and 33). Cicero's correspondence also attests to the ups and downs in his relations with his brother and his nephew (both named Quintus): in the case of his brother it goes from very affectionate terms in earlier letters to much harsher tones following their disagreements in 49 BCE over the conflict between Pompey and Caesar. Quarrels went on even longer with the younger Quintus, for various reasons. In a few years, however, they were all reconciled (see, for example, *Letters to Atticus* 16.5.2) and all suffered proscription by Mark Antony and the triumvirs in 43 BCE. Cornelius Dolabella was fiercely attacked, along with his ally Mark Antony, in Cicero's *Philippics;* yet the *Letters to Atticus* show that Cicero had a very different attitude toward him earlier on, not only because Dolabella had been his son-in-law for a few years but also because Cicero had tried political collaboration with him: see, for example, the high praises addressed to him in *Letters to Atticus* 14.17a, which Atticus himself considered a bit excessive, and 14.18, attesting how the relationship with Dolabella had become tense on several issues.

6. To Petrarca and many later students of Rome, Caesar's western conquests made him a hero. Cicero appreciated his learning and intellect but could not forgive him for overriding the Senate's authority as consul in 59 BCE and illegally invading Italy in 49 BCE. While Cicero had earlier cooperated with Caesar in public works, in 49 BCE he felt obliged to support Pompey. After Pompey's defeat at Pharsalus, Cicero refused Caesar's invitation to take part in what he considered a sham political life. Apart from a short-lived hope of renewed liberty when Caesar pardoned Marcus Marcellus in 46 BCE (thanks in part to Cicero's speech *In Defense of Marcellus*), Cicero became consistently more hostile to Caesar's autocracy and ultimately applauded his assassination. Cicero's correspondence fully

displays his progressive shifting of opinions and allegiances and above all his moments of uncertainties and weakness in choosing sides and deciding what course of action to take.

7. Cicero very frequently stresses his close relationship with Pompey in his *Letters to Atticus* (see, for example, 1.12.3, 1.17.10, 2.20.1) and he adduces it as the reason for offering himself as a mediator between him and Caesar on the eve of the civil war (see *Letters to Atticus* 9.11a).

8. The quotation comes from *Letters to Brutus* 1.16.7: this letter from Brutus to Cicero, harshly blaming him for supporting Octavian, is generally considered a spurious rhetorical exercise later merged in the collection. Cicero, in fact, had mixed feelings toward Octavian, thinking he was bright but too young to be reliable. The *Letter to Octavian*, transmitted along with those to *Atticus, Brutus, and Quintus* in the manuscripts, is spurious, but Petrarca believed its harsh criticism for Octavian's sudden siding with Antony was authentic and blamed it as the reason why Cicero was left without allies at the mercy of Antony.

9. Cicero, *Letters to Brutus* 1.17.5, another letter by Brutus, preserved within the collection but now considered spurious.

10. The allusion is to Cicero, *Letters to Atticus* 10.8.8, written in 49 BCE during the civil war conflict.

### VIII.3. To Marcus Tullius Cicero (*F.* 24.4)

This letter was composed in 1345, only a few months after VIII.2, and is intended as a sort of *amende honorable* to Cicero. It is chiefly important for its evidence of Petrarca's familiarity with Cicero's works and awareness of those that had not yet been rediscovered (§§11–14).

1. See Cicero, *On Friendship* 89: in this dialogue it is in fact Laelius who quotes this line by Terence (*The Andrian Girl* 68), calling him a friend (*familiaris meus*); both Laelius and Terence belonged to the circle of Scipio's friends and protégés.

2. In Book 2 of *On Moral Ends*, Cicero criticizes Epicurus extensively for the odd discrepancy between his austere way of life and the theory of hedonism expressed by his philosophy.

3. This is not Seneca the philosopher, but his father, the Elder Seneca: on this medieval misunderstanding, see the note on VIII.4. In *Controversies* 1, preface 11, echoed here, the Elder Seneca laments that of all the greatest orators he missed hearing only Cicero, not because he belonged to another generation but because Cicero had died too soon in the civil wars. The comparison between Cicero's and Vergil's different fields of expertise comes from *Controversies* 3, preface 8, where it is reported as an example used by the contemporary orator Cassius Severus to justify the fact of being a brilliant orator in court but a much inferior one when it came to the genre of declamatory exercises.

4. The story comes from Servius' commentary on Vergil, *Eclogues* 6.11. According to Servius, Cicero happened to be present at an alleged early public reading of Vergil's *Eclogue* 6 (the collection of *Eclogues* was in fact not finished before 39 BCE, four years after Cicero's death), and he loved it so much that he praised the poet as *magnae spes altera Romae*, a phrase Vergil himself uses in *Aeneid* 12.168 to describe Aeneas' son, Ascanius. Vergil became the Italian humanists' chief model in poetry, as Cicero was in prose.

5. See Juvenal, *Satires* 11.180–81, and Macrobius, *Saturnalia*, Books 5–6: as Dotti 2004–9, *ad loc.*, points out, both sources were also mentioned in the comparison between Latin and Greek poetry in Petrarca's *Things Worth Remembering* 2.25.3.

6. This was Petrarca's own judgment, but he had very little knowledge of the Homeric texts at the time he was writing this letter (see VIII.9).

7. Propertius salutes the *Aeneid* in *Elegies* 2.34.61–66; Petrarca probably draws the reference from Donatus' *Life of Vergil* 30.

8. The loss of many of these works by Cicero is lamented also at II.6, III.1, and III.9. Petrarca knew only the parts of *On the Republic* preserved by Macrobius' commentary on the *Dream of Scipio* (from the final book of *On the Republic*), along with some excerpts in Lactantius and in Augustine. *On Household Matters* is Cicero's lost translation of Xenophon's *Oeconomicus* (see III.1.4). *On Warfare* refers to a spurious work, abridging Vegetius' longer treatise. *On the Praise of Philosophy* refers to Cicero's lost dialogue *Hortensius*, which Petrarca knew from the excerpts quoted by

Lactantius and by Augustine (see III.9.8). Also, the *Consolation* Cicero composed after his daughter's death is lost and known only through references in Lactantius and in Jerome (see II.6.17). For *On Glory*, II.6 describes how Petrarca believed he had found two copies of this text but lost them when they were borrowed and pawned by his old teacher Convenevole da Prato.

9. Cicero's main works on oratory (*Brutus, On the Orator, Orator*) were known in Petrarca's time only from truncated manuscripts (the *mutili*). The *Academica* went through two editions while Cicero lived, but only parts of each edition survive. Three books of *On the Laws* survive out of a probable five.

10. These rivers marked the outermost boundaries of the known world in ancient times, and so did the Ocean, the Indians, and Garamantes (an ancient Libyan tribe) mentioned in the following two Vergilian quotations. Both quotations are drawn from prophetic representations of Augustus' future glory: in Jupiter's prophecy, at *Aeneid* 1.287, and Anchises' vision, at *Aeneid* 6.794–95.

11. Petrarca uses the mythical term "Erebus" to indicate a generic pagan underworld or hell, as opposed to Christian Heaven.

12. Petrarca is at Avignon.

### VIII.4. To Annaeus Seneca (*F.* 24.5)

The letter is dated from Parma in 1348, three years after the letters to Cicero, and was later revised around 1365 (see note on §17 below). Petrarca was familiar with all the texts of Seneca known to us and with other texts attributed to him that we now believe to be inauthentic; but he also shared the confusion of his time about the two Senecas (see Appendix III). Petrarca lacked a major source for Seneca's life, the sections of Tacitus' *Annals* recording the reigns of Claudius and Nero (Books 11–16) discovered by Boccaccio in 1371. Nor could he read Cassius Dio's Greek histories of Nero's reign, which were not translated until 1533. Petrarca's Seneca here depends entirely on Suetonius' imperial biographies and internal references in Seneca's own works.

1. According to Rossi 1933–42, *ad loc.*, Petrarca may here refer to a passage in Seneca the Elder (*Controversies* 1, preface 6–7).

2. Petrarca refers here to the spurious *Epistula Plutarchi instruentis Traiani,* also known as *Institutio Traiani,* excerpts of which are preserved within the work of John of Salisbury (*Policraticus* 5–6).

3. Petrarca echoes the late antique and Byzantine opinion that Plato was *theios,* Aristotle *daimonios,* that is, that Plato's spirit was divine while Aristotle's was merely super-human. Petrarca does not use the word *demonius* here in the Christian sense of an evil spirit. Fenzi has argued in the notes to his edition of Petrarca's *On His Own Ignorance and That of Many Others* (488–89, n. 519), the epithets "divine" and "demonic spirit," for Plato and Aristotle, respectively, derive from William of Moerbecke's thirteenth-century translation into Latin of Proclus' work *De providentia et fato* (Proclus' original Greek version is now lost); they reflect the late antique Platonic view that Aristotle's philosophy was more authoritative when dealing with the sublunar world, Plato's with theological questions.

4. Plutarch's *Parallel Lives* do include the coupled biographies of Demosthenes and Cicero, as well as those of Alexander the Great and Caesar, but Plutarch does not seem ever to have written biographies or essays comparing Homer with Vergil, nor comparing Varro with both Plato and Aristotle. Also, no such praise of Seneca as the one reported here by Petrarca is present anywhere in the extant corpus of Plutarch's works. So far no written Latin source is known for these dubious pieces of information. Pade, *The Reception of Plutarch's Lives,* 68–70, following a suggestion in Rossi 1933–42, *ad loc.,* argues that Petrarca's source may rather be oral, given his acquaintance with the Greeks Barlaam and Nicolas Sigeros at the time this letter was composed.

5. Seneca was brought back from exile by Agrippina in 49 CE in order to tutor her son Domitius Ahenobarbus (the future emperor, Nero). As it turned out, it was an offer he could not refuse.

6. The Great Sirte (Gulf of Sidra on the Libyan shores) was famously dangerous in antiquity for its storms and treacherous shoals.

7. A reference to the sword of Damocles, mentioned in Cicero, *Tusculan Disputations* 5.21.

8. This dream is reported by Suetonius, *Life of Nero* 7.1.

9. Cleanthes of Assus (flourished in the third century BCE) was a pupil of Zeno of Citium, the founder of Stoic philosophy, and, after Zeno's death, his first successor at the head of the school. A hymn to Zeus composed by him (see *Stoicorum Veterum Fragmenta* 1.527), from which this line is taken, is quoted with approval by Seneca in *Moral Letters* 107.11 (written around 64, late in Nero's principate).

10. See Suetonius, *Life of Nero* 35.5.

11. See Suetonius, *Life of Nero* 52.1.

12. See Ovid, *Sorrows* 2.381.

13. The *Octavia*, with its negative depiction of Nero, cannot be by Seneca, who is himself portrayed in the tragedy as trying to convert Nero to merciful behavior; more significantly, the tragedy shows knowledge of Nero's death, which occurred in 68 CE, three years after he ordered the assassination of Seneca.

14. This sentence and the entire §17 that follows were inserted into the letter at a later stage, probably after learning about Boccaccio's hypothesis on the existence of two different authors under the name of Seneca (see Dotti 2004–9, *ad loc.*). Around 1362–63 Boccaccio had in fact gotten hold of an extremely rare manuscript containing Martial's *Epigrams*, probably in Montecassino: at 1.61.7–8, while listing famous poets and writers who like himself had come from Spain, Martial mentioned the existence of two Senecas. Of course Martial's text meant to distinguish between Seneca the Elder, the "Rhetor," and his son, Seneca, the philosopher and dramatist, but Boccaccio instead interpreted the passage as distinguishing between one Seneca, who was both rhetor and philosopher, and a second and younger one, author of the tragedies. The *Octavia* is believed by modern scholarship to be an anonymous work of the late first century CE.

15. This comment reflects on Petrarca's own self-censorship in his public speeches.

16. *On Clemency*, composed in 55 CE, praises the new emperor Nero in order to show him how he should behave and the rewards mercy will gain him. *The Consolation to Polybius* was written by Seneca from exile around 43 and quotes a fictitious speech by Claudius; in fact, it was ad-

dressed to Claudius' powerful freedman Polybius, lavishing praise on the emperor in the hope of being recalled.

17. Suetonius, *Life of Nero* 19.3.

18. See Suetonius, *Life of Nero* 22.1–2.

19. See Suetonius, *Life of Nero* 12.3.

20. See Suetonius, *Life of Nero* 22.3.

21. See Suetonius, *Life of Nero* 12.4.

22. It was a common hyperbole to treat the ruling emperor as divine. For the comparison with Augustus, see Seneca, *On Clemency* 1.11.1.

23. Suetonius, *Life of Nero* 16.2.

24. Starting with the late second century (for example, Tertullian, *On the Soul* 20.1), we see attestations of a supposed conversion to Christianity by the philosopher Seneca. By the time of Jerome (*On Famous Men* 12) and Augustine (*Letters* 153.14), the legend of a friendship between the Apostle Paul and Seneca was circulating, along with a pseudonymous set of letters exchanged between the two of them. Petrarca here refers to Ps.-Seneca, *Letters to Paul* 12.

## VIII.5. To Marcus Varro (*F.* 24.6)

Marcus Terentius Varro was born in 116 and died in 27 BCE. He served as admiral under Pompey and later briefly as Pompey's legate governing Further Spain. Despite having sided with Pompey during the civil war, he received Caesar's pardon and was commissioned to establish a public library. This project was interrupted by the civil conflict after Caesar's death but later resumed by Asinius Pollio under Augustus; Varro, however, was the only living man honored by a portrait bust among the Greek and Roman writers in the library (see Pliny, *Natural History* 7.115). In fact, Varro, during his long life, had been a prolific writer, composing over seventy works in a total of over six hundred individual volumes. Yet, of this immense production, only the three books *On Farming* and six out of twenty-five books *On the Latin Language* have come down to us; the rest are only known through scattered fragments and titles. The complaint for such a great loss is the main topic of Petrarca's letter to Varro. At the time Petrarca first composed it (the original version was dated 1343 [*sic*], while the final one is of November 1, 1350), he probably did not even have direct knowledge of either of the surviving texts; according to Piras, "Nuove testimonianze," he obtained a copy of *On Farming* only in 1360, from Guglielmo da Pastrengo, and one of the extant books of *On the Latin Language* in 1355, from Boccaccio (who had found it in Montecassino); see *F.* 18.4. Here Petrarca draws his information on Varro from indirect sources (mostly Cicero, Augustine, and Lactantius).

1. Plautus, *Casina* 19.

2. On Varro's relations to Pompey and Caesar, see headnote. From Lactantius, *Divine Institutes* 1.6.7, we know that Varro had dedicated his work *On Divine Matters* (*Rerum Divinarum libri*, part of his *Antiquitates*) to Caesar in 47 BCE, at a time when Caesar had long held office as pontifex maximus.

3. For a list of Varro's works and their fortuna from antiquity to the early modern period, see the article of Virginia Brown, "Varro, Marcus Terentius," in *Catalogus Translationum et Commentariorum*, ed. F. E. Cranz (Washington, D.C., 1980), 4:451–500.

4. Varro participates as a speaker in Cicero's skeptical *Academica* and is honored in a fragment of that dialogue cited by Augustine, *City of God* 6.2.

5. See Lactantius, *Divine Institutes* 1.6.7.

6. Cicero speaks more than once of Cato's recommendation about the proper use of leisure: for example, *On the Republic* 1.27, and *In Defense of Plancius* 66.

7. Varro, like Cicero, had studied in Athens with the academic philosopher Antiochus of Ascalon. The comparison between Cicero's and Varro's styles derives from Augustine, *City of God* 6.2.

8. The quotation as well as the laudatory comment on Varro's books *On Divine Matters* and *On Human Matters* (together forming his *Antiquitates*) derive again from Augustine, *City of God* 6.2. Books 4, 6, and 7 of that

work, which deal with Roman religion, are based to a large extent on Varro's *Antiquitates*, Books 1, 14, and 16. Augustine also preserved fragments of several other works of Varro.

9. See Vergil, *Aeneid* 9.416.

10. The list of scholars who had suffered the same literary neglect as Varro probably derives from Macrobius, *Saturnalia* 3, where all these names are mentioned (along with that of Varro) in an erudite conversation on Vergil. They do not seem to be ordered by discipline or century, but represent many of the disciplines explored by Varro's broad interests: antiquarian history, philology, and sacred and secular law. As in the case of Varro (see headnote), all these ancient authors were known to Petrarca only through indirect tradition: the Elder Cato's *On Agriculture* was discovered by Coluccio Salutati only after Petrarca's death. The same goes for the work by Sextus Pompeius Festus (second–third century CE), whose abridgment of the antiquarian dictionary (*De verborum significatu*) by the Augustan scholar Verrius Flaccus was rediscovered only in the fifteenth century. Publius Nigidius Figulus (first century BCE) was a Neo-Pythagorean philosopher who also had grammatical and antiquarian interests. Gaius Julius Hyginus, a freedman of Augustus, placed in charge of the Palatine library in Rome, also had broad scholarly interests: he is not to be confused with the later mythographer Hyginus, who wrote the *Fabulae* and *On Astronomy*. Antonius Gnipho and Gavius Bassus (spelled "Gaius" here) were grammarians who lived in the first century BCE; Cloatius Verus was a lexicographer of the Augustan age. Servius Sulpicius Rufus (first century BCE), Gaius Ateius Capito (Augustan period), Masurius Sabinus (first century CE) were famous jurists. Quintus Fabius Pictor (third–second century BCE) and Lucius Cassius Hemina (second century BCE) were historians. Finally, very little is known, outside Macrobius, of Veranius (spelled "Veratius" in Petrarca's text and called *Pontificalis*, from the name of his work *Pontificales Quaestiones*), Octavius Hersennius, and Granius Flaccus (spelled "Gaius" here), who were all experts in sacred law and probably lived in the first century BCE. The same can be said of the two grammarians Lucius Cornelius Balbus (first century BCE) and Statius Tullianus (fourth century CE).

## VIII.6. To Quintilian (*F.* 24.7)

Born around 35 CE, the Spanish rhetorician Quintilian taught rhetoric at Rome for twenty years, after he was brought in with the retinue of the short-lived emperor Galba in 68, and appeared in the courts, earning the distinction of being named Rome's first public professor of rhetoric by Vespasian. Besides acting as tutor for Domitian's great-nephews, he trained future orators, including Pliny the Younger. The date of Quintilian's death is unknown but must have occurred in the late 90s. Petrarca saw and copied a manuscript of Quintilian's *Institutes* in his friend Lapo da Castiglionchio's possession at Florence in 1350 (the present letter is dated December 7 of that year). This manuscript, however, as Petrarca here complains, showed a text heavily corrupted and full of lacunae: an intact text was discovered by Poggio Bracciolini at the Abbey of St. Gall in 1416, long after Petrarca's death.

1. Quintilian's *Institutes of Oratory* is in twelve books, but the manuscript in Petrarca's possession (see headnote) did not distinguish them clearly.

2. Most of Cicero's rhetorical works were composed in his later years.

3. In the initial two books of Quintilian's *Institutes*, the ideal training of an orator begins with nursing and elementary education.

4. The quotation comes from Cicero, *On Invention* 1.6.8 (called *Rhetorica* by Quintilian, e.g., *Institutes* 3.1.20). The second-century BCE Alexandrian rhetorician Hermagoras devised the system for classifying legal issues, which was practiced and modified by Cicero and others, but was blamed for having an extremely poor style himself.

5. Petrarca is here alluding to the collection of *Greater Declamations*, which in the Middle Ages circulated under the name of Quintilian and was often referred to as the *Causae* (not to be confused with Quintilian's lost book *De causis corruptae eloquentiae* [On the Causes of Corrupt Eloquence], to which he refers in his *Institutes* at 6 proem. 3 and 8.6.76).

6. Petrarca borrows from Horace (*Art of Poetry* 304–8) the comparison of a critic with the whetstone on which warriors sharpened their swords, and poets their words, before combat.

7. On the ill will between Quintilian and Seneca, Petrarca is misled: it is Seneca the Elder who speaks contemptuously of a man called Quintilianus (*Controversies* 10, preface 2), who must have lived a generation or two before the author of the *Institutes*. However, Quintilian's own judgment on Seneca in *Institutes* 10.2.125–31 is detailed and balanced, but reflects both his distaste for Seneca's influence on his extravagant young imitators and his conviction that Seneca's influence had damaged their rhetoric. Both Quintilian and Seneca were from Spain, from Calahorra and Cordoba, respectively.

8. See Quintilian, *Institutes of Oratory* 10.1.125.

9. See Seneca the Elder, *Controversies* 10, preface 2. Petrarca can observe only the evident inconsistency of his sources, without however being able to draw the appropriate conclusion about the identity of the authors in question.

10. See Eusebius, *Chronicle* (p. 186 Helm), preserved only in Jerome's Latin translation.

11. See Quintilian, *Institutes* 4 proem. 2–3. The emperor Domitian appointed Quintilian as private tutor of his two great-nephews (born of his cousin Flavius Clemens and his niece Flavia Domitilla), whom he had chosen as heirs to the throne.

12. This comes from the spurious letter from Plutarch to the emperor Trajan (*Epistula Plutarchi instruentis Traianum*) quoted in John of Salisbury, *Policraticus* 5.1: see note on VIII.4.3.

13. That is, Florence, located on the right side of the Apennines (if looking south) and on the right bank of the Arno (if looking toward its mouth).

### VIII.7. To the historian Titus Livius (*F.* 24.8)

The shortness of this letter addressed to Livy is strange and surprising, given Petrarca's long devotion to this author (see Appendix III). Petrarca worked on the text of Livy with the detailed attention of an editor (see Introduction, vol. 1), and his work would become of tremendous significance in the history of Renaissance republicanism and Renaissance culture as a whole. Livy's history was Petrarca's only guide to the monarchy and the early and middle Republic (the extant Books 1–10 and 21–45 cover the years from Rome's origin to 293 and from 218 to 167 BCE, respectively) and the source of many of his exemplary heroes, whom Petrarca also celebrated in his biographical compendium *On Illustrious Men.* Petrarca's own unfavorable contrast between the moral decline of his times and the more honorable past, and his delight in contemplating the virtuous examples of the early Republic, go back to Livy's preface (1.5). But perhaps one reason for the brevity of this letter may be the lack of grounds for reproaching the historian. Petrarca's unconditional enthusiasm for Livy is visible also at *S.* 16.7.3–6.

1. Petrarca is recalling the story told in Jerome, *Letters* 53.1, how a man came to Rome from furthest Cadiz in Spain simply to see Livy: see *S.* 16.7.3–6.

2. Only 35 books now survive of the original 142 composed by Livy (see Introduction, vol. 1, xx–xxi).

3. These names evoke heroes of the surviving books of Livy, but they are deliberately presented out of order. Most of them had been celebrated in Petrarca's *On Illustrious Men*. He uses the rhetorical plurals to magnify the number of noble families and commanders; thus the Cornelii Scipiones cover the generations of Africanus, who defeated Hannibal, and his adopted grandson Scipio Aemilianus, as do the elder and younger Laelii. Other heroes of the Punic Wars listed here are Fabius Maximus, Caecilius Metellus, Claudius Marcellus, Claudius Nero, Livius Salinator, and Atilius Regulus. Quinctius Cincinnatus, Furius Camillus, Papirius Cursor, Manlius Torquatus, Valerius Corvinus (or Corvus), and the Decii represent the early and middle Republic. Then come the noble families of the second century, like the Aemilii, Fulvii (Nobiliores and Flacci), and Flaminii. Finally, the (Iunii) Bruti and (Porcii) Catones span five centuries, from the beginning to the end of the Republic, from Lucius Junius Brutus to M. Brutus, who killed Caesar, and from Cato the Elder to Brutus' uncle M. Porcius Cato of Utica.

4. Petrarca is here alluding to the *Periochae*, summaries of Livy's entire text, probably composed around the third or fourth century CE, that allow us to have some idea of the content of the missing books.

5. The third-century BCE Greek historian Polybius and the two Roman annalists Claudius Quadrigarius and Valerius Antias (from the early first century BCE) had all been sources for Livy's work. The histories of both Quadrigarius and Antias are lost and known only through indirect tradition. Of Polybius' original forty books, only the first five plus some substantial excerpts now survive, but of course they were unknown to Petrarca. Pliny the Elder wrote a history of Rome (*A fine Aufidii Bassi historiarum libri XXXI*), about which we know thanks to his nephew Pliny the Younger (*Letters* 3.5.6). Petrarca does not seem to have known this letter (on the controversial question of Petrarca's knowledge of Pliny's *Letters*, see Antognini, "*Placet experiri*," 69–70); yet he may have simply inferred the existence of Pliny the Elder's historical work from a misunderstood reference in Suetonius' short *Life of Pliny the Elder* (fr. 80 Reifferscheid, a biography included in Suetonius' lost *On Illustrious Men*); see Giazzi, "Un episodio," 66–67. Petrarca had probably been led to believe Pliny, who came from Como, to be Veronese from *Natural History* preface 1.1.1, where Pliny calls Catullus of Verona his fellow countryman. Sallust's *Histories* are also lost apart from fragments (while we do possess his monographs *Catiline's Conspiracy* and the *The War against Jugurtha*); Sallust was slightly older than Livy and died before Livy began his histories—hardly a "rival" to him: Petrarca probably drew the idea of their rivalry from Livy's criticism of Sallust's style reported in Seneca the Elder, *Controversies* 9.1.14.

6. A tombstone of a man called Livius in the porch of the church of Saint Justina in Padua was assumed to be a monument to the historian.

### VIII.8. To the orator Asinius Pollio (*F.* 24.9)

C. Asinius Pollio (76 BCE–4 CE) was a supporter of Mark Antony after the death of Caesar and held the consulship of 40 BCE, an honor followed by his triumph over the Parthini in Illyria in the following year. When Octavian and Antony quarreled, Pollio retired from politics and occupied himself with literature. He created Rome's first public library (anticipating the opening of the Palatine library in 28 BCE). Nothing but a few short fragments have survived of Pollio's literary production, but according to Vergil, *Eclogues* 8.10, he wrote tragedies, and Horace's *Ode* 2.1, addressed to Pollio, like Vergil's *Eclogue* 8, praises him in many ways and claims his history of the civil war started in 60 BCE. Pollio, however, remained famous above all for his oratory, recalled by many later authors: see Seneca the Elder, *Controversies* 4, preface 3; Seneca the Younger, *Moral Letters* 100.7–9; Quintilian, *Institutes* 10.113. His praises are almost always accompanied by the consideration that he was inferior to Cicero (see Seneca's and Quintilian's judgment in the passages just quoted): this, along with the testimonies of Pollio's own critcism and enmity toward Cicero (see Seneca the Elder, *Suasoriae* 6.14–15; Suetonius, *Life of Claudius* 41.3; Gellius, *Attic Nights* 17.1.1), must have inspired the second half of Petrarca's letter. The passage from Seneca the Elder's *Suasoriae* (6.14–15) in particular is followed by a much more favorable judgment on Cicero by Livy (*Suasoriae* 6.16–17): this may help to explain the juxtaposition of the letters to Livy and Pollio in this book of the *Familiares*.

1. See headnote; Petrarca is echoing these details of Pollio's life from Eusebius' *Chronicle* (p. 170–71 Helm), which is also his source for the death of Pollio's son Asinius Gallus, suspected by Tiberius of being a rival for his position (see §3 below).

2. See on §2 above; Pollio's son died in 33 CE, so quite a few years after Pollio's death in 4 CE, but Petrarca's source (Eusebius, *Chronicle* p. 171 Helm) dates it to 16 CE.

3. The reference of this allusion remains obscure; possibly unnamed authorities in Aristotle's *Ethics* 1.11.1101a20.

4. That is Augustus; see Macrobius, *Saturnalia* 2.4.21.

5. Petrarca is referring to the poet Licinius Calvus, a close friend of Catullus and a contemporary orator who advocated a plain Attic style. He was a vigorous and successful speaker, fiercely critical of Cicero (as Petrarca knew from Seneca the Elder, *Controversies* 7.4.6). For the common enmity of Calvus and the two Pollios toward Cicero, see also Quintilian, *Institutes* 12.1.22.

6. See VIII.2–3.

7. See on §6 above.

8. Alongside the three fourth-century Athenian orators, Isocrates and the rivals Demosthenes and Aeschines, Petrarca includes a few famous Romans, who were also just names to him, as their works are completely lost: L. Licinius Crassus and Marcus Antonius the Elder (both active at the beginning of the first century BCE) are the protagonists of Cicero's dialogue *On the Orator;* Pollio's contemporary M. Valerius Messala Corvinus assumed the position of an elder statesman under Augustus and was Tibullus' patron; Cicero's slightly older contemporary Q. Hortensius Hortalus had been his opponent in major trials and was the greatest exponent of the Asianic style. Here Petrarca combines the last two orators from different generations in order to display his learning, by playing off Cicero's praise of Hortensius' excellent memory (*Tusculan Disputations* 1.24.59) against the report in Eusebius' *Chronicle* (p. 170–71 Helm) about Messalla's loss of his memory two years before his death.

9. The Insubrians were a Gaulish people inhabiting northern Italy before the Roman conquest in the third-second century BCE.

### VIII.9. Reply to a long letter sent under the name of Homer (*F.* 24.12)

This letter closes the series of letters to the ancients in Book 24 and is the only one that is imagined as a response: the letter from Homer to which it replies, if it ever existed, may have been written by an intimate of Petrarca, who knew his aspirations and ideas and shared his profound desire to bring the Greek author back to life. Thus "Homer" may have been impersonated either by Pietro da Moglio, the rhetorician from Bologna to whom §32 probably alludes, or by one of the three Florentine Homer-enthusiasts mentioned in §31. Of these, according to Dotti 2004–9, *ad loc.*, following Pertusi, *Leonzio Pilato fra Petrarca e Boccaccio,* 73–111, Boccaccio is the most likely candidate, with his intimate knowledge of Petrarca, and especially with the various points of coincidence between the topics discussed in this letter and Boccaccio's own works, above all the erudite comments on Homer's work within his *Commentary* on Dante's *Comedy*. On Petrarca's frustrated attempts to learn Greek, see III.12: he first tried to learn Greek in Avignon from the learned Calabrian monk Barlaam, then, after Barlaam left to take up his promotion to the bishopric of Gerace, Petrarca turned to Barlaam's pupil Leonzio Pilato, a difficult man whom Petrarca had met at Padua around 1358 and who was soon appointed to the first chair of Greek at the University in Florence. Leonzio had also been commissioned by both Petrarca and Boccaccio to produce a Latin translation of both Homeric poems, which was finished by 1365 (see III.21 and III.22) and sent to Petrarca only in 1366 (see *S.* 6.2). Leonzio must have been the source for much of the erudite information on Homer discussed here by Petrarca and by Boccaccio in his own works. By the time Petrarca was writing this letter, dated from Milan, October 9, 1360, he already owned a complete Greek manuscript of the *Iliad,* sent to him by Nicolas Sigeros (see III.12).

1. From Petrarca's *Variae* 25 (= 46 ed. Pancheri, *Lettere disperse*), we know that he believed that Cicero had composed a translation of the *Odyssey* into Latin and that the Latin translation of *Odyssey* 1.1–2 quoted by Horace at *Ars Poetica* 141–42 came from this work.

2. Leonzio Pilato: see headnote.

3. It is unclear what Petrarca here means by "the beginnings of some books": according to Dotti 2004–9, *ad loc.*, it may allude to some translation samples by Leonzio Pilato from the proems of books, or to the *Periochae Homeri Iliadis et Odyssiae,* a work attributed to the fourth-century Latin writer Ausonius and consisting of a short outline of each book of both Homeric poems, each preceded by the book's initial couple of lines. Finally, the booklet commonly attributed to Homer but rightly considered spurious by Petrarca is a short Latin version of the *Iliad,* probably composed in the mid-first century CE and circulating in the Middle Ages under the name of *Ilias Latina.*

4. See Seneca the Elder, *Controversies* 3, preface 8.

5. Cicero's quotations and interpretations of Homer are frequent throughout his treatises and dialogues. Vergil's debt to Homer in the *Aeneid* is ubiquitous.

6. Cicero's poetic works are lost, but fragments survive and were available to Petrarca through indirect tradition. The "letters of Vergil in prose"

may refer to Vergil's letter to Augustus quoted by Macrobius, *Saturnalia* 1.24.11.

7. For Petrarca's previous negative judgment on the possibility of adequately translating Homer into Latin or even paraphrasing it in Greek prose, see his *Variae* 25 (= 46 ed. Pancheri, *Lettere disperse*), referring to Jerome's preface to his Latin version of Eusebius' *Chronicle* (p. 4 Helm).

8. This refers to Petrarca's verse letter to Vergil, *F.* 24.11.

9. This garbled tradition seems to combine myth and history: the inhabitants of Mount Helicon are Apollo and the Muses; Cadmus, son of Agenor, was a mythical Phoenician king who moved to Greece and was credited with the introduction of the alphabet there (see, for example, Herodotus, *Histories* 5.58); according to one tradition, Hercules (also called by the patronymic Alcides, from his mortal grandfather Alcaeus) had — quite unsuccessfully — learned music and poetry from the mythical poet Linus. Petrarca's source here must be the teaching of Leonzio Pilato.

10. Homer's ancient biographies reported the legend of his numerous travels (especially to Egypt and Phoenicia), which would explain the wide knowledge displayed in his poems. Petrarca was able to read about the trip to Egypt by the philosophers Pythagoras of Samos and Plato in Valerius Maximus 8.7.ext.2–3 or in Cicero, *On Moral Ends* 5.29.87. But the source here rather seems to be Diodorus Siculus, *Bibliotheca* 1.69.4 and 96.2, where Solon (of course known through Leonzio Pilato) is also mentioned along with the other two philosophers (see Pertusi, *Leonzio Pilato fra Petrarca e Boccaccio,* 89). For the Athenian legislator Solon and his late conversion to poetry, see the note on III.14.8.

11. Petrarca's source of information must have discussed the existence of works by Homer that were lost, and this gives him another occasion to complain about the fact of being surrounded by a barbaric age and by barbaric people who have destroyed classical culture.

12. On the "not honorable" deaths of Homer and Sophocles from overwhelming emotions, see Valerius Maximus 9.12.ext.3 and 5: Homer was said to have died of mortification because he could not answer a fisherman's question; Sophocles allegedly died of joy, after having won a poetic

competition. Petrarca mentions these anecdotes elsewhere; see in particular *Metrical Epistles* 2.14.161–63.

13. Petrarca is again citing Valerius Maximus' chapter (9.12.6) here on the death of the late third-century CE comic playwright Philemon of Syracuse, from laughter. He might have found a more noble version of this sudden death at Apuleius, *Florida* 16.

14. See Donatus, *Life of Vergil* 43.

15. Apollo, as the god of poetry.

16. The fifth and sixth books of Macrobius' *Saturnalia* enumerate passages that Vergil "took" from Homer; in particular, Macrobius claims Vergil's superiority over Homer at *Saturnalia* 5.11. The uncertainty on whom to assign "the palm of victory" also echoes in Juvenal, *Satires* 11.180–81.

17. See Horace, *Satires* 1.5.40–42.

18. See Macrobius, *Saturnalia* 5.3.16; see also Donatus, *Life of Vergil,* 46 ("facilius esse Herculi clavam quam Homero versum subripere" [it is easier to steal Hercules' club than a verse of Homer]).

19. See Lucan, *Pharsalia* 9.984.

20. See Horace, *Epistles* 1.2.1–4, and *Odes* 4.9.5–6.

21. References to Homer are quite common in these authors: for example, Ovid, *Loves* 1.8.61, *The Art of Love* 2.109; Juvenal, *Satires* 6.437; and Statius, at the opening of his *Achilleid* (1.1–4).

22. Like Orpheus and Linus (see on §8 above), Musaeus is another legendary Greek poet, brought up by the Muses themselves, whom Vergil sets in the Elysian Fields in *Aeneid* 6.667. Linus is mentioned by Vergil at *Eclogues* 4.55–57 and 6.67; Orpheus appears quite frequently in his works, and his famous descent to the underworld is described at *Georgics* 4.454–527.

23. Hesiod "of Ascra" is hailed by Vergil in *Georgics* 2.176 as the model of this poem (see also *Eclogues* 6.70), just as Vergil hails the poetry of "Syracusan" Theocritus in *Eclogues* 6.1; on the contrary, Homer, the evident

model for Vergil's "heroic," that is, epic, poem *Aeneid,* is never mentioned in it.

24. L. Varius Rufus (wrongly spelled "Varus" by Petrarca) and Cornelius Gallus are friends and poets whom Vergil highly praises in *Eclogues* 9.35 (Varius), and 6.64 and 10.176 (Gallus).

25. See on §21 above.

26. From Servius' short *Life of Vergil.*

27. This is again Statius (wrongly called "Pampinius," instead of "Papinius"), quoted here for his tribute to Vergil in the coda of his *Thebaid* 12.816–17, warning his poem not to challenge the "divine *Aeneid,*" and in *Thebaid* 10.445–46, for his admission that his style was inferior. The reference to Statius' courtesy of manners (*urbanitas*) recalls *De disciplina scholarium* 1, a twelfth-century treatise, circulating under the name of Boethius.

28. This is the so-called *Appendix Virgiliana,* containing short poems and a miniature epic then attributed to Vergil, the *Ciris,* which mentions Homer in verse 65.

29. Petrarca is here alluding to the fact that in antiquity Homer was also considered an authority and referred to in juridical and medical texts: for example, see *Digest* 48.5.14.1 or 32.1.65.4 for the former, and Apuleius, *Apologia* 31, for the latter.

30. See Petrarca's allusion to Horace, *Epistles* 1.2.1–4, at §20 above. For the idea of Homer "veiling" truth under the cloud of poetry, see Macrobius, *Commentary to the "Dream of Scipio"* 2.10.11, but the "rich and refined cloak (or veil)" is also the allegory that Petrarca sees as a key to the special function and sanctity of poets: see III.23.

31. The Elysian Fields is the part of the ancient underworld reserved to the righteous.

32. Solomon in Ecclesiastes 1:15.

33. Petrarca's and Homer's common friend is Leonzio Pilato, who "had brought Homer" to Florence, where Leonzio was presently working at the translation of his texts into Latin. Leonzio came from Calabria, al-

though he claimed to be from Thessaly: see III.21.1. The reason why Petrarca here calls him a Byzantine rather than a Calabrian is unclear (perhaps because Calabria's large Greek-speaking communities, still preserved in Petrarca's time, derived from the Byzantine dominion over the region that lasted until the eleventh century). As usual, Petrarca plays on the Roman name of Florence (*Florentia*), the "flowering" or "flourishing" city.

34. Ausonia was the name by which ancient Greeks called southern Italy, and by extension it indicates Italy as a whole.

35. Florence is indicated by its location, situated between the Roman colony of Fiesole and the Arno River. The three Pierian spirits who are interested in Homer are Boccaccio and perhaps Domenico Silvestri (who taught Greek in Florence after Leonzio Pilato) and Domenico Bandini (author of the encyclopedic work *Fons memorabilium universi*): see Dotti 2004–9, *ad loc.*

36. According to Dotti 2004–9, *ad loc.*, the fourth Florentine could be Petrarca's great friend Francesco Nelli, who was still in Florence in 1360, when this letter is dated. The fifth is Zanobi da Strada, who had received poetic coronation by the emperor Charles IV at Pisa in 1355 and had moved to Avignon (as usual called Babylon by Petrarca; see II.7.5) in 1359, after being appointed secretary to the pope. Zanobi's "laurel crown" is called *Peneia*, with allusion to the story of Daphne's metamorphosis into a laurel tree, hence sacred to Apollo, the god of poetry; Daphne was the daughter of the river god Peneus in Thessaly. As Dotti points out (2004–9, *ad loc.*), the crown is also called *Alpheia*, to allude to Pisa, where it was awarded; the Italian Pisa was believed to have been founded by colonists from the town of Pisa in the Greek region of Elis, in the western Peloponnese, through which the river Alpheus flows: see Vergil, *Aeneid* 10.179–80.

37. The Homer enthusiast in Bologna may be Pietro da Moglio, suspected by some scholars of being the composer of "Homer's" letter, to which Petrarca is responding.

38. The Veronese Homerists are probably the erudite jurist and politician Gugliemo da Pastrengo and the poet and grammarian Rinaldo Cavalchini from Villafranca; the one from Sulmona must be Barbato (see on III.6). The Mantuan who changed his studies in literature to astronomy cannot be identified: see Dotti 2004–9, *ad loc.* Latin *signa* is used here as a pun on two senses: the standards of the Roman army and the constellations.

39. Dotti 2004–9, *ad loc.*, could not identify either the Homerist from Rome or the one from Perugia who abandoned his studies (metonymically indicated by Mount Parnassus, sacred to Apollo) and moved to Spain, where he seems to have become rich by less honorable activities.

40. That is, Leonzio Pilato.

41. This is Petrarca's first teacher of Greek, Barlaam, who left Florence to take up a bishopric in southern Italy for which Petrarca had recommended him: see headnote.

42. See note on §13 above.

43. The Castalian Springs on Mount Parnassus and Mount Helicon were sacred to Apollo and the Muses. The nightingales, used symbolically for poets or singers, allude to the tragic story of Procne and Philomele, narrated also by Ovid (*Metamorphoses* 6.401–674).

44. This is cited by Cicero, in *Tusculan Disputations* 1.34, as the last line of Ennius' epitaph. The word *docta* ("learned," here a transferred epithet) is not in the manuscripts used in Rossi's edition but was supplied by him from modern texts of Cicero, as the sense requires.

45. The Thessalian friend is again Leonzio Pilato (see note on §30 above); on the state of Petrarca's manuscript of Homer and on his plans regarding it, see headnote.

46. Homer is imagined being in the company of the mythical poets Orpheus and Linus (on whom see on §§8 and 21 above) and the famous fifth-century Attic tragedian Euripides.

47. The source for this etymology of the Latin name of Milan, *Mediolanum,* as probably deriving from *medium amnium* (in the middle of rivers), is unknown.

## PART IX

### IX.1. To Guido Sette (*S.* 10.2)

This letter to his childhood friend Guido Sette was sent from Venice late in 1367 before Petrarca knew of Guido's death at the Benedictine monastery which he had founded at Portofino. It probably never reached him. This letter is not presented as autobiography but as an argument, identified by its heading, "On the changes in the times," and contrasting the world of their youth with its present change for the worse. Thus Petrarca's discussion is carried out through a survey of places he visited during his life in order to show how all of them have suffered a more or less evident level of decadence in recent years. But his argument is that although human individuals are changed by aging, the changes (for the worse) that he and Guido have witnessed are not the fault of their own changed perceptions, but actual deterioration in society. Indeed Petrarca had to witness, during his lifetime, the dreadful effects of the deep crisis that wracked Europe in the fourteenth century. The letter reviews all the disasters of recent times (the recurring plague, the earthquakes and the ravages of brigand companies led by condottieri), and argues that these calamities result from God's anger at the moral decline of society. The first part of the letter, however, recalling Petrarca's early years, spent mostly with or near Guido, also offers happier, more informal reminiscences: as boys and adolescents they would be unaffected by the public events that would later bring Petrarca both distress and public fame, events that, for example, had caused Petrarca's father to leave his hometown and go into exile.

1. Horace, *Art of Poetry* 173–74, describing the typical faults of old age, especially its praise for the good old days (*laudator temporis acti*).

2. Guido Sette spent his first years at Luni, where he was born in 1304, the year of Petrarca's own birth.

3. Both Petrarca and Guido moved to Avignon with their families in 1311, when they were both seven years old. The province of Arelate (which is the Latin name of the city of Arles that governed it) was the late antique designation for the region corresponding to Provence, which in classical times was instead called "Gallia Narbonensis." By "Gallia Transalpina,"

ancient Romans indicated the entire region inhabited by Gallic tribes beyond the Alps, roughly coinciding with modern-day France.

4. During the trip to Avignon, Petrarca's family traveled by sea from Genoa to Marseilles. Guido Sette's birthplace, Luni, was under Genoese control, and Guido became archbishop of Genoa in 1358. Petrarca is alluding to *F.* 14.5, the letter he addressed in 1352 to the Genoese doge and council.

5. Petrarca and Guido moved to Carpentras in 1312, when they were both eight years old, and they remained there until 1316, studying under Convenevole da Prato (see II.6).

6. Petrarca here divides his adult life into four-year periods for the sake of symmetry, and thus sometimes distorts the actual chronology of the events he mentions: after this first four-year period, in Carpentras, he spent four years in Montpelier (see §40); later, he dates his early trips around Europe with Giacomo Colonna (see §87) to the fourth year after he left Bologna (where he reckons to have spent three years, see §58), and then places his first trip to Paris after four more years (see §89); four years later he went to Rome for the first time (see §101), and after four more years he went to Naples (see §104); finally, a second trip to Naples is dated four years after the first one (see §107).

7. The text here recalls the proverbial hexameter line: "Tempora mutantur, nos et mutamur in illis" (The times change and we change with them).

8. Petrarca's source for these anecdotes about ancient miniature works is Pliny, *Natural History* 7.21.85, but see also 36.4.43 for Myrmecides and Callicrates, and Solinus, *Collectanea rerum memorabilium* 1.100, for the anecdote reported by Cicero (whose original text is lost). Myrmecides and Callicrates were two ancient Greek sculptors, the former active in Athens and the latter in Sparta, who were particularly famous for their amazing miniatures.

9. Carpentras became the capital of the Comtat Venaissin in 1320 and hence the seat of legal assizes.

10. The Comtat Venaissin was plundered by a free company of Gascons in 1357.

11. Petrarca and Guido studied in Montpellier for four years, 1316 to 1320 (on Petrarca's division of his life into four year periods, see on §22 above). Montpellier was under the rule of the kings of Majorca until it was incorporated by Philippe VI of France in 1349.

12. In 1320 Petrarca and Guido moved to the famous university of Bologna in order to continue their legal studies.

13. "Fat" is an epithet commonly attributed to Bologna from the twelfth century and refers to its wealth (and excellent produce and sausages).

14. Pope Urban V made an effort to improve Bologna's condition after the city had gone back under the Church's control in 1360; see the note on VII.7.160.

15. The pun insists on the association of the town's name "Macerata" with the Latin adjective *macer*, "thin." The author of the joke is Cardinal Androin de la Roche, whom Petrarca met in early spring 1364; Cardinal de la Roche was a *legatus a latere*, that is, a papal legate of particular importance and power (literally, "from the Pope's side," that is, from his most intimate and trusted entourage).

16. Bologna came under the tyranny first of the Pepoli family (1337–50), then of Giovanni d'Oleggio (1355–60), until Cardinal Albornoz entered the city in 1360 to reclaim it for the Church. The Visconti were Bologna's most important external enemies at the time.

17. Florence is "the city on the Arno River," which was the homeland of Petrarca's father and was always claimed by Petrarca as his own, although he was born in Arezzo and visited Florence for the first time only in 1350. "The city on the Rhône" is Avignon. Petrarca left Bologna and returned to Avignon in 1326, upon his father's death. He had arrived in Bologna in 1320, but his studies were often interrupted for various reasons: three years is the period that he was actually enrolled at the university.

18. This is Livy's verdict in his character sketch of Hannibal (21.4.9).

19. The Curia used its bureaucracy to impose new taxes. The new walls of Avignon were begun in 1360 and strengthened in 1365, after repeated raids by the free companies.

20. Bertrand du Guesclin used the pretexts of diverting the companies of condottieri and raising funds to support a crusade against the infidel in order to extort a large sum of money from Pope Urban V in 1365: as Petrarca hints, this had the merit of providing a further stimulus to Urban's desire to return the Curia to Rome (see II.6.200).

21. The neglected spouse is Rome, which Petrarca marks elsewhere (e.g., VII.6.76) as the proper consort of the papacy and also of the Holy Roman Empire of Charles IV (e.g., VII.6.338 or VI.8.27).

22. This has been interpreted as an allusion to Cardinal Guillaume Bragose, who had been one of the main opponents of moving the papal seat back to Rome (see *S.* 9.2.91–102 and 184–86). Since he died on November 11, 1367, this letter must have been composed after this date.

23. The beauty of the source of the Sorgue is frequently celebrated in Petrarca's works: see, for example, *Canzoniere* 126: *Chiare, fresche et dolci acque*.

24. Petrarca lost his mother, Eletta Canigiani, early, when he was about fifteen. He composed a Latin lament for her, *Metrical Epistles* 1.7.

25. Guido Sette had been named after his uncle.

26. Petrarca's stays at Vaucluse (1337–40, 1342–43, 1346–47, and 1351–53) alternated with his repeated journeys to Italy.

27. It was a cliché of Roman literature to associate poets with the woods and groves where they supposedly found inspiration to compose their work: see, for example, Propertius 1.18, or Horace, *Satires* 2.6. On Petrarca's way of life at Vaucluse, see especially II.12.

28. This is Philippe de Cabassoles, Petrarca's friend and bishop of Cavaillon, of whose see Vaucluse was a part.

29. See §37 above.

30. The raid probably occurred at Christmas 1353, after Petrarca had left Vaucluse in spring of the same year; it was the son of his bailiff Raymond Monet who rescued the books Petrarca had left behind and took them to safety. Laverna was a Roman goddess and the protectress of thieves. Croesus, the sixth-century king of Lydia, was a byword in ancient Greece for his enormous wealth, until he was defeated by the Per-

sian king, Cyrus the Great. We know the story from the first book of Herodotus, but Petrarca had to depend on intermediate sources.

31. "Go now" echoes the ironic taunt of Roman satirists (see, for example, Juvenal 6.306 or Martial 1.42.6): Petrarca speaks with bitter scorn.

32. *Vallis Clausa*, that is, "Enclosed Valley," is the Latinized name of Vaucluse; see the note on II.8.

33. In 1330, four years after leaving Bologna, Petrarca, along with Angelo Tosetti and Ludwig van Kempen, accompanied their friend Giacomo Colonna to Lombez in Gascony, where Giacomo had been newly appointed bishop.

34. This is Petrarca's journey of 1333, described in his letters to Cardinal Giovanni Colonna, *F.*1.4 and 5. Again, for Petrarca's division of his life in four-year periods, see on §22 above.

35. Petrarca went back to Paris in 1360–61, on a diplomatic mission for the Visconti.

36. The letter is IV.14, addressed to Pierre Bersuire in February 1361, describing the humiliation of the French king (John the Good) and wretched condition of France during the Hundred Years' War.

37. King John the Good was imprisoned by Edward III of England at Poitiers in 1356. He was released in 1360, as a result of the treaty of Brétigny, in return for a huge ransom.

38. King John the Good's son is Charles V, who succeeded his father to the throne in 1364 and ruled until 1380. Petrarca seems to be the only source for this episode of king and prince of France being forced to strike a bargain with the companies of mercenaries (see Rizzo 2006–14, *ad loc.*).

39. Petrarca went to Rome in 1337, and he describes it as still reflecting its past greatness.

40. Stefano Colonna was the father of both Petrarca's friend Giacomo, bishop of Lombez, and Cardinal Giovanni, Petrarca's powerful patron at Avignon (see Appendix III). See Petrarca's letter of consolation to the long-lived Stefano (*F.* 8.1) after the deaths of numerous members of his family, including the recent deaths of his sons, Cardinal Giovanni, who died of plague in 1348, and Pietro and Stefano the Younger (along with

Giovanni, son of Stefano the Younger), who all died in the fight against Cola di Rienzo in November 1347 (see IX.2.31).

41. This was Petrarca's journey to Naples in 1341 to pay homage to Robert, king of Sicily, and to be examined for the poetic *Laurea*. Letter VI.3 laments the sad state of Naples in the power vacuum created by Robert's death in 1343.

42. For the philosophical and consolatory classical motif of a well-timed death (*mors opportuna*), see also the case of Pierre Bersuire, who died too late, in §91, above.

43. Petrarca was sent there as envoy in 1343, upon King Robert's death, at the urging of Pope Clement VI.

44. The point of these references to the islands in the Bay of Naples and the surrounding countryside is to stress that the natural features remained unspoiled, while human society was corrupted. The *Ager Falernus*, which produced the famous Falernian wine, was the ancient designation for the area around Mount Massico, north of Naples. Baiae was an exclusive seaside resort in Roman times: it corresponds to the modern town of Bacoli (or Baia) on the northern edge of the Bay of Naples, and it is part of an area, the Phlegraean Fields, characterized by bradyseism and geothermal phenomena.

45. Petrarca alludes to his letters VI.3 and *F.* 5.3.14, both composed soon after King Robert's death in 1343. Petrarca's dark predictions proved true when Prince Andrew of Hungary, husband of Queen Joanna of Naples, was murdered after trying to overrule his wife and seize the crown (1345), which led to a war against Hungary and an endless series of devastating invasions of Naples by Hungarian troops, starting in 1348.

46. Petrarca alludes to Azzo da Correggio, who invited him to Parma, and to the ruler of Padua, Giacomo da Carrara, who also obtained a canonry there for him but was assassinated shortly after, in December 1350; see the lament for his death in *F.* 11.2, IV.13, and Appendix I.

47. Petrarca returned to Padua in the first half of 1351 and again lived there in 1361–62 and 1368–69.

48. The Great Plague of 1347–49.

49. Francesco da Carrara continued his father's favors to Petrarca and is the addressee of V.6, a personalized treatise on good government. Despite the excellent rule of both Giacomo and Francesco da Carrara, Padua could not be restored to the wealth it had before the outbreak of the plague of 1348.

50. Petrarca was invited by the Visconti to move to Milan in 1353 and lived there until 1361. He also visited Pavia (whose ancient Latin name was *Ticinum*) regularly at the invitation of Galeazzo II Visconti, after the Visconti had defeated the tyrant-monk Giacomo Bussolari in 1359 (see VI.13).

51. According to Orosius (*Histories* 4.13.15), Milan was a "most flourishing" (*florentissima*) city at the time of its capture by the Romans in 222 BCE.

52. See Ovid, *Metamorphoses* 9.38–39.

53. See Appendix I for Petrarca's early life.

54. Petrarca again indicates Florence as his homeland (see §58 above), making his customary play on the meaning of its Latin name (*Florentia*, the "flourishing" city).

55. Petrarca resided in Venice almost continuously from 1362 to 1368; see Appendix I. Dotti 2002–13, *ad loc.*, notes that this is the only reference to that youthful visit to Venice and dates it to 1321.

56. See Horace, *Odes* 1.12.56.

57. Venice's merchant trade and travelers' reports certainly were one source of Petrarca's generalizations about Egypt and the Near East. Not only were the conditions of present-day Greece dramatically inferior to what they had been in classical times, but things had gotten even worse since mid-thirteenth century, as the Byzantine Empire was progressively succumbing to the Ottomans. The Scythians were an ancient population inhabiting the regions northeast of the Black and Caspian seas, and they were pictured in antiquity as extremely barbaric, as, for example, Ovid does while talking about the Scythian city of Tomis (modern-day Constanta) in his poetry of exile. Slave trade from these regions greatly inten-

sified with the Mongol invasions since the thirteenth century, and Venice was an important hub in Italy for this kind of commerce.

58. These lines are not from Ovid's autobiographical exile poems, but from his fantasy of personified Hunger in *Metamorphoses* 8.797–800.

59. Ecclesiastes 7:11.

60. See §§36 and 130–32 above.

61. Petrarca by *societas* here probably is referring collectively to the "free companies" of unemployed mercenaries who roamed France and Italy in the later fourteenth century and made their living by plunder and holding cities to ransom. See William Caferro, *Mercenary Companies and the Decline of Siena* (Baltimore, 1998).

62. The Florentine guilds of artisans and merchants grew, since the twelfth century, into a very strong commercial and political system that allowed the city to become internationally powerful and its industry, especially that of woolen textiles, to thrive throughout Europe.

63. Associations of pilgrims were active in numerous cities.

64. As Dotti 2002–13, *ad loc.*, points out, Petrarca here may be alluding to the Great Company of Werner von Urslingen, which was formed around 1340 and caused widespread devastation in northern Italy during the years that followed.

65. For the money extorted by Bertrand du Guesclin from Pope Urban V in 1365, see on §61 above. For the pope's reaction and Petrarca's comment on it, see VII.6.200.

66. Petrarca did not know the terrifying description of the plague of Athens in Thucydides' *History of the Peloponnesian War* 2.47–58, nor the one by Lucretius at the close of his *On the Nature of the Universe* (a poem rediscovered only in 1417 by Poggio Bracciolini), but he could still read, for example, Ovid's description of a plague on the island of Aegina (*Metamorphoses* 7.523–614) and, of course, the references to epidemics attested by Latin historical writers.

67. The first onset of the plague was in late 1347 and, before the date of this letter, it had returned to Italian cities in 1361, 1362, and 1363. On the impact of the plague of 1348, see II.3.

68. Numerous earthquakes, erupting in either Italy or the Mediterranean basin, are recorded by Roman historians (e.g., Livy 22.5.6, or Suetonius, *Life of Tiberius* 48.2). Book 6 of Seneca's *Natural Questions* and also Pliny's *Natural History* 2.191–211 investigate the causes of this natural phenomenon.

69. This is the earthquake of January 25, 1348, with its epicenter in the Alpine region of Carinthia; Petrarca refers to Vergil's mention of an Alpine earthquake among the portents following Julius Caesar's death, in *Georgics* 1.475.

70. The earthquake of 1349 hit the region of Lazio as well as Campania and south Tuscany; at Rome, in particular, it heavily damaged the Torre dei Conti and the basilicas of Saint Paul Outside the Walls and the Lateran. At *F.* 11.7.3–5 Petrarca, some time after the event (in June 1351), writes about this to Ludwig van Kempen.

71. This earthquake occurred on October 18, 1356, and damaged a large area of Basel.

72. Petrarca visited Basel in 1356 because he had been commissioned by the Visconti to negotiate with the Holy Roman emperor Charles IV; when after a month Charles had still not arrived in Basel, Petrarca set off to find him in Prague ("the remotest barbarian region"), where he stayed for a month at the imperial court (see II.17.20). As Rizzo points out (2006–14, *ad loc.*), Petrarca left Basel in June, that is, almost four months—and not just a few days—before the earthquake: the deliberate inaccuracy makes the account more dramatic.

73. The bishop of Basel at the time was Johannes von Münsingen.

74. Petrarca is referring back to §§36, 130–32 and 135.

75. Petrarca contrasts his equality of age with Guido Sette with Guido's higher status. Compare *S.* 8.8, to Boccaccio, written on Petrarca's sixty-third birthday, in July 1367.

## IX.2. To posterity (*S.* 18)

Petrarca's *Letter to Posterity* is, unlike the previous letter, a straightforward autobiography, which, after the introductory paragraph, is organized in two parts: a general portrait of the author, both moral and physical, in

§§2–11, and a chronological narrative going up to 1351, in §§12–30. According to Dotti, *Vita di Petrarca*, 431–32, n. 139, and Elvira Nota in Dotti 2002–13, 5:211, a first draft of the text was composed between 1350 and 1355, then later reworked around 1371–72 (as internal references prove: see on §§3, 15, and 24), but it was never carried to completion. As Elvira Nota (in Dotti 2002–13, 5:209–11) has hypothesized, the unfinished nature of the letter and the daunting task of dealing with Petrarca's intricate drafts may explain why the posthumous editors of the *Seniles* decided to separate it from the rest of the collection, which was otherwise much more polished. Yet these editors reported the heading ("to Posterity") at the end of Book 17, which suggests that Petrarca, at least at some point, may really have meant this letter to future readers to stand at the close of his last epistolary collection. In fact, the letter "to Posterity" would match those to the ancients in the closing book of the *Familiares* and, like them, represent a human attempt to defy the barriers of death and time; it would also work as a sort of *sphragis*, as a personal seal affixed by the writer to his lifelong epistolary collections.

According to a persuasive article by Karl Enenkel, "Modeling the Humanist," Petrarca's autobiography, which is unique in its time, was certainly inspired by the tradition of classical Latin biography, particularly the lives of Vergil, Horace, and Terence, derived from Suetonius' *On Illustrious Men* and commonly used to introduce the manuscripts of these authors' works in the Middle Ages. This model, characterized by the organization of the biographical material through thematic rubrics, appears conflated with that of Ovid's poetic autobiography at *Sorrows* 4.10, which instead progresses through a chronological narrative and, like the present letter, is addressed to posterity. But above all Enenkel establishes a close relation between this letter and the biography of Petrarca written by Boccaccio in late 1341 or early 1342 under the influence of Petrarca's fame, thanks to his crowning with the laurel, even before they met. Boccaccio's brief biography, *De vita et moribus domini Francisci Petracchi* (in Boccaccio, *Vita di Petrarca*, ed. Villani), like the present letter, shows the influence of both Ovid's *Sorrows* 4.10 and the genre of Latin biography, but in particular Boccaccio draws on Suetonius' *Lives of the Twelve Caesars*, the form of which is followed in Boccaccio's text: a first chronological narrative up to "coronation" (§§1–17 Villani), followed by a second part sketching a general portrait, both moral and physical (§§18–27 Villani); to this "Suetonian" structure Boccaccio adds a third part, at §§28–30, consisting of a list of Petrarca's works. Boccaccio's biography is colored by his desire to enhance Petrarca's family and life circumstances while tracing his uninterrupted ascent to fame: it is an open eulogy composed by a great admirer. Petrarca knew this work and, as Enenkel has illustrated, he seems to be rewriting it with the aim of modifying the tone of its content to a more modest self-presentation, in keeping with a man writing about himself—especially when the man is a Christian, whose main virtues should be humility and contempt for worldly glory. Petrarca's agenda in the present letter is to leave an image of himself that fits those values of modesty without obscuring his life's achievements, an image that highlights his ability always to maintain his freedom without obscuring the great favor he had enjoyed with some of the greatest men of the time.

1. Petrarca recalls Suetonius, *Life of Augustus* 2.3.

2. See Ecclesiastes 11:10.

3. "Know thyself" was inscribed on the temple of Apollo at Delphi; see *S.* 2.1.34.

4. This would date his resort to spectacles (for reading, surely) and this letter to after 1364.

5. The Roman gourmet M. Gavius Apicius (early first century CE) was known for extravagance and is said to have committed suicide when he deemed he had not enough money left to maintain his luxurious standards: see Seneca, *Consolation to His Mother Helvia* 10.8–9. Apicius is also the author of a cookbook, titled *De re coquinaria,* that has come down to us in a late antique, expanded form.

6. Petrarca's beloved, the chaste married woman Laura, died, as Petrarca records on the flyleaf of his Vergil, in 1348, but Petrarca continued his love poetry after her death.

7. This is surely an ungrateful claim, given that he had a son and a daughter, perhaps by different women, in 1337 and 1343, respectively, shortly before this supposed repudiation of his sexuality, here dated to

around 1344 (i.e., when he turned forty); but an earlier letter (*S.* 8.1.15) claims he rejected sex after 1350.

8. In particular, Petrarca felt close to King Robert of Naples and the Holy Roman emperor Charles IV.

9. Compare III.17, probably composed in 1360, on his new preference for sacred over profane writings. Petrarca's "conversion" to sacred writing had a first realization in 1346–47, during his third stay at Vaucluse, where he composed *On Solitary Life, On Religious Leisure,* the *Bucolic Poem,* and shortly after, the *Penitential Psalms;* many of his later works reflect such renewed religious inspiration (certainly the *Secret Book,* but also the biographies of Old Testament figures added to the collection of *On Illustrious Men* or the final series of *Triumphs*); yet Petrarca never abandoned his "profane" works and kept revising many of them till the end of his life.

10. See Suetonius, *Life of Augustus* 84.2.

11. Petrarca's father, grandfather, and great-grandfather had all been notaries, roughly equivalent to English solicitors, and were given the title of respect "Ser," equivalent to "Mr.," a step below "Messer" (my lord); the latter honorific indicated a rank equivalent to a barrister, judge, chancellor, or knight.

12. See Appendix I.

13. The Rhône, flowing past Avignon.

14. Petrarca was at Carpentras from 1312 to 1316, where he received his primary education.

15. See Appendix I.

16. Much of late medieval training in civil law consisted of the study of Justinian's *Corpus Iuris Civilis,* particularly the *Digest.*

17. In III.14 Petrarca provides young Marco of Genoa, who was seeking advice about the law as a career, with his fullest treatment of the history of law as a discipline, along with a bitter complaint about the degradation of modern lawyers, who are deemed ignorant of the great classical legislators and deeply dishonest, seeking only profit that can be made from petty lawsuits.

18. The friendship contracted with Giacomo Colonna at Bologna was the most important of Petrarca's youth, just as that brief summer in Lombez (Gascony) became a blessed memory: along with his other two great friends, Ludwig van Kempen and Angelo Tosetti, Petrarca had accompanied Giacomo to his new bishopric in Lombez in 1330.

19. Petrarca remained under the protection of Cardinal Giovanni Colonna from 1330 to 1347, when their relationship grew colder, probably also as a consequence of Petrarca's support for Cola di Rienzo, who was in conflict with the Colonna family at Rome. For Petrarca's trip to France and Germany in spring 1333, see *F.* 1.4–5 and 3.1.

20. Petrarca first visited Rome in 1337, when he met Stefano Colonna the Elder. Born around 1265, Stefano was the head of the whole family; he would have been seventy-two when Petrarca met him. He lived on to lose numerous members of his family (see the note on IX.1.102 and Petrarca's belated letter of condolence, *F.* 8.1). While Petrarca's reverence for Stefano is real and born out by his letter *F.* 8.1, here he is glossing over his rupture with Cardinal Giovanni, just as in §32 below he will introduce a lament for the decline of his patrons, the Colonna, without admitting how his own behavior contributed to the rupture between them.

21. See Appendix III.

22. Augustine's *Confessions* describes his first encounter with Ambrose at 5.13.23, where Ambrose "took Augustine up" (the word used of a father acknowledging a child) in a fatherly fashion, offering the guidance and protection of a bishop.

23. See Appendix II for Petrarca's work on the *Africa*.

24. Petrarca gives his award of the laurel crown of poetry five chapters in this short unfinished biography. The letters consulting Cardinal Giovanni are III.2 and 3, dating from September 1340.

25. Petrarca met King Robert at the end of February 1341 and spent several days with him. See Appendix I.

26. Book 4 of the *Familiares* follows Petrarca's visit to and the subsequent ceremony at Rome in April 1341; on the ceremony see in particular II.5–6 and the *Metrical Epistle* 2.1.

27. Petrarca went directly from Rome to Parma, newly liberated by the da Correggio dynasty from Mastino della Scala, in May 1341 and stayed until spring 1342. Shortly after, however, the da Correggio family lost its rule over Parma again, due to internal feuds among the brothers Azzo, Simone, Giovanni, and Guido.

28. According to Dotti 2002–13, *ad loc.*, Petrarca had certainly bought his house at Parma, which is still visible, by 1344. For further details of his sojourns in Parma, see Appendix I.

29. After having begun his *Africa* at Vaucluse in 1338–39 (see on §25 above), Petrarca resumed its composition at Selvapiana, a woody area at the foot of the Apennines south of Parma, right across the river Enza, which marked the boundary between the territory of Parma and that of Reggio Emilia. Yet, contrary to what he claims here, he never finished this poem: though the *Africa* does have a properly grandiose ending, with Scipio's triumph after Zama, it clearly lacks final revision.

30. Petrarca returned to Vaucluse at the beginning of 1342 and remained there until September 1343. The narrative at this point completely skips the years 1342 to 1347, that is, Petrarca's second stay at Vaucluse (1342–43), his second trip to Naples, the period spent in Parma and Verona (1343–45), and his third stay at Vaucluse (1345–47). The account resumes, in fact, with his return to Italy in 1347. If not intentional or simply due to the unfinished nature of the text, this gap in the narrative may be the result of a lacuna in Petrarca's original draft at this point, possibly caused by the loss of a leaf from his manuscript (see Elvira Nota in Dotti 2002–13, 5:231–32).

31. Petrarca is skirting an important reason for his departure from Avignon and rupture with Cardinal Giovanni Colonna in 1347, that is, his support of Cola di Rienzo in Rome, who was fiercely opposed by the Colonna family: it was precisely the fight against Cola di Rienzo that occasioned the death of Pietro, Stefano the Younger, and his son Giovanni in that year. Cardinal Giovanni and their father (Stefano the Elder) both died in 1348, while Giacomo had died in 1341.

32. The closing sentence of §32, following the lacuna, shows elements of inconsistency that derive from the unfinished nature of the text and re-

flect the difficulties its first editors must have encountered in their attempt to impose order on a working draft full of erasures, marginalia, and insertions of uncertain placement. Elvira Nota gives the text we read in the manuscripts that preserve this letter, thus trusting the judgment of its earlier editors, but parts of this sentence may belong elsewhere (on different hypotheses by modern scholars, see Nota in Dotti 2006–14, 5:230–32 and 369 *ad loc.*). Petrarca left Avignon in November 1347, and since he was born in July 1304, he must have still been forty-three, not forty-four, at the time.

33. Giacomo II da Carrara ruled Padua from 1345 to 1350. After Giacomo's assassination in 1350, his son Francesco inherited power and continued his father's offers of hospitality, but Petrarca clearly felt less at ease with the younger generation. Petrarca would spend more and more time at Arquà in his last years, where he wrote V.6, addressed to the younger ruler.

34. In April 1349 Petrarca accepted Giacomo da Carrara's offer of a rich canonry in the city of Padua and a house near the cathedral. Though he never became a priest, Petrarca had for a long time been in minor orders, which enabled him to hold such benefices.

35. Petrarca returned to Vaucluse in the summer of 1351. For changing places as a mark of human restlessness, see Horace, *Epistles* 1.11.27.

# *Concordances (Volumes 1 and 2)*

## a. *Between this edition and standard order of the* Epistulae familiares *and* Epistulae seniles*

| This edition | *Familiares/Seniles* |
|---|---|
| I.1 | F. 1.1 |
| I.2 | F. 18.8 |
| I.3 | F. 24.13 |
| I.4 | S. 1.1 |
| | |
| II.1 | F. 4.1 |
| II.2 | F. 6.2 |
| II.3 | F. 8.7 |
| II.4 | F. 16.2 |
| II.5 | S. 3.1* |
| II.6 | S. 16.1* |
| II.7 | F. 11.6 |
| II.8 | F. 11.4 |
| II.9 | F. 15.11 |
| II.10 | F. 15.12 |
| II.11 | F. 15.13 |
| II.12 | F. 13.8 |
| II.13 | F. 15.7 |
| II.14 | F. 19.16 |
| II.15 | F. 22.7 |
| II.16 | S. 13.10 |
| II.17 | S. 17.2 |

* Letters marked with an asterisk (*) are abridged.

| This edition | *Familiares/Seniles* |
|---|---|
| III.1 | F. 3.18 |
| III.2 | F. 4.4 |
| III.3 | F. 4.5 |
| III.4 | F. 4.6 |
| III.5 | F. 4.7 |
| III.6 | F. 4.8 |
| III.7 | F. 4.15 |
| III.8 | F. 4.16 |
| III.9 | F. 12.8 |
| III.10 | F. 13.5* |
| III.11 | F. 13.7 |
| III.12 | F. 18.2 |
| III.13 | F. 18.4 |
| III.14 | F. 20.4* |
| III.15 | F. 21.10 |
| III.16 | F. 21.15 |
| III.17 | F. 22.10 |
| III.18 | F. 22.2 |
| III.19 | F. 23.19 |
| III.20 | S. 3.1* |
| III.21 | S. 3.6 |
| III.22 | S. 6.1 |
| III.23 | S. 4.5 |
| | |
| IV.1 | F. 7.14 |
| IV.2 | F. 9.4 |
| IV.3 | F. 9.9 |
| IV.4 | F. 3.11 |
| IV.5 | F. 9.11 |
| IV.6 | F. 12.16 |
| IV.7 | F. 22.1 |
| IV.8 | S. 15.3* |
| IV.9 | F. 7.3 |
| IV.10 | F. 16.3 |

| This edition | *Familiares/Seniles* |
|---|---|
| IV.11 | F. 8.4 |
| IV.12 | S. 2.2 |
| IV.13 | F. 11.3 |
| IV.14 | F. 22.14* |
| IV.15 | F. 4.12 |
| IV.16 | F. 17.10 |
| | |
| V.1 | F. 1.9 |
| V.2 | F. 6.4 |
| V.3 | F. 7.17 |
| V.4 | F. 3.7 |
| V.5 | F. 12.2 |
| V.6 | S. 14.1* |
| | |
| VI.1 | F. IV.2 |
| VI.2 | F. IV.3 |
| VI.3 | F. V.1 |
| VI.4 | F. 7.7 |
| VI.5 | F. 13.6 |
| VI.6 | F. 11.16 |
| VI.7 | F. 15.9 |
| VI.8 | F. 11.8 |
| VI.9 | F. 10.1 |
| VI.10 | F. 19.1 |
| VI.11 | F. 19.3 |
| VI.12 | F. 23.2* |
| VI.13 | F. 19.18 |
| | |
| VII.1 | F. 6.1 |
| VII.2 | F. 10.3 |
| VII.3 | F. 16.4 |
| VII.4 | F. 17.1 |
| VII.5 | S. 1.5* |
| VII.6 | S. 7* |

| This edition | *Familiares/Seniles* |
|---|---|
| VII.7 | S. 9.1* |
| | |
| VIII.1 | F. 24.2 |
| VIII.2 | F. 24.3 |
| VIII.3 | F. 24.4 |
| VIII.4 | F. 24.5 |
| VIII.5 | F. 24.6 |
| VIII.6 | F. 24.7 |
| VIII.7 | F. 24.8 |
| VIII.8 | F. 24.9 |
| VIII.9 | F. 24.12 |
| | |
| IX.1 | S. 10.2 |
| IX.2 | S. 18 |

b. *Between the standard order of the* Epistulae familiares and Epistulae seniles *and this edition*

| *Epistulae familiares* | This edition |
|---|---|
| F. 1.1 | I.1 |
| F. 1.9 | V.1 |
| F. 3.7 | V.4 |
| F. 3.11 | IV.4 |
| F. 3.18 | III.1 |
| F. 4.1 | II.1 |
| F. 4.2 | VI.1 |
| F. 4.3 | VI.2 |
| F. 4.4 | III.2 |
| F. 4.5 | III.3 |
| F. 4.6 | III.4 |
| F. 4.7 | III.5 |
| F. 4.8 | III.6 |
| F. 4.12 | IV.15 |

| *Epistulae familiares* | This edition |
|---|---|
| *F.* 4.15 | III.7 |
| *F.* 4.16 | III.8 |
| *F.* 5.1 | VI.3 |
| *F.* 6.1 | VII.1 |
| *F.* 6.2 | II.2 |
| *F.* 6.4 | V.2 |
| *F.* 7.3 | IV.9 |
| *F.* 7.7 | VI.4 |
| *F.* 7.14 | IV.1 |
| *F.* 7.17 | V.3 |
| *F.* 8.4 | IV.11 |
| *F.* 8.7 | II.3 |
| *F.* 9.4 | IV.2 |
| *F.* 9.9 | IV.3 |
| *F.* 9.11 | IV.5 |
| *F.* 10.1 | VI.9 |
| *F.* 10.3 | VII.2 |
| *F.* 11.3 | IV.13 |
| *F.* 11.4 | II.8 |
| *F.* 11.6 | II.7 |
| *F.* 11.8 | VI.8 |
| *F.* 11.16 | VI.6 |
| *F.* 12.2 | V.5 |
| *F.* 12.8 | III.9 |
| *F.* 12.16 | IV.6 |
| *F.* 13.5* | III.10 |
| *F.* 13.6 | VI.5 |
| *F.* 13.7 | III.11 |
| *F.* 13.8 | II.12 |
| *F.* 15.7 | II.13 |
| *F.* 15.9 | VI.7 |
| *F.* 15.11 | II.9 |
| *F.* 15.12 | II.10 |
| *F.* 15.13 | II.11 |

| *Epistulae familiares* | This edition |
|---|---|
| F. 16.2 | II.4 |
| F. 16.3 | IV.10 |
| F. 16.4 | VII.3 |
| F. 17.1 | VII.4 |
| F. 17.10 | IV.16 |
| F. 18.2 | III.12 |
| F. 18.8 | I.2 |
| F. 18.14 | III.13 |
| F. 19.1 | VI.10 |
| F. 19.3 | VI.11 |
| F. 19.16 | II.14 |
| F. 19.18 | VI.13 |
| F. 20.4* | III.14 |
| F. 21.10 | III.15 |
| F. 21.15 | III.16 |
| F. 22.1 | IV.7 |
| F. 22.2 | III.18 |
| F. 22.7 | II.15 |
| F. 22.10 | III.17 |
| F. 22.14* | IV.14 |
| F. 23.2* | VI.12 |
| F. 23.19 | III.19 |
| F. 24.2 | VIII.1 |
| F. 24.3 | VIII.2 |
| F. 24.4 | VIII.3 |
| F. 24.5 | VIII.4 |
| F. 24.6 | VIII.5 |
| F. 24.7 | VIII.6 |
| F. 24.8 | VIII.7 |
| F. 24.9 | VIII.8 |
| F. 24.12 | VIII.9 |
| F. 24.13 | I.3 |

| *Epistulae seniles* | This edition |
|---|---|
| S. 1.1 | I.1 |
| S. 1.5* | VII.5 |
| S. 2.2 | IV.12 |
| S. 3.1* | II.5 |
| S. 3.1* | III.20 |
| S. 3.6 | III.21 |
| S. 4.5 | III.23 |
| S. 6.1 | III.22 |
| S. 7* | VII.6 |
| S. 9.1* | VII.7 |
| S. 10.2 | IX.1 |
| S. 13.10 | II.16 |
| S. 14.1* | V.6 |
| S. 15.3* | IV.8 |
| S. 16.1* | II.6 |
| S. 17.2 | II.17 |
| S. 18 | IX.2 |

# *Bibliography*


## I. EDITIONS AND TRANSLATIONS OF PETRARCA'S WORKS

### A. Letters

#### FAMILIAR LETTERS

*Epistole Familiares*. Edited by Sebastiano Manilio. Venice: Giovanni and Gregorio de Gregori, 1492. *Editio princeps* of *Familiares* 1–8.

*Librorum Francisci Petrarche impressorum annotatio*. 2 vols. Venice: Simone da Lovere for Andrea Torresano da Asola, 1501. *Editio princeps* of five letters from Book 24 in vol. 1 (printed after Books 1–8).

*Francisci Petrarchae . . . Epistolarum familiarium libri XIV. Variarum liber I. Sine titulo liber I. Ad quosdam ex veteribus illustriores liber I*. Lyon: Samuel Crispin, 1601. *Editio princeps* of Books 18–21 and part of 23 (here numbered as Books 9–14), as well as of seven more letters from 24.

*Epistolae de rebus familiaribus et variae*. Edited by Giuseppe Fracassetti. 3 vols. Florence: Le Monnier, 1859–63. First complete edition of the twenty-four books of the *Familiares*, thus including the *editio princeps* of Books 9–17, 22, most of 23 and *F.* 24.12; only a few isolated letters from these books had previously circulated in print.

*Lettere di Francesco Petrarca: delle cose familiari libri ventiquattro, lettere varie libro unico*. Italian translation and notes by Giuseppe Fracassetti. 5 vols. Florence: Le Monnier, 1863–67. Based on Latin text by Fracassetti, *Epistolae de rebus familiaribus et variae*.

*Le Familiari*. Edited by Vittorio Rossi (vols. 1–3) and Umberto Bosco (vol. 4). 4 vols. Florence: Sansoni (Edizione Nazionale delle Opere di Francesco Petrarca), 1933–42.

*Letters on Familiar Matters*. English translation by Aldo S. Bernardo. 3 vols. Albany: State University of New York Press, 1975–85. Based on Latin text of Rossi-Bosco, *Le Familiari*.

*Lettres Familières*. Edited and annotated by Ugo Dotti; French translation by André Longpré. 6 vols. Paris: Les Belles Lettres, 2002–5. Based on Rossi-Bosco, *Le Familiari*.

*Le Familiari*. Edited with Italian translation and notes by Ugo Dotti in collaboration with Felicita Audisio. 5 vols. Turin: Aragno, 2004–9. Based on Rossi-Bosco, *Le Familiari*.

LETTERS OF OLD AGE

*Librorum Francisci Petrarche impressorum annotatio*. 2 vols. Venice: Simone da Lovere for Andrea Torresano da Asola, 1501. *Editio princeps* of the *Seniles* in vol. 2.

*Lettere senili di Francesco Petrarca*. Italian translation and notes by Giuseppe Fracassetti. 2 vols. Florence: Le Monnier, 1869–70. Books 1–17 only (thus excluding the letter *To Posterity*, which was instead published in Fracassetti, *Epistolae de rebus familiaribus et variae*, 1:1–11); based on early printed editions.

*Letters of Old Age*. English translation by Aldo S. Bernardo, Saul Levin, and Reta A. Bernardo. 2 vols. Baltimore: Johns Hopkins University Press, 1992. Based on the 1501 *editio princeps*.

*Lettres de la vieillesse*. Edited by Elvira Nota, with introduction and notes by Ugo Dotti. French translation by Frédérique Castelli, François Fabre, Antoine de Rosny, Laure Schebat, Claude Laurens, and Jean-Yves Boriaud. 5 vols. Paris: Les Belles Lettres, 2002–13.

*Le Senili*. Edited by Elvira Nota, with an Italian translation and notes by Ugo Dotti in collaboration with Felicita Audisio. 3 vols. Turin: Aragno, 2004–10.

*Res Seniles*. Edited with Italian translation and notes by Silvia Rizzo in collaboration with Monica Berté. 3 vols. Florence: Le Lettere (Edizione Nazionale delle Opere di Francesco Petrarca), 2006–14. Books 1–12 only to date.

Refe, Laura. *I "Fragmenta" dell'Epistola "Ad Posteritatem" di Francesco Petrarca*. Messina: Centro internazionale di studi umanistici, 2014. Includes a commented edition of *Seniles* 18.

### METRICAL EPISTLES

*Epistulae metricae*. Edited with German translation and notes by Otto and Eva Schönberger. Würzburg: Königshausen and Neumann, 2004. Based on early printed editions.

*Petrarch at Vaucluse: Letters in Verse and Prose*. English translation by Ernest Hatch Wilkins. Chicago: University of Chicago Press, 1958. Selection of letters, including *Metrical Epistles* 1.4, 6, 10, 12 and 3.1, 4, 5, 30, 33; based on Latin text by Enrico Bianchi [in *Rime, Trionfi e Poesie Latine*. Milan and Naples: Ricciardi, 1951] and, for *Epistles* 1.12 and 3.30, the text of Domenico Rossetti [in *Poesie minori del Petrarca*. Milan: Società Tipografica de' Classici Italiani, 1829–34].

### THE BOOK WITHOUT A NAME

Piur, Paul. *Petrarcas "Buch ohne Namen" und die päpstliche Kurie, ein Beitrag zur Geistesgeschichte der Frührenaissance*. Halle, Saale: M. Niemeyer, 1925. Study containing text edition of the *Liber sine nomine* in pt. 2, 161–238.

*Petrarch's Book without a Name: A Translation of the Liber sine nomine*. English translation by Norman P. Zacour. Toronto: Pontifical Institute of Mediaeval Studies, 1973. Based on the Latin text of Piur, *"Buch ohne Namen."*

*Sine nomine: Lettere polemiche e politiche*. Edited by Ugo Dotti. Bari: Laterza, 1974. Latin text based on Piur, *"Buch ohne Namen,"* with facing Italian translation.

*Libro senza titolo*. Edited by Laura Casarsa, with Italian translation and notes; introduction by Ugo Dotti. Turin: Aragno, 2010. Latin text based on Piur, *"Buch ohne Namen,"* with revisions.

*Liber sine nomine*. Edited with Italian translation by Giovanni Cascio. Florence: Le Lettere (Edizione Nazionale delle Opere di Francesco Petrarca), 2015. New critical edition.

### UNCOLLECTED LETTERS

*Epistulae de rebus familiaribus et variae*. Edited by Fracassetti, vol. 3, pp. 309–409. See *Familiar Letters*, above. Including a total of seventy-three uncollected letters attributed to Petrarca in manuscripts and early printed editions (sixty-five *Variae* and eight more letters in an appendix).

Wilkins, Ernest Hatch, and Giuseppe Billanovich. "Miscellaneous Letters." *Speculum* 37.2 (1962): 226–43. Edition of eighteen uncollected letters and fragments (mostly not included in Fracassetti, *Epistolae de rebus familiaribus et variae*).

*Lettere disperse: Varie e miscellanee*. Edited by Alessandro Pancheri, with Italian translation and notes. Parma: Fondazione Pietro Bembo-U. Guanda, 1994. Including seventy-six letters, based on Fracassetti, *Epistolae de rebus familiaribus et variae*, Wilkins-Billanovich, "Miscellaneous Letters," and other modern editions.

*Epistole tardive di Francesco Petrarca: Edizione critica con introduzione e commento*. Edited by Gunilla Sävborg. Stockholm: Alqvist and Wiksell International, 2004. Including thirty-three uncollected letters, dated 1361–73.

#### LETTERS ADDRESSED TO PETRARCA

Cochin, Henry. *Un amico di Petrarca: lettere del Nelli al Petrarca*. Florence: Le Monnier, 1901.

*Lettere a Petrarca*. Edited with Italian translation and notes by Ugo Dotti. Turin: Aragno, 2012. Based for most texts on earlier modern editions.

### B. Latin Poetry

#### PHILOLOGIA PHILOSTRATI

Mariotti, Scevola. "La *Philologia* del Petrarca." *Humanitas. Revista do Instituto de estudios clássicos da Faculdade de letras da Universidade de Coimbra* 3 (1950–51): 191–206. Fundamental study on this lost comedy.

#### AFRICA

*L'Africa*. Edited by Nicola Festa. Florence: Sansoni (Edizione Nazionale delle Opere di Francesco Petrarca), 1926. Reprint, Florence: Le Lettere, 1998.

*Petrarch's Africa*. English translation and notes by Thomas G. Bergin and Alice S. Wilson. New Haven: Yale University Press, 1977. Based on Latin text by Festa, *L'Africa*.

*L'Afrique: 1338–74*. Edited with French translation and notes by Rebecca Lenoir; introduction by Henri Lamarque. Grenoble: Millon, 2002. Latin text based on Festa, *L'Africa*, with revisions.

*L'Afrique = Africa*. Edited with French translation and notes by Pierre Laurens. Paris: Les Belles Lettres, 2006. Only vol. 1, including Books 1–5 to date; Latin text based on ms. Florence, Biblioteca Laurenziana Acquisti e Doni 441, unknown to Festa, *L'Africa*.

BUCOLIC POEM

Avena, Antonio. *Il Bucolicum Carmen e i suoi commenti inediti*. Bologna: Forni, 1906. Study containing a text edition at pp. 95–165.

*Petrarch's Bucolicum Carmen*. Edited with English translation and notes by Thomas G. Bergin; illustrations by Deane Keller. New Haven: Yale University Press, 1974. Latin text follows Avena, *Il Bucolicum Carmen e i suoi commenti inediti*.

*Bucolicum Carmen*. Edited with French translation and notes by Marcel François and Paul Bachmann, with the collaboration of François Roudant. Paris: Champion, 2001.

*Bucolicum Carmen*. Edited with Italian translation by Luca Canali, notes by Maria Pellegrini. Lecce: Manni, 2005. Latin text reproduces Avena, *Il Bucolicum Carmen e i suoi commenti inediti*.

PENITENTIAL PSALMS

*Les Psaumes pénitentiaux*. Edited with a French translation by Henry Cochin; preface by Pierre de Nolhac. Paris: L. Rouart, 1929.

*Salmi penitenziali*. Edited with Italian translation and notes by Roberto Gigliucci. Rome: Salerno, 1997. Latin text based on Cochin's edition.

*Psalmi penitentiales; Orationes*. Edited with Italian translation and notes by Donatella Coppini. Florence: Le Lettere (Edizione Nazionale delle Opere di Francesco Petrarca), 2010.

#### UNCOLLECTED LATIN POEMS

Feo, Michele. "Poesie Latine Disperse." In *Petrarca nel Tempo: Tradizioni, lettori e immagini delle opere*, edited by Michele Feo, 308–16. (Comitato Nazionale per le celebrazioni del VII Centenario della nascita di Francesco Petrarca.) Pontedera: Bandecchi e Vivaldi, 2003. Study containing a comprehensive overview of Petrarca's uncollected Latin poems.

*Gabbiani*. Edited with introduction and notes by Francisco Rico; Italian translations by various authors. Milan: Adelphi, 2008. Includes twelve Latin poems, mostly based on earlier editions.

*Improvvisi: un'antica raccolta di epigrammi*. Edited with Italian translation and commentary by Monica Berté. Rome: Salerno, 2014. Includes twenty Latin poems.

### C. Latin Prose Works: Biographical and Historical

#### LIFE OF TERENCE

Villa, Claudia. "La *Vita Terentii* di Francesco Petrarca." In *Estravaganti, disperse, apocrifi petrarcheschi*, edited by Claudia Berra and Paola Vecchi Galli, 573–79. Milan: Monduzzi, 2007.

*La Vita Terrentii de Petrarca*. Edited by Iñigo Ruiz Arzálluz with Spanish translation and notes. Rome: Antenore (Studi sul Petrarca 39), 2010.

#### ON FAMOUS MEN

*De viris illustribus*. Edited by Guido Martellotti. Florence: Sansoni (Edizione Nazionale delle Opere di Francesco Petrarca), 1964. Contains Book 1 of *On Illustrious Men*.

*De gestis Caesaris*. Edited by Giuliana Crevatin. Pisa: Scuola Normale Superiore (Testi e saggi rinascimentali 2), 2003.

*De viris illustribus*. Edited with Italian translation by Silvano Ferrone. Florence: Le Lettere (Edizione Nazionale delle Opere di Francesco Petrarca), 2005. Includes Book 1 of *On Illustrious Men*, based on Martellotti, *De viris illustribus*, with revisions.

*De viris illustribus IV: Compendium.* Edited with Italian translation by Paola de Capua. Firenze: Le Lettere (Edizione Nazionale delle Opere di Francesco Petrarca), 2007.

*De viris illustribus II: Adam-Hercules.* Edited with Italian translation by Caterina Malta. Firenze: Le Lettere (Edizione Nazionale delle Opere di Francesco Petrarca), 2007.

*Gli uomini illustri; Vita di Giulio Cesare.* Italian translation and notes by Ugo Dotti. Turin: Einaudi, 2007. Includes Books 1 and 2 of *On Illustrious Men*, the *Vita Julii Caesaris* (*De gestis Cesaris*), and the *Collatio inter Scipionem, Alexandrum, Annibalem et Pyrhum.*

*De viris illustribus: Adam-Hercules.* Edited with Italian translation and notes by Caterina Malta. Messina: Centro interdipartimentale di studi umanistici dell'Università di Messina, 2008. Includes Book 2 of *On Illustrious Men;* more detailed edition than Malta, *De viris illustribus II.*

*De viris illustribus III: De gestis Cesaris.* Italian translation by Giacinto Namia. Firenze: Le Lettere (Edizione Nazionale delle Opere di Francesco Petrarca), 2012. Translation based on text to be publishsed in Namia's forthcoming edition for the Edizione Nazionale.

### THE ENCOUNTER BETWEEN SCIPIO, ALEXANDER, HANNIBAL, AND PYRRHUS

Martellotti, Guido. "La *Collatio inter Scipionem, Alexandrum, Annibalem et Pyrhum,* un inedito del Petrarca nella Biblioteca della University of Pennsylvania." In *Classical, Mediaeval and Renaissance Studies in Honor of Berthold Louis Ullman,* edited by Charles Henderson, Jr., 2:145–68. Rome: Edizioni di storia e letteratura, 1964. Possibly a fragment of *On Famous Men.*

### GUIDE THE HOLY LAND

*Itinerario in Terra Santa.* Edited with Italian translation by Francesco Lo Monaco. Bergamo: P. Lubrina, 1990. Edition of this historical geography based on the two most relevant manuscripts.

*Itinéraire de Gênes à la Terre Sainte: 1358.* Edited with French translation by Christophe Carraud and Rebecca Lenoir, with notes by Rebecca

Lenoir. Grenoble: Millon, 2002. Latin text reproduces Lo Monaco, *Itinerario in Terra Santa*.

*Petrarch's Guide to the Holy Land. Itinerary to the Sepulcher of Our Lord Jesus Christ; Facsimile Edition of Cremona, Biblioteca Statale, Deposito Libreria Civica, Manuscript BB.1.2.5*. Edited with English translation and notes by Theodore J. Cachey, Jr. Notre Dame: University of Notre Dame Press, 2002. Containing both a facsimile edition and a transcription of the manuscript's text.

## D. Latin Prose Works: Moral and Religious

### THINGS WORTH REMEMBERING

*Rerum Memorandarum Libri*. Edited by Giuseppe Billanovich. Florence: Sansoni (Edizione Nazionale delle Opere di Francesco Petrarca), 1943.

*Rerum Memorandarum Libri*. Edited with Italian translation by Marco Petoletti. Florence: Le Lettere (Edizione Nazionale delle Opere di Francesco Petrarca), 2014. Based on Billanovich, *Rerum Memorandarum Libri*, with revisions.

### ON THE LIFE OF SOLITUDE

*The Life of Solitude*. English translation by Jacob Zeitlin. Urbana: University of Illinois Press, 1924. Based on texts from early printed editions.

*De vita solitaria* in *Francesco Petrarca: Prose*, pp. 285–591. Edited with Italian translation and notes by Guido Martellotti et al. Milano: Ricciardi, 1955. Edition based on ms. Vaticanus Latinus 3357; revised edition by Antonietta Bufano, in *Opere Latine*, 1:261–565. Turin: UTET, 1975.

*De vita solitaria. Buch 1*. Edited with commentary by Karl Enenkel. Leiden and New York: Brill, 1990.

*De vita solitaria = La vie solitaire: 1346–1366*. Edited with French translation and notes by Christophe Carraud; preface by Nicholas Mann. Grenoble: Millon, 1999. Latin text based on Enenkel, *De Vita Solitaria*, with revisions, for Book 1, and Martellotti, *De Vita Solitaria* in *Prose*, and Bufano, *Collatio coram domino Iohanne Francorum rege*, for Book 2.

### ON RELIGIOUS RETIREMENT

*On Religious Leisure*. Edited with English translation by Susan S. Schearer; introduction by Ronald G. Witt. New York: Italica Press, 2002. Based on Giuseppe Rotondi's edition (*Il "De otio religioso" di Francesco Petrarca*. Città del Vaticano: Biblioteca Apostolica Vaticana, 1958).

*De otio religioso*. Edited with Italian translation by Guido Goletti. Florence: Le Lettere (Edizione Nazionale delle Opere di Francesco Petrarca), 2006.

### MY SECRET BOOK

*Secretum* in *Prose*, pp. 21–215. Edited with Italian translation and notes by Enrico Carrara. Milan: Ricciardi, 1955. Edition based on ms. Laurenziana XXVI sin. 9; revised edition by Antonietta Bufano, in *Opere Latine*, 1:43–259. Turin: UTET, 1975.

*Secretum*. Edited with Italian translation and notes by Enrico Fenzi. Milan: Mursia, 1992. Latin text follows the editions of Carrara, *Secretum* in *Prose*, and Bufano, *Collatio coram domino Iohanne Francorum rege*.

*The Secret*. English translation by Carol E. Quillen. Boston and New York: Bedford/St. Martin's, 2003. Latin text by Carrara, *Secretum* in *Prose*.

*My Secret Book*. Edited and translated by Nicholas Mann. (I Tatti Renaissance Library 72.) Cambridge, MA: Harvard University Press, 2015. Latin text follows the editions of Carrara, *Secretum* in *Prose*, and Bufano, *Collatio coram domino Iohanne Francorum rege*.

### ON THE REMEDIES FOR FORTUNE FAIR AND FOUL

*Petrarch's Remedies for Fortune Fair and Foul*. English translation and notes by Conrad Rawski. 5 vols. Bloomington: Indiana University Press, 1991.

*De remediis utriusque fortune = Les remèdes aux deux fortunes: 1354–1366*. Edited with French translation and notes by Christophe Carraud; preface by Giuseppe Tognon. 2 vols. Grenoble: Millon, 2002. Latin text based on early printed editions.

*Petrarca e le arti figurative: De remediis utriusque Fortune, I 37–42*. Edited with Italian translation and commentary by Giulia Perucchi. Florence: Le Lettere (Materiali per l'Edizione Nazionale delle Opere di Francesco Petrarca), 2014.

### INVECTIVES

*De ignorantia: Della mia ignoranza e di quella di molti altri*. Edited with Italian translation and notes by Enrico Fenzi. Milan: Mursia, 1999. Latin text based on Pier Giorgio Ricci's edition (in *Opere Latine*, pp. 1025–51. Edited by Antonietta Bufano. Turin: UTET, 1975), with revisions.

*Invectives*. Edited with English translation and notes by David Marsh. (I Tatti Renaissance Library 11.) Cambridge, MA: Harvard University Press, 2003. Texts based, with minor revisions, on Pier Giorgio Ricci's edition (Rome: Edizioni di storia e letteratura, 1978) for *Contra medicum;* Pier Giorgio Ricci's edition (Florence: Le Monnier, 1949) for *Contra quendam magni status hominem;* Giuliana Crevatin's edition (Venice: Marsilio, 1995) for *Contra eum qui maledixit Italiae*. The text of *De ignorantia* was edited for this volume by James Hankins from the two autograph manuscripts in Berlin and the Vatican.

Berté, Monica. *Jean de Hesdin e Francesco Petrarca*. Messina: Centro interdipartimentale di studi umanistici, 2004. Study containing edition, with Italian translation and notes, of de Hesdin's pamphlet (against which Petrarca wrote his *Contra eum qui maledixit Italie*), at pp. 115–63.

*Contra eum qui maledixit Italie*. Edited with Italian translation by Monica Berté. Florence: Le Lettere (Edizione Nazionale delle Opere di Francesco Petrarca), 2005.

*Invective contra medicum; Invectiva contra quendam magni status hominem sed nullius scientiae aut virtutis*. Edited with Italian translation by Francesco Bausi. Florence: Le Lettere (Edizione Nazionale delle Opere di Francesco Petrarca), 2005.

## E. Speeches and Other Short Latin Writings

Hortis, Attilio. *Scritti inediti di Francesco Petrarca*. Trieste: Tipografia del Lloyd Austro-Ungarico, 1874. Study containing edition of *Collatio lau-*

*reationis*, at pp. 311–28; *Arenga facta Veneciis*, at pp. 329–33; *Arringa facta Mediolani*, at pp. 335–40; *Arenga facta in civitate Novarie*, at pp. 341–58.

Lazzarini, Vittorio. "La seconda ambasceria di Francesco Petrarca a Venezia." In *Miscellanea di studi critici in onore di Guido Mazzoni*, edited by A. Della Torre and P. L. Rambaldi, 1:173–83. 2 vols. Florence: Tipografia Galileiana, 1907.

Wilkins, Ernest Hatch. "Petrarch's Coronation Oration." *Publication of the Modern Language Association of America* 68 (1953): 1241–50. (Reprint in Wilkins, *Studies in the Life and Works of Petrarch*, 300–13.) English translation of *Collatio laureationis*, based on the Latin text of Hortis, *Scritti inediti di Francesco Petrarca*.

D'Alessio, Nicoletto. *La storia della guerra per i confini*. In *Rerum Italicarum Scriptores* 17.1.3, edited by Roberto Cessi, 160. Bologna: Zanichelli, 1965. Edition including the text of Petrarch's "Oration for the Second Venetian Embassy."

Godi, Carlo. "L'orazione del Petrarca per Giovanni il Buono." *Italia Medievale e Umanistica* 8 (1965): 45–83. Study containing edition of *Collatio coram domino Iohanne*, at pp. 73–83.

———. "La *Collatio Laureationis* del Petrarca." *Italia Medievale e Umanistica* 13 (1970): 1–27. Study containing edition of *Collatio laureationis*, at pp. 13–27. A second edition of the *Collatio laureationis* was published by Godi in 1988, based on the collation of a new manuscript ("La *Collatio Laureationis* del Petrarca nelle due redazioni"), in *Studi Petrarcheschi* 5 (1988): 1–58.

———. "Il Petrarca 'inutilis orator' a Venezia: l'arringa per la pace tra Genovesi e Veneziani." In *Vestigia: Studi in onore di Giuseppe Billanovich*, edited by Rino Avesani, Mirella Ferrari, Tino Foffano, Giuseppe Frasso, and Agostino Sottili, 1:399–416. 2 vols. Rome: Edizioni di storia e letteratura, 1984. Study containing edition of *Arenga facta Veneciis*, at pp. 412–16.

Dotti, Ugo. *Petrarca a Milano. Documenti milanesi 1353–1354*. Milan: Ceschina, 1972. Study containing an edition of the *Arenga facta Veneciis* (based on Hortis, *Scritti inediti di Francesco Petrarca*), at pp. 176–79, and Italian translation at pp. 115–17.

*Collatio coram domino Iohanne Francorum rege* in *Opere Latine*. Edited with Italian translation and notes by Antonietta Bufano. Turin: UTET, 1975, 2:1285–1309. Based on Godi's 1965 edition of *Collatio coram domino Iohanne*.

Mertens, Dieter. "Petrarcas Privilegium laureationis." In *Litterae Medii Aevi. Festschrift für Johanne Autenrieth zu irhem 65. Geburstag*, edited by Michael Borgolte and Herrad Spilling, 225–47. Sigmaringen: Jan Thorbecke Verlag, 1988. Study containing edition of *Privilegium laureationis*, at pp. 236–47.

Rawski, Conrad H. "Petrarch's Oration in Novara: A Critical Transcription of Vienna, Oesterreichische Nationalbibliothek, MS Pal. 4498, fols. 98r–104v." *The Journal of Medieval Latin* 9 (1999): 148–93. Study containing edition of *Arenga facta in civitate Novarie*, at pp. 174–93.

*Petrarca a Novara: 18 Giugno 1358*, pp. 17–27. Italian translation by Dorino Tuniz; introduction by Francesco Cognasso. Novara: Interlinea, 2004. Latin text of *Arenga facta in civitate Novarie* in appendix, reproducing Hortis, *Scritti inediti di Francesco Petrarca*.

#### UNCOLLECTED PRAYERS

*Orationes*. Edited with Italian translation by Donatella Coppini. See *Penitential Psalms*.

#### TESTAMENT

*Petrarch's Testament*. Edited with English translation by Theodor Ernst Mommsen. Ithaca: Cornell University Press, 1957.

### F. Poetry in Italian

#### CANZONIERE

*Il Canzoniere di Francesco Petrarca riprodotto letteralmente dal Cod. Vat. Lat. 3195 con tre fotoincisioni*. Edited by Ettore Modigliani. Rome: Società Filologica Romana, 1904. Diplomatic edition.

*Canzoniere*. Edited with an introduction by Gianfranco Contini; notes by Daniele Ponchiroli. Turin: Einaudi, 1964. Revision of original edition published in Paris: Tallone, 1949.

*Petrarch's Lyric Poems: The Rime Sparse and Other Lyrics*. Edited with English translation by Robert M. Durling. Cambridge, MA: Harvard University Press, 1976. Based on Modigliani 1904, with sligthly modernized orthography and punctuation; it also includes fourteen of the uncollected poems.

*Il Codice degli abbozzi: edizione e storia del manoscritto Vaticano latino 3196*. Edited by Vinicio Pacca and Laura Paolino; introduction by Marco Santagata. Milan: Mondadori, 1996 (esp. pp. 627–754). Milan and Naples: Ricciardi, 2000. Diplomatic edition.

*Canzoniere*. Edited and annotated by Marco Santagata. Milan: Mondadori, 2004. Revision of original 1996 edition.

*Canzoniere = Rerum Vulgarium Fragmenta*. Edited with commentary by Rosanna Bettarini. 2 vols. Turin: Einaudi, 2005. Based on Contini, *Canzoniere*, and Santagata, *Canzoniere*,with further revisions.

Savoca, Giuseppe. *Il Canzoniere di Petrarca tra codicologia ed ecdotica*. Florence: Olschki, 2008. Introduction to Savoca's edition.

*Rerum vulgarium fragmenta*. Edited by Giuseppe Savoca. Florence: Olschki, 2008.

## TRIUMPHS

*Die Triumphe*. Edited by Carl Appel. Halle an der Saale: Niemeyer, 1901.

*The Triumphs of Petrarch*. English translation by Ernest Hatch Wilkins. Chicago: Chicago University Press, 1962.

*Trionfi, Rime estravaganti, Codice degli abbozzi*. Edited by Vinicio Pacca and Laura Paolino; introduction by Marco Santagata. Milan: Mondadori, 1996. Edition of *Triumphs* by Vinicio Pacca, at pp. 3–626, based on Appel, *Die Triumphe*, and later studies.

## UNCOLLECTED ITALIAN POEMS

*Rime disperse di Francesco Petrarca o a lui attribuite*. Edited by Angelo Solerti. Florence: Sansoni, 1909. Includes 214 poems that were traditionally attributed to Petrarca.

*Rime disperse*. Edited with English translation, notes, and introduction by Joseph A. Barber. New York: Garland, 1991. Includes seventy poems deemed authentic; based on manuscripts and early printed editions.

*Trionfi, Rime estravaganti, Codice degli abbozzi*. Edited and annotated by Vinicio Pacca and Laura Paolino; introduction by Marco Santagata. Milan: Mondadori, 1996. Edition of *Rime estravaganti* by Laura Paolino, at pp. 647–754, including twenty-one poems deemed authentic.

Vecchi Galli, Paola. "Voci della dispersione." In *Estravaganti, disperse, apocrifi petrarcheschi*, edited by Claudia Berra and Paola Vecchi Galli, 1–24. Milan: Monduzzi, 2007. Study anticipating a critical edition and including, at pp. 23–24, a list of thirty-three poems deemed authentic.

## II. SECONDARY LITERATURE

Antognini, Roberta. *'Placet experiri': Il progetto autobiografico delle* Familiares *di Petrarca*. Milano: LED, 2008.

Armstrong, Guyda, Rhiannon Daniels, and Stephen J. Milner. "Boccaccio as Cultural Mediator." In *The Cambridge Companion to Boccaccio*, edited by G. Armstrong, R. Daniels, and S. J. Milner, 3–19. Cambridge: Cambridge University Press, 2015.

Ascoli, Albert R. "Petrarch's Middle Age: Memory, Imagination, History and the 'Ascent of Mt. Ventoux.'" In idem, *A Local Habitation and a Name: Imagining Histories in the Italian Renaissance*, 21–58. New York: Fordham University Press, 2011.

———. "Petrarch's Private Politics: *Rerum familiarium libri XIX*." In idem, *A Local Habitation*, 118–58.

———. "Epistolary Petrarch." In *The Cambridge Companion to Petrarch*, 120–37.

Bianchi, Lorenzo. *Ad limina Petri: spazio e memoria della Roma cristiana*. Roma: Donzelli, 1999.

Billanovich, Giuseppe. *Petrarca letterato*. Vol. 1, *Lo scrittoio del Petrarca*. Rome: Edizioni di Storia e Letteratura, 1947 (esp. pp. 1–55: "Dall' *Epystularum mearum ad diversos liber* ai *Rerum Familiarium libri XXIV*").

———. *Petrarca e il primo Umanesimo*. Padua: Antenore, 1996 (esp. pp. 168–84: "Petrarca e il ventoso").

Boccaccio, Giovanni. *Vita di Petrarca*. Edited with Italian translation by Gianni Villani. Rome: Salerno, 2004.

Boriaud, Jean-Yves. "L'Image de Rome dans la Lettre Familière VI.2." In *Pétrarque epistolier*, 57–66.

*The Cambridge Companion to Petrarch*. Edited by Albert Russell Ascoli and Unn Falkeid. Cambridge: Cambridge University Press, 2015.

Dotti, Ugo. *Vita di Petrarca*. Bari: Laterza, 1987.

——. *Petrarca civile: alle origini dell'intellettuale moderno*. Rome: Donzelli, 2001.

Enenkel, Karl. "Modelling the Humanist." In *Modelling the Individual: Biography and Portrait in the Renaissance, with a Critical Edition of Petrarch's Letter to Posterity*, edited by Karl Enenkel, Betsy de Jong-Crane, and Peter Liebregts, 11–49. Amsterdam: Rodopi, 1998.

*Estravaganti, disperse, apocrifi petrarcheschi: Gargnano del Garda (25-27 settembre 2006)*. Edited by Claudia Berra and Paola Vecchi Galli. Milan: Cisalpino, 2007.

Fenzi, Enrico. *Saggi Petrarcheschi*. Fiesole: Cadmo, 2003.

Feo, Michele. "Petrarca." *Enciclopedia Virgiliana*, 4:53–78. 5 vols. Roma: Enciclopedia italiana, 1973. Also online.

Foresti, Arnaldo. *Aneddoti della vita di Francesco Petrarca*. Brescia: Vannini, 1928. New edition, corrected and enlarged by the author, with a preface by Giuseppe Billanovich. Padua: Antenore, 1977.

Gaisser, Julia Haig. *The Fortunes of Apuleius and the* Golden Ass: *A Study in Transmission and Reception*. Princeton: Princeton University Press, 2008 (esp. chaps. 3–4).

Giazzi, Emilio. "Un episodio della fortuna dei due Plinii tra Trecento e Quattrocento: Domenico Bandini di Arezzo." In *Analecta Brixiana*, edited by Alfredo Valvo and Gian Enrico Manzoni, 49–74. Milan: Vita e Pensiero, 2004.

Hankins, James. "Petrarch and the Canon of Neo-Latin Literature." In *Petrarca, l'Umanesimo e la civiltà europea*, 2:905–22.

*Le postille al Virgilio Ambrosiano*. Edited and commented by Marco Baglio, Antonietta Nebuloni Testa, and Marco Petoletti; introduction by Giuseppe Velli. 2 vols. Padua: Antenore, 2006.

Lokaj, Rodney. "Gherardo dans le *Familiares* de Pétrarque." In *Pétrarque epistolier*, 45–56.

Mazzotta, Giuseppe. *The Worlds of Petrarch*. Durham, NC: Duke University Press, 1993.

———. "Petrarch's Epistolary Epic." In *Petrarch: A Critical Guide*, 309–19.

McLaughlin, Martin. "Petrarch and Cicero: Adulation and Critical Distance." In *Brill's Companion to the Reception of Cicero*, edited by William H. F. Altman, 19–38. Leiden-Boston: E. J. Brill, 2015.

*Motivi e forme delle* Familiari *di Francesco Petrarca: Gargnano del Garda, 2–5 ottobre 2002*. Edited by Claudia Berra. Milano: Cisalpino, 2003.

Musto, Ronald G. *Apocalypse in Rome: Cola di Rienzo and the Politics of the New Age*. Berkeley: University of California Press, 2003.

Nardella, Cristina. *Il fascino di Roma nel Medioevo: Le "Meraviglie di Roma" di maestro Gregorio*. Roma: Viella, 1997.

Nolhac, Pierre de. *Pétrarque et l'Humanisme*. 2 vols. Paris: Champion, 1907. Reprint, 1965.

Pade, Marianne. *The Reception of Plutarch's Lives in Fifteenth-Century Italy*. Copenhagen: Museum Tusculanum Press (University of Copenhagen), 2007.

Pertusi, Agostino. *Leonzio Pilato fra Petrarca e Boccaccio: le sue versioni omeriche negli autografi di Venezia e la cultura greca del primo Umanesimo*. Venice: Istituto per la collaborazione culturale, 1964.

*Petrarca, l'umanesimo e la civiltà europea: Atti del Convegno Internazionale Firenze, 5–10 dicembre 2004*. Edited by Donatella Coppini and Michele Feo. 2 vols. Florence: Le Lettere (Quaderni Petrarcheschi 17–18), 2007–8.

*Petrarca e il mondo greco: Atti del Convegno internazionale di studi, Reggio Calabria, 26–30 novembre*. Edited by Michele Feo, Vincenzo Fera, Paola Megna, Antonio Rollo. Florence: Le Lettere (Quaderni Petrarcheschi 12–13), 2002–3.

*Petrarca nel tempo: Tradizioni, lettori e immagini delle opere; catalogo della mostra, Arezzo, Sottochiesa di San Francesco, 22 novembre 2003–27 gennaio 2004*. Edited by Michele Feo. Pontedera: Bandecchi e Vivaldi, 2003.

*Petrarch. A Critical Guide to the Complete Works*. Edited by Victoria Kirkham and Armando Maggi. Chicago: University of Chicago Press, 2009. See esp. pt. 6, on Petrarch's various epistolary collections.

*Pétrarque épistolier: Actes des Journées d'études, Université de Toulouse-Le Mirail, Toulouse, 26–27 mars 1999*. Edited by Jean-Yves Boriaud and Henri Lamarque. Paris: Les Belles Lettres, 2004.

Piras, Giorgio. "Nuove testimonianze dalla biblioteca di Petrarca: le annotazioni al *De lingua latina* di Varrone." In *Petrarca, l'umanesimo e la civiltà europea*, 2:829–56.

Rico, Francisco, and Luca Morozzi. "Petrarca, Francesco." In *Dizionario biografico degli italiani Treccani*. Vol. 82 (2015). Available online, http://www.treccani.it/enciclopedia/francesco-petrarca_(Dizionario-Biografico)/.

Rizzo, Silvia. "Il Latino del Petrarca nelle *Familiari*." In *The Uses of Greek and Latin: Historical Essays*, edited by A. C. Dionisotti, Anthony Grafton, and Jill Kraye, 41–56. London: The Warburg Institute, University of London, 1988.

——. *Ricerche sul Latino umanistico*. Vol. 1. Rome: Edizione di storia e letteratura, 2002.

Stock, Brian. "Reading, Writing, and the Self: Petrarch and His Forerunners." *New Literary History* 26 (1995): 717–30.

Volk, Katharina. *Manilius and His Intellectual Background*. Oxford and New York: Oxford University Press, 2009.

Wilkins, Ernest Hatch. *The Making of the "Canzoniere" and Other Petrarchan Studies*. Rome: Edizioni di storia e letteratura, 1951.

——. *Studies in the Life and Works of Petrarch*. Cambridge, MA: The Mediaeval Academy of America, 1955.

——. *The* Epistolae metricae *of Petrarch: A Manual*. Roma: Edizioni di storia e letteratura, 1956.

——. *Petrarch at Vaucluse*. Chicago: University of Chicago Press, 1958.

——. *Petrarch's Eight Years in Milan*. Cambridge, MA: The Mediaeval Academy of America, 1958.

——. *Petrarch's Later Years*. Cambridge, MA: The Mediaeval Academy of America, 1959.

——. *Petrarch's Correspondence*. Padua: Antenore, 1960.

——. *Life of Petrarch*. Chicago: University of Chicago Press, 1961.

——. *Studies on Petrarch and Boccaccio*. Edited by Aldo S. Bernardo. Padua: Antenore, 1978.

Witt, Ronald. *In the Footsteps of the Ancients: The Origins of Humanism from Lovato to Bruni*. Leiden and Boston: Brill, 2000.

——. "La concezione della storia in Petrarca." In *Petrarca: canoni, esemplarità*, edited by Valeria Finucci, 211–28. Rome: Bulzoni, 2006.

Ziolkowski, Jan M., and Michael C. J. Putnam, eds. *The Virgilian Tradition: The First Fifteen Hundred Years*. New Haven: Yale University Press, 2008.

# *Cumulative Index to Volumes I and II*

*Publication of this volume has been made possible by*

The Myron and Sheila Gilmore Publication Fund at I Tatti
The Robert Lehman Endowment Fund
The Jean-François Malle Scholarly Programs and Publications Fund
The Andrew W. Mellon Scholarly Publications Fund
The Craig and Barbara Smyth Fund
for Scholarly Programs and Publications
The Lila Wallace–Reader's Digest Endowment Fund
The Malcolm Wiener Fund for Scholarly Programs and Publications